D0205729

FORBIDDEN FILMS

CENSORSHIP HISTORIES OF
125 Motion Pictures

Dawn B. Sova

Foreword by
Marjorie Heins

Facts On File, Inc.

Forbidden Films

Copyright © 2001 by Dawn B. Sova

Checkmark Books
An imprint of Facts On File, Inc.
132 West 31st Street
New York NY 10001

Library of Congress Cataloguing-in-Publication Data

Sova, Dawn B.
Forbidden films : censorship histories of 125 motion pictures / Dawn B. Sova;
foreword by Marjorie Heins.
p. cm.
Includes bibliographical references and index.
ISBN 0-8160-4017-6 (alk. paper)—ISBN 0-8160-4336-1 (pbk.: alk. paper)
1. Motion pictures—Censorship—United States—History. I. Title.

PN1995.62.S67 2001
363.3'1—dc21   2001023154

Facts On File books are available at special discounts when purchased in bulk quantities for businesses, associations, institutions or sales promotions. Please call our Special Sales Department in New York at 212/967-8800 or 800/322-8755.

You can find Facts On File on the World Wide Web at http://www.factsonfile.com

Text design by Cathy Rincon
Cover design by Catherine Lau Hunt

Printed in the United States of America

MP FOF 10 9 8 7 6 5 4 3 2 1
(pbk) 10 9 8 7 6 5 4 3 2 1

This book is printed on acid-free paper.

Contents

Acknowledgments

IV

Foreword

V

Introduction

X

List of Entries

XIV

FORBIDDEN FILMS

1

Bibliography

313

Appendixes
I. Directors' Profiles
327

II. Reasons for Banning
347

III. 125 Additional Challenged, Censored,
and Banned Films
349

Index
351

ACKNOWLEDGMENTS

This book would never have been written had not so many courageous filmmakers taken risks and dared to value art over propriety and creativity over conformity. I owe a debt of gratitude to the thousands of producers, directors, cinematographers, screenwriters, actors and many more in the film industry who braved the censors and challengers and who chose to make magic on screen rather than to produce conventional images that offend no one and, so often, entertain very few. I also owe many debts of gratitude to the archivists in libraries across the United States who have courageously maintained records of their states' shame, of proceedings by boards of censors that denied tens of thousands of potential viewers access to provocative and informative films or by censors who mutilated films beyond recognition in the name of morality.

More personally, I must express my deepest appreciation and admiration to my agent, Bert Holtje, of James Peter Associates, who supported this effort and found it a home, and to Anne Savarese, editor at Facts On File, Inc., who offered this project a home and then waited patiently as it slowly made its way to her desk.

A very heartfelt appreciation must go to Robert Gregor, a master at research and at ferreting out hidden websites, as well as a meticulous writer who stepped up to help place this project back on track when it appeared about to derail.

I cannot imagine embarking upon a writing project without first consulting with I. Macarthur Nickles, director of the Garfield (New Jersey) Library, whose professional expertise and remarkable insight always help to clarify the possibilities of a project. He has created in my hometown library an intellectual center filled with possibilities and the means of obtaining anything and everything that I require in regard to research.

My parents, Emil and Violet Sova, have earned my greatest appreciation for giving me the thirst to know and to explore the world around me. What greater gift can someone receive?

FOREWORD

Movies are "a business, pure and simple"—so said the U.S. Supreme Court in 1915 when it denied constitutional protection to this intriguing new medium of entertainment. Upholding an Ohio law that created a state board of film censors, the Court acknowledged that movies had many useful purposes but warned that they could also "be used for evil" by arousing a "prurient interest."[1] Although the justices eventually did reverse themselves and rule that the immensely powerful art of cinema was a form of expression protected by the First Amendment,[2] the very power of film also made those flickering images on the giant screen a continuing flash point for censorship.

In the early part of the 20th century, cinema was not alone: The creative arts in general were low on the list of free-speech causes. Even the fledgling American Civil Liberties Union refused to protest the 1923 prosecution of Sholem Asch's play *God of Vengeance* because the issue, according to then-ACLU director Roger Baldwin, was "not primarily one of freedom of opinion," but "of censorship on the ground of morality."[3] By the 1930s, the ACLU had changed its tune and actively supported efforts to bring James Joyce's sprawling, obscure and undoubtedly vulgar masterpiece *Ulysses* into the United States in defiance of prevailing standards of obscenity law. Although the decision in *United States v. One Book Called "Ulysses"* in 1933 went a long way toward bringing literature under the First Amendment's protective umbrella,[4] cinema lingered in murky constitutional terrain for another 19 years.

Film licensing boards during these years wielded wide discretionary powers. Indeed, the numerous grounds on which they relied to deny exhibition permits testify to the increasing dramatic and artistic power of the medium—its ability not only to entertain, amuse and provoke emotions, but also to address social issues in compelling ways. Chief Justice Earl Warren, dissenting in a 1961 case that rejected a constitutional challenge to these "prior restraint" licensing schemes for cinema, nicely summed up the breadth of American film censorship. Chicago's licensing board, Warren recounted, had banned newsreels of police officers shooting at labor pickets; "ordered the deletion of a scene depicting the birth of a buffalo in Walt Disney's *Vanishing Prairie*"; refused a license for *Anatomy of a Murder* "because it found the use of the words 'rape' and 'contraceptive' to be objectionable"; and banned Charlie

Chaplin's *The Great Dictator*, "apparently out of deference to its large German population." Memphis banned the film *Curley* "because it contained scenes of white and Negro children in school together," and likewise suppressed *The Southerner*, a film about poor tenant farmers, because it reflected badly on the South. Kansas "ordered a speech by Senator Wheeler opposing the bill for enlarging the Supreme Court to be cut from the *March of Time* as 'partisan and biased.'" A film version of *Carmen* was condemned in Ohio "because cigarette-girls smoked cigarettes in public" and in Pennsylvania because of "the duration of a kiss."[5]

The Supreme Court was not altogether comfortable with this state of affairs, and beginning in 1952, it found reasons to overturn a number of film bans. The watershed case was *Burstyn v. Wilson*, involving a short film, *The Miracle*, by the Italian neorealist director Roberto Rossellini—an intensely focused, gritty parable of a simpleminded peasant woman who believes she has been divinely impregnated by her favorite saint. The film initially received an exhibition permit from the State of New York as part of a trilogy of foreign movies called *The Ways of Love*, but a campaign of protest soon began. It culminated in a fiery condemnation of *The Miracle* by New York City's Francis Cardinal Spellman that was read at all masses in St. Patrick's Cathedral. New York's censors revoked the film's permit on grounds of sacrilege. The distributor, Joseph Burstyn, sued, and the case eventually made its way to the Supreme Court.

Squarely announcing what they had only noted in passing in a case four years before, the justices this time proclaimed that movies *were* protected by the First Amendment and that New York's ban on "sacrilegious" films was unconstitutional. "The censor is set adrift upon a boundless sea," wrote Justice Tom Clark for the Court, "amid a myriad of conflicting currents of conflicting views, with no charts but those provided by the most vocal and powerful orthodoxies." The Court ruled that the state had no business favoring "any or all religions" in this way. Clark acknowledged that films may "possess a greater capacity for evil, particularly among the youth of a community, than other modes of expression," but this was not sufficient reason to deny them First Amendment protection.[6]

Cinema's moral guardians were frustrated once again in 1959 when the Supreme Court invalidated New York's demand for cuts in a film version of D.H. Lawrence's classic novel *Lady Chatterley's Lover*. The state argued that the film, by portraying Lady Chatterley's adultery in sympathetic terms, encouraged "sexual immorality." But in one of those timeless passages that punctuate the literature of censorship, the Supreme Court said that the First Amendment's "guarantee is not confined to the expression of ideas that are conventional or shared by a majority. It protects advocacy of the opinion that adultery may sometimes be proper, no less than advocacy of socialism or the single tax."[7] It was not accidental that here, as in *The Miracle* case, the Court announced a fundamental First Amendment principle—that government cannot suppress ideas it doesn't like—in the context of film censorship. For just as film's ability to challenge conventional ideas in striking and powerful ways inspired censorship, it also inspired advances in free-expression law.

Still, all was not resolved in favor of cinematic freedom. The Court still had not questioned the basic validity of "prior restraint" movie licensing schemes. In fact, it upheld such a scheme in the 1961 case that inspired Chief Justice Warren's impassioned recitation of film censorship highlights. Although prior licensing, by this point in American constitutional history, would not have been upheld for newspapers or books, the seductive visuals, narrative drive and mythmaking capability of cinema were still thought to pose particular dangers. (Today, although film is still attacked, the most fervid pro-censorship rhetoric is reserved for newer media like video games and the Internet.)

The Supreme Court did finally invalidate a prior censorship scheme for cinema in 1965. But the Court still held back from ruling that a state could never have a licensing system. Instead, by requiring censorship boards to go to court promptly for adjudications of obscenity if they wanted to deny exhibition licenses, it stripped the remaining boards of their formerly freewheeling powers.[8] The back of America's film censorship system was now seriously bent, if not completely broken, and three years later, the Court invalidated licensing standards in Dallas, Texas, that barred anyone under 16 from viewing any movie that the local censors deemed to contain "brutality, criminal violence or depravity," "nudity beyond the customary limits of candor" or "sexual promiscuity or extra-marital relations or abnormal sexual relations." (The city had classified Louis Malle's *Viva Maria!* as "not suitable for young persons.")[9]

Official film censorship in the United States is now largely a relic of the past, save for our still-extant obscenity laws and for occasional attempts to ban the distribution of "violent" videos to minors. Films like Louis Malle's *The Lovers* and Mike Nichols's *Carnal Knowledge* were found obscene by state courts in the 1960s and '70s but were rescued in Supreme Court decisions that found them not sufficiently "offensive" or lacking in value to meet the Court's shifting obscenity test.[10]

Movie censorship today has thus shifted almost completely to the realm of private industry "self-regulation" (the Motion Picture Association of America's rating system, which replaced the more restrictive Hays Production Code in the 1960s) and to indirect but still potent venues for suppression like schools and libraries. In 1998, for example, Oklahoma City police seized all available videotapes of an Academy Award-winning film version of Günter Grass's novel *The Tin Drum* on the ground that three scenes in the film contained child pornography. (The courts later disagreed.)[11] The dispute arose because the video had been available at the local library. In a Colorado public school, a teacher was fired for showing his classes the historical film *1900* by Bernardo Bertolucci[12]; and in Kenosha, Wisconsin, the school board barred students from viewing any R-rated film, including Steven Spielberg's powerful Holocaust drama, *Schindler's List*. A federal judge upheld the school district, ruling that students had no First Amendment right to see the film as part of the school curriculum and that the board's reliance on the MPAA's ratings was "reasonably related to legitimate pedagogical concerns."[13]

When, shortly afterward, Congress passed a law requiring most new TV sets to have a "v-chip," designed to block programs containing sexual, violent or "indecent" material, Congressman Tom Coburn likewise relied on the MPAA's rating system to denounce a recent NBC broadcast of *Schindler's List.* "I cringe," Coburn said, "when I realize that there were children all across the nation watching this program. They were exposed to the violence of multiple gunshot head wounds, vile language, full frontal nudity and irresponsible sexual activity." Displaying mind-boggling blindness to the artistic and historical justifications for violence and nudity in the film, Coburn said the broadcast was proof that the new TV ratings, created by the industry in response to the v-chip law, would "only encourage" more sex and violence on television.[14]

MPAA ratings, although certainly not equivalent to official government censorship, are also not simply benign information for parents. Film critics became painfully aware of this in 1999 when the MPAA forced the director Stanley Kubrick to mask a few fleeting moments of explicit sex during a lugubrious orgy scene in his last film, *Eyes Wide Shut,* in order to obtain an R rating. "How is it possible," the critics asked, "that a serious movie about human sexuality, made by one of the world's master filmmakers, cannot be seen by American adults in its intended form?"[15]

Their question was a good one and suggests that the colorful history of American film censorship is not yet at an end. Given the substantial political and emotional satisfactions of censorship—its perennial use as a symbolic club to hammer home prevailing moral values—its persistence is not surprising. Cinema may not be a novelty any more, but it is still a brilliantly versatile medium with astounding power to startle, amuse, inform, provoke and offend. From the spirituality of *The Miracle* to the inspired political commentary of Chaplin's *The Great Dictator,* it has been precisely this versatility that has made film both a target of censorship and an inspiration for some of the Supreme Court's most important pronouncements on freedom of speech.

—Marjorie Heins, Director of the Free Expression
Policy Project at the National Coalition Against Censorship
and author of *Not in Front of the Children: "Indecency," Censorship,
and the Innocence of Youth* (New York: Hill & Wang, 2001)

---

1. *Mutual Film Corp. v. Industrial Comm'n*, 236 U.S. 230, 242 (1915).
2. *U.S. v. Paramount Pictures*, 334 U.S. 131 (1948). This was an antitrust case in which Justice William O. Douglas noted in passing that movies, "like radio and television, are included in the press whose freedom is guaranteed by the First Amendment." The Court squarely overruled *Mutual Film* four years later in *Joseph Burstyn, Inc. v. Wilson*, 343 U.S. 495 (1952).
3. See David Rabban, *Free Speech in Its Forgotten Years* (Cambridge, U.K.: Cambridge University Press, 1997), pp. 311–12.

4. *United States v. One Book Called "Ulysses,"* 5 F. Supp. 182, 183–85 (S.D.N.Y. 1933), affirmed, 72 F.2d 705 (2d Cir. 1934).
5. *Times Film Corp. v. Chicago,* 365 U.S. 43, 69–72 (1961) (Warren, C.J., dissenting). See the entry on *Don Juan* for more on this case.
6. *Joseph Burstyn, Inc. v. Wilson,* 343 U.S. 495, 504–05, 502 (1952). See the entry on *The Miracle.*
7. *Kingsley Int'l Pictures v. Regents of the Univ. of the State of New York,* 360 U.S. 684, 689 (1959). See the entry for *Lady Chatterley's Lover.*
8. *Freedman v. Maryland,* 380 U.S. 51 (1965).
9. *Interstate Circuit v. Dallas,* 390 U.S. 676, 688–89 (1968). See the entry for *Viva Maria!*
10. *Jenkins v. Georgia,* 418 U.S. 153 (1974); *Jacobellis v. Ohio,* 378 U.S. 184 (1964). See the entries for *Carnal Knowledge* and *The Lovers.*
11. *Oklahoma ex rel. Macy v. Blockbuster Videos,* No. CIV–97–1281–T (W.D. Okla. 1998); *Video Software Dealers Ass'n v. Oklahoma ex rel. Oklahoma Dep't of Libraries,* No. CIV–97–1150–T (W.D. Okla. 1998).
12. *Board of Education v. Wilder,* 960 P.2d 695 (Colo. 1998).
13. *Borger v. Bisciglia,* 888 F. Supp. 97, 100 (E.D. Wis. 1995).
14. David Bianculli, "Does Schindler's List Critic See the Same Film as the Rest of Us?" *Charlotte Observer,* Mar. 5, 1997, p. 14E; *Television Rating System: Hearings Before the Senate Comm. on Commerce, Science and Transp.,* 105th Cong., 1st Sess. (Feb. 27, 1997), p. 31; "Censorship and 'Schindler's List,'" *Boston Globe,* Mar. 4, 1997, p. A14.
15. Bernard Weinraub, "Critics Assault Ratings Board Over 'Eyes,'" *New York Times,* July 28, 1999, p. E3.

INTRODUCTION

No one book can fully cover the history of film censorship. Nor can one book adequately identify all of the films that have been banned, censored, or challenged in the United States, let alone around the world. Even extensive lists prove to be inadequate, for analyses of the films and of their suppression are missing. Therefore, the best effort—the one that is, at least, realizable—is a book such as *Forbidden Films*, which analyzes representative films and the means by which they have been suppressed in whole or in part by mechanisms that have varied over more than a century of film history.

The call for film censorship in the United States began soon after the power of the medium was unleashed on an eager viewing public. Even though early films were silent, one picture usually was more expressive than a thousand words, and that fact was not lost on would-be moralists. In 1915, D.W. Griffith's *The Birth of a Nation* shocked and titillated audiences with its scenes of racial strife and deification of the Ku Klux Klan. After viewing it in a private screening at the White House, President Woodrow Wilson said "it is like writing history in lightning. . . . My only regret is that it is all so terribly true." Despite Wilson's reaction, the film would become the most frequently banned in history, in more than one hundred incidents and as recently as 1980.

Efforts to suppress the film in 1915 led to a key decision by the United States Supreme Court, which ruled in *Mutual Film Corporation v. Industrial Commission of Ohio*, 236 U.S. 230 (1915), that a film must be treated as a commercial enterprise and, as such, could not claim protection of such constitutional guarantees as freedom of speech and press. That one judgment not only denied constitutional protection to movies, but also left films open to censorship and banning by city and state boards of censors nationwide, with no recourse in the courts until the early 1950s.

At the time of the *Mutual Film Corporation v. Industrial Commission of Ohio* decision, plans were underway for a federal censorship body. A group called the National Board of Review of Motion Pictures had existed since 1909, but studios voluntarily submitted their films for review and its role was to offer "selection," not censorship, and to classify movies for theater owners according to the levels of vulgarity and crime. The proposals for a Federal Motion Picture Commission, which would be under the aegis of the Bureau of Education in the Department of the Interior, sought to establish a nationwide censoring group that would have set policy for the nation. The movie industry and the individual states were understandably upset by this possibility.

In response, the movie industry, represented by the Motion Picture Producers and Distributors Association (MPPDA) headed by former U.S. postmaster Will Hays, created a code to which all members were expected to adhere. The MPPDA, which included both studio and theater owners, created a series of self-regulating agencies, beginning with the creation of the Studio Relations Committee (SRC) in 1927, which led to the development of the Production Code Administration (PCA) in June 1934 that issued or denied a "seal of approval" for movies. Theater owners who were members of the MPPDA—and most were—agreed to exhibit only films that carried the seal. Such groups as the Catholic Legion of Decency (LOD) organized formally in April 1934 found the SRC too lax. The American Catholic Church had long attempted to control the content of films, beginning with its ban of *Power of the Cross* in 1916 and its threat to excommunicate the film's director, A. M. Kennelly. In 1922, representatives of the church began to publish lists of recommended films, which led Hollywood to court the opinions of such prominent Catholics as Martin Quigley and Daniel Lord in drafting the Motion Picture Production Code in 1930. When these standards also appeared to be too lax, Catholic bishops and priests created a vigorous national campaign to purify the cinema, leading to the creation of the LOD. Their threats and actions forced the movie industry to create the more stringent PCA code in 1934, which suppressed many previously released films and resulted in the wholesale mutilation of others to fit the new requirements. Thus began a war among the censors.

Films suffered scrutiny at numerous points, from the excisions made in screenplays at the suggestion of the SRC before production even began, to frames and even whole segments cut from films before the PCA would grant a film the seal of approval, to the later cuts made by city and state censorship boards. Even after a film concept had been altered at three or four checkpoints, the movie might still be suppressed if the LOD were particularly vocal. In Chicago, for example, many films that had received the industry seal received a "C" (condemned) rating from the LOD and were boycotted. Some films might later be restored if master copies in tolerable condition could be found, while others were lost forever. The most fortunate films were those pulled from circulation "forever" by SRC head Joseph Breen in 1934 and locked away in a vault. Although they were not unearthed until the early 1980s, they at least emerged intact.

Movies were finally granted constitutional protection in 1952, when the United States Supreme Court decided in *Burstyn v. Wilson*, 343 U.S. 495 (1952), a case brought in relation to the movie *The Miracle*, that "Expression by means of motion pictures is included within the free speech and free press guaranty of the First and Fourteenth Amendments." This did not end the censorship of films, but it was the beginning of greater freedom for filmmakers. Vague language had to be removed from state censorship laws, and the basis for censorship was narrowed to "obscenity." Thus, film censorship laws that stated as their authority "immorality" or "sacrilegious" content were deemed unconstitutional. The burden was placed on the censors to prove that a film was "obscene" within the limits of the law. Censors had to change their tactics, and this in turn marked the decline of formal, official film censorship. At the same time, Hollywood experienced a moral and personal attack from Washington, D.C., as the House Un-American Activities Committee investigated Communist activities in the film capital. Informers named members of the film community with Communist Party affiliation, who were then blacklisted and no longer able to find film work. Film content was also affected, as filmmakers toned down the intellectual content and social messages in movies.

Today, the Code and Rating Administration (CARA) of the Motion Picture Association of America (MPAA) is not a censoring but a rating body. Potential audiences are alerted to film content by the rating given to a film: "G" (suitable for general audiences), "PG" (parental guidance suggested/ some material may not be suitable for children), "PG-13" (parents strongly cautioned/some material may be inappropriate for children under 13), "R" (restricted viewing and people under 17 not admitted without an adult), "NC-17" (no children under 17 admitted). In 1990, CARA replaced the "X" by "NC-17," a rating that many filmmakers fight to avoid, knowing that their strongest audiences are usually under the age of 17. The MPAA instituted the NC-17 rating so that certain films could be rated "for adults only" without making theater owners subject to the restraints of local ordinances that prevented newspaper advertisements for X-rated films and their exhibition.

The censorship of films was ruled unconstitutional by the Supreme Court in 1952, but efforts of religious, political, and other groups to prevent others from viewing films of which they disapprove continues. In some cases, historically marginalized groups who have experienced racial, religious, ethnic, and social bias have stepped forward to attempt to halt the showing of such films as *Basic Instinct*, *Monty Python's Life of Brian*, and *Cruising*. Censorship today now rests less with federal, state, or local ordinances that dictate appropriate film content than with force of opinion by smaller groups with more specialized agenda.

Although the main focus of this book is on acts of film censorship in the United States, some entries include discussion of censorship in other nations, to provide either a context for concurrent censorship in the United States or to exhibit how other nations perceive materials deemed acceptable here.

Entries in this volume offer only a sampling of the many films that have been banned, censored and challenged in the barely 100 years of film history, as the supplemental list in the appendix attests. To aid both the scholarly researcher and the casual browser, entries are arranged alphabetically and include complete production data, cast information, plot summary and censorship history. Each entry also contains a list of further readings for in-depth examination of the attempts to suppress the film. Works whose titles appear in SMALL CAPITAL LETTERS have their own entries in the volume. Appendixes contain brief biographies of the directors and categorization of the profiled films based on the reasons for which attempts to suppress them occurred.

LIST OF ENTRIES

The Affairs of Cellini
L'Âge d'Or
The Alibi
The Alimony Lovers
All Quiet on the Western Front
Amistad
Amok
Anatomy of a Murder
And God Created Woman
Anna and the King
Ann Vickers
Baby Doll
Baby Face
Basic Instinct
The Bedford Incident
Behind the Green Door
Belle of the Nineties
The Birth of a Baby
The Birth of a Nation
Blockade
Blonde Venus
The Blue Angel
Blue Movie
Body of a Female
The Brand
Bunny Lake is Missing
Caligula
Candy
Carmen, Baby
Carnal Knowledge

Un Chant d'Amour
Cindy and Donna
The Connection
Cruising
Curley
Damaged Goods
December 7th
Deep Throat
Desire Under the Elms
The Devil in Miss Jones
La Dolce Vita
Don Juan
Dracula
Dressed to Kill
The Easiest Way
Ecstasy
Emmanuelle
The Exorcist
491
A Farewell to Arms
Flaming Creatures
The Fox
Frankenstein
Freaks
The Game of Love
Garden of Eden
The Great Dictator
I, A Woman
I Am Curious—Yellow
Idiot's Delight

I'm No Angel
The James Boys in Missouri
The Killing of Sister George
Lady Chatterley's Lover
The Last Picture Show
Last Tango in Paris
The Last Temptation of Christ
Lolita (1962)
Lolita (1997)
Lorna
The Lovers
M
The Man With the Golden Arm
Martin Luther
The Miracle
Miss Julie
Mom and Dad
Monty Python's Life of Brian
The Moon is Blue
Naked Came the Stranger
The Naked Truth
Native Son
Natural Born Killers
Never On Sunday
The Newcomers
The North Star
October
Of Human Bondage
The Ordeal
The Outlaw
Pattern of Evil
Pinky
Professor Mamlock

Purity
Red-Headed Woman
Reefer Madness
Revenge at Daybreak
The Road to Ruin
La Ronde
Room at the Top
Scarface: The Shame of a Nation
Schindler's List
The Sex Lure
She Done Him Wrong
The Sign of the Cross
Spain in Flames
Spartacus
The Spirit of '76
The Spy
A Stranger Knocks
A Streetcar Named Desire
Therese and Isabelle
The Tin Drum
Titicut Follies
Tomorrow's Children
Toto Who Lived Twice
The Virgin Spring
Viva Maria!
The Vixen
Whirlpool
Wild Weed
Windows
Women of the World
Woodstock
The Youth of Maxim

FORBIDDEN FILMS

THE AFFAIRS OF CELLINI

Country and date of production: United States, 1934
Production company/distributor: Twentieth Century Pictures/United Artists
Format: Sound, black and white
Running time: 80 minutes
Language: English
Producer: Darryl F. Zanuck
Director: Gregory La Cava
Screenwriters: Edwin Justus Mayer (play, *The Firebrand*), Bess Meredyth
Awards: None
Genre: Comedy
With: Constance Bennett (Duchess of Florence), Fredric March (Benvenuto Cellini), Frank Morgan (Duke of Florence), Fay Wray (Angela), Vince Barnett (Ascanio), Jessie Ralph (Beatrice), Louis Calhern (Ottaviano), Jay Eaton (Polverino), Paul Harvey (Emissary), Jack Rutherford (Captain of the Guards), Irene Ware (Girl)

SUMMARY

Set in 16th-century Florence, Italy, the film, which is based on the play *The Firebrand* by Bess Meredyth, purports to relate the love life of the goldsmith and sculptor Benvenuto Cellini (1500–71). The film focuses on the Renaissance artist's sexual liaisons with women. The plot involves what might be called a love quadrangle involving Cellini, a peasant girl named Angela, the duke of Florence, and the duke's wife, the duchess of Florence. Cellini is in love with Angela, who is the mistress of the duke. The duchess of Florence is in love with Cellini. Despite his profession of love for Angela, Cellini also is engaged in an affair with the duchess. As the four characters move from one romantic engagement to the next, the film contains numerous scenes of swashbuckling swordplay, with characters jumping from balconies and swinging from chandeliers. In the end, the duke and duchess reunite, and Cellini appears to be headed for bliss with the peasant girl.

CENSORSHIP HISTORY

The film was one of the first produced by Darryl F. Zanuck after he left Warner Bros. and founded Twentieth Century Pictures, which would release many of its films through United Artists. As an act against what he saw as an increasingly restrictive climate of studio self-censorship, Zanuck chose not to associate his new studio with either the nationwide Motion Picture Producers and Distributors Association (MPPDA) or with the Association of Motion Picture Producers (AMPP), MPPDA's West Coast branch. By not joining either group, Zanuck could avoid having to submit the script to the Studio Relations Committee (SRC), which could either approve it or suggest changes that would delay production. Unlike member studios, which attempted to second-guess the various state censor boards and, before releasing a film, removed all scenes that might possibly offend the diverse populations, Zanuck made the film according to his own standards. He eventually had to submit to demands by the Studio Relations Committee (SRC) for modifications, however: Without the Production Code Administration (PCA) seal of approval, United Artists could not distribute the film. Most first-run theaters belonged to the MPPDA and had agreed not to show a film unless it carried the seal.

SRC head Joseph Breen lambasted *The Affairs of Cellini* as filled with "lascivious" and "depraved" behavior and declared its characters "libidinous persons who engage themselves in promiscuous sexuality." Before the film could receive a PCA seal of approval, Zanuck had to cut scenes of passionate embraces and scenes that placed characters suggestively near or in bedrooms. Upon receiving the purity seal the film played full runs on the East and West coasts and in first-run theaters, but it was blacklisted by the Catholic diocese of Chicago. In 1934, Chicago contained the most powerful of the local censor boards nationwide as well as one of the largest Roman Catholic populations. The Legion of Decency, headed by Cardinal George W. Mundelein, condemned the film as immoral, issued it a "C" ("Condemned") rating and warned Catholics that they faced eternal damnation if they saw the film. The ban, while not municipally imposed, was effective: The large number of Catholics who boycotted the film brought it national attention and made it financially unsuccessful in Chicago and elsewhere. The film, which cost Zanuck a little over a half-million dollars to make, eventually proved a loss.

FURTHER READING

Black, Gregory D. *Hollywood Censored: Morality Codes, Catholics, and the Movies.* New York: Cambridge University Press, 1994.
Maltby, Richard. "The Genesis of the Production Code." *Quarterly Review of Film and Video* 15, no. 4 (March 1995): 5–57.
Viera, Mark A. *Sin in Soft Focus: Pre-Code Hollywood.* New York: Harry N. Abrams, 1999.

L'ÂGE D'OR

Country and date of production: France, 1930; released in the United States as *The Age of Gold*
Production company/distributor: Les Films Sonores Tobis/Corinth Films (United States, 1979)
Format: Sound, black and white
Running time: 60 minutes
Language: French
Producer: Comte Charles de Noailles

Director: Luis Buñuel
Screenwriters: Luis Buñuel, Salvador Dalí
Awards: None
Genre: Drama
With: Gaston Modot (The Man), Lya Lys (Young Woman), Caridad de Laberdesque (Chambermaid and Little Girl), Max Ernst (Leader of men in cottage), Joseph Llorens Artigas (Governor), Lionel Salem (Duke of Blangis), Germaine Noizet (Marquise), Duchange (Conductor), Ibanez (Marquis)

SUMMARY

One of Luis Buñuel's legendary films, *L'Âge d'Or* would seem, at first glance, to be a story of sexual frustration in a repressed society. A man and a woman in love attempt to consummate their passion but are thwarted by their families, the Roman Catholic Church and their middle-class society. As the film continues, however, the radical nature of Buñuel's work emerges through numerous attacks on organized religion and his uncompromising criticism of society. To add irony to the already disturbing and contradictory images, Buñuel scores the film with classical music by Richard Wagner, Ludwig von Beethoven and Claude Debussy.

Written in collaboration with the surrealist painter Salvador Dalí, the film is extremely disjointed and bombards viewers with bizarre and irrational images. When the couple first appear, they attempt to make love rolling around in the mud while a crowd, representing society, has its back turned. Members of the culturally varied crowd, situated according to their social class, are fascinated as they watch a humorous commemoration of four holy men who died in the most meaningless fashion. Nearest to the spectacle are the representatives of the upper class, wearing bow ties, top hats and jewelry. Members of the middle class are farther back and are dressed more modestly. The working class members are poorly dressed and standing in the background, where they can barely see the events.

When members of the upper classes notice the lovers, they shake their fists and call for the police, who imprison the man. The loosely structured plot also contains a dream sequence in which a well-dressed, archetypal father figure carrying a rifle shoots his similarly archetypal son after the boy commits a minor offense in the garden. Viewers are expected to associate the father with all of the teachings of the Catholic Church and society that have gotten in the way of the man's natural enjoyment of his life and of his love. The boy in the dream represents the man, who has naively challenged society's outdated values. The father is angered to such an extent by the child's mockery of his seriously given advice that he shoots the boy twice with the rifle. The dark sequences come to a climax in which a meek Christ is equated with a participant in a murderous orgy in the marquis de Sade's *120 Days of Sodum*, an ending that led to changes of egregious blasphemy.

CENSORSHIP HISTORY

When first released in 1930, *L'Âge d'Or* was criticized for appearing to lack morals. The sexual innuendo and nature of the film were topics of heated debate. The film played to packed audiences during the first six nights after it debuted in Paris at the Studio 28 theater. After the first week, conservative groups sponsored by the Catholic Church and right-wing pressure groups such as Les Camelots du Roi and Les Jeunesses Patriotiques protested in front of the theater and publicly attacked Luis Buñuel and Salvador Dalí in the press. The aristocratic producer, Charles de Noailles, who had provided financial support to the film as a gift to his wife, was publicly condemned by the church, which threatened him with excommunication. The protesters became physically violent, destroying exhibits and seats in the theater and splattering ink on the screen. This destruction led police to close the theater and to remove the film, thus beginning an official ban on the film in France.

The protesters railed against the film's treatment of sexuality and noted especially their distaste for a scene in which a woman simulates fellatio with the toe of a statue. What led to the banning of the film for 49 years, however, was the disdain that Buñuel and Dalí showed toward the church in their support of premarital sex, their depiction of Jesus as a murderous impostor and the anti-Catholic messages projected by a slide show in the film, such as an aerial view of the Vatican with the caption, "The ancient city of Rome/Mistress to Pagan Times." Even de Noailles could not rally support among his peers, because the film depicted members of the upper-class culture as too sexually inhibited and frightened by the status quo to break free of society's restraints or to oppose the restrictions of religion.

Although copies of the film circulated to film clubs and among private patrons, it was not publicly screened in France nor in the United States until 1979, when the influence of the Roman Catholic Church had diminished greatly.

FURTHER READING

Abel, Richard. *French Film Theory and Criticism: A History/Anthology, 1907–1939.* Vol. 2. Princeton: Princeton University Press, 1988.

Crispin, Colin. *The Classic French Cinema, 1930–1960.* Bloomington: Indiana University Press, 1994.

Gangas, Spiros. "L'Âge d'Or." *Edinburgh University Film Society Programme,* 1993–1994.

Hammond, Paul. *L'Âge d'Or.* Bloomington: Indiana University Press, 1997.

Williams, Linda. *Figures of Desire: A Theory and Analysis of Surrealist Films.* Berkeley: University of California Press, 1992.

THE ALIBI

Country and date of production: United States, 1929; released in United Kingdom as *The Perfect Alibi,* 1929

Production company/distributor: Feature Productions/United Artists
Format: Sound, black and white
Running time: 90 minutes
Language: English
Producer: Roland West
Director: Roland West
Screenwriters: Elaine S. Carrington, J. C. Nugent, John Griffith Wray
Awards: None
Genre: Drama
With: Chester Morris (Chick Williams), Harry Stubbs (Buck Bachman), Mae Busch (Daisy Thomas), Eleanore Griffith (Joan Manning Williams), Irma Harrison (Toots), Regis Toomey (Danny McGann), Al Hill (Brown), James Bradbury, Jr. (Blake), Elmer Ballard (Soft Malone), Kernan Cripps (Trask), Purnell Pratt (Sergeant Pete Manning), Pat O'Malley (Detective Sergeant Tommy Glennon), DeWitt Jennings (O'Brien)

SUMMARY

Based on the play *Nightstick*, written by Elaine S. Carrington, J. C. Nugent and John Griffith Wray, this crime melodrama appears dated to contemporary audiences. The plot focuses on Joan Manning, the daughter of a tough police sergeant and a rebel against her father's strict adherence to the law. When she meets Chick Williams, recently released from prison and claiming his innocence and unfair treatment at the hands of the police, Joan loses her head and her heart to him. Her sympathy for what Chick says he suffered while incarcerated leads Joan to disobey all of her father's warnings. She and Chick date and then marry in secret. After their hasty wedding the newlyweds go to a movie, where Chick tells Joan that he must leave her at the intermission to "take care of something." His mission is to join members of a gang in a warehouse robbery, during which he accidentally kills a policeman before returning to his new wife in the theater. When the police later question Chick, whom they suspect of the robbery and murder based on observations made by witnesses, Joan serves as his alibi and states that Chick was with her in the theater when the crimes were committed. The police remain unconvinced and assign an undercover agent to watch Chick, who becomes friendly with the man and reveals the crimes to him. After Joan sees the undercover police officer and tells Chick that the man is a friend of her father's, Chick kills his new "friend." Soon after, the police appear at the Williams' home to arrest Chick and find him hiding in the closet. Detective Sergeant Tommy Glennon, a police officer who has always been in love with Joan, seeks to show her Chick's cowardice. He fires a gun containing blanks at the closet. Unsure why he has not been killed by the shots, Chick bolts from the closet and jumps out of the window, where he falls to his death. As the police take away the body, Joan realizes how mistaken she was in rebelling against her law-abiding father by marrying Chick. The film ends with the suggestion that her future will probably include Detective Sergeant Glennon.

CENSORSHIP HISTORY

The city of Chicago banned this film from theaters in 1929 when the superintendent of police denied film distributors a permit to exhibit. Authority for the denial was based on a city censorship statute that provided grounds for the superintendent's claim that *The Alibi* portrayed police methods that "are brutal and revolting, and would tend, in the opinion of the censor board, to create contempt and hatred for the entire police force." The denial charged further that the film contained "immorality, criminality, and depravity," based on scenes depicting the robbery, the fatal shooting of the police officer at the robbery site, the murder of the undercover police officer, the brutal interrogation methods of the police, and the ability of the gang members to use the daughter of a member of the police force to provide an alibi for the crime. The distributor of the film appealed the denial in a hearing that took place in the Circuit Court of Cook County. Judge Harry M. Fisher granted a temporary injunction against the denial until after he had viewed the film to make his own decision. To make its case, the city submitted the film script, but Judge Fisher declared that the script represented only "a part of the story told, and that so inaptly told that it can have no probative value." After viewing the film, Judge Fisher issued a permanent injunction that prevented the city from interfering further with exhibition of the film.

The Chicago censorship board then filed an appeal with the Supreme Court of Illinois, which reversed the lower court ruling after determining that the distributor had not shown "by competent evidence" that the city had acted "unreasonably and arbitrarily" in denying the exhibition permit. In rendering the decision, the court declared that the film portrayed violent actions and brutal behavior on the part of both gang members and the police and "contains threats of unlawful killings, made both by the criminals and by the police." The court wrote with particular disdain of a scene in the film that depicts "an attempt by the police officers to extort evidence from prisoners by the use of what is known as the 'sweating process,' which practice has been most severely condemned by this court." The decision concluded that the Chicago censorship board was "fully justified in refusing a permit for its [the film's] exhibition" and declared that it "could not fail to have a tendency to cheapen the value of human life in the minds of youthful spectators."

In an assessment of the 1930 decision made by the Supreme Court of Illinois, Edward de Grazia observes that, based on constitutional law today, "the court was decidedly in error" in placing the burden of proof on the distributor rather than requiring the censor to establish grounds for refusing a permit for showing a film. De Grazia also takes issue with the court's decision that "the portrayal of immorality and of 'disrespect for the law and its officers' are valid grounds for censorship. There is no question today that such grounds present constitutionally defective bases for interfering with the circulation of films."

FURTHER READING

Black, Gregory D. *Hollywood Uncensored: Morality Codes, Catholics, and The Movies.* New York: Cambridge University Press, 1994.

de Grazia, Edward. *Banned Films: Movies, Censors and the First Amendment.* New York: R. R. Bowker, 1982.

MacQueen, Scott. "Alibi: Gangsters Take On Talkies." *American Cinematographer* 72, no. 4 (April 1991).

United Artists Corporation v. Thompson, 171 N.E. 742, 339 Ill. 595 (1930).

THE ALIMONY LOVERS

Country and date of production: United States, 1969
Production company/distributor: Clover Films
Format: Sound, color
Running time: 74 minutes
Language: English
Producer: William Dancer
Director: Harold Perkins
Screenwriters: Not credited
Awards: None
Genre: Adult
With: Sebastian Gregory (Roger Rose)

SUMMARY

The plot of *The Alimony Lovers* revolves around the activities of an enterprising, recently divorced character named Roger Rose who has just moved into a luxury apartment complex. The complex is populated mainly with divorced women who are enjoying life while collecting alimony. After discovering that considerable sexual activity takes place among the residents, and after sampling some of the activity firsthand, Rose decides that he has found a way to make a fortune. He convinces women in the apartment complex that they are wasting their talents by keeping their sexual activities private. He makes them a business proposition to serve as their agent and arrange for them to perform with him in front of audiences for a fee, of which he would keep a large part. The women agree, and the business thrives until the police intervene and close down Rose's operation. Despite the setback, Rose's ardor does not appear to have cooled because he immediately turns his sexual attentions to the female lawyer assigned to the case.

CENSORSHIP HISTORY

The Alimony Lovers would be of little interest if it had not been the subject of the first film censorship case to be heard by the Maryland Court of Appeals following the passage of a new law by the state legislature, which had aligned the state censorship statute with the procedural guidelines for constitutional licensing of motion pictures established by the United States Supreme Court in the 1965 case of *Freedman v. Maryland, 380 U.S. 51 (1965)*, involving REVENGE AT DAYBREAK. As written in *Hewitt v. Maryland State Board of Censors*, the board had "five days to approve or disapprove a film for licensing following its submission to it, three additional days after any disapproval to petition the court for an order affirming the disapproval, another five days for the court to commence a hearing on the film, and two days from the hearing for the court to reach a decision on whether the film should be licensed or not." Under the old law, no time limits were placed on the censorship board, thus permitting greater abuses of the law. After the board of censors judged *The Alimony Lovers* to be obscene and the Baltimore City circuit court affirmed the decision, the distributor appealed the decision to the Maryland Court of Appeals, arguing that he had the right to exhibit the film because the censors had not followed the required procedures and "the circuit court had not tried the matter within the statutorily specified five days." The distributor argued further that because the board's petition was heard and decided on the seventh day, the judge "had so much less time for consideration that his decision is subject to suspicion." In the Maryland Court of Appeals decision, Chief Justice Hall Hammond refused to consider this reasoning and wrote, "This argument leaves us cold." The court affirmed the decision of the lower court.

FURTHER READING

Carmen, Ira H. *Movies, Censorship and the Law.* Ann Arbor: University of Michigan, 1966.

De Grazia, Edward, and Roger K. Newman. *Banned Films: Movies, Censors and the First Amendment.* New York: R. R. Bowker, 1982.

Hewitt v. Maryland State Board of Censors, 258 A. 2d 217 (1969).

Maryland Board of Censors. Annual Reports. Baltimore, Md.: The Board, 1969.

Scott, Barbara. "Motion Picture Censorship and the Exhibitor." *Film Comment* 2, no. 4 (Fall 1965): 56–60.

ALL QUIET ON THE WESTERN FRONT

Country and date of production: United States, 1930
Production company/distributor: Universal Pictures
Format: sound, black and white
Running time: 131 minutes
Language: English
Producer: Carl Laemmle, Jr.
Director: Lewis Milestone
Screenwriters: George Abbott, Maxwell Anderson, Del Andrews
Awards: 1930 Academy Awards, Best Director (Lewis Milestone), Best Picture

1930 Photoplay Awards, Medal of Honor awarded to Carl Laemmle, Jr.
Genre: War
With: Lew Ayres (Paul Baumer), Louis Wolheim (Katczinsky), John Wray (Himmelstoss), Arnold Lucy (Kantorek), Slim Summerville (Tjaden), Ben Alexander (Kemmerick), William Bakewell (Albert), Scott Kolk (Leer), Owen Davis, Jr. (Peter), Russell Gleason (Muller), Walter Rogers (Behm), Richard Alexander (Westhus), Harold Goodwin (Detering), G. Pat Collins (Lieutenant Bertinck), Beryl Mercer (Mrs. Baumer), Edmund Breese (Herr Meyer), Yola D'Avril (Suzanne)

SUMMARY

The first major antiwar film in the sound era, made only 12 years after the end of World War I, *All Quiet on the Western Front* (1930) is based closely upon the 1929 novel by Erich Maria Remarque, whose experiences as a young German soldier in the Great War are portrayed through the main character, Paul Baumer. The novel begins with the young men already at war, with flashbacks to their schooldays and prewar experiences, but the film presents their lives in a chronological manner through a series of scenes that portray the senseless nature of war from the point of view of the young German soldiers in the trenches. Contrary to the romanticized view of war popular at the time, the young soldiers find no glory on the battlefield, only death and disillusionment. Critically acclaimed and financially successful in its first release, the film is still considered among the greatest of antiwar movies, despite a lack of the special effects that contemporary audiences have come to expect in an action movie.

The film opens with a prologue that is taken from the foreword to Remarque's novel:

> This story is neither an accusation nor a confession, and least of all an adventure, for death is not an adventure to those who stand face to face with it. It will try simply to tell of a generation of men who, even though they may have escaped its shells, were destroyed by the war . . .

The film opens in a small German town. As martial music plays, spike-helmeted German soldiers march in sight of flags and cheering crowds. Viewers are introduced to characters who will play significant roles later in the film, especially the students of Professor Kantorek, who rouses his entire class of boys, "the iron men of Germany," to fight for "the glory of the Fatherland." Seven of the boys enlist immediately, expecting a great adventure, but they find only the realities of war: One after another, they are maimed and killed.

Although the film contains brief comic moments and four of the young men experience a night of romance with French peasant girls, the focus is on the horrors of war and the gradual hopelessness the recruits feel as the war progresses. The cinematography emphasizes the haunted looks on the faces of the soldiers as they march to carry out their duties and, later, as they sit terrified, hungry, tired and disheveled in an underground bunker, hearing the ever-present sound of bombs exploding above them. The antiwar message is clear throughout the film, from the soldiers' first experiences under fire through Paul's all-night vigil in a trench with a dead French soldier and his eventual realization that the original class of German schoolboys has been decimated: "Out of 20, three are officers, nine dead, Muller and three others wounded, and one in the mad house."

Even a brief return to his hometown offers Paul no solace because no one understands the horrors that he has endured. He returns early to duty, only to find that more friends have died. Germany is struggling, supplies are short and the situation feels lost. On a seemingly peaceful day—and with an armistice scheduled for 11 A.M.—Paul sits alone and reaches for a butterfly. A shot rings out. The audience sees Paul's hand jerk back, twitch for a moment and go limp in death. In the epilogue, the camera sweeps across a dark, battle-scarred hillside covered with white crosses and corpse-strewn fields, on which is superimposed a ghostly view of Paul and other soldiers marching away from the camera. One by one, the ghostly soldiers look back with accusation in their eyes.

CENSORSHIP HISTORY

Colonel Jason S. Joy, director of the Studio Relations Committee (SRC), described *All Quiet on the Western Front* as filled with "boldness and truthfulness." To prevent what he referred to as "the often picayune and petty concerns" of local censor boards, he tried to obtain advance support for the film in the United States through various groups, including the Boy Scouts of America, and even attempted to rally the support of women's organizations in Germany but to little success. Censor boards were upset by a scene of naked men bathing in a river, "turning somersaults, or otherwise unduly exposing themselves," and demanded that it be cut from the film.

When SRC staffer James B. Fisher reviewed the film for the SRC with a preview audience, he looked specifically for audience reaction to two other scenes. In one, a young recruit experiences his first bombardment and loses control of his bowels, and his platoon sergeant orders him to change his "drawers." Fisher found that the audience seemed oblivious to the indelicate implications of the line that meant a man had experienced a bowel movement in his pants in full view of the audience, aside from two or three men in the audience who laughed briefly. In the other, more prolonged scene, the main character and two other soldiers take food to the farmhouse of three French girls and spend the night. Although no sexual activity is shown nor spoken of, the scene ends with the silhouetted images of Paul and one of the girls projected on what the audience knows to be a bedroom wall. Paul tells the girl that he will probably never see her again and would not recognize her if he did, but that he will always remember her: "*Toujours*. Oh, if only you could know how different this is from the women we soldiers meet." Fisher waited for the audience to react with snickers or with off-color remarks and laughter, but none did, so the scene stayed in. When the Ohio board of censors later screened the film, however, members offered the ultimatum that either this scene be cut or the film would not play in Ohio. Universal Pictures allowed the cut for exhibition in that state.

In 1938, when Universal sought to re-release the film, Production Code Administration (PCA) head Joseph Breen demanded that the studio excise the same love scene, which had been included in the 1930 release of the film, as had been the scene of the soldiers bathing in a river. He expressed the belief that the scenes were "dangerous" to viewers and refused to issue the PCA seal of approval without the cuts. Unlike the Ohio board of censors, however, Breen demanded that the studio make the cuts on the master negatives and not just on prints, fine-grain positives or duplicate negatives.

When *All Quiet on the Western Front* was re-released in November 1939, the "offensive" scenes were missing, but several scenes were added to project "a strongly anti-Nazi (but pro-German people)" statement. New material included voiceover commentary and the insertion of documentary film containing scenes of prewar and postwar Germany.

In 1998, the film was returned approximately to its original state. The documentary scenes were removed and the censored love scene was restored through the use of fine-grain positives.

FURTHER READING

"All Quiet on the Western Front: Screenplay by George Abbott, Maxwell Anderson, and Dell Andrews; Adaptation by Dell Andrews; Dialogue by Maxwell Anderson and George Abbott (Abbott Version, November 19, 1929)" in *Best American Screenplays: First Series: Complete Screenplays*, ed. Sam Thomas. New York: Crown Publishers, 1986; pp. 13–72.

Jowett, Garth. *Film: The Democratic Art—A Social History of American Film.* Boston: Little, Brown and Company, 1976.

Remarque, Erich Maria. *All Quiet on the Western Front.* Berlin, Germany: Impropylaen-Verlag, 1928. Eng. trans. by A. W. Wheen. Boston: Little Brown and Company, 1929.

Viera, Mark A. *Sin in Soft Focus: Pre-Code Hollywood.* New York: Harry N. Abrams, 1999.

AMISTAD

Country and date of production: United States, 1997
Production company/distributors: DreamWorks SKG/DreamWorks Distribution, L.L.C. (United States); Lusomundo (Portugal); United International Pictures (UIP) (Finland, France, Spain)
Format: Sound, color (Technicolor)
Running time: 152 minutes (United States and Canada), 155 minutes (Europe)

Language: English
Producers: Debbie Allen, Robert M. Cooper, Laurie MacDonald, Walter F. Parkes, Tim Shriver, Steven Spielberg, Colin Wilson
Director: Steven Spielberg
Screenwriters: William Owens (book, *Black Mutiny*), David H. Franzoni
Awards: 1999 Academy Awards, Best Cinematography (Janusz Kaminski), Best Costume Design (Ruth E. Carter).
1998 Broadcast Film Critics Association Awards, Best Supporting Actor (Anthony Hopkins).
1998 European Film Awards, Outstanding European Achievement in World Cinema (Stellan Skarsgård).
1998 Golden Globes, USA, Best Director of a Motion Picture (Steven Spielberg), Best Motion Picture–Drama.
1998 Golden Satellite Awards, Outstanding Cinematography (Janusz Kaminski), Best Director of a Motion Picture–Drama (Steven Spielberg), Best Producer of a Motion Picture–Drama (Debbie Allen, Steven Spielberg, Colin Wilson), Best Motion Picture Screenplay–Adapted (David H. Franzoni).
1998 Image Awards, Outstanding Lead Actor in a Motion Picture (Djimon Hounsou), Outstanding Supporting Actor in a Motion Picture (Morgan Freeman).
1998 PGA Golden Globe Laurel Awards: Vision Award for Theatrical Motion Pictures (Debbie Allen, Steven Spielberg, Colin Wilson).
Genre: Drama
With: Morgan Freeman (Theodore Joadson), Nigel Hawthorne (Martin Van Buren), Anthony Hopkins (John Quincy Adams), Djimon Hounsou (Cinqué), Matthew McConaughey (Baldwin), David Paymer (Secretary Forsyth), Pete Postlethwaite (Holabird), Stellan Skarsgård (Tappan), Razaaq Adoti (Yamba), Abu Bakaar Fofanah (Fala), Anna Paquin (Queen Isabel II), Tomas Milian (Calderón), Chjwetel Ejiofor (Ensign Covey), Derrick N. Ashong (Bukei), Geno Silva (Ruiz), John Ortiz (Montes), Ralph Brown (Lieutenant Gedney), Darren Burrows (Lieutenant Meade), Allan Rich (Judge Juttson), Paul Guilfoyle (Attorney), Peter Firth (Captain Fitzgerald), Xander Berkeley (Hammond), Jeremy Northam (Judge Coglin), Arliss Howard (John C. Calhoun)

SUMMARY

This film, which takes its name from the Spanish slave ship *La Amistad*, is based on a historical event that took place in the summer of 1839 off the coast of Cuba. Held captive in the cramped cargo hold of the ship, 53 Africans, who had been kidnapped from three different tribes, broke free of their chains and shackles and tried to take back their freedom.

The film begins in darkness. Lightning flashes briefly illuminate what is only barely recognizable as a human face, with wildly rolling eyes and the expression of a desperate animal. The camera then focuses on the clawing actions of the man, Cinqué, who is struggling to remove shackles, and blood is shown seeping slowly from his hand. Once free, Cinqué helps the other 52 men remove their shackles and assumes leadership over the group. The men arm themselves with machetes and kill all but two crew members to take control of the ship. The uprising is violent and bloody, and the film makes clear that Cinqué and his followers are desperate men who will do anything to attain their freedom. The two survivors of the crew are ordered to steer the ship and its human cargo back to Africa, but the two trick the Africans by maneuvering the ship up the Eastern seaboard.

An American naval vessel eventually sees the *Amistad* and captures it off the coast of Long Island, after which United States officials charge the Africans with murder and piracy. The issue of property rights also arises as the captured Africans become the focus of a three-way property dispute. Queen Isabella and Spain want their ship returned; the slave owners want what they consider their property returned; and the two crew members and the captain of the American ship that captured the Africans claim salvage rights. The ensuing three trials that the African men must endure before they are eventually freed by a Supreme Court decision show the great geographical schism of the United States, when the economic interests of the agricultural, slave-dependent South were in opposition to those of the industrialized North. In defending the men, the Abolitionists and their inexperienced young attorney argue that the Africans are human beings who defended themselves against their captors, not simply goods to be shuffled from one nation to another or from one owner to another. The breadth of the case draws in the aged former president John Quincy Adams, who sides against slavery and eloquently debates President Martin Van Buren, who is running for re-election and who appears willing to ignore justice in order to appease the slave-owning states whose votes he needs.

CENSORSHIP HISTORY

Nominated for Academy Awards in the United States, *Amistad* was received less than enthusiastically by Jamaica's government-appointed Jamaican Cinematographic Authority (CA) in 1998. After previewing the film, the authority determined that the opening scene, in which the mutinying slaves free themselves and then use machetes to kill the white slave traders was too violent and bloody for Jamaican audiences. The five-member group, which includes only one person who is employed in the film industry, demanded that the scene be cut from the film, arguing that more than 90% of the people living on Jamaica are descended from West African slaves and that the violent actions insulted their heritage. In defending this action, Reverend Stanford Webley, president of the authority, said that the board applied long-existing standards to the film and decided that *Amistad* is "an adult movie" and should be restricted to audiences aged 18 or older. Despite significant outcry from critics, who asserted that to censor the scene was to dilute the Carribean black history depicted in the film, the CA held its ground and Jamaican audiences viewed only the censored version.

In the United States, the Mormon Church-owned Brigham Young University in Provo, Utah, banned *Amistad* from the campus theater for its violence and nudity. Campus officials claimed *Amistad* would be too hard for them to edit, as they had done for SCHINDLER'S LIST in 1994, to provide a suitable version for campus viewing.

FURTHER READING

"Because It's Not Nice." *The Star-Ledger* (New Jersey), January 23, 1998, p. 3.

"Brigham Young University Bans Movie Amistad." *Jet*, February 9, 1998, p. 29.

Campbell, Howard. "Jamaican Censors Cut Opening Slave Ship Scenes from *Amistad*." Associated Press, February 17, 1998.

"Censors Cut Opening of *Amistad*." *Calgary Herald*, February 18, 1998, p. E3.

Hemblade, Christopher. "Chain Reaction." *Empire* (U.K.) 105 (March 1998): 74–79.

Jeffries, Neil. "Amistad." *Empire* (U.K.) (October 1998): 131.

Lemisch, Jesse. "Black Agency in the Amistad Uprising: or, You've Taken Our Cinque and Gone." *Souls: A Critical Journal of Black Politics, Culture, and Society* 1, no. 1 (Winter 1999): 57–70.

Schickel, Richard. "Amistad: A Paean to Past Agony." *The Arts/Culture* 150, no. 25 (December 15, 1997).

AMOK

Country and date of production: France, 1934

Production company/distributor: Pathé-Natan (France)/Pathé-Natan (France); Distinguished Films (United States, 1947)

Format: Sound, black and white

Running time: 92 minutes

Language: French

Producer: None identified

Director: Fyodor Otsep (as Fedor Ozep)

Screenwriters: André Lang, H. R. Lenormand, Stefan Zweig

Awards: None

Genre: Drama

With: Claude Barghon, Marcelle Chantal, Hubert Daix, Fréhel, Jean Galland, Madeleine Guitty, Soura Hari, Valéry Inkijinoff, Toshi Komori, Pierre Magnier, Jean Servais, Jean Yonnel

SUMMARY

Amok is a French adaptation of the short story "Der Amokläufer" ("The Madness Lover"), written by German author Stefan Zweig and directed by Russian emigré Fyodor Otsep. Although the early scenes are romantically surreal, the story explores the consequences of compulsive love and shows with harsh realism the manner in which an irrational madness can sometimes take hold beneath the surface of respectable society. The first 11 minutes of the film, during which the characters and their obsessions are revealed, provide only a visual story, with no dialogue. The film takes place on a French colonial island and revolves around a physician's obsessive passion for the wife of a wealthy landowner who has been away from the island for a year. The wife has had an affair and become pregnant, and she asks the physician to perform an abortion before her husband returns. At first the physician refuses, but then later hints that he will do what she asks if they can become lovers. Unwilling to meet his terms, the wife visits a native herb doctor in desperation, and the attempted abortion ends her life. As the physician treats the dying woman and tries to save her, he promises to keep her secret and later tells her husband that she died of a heart attack. The husband decides to take the body to Europe to have an autopsy performed, but the physician thwarts this plan. Determined to keep his promise, the physician arrives at the ship as the casket is being raised to the deck by a rope and pulley. He darts forward and cuts the rope and then falls into the water with the casket to die.

CENSORSHIP HISTORY

In 1946, the New York State Board of Censors reviewed the film and denied the American distributor, Distinguished Films, a license to exhibit unless the company would agree to cut several minutes containing dialogue between the physician and the wife regarding the proposed abortion and the scenes immediately preceding, during and after the abortion performed by the herb doctor. The board determined that the film was "indecent, immoral, tends to corrupt morals," and required that the changes be made before it would reconsider granting the film a license. Distinguished Films appealed the decision in a case heard before the New York State Supreme Court, Appellate Division, arguing that the film was "no more sordid or gross than many which have been approved." The court failed to agree, noting instead that the "standard in matters of this kind is flexible," and affirmed the decision to ban the film. In a written decision, Justice James P. Hill expressed a view that even the suggested cuts would not improve the chances that the film would be granted a license because the theme of the film would remain clear, and the court found "understandable that some reviewing bodies would think this film offended."

FURTHER READING

Carmen, Ira H. *Movies, Censorship and the Law.* Ann Arbor: University of Michigan Press, 1966.
De Grazia, Edward, and Roger K. Newman. *Banned Films: Movies, Censors and the First Amendment.* New York: R. R. Bowker Company, 1982.
Distinguished Films v. Stoddard, 68 N.Y.S. 2d 737 (1947).

ANATOMY OF A MURDER

Country and date of production: United States, 1959
Production company/distributor: Carlyle Productions/Columbia Pictures
Format: Sound, black and white
Running time: 160 minutes
Language: English
Producer: Otto Preminger
Director: Otto Preminger
Screenwriters: Robert Traver (novel), Wendell Mayes
Awards: 1960 British Academy Awards, Best Film from any Source (Otto Preminger).
1960 Grammy Awards, Best Sound Track Album–Background Score from Motion Picture or Television (Duke Ellington).
1959 New York Film Critics Circle Awards, Best Actor (James Stewart), Best Screenplay (Wendell Mayes).
1959 Venice Film Festival, Volpi Cup for Best Actor (James Stewart).
Genre: Drama
With: James Stewart (Paul Biegler), Lee Remick (Laura Manion), Ben Gazzara (Lieutenant Manion), Arthur O'Connell (Parnell McCarthy), Eve Arden (Maida Rutledge), Kathryn Grant (Mary Pilant), George C. Scott (Claude Dancer), Orson Bean (Dr. Smith), Russ Brown (Mr. Lemon), Murray Hamilton (Paquette), Brooks West (Mitch Lodwick), Ken Lynch (Sergeant Durgo), John Qualen (Sulo), Howard McNear (Dr. Dompierre), Alexander Campbell (Dr. Harcourt), Ned Wever (Dr. Raschid), Jimmy Conlin (Madigan), Royal Beal (Sheriff Battisfore)

SUMMARY

The movie is based on the best-selling 1958 novel written by Robert Traver, the nom de plume of a Michigan judge who insisted that the story was fiction, although the details in the novel strongly resemble an actual murder that took place in Michigan in 1952. The story, set primarily in a courtroom, revolves around the killing of a bar owner by an army lieutenant, Manion, who claims that he acted in a passionate rage following the rape of his wife by the bar owner. The defense of Manion falls to Paul Biegler who, since being voted out of office as local prosecutor, has spent more time fishing than keeping up his law practice. Biegler agrees to defend the lieutenant, who is an uncooperative, crude hothead. The case is further complicated by the behavior of Laura Manion; although she claims to have been recently raped, she acts seductively toward most of the men around her and flirts openly with her husband's attorney. Biegler appears to face insurmountable odds. The presiding judge is from out of town; the prosecution uses both the local district attorney and a sharp district attorney from a large city elsewhere in the state, both of whom confidently expect to demolish the defense of the less-sophisticated Biegler. As the story unfolds, the audience soon begins to question the motivations of the murderer, his wife and the victim. The story of rape and revenge seems plausible enough on the surface, and the testimony of an army psychiatrist seems to support the claim that Manion was temporarily insane. Yet, as details of the characters' lives emerge, whether Laura really was raped is called into question, as is the contention about her husband's mental state.

CENSORSHIP HISTORY

In 1959, the city of Chicago invoked an ordinance inaugurated in 1907 to refuse Columbia Pictures a license to exhibit *Anatomy of a Murder*. The city board of censors, headed by the superintendent of police, objected to the film because of its use of such terms as "rape," "sperm," "penetration" and "contraception" in the testimony at the trial. The board members also objected to Laura Manion's account of the rape and argued that the combination of such terminology with the description of the forced act made the film obscene according to the city ordinance. Representing Columbia Pictures, producer and director Otto Preminger brought suit against the city in the United States District Court for the Northern District of Illinois. He petitioned the court to direct Chicago to grant a license to exhibit the film and to end all further attempts to block the showing of the film.

In rendering a decision, the court determined that the board of censors had "exceeded constitutional bounds" and it reversed the decision of the board. In making a determination, Judge Julius H. Miner applied the measure established by *Roth v. United States*, 354 U.S. 476 (1957) in regard to books and plays, requiring that the work must "be judged as a whole in terms of its effect on the average, normal reader or viewer." He determined that the medical terminology used in the trial was unlikely to "so much arouse the salacity of the normal and average viewer as to outweigh its artistic and expert presentation." In contrast to the objections voiced by the city censors in regard to Laura Manion's description of the rape, Judge Miner wrote that it "has the effect of arousing pity and revulsion rather than desire or sexual impure thoughts."

FURTHER READING

Carmen, Ira H. *Movies, Censorship and the Law*. Ann Arbor: University of Michigan Press, 1966.
Columbia Pictures Corp. v. Chicago, 184 F. Supp. 817 (1959).
Schumach, Murray. *The Face on the Cutting Room Floor*. New York: William Morrow, 1964.
"Too Much Anatomy." *Richmond News Ledger*, August 5, 1959, p. 50.
Traver, Robert. *Anatomy of a Murder*. New York: St. Martin's Press, 1958.

AND GOD CREATED WOMAN

Country and date of production: France, 1956 (as *Et Dieu créa la femme*); released in United Kingdom as *And Woman Was Created*, 1956; in United States as *And God Created Woman*, 1957

Production company/distributor: Cocinor (France)/Kingsley International

Format: Sound, color

Running time: 95 minutes

Language: French

Producer: Raoul J. Lévy

Director: Roger Vadim

Screenwriters: Roger Vadim, Raoul Lévy

Genre: Drama

With: Brigitte Bardot (Juliette Hardy), Curt Jürgens (Eric Carradine), Jean-Louis Trintignant (Michel Tardieu), Christian Marquand (Antoine Tardieu), Marie Glory (Mme. Tardieu), Georges Poujouly (Christian Tardieu), Jane Marken (Madame Morin), Jean Tissier (M. Vigier-Lefranc), Isabelle Corey (Lucienne), Jacqueline Ventura (Mme Vigier-Lefranc), Jacques Ciron (Roger), Paul Faivre (M. Morin), Jany Mourey (Jeune femme), Philippe Grenier (Perri), Jean Lefebvre (Rene, as Jean Lefèvre), Léopoldo Francès (Danseur), Jean Toscano (Rene, as Toscano)

SUMMARY

And God Created Woman, by director Roger Vadim's own admission, cast Brigitte Bardot as "every married man's fantasy" in the role of Juliette, an 18-year-old orphan who becomes the sexy and amoral girl-wife of one man and the object of desire for two others. Working at a newsstand and living in St. Tropez with a couple who have threatened to send her back to the orphanage if she doesn't conform to accepted behavior, she seems unaware of the power that her physical attractiveness has over men. Juliette and Antoine, the elder son of a fishing family, are sexually attracted to each other, but before any intimacy takes place, she overhears him telling other men in the washroom that she is the type of woman for a one-night stand, not someone with whom to build a life. When he later tries to make love to her, Juliette rebuffs him. When Antoine is away, his younger brother Michel, who worships Juliette, asks her to marry him and she accepts because she likes him, even if she does not feel passion for him. The marriage also will give her a home of her own and eliminate the threat of being sent away. The two seem happy for a time, but Antoine returns and begins to prey upon Juliette. He continuously tries to be alone with her, and he finally succeeds. The two are discovered embracing passionately on the beach and express no regret at their actions, leading Michel to become deeply depressed. Eric Carradine, a rich businessman who has tried to buy the property that the brothers live on so he can build a casino, has witnessed Juliette sunbathing in the nude and has also waited for his chance with her. He approaches her while she is vulnerable and offers her sympathy and liquor. She becomes drunk and begins to dance sensuously and without inhibition, until her husband grows angry and beats her.

CENSORSHIP HISTORY

And God Created Woman joined THE LOVERS (1958) and LADY CHATTERLEY'S LOVER (1957) in providing American audiences with new forms of artistic vision and frank sensuality previously unseen in Hollywood productions. Even more important, their popularity led to more films that dealt with human sexuality on an adult level and, in turn, a greater number of challenges that would land in the courts and eventually provide victories for film distributors and the public. *And God Created Woman* was challenged by the Legion of Decency in every city in which it was distributed, but it nonetheless managed to obtain licensing for exhibition in the states of New York, Maryland and Virginia. Despite protests, it was also shown in various cities in the states of California, Illinois, Kentucky, Missouri, Ohio, Oregon, Pennsylvania, Texas and Washington. In 1958, a city-appointed board in Philadelphia conducted a private viewing of the film three weeks before it was scheduled to begin public exhibition in the city. After the showing, theater owners in Philadelphia received a denial of the right to exhibit from a city assistant district attorney who wrote that state law declared illegal the showing of any film "of lascivious, sacrilegious, obscene, indecent, or immoral nature," and that *And God Created Woman* met four of the five objections. The warning cautioned theater owners that exhibiting the film could result in their arrest and in seizure of the film. Two theater owners who had planned to show the film took the caution seriously: They informed both the district attorney and the United States distributor of the film, Kingsley International, that they would break their contract and not show the film.

When this occurred, Kingsley International filed suit with the Philadelphia Court of Common Appeals and argued that the requirements of constitutional due process had not been satisfied because the statute was too vague and that the movie had not been proved obscene in a court of law. Lawyers for the distributor asked for an injunction to allow the showing of the film without interference from the office of the district attorney and asserted that without the injunction the distributor would suffer "irreparable injury." Theater owners were permitted to show the film during the week that the court took to consider the distributor's request, and the film played to packed audiences who were aware that they might not have the same opportunity the following week.

When the Philadelphia Court of Common Appeals denied the request by Kingsley International for the injunction, the office of the district attorney sent law enforcement officers to the theaters to seize the film and to arrest the theater managers. In response, lawyers for Kingsley International filed an appeal with the Supreme Court of Pennsylvania, which reversed the decision of the lower court. While acknowledging that the office of the district attorney "is required to enforce the obscenity statutes," the court wrote that the district attorney had directed criminal prosecution proceedings against the theater owners and not the distributor, thus leaving the distributor open to "irreparable injury" because he was not a party in the criminal proceeding and, thus, had no legal right nor means of protecting his interests.

FURTHER READING

Giglio, Ernest David. *The Decade of the Miracle, 1952–1962: A Study in the Censorship of the American Motion Picture.* Doctoral dissertation, Syracuse University, 1964. Ann Arbor: University Microfilms International.
Kingsley International Pictures Corporation v. Blanc, 153 A. 2d 243 (1959).
Miller, Frank. *Censored Hollywood: Sex, Sin and Violence on Screen.* Atlanta, Ga.: Turner Publishing, 1994.
Schumach, Murray. *The Face on the Cutting Room Floor.* New York: William Morrow, 1964.

ANNA AND THE KING

Country and date of production: United States, 1999
Production company/distributor: Fox 2000 Pictures/20th Century Fox Film Corporation (United States)
Format: Sound, color (Technicolor)
Running time: 147 minutes
Language: English
Producers: Lawrence Bender, G. Mac Brown, Terence Chang, Ed Elbert, Jon J. Jashni, Julie Kirkham, Wink Mordaunt
Director: Andy Tennant
Screenwriters: Steeve Meerson, Peter Krikes
Awards: 2000 Academy Awards, Best Art Direction (Luciana Arrighi), Best Set Direction (Ian Whittaker).
2000 Golden Globes, Best Original Musical Score (George Fenton).
2000 Golden Satellite Awards, Best Art Direction/Production Design (Luciana Arrighi, Lek Chaiyan Chunsuttiwat, Paul Ghirardani, John Ralph).
2000 Young Artist Awards, Best Family Feature (Drama).
Genre: Drama/romance
With: Jodie Foster (Anna Leonowens), Chow Yun-Fat (King Mongkut), Ling Bai (Tuptim), Tom Felton (Louis), Syed Alwi (The Kralahome), Randall Duk Kim (General Alak), Lim Kay Siu (Prince Chowfa), Melissa Campbell (II) (Princess Fa-Ying), Keith Chin (Prince Chulalongkorn), Mano Maniam (Moonshee), Shanthini Venugopal (Beebe), Deanna Yusoff (Lady Thiang)

SUMMARY

This is the fourth film that has been made based on events in Bangkok, Siam, in 1862 when a British governess was hired by the king's court to teach his many children (more than 50, from his many wives and concubines). The first two films, *Anna and the King of Siam* (1946), starring Irene Dunne and Rex Harrison, and *The King and I* (1956), a musical starring Deborah Kerr and Yul Brynner, are classics. The plot focuses on a widowed British schoolteacher, Anna Leonowens, who goes to Siam (now Thailand) with her young son after spending 20 years in India. She hasn't forgotten her British ways because, as she says, "India is English. That's what being colonized is all about." In a reflection of her times, she believes "the ways of England are the ways of the world." Anna is a strong woman who cares little about protocol around King Mongkut and insists on being treated as his equal—quite an aberration in a court where all subjects are required to drop to their knees and touch their foreheads to the ground when the king appears. Anna is not intimidated by the king's presence and he, having never encountered such insolence, is intrigued by her. He learns to admire Anna when she reprimands both her own son and the king's for fighting in class. Sparks begin to ignite between Anna and the king, and even the restrictions by which they are bound at that time in history and in that society do not diminish the emotion they feel. The plot also includes a political storyline about a traitor in the Siamese army who tries to overthrow the king, as well as a diversion about young lovers whose lives are affected by Anna's meddling.

CENSORSHIP HISTORY

When *Anna and the King* was released, the government of Thailand sent informational releases to its diplomatic and consular representatives around the world informing them that citizens of Thailand could face jail for owning a copy of the movie. The chairman of the Thailand Board of Censors, the body that banned the Hollywood film, urged police to prosecute anyone in Thailand who sold, owned or screened a copy of the film. Anyone convicted of the offense would face up to one year in jail or a heavy fine, or both. Informed of Thailand's stance, 20th Century Fox decided not to appeal the ban on the movie, but Thai police were forced to deal with an influx of illegal videocassettes and videodisks. In one day, police arrested a man and a woman in the Pratunam area and seized 400 videocassettes of the film. The basis for the ban, according to Thai film censors, was the film's irreverent and historically inaccurate portrayal of the country's beloved monarchy, especially King Mongkut, which they claimed was insulting to the royal family.

The ruling is based on the 1930 censorship law which prohibits filmmakers from portraying the Thai monarchy in a way that does not give it due respect, the censor board chairman, Police Maj. Gen. Prakat Sataman, said at a news conference. He declared the movie illegal and ordered police to aggressively pursue confiscation of pirated video disks and tapes that were available in Bangkok. The Thai board of censors, comprised of 19 people, including historians, journalists and Thai film industry representatives, found 30 objections in the film. Such scenes as the king angrily hitting his crown so hard that it falls to the ground were deemed "extremely unacceptable" because they show the monarch mistreating a symbol of his authority. Censors also objected to a scene in which Anna kisses one of the king's daughters on the lips to say good night, as well as to scenes that imply that Anna and Mongkut were romantically involved. One member of the board of censors, a university history lecturer named Thepmontree Limphapayom, claimed that "the film could be shown here if it was cut, but after the cutting it would probably last only about 20 minutes."

The royal family, which screened the film, claimed to have had no major quibbles with it or with any of the three previous versions, all also banned in Thailand, aside from historical inaccuracy. Prince Chatri, a nephew of the current king Bhumibol, dismissed the background story as the result of flights of fancy by a highly imaginative Anna Leonowens, and censors contended that King Mongkut was a refined scholar, not the dancing despot he has been portrayed.

FURTHER READING

Delorme, Gérard. "Anna and the King." *Première* (France), February/March 2000, p. 56.
Gleiberman, Owen. "Anna And The King (C+)." *Entertainment Weekly* 520, no. 1, January 7, 2000, p. 42.
Khaikaew, Thaksina. "'Anna and the King' Challenged." *Associated Press,* September 28, 1999.
Levy, Emanuel. "'King' and Eye-Popping Pageantry." *Variety* 377, no. 4A (December 1999): 83–84.
"Reasons for Banning 'Anna and the King'." *The Nation,* January 7, 2000, p. 11.
Sangster, Jim. "Anna and the King." *Film Review* (U.K.), January 2000, p. 24.
Sauter, Michael. "Video: Anna And The King." *Entertainment Weekly* 1, no. 546, June 23, 2000, p. 76.

ANN VICKERS

Country and date of production: United States, 1933
Production company/distributor: RKO Radio Pictures Inc./RKO Pictures
Format: Sound, black and white
Running time: 72 minutes
Language: English
Producers: Pandro S. Berman, Merian C. Cooper
Director: John Cromwell
Screenwriters: Sinclair Lewis (novel), Jane Murfin
Awards: None

Genre: Drama
With: Irene Dunne (Ann Vickers), Walter Huston (Barney Dolphin), Conrad Nagel (Lindsay Atwell), Bruce Cabot (Captain Resnick), Edna May Oliver (Malvina Wormser), Mitchell Lewis (Captain Waldo), Murray Kinnell (Dr. Slenk), Helen Eby-Rock (Kitty Cognac), Gertrude Michael (Mona Dolphin), J. Carrol Naish (Dr. Sorell), Sarah Padden (Lil), Reginald Barlow (Chaplain), Rafaela Ottiano (Feldermus)

SUMMARY

A review in *Variety* in 1933 blithely predicted that the tried-and-true plot would make *Ann Vickers* profitable at the box office, for "her [the heroine's] sufferings are bearable and her ultimate happiness is assured, so this is vicarious enjoyment for any woman. Lovely romance, moderate penance, final respectability. All of which suggests that *Ann Vickers* should do moderately good biz." Based on the best-selling novel by Sinclair Lewis, the film tells the story of Ann Vickers, a young woman who graduates from an elite liberal arts college and moves to New York City to become a social worker in a settlement house shortly before World War I. She meets and falls in love with a young army captain, by whom she becomes pregnant. After Ann sees him with another woman, she realizes that he does not love her, so she has an abortion. Although she vows to devote herself solely to her work, Ann later marries a man who is good to her but whom she finds very dull. She begins to build a reputation as a reformer, advocating for birth control, improved welfare and better housing for the poor.

Tammany Hall judge Barney Dolphin arranges a job in a prison for Ann, and she is caught in an uprising in which the women inmates rebel and riot. In the aftermath, she becomes radicalized after seeing one inmate hanged and another whipped. When Ann protests such abuse of inmates she is told to resign, but she refuses until she is framed and blackmailed. The experience inspires her to write a successful book on prison life in which she exposes the prevalence of drugs and sex and the brutal abuse of prisoners by their jailers. The success of the book leads to the offer of a top position in a prison that she can reform. When the prison board learns that she is having an affair with Dolphin while continuing to live with her husband, however, it tries to remove Ann from her job. She fights for and wins the right to stay, but tragedy strikes again when Dolphin is jailed for corruption just as Ann discovers that she is pregnant with his child. While the former judge serves time in prison, Ann leaves her husband and gives birth to a son. When Dolphin is pardoned after three years, he and Ann resume their relationship without concern for conventional morality.

CENSORSHIP HISTORY

The film was one of many that were made after Father Daniel J. Lord, S.J., the architect of the Hays Code and a leader of the Catholic Legion of

Decency (LOD), urged Will Hays to make films about American heroes, but the screen portrayal of a reformer who advocates birth control and carries on a torrid extramarital love affair was not what they had in mind. RKO Radio Pictures knew before filming began that *Ann Vickers* would excite controversy because the novel had been openly attacked in the Catholic press and was forbidden reading for American Catholics. In 1933, the Jesuit publication *America* labeled the novel "obscene," while *Catholic World* had warned readers to "stay at a safe distance from this book" and charged Lewis with delighting in portraying "the refuse, the garbage, the dumps, the cesspools." As Mark Schorer wrote in *Sinclair Lewis: An American Life*, other readers with no specific religious affiliation labeled Lewis a "disgusting, obscene maggot" for writing the "stinking and filthy" novel *Ann Vickers*.

The reputation of the story was well known by the time that RKO submitted the script to the Studio Relations Committee (SRC) in May 1933. SRC head James Wingate and his assistant Joseph Breen condemned that script at the outset for being "vulgarly offensive" and for its "patent attempt to build up sympathy for the leading character," whom they considered to be immoral, while it also violated the "sanctity of marriage" clauses of the SRC agreement with the studios. Wingate and Breen informed RKO that the script offered no "moral lesson," nor did it put the heroine through a "moral struggle." According to the production code, a major character who shows such "utter disregard for the conventions of society" must suffer the "condemnation of this flaunting of the laws of convention," but Ann Vickers is an intelligent, attractive and well-educated professional who shows no remorse for her actions. These objections led the SRC to deny approval to the script and to offer, instead, the "unanimous opinion of our staff that the present treatment violates the spirit and the letter of the code."

Merian Cooper, RKO vice president in charge of production, defended the integrity of the script. He admitted that the material was controversial but vowed that the movie would not "pander to cheap sex, nor to cheap and vulgar emotions." Although RKO head B. B. Kahane protested in writing to Will Hays, president of the Motion Picture Producers and Distributors Association, that the attitude of the SRC was "quite discouraging and disturbing," the studio suggested that it might be willing to rewrite the script to make the main character suffer for her sexual transgressions and to eliminate the threat of adultery by making Ann Vickers unmarried when she has her affair. She would be made to suffer further by losing from her job because of the scandal over one of her affairs, after which she would live life of poverty and be shunned by her friends. When Wingate and Breen reviewed the modified script, they made further demands that the film include "a definite affirmative denouncement" of the character's transgressions made by a "spokesman for accepted morality." Angry at this demand, Kahane argued that Hays should assemble a jury to assess the original script because the SRC seemed to hold too narrow an interpretation of the Production Code.

Hays backed away from that demand and wrote what he thought was a mollifying letter to RKO. He reminded the studio that the Code was clear in stating the necessity "to establish in the minds of the audience that adultery is *wrong, unjustified* and *indefensible.*" RKO revolted and Kahane bluntly told the SRC that the studio did not feel compelled to make any changes with which it did not agree, although scriptwriters did modify the material sufficiently to earn the Production Code Administration seal of approval. By making Ann unmarried at the time she has the affair, the threat of adultery was eliminated.

Upon release, the film was immediately placed upon the condemned list of the Catholic Legion of Decency (LOD), which launched a national crusade and gained the signatures of millions of Catholics in the United States who pledged to boycott all movies that Catholic Church officials judged to be immoral.

FURTHER READING

"Ann Vickers." Catholic World 36 (February 1933): 622.

Black, Gregory D. *Hollywood Censored: Morality Codes, Catholics, and the Movies.* New York: Cambridge University Press, 1994.

Doherty, Thomas. *Pre-Code Hollywood: Sex, Immorality, and Insurrection in American Cinema, 1930–1934.* New York: Columbia University Press, 1999.

McLaughlin, Mary L. "A Study of the National Catholic Office for Motion Pictures." Ph.D. dissertation in speech, Indiana University, 1974.

Schorer, Mark. *Sinclair Lewis: An American Life.* New York: McGraw-Hill, 1961.

Talbot, Francis X., S.J. "More on Smut." *America* 48 (February 25, 1933): 500–501.

BABY DOLL

Country and date of production: United States, 1956
Production company/distributor: Newtown Productions/Warner Bros.
Format: Sound, black and white
Running time: 114 minutes
Language: English
Producers: Elia Kazan, Tennessee Williams
Director: Elia Kazan
Screenwriter: Tennessee Williams
Awards: 1957 British Academy Awards, Most Promising Newcomer (Eli Wallach), Best Film From Any Source.
1957 Golden Globes, Best Motion Picture Director (Elia Kazan)
Genre: Drama/tragicomedy
With: Karl Malden (Archie Lee Meighan), Carroll Baker (Baby Doll), Eli Wallach (Silva Vacarro), Mildred Dunnock (Aunt Rose Comfort), Lonny Chapman (Rock), Eades Hogue (Town Marshal), Noah Williamson (Deputy)

SUMMARY

Baby Doll is the result of the combination and expansion of two one-act plays written by Tennessee Williams, *Twenty-Seven Wagons Full of Cotton* and *An Unsatisfying Supper*. The film begins with the view of a young, scantily dressed blonde woman lying in a crib with the side down, as a middle-aged balding man peeks lecherously at her through a hole in the wall. Curled up and sucking her thumb, she is peacefully asleep until she hears the scraping sound of the man's attempt to enlarge the hole so that he can gain a better view of her provocatively posed body. She sneaks out of the crib and walks quietly into the adjacent room, where she confronts Archie Lee Meighan, her husband. A failed cotton-gin owner, Meighan eagerly awaits the following day when his childish bride, whom he calls "Baby Doll," will turn 20 years of age. When they married two years earlier, Meighan had promised her now-deceased father that he would not consummate the marriage until she reached that age.

After Baby Doll berates her husband for his peeping, he receives a telephone call from the furniture company threatening repossession and engages in an argument with Baby Doll's simpleminded Aunt Rose Comfort, who also lives in his decrepit mansion. Frustrated with his failures, Meighan shouts for his wife to join him as he heads for a doctor's appointment in town. On their way home, they pass one of the furniture repossession trucks filled with their furniture, and he finds that Syndicate Cotton Gin, a new competitor that forced him and other local gin owners out of business, is holding a celebration after its first successful year. Later that night, Meighan retrieves a can of kerosene from his pickup truck and sets the Syndicate Cotton Gin building on fire.

The following day, Silva Vacarro, manager of the burned-down gin, arrives at Meighan's dilapidated property. He arranges for Meighan to gin his cotton until the Syndicate Gin can be rebuilt and promises to bring 27 wagons of cotton later in the day. Vacarro suspects Meighan of having set the fire and pursues Baby Doll, hoping to convince her to sign a statement attesting that her husband committed arson. After teasing and taunting Baby Doll, who writhes sensually in her swing seat, Vacarro reminds her that her husband has said the world runs on the principle of "tit for tat." He prepares to pay Meighan back for the burned-down gin by seducing Baby Doll. She is aroused by his attentions, but she makes one last attempt to resist the new sensations that he has excited in her and goes to the gin, where her husband is repairing broken machinery. Aggravated that she has entered the work area against his orders not to do so when the workers are around, Meighan slaps and shouts at her. After Meighan goes to town to obtain parts, Vacarro makes his move in the empty house. He first terrorizes Baby Doll into signing a statement that identifies Meighan as the arsonist and then pretends to leave but returns when Baby Doll expresses disappointment.

The two are still in Baby Doll's crib when Meighan returns, but Baby Doll descends the staircase alone, wearing only a silk slip. Newly awakened to her sexuality, she is not intimidated when her husband verbally assaults her. She ignores him and walks onto the porch in full view of several men working across the road. When Vacarro also descends the staircase, Meighan realizes what has occurred and threatens him. Vacarro coolly tells Meighan that he came to obtain proof of the arson and that is all, although he admits to being attracted by Baby Doll. Meighan grabs a shotgun and runs after Vacarro while Baby Doll calls the police, who arrive to handcuff Meighan and take him away. As the sheriff's car leaves, the clock strikes midnight and Meighan calls out: "Today's my Baby Doll's birthday." Before Vacarro leaves, he tells Baby Doll that he will return the next day, but she is not sure that he will—and neither is Aunt Rose, whom Vacarro promised a job. The movie ends with a view of the sheriff's car driving into the night with Archie and a silhouette view of the decaying mansion.

CENSORSHIP HISTORY

When first released, *Baby Doll* was denounced as salacious, revolting, dirty, steamy, lewd, suggestive, morally repellent and provocative. A review in *Time* magazine stated that it was "the dirtiest American-made motion picture that has ever been legally exhibited." So strong was the public outcry against the film that many theaters were forced to cancel their showings. Despite such opposition, the movie did well at the box office because the film themes of sexual repression, lust, seduction, moral decay and human corruption appealed to a large number of theatergoers. The screenplay experienced a lengthy delay of three years from the initial objections to the original script raised by the Production Code Administration (PCA) to the final writing of the screenplay for the movie, which eliminated overt implications that Vacarro had seduced Baby Doll and treated with greater delicacy Meighan's sexual frustration. Elia Kazan refused to make one of the major changes suggested, the swing scene, which the PCA claimed exhibited too clear a seduction to the point of suggesting that Baby Doll is having orgasmic physical reactions.

Although the PCA eventually granted the movie its seal of approval, the Catholic Legion of Decency (LOD) attacked the film fiercely. When the movie was released in New York City, the leader of the New York archdiocese, Francis Cardinal Spellman, denounced it from the pulpit of St. Patrick's Cathedral midway through a solemn mass on December 16, 1956. Spellman expressed shock that the film industry would approve such a film that represented a "definitive corruptive moral influence" on American society. He also reminded churchgoers that the film had been condemned by the Legion of Decency (LOD) and that viewing the movie would constitute a sin that would threaten their souls.

Although Protestant leaders challenged Spellman's view and defended the "essential morality" of the film, all religious groups agreed that the manner in which Warner advertised the film was objectionable. Posters portrayed a pouting, scantily clad Carroll Baker posed seductively either standing against a doorframe or curled in her crib and sucking her thumb. An editorial published in *Commonweal* stated that "if, in the case of *Baby Doll*, its producers consider it a serious and artistic treatment of an adult theme, they have no business advertising it in the way they have. If Hollywood wants to make adult pictures and be taken seriously as an artistic medium, movie advertising should not suggest that the industry is simply a highly organized scheme to merchandise French postcards that talk." Catholics picketed theaters that exhibited the film, and many theaters throughout the United States also received bomb threats. In some cities, priests waited in theater lobbies to identify and write the names of parishioners who defied the LOD condemnation. When the bishops and archbishops representing the LOD demanded six-month boycotts against the theaters, the American Civil Liberties Union (ACLU) intervened. The ACLU declared that the action was "contrary to the spirit of free expression in the First Amendment. It can threaten theater's existence, and may deny to other groups within the community a chance to see films of their choice."

In Aurora, Illinois, city residents attended a large meeting at the city hall to demand that city officials put a halt to the showing of *Baby Doll*. The city entered a complaint with the Circuit Court of Kane County, claiming that the scene in which Baby Doll lies on the floor and Vacarro stands above her with one foot moving in a circular motion on her stomach was "scandalous, indecent, immoral, lewd, and obscene . . . [and] displays an arousal of her sexual passion." A court affidavit condemned the film as "an open and flagrant violation of public morals and decency" and found that the suggested "infidelity of an underaged wife is most dangerous and revolting." The court granted a request by the city for a temporary injunction to prevent exhibition of the film in Aurora. Warner Bros. appealed the decision, but the Appellate Court of Illinois affirmed the decision of the lower court.

FURTHER READING

"Baby Doll." *Commonweal*, 65 (January 11, 1957): 372.
"Baby Doll." *Variety*, January 9, 1957, p. 13.
"Cinema." *Time* 68 (December 24, 1956): 61.
City of Aurora v. Warner Bros. Pictures Distributing Corporation, 147 N.E. 2d 694 (1958).
Jowett, Garth. *The Democratic Art: A Social History of the American Film*. Boston: Little, Brown, 1976.
Miller, Frank. *Censored Hollywood: Sex, Sin and Violence on Screen*. Atlanta, Ga.: Turner Publishing, 1994.
Schumach, Murray. *The Face on the Cutting Room Floor*. New York: William Morrow, 1964.

BABY FACE

Country and date of production: United States, 1933
Production company/distributor: Warner Bros.

Format: Sound, black and white
Running time: 70 minutes
Language: English
Producer: Raymond Griffith
Director: Alfred E. Green
Screenwriters: Gene Markey, Kathryn Scola, Darryl F. Zanuck (as Mark Canfield; story)
Awards: None
Genre: Drama
With: Barbara Stanwyck (Lily Powers), George Brent (Trenholm), Donald Cook (Stevens), Alphonse Ethier (Cragg), Henry Kolker (Carter), Margaret Lindsay (Ann Carter), Arthur Hohl (Sipple), John Wayne (Jimmy McCoy), Robert Barrat (Nick Powers), Douglass Dumbrille (Brody), Theresa Harris (Chico)

SUMMARY

Baby Face relates the manner in which an ambitious small-town girl uses her sexual power to manipulate men as she moves from tending bar in her father's Prohibition-era speakeasy to a life of luxury in New York City. Lily Powers wants more from life than she will receive by working in a basement speakeasy in an industrial town. When her father dies after an illegal still explodes, she moves to New York with Chico, a young African-American woman from the town who will serve as her maid. Lily looks for work in a bank despite her apparent lack of education and business skills. Although untrained in office work, Lily uses her physical attractiveness to convince bank personnel manager Jimmy McCoy to approach his boss, Brody, to provide a job for her at the bank. Once hired, Lily begins to use her physical assets to move up in the bank hierarchy, pushing McCoy aside as she meets and charms increasingly more powerful men. She first works for Brody, who is later fired, after which Lily convinces his successor Stevens to make her his receptionist. Brody calls her and attempts to maintain the relationship that he thinks he has had with Lily, but she has moved on to a more powerful prey. Stevens is engaged to another woman, but he cannot resist Lily's seductiveness, which leads to a night out during which they drink a little too much and kiss passionately. A few days later at the office, Lily hugs Stevens as his fiancée Ann Carter, daughter of the bank president, walks in sees them, and then runs to cry on her father's shoulder. As a man of the world, Carter understands the power that women like Lily exude, so he tells Stevens to fire her. He implies that Stevens will suffer no repercussions for his misstep but directs him to take some time off. When Stevens fires Lily but suggests that their relationship continue, she kisses him and tells him that the firing will end their relationship. On the pretense of making his position clear, Carter tells Lily that Stevens is engaged, a fact she pretends not to have known as she cries and claims she loves Stevens. Carter asks Lily to join him for dinner, during which

Lily exerts more of her charm and suggests that he give her money. She and Carter begin a relationship.

The film implies that Lily becomes Carter's mistress: Carter moves Lily, with her maid, into a penthouse apartment, and she begins to wear furs and diamonds. Meanwhile, Stevens continues to love Lily and tries to see her, but she refuses. Finally, a deranged Stevens barges into Lily's apartment, shouting that he will kill himself if Lily won't marry him, but he finds only Carter. The camera leaves the scene, and shots are heard. When Lily appears, she finds both men dead, and the newspapers report the incident as a murder-suicide. When the police arrive, Lily claims that she is simply "a victim of circumstance."

But Lily has one more conquest to make. The newspapers offer her $15,000 for her story, and the bank, hoping to maintain dignity by keeping the story out of the papers, offers to match whatever the papers are offering. During a meeting with the bank board of officers, Lily meets Trenholm, the new president, who suggests that the bank send her to France to work at the Paris branch. Lily accepts the offer, and when Trenholm visits the Paris branch, the two enjoy dining and dancing. Trenholm confesses his love for her, and they are married. To keep Lily in furs and diamonds, Trenhold skims money from the bank, which leads to its collapse. Trenholm is indicted and must make up for the losses. When he asks Lily for the money he gave her, she refuses and prepares to travel; then she changes her mind, only to find that Trenholm has attempted suicide. Chastened, Lily cries and promises to give him everything. The film ends with the board announcing that Lily has provided money to save the bank and that she and Trenholm have gone to work in the industrial town she had fought so hard to escape. The ending was not part of the original film script, which left Trenholm dead, and Lily unrepentant and poised to find yet another wealthy man as a victim.

CENSORSHIP HISTORY

According to Frank Miller, author of *Censored Hollywood*, *Baby Face* is "the most notorious of the sex-in-the-workplace films of the pre-Code era." Joe Breen, head of the Production Code Administration (PCA), categorized the film as a "Class I" movie when the PCA was fully operational in July 1934, which meant that it was removed from current release and was designated never to be re-released. Because of these actions, *Baby Face* was not seen again until the fine grain original prints were transferred to videotape in the late 1980s. The overall objection to the film was that it glorifies vice in a number of instances. In the original script, Lily's father, owner of a speakeasy, forces her to dance at all-male parties, to have sexual relationships with various men who can benefit him and to dance almost nude for the cash that men in the speakeasy are willing to pay. When she turns to an old German cobbler in her town, he quotes the philosopher Friedrich Nietzsche and counsels her to use her youth and beauty and to "use men, not let them use you." Once Lily has escaped to New York City, she begins a series of affairs with men of increasing professional power and eventually becomes the mistress of a bank president.

James Wingate, head of the Motion Picture Producers and Distributors Association (MPPDA), advised Darryl Zanuck, head of production at Warner Bros., to downplay "the element of sex" and to punish Lily by having her lose her money and her husband, whom she loves. Wingate also suggested that the script would not pass if the studio did not strengthen the "moral value" of the film by making Lily lose all of her money and jewels and return to the small industrial town from which she had escaped. Zanuck was also directed to delete several "objectionable" lines, such as "Is it your first [sexual experience]?" and "I know you have had many lovers before." The studio was also told to tone down the suggestions that Lily's father had forced her into prostitution and that she was using sex to make her way in New York City. It was finally told to make the ending more wholesome, so Lily was forced to return to where she began.

During the shooting of the film, Zanuck left Warner Bros. after a disagreement with Jack Warner over a separate issue. *Baby Face* became the responsibility of Hal Wallis, the new head of production. Although the MPPDA had approved the modified script, it did not approve the finished movie, and Wallis was forced to remove several scenes, including several rough exchanges between Lily and her father and her seduction of a brakeman to receive a free train ride out of town. Joe Breen demanded that the film exhibit "morally compensating values," which would become a key phrase in the final draft of the 1934 Production Code. To do this, Breen demanded that the cobbler's lines be changed so that his advice to Lily would remind her of the need to act morally. As a result, instead of advising her to follow Nietzsche and use whatever she might to achieve goals, in the approved version he tells her: "A woman, young, beautiful, like you are, can get anything she wants in the world. But there is a right and a wrong way. Remember the price of the wrong way is too great."

Even with these changes, *Baby Face* became the target of the Catholic Legion of Decency (LOD), which placed it on the banned list in Chicago. The film was also banned from exhibition in Ohio and Virginia because the board of censors in both states found it "morally objectionable" and determined that it would lead to "corruption of youth." In 1934, as a result of the great pressure exerted by the LOD, the Hays office worked with LOD official Martin Quigley to construct a production code stronger than the one passed in 1930, which would incorporate Joe Breen's "compensating moral values" that required films to contain "at least sufficient good to compensate any evil they relate." When the new code went into effect on July 11, 1934, *Baby Face* was listed as a "Class I" production and pulled from circulation, as Breen vowed that it would never again be released. The film was never again released in theaters but is seen on television and videotape.

FURTHER READING

Doherty, Thomas. *Pre-Code Hollywood: Sex, Immorality, and Insurrection in American Cinema, 1930–1934.* New York: Columbia University Press, 1999.

Leff, Leonard J., and Jerold L. Simmons. *The Dame in the Kimono: Hollywood, Censorship, and the Production Code from 1920 to the 1960s.* New York: Grove Weidenfeld, 1990.

Miller, Frank. *Censored Hollywood: Sex, Sin, and Violence on Screen.* Atlanta, Ga.: Turner Publishing, 1994.

Vieira, Mark. *Sin in Soft Focus: Pre-Code Hollywood.* New York: Harry N. Abrams, 1999.

BASIC INSTINCT

Country and date of production: United States, 1992
Production company/distributor: Carolco; TriStar Pictures/Columbia TriStar Film Distributors
Format: Sound, color
Running time: 123 minutes
Language: English
Producers: Mario Kassar, Alan Marshall IV
Director: Paul Verhoeven
Screenwriter: Joe Eszterhaus
Awards: 1993 Academy Awards, Best Film Editing (Frank J. Urioste).
1993 Golden Globes, USA, Best Original Score–Motion Picture (Jerry Goldsmith).
1993 MTV Movie Awards, Best Female Performer (Sharon Stone), Most Desirable Female (Sharon Stone), Best Male Performer (Michael Douglas).
Genre: Mystery/crime thriller
With: Michael Douglas (Detective Nick Curran), Sharon Stone (Catherine Tramell), George Dzundza (Gus), Jeanne Tripplehorn (Doctor Beth Garner), Denis Arndt (Lieutenant Walker), Leilani Sarelle (Roxy), Bruce A. Young (Andrews), Chelcie Ross (Captain Talcott), Dorothy Malone (Hazel Dobkins), Wayne Knight (John Correli), Daniel von Bargen (Lieutenant Nilsen), Stephen Tobolowsky (Doctor Lamott), Benjamin Mouton (Harrigan), Jack McGee (Sheriff), Bill Cable (Johnny Boz), Stephen Rowe (Internal Affairs Investigator), Mitch Pileggi (Internal Affairs Investigator)

SUMMARY

When this film opens, a former rock star and San Francisco nightclub owner, Johnny Boz, is found in bed, brutally stabbed to death with an ice pick, apparently killed while engaging in sex. When the police investigators discover that Johnny's murder is identical to a scene described in a murder mystery novel written by one of the victim's girlfriends, they bring in a psychiatrist to help with the case. The chief investigator is San Francisco detective Nick Curran, who is burdened with a multitude of personal problems. He is recovering from bouts with alcoholism and drug addiction; also, an unjustified shooting of several tourists whom he mistook for perpetrators has earned him the nickname of "Shooter" among his enemies and forced him to either enter counseling with the police psychiatrist or lose his job. To complicate his life further, Curran becomes involved in a sexual relationship with the police psychiatrist treating him.

Police question the dead man's girlfriend, novelist Catherine Tramell, and her direct answers and overtly sexual nature strike a nerve with Curran. The sultry Catherine leads the investigator into believing that she may have indeed committed the crime. She teases the officers who question her by shifting about seductively on her chair, crossing and uncrossing her legs and making it clear that she isn't wearing underwear. Her behavior deflects attention from the facts in the case and suggests that she is the prime suspect. The police don't have enough evidence to arrest Catherine, however, so she remains free and begins to pursue Curran sexually, who keeps her under surveillance. He knows she is dangerous but is powerfully attracted to her because she stirs up the self-destructive tendencies he has controlled so carefully in recent months. The police hierarchy soon have reason to question Curran's judgment when he starts to drink again and appears to have fallen in love with his number-one suspect. All is not as it seems, and eventually Catherine's past and present sexual relationships with two women, both very jealous, complicate the assumptions of the police. The bisexual Catherine and her two female lovers each have the motives and the means to have committed the murder. Further, one or more of the three may have killed before, and Curran discovers that Catherine is linked to other unsolved deaths. The audience wonders whether Curran will be able to prove that Catherine committed the murder or if he will die in the same way as Johnny Boz.

CENSORSHIP HISTORY

Basic Instinct attracted protest from liberal and conservative groups alike. The loudest and most vigorous protests and the greatest efforts to halt its filming emerged not because of the violence nor the overtly sexual nature of the film, but instead for political reasons. When filming began at the Tosca Café in San Francisco, members of the militant homosexual activist groups ACT UP and Queer Nation threw paint bombs on the set, blew whistles and encouraged drivers in the area to honk their horns. *U.S. News & World Report* also described the groups' protests against Ray Chalker, publisher of a gay newspaper and owner of a gay bar rented out to the film company as a site. Group members picketed the bar, jammed his answering machine with threatening calls, poured glue into the locks of his home and vandalized his car. They later demonstrated at the opening of the film, claiming that its murderous lesbian character caters to public homophobia and incites gay-bashing. Advocacy groups for gays and lesbians asserted that although the movie provided representation of homosexuals, a formerly hidden or invisible segment of the population, movies such as *Basic Instinct* perpetuate homophobic stereotypes through negative depictions without providing a balance by including positive depictions as well. Hollywood attempted to counter such arguments by citing the First Amendment, but Charles Lyons says, in the words of a protester against CRUISING (1980), that it is "'absurd to argue the First Amendment in this case because it presumes equality. There's no equality as long as we haven't the economic power or economic base that Hollywood has. . . .'"

Shortly after filming began, members of Queer Nation met with the director and producer to ask for script revisions and to propose the role of Nick Curran be changed to a female character, in order to correct what *Time* quoted the group as labeling a "clearly homophobic, lesbophobic film that once again inverts the reality of our lives." They also demanded that the film feature the murders of women as well as men, to avoid labeling lesbians and female bisexuals as hating men. Executives at both Carolco and Tri-Star refused to consider what they called "vetting of entertainment by special-interest groups." In March 1992, when the movie opened in theaters across the United States, demonstrators representing feminist and gay rights groups picketed with signs and handed out leaflets, and they also threatened to disrupt the Academy Awards ceremony, scheduled for the following week. (The film was released too late to be nominated for the 1992 awards, but the lead actors, Michael Douglas and Sharon Stone, were scheduled to be Oscar presenters.) In press notices released in the week preceding the awards ceremony, the Los Angeles chapter of Queer Nation threatened to blockade limousine traffic and to disrupt the ceremonies. They were supported in the protest by the National Organization for Women (NOW), whose Los Angeles branch expressed strong disapproval of the way in which the movie portrayed women and released to *Maclean's* magazine the statement, "We were expecting it to be homophobic, but it also is one of the most misogynistic films in recent memory."

Protests occurred in numerous cities. In Toronto, gay activists converged on lines of theatergoers and shouted out the name of the killer in the movie. In Los Angeles, members of Queer Nation formed a committee named "[the killer's name] did it," and the San Francisco *Bay Times* printed the group's slogan and protest in a full-page advertisement, including the admonition, "Hollywood consistently portrays us as victims or psychotics. We're saying don't spend your money to see homophobia and misogyny."

The uproar led screenwriter Joe Eszterhaus to reject his support of the movie, for which he was paid $3.3 million—the highest sum ever paid for a screenplay at that time. Although the final release of the film closely follows his original script, Eszterhaus sought to make changes after the film was nearly complete to accommodate the demands of gay protesters, but the director refused. In another attempt to defuse the issue, the writer asked that the producer run a disclaimer at the opening of the film, stating "The movie you are about to see is fiction." When the director Paul Verhoeven refused and stayed with the original script, Eszterhaus announced publicly that he no longer supported it.

The movie also drew protests from conservative groups and led Cardinal Roger Mahoney, leader of the Los Angeles Roman Catholic archdiocese, to call for a new morality code to ban nudity, "lustful embraces," foul language, and blasphemy in movies and on television. Michael Medved, the co-host of *Sneak Peeks*, a weekly, nationally syndicated television show, publicly agreed with Cardinal Mahoney and charged that film in the United States was threatening traditional American values and had become the enemy of decency. The threat of an NC-17 rating, which would have denied admission to anyone under the age of 17, would have severely damaged profits for the $50 million film because many newspapers refuse to advertise films with this rating. Verhoeven admitted to having shot several of the scenes from different angles, from the discreet to the revealing, to provide footage for a version that he was sure the ratings board would reject. He then used outtakes to produce a less graphic version that the board did approve and grant an "R" rating, which allows teenagers accompanied by an adult to view the movie in the United States. In Canada, even the revised version was rated to restrict viewing of *Basic Instinct* to people over the age of 18.

FURTHER READING

Battistini, Robert. "Basic Instinct: Revisionist Hard-On, Hollywood Trash, or Feminist Hope?" *Cinefocus* 2, no. 2 (Spring 1992): 38–43.

Bowman, James. "To Die in Bed (The Sex-Death Complex in Motion Pictures)." *American Spectator* 25, no. 1 (June 1992): 47–49.

"Censors on the Street (Gay Activists Protest Against *Basic Instinct*)." *Time*, May 13, 1991, p. 70.

Danziger, Marie. "*Basic Instinct:* Grappling for Post-Modern Mind Control." *Literature/Film Quarterly* 22, no. 1 (1994): 7–10.

Deleyto, Celestino. "The Margins of Pleasure: Female Monstrosity and Male Paranoia in *Basic Instinct*." *Film Criticism* 21, no. 3 (Spring 1997): 20–42.

Hoberman, J. "Fantastic Projections (Criticism of Director Paul Verhoeven's Movie *Basic Instinct*)." *Sight and Sound* 2, no. 1 (May 1992): 4.

Holmlund, Chris. "Cruisin' for a Bruisin': Hollywood's Deadly (Lesbian) Dolls." *Cinema Journal* 34, no. 1 (Fall 1994): 31–51.

Johnson, Brian D. "Killer Movies (Violence in Motion Pictures)." *Maclean's*, March 30, 1992, pp. 48–51.

Kauffman, L. A. "Queer Guerrillas in Tinseltown (Protesting Movie Portrayals of Gays and Lesbians)." *Progressive* 56:7 (July 1992): 36–37.

Leo, John. "The Politics of Intimidation." *U.S. News & World Report*, April 6, 1992, p. 24.

Lyons, Charles. *The New Censors: Movies and the Culture Wars.* Philadelphia: Temple University Press, 1997.

Picardie, Ruth. "Mad, Bad and Dangerous (Gay Film Makers and Gay Opposition to the Film *Basic Instinct*)." *New Statesman & Society*, May 1, 1992, p. 36.

Sharrett, Christopher. "Hollywood Homophobia" (Column). *USA Today* (Magazine), July 1992, p. 93.

Simpson, Janice C. "Out of the Celluloid Closet: Gay Activists Are on a Rampage Against Negative Stereotyping and Other Acts of Homophobia in Hollywood." *Time*, April 6, 1992, p. 65.

THE BEDFORD INCIDENT

Country and date of production: United States and Great Britain, 1965
Production company/distributor: Columbia Pictures Corporation/Columbia Pictures
Format: Sound, black and white
Running time: 102 minutes
Language: English
Producers: James B. Harris, Richard Widmark
Director: James B. Harris
Screenwriters: James Poe, Mark Rascovitch (novel)
Awards: None
Genre: Thriller
With: Richard Widmark (Capt. Eric Finlander), Sidney Poitier (Ben Munceford), James MacArthur (Ensign Ralston), Martin Balsam (Lieutenant Commander Chester Potter, M.D.), Wally Cox (Seaman Merlin Queffle), Eric Portman (Commodore Wolfgang Schrepke, Deutsche Marine), Michael Kane (Commander Allison, Executive Officer), Colin Maitland (Seaman Jones)

SUMMARY

The Bedford Incident portrays a clash of national wills during the cold war and the results of a confrontation between United States and Russian forces. Captain Eric Finlander, an experienced naval captain, has earned a reputation as a confident commander who can be hard on his troops at times. He is especially demanding on the performance of Ensign Ralston, a young officer new to the destroyer, whom Finlander believes may have potential if he is trained in the correct manner—his manner. Finlander's newest assignment is the command of the USS *Bedford*, a newly launched naval destroyer, whose mission is to root out hostile submarines in the North Atlantic.

Due to heightened media attention over the cold war, the United States government has given a newspaper permission to interview the captain and to document the ship's activities on this deployment. Ben Munceford is the civilian selected to accompany the ship along its routine patrols. He is a veteran newspaperman who seems slightly hesitant about the duty, and the captain makes clear from the beginning that he views Munceford as an unnecessary distraction. Finlander is also upset with another decision of the high command, whom he feels has done a disservice to his crew and to his ship by sending along a replacement doctor.

While on maneuvers, the Bedford tracking devices detect a Russian submarine operating inside the territorial waters of Greenland, and Finlander intends to make the submarine come to the surface, using any tactic possible. The dogged chase puts the crew under extreme tension, adding to the suspense and causing the viewer to wonder which side is going to yield first. Finlander is relentless in his decision to hunt the submarine and attempt to destroy it. After what seems like an eternity of cat-and-mouse, the *Bedford* finally corners the submarine. Ralston, who is shaken by his captain's constant needling, accidentally launches a nuclear missile. The audience realizes, however, that the Russian also launched a missile just before being hit, so the crews of both vessels will die.

CENSORSHIP HISTORY

The Bedford Incident is one of two films (see also BUNNY LAKE IS MISSING) selected by Columbia Pictures to serve as test cases in an effort to prove the Kansas censorship laws unconstitutional. Despite informal condemnation of the film as exhibiting a too-liberal bias in portraying the confrontation of a U.S. Navy destroyer with a Russian submarine as a no-win situation, the film was not banned nor censored for content in any city or state nationwide. In November 1965, seven months after the United States Supreme Court struck down the censorship law in the state of Maryland (in a case involving the film REVENGE AT DAYBREAK), Columbia Pictures chose to test the law in Kansas by distributing this film and *Bunny Lake Is Missing* without seeking approval by the Kansas Board of Reviews (BOR) and by informing the BOR that it would no longer submit future films that the company intended to exhibit in the state, nor would it seek a certificate of approval. State Attorney General Robert Londerholm brought suit against Columbia Pictures in Shawnee County district court to prevent the distributor from "selling, leasing, exhibiting or using" the films without first obtaining permission from the BOR. The distributor retained for its defense former Kansas governor John Anderson, Jr., who defended the action of the company on the grounds that the Kansas statute required the exhibitor to prove that the film was protected expression, but the constitutional standards required the opposite: that the BOR prove the film to be unprotected expression.

Citing the ruling in *Freedman v. Maryland* in regard to *Revenge at Daybreak*, the presiding judge Marion Beatty refused to concur with the state and ruled that the system of censorship practiced by the Kansas BOR was unconstitutional because it "abridged the freedom of expression." State Attorney General Londerholm appealed the ruling to the state supreme court, which affirmed the decision of the lower court that the state motion picture censorship law was unconstitutional and that the law "violated the constitutional guaranty of freedom of expression." The court gave the BOR 60 days to complete operations and to turn over all money and properties to designated state agencies, $20,000 in the BOR account was turned over to the general revenue fund.

FURTHER READING

Gaume, Thomas Michael. *Suppression of Motion Pictures in Kansas, 1952–1975.* Unpublished thesis, University of Kansas, Lawrence, 1976.
Kansas State Board of Review. *Complete List of Motion Picture Films Submitted.* Topeka: Kansas State Board of Review, 1966.
State ex rel. Londerholm v. Columbia Pictures Corporation, 417 P. 2d 255 (1966).
Warner, Linda K. *Movie Censorship in Kansas: The Kansas State Board of Review.* Unpublished thesis, Emporia State University, 1988.

BEHIND THE GREEN DOOR

Country and date of production: United States, 1973
Production company/distributor: Mitchell Brothers Pictures/Jartech
Format: Sound, color
Running time: 72 minutes
Language: English
Producers: Artie Mitchell, Jim Mitchell
Directors: Artie Mitchell, Jim Mitchell
Screenwriters: Anonymous, Jim Mitchell
Awards: None
Genre: Drama/Adult
With: Marilyn Chambers (Gloria Saunders), Artie Mitchell (Kidnapper), Jim Mitchell (Kidnapper), Ben Davidson (Porter), Johnny Keyes (Stud), Yank Levine (Truck Driver), George S. MacDonald (Barry Clark, a Truck Driver)

SUMMARY

Among the pioneer efforts of "porno art," crossover films that attempted to bring explicitly sexual stories to mainstream film audiences, *Behind the Green Door* also capitalized on the interest generated the previous year by DEEP THROAT. The story line is simple: Gloria, a young and beautiful woman, is kidnapped and taken to a private sex club in the North Beach section of San Francisco, where she becomes the central attraction as she enthusiastically participates in a range of sexual activity. In the audience is Barry Clark, a bachelor truck driver from a small town whose friend has brought him to the sex club to broaden his sexual experience. At first, Gloria seems bewildered and hesitant, but she soon performs sexually onstage with other people for an audience of voyeurs who move from self-manipulation to direct sexual inter-actions that turn the behavior of the crowd into an orgy. At one point Gloria engages in sexual activity with three men at once, while members of the audi-ence become so sexually excited that they join the performers on stage. In the middle of the confusion, Barry takes the exhausted Gloria from the stage and the two leave on their own.

CENSORSHIP HISTORY

The film offered audiences shocks beyond the depiction of graphic sexual activity. Unlike the deliberately provocative and sultry actresses of previous sexually explicit films Marilyn Chambers projected a fresh-faced and inno-cent beauty that had won her a previous role as a demure young mother whose face appeared in Ivory Snow commercials and on boxes of the baby clothes detergent. Further, the film was not created to be shown in the back-rooms of bars and at stag parties but in feature film theaters as the new-styled "porn chic." The film was banned in Suffolk County, New York, after the owner of a 600-seat movie theater located in a shopping center exhibited the film and was charged with violating section 1141 of the state penal law, which prohibits the exhibition of any film that "appeals to prurient interest in sex, goes substantially beyond the customary limits of candor, and has utterly no redeeming social value." The judge in the case refused the defendant's offer to view the film, rejected expert testimony regarding the film's "art quality," and banned the film from exhibition in Suffolk County.

Edward De Grazia reports that in the same year the film was also the tar-get of a civil action brought by the corporation counsel for New York City and the New York County district attorney, who sought to prevent its exhibi-tion at theaters in New York City. In its case, the New York City prosecution charged that the "multiple and variegated ultimate acts of sexual perversion would have been regarded as obscene by the community standards of Sodom and Gomorrah" and called for an injunction against exhibiting the movie. The distributors of the film filed an appeal of the decision with the Supreme Court's appellate division, which upheld the constitutionality of the action in *Redlich v. Capri Cinema* and declared that the New York statute was not overly broad within the meaning of the Supreme Court's holding in the landmark case of *Miller v. California* (see CARNAL KNOWLEDGE), De Grazia and Jonathan Green also report that the film was banned from exhibition without incident in the following states: Texas, from 1974 to 1982; Colorado, 1975; Georgia, 1976; and California, 1979.

FURTHER READING

De Grazia, Edward. *Banned Films: Movies, Censors, & the First Amendment.* New York: R. R. Bowker, 1982.
Green, Jonathan. *The Encyclopedia of Censorship.* New York: Facts On File, 1990.
Miller v. California, 413 U.S. 15 (1973).

Redlich v. Capri Cinema, 349 N.Y.S. 2d 697 (1973).
Trillin, Calvin. "Trying *Green Door.*" *The New Yorker*, February 11, 1974, pp. 23–24.

BELLE OF THE NINETIES

Country and date of production: United States, 1934
Production company/distributor: Paramount Pictures
Format: Sound, black and white
Running time: 73 minutes
Language: English
Producer: William LeBaron
Director: Leo McCarey
Screenwriter: Mae West
Awards: None
Genre: Comedy/western
With: Mae West (Ruby Carter), Roger Pryor (Tiger Kid), Johnny Mack Brown (Brooks Claybourne), John Miljan (Ace Lamont), Katherine DeMille (Molly Brant), James Donlan (Kirby), Stuart Holmes (Dirk), Harry Woods (Slade), Edward Gargan (Stogie), Libby Taylor (Jasmine)

SUMMARY

Mae West wrote the screenplay for this film, titled *It Ain't No Sin* when submitted to the Production Code Administration (PCA) for approval but later changed to *Belle of the Nineties*. The story is about Ruby Carter, a vaudeville star with a notorious past who has fallen in love with Tiger Kid, a young boxing star. The movie opens with the police reviewing the records on Ruby. Viewers learn that she has been suspected of a range or crimes, including murder and possessing stolen bonds, but lack of evidence or the refusal by victims to prosecute have kept her out of jail. Tiger Kid loves Ruby and tells her that he would do anything for her, but his manager, Kirby, wants Ruby out of the boxer's life because he fears his fighter will lose his focus if the relationship continues. To make Tiger jealous, Kirby pays a man to call Ruby and pretend that he knows her. This leads Tiger to believe that Ruby has been unfaithful to him, so he leaves her.

The disappointed Ruby takes a singing job in a New Orleans club. She meets and has an affair with a wealthy younger man, who gives her a diamond necklace. This angers Ace Lamont, the club owner, who is infatuated with Ruby despite having a girlfriend, but Ruby's principles keep her from returning his interest. When Tiger arrives in New Orleans for a boxing match with a fighter financed by Lamont, he and Ruby meet again. Lamont knows of Tiger's criminal past and uses the knowledge to blackmail Tiger into stealing Ruby's jewels. After Ruby realizes that Tiger is the thief, she attends the fight and surreptitiously slips a sedative into Tiger's water bottle, causing him to lose the fight in the 28th round and bankrupting Lamont, who had bet heavily that Tiger would win.

After the match, Lamont prepares to burn down his club so he can avoid paying off the debts. After he has locked Ruby in and is busy pouring kerosene throughout the place, Ruby opens his safe and takes her jewelry and most of Lamont's cash. Tiger appears and expresses anger that Ruby bet against him, but she reminds him that Lamont gave him the water bottle. Tiger knocks out Lamont and accidentally kills him. To cover their tracks, Ruby throws down a cigarette and starts a fire. Tiger rushes to save Molly from the inferno while Ruby nonchalantly calls the Fire Department. In the final scenes, Tiger explains to Ruby why he stole her jewelry, and the two marry.

CENSORSHIP HISTORY

It Ain't No Sin was Mae West's third starring vehicle and the one that created the most difficulty with the censors. Paramount had seen the economic success of her racy formula in I'M NO ANGEL (1933) and SHE DONE HIM WRONG (1933) and would make every effort to have a third success. The PCA scrupulously reviewed the script. On March 7, 1934, PCA head Joe Breen wrote a four-and-a-half-page letter to the producers criticizing the title for being "sacrilegious" and warning them that the script was a "glorification of prostitution and violent crime without any compensating moral values of any kind," and that the characterization was "certain to throw the sympathy of the audience with sin, crime, wrongdoing, and evil." Despite the producers' reminders of the script's comic aspects, Breen was adamant that the script was in total violation of the code, but Paramount began to film two weeks later after making only minimal changes in dialogue. At the same time, Paramount mounted a preliminary advertising campaign by ordering the erection of huge billboards on Broadway, proclaiming *"It Ain't No Sin."* The billboards also contained the line that has long been associated with West, "Come up and see me some time," which Paramount told a *Variety* reporter was intended to be taken as "an invitation to tea." Catholic priests and members of the Catholic Legion of Decency (LOD) picketed the billboards and carried placards stating "IT IS!"

The finished film arrived at the SRC in late May 1934, and, after it was passed to the approval arm the PCA on June 1, Breen rejected the film, largely because of the "violent and lustful kissing" that occurred throughout most of it. The PCA also demanded that the studio change the title and soften Ruby Carter's criminality and seductiveness. The studio appealed the decision and the film was sent to the New York censors, who rejected the film on June 28 and made additional demands that were meant to appease the increasingly vocal Legion of Decency. West reluctantly made the suggested cuts, including an ending to include the marriage of Tiger and Ruby. She and the Paramount producers also decided to change the name of the film, first selecting *St. Louis Woman*, then rejecting it when they learned that another film had that title. On August 6, the film received the PCA certificate of approval, and the marks of the censor were clear in the sometimes disjointed scenes and in the ending. Of the several scene cuts demanded by the censors, one had to be refilmed with a narrower angle so that West could not be seen "manipulating her torso" more than the standards of the PCA allowed. The final version of the film was eventually released throughout the United States, but the Chicago Legion of Decency condemned the film in total and forbade all Catholics in the archdiocese from seeing it in any form.

FURTHER READING

Black, Gregory D. "Hollywood Censored: The Production Code Administration and the Hollywood Film Industry, 1930–1940." *Film History* 3, no. 3 (1989): 167–189.
"It Ain't No Sin." Variety, June 13, 1934, p. 1.
Leff, Leonard J., and Jerold L. Simmons. *The Dame in the Kimono.* New York: Grove Weidenfeld, 1990.
Miller, Frank. *Censored Hollywood: Sex, Sin, and Violence on Screen.* Atlanta, Ga.: Turner Publishing, 1994.
"Miss West Talks Shop." *The New York Times,* February 3, 1935, p. 5.
Rorty, James. *"It Ain't No Sin." Nation,* August 1, 1934, pp. 124–27.
Vieira, Mark A. *Sin in Soft Focus: Pre-Code Hollywood.* New York: Harry N. Abrams, 1999.

THE BIRTH OF A BABY

Country and date of production: United States, 1938
Production company/distributor: Special Pictures Corporation
Format: Sound, black and white
Running time: 72 minutes
Language: English
Producer: Jack H. Skirball
Director: Al Christie
Screenwriters: Arthur Jarrett, Burk Symon
Awards: None
Genre: Educational
With: Kathleen Comegys (Mrs. Wilson), Josephine Dunn (Mrs. Bromley), Walter Gilbert (Mr. Perry), Frederica Going (Mrs. Perry), Richard Gordon (Dr. Wilson), Edith Gresham (Mrs. Case), Helen Hawley (Mrs. Burgess), Eleanore King (Mary Burgess), Ruth Matteson (Julia Norton), Robert Ober (Mr. Case), William Post, Jr. (John Burgess)

SUMMARY

The Birth of a Baby is a dignified health education film, produced with funds provided by the American Committee on Maternal Welfare, that dramatizes the lives of a couple through the various stages of pregnancy and the birth of a child. The film emphasizes the importance of consulting a physician early in the pregnancy and explains the various physical changes that the mother-to-be can expect, as well as the emotional changes that will affect the couple. Throughout the film, the couple repeatedly is advised of the importance of good communication between the pregnant woman and her doctor and of the need for good health care during this time.

Although *The Birth of a Baby* was produced as an educational film, the American Committee on Maternal Welfare sought to show it in commercial movie theaters to reach relevant audiences in great numbers. This goal was endorsed enthusiastically by the American Medical Association, the United States Public Health Service, the American Hospital Association and a dozen state health societies, as well as by First Lady Eleanor Roosevelt, who said that the film "could not be harmful because it is honest." Even the Catholic Legion of Decency (LOD) acknowledged the sincere purposes of the film sponsors, although it denied approval for the film and deemed it "unsuited for entertainment and inappropriate for general theatrical exhibition."

CENSORSHIP HISTORY

The film was the object of censors' attention despite the many endorsements it garnered. Public officials in such states as Ohio, Nebraska, New York and Virginia determined that the scene of a baby being born violated their statutes against indecent or immoral movies. In Cincinnati, Ohio, the chief of police reported to the city manager, "The picture is positively terrible, and I can see nothing educational in it." As a result, the city council, acting at the direction of the city manager, banned the film from exhibition in the city. In Omaha, Nebraska, the city welfare board, with a vote of two in favor, one against and two abstentions, approved general exhibition of the film, but the mayor reversed the decision of the board after receiving complaints. Claiming that he was not influenced by his opinion that the film was unnecessary because "it commercializes the most sacred thing in life," the mayor ruled that the film could be shown only if the vote of the city welfare board were unanimous. When the vote remained the same, the mayor banned any showing of the film.

State censors in Virginia refused to allow the exhibition of *The Birth of a Baby*, but they reversed themselves after a theater operator appealed the decision in the Circuit Court of Richmond, which ordered the board of censors to issue a permit for statewide exhibition. The city of Lynchburg challenged the ruling, and the city manager, backed by the city council, told a theater operator that the film could not be exhibited within the city limits. Citing a city ordinance that prohibited "obscene and indecent films," the manager asserted that *The Birth of a Baby* violated the ordinance and directed that the theater operator would not be permitted to exhibit the film. The operator appealed to the Corporation Court of Lynchburg and asked for an injunction to prevent the city from preventing the theater from showing the film. Presiding Judge Aubrey E. Strode granted the injunction, and the city of Lynchburg challenged the decision in an appeal to the Virginia Supreme Court of Appeals, which affirmed the decision of the lower court. In the decision, the state court of appeals said that the city of Lynchburg could not prevent the exhibition of a film after the state board had licensed it for statewide showing. President Judge Herbert B. Gregory wrote in his decision, "The State by its statute having occupied the entire field of moving picture censorship, municipalities are thereby excluded therefrom as to matters comprehended by the statute." He concluded that giving municipalities the power to censor films and to determine the rights of owners to exhibit them would render the state unified control plan "ineffectual and inoperative to carry out the expressed intention of the legislature."

In New York State, the state censorship board denied the film a license for exhibition after determining that it "would tend to corrupt morals" on the grounds that it was "indecent" and "immoral." The board refused to license the film to be shown in "places of amusement" but did grant it a special permit to be shown for educational purposes. The film sponsors filed a complaint with the state supreme court, which confirmed the decision of the board. Justice Gilbert V. Schenck wrote:

> This picture may have its scientific value. It is not inherently indecent in the ordinary accepted sense of the word, but it becomes indecent when presented in places of amusement. For clinical purposes the picture may be shown under a special permit authorizing the showing of educational pictures of this character under certain restrictions. But a picture depicting the actual birth of a child becomes indecent when presented to patrons of places of public entertainment.

The matter was sent to the New York Court of Appeals, which affirmed the decision of the lower court without opinion.

Photographs from the film appeared as a centerfold in the April 11, 1938, issue of *Life* magazine. After readers complained, publisher Ralph Larsen was arrested and charged with selling an obscene magazine. He was acquitted by Justice Nathan D. Perlman in the Court of Special Sessions, who determined that the pictures were "based on a film produced under the auspices of a responsible medical group. There is no nudity or unnecessary disclosure. The subject has been treated with delicacy."

FURTHER READING

American Committee on Maternal Welfare v. Cincinnati, 26 Ohio L. Abs. 533 (C. P. 1938).
American Committee on Maternal Welfare v. Mangan, 14 N.Y.S. 2d 39, 257 App. Div. 570 (1939), affirmed 283 N.Y. 551 (1940).
City of Lynchburg v. Dominion Theaters, 7 S.E. 2d 157 (1940).
Eberwein, Robert. *Sex Education: Film, Video, and the Framework of Desire.* New Brunswick, N.J.: Rutgers University Press, 1999.

Ernst, Morris L., and Alexander Lindey. *The Censor Marches On.* Garden City, N.Y.: Doubleday, 1940.

People v. Larsen, 5 N.Y.S. 2d 55 (1938).

THE BIRTH OF A NATION

Country and date of production: United States, 1915 (premiered as *The Clansman*)

Production company/distributor: David W. Griffith Corp./Epoch Producing Corporation

Format: Silent, black and white

Running time: ca. 165 minutes

Language: English

Producer: D. W. Griffith

Director: D. W. Griffith

Screenwriters: Thomas F. Dixon, Jr. (novels, *The Clansman* and *The Leopard's Spots*), D. W. Griffith, Frank E. Woods

Awards: None

Genre: Drama

With: Lillian Gish (Elsie Stoneman), Mae Marsh (Flora Cameron), Henry B. Walthall (Colonel Ben Cameron), Miriam Cooper (Margaret Cameron), Mary Alden (Lydia Brown), Ralph Lewis (Austin Stoneman), George Siegmann (Silas Lynch), Walter Long (Gus), Robert Harron (Tod Stoneman), Wallace Reid (Jeff, the blacksmith)

SUMMARY

The Birth of a Nation was director D. W. Griffith's personal interpretation of the Reconstruction era in the South, which he adapted from two popular novels, *The Clansman* and *The Leopard's Spots*, written by North Carolina preacher Thomas Dixon, Jr., whose uncle was a Grand Titan in the Ku Klux Klan. The picture is prefaced by "A Plea for the Art of the Motion Picture": "We do not fear censorship, for we have no wish to offend with improprieties or obscenities, but we do demand, as a right, the liberty to show the dark side of wrong, that we may illuminate the bright side of virtue—the same liberty that is conceded to the art of the written word—that art to which we owe the Bible and the works of Shakespeare." Another message concerning the horror of war precedes the film: "If in this work we have conveyed to the mind the ravages of war to the end that war may be held in abhorrence, this effort will not have been in vain." Typically, for the period, the film's major black roles, played as stereotypes, were performed by white actors in blackface, while the black actors in the film played only in minor roles.

Part one of the movie opens in the South before the American Civil War with the descriptions of two families: the Stonemans, a Northern family led by an Abolitionist congressman Austin Stoneman, who has a daughter, Elsie, and two sons; and a Southern family, the Camerons, who have two daughters, Margaret and Flora, and three sons, including the central character, Ben Cameron. The Stoneman boys are friends with the slave-owning Camerons and visit their opulent South Carolina plantation, where, in the first 15 minutes of the film, numerous images suggest that the Camerons are kindly and tolerant. The Cameron patriarch is surrounded by playful puppies and kittens, and his son Ben shakes hands with one of the slaves who has just danced for the visitors from the North. The eldest boy, Phil Stoneman, becomes enamored with Margaret Cameron, and Ben Cameron is given a picture of Elsie Stoneman, whom he begins to idealize.

The Civil War begins, and all of the sons from both families join their respective sides. In one scene, the Cameron house is ransacked by a black Northern militia led by a white captain. A Confederate unit eventually shows up to drive off these intruders, but later the family loses everything anyway. As the war drags on, the youngest Stoneman boy is killed, as are two of the Cameron sons. Although Ben Cameron survives, he is seriously injured and recuperates in a Northern hospital where Elsie is a nurse. Ben faces a death warrant because of his loyalties, but Mrs. Stoneman and Elsie intercede with President Lincoln to save him, and Ben is soon able to return home to help his family rebuild. After Lincoln is assassinated, a scene that is dramatized in the film, Northern political leaders such as Austin Stoneman pursue their own agendas to implement programs of black equality and punish the South for seceding.

Part two attempts to illustrate the period of Reconstruction following the Civil War and begins with the following preface: "This is an historical presentation of the Civil War and Reconstruction Period, and is not meant to reflect on any race or people of today."

Austin Stoneman and his protege Silas Lynch, who is half African American, go to South Carolina to organize Southern blacks to vote. They are pleased as their factions elect a largely black legislature, with Lynch as lieutenant governor. Fearing black supremacy, Ben Cameron joins others in striking back against what they perceive as the powerlessness of Southern whites by forming the Ku Klux Klan. Elsie Stoneman, who is loyal to her father's efforts, distances herself from Ben because of his participation in this group, but she changes her mind as she understands the purpose of the Ku Klux Klan. When a former slave, Gus, becomes romantically interested in Flora Cameron and pursues her into the forest, then traps her on a precipice, Flora jumps to her death rather than let him catch her. Klan members, led by Ben, track down Gus, hang him, and leave his body on the doorstep of Lieutenant Governor Silas Lynch, who in turn retaliates by ordering his militiamen to capture and execute Klan members. The Cameron household escapes his militia and takes refuge in their isolated country home, but black militiamen surround them. At another site, Lynch attempts to force Elsie to marry him and to become the queen of his Black Empire. As Elsie screams for help, members of the Klan send for reinforcements that speed to her rescue. The Klan later saves the trapped Cameron family, then overcomes all of the blacks and forces a collapse of the Black Empire. In the celebration that follows, the white-robed heroes triumphantly ride through the streets. A short time later, on election day, Klan members supervise the proceedings and prevent blacks from voting. As the film draws to a close, Phil Stoneman and Margaret Cameron marry, as do Ben Cameron and Elsie Stoneman. The epilogue prophesies the coming of the Prince of Peace: "Dare we dream of a golden day when the bestial War shall rule no more. But instead—the gentle Prince in the Hall of Brotherly Love in the City of Peace." The film ends with a final image of large numbers of suffering people under a warlike ruler transformed into seemingly angelic figures under the rule of a glowing, Christlike figure.

CENSORSHIP HISTORY

Film scholars consider *The Birth of a Nation* to be among the most important films of all time for its many cinematic innovations and refinements, technical effects and artistic advancements. The film had a formative impact on film history and the development of film as art. At almost three hours in length, it was longer than any previous film and, as such, established the feature film instead of the 10 or 20-minute length of most other early films as the norm. *The Birth of a Nation* was released in the largest movie theaters in cities such as Los Angeles and New York and became one of the most profitable films of the 20th century, making $18 million for its original producers. It was the first film to be aggressively marketed internationally, not only to England but also to all of Europe in country-by-country negotiations. *The Birth of a Nation* was also the first American movie to be released with its own musical score, written for a 40-piece orchestra.

The film may have been technically and artistically innovative, but it also represented the entrenched racism of the plantation genre of film at its pinnacle. The overt racist message was clearly stated in one of the titles that appeared on screen to describe the Ku Klux Klan members marching forward "in defence [*sic*] of the Aryan birthright." The subject matter of this film created the first major U.S. censorship battle over a movie. Even President Woodrow Wilson, during a private screening at the White House, is reported to have exclaimed: "It's like writing history with lightning. And my only regret is that it is all terribly true." Immediately upon release, the film was criticized by the newly formed National Association for the Advancement of Colored People (NAACP) for its racist portrayal of blacks. The group denounced the film as providing "the meanest vilification of the Negro race." The NAACP asked the National Board of Censorship of Motion Pictures, created by New York theater owners on March 26, 1909, to deny approval to the film, but the board approved the film in a divided vote. This failure of the board to act effectively in the case of *The Birth of a Nation* led to its loss of authority and demise.

When the film was released, protests occurred in major cities, and in subsequent years the film has been the target of picketing and numerous lawsuits. In New York City, editorials called for the creation of an official local censor and commented on the widespread indignation and racial hatred that the film had aroused. In Boston, protesters picketed theaters and attempted to stop patrons from seeing the film, and 10 days after the film was released, nearly 3,000 people marched on the state capitol to demand an end to the exhibition of the film. In Chicago the mayor refused to allow the film to open until the state legislature passed a statute banning racially inflammatory materials in all media. The governor of Ohio banned the film outright throughout the state upon recommendation of the state board of censors, and the film also was banned in the cities of Denver, Pittsburgh, St. Louis and Minneapolis. The banning did not hurt ticket sales but instead increased interest in the film, which became the first blockbuster success of the silent screen. In New York City alone, even at the then-outrageous price of two dollars per ticket, the film was exhibited in a Broadway theater for 44 continuous weeks, and an estimated 825,000 people saw it in 1915 during its run.

In Kansas in 1915, the newly incorporated Kansas State Board of Review (BOR) refused to approve *The Birth of a Nation* for exhibition in the state although it received critical acclaim from all three board members. The BOR questioned the historical accuracy of the film and argued to ban it in total for "inciting racial hatred and sectional bias." The distributor entered a request for review to the Appeal Board, which concurred with the BOR decision and refused to reverse the rejection. The decision to ban the film resulted in mixed public opinion among Kansas residents. Members of the Union veterans' group Grand Army of the Republic (GAR), which had openly condemned the film based only on reviews, applauded the decision and stated that the production was disrespectful because "it suggested that the North was wrong and the South was right in the Civil War" and it glorified the Ku Klux Klan. In contrast, wives of many state officials spoke out against banning the film, and some who had managed to view it emphasized that they experienced no feelings of "race hatred" after doing so. The decision of the Kansas State BOR regarding *The Birth of a Nation* stood firm until 1923, when the BOR reviewed the film once again, made suggestions for editing, and passed it for exhibition.

In Minneapolis, the banning of *The Birth of a Nation* did not raise issues of constitutionality nor of the freedom of the press; instead, it was a test of the right of the mayor to exercise the power to revoke licenses, delegated to him by law. The city charter stated that any license granted by authority of the city council could be revoked by the mayor or the council at any time. Mayor W. G. Nye asserted this power in 1915, after seeing the disruptions that other cities nationwide had endured, and told the theater operator that he would revoke the theater's license if *The Birth of a Nation* were shown. When the theater operator filed a request with the District Court of Hennepin County asking that the court enjoin this censorship, Nye defended the ban by calling for a panel of "unprejudiced people of diverse callings" to view the film and to determine its "fitness." He later reported to the court that the results of the film showing revealed that it "tended to bring reproach upon the negro race" and he expressed fear that having the general population view the film "would invite race hatred and riots." Nye further charged the movie with tending "to inculcate in the public mind a distrust of public officials and law" and to justify "lawless citizens in their attempts to organize themselves into bands to avenge real or fanciful wrongs with the avowed purpose to override public authority and take into their own hands the punishment of officers in such a manner as they shall decide, irrespective of courts, public officers, and the government itself." The mayor also questioned the historical accuracy of the film and suggested that such inaccuracies "prejudiced the public mind." The district court in *Bainbridge v. City of Minneapolis* refused to reverse the mayor's ban. The theater operator took the matter before the Supreme Court of Minnesota, which affirmed the decision of the lower court.

The controversy did not die with the silent era, for censorship battles erupted when the film was reissued in 1924, 1931 and 1938, although, as Miller states, "in later years, local censors usually banned the film to prevent the KKK from using it as a recruiting tool." In 1978, a riot resulted when the film was screened in Oxnard, California. The controversy has extended even to its role as a classic American film. In 1993, the film was added to the National Film Registry, and black leaders tried to stop the honor as they protested its racial content.

FURTHER READING

Aitken, Roy E., as told to Al P. Nelson. *The Birth of a Nation Story.* Middleburg, Va.: Denlinger Publishing, 1965.
Bainbridge v. City of Minneapolis, 154 N.W. 964 (1915); affirmed 242 U.S. 353 (1916).
"Films and Birth and Censorship." *Survey* 34 (April 3, 1915): 4–5.
Fleener-Marzec, Nickieann. *D. W. Griffith's "The Birth of a Nation": Controversy, Suppression, and the First Amendment as It Applies to Filmic Expression, 1915–1973.* Madison, Wisc.: University of Wisconsin, 1977.
Gish, Lillian. "The Making of *The Birth of a Nation*," in *The Movies, Mr. Griffith, & Me.* Englewood Cliffs, N.J.: Prentice-Hall, 1959.
Henderson, Robert M. *D. W. Griffith: His Life and Work.* New York: Oxford University Press, 1972.
Jacobs, Lewis. "D. W. Griffith: *The Birth of a Nation* and *Intolerance*," in *The Rise of the American Film.* New York: Harcourt Brace, 1939.
Lamont, Corliss. *Freedom Is as Freedom Does: Civil Liberties Today.* New York: Horizon Books, 1956.
Lang, Robert, ed. *The Birth of a Nation: D. W. Griffith, Director.* New Brunswick, N.J.: Rutgers University Press, 1994.
Miller, Frank. *Censored Hollywood: Sex, Sin and Violence on Screen.* Atlanta, Ga.: Turner Publishing, 1994.
"The Regulation of Film." *Nation*, 100 (May 6, 1915): 486–487.
Silva, Fred, ed. *Focus on The Birth of a Nation.* Englewood Cliffs, N.J.: Prentice-Hall, 1971.

Wedin, Carolyn. "How The NAACP Fought the Worst Great Movie." *American Legacy* 2, no. 4 (Winter 1997): 37–42.

BLOCKADE

Country and date of production: United States, 1938
Production companies/distributor: Walter Wanger Productions, Inc./ United Artists
Format: Sound, black and white
Running time: 85 minutes
Language: English
Producer: Walter Wanger
Director: William Dieterle
Screenwriter: John Howard Lawson
Awards: None
Genre: War
With: Madeleine Carroll (Norma), Henry Fonda (Marco), Leo Carrillo (Luis), John Halliday (Andre Gallinet), Vladimir Sokoloff (Basil, Norma's Father), Robert Warwick (General Vallejo), Reginald Denny (Edward Grant), Peter Godfrey (Magician), Katherine DeMille (Cabaret Girl), William B. Davidson (Commandant)

SUMMARY

Blockade is a fictional treatment of the Spanish Civil War, which began when the fascist leader General Francisco Franco led the Spanish army in rebellion against the freely elected, legally constituted Republican government (known as the Popular Front or the Loyalists) of Spain on July 17, 1936. The ensuing civil war became one of the most fervent humanitarian causes in Hollywood during the 1930s, despite the official position of neutrality held by the United States government. Among the many films about the Popular Front that producers contemplated, and despite the efforts by Ernest Hemingway to release *The Spanish Earth*, a film for which he had co-written the script with Lillian Hellman and Archibald MacLeish, only *Blockade* was ever released. Distributors, as well as the leading producers and directors, were reluctant to commit themselves publicly. The film goes to great lengths to disguise the names of real people and places, but it still provides an accurate portrayal of the conflict so that viewers will condemn the bombing and starvation of women and children that occurred in Spain.

Producer Walter Wanger first assigned the task of writing a script about Spain in 1937 to the radical playwright Clifford Odets, a member of the Communist Party, but the resultant screenplay was technically impossible to film. Desperate to meet his shooting schedule, Wanger turned to John Howard Lawson, another member of the Communist Party, to rewrite the script. A Hollywood veteran and vocal pro-Loyalist (advocate for the Popular

Front), Lawson knew that a film that was overtly sympathetic to the Spanish Loyalists, who counted communists among their supporters, could not be made, so he would have to use subterfuge: "We could not call the Loyalists by name, we could not use the actual Loyalists' uniform." Although the screenwriter sought to warn the American people that the Spanish Civil War pointed ominously to a greater war, as well as to reveal the horrifying conditions that the bombing of cities and the starvation of the civilian population had caused, the message had to be muted. The resulting screenplay depicts clearly occurring events in Spain, but the opposing sides are not identified in the film. The political leanings of Marco, the hero of the film, are not identified, although any politically active viewer would know that he is a Loyalist. As finally released, the film is a spy caper and romance that carries a diluted examination of the issue of fascism versus democracy.

CENSORSHIP HISTORY

Film censorship of commercial "entertainment" films for blatantly political reasons became prominent in the late 1930s in the United States as filmmakers walked the fine line between portraying accurately the events in Europe and meeting the pressure exerted by the U.S. government to maintain the air of American neutrality to these events. Political scientists such as Larry Ceplair and Steven Englund maintain that "Roosevelt feared alienating the large Catholic voting bloc in the United States (the Catholic hierarchy, of course, staunchly supported Franco) as well as the numerous proponents of traditional American isolationism." Although the Hays Office had given the script prior approval, later angry reactions by American supporters of General Franco, who viewed the film as pro-Loyalist and anti-Franco, led to industry and government involvement in undermining the economic success of the film.

When the movie opened at Radio City Music Hall in 1938, Catholic groups supported by the Catholic Legion of Decency (LOD) set up pickets around Radio City and displayed what Winchell Taylor wrote in *The Nation* were "fantastic accusations of 'war propaganda.'" Parish priests ordered members of their churches to boycott the film, and the Knights of Columbus and other Catholic groups supported by the LOD made noisy protests to the Hays Office. Martin Quigley, an influential Catholic publisher whose *Motion Picture Herald* wielded substantial influence, directed his publications to attack the film for its perceived propagandist bias and to urge Catholics of conscience to boycott the movie. Even after the film was heavily edited and shorn of almost all its political content, the LOD continued to protest showing of the film because they claimed that it "sided with the anticlerical Republicans."

To avoid disruptions, Fox West Coast Theatres refused to show the film as a first-run release. The International Alliance of Theatrical Stage Employees (IATSE), Hollywood's largest trade union, denounced the film at its national convention and passed a resolution to inform producers that union projectionists "will not be responsible for the handling of propaganda films by its members." After an initially good financial record for its first release, the film was denied bookings for a second-run release in theater chains along the West Coast. Taylor wrote that the hysteria directed at *Blockade* was "fundamentally an attack not so much on an inferentially pro-Loyalist film, as on the whole idea of making films on serious social and political themes."

FURTHER READING

"Censorship Fight Over Movie Morals." *Life* 5 (July 18, 1938): 50–55.

Ceplair, Larry. "The Politics of Compromise in Hollywood: A Case Study." *Cineaste* 8, no. 4 (1982): 2–7.

Ceplair, Larry, and Steven Englund. *The Inquisition in Hollywood: Politics in the Film Community, 1930–1960.* Garden City, N.Y.: Doubleday, 1980.

Davis, Dave, and Neal Goldberg. "Organizing the Screen Writers Guild—An Interview with John Howard Lawson." *Cineaste* 8, no. 2 (1982): 10.

Miller, Frank. *Censored Hollywood: Sex, Sin and Violence on Screen.* Atlanta, Ga.: Turner Publishing, 1994.

Taylor, Winchell, "Secret Movie Censors." *Nation* 124 (July 9, 1938): 38–40.

BLONDE VENUS

Country and date of production: United States, 1932
Production company/distributor: Paramount Pictures
Format: Sound, black and white
Running time: 92 minutes
Language: English
Producer: Josef von Sternberg
Director: Josef von Sternberg
Screenwriters: Jules Furthman, S. K. Lauren
Awards: None
Genre: Drama
With: Marlene Dietrich (Helen Faraday), Herbert Marshall (Edward Faraday), Cary Grant (Nick Townsend), Dickie Moore (Johnny Faraday), Gene Morgan (Ben Smith), Rita La Roy (Taxi Belle), Robert Emmett O'Connor (Dan O'Conner), Sidney Toler (Detective), Morgan Wallace (Dr. Pierce)

SUMMARY

Blonde Venus was one of a number of films appearing from 1930 to 1933 that dealt with the subjects of divorce, adultery, prostitution and promiscuity. Many critics have viewed these movies as a reflection of conditions during the Great Depression that were causing people to make difficult moral decisions. In this movie, although the leading woman character commits adultery, she does so in order to obtain money for a treatment that will save her husband's life. He rejects her when he learns of her infidelity, without attention to her reasons.

Ned Faraday, an American chemist, falls in love with and marries a German entertainer, but tragedy strikes soon after they begin a family. He learns that he has become poisoned with radium and will need an expensive treatment if he is to become well again. Hoping to raise enough money for her husband's procedure, his beautiful wife Helen returns to her old profession of singing in nightclubs and becomes very popular as the Blonde Venus. When she realizes that she will not make the large sum of money needed in enough time to save her husband's life, she prostitutes herself to a millionaire named Nick Townsend. Once she has acquired the amount of money needed for treatment, Ned goes to Europe without questioning too strenuously how Helen managed, and Helen continues the affair with Townsend. When Ned returns from Europe, cured of radium poisoning, he discovers that his loving wife has been unfaithful and begins to hate her. He is unable even to look at the woman whom he believes has betrayed him emotionally and physically. Made to feel ashamed and panicked, Helen flees with her son Johnny. The two begin a covert life of running from the authorities, with the Missing Persons Bureau in relentless pursuit of Helen. When they finally catch her, they return Johnny to Ned and leave Helen to fend for herself. With nowhere to go and no family, she leaves for Paris. Since she is not trained in any other profession, she revives her career as a nightclub entertainer and, once again, becomes quite famous. Still infatuated with Helen, Nick Townsend follows her to Paris and the two discover that they both still care deeply for each other. They resume their affair, then become engaged and return to America to start a life together. Once Helen is back in the United States she becomes unhappy, for her heart is drawn back to her former life. She misses her son and wonders what has become of her former husband, Ned. The remainder of the film presents Helen's attempts to decide in which life she truly belongs.

CENSORSHIP HISTORY

Controversy over *Blonde Venus* began in the script stage, when Paramount production head Ben P. Schulberg rejected the original script written by Josef von Sternberg as "too raw" to produce and demanded that a "safe version" of the script be written. Sternberg's first version ended with Helen giving up her glamorous career and her wealthy lover to return to her modest marriage and her family. The Motion Picture Producers and Distributors Association censor in charge of the project, Lamar Trotti, rejected the script because Helen's affair is "justified in the minds of the audience by tearing down the character of the husband, who, up to this point, has been a decent man who was deceived by his wife." To reunite the husband and wife at the end of the film, as occurred in the first version, removed the possibility of the "compensating moral values" demanded by the industry censors. The second version of the script, written largely by Paramount production head Ben P. Schulberg, modified the ending to show Helen alone; yet it retained the adulterous affair and Helen's move into prostitution and other objectionable behavior. The industry censor finally approved the third version of the script, which was the result of a compromise between the two earlier scripts.

The movie filmed from the modified script received the approval of the Studio Relations Committee (SRC) because, as Jason Joy, the SRC head, explained, "Never are infidelity and prostitution themselves made attractive." In reality, the film moves Helen Faraday up and down the socioeconomic ladder. She begins as a singer in a Berlin cabaret; moves to a life of near-poverty as the American wife of a dying man; enters an affair that takes her to an opulent Manhattan apartment; falls into the depths as a low-class prostitute in the Deep South; then resurrects herself as a star nightclub attraction in France.

Those who objected to exhibiting the film were concerned with more than the story line; they also focused on the nature of Helen's nightclub act. Appearing as the "Blonde Venus," Helen's nightclub act has her wearing a gorilla suit and bushy, platinum blonde wig while she dances in front of an undulating chorus line of dancers who are in blackface and wearing bushy black wigs. When Helen removes the suit to reveal her skimpy costume beneath, she begins to undulate to the song "Hot Voodoo," which hints of her own dark desires:

> Hot voodoo—black as mud
> Hot voodoo—in my blood
> That African tempo has made me a slave
> Hot voodoo—dance of sin
> Hot voodoo—worse than gin
> I'd follow a cave man right into his cave.

In 1934, as a result of great pressure exerted by the Catholic Legion of Decency (LOD), the Hays office worked with LOD official Martin Quigley to construct a production code stronger than the one passed in 1930. The new code would incorporate production code administration head Joe Breen's "compensating moral values," which required films to contain "at least sufficient good to compensate any evil they relate." When the new code went into effect on July 11, 1934, *Blonde Venus* was reclassified by the Production Code Administration as a "Class I" production and pulled from circulation. Breen vowed that it would never again be released in its original form.

FURTHER READING

Black, Gregory D. *Hollywood Censored: Morality Codes, Catholics, and the Movies.* Cambridge, England: Cambridge University Press, 1994.

Doherty, Thomas. *Pre-Code Hollywood: Sex, Immorality, and Insurrection in American Cinema, 1930–1934.* New York: Columbia University Press, 1999.

Jacobs, Lea. "The Censorship of the Blonde Venus." *Cinema Journal* 27 (Spring 1988): 21–31.

Vieira, Mark A. *Sin in Soft Focus: Pre-Code Hollywood.* New York: Harry N. Abrams, 1999.

THE BLUE ANGEL

Country and date of production: Germany, 1930 (*Der Blaue Engel*)

Production company/distributor: Universum Film A.G. (UFA) (Germany)/Paramount (United States, 1931)

Format: Sound, black and white

Running Time: 99 minutes (Germany); 93 minutes (United States)

Language: German, English

Producer: Erich Pommer

Director: Josef von Sternberg

Screenwriters: Heinrich Mann (novel, *Professor Unrat*), Carl Zuckmayer, Karl Vollmöller, Heinrich Mann, Robert Liebmann, Josef von Sternberg (uncredited)

Awards: None

Genre: Drama

With: Emil Jannings (Prof. Immanuel Rath), Marlene Dietrich (Lola Lola), Kurt Gerron (Kiepert, the Magician), Rosa Valetti (Guste, his wife), Hans Albers (Mazeppa, the Strong Man), Reinhold Bernt (the Clown), Eduard von Winterstein (Headmaster)

SUMMARY

The Blue Angel, Germany's first sound film, was filmed simultaneously in German and English. Von Sternberg constructed the film around Marlene Dietrich, and he intended to use it to bring her fame. The cabaret set was specially designed to place it in the time of von Sternberg's own adolescence. The songs, which have very few notes, were especially chosen to suit Dietrich's limited voice. The story portrays the fall and humiliation of Professor Immanuel Rath, a high school literature teacher. His students mock him and show no interest in their studies, preferring to spend class time talking and passing around pictures of a local nightclub singer, which Rath confiscates. Determined to save the students from what he believes to be the singer's negative influence, he decides to speak with her and goes to the Blue Angel nightclub. While waiting in Lola's dressing room, the stodgy teacher becomes fascinated with the life that she leads, as it is so unlike his conservative, scholarly existence. He sees many of his students at the nightclub, where one boy sneaks a pair of Lola's underpants into the professor's coat pocket. Discovering the item later, Rath is embarrassed and goes to the club the next night to return them. He begins to drink as he listens to Lola sing. He is soon seduced by her smoky voice and the sensuality of her song in which she proclaims that she is "made for love from head to toe." Helpless against Lola's aggressive sexuality, Rath spends the night with her and is late to class the next morning. After his administrator reprimands him for jeopardizing his respected pedagogical career for a woman of Lola's sort, Rath announces that Lola will be his wife. The professor is further humiliated by the students, who rebel even more strenuously, call him "garbage," and make fun of his infatuation.

Rath and Lola do marry and, because his teaching career is now destroyed, the professor becomes a peddler of sorts, selling to anyone interested the provocative photographs of Lola that he once hated. After five years of marriage, his dignity is gone. He is reduced to the level of a pathetic clown who works as an assistant to a sleight-of-hand magician. He experiences complete humiliation when he must appear in an act in his clown guise at the Blue Angel nightclub in front of his former colleagues and students while Lola is romanced onstage by a young, virile-looking strongman. Barely able to make it through the act, the professor-turned-clown staggers back to his old school classroom where he is last seen slumped over and clutching his desk.

CENSORSHIP HISTORY

The Blue Angel is an erotic parable that expresses the plight of German intellectuals between the two world wars. In part, it explores the manner in which the educated mind may look down on sensual pleasures, partly from the fear that such desires will make a fool of even the most intellectual man, as Lola Lola does to Rath. Such insecurity may often account for the zeal with which some attempt to suppress such basic instincts. The sexuality in the film has been frequently discussed. In one scene, as Lola Lola leaves her dressing room to perform, she brazenly adjusts her underpants and gives a provocative look backward at a surprised Rath. Lola Lola is the schoolboy's fantasy, with stockings, makeup and a top hat. She is responsible for the downfall of a middle-class professor who becomes infatuated with her while trying to save his students from her influence. By marrying her and becoming an act in the cabaret, he gives the cabaret respectability while losing his own when he joins the lineup.

The Blue Angel was criticized when it first appeared in Germany. It was a very personal film for von Sternberg, who treated the scenario as a base for his own interest in and obsession with Marlene Dietrich, with whom he was in love. However personal the film was, Alfred Hugenberg, a right-wing nationalist politician and the head of UFA, the studio that produced the film, viewed it as an attack on the middle class, although he did not direct von Sternberg to make changes. Dietrich claimed in her autobiography to have been shocked by *The Blue Angel:* "Remember I was a well brought up German girl."

The film was one of the first to be judged by Jason Joy when he was appointed to head the Studio Relations Committee. Because of the raw sexuality that Lola Lola exudes on screen, as Gregory Black observes, "the film certainly violated the code both in specific provisions and spirit." Despite this, when Paramount invited Joy to view the film in order to solicit the approval of the SRC to exhibit the film in the United States, Joy found nothing objectionable and, instead, pronounced the film "superb."

Local censors were not as impressed. In Pasadena, California, city censor C. V. Cowan charged that he would not allow a film with such "blatant sexuality" to be exhibited, and he banned the film from the city. After the owner of the Colorado Theatre begged him to reconsider, Cowan edited the film to remove scenes that he found offensive and then attached a statement indicating that the film had been censored to receive approval. At the first showing, the audience expected to see a darkly sensual film; instead, they were subjected to drastically condensed and poorly edited version that led the audience to show its disapproval with "a terrific razzing." To prevent further audience response of the same sort, the theater owner removed the statement.

All of Dietrich's movies, including *The Blue Angel*, were banned in Germany during World War II. Despite personal appeals made by Adolf Hitler, she refused to work in Germany and refused to make the pro-Nazi statements that he requested. Dietrich became a U.S. citizen in 1937 and from 1943 to 1946 made more than 500 personal appearances before Allied troops.

FURTHER READING

Black, Gregory D. *Hollywood Censored: Morality Codes, Catholics, and the Movies*. New York: Cambridge University Press, 1994.

Riva, Maria. *Marlene Dietrich (by her daughter)*. New York: Alfred A. Knopf, 1993.

Spoto, Donald. *The Blue Angel: The Life of Marlene Dietrich*. Boston: G. K. Hall, 1993.

Vieira, Mark. *Sin in Soft Focus: Pre-Code Hollywood*. New York: Harry N. Abrams, 1999.

Wyman, Mark. "The Blue Angel." *Film Review* (U.K.), November 1997, p. 26.

BLUE MOVIE

Country and date of production: United States, 1969 (original title *Fuck*)
Production company/distributor: Andy Warhol Films
Format: Sound, color
Running time: 90 minutes
Language: English
Producer: Paul Morrissey
Director: Andy Warhol
Screenwriter: Andy Warhol
Awards: None
Genre: Drama
With: Viva (Herself), Louis Waldon (Himself)

SUMMARY

Blue Movie, originally titled *Fuck* but retitled when it was released in New York City, debuted at the New Garrick Theater on Bleecker Street that had been renamed the Andy Warhol Garrick Theater soon after Warhol was shot and critically wounded in 1968 by Valerie Solanis, who had held a minor role in his movie *I, a Man*. The movie is part of a larger compendium of material that Warhol filmed between the summer of 1966 and the autumn of 1967, which he named **** [*sic*]. The entire 25-hour movie **** was shown only once intact, on December 15 and 16, 1967 and then dismantled. In his memoir *POPism*, Warhol said of **** that it "brought back all our early days of shooting movies just for the fun and beauty of getting down what was happening with people we knew . . . **** was like life, our lives, flashing in front of us—it would just go by once and we'd never see it again." The 90-minute segment that was first screened as *Blue Movie* covers the same amount of time during an afternoon a couple spends lying in bed in their Manhattan apartment, discussing social issues; engaging first in sexual foreplay, then in coitus; taking a shower; and watching television. At first, they discuss the Vietnam War, the garbage strike, and New York City's Mayor John Lindsey as if they are alone, but they express increasing awareness of the camera as the film nears an end, until Viva finally stares at the camera and asks, "Is it on?"

CENSORSHIP HISTORY

The film played for several weeks at the Andy Warhol Theater, and it was viewed at several different times by members of the New York Police Department before two police officers asked a New York County assistant district attorney to assist them in obtaining a warrant to stop the exhibition of the film. Armed with a search warrant and three "John Doe" warrants for the theater operator, the ticket taker and the projectionist, the two police officers made the arrests and impounded the film "to preserve it as evidence." The charges against the projectionist and the ticket taker were dropped, but the theater operator faced criminal charges for promoting obscene material. The New York State Supreme Court, Appellate Term, affirmed the conviction, which was later reaffirmed in *People v. Heller* when the case was brought before the New York Court of Appeals. The court of appeals concurred that the film was obscene and refuted the contention of the theater operator that a constitutional need existed for the court to hold an adversary hearing to determine if the film were obscene before issuing warrants to seize the film. When the case was later heard in 1973 by the U.S. Supreme Court in *Heller v. New York*, the justices voted to remand the case to the New York court for the "sole purpose of affording an opportunity to reconsider substantive issues" of obscenity and to apply the newly established Miller Standard to assess it. The Miller Standard replaced the old application of a national consensus to determine what is obscene with a new approach that was based on the standards of each community. When the New York courts reconsidered *Blue Movie* using the standards set down in *Miller v. California*, the film was found obscene and was banned once again.

FURTHER READING

Hoberman, J., and Jonathan Rosenbaum. *Midnight Movies.* New York: Harper & Row, 1983.

Krafsur, Richard, ed. *American Film Institute Catalog of Motion Pictures: Feature Films 1961–1970.* New York: R. R. Bowker, 1976.

Miller v. California, 413 U.S. 15 (1973).

People v. Heller, 277 N.E. 2d 651 (1971).

Heller v. New York, 413 U.S. 483 (1973).

Warhol, Andy. *Blue Movie—Screenplay.* New York: Grove Press, 1970.

BODY OF A FEMALE

Country and date of production: United States, 1964
Production company/distributor: Amlay Pictures/Joseph Brenner Associates, Inc.
Format: Sound, black and white
Running time: 71 minutes
Language: English
Producer: Michael Findlay (credited as Julian Marsh and J. Ellsworth)
Director: Michael Findlay (credited as Julian Marsh and J. Ellsworth)
Screenwriter: Francis Ellie
Awards: None
Genre: Thriller
With: Lem Amer (Spencer), Michael Findlay (Bruno), Roberta Findlay (Cindy), Kate Swanson (Mrs. Arnold), Sally Wood (Norma)

SUMMARY

In *Body of a Female*, a young striptease dancer named Cindy is kidnapped by Bruno, a drifter who has been ordered to deliver her to an opulent New England mansion owned by Spencer, a man whose tastes run to whips and bondage. When Cindy arrives at the mansion, Spencer offers a substantial amount of money for her to stay and perform her striptease act, and she agrees. While she dances, Spencer's body twitches with his desire to whip her, but he restrains himself, hoping to have his pleasure later. After Spencer goes into town for a while, Bruno appears at the mansion to see Cindy. He speaks first with the housekeeper, who tells him what Cindy already has been compelled to do and what Spencer probably will do to Cindy when he returns. Before Bruno can warn Cindy, she runs into the house, to be met a short time later by Spencer, who has returned to tie her up and whip her. The infatuated Bruno rushes into the mansion, frees Cindy and runs away with her. A desperate Spencer follows the two, knowing that his reputation will be ruined if Cindy tells anyone about his obsessions. He determines that he must kill both Cindy and Bruno. Spencer finds the couple on the beach acting out their sexual infatuation with each other. He and Bruno struggle, but the young drifter is stronger. The movie ends with Spencer dead by drowning and Cindy about to begin a new life with Bruno.

CENSORSHIP HISTORY

This film was not widely distributed, nor was it widely banned, but the importance of *Body of a Female* is that a challenge to its banning led the United States Supreme Court to declare the Chicago motion picture censorship ordinance unconstitutional as applied to the manner in which this film and one even less known, *Rent-a-Girl* (1965), were banned. In 1967, the Chicago board of censors refused the distributor a license to exhibit the film, and applied to the Circuit Court of Cook County to enjoin Teitel Film Corp. permanently from publicly exhibiting the film in Chicago. The distributor challenged the ruling, but the Supreme Court of Illinois affirmed the ruling of the lower court in *Cusack v. Teitel Film Corp.* and wrote that their "examination of these films shows that they deal not merely with sex, but with sexual deviations which can only appeal to those with a shameful and morbid interest in nudity and sex . . . and the producers have apparently spared no effect to see that the spectator searching for the erotic is not disappointed." The distributor challenged the decision, and the case was heard by the United States Supreme Court, which in *Teitel Film Corp. v. Cusack* reversed the decision of the Illinois Supreme Court and declared the Chicago ordinance unconstitutional. The higher court pointed out that the ordinance failed to provide sufficient time to complete the administrative process before initiating a judicial proceeding and the ordinance did not contain a provision to assure a prompt final judicial decision.

FURTHER READING

Cusack v. Teitel Film Corp., 230 N.E. 2d 241 (1967)
De Grazia, Edward, and Roger K. Newman. *Banned Films: Movies, Censors & The First Amendment.* New York: R. R. Bowker, 1982.
Teitel Film Corp. v. Cusack, 390 U.S. 139 (1968).

THE BRAND

Country and date of production: United States, 1919
Production company/distributor: Rex Beach Film Corporation/Goldwyn Distributing Corporation
Format: Silent, black and white
Running time: 105 minutes
Language: English
Producer: Rex Beach
Director: Reginald Barker
Screenwriter: Rex Beach

Awards: None
Genre: Adventure
With: Kay Laurel (Alice Andrews), Russell Simpson (Dan McGill), Robert McKim (Bob Barclay), Robert Kunkel (Hopper), Mary Jane Irving (The Child)

SUMMARY

The Brand is based on a short story written by Rex Beach, who adapted it for the screen. Set in Alaska during the gold rush, this uncomplicated period piece features numerous camera views of a snow-covered landscape of mountains and open spaces, sparsely punctuated by picturesque miners' cabins. The dance halls offer the only relief from this barrenness, and the miners cluster in these dance halls each night to drink, listen to the piano music and watch the women dance. The plot centers on one of the dance hall girls, Alice Andrews, who is living with her lover and her child in the mining camp. She has left her husband to live with her lover, and the movie appears to leave deliberately unclear whether the child was fathered by Alice's husband or by her lover. Her indiscretion leads to disaster when her husband reappears and threatens Alice and then attacks her lover with a knife, cutting into his forehead "the brand," a deep cut that seems likely to permanently scar him.

CENSORSHIP HISTORY

The Pennsylvania State Board of Censors refused the application for a license to exhibit this film, which was submitted in 1919 by Goldwyn Distributing Corporation. The censors believed that no amount of editing could make the film conform to its requirements because the plot was largely about the dancer and her lover who are, in the words of the board, "living together without marriage, and in adultery," an action that was designed to "debase or corrupt the morals." Board members also charged that *The Brand* contained material that was "designed to inflame the mind to improper adventures." Goldwyn appealed the board's decision in a common pleas court in Philadelphia, charging that the decision of the board of censors was "an arbitrary and oppressive abuse of discretion" and that the film was "moral and proper." The common pleas court reviewed the film and reversed the decision of the censors, using as its justification provision in the Pennsylvania motion picture licensing law that granted the court the reversal power without specifying the grounds permitting it to do so.

The board of censors then appealed the decision of the lower court to the Pennsylvania Supreme Court, which reversed the opinion of the common pleas court and reprimanded the lower court for not placing the burden of proof on the distributor, who would have to show that the censors had made their decision based on grounds that were not authorized by the statute. The Pennsylvania Supreme Court reminded the lower court that the moral standard set by the statute "pays high deference and respect to the sanctity and purity of the home and family relation between husband and wife, upon which the home rests." The film, the court concluded, conflicts with this standard because it depicts an "adulterous relationship, long continued, between a libertine and an immoral married woman, the legal wife of another, with no moral to be derived therefrom other than that the man who debauched the wife of another runs the risk . . . of having his brow scarred with a knife."

FURTHER READING

Pennsylvania, State Board of Censors (Motion Pictures). *Notice [concerning rule change].* Harrisburg, Penn.: The Board, 1919.
Pennsylvania, State Board of Censors (Motion Pictures). *Legal Briefs, 1915–1921.* Pennsylvania State Archives, Pennsylvania Historical and Museum Commission, RG-22, Series #22.28.

BUNNY LAKE IS MISSING

Country and date of production: United States, 1965
Production company/distributor: Columbia Pictures
Format: Sound, black and white
Running time: 107 minutes
Language: English
Producer: Otto Preminger
Director: Otto Preminger
Screenwriters: Marryam Modell (from her Evelyn Piper novel), John Mortimer, Evelyn Mortimer
Awards: 1967 British Academy Awards, Best British Art Direction (Donald M. Ashton).
Genre: Mystery/thriller
With: Keir Dullea (Stephen Lake), Carol Lynley (Ann Lake), Lucie Mannheim (Cook), Noel Coward (Wilson), Delphi Lawrence (First Mother at School), Martita Hunt (Ada Ford), Anna Massey (Elvira), Jill Melford (Teacher), Victor Maddern (Taxi Driver), Laurence Olivier (Superintendent Newhouse), Clive Revill (Andrews)

SUMMARY

Filmed from a screenplay adapted from the novel by Marryam Modell, writing as Evelyn Piper, *Bunny Lake Is Missing* is an eerie film that suggests that the main character lives in a fantasy world. Ann Lake, a young, unmarried American mother, has recently settled in London with her daughter, Bunny, and Ann's brother, Stephen. Almost immediately after their arrival, Ann enrolls her daughter in a British day school. When she goes to retrieve her daughter after the girl's first day at school, no one has any record of Bunny having been registered, and no one admits to having seen the child. The English detective summoned to trace the missing child questions everyone, including Ann, but the police can find no trace that the girl ever existed. They voice suspicions to Ann's brother that Ann may be mentally unhinged. When Stephen provides responses that back up the suspicions of the police, they give up the search. Ann later learns that Stephen is mentally disturbed and that he has kidnapped and drugged Bunny and intends to strangle her. To keep her daughter alive, Ann humors Stephen and plays children's games with him as she waits for the police to come to her rescue.

CENSORSHIP HISTORY

Bunny Lake Is Missing is one of two films (also THE BEDFORD INCIDENT) selected by Columbia Pictures to serve as test cases in an effort to prove the censorship laws in Kansas unconstitutional. Despite informal condemnation of the film for the portrait of Ann as an unwed mother and the suggestion of an incestuous relationship between Ann and Stephen, the film was not banned nor censored for content in any city or state nationwide. Instead, in November 1965, seven months after the United States Supreme Court struck down the censorship law in the state of Maryland (in a case involving the film *Revenge at Daybreak*), Columbia Pictures chose to test the law in Kansas by distributing this film and *The Bedford Incident* without seeking prior approval by the Kansas Board of Reviews (BOR) and by informing the Kansas BOR that it would no longer submit future films that the company intended to exhibit in the state, nor would it seek a certificate of approval.

State attorney general Robert Londerholm brought suit against Columbia Pictures in Shawnee County district court and sought to prevent the distributor from "selling, leasing, exhibiting or using" the films without first obtaining permission from the board of reviews. The distributor retained for its defense former Kansas governor John Anderson, Jr., who defended the action of the company on the grounds that the Kansas statute required the exhibitor to prove that the film was protected expression but federal constitutional standards required the opposite—that the BOR prove the film to be unprotected expression. Citing the ruling in *Freedman v. Maryland*, in regard to *Revenge at Daybreak*, the presiding judge Marion Beatty refused to concur with the state and ruled that the system of censorship practiced by the Kansas BOR was unconstitutional because it "abridged the freedom of expression." Attorney General Londerholm appealed the ruling to state supreme court, which affirmed the decision of the lower court in holding the state motion picture censorship law to be unconstitutional because it "violated the constitutional guaranty of freedom of expression." The court gave the BOR 60 days to complete operations and to turn over all money and properties to designated state agencies, and $20,000 in the BOR account was turned over to the general revenue fund.

FURTHER READING

Gaume, Thomas Michael. *Suppression of Motion Pictures in Kansas, 1952–1975.* Unpublished thesis, University of Kansas, 1976.

Kansas State Board of Review. *Complete List of Motion Picture Films Submitted.* Topeka: Kansas State Board of Review, 1966.

State ex rel. Londerholm v. Columbia Pictures Corporation, 417 P. 2d 255 (1966).

Walker, Alexander. "Bunny Lake is Missing." *The London Evening Standard,* December 8, 1999.

Warner, Linda K. *Movie Censorship in Kansas: The Kansas State Board of Review.* Unpublished thesis, Emporia State University, 1988.

CALIGULA

Country and date of production: United States and Italy, 1980 (also known as *Io, Caligula* in Italy and *Caligula, My Son* in United Kingdom)

Production company/distributor: Felix Cinematografica; Penthouse Films/Analysis Releasing

Format: Sound, color

Running time: 156 minutes

Language: English

Producers: Bob Guccione, Franco Rossellini, Jack H. Silverman

Directors: Tinto Brass, Bob Guccione (additional scenes), Giancarlo Lui (additional scenes)

Screenwriters: Bob Guccione (additional dialogue), Giancarlo Lui (additional dialogue), Gore Vidal (earlier screenplay)

Awards: None

Genre: Adult

With: Malcolm McDowell (Caligula), Teresa Ann Savoy (Drusilla), Helen Mirren (Caesonia), Peter O'Toole (Tiberius), John Steiner (Longinus), Guido Mannari (Macro), Paolo Bonacelli (Chaerea), Leopoldo Trieste (Charicles), Giancarlo Badessi (Claudius), Mirella D'Angelo (Livia), Anneka Di Lorenzo (Messalina), Lori Wagner (Agrippina), Adriana Asti (Ennia), John Gielgud (Nerva)

SUMMARY

The film *Caligula* relates in a straightforward manner the story of the rise and death of Emperor Caligula Caesar, the fourth of the 12 Caesars of the Roman Empire and the most widely recognized after Julius Caesar. History relates that Caligula was one of the most evil rulers ever to control Rome and that his reign was bloody, violent and corrupt. These facts colored the artistic vision of Gore Vidal, who wrote the original screenplay for the film. Vidal sought to convey Caligula's personality and actions in the context of a biographical film; the producer and director, however, sought to alter the focus by graphically illustrating the ruler's decadent and libertine behavior. *Caligula* chronicles the young emperor's rise to power after the death of his great-grandfather, Tiberius. Caligula, who ruled from A.D. 37 to 41, began his reign as a seemingly popular and fair ruler. Involved in an incestuous relationship with his sister Drusilla, he at first enjoys the allure of absolute power, but it soon overwhelms him, and he begins a descent into madness. Caligula orders family members and advisers murdered; forces the wives of his senators to work in a brothel of his own construction; sleeps with his horse; licks his dead sister's naked corpse; declares himself a god; and rapes both a bride and a groom at their wedding reception, before becoming the object of a bloody assassination.

CENSORSHIP HISTORY

Caligula was widely discussed before its release. Much of the attention was given to the anticipated sexual scenes that would later dominate all critical consideration of the work. The film was funded by Bob Guccione, publisher of *Penthouse* magazine, and cost $15 million to make in 1980. Gore Vidal rejected Guccione's suggestions to write sexually graphic scenes into the screenplay; he then sued to have his name removed from the credits when Guccione ignored Vidal's objections and adapted the material to include diverse sexual acts. After viewing the final version of the film, Sir John Gielgud, Malcolm McDowell and Peter O'Toole sought to disassociate themselves from the production, but their names remained in the credits. Guccione knew that *Caligula* would not receive approval from the Motion Picture Association of America (MPAA), so he did not submit it. Instead, he labeled the film as for mature audiences only, assigned it an "MA" rating and instructed theater owners that the film was not to be shown to anyone under the age of 18. The movie was filmed in Italy. When it arrived in the United States in April 1980, U.S. Customs agents at New York's Kennedy Airport declared the film obscene under the guidelines created by the 1973 *Miller v. California* decision and asked the U.S. Department of Justice Criminal Division to prosecute the distributors. In *Miller v. California*, the U.S. Supreme Court decided that to judge a work obscene, the courts must apply the following three-pronged test to determine (1) whether the average person, applying contemporary community standards, would find that the work, taken as a whole, appeals to the prurient interest; (2) whether the work depicts or describes, in a patently offensive way, sexual conduct specifically defined by the applicable state laws; and (3) whether the work, taken as a whole, lacks serious literary, artistic, political, or social value. After viewing the film, the department, led by Deputy Attorney General Benjamin R. Civiletti, claimed its right of administrative discretion, refused the request by customs agents and allowed *Caligula* to enter the United States.

When the film opened in New York City on February 1, 1981, members of Morality in Media, a group that sought to remove what is termed obscene from films, books and other media, attempted to bring a class action suit against distributors of the film. One hour after the film began its run, the theater manager was handed a warrant of arrest based "upon an admiralty and maritime claim," because the film had been brought into the country. Lead claimants in the suit were the head of the Morality in Media movement, Father Hill, and the solicitor general of Fulton County, Georgia, who had long been involved in the anti-obscenity movement. The petition for the class action suit claimed to also represent 3,300 Roman Catholic priests in New York, Los Angeles and Chicago—who had the responsibility "to protect and maintain public morality consistent with the work and family ethic" of 3 million parishioners—and 2,200 prosecutors nationwide. The suit charged that the Criminal Division of the Justice Department had "failed to perform their non-discretionary duty" by allowing the film to enter the United States. The court did not agree with the group, and Judge Vincent L. Broderick dismissed the complaint, declaring that no mandatory duty existed under the Customs Act to compel either the United States attorney or the attorney general "to proceed judicially against the film."

The Court of Appeals for the Second Circuit affirmed the ruling and stated that the private right of action called for by the suit would frustrate one of the purposes of the Customs Act, which is "to screen imported materials for obscenity at the border under rigorous procedural safeguards." The group then moved its efforts to Boston, where its suit met similar failure after complaints from citizens and religious groups that *Caligula* was obscene moved police to seize the film from the theater where it was being shown. The trial in Boston Municipal Court lasted two weeks, during which portions of the proceedings were televised and viewers heard a diverse group of witnesses testify. Chief Judge Harry Elam applied the standards established by *Miller v. California* and determined that the movie did lack serious literary, artistic and scientific content. He characterized the film as "highly prurient," but he also agreed with the views of the political scientist Andrew Hacker, whom Elam felt "articulated rather effectively" that throughout the script ran a political truth: "absolute power corrupts absolutely." Judge Elam wrote of Hacker's testimony:

> He was able to show the frightening effect of power in the hands of a single person, how power was used to emasculate, debase, and exploit sexually. And he was able to relate convincingly all of this to its historical context, as reported by ancient Roman historians. He projected the sobering thought that it was important to be aware of this and other such degrading periods in the history of our world, lest they are allowed to repeat themselves.

As a result, the court ruled that *Caligula* satisfied the standard laid down in *Miller v. California*.

After this failure, Hinson McAuliffe, solicitor general of Fulton County, Georgia and co-leader of Morality in Media, vowed openly that he would bring criminal charges against theater owners and against *Penthouse* magazine if attempts were made to show the film in his county. Hoping to avert further legal proceedings, *Penthouse* filed a request with the federal court in Atlanta for an order that would grant *Caligula* protection under the First Amendment and prevent prosecution of distributors and of theater owners in Georgia who would exhibit the film. The action was hailed by McAuliffe, because the film could not be shown in Atlanta or anywhere else in the county until after a trial could be held, which the prosecution intended to win. Documents filed with the federal district court in the Northern District of Georgia related that the film already had been exhibited in more than 100 U.S. cities. *Penthouse* called as its expert witness Dr. Robert Sklar, chairman of the department of film studies at New York University and the author of numerous works of film theory and criticism.

In testimony, Dr. Sklar, quoted in De Grazia, praised the "serious artistic value" of the work and pointed to the manner in which it conveyed ideas of "corruptive power, indifference to human life, terror, the relationship of mortality and immortality," as well as the "effective use" that the film makes of "elements of the cinematic art," such as set design, music, acting and cinematography. An advisory jury impaneled by the court viewed the film and determined that it was not obscene. The court record relates that both the court and the jury agreed that the film did not appeal to, but instead tended to inhibit, sexual arousal. While the film was ruled to be "patently offensive . . . an affront to contemporary community standards," and lacking serious literary and scientific value, the court records also show that it was thought to have serious political and artistic value. The decision in *Penthouse v. McAuliffe* cleared the way for *Caligula* to be shown throughout the South. Buoyed by the victory in Atlanta, Guccione edited out several of the more blatantly sexual and violent scenes and then submitted the film to the MPAA, which assigned it an "X" rating.

FURTHER READING

De Grazia, Edward, and Roger K. Newman. *Banned Films: Movies, Censors & the First Amendment.* New York: R.R. Bowker, 1982.

Green, Jonathan. *The Encyclopedia of Censorship.* New York: Facts On File, 1990.

Miller, Frank. *Censored Hollywood: Sex, Sin and Violence on Screen.* Atlanta, Ga.: Turner Publishing, 1994.

Morality in Media v. One Motion Picture Entitled "Caligula," No. 80–0640 (Southern District of New York), No. 80–6037 (Court of Appeals for the Second Circuit), Federal Court House, New York. [Files]

"Penthouse v. McAuliffe." Media Law Reporter 7 (1981): 1978.

Scott, Michael. "The Highbrow Railings of Gore Vidal." *Rolling Stone,* May 15, 1980.

CANDY

Country and date of production: United States, 1968
Production company/distributor: American Broadcasting Company/ Cinerama

Format: Sound, color
Running time: 119 minutes
Language: English
Producers: Robert Haggiag, Selig Seligman, Peter Zoref
Director: Christian Marquand
Screenwriters: Buck Henry, Terry Southern and Mason Hoffenberg
(based on Southern and Hoffenberg's "Maxwell Kenton" novel)
Awards: None
Genre: Comedy
With: Charles Aznavour (Hunchback), Marlon Brando (Grindl), Richard
Burton (McPhisto), James Coburn (Dr. Krankheit), John Huston (Dr.
Dunlap), Walter Matthau (General Smight), Ringo Starr (Emmanuel),
Ewa Aulin (Candy), John Astin (Daddy, Uncle Jack), Elsa Martinelli
(Livia), Sugar Ray Robinson (Zero), Anita Pallenberg (Nurse Bullock),
Lea Padovani (Silvia), Florinda Bolkan (Lolita), Marilù Tolo (Conchita),
Nicoletta Machiavelli (Marquita), Umberto Orsini (Hood), Enrico Maria
Salerno (Jonathan J. John)

SUMMARY

The film is based on the classic novel of the same name, written by Terry
Southern and Mason Hoffenberg under the pseudonym of Maxwell Kenton.
The fast-moving story features a lively soundtrack of contemporary music
and mocks the fads of the United States in the 1960s, such as LSD use, Eastern religions, antimilitary protests and hippies. Critics denigrated *Candy*,
contending that it lacked a coherent story line, but audiences enjoyed the
social satire and the self-spoofing by such established actors of the periods as
Charles Aznavour, Richard Burton, Marlon Brando, John Astin, Ringo Starr,
Walter Matthau, James Coburn and John Huston.

The movie is based on a satirical novel, a send-up of Voltaire's *Candide*. In
its most basic sense, the film is about the sexual awakening of a young woman
who embarks on a number of bizarre sexual escapades with a bevy of strange
and disturbing characters. Along the road to becoming a woman, Candy
encounters a doctor who encourages prolific and frequent masturbation, an
exhibitionist gynecologist who examines Candy publicly, and a hunchbacked
thief with a penchant for rubbing himself against police officers.

The first escapade begins with a young Candy being taken advantage of
by a pretentious poet named McPhisto, played by Richard Burton. The poet,
a self-absorbed alcoholic, spills his drink on himself, causing the sympathetic
Candy to take him home and dry him off. This leads to another sexual scene
involving Candy and a Mexican gardener, played by Ringo Starr, while
McPhisto the poet has sex with a doll that is a Candy lookalike. This scene is
interrupted when Candy's father, played by John Astin, walks into the house.
Her father, uncle and aunt decide to move away to save the family's reputation and name. In their attempts to escape, the family is harassed by the

gardener's sister, who knocks Candy's father unconscious. Finally, the family boards a war plane flown by a seemingly psychotic pilot, played by Walter Matthau, who refuses to land the plane because "war can happen at any time." Matthau then attempts to rape Candy. After this scene, any semblance of realism is lost, and the film degenerates into myriad sexual exploits, with each encounter more bizarre than the last.

While the bulk of the film plays like a pornographic movie with a plot, a subtle subplot does emerge. Through her strange sexual exploits, Candy becomes a self-reliant adult capable of emotion and independent decision making. The subplot functions as an analogy for the turbulent era in which the film was made: Only through thumbing her nose at conventional society and perceived decency can our heroine attain true inner freedom and personal satisfaction.

CENSORSHIP HISTORY

The film, which advocates sexual freedom and experimentation, was censored when it was released in France and in the United States. As reported in *The American Film Institute Catalog of Motion Pictures: Feature Films, 1961–1970*, the original version of the movie was 124 minutes long, but 14 minutes were cut to permit exhibition in France. In the United States, the reputation of the novel on which the film was based, published a decade earlier, led many theaters to reject the film, even though it received an "R" rating from the classification board of the Motion Picture Association of America (MPAA). In Jackson, Mississippi, the manager of the Paramount Theater decided to show *Candy* and was arrested with his projectionist on a charge of exhibiting an obscene film: Three police officers dressed in civilian clothes bought tickets and viewed the film, then arrested the two men and seized the print of the film as evidence. The defendants were brought to criminal trial, where they were charged with and found guilty of "exhibiting to public view an obscene picture." Attorneys representing the manager and the projectionist of the Paramount Theater appealed the verdict to the county court and asked the United States District Court for the Southern District of Mississippi to prevent law-enforcement officials from blocking exhibition of the film and to order that the print of the film be returned to the theater, which should then be permitted to exhibit it. In a decision in *Hosey v. City of Jackson*, 309 F. Supp. 527 (1970), the court declared the censorship statute constitutional; it also ruled that the seizure of the film was constitutional because it was authorized under the statute and because, in the eyes of the court, the film was obscene.

De Grazia observes that the importance of the case lies in "illustrating how a court was able to apply the *Memoirs* test of obscenity to a 'Hollywood-type' movie rated 'R' by the MPAA classification board and conclude that the film was obscene." (The case to which de Grazia refers is *Memoirs vs. Massachusetts*, 383 U.S. 413 (1966) involving the novel *Fanny Hill: Memoirs of a Woman of Pleasure*.) In the resulting decision, the court wrote, "The film is devoid of any literary or artistic merit and presents nothing more than a vivid portrayal of hard-core pornography. The film has no discernible theme or plot and involves a disconnected series of scenes depicting sexual gratification in a shocking and shameful manner." Prosecutors took the case before the United States Supreme Court, which reversed the ruling in *Hosey v. City of Jackson*, 401 U.S. 987 (1971).

FURTHER READING

Aronson, Charles S. "Candy." *Daily Variety*, January 14, 1969.
"Candy." *Newsweek*, December 30, 1968.
De Grazia, Edward, and Roger K. Newman. *Banned Films: Movies, Censors & the First Amendment.* New York: R. R. Bowker, 1982.
Krafsur, Richard. *American Film Institute Catalog of Motion Pictures: Feature Films, 1961–1970.* New York: R. R. Bowker, 1982.
Sova, Dawn B. *Banned Books: Literature Suppressed on Sexual Grounds.* New York: Facts On File, 1998.

CARMEN, BABY

Country and date of production: Netherlands/United States, 1967
Production company/distributor: Amsterdam Film Cie./Audubon Films
Format: Sound, color
Running time: 90 minutes
Language: English
Producer: Radley Metzger
Director: Radley Metzger
Screenwriters: Prosper Mérimée (novel), Jesse Vogel
Awards: None
Genre: Drama
With: Uta Levka (Carmen), Claus Ringer (Jose), Barbara Valentine (Dolores), Walter Wilz (Baby Lucas), Christiane Rücker (Misty), Arthur Brauss (Garcia), Doris Arden (Darcy), Michael Münzer (Magistrate), Christian Fredersdorf, Nino Korda, Carl Möhner (Medicio)

SUMMARY

Carmen, Baby integrates a feminist sensibility with counterculture motifs to create a contemporary version of the classic Prosper Mérimée novel *Carmen*, the inspiration for George Bizet's opera *Carmen* and numerous other movies. This film portrays as its heroine a prostitute who casts a spell on a rookie police officer in a small Spanish port town. The man wants to possess the mind, body and soul of the free-spirited Carmen, but she insists on freedom from emotional entanglements and control. Adding to the troubles of the young police officer is Carmen's reliance on astrology and her full faith in her horoscope. Carmen believes that she must be free because her horoscope tells her so, not because she actually feels the need for freedom.

Carmen, Baby was made at the height of the 1960s sexual revolution, and Carmen's desire to explore and define her emerging sexuality reflects the feelings of many young women of that time. In addition, the fact that a police officer, a societal figure of authority, attempts to control and possess her is an extra piece of social commentary that taps into the prevailing countercultural beliefs. The main paradox, however, is that while Carmen seems intent on maintaining her freedom from control and remaining in charge of her own destiny, she remains controlled by the stars and relies on astrology to chart her destiny. Carmen is a mystery even to her many admirers. The Baron, who is enthralled with her, says, "I know her intimately . . . but not well." The police officer, José, refers to her with apparent despair as "that strange and wild girl," whom he marries. Much of the film is concerned with the on-again, off-again relationship between Carmen and José. When he one day finds Carmen with his superior officer, José goes mad and kills the other man in a fit of jealousy. They run away, but the law eventually catches them, and José is sent to prison for the murder. Carmen seeks to free him by seducing the head of the parole board. In turn, he wins freedom for her husband. Carmen soon becomes the lover of a rock-and-roll star, and José follows her to the nightclub where she is watching her lover sing. They begin to quarrel, then leave the club and go to the town square, where José pulls out a knife and stabs Carmen to death.

CENSORSHIP HISTORY

Carmen, Baby has a strong woman at the center; an exotic setting; artful, discreet sex scenes; and a party sequence that showed American audiences the director's perception of the good life—all of which spelled a sexy movie for audiences of the 1960s. Carmen's aggressive lovemaking and Jose's submission—Carmen is usually on top of him—adds some life to these sequences, and the camera angles and sexual scenes help to develop the plot. Despite what censors might have asserted, however, the direction of Radley Metzger suggests all sexual acts, rather than showing explicit camera shots, and no love scene goes below the necks of the lovers. Such efforts at discretion did not protect the film being called objectionable, nor did it protect those who exhibited the film from prosecution. The difference in this case is that the exhibition site and not the exhibition itself became the basis upon which would-be censors brought their case.

On August 28, 1968, a police officer in Richland, Washington, learned that while standing outside of the fence of the Park Y drive-in theater, he could view the film playing on the screen, which that night happened to be *Carmen, Baby.* He also found that people living in homes nearby could also view the screen clearly, as could passing motorists. He asked the city attorney of Richland to accompany him the following evening and to corroborate his observations. The two next approached the Richland justice of the peace, to whom they described several of the more "objectionable" scenes in the movie, and urged him to order the theater manager arrested. Law enforcement officers carried out the arrest and also confiscated several reels of the film as evidence. The manager was charged with violating the Washington State obscenity statute by causing "to be exhibited an obscene, indecent and immoral show," a charge of which he was later convicted in the Richland District Court. He appealed the conviction to the Benton County Superior Court, which also found him guilty of the stated charges, as did the Supreme Court of Washington.

In affirming his conviction, the Washington Supreme Court stated that the film was obscene only in "the context of its exhibition at a drive-in" but that the statute proscribing the knowing display of "obscene" films did not mention the location of the exhibition as an element of the offense. The attorney for the theater manager argued the case before United States Supreme Court on February 29, 1972, and in the decision handed down on March 20, 1972, the body held that "A State may not criminally punish the exhibition of a motion picture film at a drive-in theater where the statute assertedly violated has not given fair notice that the location of the exhibition was a vital element of the offense." William L. Dwyer argued the cause and filed briefs for petitioner, the manager of the Park Y Drive-in Theater in Richland, Washington, and Curtis Ludwig argued the cause for respondent. Other organizations were also involved in the proceedings. The cause of the theater manager was backed by the National Association of Theatre Owners, Inc. (NATO), whose representatives Stanley Fleishman and Sam Rosenwein filed briefs of amici curiae [friends of the court] to urge a reversal of the conviction, as did Louis Nizer and James Bouras, representing the Motion Picture Association of America, Inc. (MPAA). Constantine Regusis, a representative of the group Morality in Media, Inc., also filed a brief as amicus curiae, but the group urged that the earlier conviction stand.

The original statute under which the petitioner was convicted is *Wash. Rev. Code* 9.68.010, which made criminal the knowing display of "obscene" motion pictures:

> Every person who - (1) Having knowledge of the contents thereof shall exhibit, sell, distribute, display for sale or distribution, or having knowledge of the contents thereof shall have in his possession with the intent to sell or distribute any book, magazine, pamphlet, comic book, newspaper, writing, photograph, motion picture film, phonograph record, tape or wire recording, picture, drawing, figure, image, or any object or thing which is obscene; or (2) Having knowledge of the contents thereof shall cause to be performed or exhibited, or shall engage in the performance or exhibition of any show, act, play, dance or motion picture which is obscene; Shall be guilty of a gross misdemeanor.

When the Supreme Court of Washington affirmed the conviction of the theater owner, it did not hold that *Carmen, Baby* was obscene under the test laid down by this Court's prior decisions. e.g., *Roth v. United States*, 354 U.S. 476 or *Memoirs v. Massachusetts*, 383 U.S. 413, in that community standards were not violated, nor did the work, taken as a whole, appeal to prurient interests. The court expressed uncertainty as to "whether the movie was offensive to the standards relating to sexual matters in that area and whether the movie advocated ideas or was of artistic or literary value" and concluded that if it "were to apply the strict rules of *Roth*, the film 'Carmen, Baby' probably would pass the definitional obscenity test if the viewing audience consisted only of consenting adults." Thus, even as the court agreed that the film had "redeeming social value" and it was not, by itself, "obscene" under the *Roth* standard, it nonetheless upheld the conviction, reasoning that in "the context of its exhibition," *Carmen, Baby* was obscene.

The statute under which the petitioner was prosecuted made no mention of the "context" or location of the exhibition in determining whether a film is considered "obscene." Therefore, the Supreme Court justices wrote, "It is as much a violation of due process to send an accused to prison following conviction of a charge on which he was never tried as it would be to convict him upon a charge that was never made. . . . Petitioner's conviction cannot, therefore, be allowed to stand. *Gregory v. City of Chicago*, 394 U.S. 111; *Garner v. Louisiana*, 368 U.S. 157." The Court further decided that "the petitioner is criminally punished for showing *Carmen, Baby* in a drive-in but he may exhibit it to adults in an indoor theater with impunity. The statute, so construed, is impermissibly vague as applied to petitioner because of its failure to give him fair notice that criminal liability is dependent upon the place where the film is shown." In its final decision, the justices stated, "We hold simply that a State may not criminally punish the exhibition at a drive-in theater of a motion picture where the statute, used to support the conviction, has not given fair notice that the location of the exhibition was a vital element of the offense. The judgment of the Supreme Court of Washington is Reversed."

FURTHER READING

Morris, Gary. "Carmen, Baby." *Bright Lights Journal* 26 (1999). http://www.bright-lightsfilm.com
Rabe v. Washington, 405 U.S. 313 (1971).
State v. Rabe, 484 P. 2d 917, 79 Wash. 2d 254 (1971).

CARNAL KNOWLEDGE

Country and date of production: United States, 1971
Production company/distributor: AVCO Embassy Pictures, Cosmos Films/AVCO Embassy Pictures

Format: Sound, color (Technicolor)
Running time: 98 minutes
Language: English
Producers: Joseph E. Levine, Mike Nichols
Director: Mike Nichols
Screenwriter: Jules Feiffer
Awards: 1972 Golden Globe Awards, Best Supporting Actress–Motion Picture (Ann-Margret).
Genre: Dark comedy
With: Jack Nicholson (Jonathan Fuerst), Candice Bergen (Susan), Art Garfunkel (Sandy), Ann-Margret (Bobbie), Rita Moreno (Louise), Cynthia O'Neal (Cindy), Carol Kane (Jennifer)

SUMMARY

Carnal Knowledge relates the story of two male college roommates, Sandy and Jonathan, and their troubled relationships with a range of women from the late 1940s through the 1960s. Critics reviewing the film frequently commented that this is an uncomfortable film for many men to watch because so many of the romantic interactions are so common, yet they are also so dysfunctional. Sandy and Jonathan each approach women in different ways. Sandy is shy, bumbling and awkward, and he claims to be attracted to women because of their sensitivity and intelligence. In contrast, Jonathan is brash and misogynistic, and he selects women based on their physical assets. When both men meet a beautiful young woman named Susan at a college mixer, Jonathan decides that she is not his type because her breasts are too small. Sandy dates her and learns that she is sexually passionate, although a virgin. When Jonathan learns this from Sandy, he asks her out and seduces her, then Sandy does the same, and they both date her for a while. After a time, Jonathan asks Susan to choose between him and Sandy. She chooses Sandy because she believes he would be less capable of dealing with her rejection.

A decade later, Sandy, now a well-established physician in New York City, is married to Susan, but Jonathan has spent those years dating a large number of women. He believes that a 29-year-old model named Bobbie is the woman for whom he has been searching, but their relationship soon becomes destructive: She barely survives an overdose of pills after Jonathan refuses her proposal that they marry and have a child. Another decade passes: Sandy is now divorced from Susan and living with an 18-year-old hippie named Jennifer, whom he claims loves him purely and without limits. They visit Jonathan in his opulent bachelor apartment. Jonathan brings Jennifer to tears by showing slides of the many women in his life. He also reveals that he did marry Bobbie and have a child with her, but they had a bitter divorce and he is now paying a high alimony. After Sandy and Jennifer leave, an expensive prostitute visits Jonathan. She goes through what appears to be a regular ritual, assuring him that he is sexy and that she finds him to be very masculine.

As the film ends, the audience is left with the message that these are two self-involved and juvenile men with a decidedly vicious attitude toward sexual involvement with women.

CENSORSHIP HISTORY

Carnal Knowledge was acclaimed by critics as one of the 10 best films of 1971, yet in March 1972 a criminal jury in Albany, Georgia, declared that the film was obscene and convicted theater operator Billy Jenkins of distributing obscene material. On January 13, 1972, local law-enforcement officers in Albany, Georgia, executing a search warrant, seized the film and arrested the theater manager. The case went to trial in the superior court of Dougherty County, where on March 23, 1972, the jury declared Jenkins guilty. The judge fined him $750 and sentenced him to 12 months probation. The jury based its decision on the Georgia obscenity statute, Ga. Code Ann. 26–2101 (b) (1972), which contained language similar to that expressed in the opinion of the United States Supreme Court in *Memoirs v. Massachusetts*, 383 U.S. 413 (1966), to define obscene material:

> Material is obscene if considered as a whole, applying community standards, its predominant appeal is to prurient interest, that is a shameful or morbid interest in nudity, sex or excretion, and utterly without redeeming social value and if, in addition, it goes substantially beyond customary limits of candor in describing or representing such matters.

The theater owner then appealed the conviction to the Supreme Court of Georgia, which on July 2, 1973, upheld the decision of the lower court. The court stated that the theater owner had been convicted under a Georgia statute containing a definition of obscenity that was "considerably more restrictive" than the definition that had emerged recently in *Miller v. California*, a case that had been decided after the first conviction of Jenkins, and warned that the First Amendment does not permit the commercial exhibition of "hardcore pornography."

Jenkins then appealed the decision to the United States Supreme Court, which declared that convictions that were being appealed at the time of the Miller decision "should receive any benefit available to them from those decisions." Louis Nizer, who argued the case for Jenkins on April 15, 1974, was joined on the briefs by Tench C. Coxe, William H. Schroder, Jr., and James Broder. The defense was supported by briefs of *amici curiae* [friends of the court] filed by representatives of the National Association of Theatre Owners; Adult Film Association of America, Inc.; Directors Guild of America, Inc.; American Library Association; American Booksellers Association, Inc.; Council for Periodical Distributors Association, Inc.; Association of American Publishers; and Authors League of America, Inc. The U.S. Supreme Court reversed the decision of the Supreme Court of Georgia, rendering a decision on June 24, 1974, that *Carnal Knowledge* was protected by the guarantee of free expression given by the First and Fourteenth Amendments to the United States Constitution. The film could not reasonably be found to be obscene as defined under the standards established by *Miller v. California*, for it does not depict sexual behavior "in a patently offensive way," nor is it a "public portrayal of hard core sexual conduct for its own sake, and for the ensuing commercial gain." The nine justices agreed that the film was not obscene and concurred to reverse the conviction.

In delivering the opinion of the court, Justice William H. Rehnquist wrote that the court acknowledged the following:

> While the subject of the picture is, in a broader sense, sex, and there are scenes in which sexual conduct including "ultimate sexual acts" is to be understood to be taking place, the camera does not focus on the bodies of the actors at such times. There is no exhibition whatever of the actors' genitals, lewd or otherwise, during these scenes. There are occasional scenes of nudity, but nudity alone is not enough to make material legally obscene under the *Miller* standards.

Justice Brennan concurred:

> . . . it is clear that as long as the Miller test remains in effect "one cannot say with certainty that material is obscene until at least five members of this Court, applying inevitably obscure standards, have pronounced it so." . . . Because of the attendant uncertainty of such a process and its inevitable institutional stress upon the judiciary, I continue to adhere to my view that, at least in the absence of distribution to juveniles or obtrusive exposure to unconsenting adults, the First and Fourteenth Amendments prohibit the State and Federal Governments from attempting wholly to suppress sexually oriented materials on the basis of their allegedly "obscene" contents. During its run as a feature film, *Carnal Knowledge* played in every state in the United States, appearing in nearly 5,000 theaters, and was viewed by nearly 20 million people.

FURTHER READING

Alpert, Hollis. "Carnal Knowledge." *Saturday Review*, July 3, 1971, p. 18.
Jenkins v. State, 199 S.E. 2d 183, 230 Ga. 726 (1973).
Jenkins v. Georgia, 418 U.S. 153 (1974).
Miller v. California, 413 U.S. 15 (1973).

UN CHANT D'AMOUR

Country and date of production: France, 1947 (released as *A Song of Love*, United States, 1950)
Production company/distributor: Film-Maker's Cooperative
Format: Silent, black and white
Running time: 26 minutes

Language: None
Producer: Jean Genet
Director: Jean Genet
Screenwriter: Jean Genet
Awards: None
Genre: Short subject
With: Java, André Reybaz, Lucien Senemaud

SUMMARY

Written and directed by Jean Genet in 1947, *Un Chant d'Amour,* his only film, transposes his ideas and writing into visual images. The avant-garde work, which contains no music or sound of any kind, has been compared to the films of Jean Cocteau, Kenneth Anger, Maya Deren and Nagisa Oshima, and its lyrical story of gay passion and romance is regarded by critics as one of the most intensely physical films ever made.

The film begins with a prison guard walking outside the prison walls. The camera shows each prisoner alone in his cell, most engaging in masturbation. Prisoners are also shown knocking on the walls to communicate, and two prisoners are blowing smoke to each other through a straw placed in a hole in the wall between their cells. The guard looks into each cell through the peephole and sees the prisoners' acts of autoeroticism. His attention is captured by the conduct of one particularly hairy-chested prisoner, who seems to arouse homoerotic desire in him. Visibly disturbed, the guard enters the cell of the hairy-chested prisoner and beats him fiercely, after which the camera shifts to show the guard again walking his rounds outside the prison walls.

The film contrasts fantasy scenes with the realistic, harsh depiction of the prison, and the viewer is left to determine where reality ends and fantasy begins. In the opening scenes of the film, the guard sees the strange sight of a bouquet of flowers repeatedly swung from one barred cell window to another, each time failing to be grasped by an emerging hand until the very end of the film, when the guard leaves the prisoners and returns to his duties. The second fantasy involves two prisoners, an agitated North African prisoner and his neighbor, a young, disinterested, tattooed convict, who are pictured in a sunlit, romantic forest in which the younger convict holds a bouquet of flowers in front of his groin. The sight of their erotic exchange of cigarette smoke through a straw in the prison wall sets off a series of fantasies for the warder and seems to bring to the surface his own homoerotic desires, which lead him to beat the older prisoner brutally. While he administers the beating, fantasies that appear to be those of the guard appear. These include what appear to be two male heads kissing and the bodies of two males in various positions performing fellatio and anal intercourse. Afterward, the guard leaves the cell but returns once more to insert his gun into the mouth of the beaten prisoner. As the guard leaves the prison, he looks back over his shoulder only to see the bouquet of flowers once more relentlessly swinging, but as he walks away he does not see that the flowers are finally caught.

CENSORSHIP HISTORY

One of the most memorable of short films, *Un Chant d'Amour* is also among the most controversial. The risqué content of the film prevented widespread attempts to exhibit it. Although much silence and confusion surrounded this hidden treasure, it has become the most famous gay short film in European history, and film historians consider the film to be emblematic of the gay film culture. As Nowell-Smith suggests, the film "inspired a new 'cinema of transgression.'"

In 1965, Film-Maker's Cooperative authorized Saul Landau to exhibit the film in the San Francisco Bay area, where he was to share the proceeds with the San Francisco Mime Troupe, an unincorporated association. His agreement stipulated that the film was not to be shown in commercial movie houses that catered to general audiences. Before the police threatened Landau with arrest, he exhibited the film a number of times—in Santa Barbara before an audience comprised mainly of members of the Center for the Study of Democratic Institutions; at several private showings in San Francisco; in several art movie houses in San Francisco; at San Francisco State College; and at Stiles Hall at the University of California, Berkeley. Director Bergfield of the special investigations bureau of the Berkeley Police Department, acting under orders from Police Chief Fording, advised Landau's agent not to exhibit the film again, for to do so would be to risk confiscation of the film and the arrest of "all persons responsible."

Attorneys representing Landau instituted an action in the Alameda County Superior Court, asking that the case be dismissed because the film possessed "artistic value" and "social importance." The court permitted Landau to call seven expert witnesses, who included authorities on drama, literature, film, criminology and law, while the court called as its own expert witness Dr. Charles W. Merrifield, a professor of social science and the head of the social behavioral sciences department at California State College, Hayward. All of Landau's witnesses expressed the theme of the film in different ways, but they all agreed that it was not hard-core pornography. Members of the trial court viewed the film twice and concluded that the average person who applied contemporary community standards would find that the predominant appeal of the film as a whole was to prurient interests. Judge George W. Phillips, Jr., wrote that the film lacked "any ideas of social importance" and had no value as art. He added that the scenes of "vividly revealed acts of masturbation, oral copulation, the infamous crime against nature (sodomy), voyeurism, nudity, sadism, masochism, and sex" rendered the work as "'nothing more than cheap pornography calculated to promote homosexuality, perversion, and morbid sex practices' and that it fell "'far short of dealing with homosexuality, per-version, masturbation or sex from the scientific, historical, or critical point of view'" (245 Cal.App.2d 822).

The court determined that *Un Chant d'Amour* was obscene within the meaning of section 311, subdivision (a) of the California Penal Code, which contained a version of the definition of obscenity created by the United States Supreme Court in *Roth v. United States*. Section 311 asserts: "'Obscene' means that to the average person, applying contemporary standards, the pre-dominant appeal of the matter, taken as a whole, is to prurient interest, i.e., a shameful or morbid interest in nudity, sex, or excretion, which goes substan-tially beyond customary limits of candor in description or representation of such matters and is matter which is utterly without redeeming social impor-tance." The Alameda County Superior Court concluded that *Un Chant d'Amour* was obscene and could not be exhibited.

Landau then appealed the ruling to the District Court of Appeal of Cal-ifornia, which affirmed the ruling of the lower court. Considering only the question of whether or not the film was obscene, the district court of appeal wrote in its decision that the film "goes far beyond customary limits of can-dor in offensively depicting certain unorthodox sexual practices and rela-tionships. . . . Because of the nature of this medium, we think a motion pic-ture of sexual scenes may transcend the bounds of the constitutional guarantee long before a frank description of such scenes in the written word. We cannot here disregard the potent visual impact of the movie in depicting acts of male masturbation, fellatio, oral copulation, voyeurism, nudity, sadism, and sodomy without any clear reference or relation to a dominant theme. We conclude that measured in terms of the sexual interests of its intended and probable recipient group . . . or to the average person, applying contemporary standards, the predominant appeal of the film taken as a whole is to the prurient interest." The court refused to sanction Landau's argument that the film had artistic merit because Jean Genet, the writer, producer and director *Un Chant d'Amour*, was a French writer of renown and wrote, instead, "the artistic merit of Genet's other works does not provide a carte blanche when he chooses to venture into the fields covered by the film" (245 Cal.App.2d 828). The case was taken before the United States Supreme Court, which in *Landau v. Fording*, 388 U.S. 456 (1967), affirmed the judg-ment of the Court of Appeal of California, First Appellate District, and con-demned the film as obscene. Justices Black, Douglas, Stewart and Fortas dis-sented. The justices gave no reasons for their decision, which was rendered on June 12, 1967.

FURTHER READING

Landau v. Fording, 245 Cal. App. 2d 820 (1966).
Landau v. Fording, 388 U.S. 456 (1967).
Mekas, Jonas. "Un Chant d'Amour." *Village Voice*, December 10, 1964.

Nowell-Smith, Geoffrey, ed. *The Oxford History of World Cinema.* New York: Oxford University Press, 1996.

CINDY AND DONNA

Country and date of production: United States, 1970
Production company/distributor: Tempo Enterprises/Crown International Pictures
Format: Sound, color
Running time: 84 minutes
Language: English
Producers: Robert Anderson, Terry Anderson
Director: Robert Anderson
Screenwriter: Barry Clark
Awards: None
Genre: Adult
With: Sue Allen, Nancy Ison, Tom Koben, Max Manning, Debby Osborne (Cindy), Cheryl Powell (Donna)

SUMMARY

The film relates the adventures of two suburban half-sisters, 15-year-old Cindy and 17-year-old Donna, who have the same mother but different fathers. When the film opens, Cindy is shy about exploring her sexuality and remains hesitant until she sees Donna having sex with Cindy's father after both have been smoking marijuana. Cindy loses her inhibitions and smokes marijuana with her friend Karen, after which the two share a sexual experience while Donna has group sex with three young men. Donna later discovers Cindy about to have sex with Donna's boyfriend; he becomes angry and throws Donna out of the house. As Donna runs into the street, she is hit by a car, and Cindy's shock at losing her sister puts an end to her sexual experimentation.

CENSORSHIP HISTORY

Cindy and Donna is an obscure film that has entered censorship history because of the legal decision of the United States Supreme Court that afforded films protection from precipitous police seizure. On September 29, 1970, the sheriff and the district attorney of Pulaski County, Kentucky, bought tickets for a showing of the film at the local drive-in theater. After viewing the film in its entirety, the two men concluded that the film was obscene and that by exhibiting the film, the theater manager was violating Ky. Rev. Stat. 436.101, a state statute that prohibited the exhibition of obscene films to the public. At the same time, the deputy sheriff viewed most of the film from a place on the road outside the drive-in theater. When the film was over, the sheriff entered the projection booth and arrested the manager of the theater on the charge of exhibiting an obscene film and seized one copy of the film to use as evidence. The sheriff did not possess a warrant when he made the arrest and seized the film nor had a judge determined the film obscene. Instead, the arrest was based solely on the sheriff's viewing and perception of the film.

The theater manager was brought to trial in Pulaski circuit court, where he pleaded not guilty to the charge of exhibiting an obscene film. The attorney for the manager filed a motion to suppress the film as evidence and to dismiss the indictment on the grounds that the film was "improperly, unlawfully and illegally seized, contrary to . . . the laws of the land." The motion was denied four days later. When the case came to trial, the sheriff testified that he had judged the film to be obscene and that it violated the state statute because it contained nudity and "intimate love scenes." The deputy sheriff, who testified that he had viewed 30 minutes of the film while standing outside the theater, concurred with the sheriff's assessment of the film, after which the jury viewed the film. Despite the testimony of the theater manager that no juveniles had been allowed entrance to the theater to view the film and that he had received no complaints about the film until it was seized by the sheriff, the jury found him guilty and rendered a special verdict that the film was obscene under the wording of Ky. Rev. Stat. 436.101.

Attorneys for the theater manager appealed the conviction before the Court of Appeals of Kentucky and asked that the film be suppressed as evidence because it had been illegally seized. The court affirmed the previous ruling and emphasized that the manager's counsel conceded in the closing argument to the jury that the film was obscene. The court stated, "No issue is presented on appeal as to the obscenity of the material," and it upheld the conviction of the manager. The United States Supreme Court, which heard the case on November 14, 1972, delivered the following opinion: "The question presented in this case is whether the seizure of allegedly obscene material contemporaneous with and as an incident to an arrest for the public exhibition of such material in a commercial theater may be accomplished without a warrant." In a decision rendered on June 25, 1973, the Court reversed the decision of the Court of Appeals of Kentucky and directed that the case be remanded for further proceedings. In the decision, the justices wrote:

> Seizing a film then being exhibited to the general public presents essentially the same restraint on expression as the seizure of all the books in a bookstore. Such precipitate action by a police officer, without the authority of a constitutionally sufficient warrant, is plainly a form of prior restraint and is, in those circumstances, unreasonable under Fourth Amendment standards. The seizure is not unreasonable simply because it would have been easy to secure a warrant, but rather because prior restraint of the right of expression, whether by books or films, calls for a higher hurdle in the evaluation of reasonableness.

Justice Brennan was joined by Justices Stewart and Marshall in agreeing to consider the holding of the Court of Appeals of Kentucky that the Constitution does not require an adversary hearing on obscenity prior to the seizure of reels of film, where the seizure is incident to the arrest of the manager of a drive-in movie theater. Justice Brennan, with the concurrence of Justices Stewart and Marshall, expressed disapproval of the Kentucky obscenity statute: "The statute under which the prosecution was brought is, in my view, unconstitutionally overbroad and therefore invalid on its face."

FURTHER READING

Farber, Stephen. *The Movie Rating Game.* Washington, D.C.: Public Affairs Press, 1972.
Roaden v. Kentucky, 473 S.W. 2d 814 (1971).
Roaden v. Kentucky, 413 U.S. 496 (1973).

THE CONNECTION

Country and date of production: United States, 1961
Production company/distributor: Films Around the World/The Connection Company–Allan Hodgon Productions
Format: Sound, color/black and white
Running time: 110 minutes
Language: English
Producers: Lewis M. Allen, Shirley Clarke
Director: Shirley Clarke
Screenwriter: Jack Gelber
Awards: None
Genre: Drama
With: Warren Finnerty (Leach), Jerome Raphael (Solly), Garry Goodrow (Ernie), James Anderson (Sam), Carl Lee (Cowboy), Barbara Winchester (Sister Salvation), Henry Proach (Harry), Roscoe Browne (J. J. Burden), William Redfield (Jim Dunn), Freddie Redd (Piano player), Jackie McLean (Sax player), Larry Richie (Drummer), Michael Mattos (Bass player), Georgia Moll (Francesca Vanini), Linda Veras (Siren)

SUMMARY

Shot in *cinéma vérité* style in a mixture of color and black-and-white images, *The Connection* takes place in an apartment belonging to one of eight addicts who are awaiting a delivery of heroin by their "connection," the mysterious "Cowboy." The premise for the film is framed by the character of Jim Dunn, a novice filmmaker who has convinced the addicts to let him film them making their connection. In return, he will pay for their fix. Although he claims to have never before experimented with heroin, Dunn is talked into trying the drug when the others question how he can understand the subjects of his film without sharing their experience. Dunn joins the men in shooting heroin. He becomes ill but recovers with the assistance of the connection. After learning that Leach, one of the eight heroin addicts, has taken an overdose that has placed him in a coma, Dunn decides to abandon the film. Several of the characters are jazz musicians, and a jazz score punctuates the film.

CENSORSHIP HISTORY

Critics praised *The Connection* for its honest portrayal of heroin addiction. Instead of glamorizing the lifestyle or moralizing against it, the film simply presents images that are not retouched and leaves the viewer to make the assessment. The subject matter of drug addiction and use in the film raised no formal objections, but the New York State Board of Regents, the board of censors, refused to grant the distributor a license to exhibit the film in the state based on its language. The censors claimed that the film contained obscenity and objected to the repetition of the term *shit*, used as slang for heroin. Attorneys representing the distributor appealed the decision before the appellate division of the state supreme court, which reversed the decision in *Connection Company v. Regents of the University of the State of New York*, 230 N.Y.S. 2d 103 (1962) and granted a license to exhibit *The Connection*. The board of censors then appealed this decision to the New York Court of Appeals in *Regents v. Connection Company*, 234 N.Y.S. 2d 722 (1962). While the case was being heard, the distributor attempted to show the film at a theater in New York, but the censors obtained a court injunction barring such exhibition until the court of appeals had rendered a decision. In determining to uphold the decision of the lower court, the court of appeals studied the use of the word *shit* in the context of the film and made a deliberate distinction between that use and the more colloquial usage. In its decision, the court wrote, "the word is not used in its usual connotation but as a definite expression of the language of the narcotic" and asserted that while the term might be "vulgar," it was not obscene.

FURTHER READING

Carmen, Ira H. *Movies, Censorships and the Law.* Ann Arbor: University of Michigan Press, 1966.
Connection Company v. Regents of the University of the State of New York, 230 N.Y.S. 2d 103 (1962).
Regents v. Connection Company, 234 N.Y.S. 2d 722 (1962).

CRUISING

Country and date of production: United States, 1980
Production company/distributor: Lorimar Film Entertainment/United Artists
Format: Sound, color

Running time: 106 minutes
Language: English
Producer: Jerry Weintraub
Director: William Friedkin
Screenwriters: William Friedkin, Gerry Walker (novel)
Awards: None
Genre: Thriller/crime drama
With: Al Pacino (Steve Burns), Paul Sorvino (Captain Edelson), Karen
   Allen (Nancy), Richard Cox (Stuart Richards), Don Scardino (Ted Bai-
   ley), Joe Spinell (Patrolman DiSimone), Jay Acovone (Skip Lea), Randy
   Jurgensen (Detective Lefronsky), Barton Heyman (Dr. Rifkin), Gene
   Davis (DaVinci), Arnaldo Santana (Loren Lukas), Larry Atlas (Eric Ross-
   man), Allan Miller (Chief of Detectives), Sonny Grosso (Detective
   Blaisia), Edward O'Neill (Detective Schreiber)

SUMMARY

Cruising is a unique film in that, although it is a thriller based on actual murders of gay men in the Greenwich Village neighborhood of New York City in
the late 1970s, viewer interest lies in the mental state of the central character
rather than in the resolution of the crimes. The film portrays a gay population characterized by a vast undercurrent of restlessness as they seek satiating
experiences. Men are portrayed as constantly on the go, moving in and out of
erotic clubs, tunnels in the park, rented rooms, and private booths in porn
shops. When Steve Burns, a heterosexual, inexperienced New York Police
Department beat officer, is recruited by the NYPD Homicide Unit to go
undercover in the gay subculture in search of a brutal killer, he acquires this
restlessness as well. The murder victims are all gay men known to frequent
"leather," S&M (sadism and masochism) and B&D (bondage and dominance)
clubs, so Burns must operate in "deep cover" and pass as gay in order to
attract the killer. He is selected by the NYPD because he fits the victims' profiles: dark hair, dark complexion, dark eyes. Working in almost complete iso-
lation from his department, he has to learn and practice complex rules and
signals of this little society. He begins to change because of his work and
barely sees his girlfriend Nancy anymore. At first, he finds the gay social
scene repellent and shocking; yet he soon begins to understand its power to
take him nightly to an edge he might never have explored—a primal male
universe.

   The killer, who has been picking up gay men, then tying them up and
hacking them to death, is tall and thin and wears sunglasses, chains, biker
jacket and hat. Late in the film, viewers learn that he is a graduate student
doing his thesis on the roots of the American musical theater. The crime
story doesn't have much impact, but the focus of the movie, on the gradual
descent of Burns into the subculture, and his friendship with a gentle gay
neighbor, Ted Bailey, lead to an eerie and ambiguous ending: Viewers learn of

Bailey's violent death and then see a chilling close-up of Burns staring at his own reflection with a strange look of cold satisfaction.

CENSORSHIP HISTORY

William Friedkin's *Cruising* was released with a disclaimer intended to defuse the fierce antagonism of the gay community, which had been voiced strongly in protests during the making of the film. The disclaimer stated, "This film is not an indictment of the homosexual world. It is set in one small segment of that world, which is not meant to be representative of the whole." From the outset, the film provoked a range of reactions. A reporter for the *San Francisco Chronicle* has called it "a lurid, twisted film that brings you into its world and completely works you over." Mainstream gays lamented, as did other protesters of the film at the time of its release, that it shows a homophobic, sex-obsessed image of gay life. In contrast, some viewers involved in the leather/SM subculture at the time this film was made have praised its accurate portrayal of a pre-AIDS lifestyle concentrated on quick sex that was (and still is) pursued by a segment of the gay community. Gay protesters passed out leaflets during filming in New York City that warned, "People will die because of this film." Vito Russo wrote in *The Celluloid Closet* that the warning was prophetic, for in November 1980, outside the Ramrod Bar where *Cruising* had been filmed, "a minister's son emerged from a car with an Israeli submachine gun and killed two gay men." Protests of the film, spearheaded by the National Gay Task Force, began at sites of filming in New York City during the summer of 1979. At first gay leaders attempted to persuade the film's producer to create a balance within the film among the types of gay characters portrayed. When Weintraub ignored their request, they led protests at nearly 80 filming sites. In July 1979, a several hundred protesters marched on the local police station in Greenwich Village the day before the film crew was scheduled to shoot there.

On July 26, 1979, the National Gay Task Force filed a demand with the mayor's office that the city revoke the permit to film. The *New York Times* reported that the group asserted in its demand that *Cruising* would cause "a potentially inflammatory and explosive" reaction from the gay community. Mayor Ed Koch characterized the demands of the group as a call for censorship, which he rejected as he defended the rights of Weintraub to film in New York. The *New York Times* quotes Koch as stating that license to film did not mean that the city "accords approval or disapproval of the film content." The protesters organized a violent march on the evening of July 27, 1979, in which over a thousand people blocked traffic in Sheridan Square, Greenwich Village, for half an hour. They shouted at, harassed and intimidated men who had taken work as extras on the film, and several hundred demonstrators violently confronted the filmmakers as the crew shot a scene at the intersection of Christopher and West Streets.

In a September 1979 interview, Friedkin recalled, "When I looked into that mob that night, I saw a gang of unruly fanatics; blowing whistles, throwing bottles and cans at the trucks, at the actors and at me. . . . A legitimate group with legitimate interests does not threaten to kill you." The National Gay Task Force claimed that it was not calling for censorship of the film. Instead, "we are asking Hollywood to use the same system of self-censorship they apply to other minorities." Bill Krause of the Harvey Milk Gay Democratic Club in San Francisco rejected Friedkin's appeal to the First Amendment in making *Cruising* and said it is "absurd to argue the First Amendment in this case, because it presumes equality. There's no equality as long as we haven't the power of economic base that Hollywood has to make films on the scale of *Cruising*. We haven't the means to respond in kind."

The release of *Cruising* in theaters on February 15, 1980, was preceded by significant plans for protests in cities around the United States. In response, General Cinema Corporation asserted that the "R" rating of the film by the Motion Picture Association of America (MPAA) was too liberal— that it deserved an "X"—and canceled plans to exhibit the film at 30 of its sites. The film was scheduled to open in San Francisco at the Ghirardelli Theatre near sites that had suffered significant spraying of anti-*Cruising* graffiti, but in an effort to maintain public peace, Mayor Diane Feinstein asked United Artists to move the opening to the Market Street Theatre. Pickets and protests marked the opening of *Cruising* in nearly 300 theaters around the United States on February 15, 1980. In New York City, protesters in the National Theatre on Broadway carried banners and chanted, and in Hollywood picketers carried signs and shouted "Close *Cruising* down" and "Don't support lies." The film that premiered was not the film that Friedkin had originally conceived, nor was it faithful to the Gerald Walker novel on which Friedkin had based the screenplay. Edward Guthmann suggests that the protests had a censorious effect on the final product: "It has been widely suggested that Friedkin yielded to community pressure, that his final package was far tamer, and less inflammatory, than his original idea." In the novel, Burns is clearly identified as the killer of the gentle Bailey, but Friedkin's ending is ambiguous. He also added the disclaimer noted at the beginning of this entry that shows the extent to which he had been influenced by the outcry. The efforts to suppress the film appeared wasted after exhibitors watched it fail to make a significant profit at the box office, not due to a lack of support as a result of protest, but due to what critics agree was a generally uninteresting and uninspired film.

FURTHER READINGS

"*Cruising* in New Ratings Rumpus; 'R' Taken, Given." *Variety*, June 11, 1980, pp. 4, 30.
"Did *Cruising* Respect Ratings?" *Variety*, June 25, 1980, p. 4.
Guthmann, Edward. "The *Cruising* Controversy: William Friedkin vs. the Gay Community." *Cineaste* 10, no. 3 (Summer 1980): 2–4.

LaSalle, Mick. "*Cruising* Back From the '80s." *San Francisco Chronicle*, May 12, 1995, p. C12.

Ledbetter, Les. "1,000 in 'Village' Renew Protest Against Movie on Homosexuals." *New York Times*, July 27, 1979, p. II.1.

Lyons, Charles. *The New Censors: Movies and the Culture Wars.* Philadelphia: Temple University Press, 1997.

Maslin, Janet. "Friedkin Defends His *Cruising.*" *New York Times*, September 18, 1979, p. C12.

Pollack, Dale. "*Cruising* Protests Intensify." *Los Angeles Times*, February 1, 1980, p. V1.

"Protestors Call the Film *Cruising* Anti-homosexual." *New York Times*, July 26, 1979, p. C1.

Russo, Vito. *The Celluloid Closet: Homosexuality in the Movies.* New York: Harper & Row, 1981.

Stephens, Bob. "Lasting Images of *Cruising.*" *San Francisco Examiner*, May 12, 1995, p. C2.

CURLEY

Country and date of production: United States, 1947
Production company/distributor: Hal Roach Studios/United Artists
Format: Sound, color
Running time: 53 minutes
Language: English
Producers: Hal Roach, Robert F. McGowan
Director: Bernard Carr
Screenwriters: Mary McCarthy, Dorothy Reid
Awards: None
Genre: Comedy
With: Frances Rafferty, Larry Oslen (Curley), Eilene Janssen, Dale Belding, Peter Miles, Kathleen Howard

SUMMARY

Produced by Hal Roach Studios, renowned for the "Little Rascals" and "Our Gang" short comedy films, *Curley* is a lighthearted film about the adventures of a group of white and African-American children in an American small town. The plot relates the apprehension that the children feel as they wait for the new teacher to appear. Their former teacher, Miss Evans, has left town to marry. When they mistake a rather bad-tempered, middle-aged woman for their new teacher, the group of children led by the mischievous but likable Curley immediately begins to concoct schemes to make her leave the job, unaware that the real teacher is the young and pretty Mildred, the niece of their target. Before Curley is aware of her identity, Mildred gives him a ride to school during which he brags about the various tricks that he and his classmates plan to play on their new teacher. When Mildred is later able to turn all of their pranks back on the children, they become angry with Curley, for they suspect that he revealed their plans on purpose to impress the new teacher, and they shun him. When Mildred shows at the school picnic that she can keep up with the most athletic of the students, she wins their respect, and Curley is eventually forgiven his indiscretion. The movie ends on a happy note, with the children becoming, once again, a happy group.

CENSORSHIP HISTORY

The banning of *Curley* from exhibition in the Memphis, Tennessee, theaters was due solely to the racial composition of the group of children in the movie, which included Caucasian and African-American children sharing a class-room and pursuing friendship outside school. In 1949, United Artists challenged the long-held censorship authority of Lloyd Binford, who had headed the Memphis, Tennessee, Board of Censors since 1928 and had "a reputation for movie censorship 'so severe and so unpredictable that pictures shown without a ripple elsewhere . . .' were often banned or cut without mercy." Although the censors in Memphis had rejected films such as *The Southerner* for showing poor whites in a negative light and *King of Kings* because they did not agree with the producer's interpretation of the Bible, "the chief victim of Binford's sallies was the Negro entertainer." When interviewers asked Binford to define the standards against which he and the Board of Censors assessed films, he replied that the law had given the board the power to ban what was "inimical to public safety, health, morals and welfare" of Memphis, and for anything further "it's just our own opinion."

When United Artists sought approval from the board of censors to exhibit *Curley* in Memphis, the board informed the distributor that it was "unable to approve your picture with the little negroes as the South does not permit negroes in white schools nor recognize social equality between the races even in children." The studio challenged the decision of the board and brought suit against the board in circuit court, claiming that the decision of the board to deny the license to exhibit "solely on the ground that members of the colored race appear" denied the rights of freedom of speech and due process guaranteed under the First and Fourteenth Amendments of the U.S. Constitution, and that such action also denied the distributor "equal protection under the law." In rendering his decision on *United Artists Corporation v. Board of Censors of City of Memphis*, Circuit Court Judge Floyd M. Henderson agreed that race or color should not be the sole legal basis for censoring a motion picture. He also ruled, however, that the First Amendment applied only where someone had been denied the right to speak; this did not apply in the case of a motion picture, so the circuit court denied the petition to the court.

The distributor appealed the decision to the Supreme Court of Tennessee, which asserted that the right to show the film was not violated in this case because the distributor had not contracted with any Memphis theater to show the picture. In its decision, the state supreme court affirmed the decision of the lower court that the statutes and ordinances in question only applied to someone whose legal right to speak is denied. The court did not feel that out-of-state corporations had authority to strike down local laws and ordinances in some other state.

FURTHER READING

Carmen, Ira H. *Movies, Censorship, and the Law.* Ann Arbor: University of Michigan, 1966.

Green, Jonathan. *The Encyclopedia of Censorship.* New York: Facts On File, 1990.

Kupferman, Theodore R., and Philip J. O'Brien. "Motion Picture Censorship—The Memphis Blues." *Cornell Law Quarterly* 36 (1951): 273–300.

United Artists Corporation v. Board of Censors of City of Memphis, 225 S.W. 2d 550 (1949).

Velie, Lester. "You Can't See That Movie: Censorship in Action." *Collier's,* May 6, 1950, pp. 11–13, 66.

DAMAGED GOODS

Country and date of production: United Kingdom, 1919
Production company/distributor: Wolf & Friendman Film Service
Format: Silent, black and white
Running time: 105 minutes
Language: English
Producer: G. B. Samuelson
Director: Alexander Butler
Screenwriter: Eugène Brieux
Awards: None
Genre: Drama
With: Campbell Gullan (George Dupont), Marjorie Day (Henrietta Louches), J. Fisher White (Doctor), James Lindsay (Rouvenal), Joan Vivian Reese (Edith Wray), Bassett Roe (Henry Louches), Annie Esmond (Marie Dupont), Winifred Dennis (The Wife).

SUMMARY

Damaged Goods, a drama written by Eugène Brieux, appeared on Broadway for one year before the American stage actor and director Richard Bennett made arrangements with the American Film Manufacturing Company to adapt it for the motion picture screen in 1915. The movie, which portrays the horrible effects of venereal disease on one man and his family, was praised by critics in the United States as a feature film of considerable educational appeal, although some suggested that the clinic scenes could be shorter. The original film, for which no prints have survived, was distributed to U.S. Army bases to be used as an entertaining way to warn soldiers of the dangers of sexual promiscuity. Contemporary movie magazines such as *Motography* praised the film for its cinematic qualities in which "artistic settings, effective lighting, and fine photography—in fact, all the essentials of a high-class presentation—play their important parts" (October 9, 1915). The film was remade in Britain in 1919, in a version that does survive, but British censorship was much harsher than American censorship at the time, so, as Kevin Brownlow observes, the British version of *Damaged Goods* "came dangerously close to being a series of subtitles interrupted by shots of appropriate characters."

The film relates the story of George Dupont, who has had a casual sexual encounter with Edith, a prostitute who plies her trade in order to support her baby. Dupont, engaged to be married to the virtuous Henriette Louches, begins to experience symptoms of syphilis and consults a physician, who begins treatment that will take three or four years to be fully effective. The doctor warns Dupont not to marry during that time for fear of infecting his wife. Dupont does not have the strength of character to tell his wife-to-be why he wants to delay the wedding, so he visits another doctor who promises him a quick cure that will allow him to marry within six months. The doctor turns out to be a quack whose cure does not work, but Dupont does not learn this until after he is married and he and Henriette have had their first child. The baby is born with syphilis, and Dupont's secret is soon revealed. Henriette takes their child and leaves him while he embarks on a proper cure of three years' duration. After he is free of the disease, a chastened Dupont reunites with his wife and child. As the film draws to a close, Edith appears as one of the doctor's cases, telling her story—she had been an employee in a couture house where her boss had raped her and then fired her when she became pregnant—and vowing to reform.

CENSORSHIP HISTORY

The British version of *Damaged Goods* produced in 1919 was a propaganda film about venereal disease, one of a number of such films produced in both the United States and Britain. Propaganda films were intended to be shown in the commercial cinema, but they also claimed to be educational and the producers claimed that they were made "to inform the public about the nature, incidence and consequences of venereal disease." Unlike the documentary or "lecture" films, propaganda films were usually short fictional narratives that were aimed at broad sections of the cinema-going public. Unlike the play and the U.S. version, in the 1919 version of *Damaged Goods* the characters are constructed as types. As in other films of its sort, sexually active women and promiscuous men are counterposed against "chaste and pure" women and men to create moral tales. In *Damaged Goods*, Dupont has his moment of dangerous sexuality, but "his stricken conscience and moral vacillation are underscored in many an anguished close-up."

When the British version of the film appeared, numerous comparisons were made to the 1915 American version, and most critics discussed the "vulgarity" of the American version in contrast with the "tastefulness" of the British view. In the American version, Dupont is shown illustrations in a medical textbook of the devastating effects of syphilis. "By contrast with the alleged sensationalism of the American VD films, the British *Damaged Goods* aspired to sell itself as a piece of 'quality' cinema." The educational focus is emphasized to the detriment of Brieux's original play, and the film was seen mostly in private screenings sponsored by "social purity" groups rather than in public cinemas.

To ensure that the film appeared only in its approved venue, the British Board of Film Censors (BBFC) refused to issue it and other propaganda films a certificate to exhibit in commercial theaters on the grounds that "the cinema was, according to the board, not a suitable place to air matters of potential controversy." The BBFC suggested that, instead, these films should be seen in halls that were specially rented for that purpose, where, as it suggested in its 1919 annual report, "securities could be taken for choosing the audience which are impossible in the ordinary cinema." The National Council for Combating Venereal Disease (NCCVD) had originally supported a film version of *Damaged Goods*, and Lord Sydenham of the NCCVD had argued that the film could reach a much larger audience than the play, but the censors worried that "the Cinema differs greatly from the Theatre: the audience is less intelligent and educated and includes far more children and young people." Despite efforts by the BBFC to limit viewing of *Damaged Goods*, the film was widely viewed because the board had only limited powers to discourage local authorities from allowing public showings. The Cinematograph Exhibitors' Association (CEA) also encouraged its members not to book the film, but these efforts had little success because less than half of the British theater owners belonged to the CEA.

FURTHER READING

Brownlow, Kevin. *Behind the Mask of Innocence.* New York: Alfred A. Knopf, 1990.
Bush, W. Stephen. "Damaged Goods." *Moving Picture World*, October 2, 1915.
"Damaged Goods." *Motography*, September 5, 1915.
"Film Censorship and Health Propaganda." *Bioscope*, December 18, 1919, p. 89.
Hunnings, Neville March. *Film Censors and the Law.* London: Allen & Unwin, 1967.
Thompson, Frank. *Lost Films: Important Movies That Disappeared.* New York: Carol Publishing, 1996.

DECEMBER 7TH

Country and date of production: United States, 1942
Production company/distributor: United States War Department
Format: Sound, black and white
Running time: 82 minutes (not released until 1991); 34 minutes (as released in 1942)

Language: English
Producer: John Ford
Directors: John Ford, Gregg Toland
Screenwriter: Budd Schulberg
Awards: 1943 Academy Award, Best Documentary–Short Subject
Genre: Drama/documentary
With: Walter Huston (Uncle Sam), Harry Davenport (Mr. "C"), Dana Andrews (World War II Ghost Soldier), Paul Hurst (World War I Ghost Soldier), George O'Brien (Narrator), James Kevin McGuinness (Narrator), Philip Ahn (Shinto Priest)

SUMMARY

John Ford had assembled in Hollywood a naval reserve film unit to be deployed should war break out in the Pacific. After the attack on Pearl Harbor on December 7, 1941, the U.S. government ordered Ford to make newsreels at various locations, including Hawaii. *December 7th* was meant to show as accurately as possible the attack on Pearl Harbor. Ford oversaw the project, but decisions for the content lay with Gregg Toland, who was assigned the work because Ford was busy with other project; it was Toland who expanded the project from a newsreel to a feature-length film. Few cameras had been on hand to record the original attack, so Toland recreated many of the major scenes using Hollywood sound stages. He also incorporated available footage of the attack into staged scenes filmed months after the bombing. The film was designed to examine the bombing and its results: the recovering of ships, the improving of defenses in Hawaii and the efforts of the United States to overcome Japanese forces at war.

The full-length version of the film that Ford produced contains fictional sequences, including an introductory segment showing Uncle Sam on the beach, vacationing in Hawaii on December 6, 1941. As he relaxes, a character representing the Voice of Responsibility tells him to be concerned about the Japanese Fifth Column-Immigrants and warns that to ignore them is to risk disaster. The indolent and overconfident Uncle Sam seems unconcerned as Japanese civilians appear everywhere in Hawaii, gathering intelligence. They listen as a servicemen carry on conversations: Japanese barbers, for example, listen intently as their American patrons converse. This is followed by a re-creation of the Japanese attack on Pearl Harbor and scenes of its aftermath—scenes that formed the core of the shorter, 34-minute version that earned the 1943 Academy Award for best documentary-short subject film. The original version concludes with a sequence in which a ghost of one of the U.S. servicemen killed at Pearl Harbor speaks with the ghost of a Revolutionary War soldier in Arlington Cemetery about how the United States will beat the Japanese in the war.

CENSORSHIP HISTORY

Considered the greatest propaganda failure of World War II, the original, 82-minute version of *December 7th* was shelved by the U.S. government in 1942 as "damaging to morale," and this version was not seen for nearly 50 years. After filming was completed, Ford and Toland presented the final product to the navy for inspection and saw it promptly denounced. Chief of Naval Operations Admiral Harold Stark wrote the following evaluation of the film that led to its banning: "This picture leaves the distinct impression that the Navy was not on the job, and this is not true." Ford was ordered to shorten the film by cutting scenes that exposed the faults of the government and emphasizing the battle scenes that showed the courage and bravery of the U.S. servicemen. The shorter film also omitted the fictional introduction and conclusion. The censored version won an Academy Award while the original, uncut version was kept from public view for nearly 50 years.

FURTHER READING

Dare, Michael. "2nd Features: *December 7th:* The Movie, Directed by John Ford/Target: Pearl Harbor." *Billboard* 103, October 19, 1991, 62.

Lombardi, Fred. "Reviews—*December 7th: The Movie,* Directed by Gregg Toland and John Ford." *Variety* 345 December 2, 1991, p. 91.

Pittman, Randy. "Video Movies—*December 7th:* The Movie." *Library Journal* 116 November 15, 1991, p. 127.

Rabinowitz, Dorothy. "TV: A Month of Classic Documentaries—from the South Pole to the Frozen North Via the Dust Bowl." *The Wall Street Journal*, November 8, 1999, p. A48.

Smith, Mark Chalon. "War Film a Morale Dilemma Movie: *December 7th* Was Deemed a Propaganda Failure and Shelved." *The Los Angeles Times*, December 6, 1991, p. 28.

DEEP THROAT

Country and date of production: United States, 1972
Production company/distributor: Vanguard Films Productions/Aquarius
Format: Sound, color
Running time: 61 minutes
Language: English
Producers: William J. Links, Lou Peraino (as Lou Perry)
Director: Gerard Damiano
Screenwriter: Gerard Damiano
Awards: None
Genre: Adult
With: Linda Lovelace (Herself), Harry Reems (Dr. Young), Dolly Sharp (Helen), Bill Harrison (Mr. Maltz), William Love (Wilbur Wang)

SUMMARY

Deep Throat is extremely important in film history as one of the first hard-core pornographic films to be seen by mainstream audiences. The story itself is rather thin, mainly because the director originally created individual segments, or "loops," that were intended to be sold as individual short sex films. Damiano later decided to create a loose plot line that connected the loops into a feature-length film that became *Deep Throat*. Linda Lovelace plays a woman unsatisfied with her sex life even after many sexual encounters, which include an attempt to have sex with 14 men at once. She consults a doctor, who discovers that her clitoris is deep in her throat. In order to experience pleasure, she must give "deep throat" oral sex to her partner. She practices on the doctor, for whom she then agrees to work as a nurse, and she also helps his male patients with their sexual problems. The doctor also has sex with his nurses, and Linda's friend is shown having group sex.

CENSORSHIP HISTORY

Film historians credit *Deep Throat* for having set in motion the modern sexually explicit film genre and for bringing pornography into the mainstream. Filmed in Miami, Florida, at a cost of only $24,000, *Deep Throat* eventually grossed over $25 million and was exhibited in 73 cities. It is also the only film to be attacked on such a grand scale by the federal government. Despite its current historic status, the film was banned in numerous states and became the subject of a large number of local and federal challenges. Although *Deep Throat* was produced before the United States Supreme Court decision in *Miller v. California*, which applied community standards to determine whether a film was obscene, most of the challenges directed toward *Deep Throat* were judged based on the local standards and objections—yet viewers in different locations did not always agree if the film was obscene. In New York City, a Manhattan criminal court judge determine that the film was "a feast of carrion and squalor . . . a Sodom and Gomorrah gone wild before the fire" and declared it too obscene to exhibit. The New York distributor cut scenes from the film and released it a second time without incident.

The film was also involved in court cases in numerous cities and states, including California, Colorado, Florida, Georgia, Illinois, Iowa, Kentucky, Louisiana, Maryland, Massachusetts, Michigan, Mississippi, Missouri, Nebraska, New Hampshire, New Jersey, North Dakota, Ohio, Pennsylvania, South Dakota, Tennessee and Texas, from 1972 through 1981. In Texas in 1975, a landlord threatened to terminate the lease of a movie theater operator, claiming that he had been warned by the county attorney that the county would "abate the theater as a public nuisance in order to prevent the future showing of allegedly obscene motion pictures." In *Universal Amusement Co. v. Vance*, 404 F. Supp. 33 (19745), the theater operator asked to have the actions of the county attorney declared unconstitutional and to enjoin the attorney from invoking the Texas public nuisance statutes to prevent the exhibition of

Deep Throat. The court declared the statutes to be invalid prior restraints on the exercise of First Amendment rights, which invalidated the county attorney's power to close the movie theater. The decision was upheld by the federal court of appeals in *Universal Amusement Co. v. Vance*, 559 F. 2d 1286 (1977). The case was then taken before the United States Supreme Court, which upheld the decision in *Vance v. Universal Amusement Co.*, 446 U.S. 947 (1980).

In contrast, a print of the film imported from Canada was seized by U.S. Customs in Boston, and a Massachusetts federal court upheld the forfeiture of the film in *United States v. One Reel of Film*, 481 F. 2d 206 (1973). The importer brought expert witnesses to testify at the trial that the movie "puts forth an idea of greater liberation with regard to human sexuality and to the expression of it" and argued further that viewing the movie would have a therapeutic value because "many women have an unreasonable fear of the penis." The decision in *Miller v. California* led the federal government to launch a nationwide crackdown on the interstate transportation of allegedly pornographic materials; they used *Deep Throat* and federal transportation and conspiracy statutes, specifically the statute that permitted the government to initiate a criminal action in any location through which the film had been transported.

In 1972, Assistant United States Attorney Larry Parrish filed conspiracy charges in Memphis, Tennessee. Although devoutly evangelical, Parrish disclaimed any religious basis for the prosecution and asserted that he was taking action to defend federal law against the transport and distribution of pornographic materials. De Grazia reports, however, that Parrish also told the Adult Film Association, "If you want to know why I am a prosecutor, you can read Romans 13," a chapter in the New Testament that speaks of ministers placed by God on Earth to carry out his wrath against evildoers. Parrish claimed that everyone and every organization connected with the production, promotion and exhibition of *Deep Throat* was a participant in the conspiracy. In his opening statement to the jury, Parrish asserted: "Once a person joins a conspiracy, he is liable for everything that happens in that conspiracy until it is ended. You must cease doing anything to further the conspiracy but, more than that, you have to take up affirmative actions to defeat and destroy the conspiracy."

To achieve his end, Parrish indicted Harry Reems, who played the doctor in the film, as well as 11 other people and five corporations, and identified 98 co-conspirators, including theater employees such as the ticket taker at a theater in Vermont, a lighting technician in Miami, projectionists at various sites where the film was exhibited and others associated peripherally with the film. Two-and-a-half years after completing his one day of work on the film and receiving his pay of $100, Harry Reems was awakened in the middle of the night in New York City by agents from the Federal Bureau of Investigation, who arrested him. He was indicted on Parrish's charge that he was part of the nationwide conspiracy to transport across state lines "an obscene, lewd, lascivious, and filthy motion picture." Federal District Judge Harry W. Wellford refused to accept the defense of First Amendment protection and told the jury that what Reems had done was not protected expression. He also pointed out that "if it weren't for Mr. Reems, we wouldn't have movies like *Deep Throat*." The jury viewed the movie and voted to convict the defendants. When Reems tried to appeal, several lawyers refused to represent him, even Roy Grutman—who had successfully defended *Penthouse* magazine—because he believed that the film "went too far . . . I couldn't defend it." Harvard law professor Alan Dershowitz eventually took the case and the convictions were overturned, largely because the court agreed that the film had been made before the decision in *Miller v. California*. (See also THE DEVIL IN MISS JONES.)

FURTHER READING

Colorado v. Tabron, 544 P. 2d 372 (1975).
De Grazia, Edward, and Roger K. Newman. *Banned Films: Movies, Censors & the First Amendment*. New York: R. R. Bowker, 1982.
Dershowitz, Alan M. *The Best Defense*. New York: Random House, 1982.
Marro, Anthony. "Prurient Interest in Memphis." *New Republic*, April 24, 1976.
Miller v. California, 413 U.S. 15 (1973).
Miller, Frank. *Censored Hollywood: Sex, Sin and Violence on Screen*. Atlanta, Ga.: Turner Publishing, 1994.
People v. Mitchell Brothers, 101 Cal. App. 3d 298 (1980).
State ex rel. Cahalan v. Diversified Theatrical Corp., 229 N.W. 2d 389 (1975).
State ex rel. Cahalan v. Diversified Theatrical Corp., 240 N.W. 2d 460 (1976).
United States v. Battista, 646 F. 2d 237 (1981).
United States v. Marks, 520 F. 2d 913 (1975).
United States v. One Reel of Film, 481 F. 2d 206 (1973).
United States v. Peraino, 21 *Criminal Law Reporter* 2125 (W. D. Tenn. Apr. 11, 1977).
Universal Amusement Co. v. Vance, 404 F. Supp. 33 (1975).
Universal Amusement Co. v. Vance, 559 F. 2d 1286 (1977).
Vance v. Universal Amusement Co., 446 U.S. 947 (1980).
Wolf, William. *Landmark Films: The Cinema and Our Century*. New York: Paddington Publishers, 1979.

DESIRE UNDER THE ELMS

Country and date of production: United States, 1958
Production company/distributor: Don Hartman Productions/Paramount Pictures Corporation
Format: Sound, black and white
Running time: 111 minutes
Language: English
Producer: Don Hartman
Director: Delbert Mann
Screenwriters: Eugene O'Neill (play), Irwin Shaw

Awards: None
Genre: Drama
With: Sophia Loren (Anna Cabot), Anthony Perkins (Eben Cabot), Burl
Ives (Ephraim Cabot), Frank Overton (Simeon Cabot), Pernell Roberts
(Peter Cabot), Rebecca Welles (Lucinda), Jean Willes (Florence), Anne
Seymour (Eben's mother), Roy Fant (Fiddler)

SUMMARY

Eugene O'Neill's 1924 play of the same name was the basis for this adaptation
by Irwin Shaw. *Desire Under the Elms* is essentially the story of people whose
lives are tinged with loneliness and shaken with thwarted passion; for them,
the only redemption is through love. Vehement family dissension has en-
veloped the Cabot farm for years. The children of old Cabot hate him. Eben,
Cabot's youngest child and the son of the second wife, remembers his dead
mother as having been worked to death, and he believes that he sees her
around the place, as if she were risen from her grave. When their father
brings home third wife, Anna, the two older sons go away to California, but
the younger son stays and hopes to avenge his mother. To Eben's surprise, his
ardent loathing for Anna unexpectedly turns to heated passion and love.
Their love affair is doomed from the beginning, and not even the serene
beauty and peace of the land can calm the storm. When Anna gives birth to a
son, fathered by Eban but whom old Cabot believes to be his, the old man
declares the infant the heir to his farm. His action is intended to punish his
three older sons, and he leaves Eban adrift in the world. While a dance in
honor of the newborn child takes place in the home, Old Cabot and Eban
quarrel outside. The old man convinces his youngest son that Anna wanted a
son only to cheat Cabot's older sons out of the farm. Eban confronts Anna
and reviles her. To prove that she truly loves Eban and was not using their
affair to gain possession of the farm, she kills the child. While Eban contacts
the sheriff, Old Cabot turns the livestock loose in the woods and plans to go
away, but he realizes that he will have to stay when he finds the money gone
from its hiding place. When Eban returns with the sheriff, he falls to his
knees in front of Anna and takes part of the blame for their child's death. The
two are taken away by the sheriff.

CENSORSHIP HISTORY

The Chicago board of censors granted Paramount a license to exhibit the
film in the city but only to people over the age of 21. The distributor filed a
request with the United States District Court for the Northern District of
Illinois for an injunction to prevent the city from blocking exhibition of the
film to audiences of all ages. Legal representatives of Paramount argued with
Paramount Film Distributing Corporation v. City of Chicago that the municipal
code of Chicago clearly established the basis for the granting of permits
for exhibition and that only films determined to be "immoral" or "obscene"

would be denied permits. The code also allowed for a limited permit to allow exhibition of a film "to persons over twenty-one" if the board of censors determined that it "tends toward creating a harmful impression on the minds of children, where such tendency as to the minds of adults would not exist." Judge Sullivan, who presided in the case, wrote, "Like any other censorship statute, this one must be approached with a caution dictated by the fact that it is a patent invasion of the right to freedom of speech guaranteed by the First Amendment." The court declared the censorship ordinance to be "hopelessly indefinite" and wrote that it violated the principles established in *Butler v. Michigan,* in which a Michigan statute that sought to limit reading material available in the state to only what was appropriate for children was struck down by the U.S. Supreme Court as being "invalid . . . unconstitutional, and void," as well as "an insufficient guide to either the censors or those who produce motion pictures." Paramount was granted the injunction and a permit for general exhibition of the film.

FURTHER READING

Butler v. Michigan, 352 U.S. 380 (1957).
DeGrazia, Edward, and Roger K. Newman. *Banned Films: Movies, Censors & the First Amendment.* New York: R. R. Bowker, 1982.
Paramount Film Distributing Corporation v. City of Chicago, 172 F. Supp. 69 (1959).

THE DEVIL IN MISS JONES

Country and date of production: United States, 1973
Production company/distributor: VCA Pictures/Marvin Films
Format: Sound, color
Running time: 74 minutes
Language: English
Producer: Gerard Damiano
Director: Gerard Damiano
Screenwriter: Gerard Damiano
Awards: None
Genre: Adult
With: Georgina Spelvin (Justine Jones), Harry Reems (Instructor), Clair Lumiere, Sue Flaken, Marc Stevens, Levi Richards, Gerard Damiano

SUMMARY

The Devil in Miss Jones was directed, written and produced by Gerard Damiano, who had made DEEP THROAT in 1972. The film tells the story of Miss Justine Jones, a lonely and frustrated virgin who becomes tired of her life and kills herself. Despite having led an exemplary life, she goes to hell because of her suicide. She argues with a clerk that if she is to spend eternity in hell, she wants to be deserving of such damnation. Wishing that she had lived a more sinful life, Miss Jones asks to return to Earth for a short time to pursue one of the seven deadly sins, lust. The clerk grants this wish and assigns her a teacher on earth who tells her to focus on pleasure even as he dispenses pain. After time with him, Miss Jones becomes sexually insatiable and pursues every possible form of sexual pleasure. She experiments sexually with a woman, with a man and a woman together and with two men. She also masturbates with a stream of water from a bathtub hose and with various fruits. When her time on Earth ends, her eternal punishment mocks her brief experiments with lust: She is sentenced to spend eternity with a man who is too insane to become sexually aroused.

CENSORSHIP HISTORY

Considered by critics to be one of the classics of sexually explicit films, *The Devil in Miss Jones* differs considerably from similar films of the 1970s and earlier in its coherent story and specially composed musical score. The emphasis on sensuality over sexuality is also unusual. The movie is also filmed on celluloid, as were feature films—but not stag films—of the period. The dialogue is pertinent to the plot, and the editing is relatively smooth, characterized by clear transitions. Despite the efforts of its creators to market *The Devil in Miss Jones* as one of the "art porn" movies that became popular in the early 1970s, the film met resistance from censors and was banned in numerous states, including California, Florida, Georgia, Kansas, Massachusetts, Michigan, Missouri, New York, South Dakota, Texas and Virginia. At the same time, viewers made such movies as *Deep Throat* and *The Devil in Miss Jones* successes at the box office. In *The Dame in the Kimono*, Leff and Simmons point out:

> *Deep Throat, The Devil in Miss Jones,* and other "triple-X" pictures went well beyond the valley of the dolls; they went beyond nude couples and pantomimed intercourse to show close-ups of genitals as well as oral and anal penetration, heterosexual and homosexual sex. Screen sex had become so popular that both *Deep Throat* and *The Devil in Miss Jones* popped up among the twelve top-grossing pictures of 1973, while *I Am Curious* became an art house smash.

Most of the challenges or bannings of the film occurred at the local level when theater operators complied with suggestions by local law enforcement and censor boards that the film not be shown. A more extensive challenge occurred in Wayne County, Michigan, where the prosecutor brought civil actions against several theaters for exhibiting "lewd" films, including *The Devil in Miss Jones.* Asserting that the terms *lewd* and *obscene* were synonymous, the prosecutor determined that *The Devil in Miss Jones* and three other films playing at the time in these theaters—*Little Sisters, It Happened in Hollywood* and *Deep Throat*—were legally obscene according to the 1973 definition of *obscene* that emerged in the landmark Supreme Court case, *Miller v. California.* He then asked the trial court to declare the theaters "public nuisances," according to a state nuisance statute that applied to "any building, vehicle, boat, aircraft, or place" that was used for the purpose of "lewdness, prostitution, gambling, etc." The trial court ordered the closing of the theaters for one year and enjoined their use "for the purposes of lewdness" for perpetuity. In its decision, the court characterized its actions as morally justified, given the nature of the films and declared the films to be

> an example of the trash that a few sick, demented minds are spewing out across our country in search of the easy dollar. . . . These films can greatly weaken, if not destroy, the moral and wholesome fiber which the citizens of this country possess in abundance. To permit this moral sabotage to continue would be to ignore the spreading of a deadly plague. . . . we are not about to permit this disease to spread.

The Michigan Court of Appeals concurred with the decision to declare the theaters in which the films were shown to be "public nuisances," but it modified the decision and prohibited the theaters from showing only those films that had been found at trial to be obscene. The ruling was overturned the following year when the supreme court of Michigan declared that only houses of prostitution, not movie theaters, could be declared "public nuisances."

FURTHER READING

De Grazia, Edward, and Roger K. Newman. *Banned Films: Movies, Censors & the First Amendment.* New York: R. R. Bowker, 1982.
Green, Jonathan. *The Encyclopedia of Censorship.* New York: Facts On File, 1990.
Leff, Leonard J., and Jerold L. Simmons. *The Dame in the Kimono: Hollywood, Censorship, & the Production Code From the 1920s to the 1960s.* New York: Grove Weidenfeld, 1990.
Miller v. California, 413 U.S. 15 (1973).
State ex rel. Cahalan v. Diversified Theatrical Corp., 229 N.W. 2d 389 (1975).
State ex rel. Cahalan v. Diversified Theatrical Corp., 240 N.W. 2d 460 (1976).

LA DOLCE VITA

Country and date of production: Italy/France, 1959
Production company/distributor: Pathé Consortium Cinéma (France), Riama Film (Italy)/Astor Pictures Corporation (United States, subtitled, 1960)
Format: Sound, black and white
Running time: 176 minutes
Language: Italian
Producers: Giuseppe Amato, Franco Magli, Angelo Rizzoli
Director: Federico Fellini
Screenwriters: Federico Fellini, Ennio Flaiano, Tullio Pinelli, Brunello Rondi

Awards: 1961 Academy Awards, Best Costume Design, Black and White (Piero Gherardi).
1961 Cannes Film Festival, Golden Palm (Federico Fellini).
1961 Italian National Syndicate of Film Journalist, Best Actor (Marcello Mastroianni), Best Original Story (Federico Fellini, Ennio Flaiano, Tullio Pinelli), Best Production Design (Piero Gherardi).
1961 New York Film Critics Circle Awards, Best Foreign Language Film.
Genre: Drama
With: Marcello Mastroianni (Marcello Rubini), Anita Ekberg (Sylvia), Anouk Aimée (Maddalena), Yvonne Furneaux (Emma), Magali Noël (Fanny), Alain Cuny (Steiner), Annibale Ninchi (Marcello's father), Walter Santesso (Paparazzo), Valeria Ciangottini (Paola), Audrey McDonald (Sonia)

SUMMARY

La Dolce Vita is a powerful and profound film that follows a series of events in the life of a journalist, Marcello Rubini. As it explores Rubini's dissatisfaction in his work and his loves, the film ultimately becomes a reflection on where one finds—or fails to find—meaning in life. Fellini shot the movie in 1959 on the Via Veneto, the Roman street of nightclubs, sidewalk cafés and streetwalkers. His hero, a gossip columnist, chronicles "the sweet life" of fading aristocrats, second-rate movie stars, aging playboys, and prostitutes. At the end of the film, Rubini is no longer an observer and reporter of the scene, but instead a participant.

This film also gave the world of entertainment the term *paparazzi*. In searching for a suitable name for the blond, weasel-like character who accompanies Rubini in his hunt for sensational stories and celebrity news, Fellini chose the name "Paparazzo" from that of a character in a libretto in an Italian opera. The term denoted the character, but his behavior signaled the new approach of hunting celebrities as if they were prey that was gaining popularity in the early 1960s, and the name soon was used to designate the whole class of limousine-chasing reporters.

The setting is Rome in the 1950s where Rubini covers the more sensational side of the news: movie stars, religious visions, the decadent aristocracy. Rubini is living with Emma, who loves him and wants a traditional marriage, but is possessive and shows little ability to understand his search for value and meaning in his life. In this search, Rubini has sexual encounters with many other women, including Anouk Aimée as a stunningly beautiful, wealthy and jaded friend and lover, and Anita Ekberg as an American movie star, also beautiful and alluringly sexy in a simple, mindless way. Rubini briefly meets an unspoiled and charming girl from the country working at a beachside restaurant. In the final scene of the film they meet again at the beach, separated not only by the tides but also more profoundly by the emotional distance between his cynicism and her innocence.

Fellini explores religious fervor throughout the film, from the opening scenes of helicopters airlifting an enormous plaster figure of Christ, to the fakery Rubini finds as he covers a claimed sighting of the Virgin Mary by two children. With other reporters, Rubini races to the site, which is surrounded by television cameras and a crowd of the devout. The children lead the faithful on a chase, claiming they see the Virgin in one place after another, as the lame and the blind hobble after them and their grandfather cadges for tips, until everyone collapses, exhausted, at dawn.

The film also explores Rubini's relationship with his father in a bittersweet sequence, and the life of intellect comes under Fellini's scrutiny at a party with artists, poets and philosophers, given by Rubini's friend Steiner. Despite all appearances, Steiner, who has a loving family, money, success and creative friends, is suffering the same boredom in which Rubini is trapped. He is not happy, but he cannot explain or find reason for his unhappiness. Later in the film, Rubini returns to Steiner's apartment to find that Steiner has shot his children and committed suicide. This ultimate expression of despair, the inability of this paragon to love enough, pushes Rubini over the edge. Instead of moving from journalism to the higher realm of literary writing, which he has been contemplating throughout the film, he sells out to become a public relations hack, a drunk and a decadent party boy. Rubini is now immersed in the world that he previously saw from the vantage of a reporter, and the film ends with a wild, now-famous orgy scene.

CENSORSHIP HISTORY

La Dolce Vita was banned by the Roman Catholic Church in predominantly Catholic countries, but the bans occurred more because of the religious criticism in the film than the sexuality. In the United States, the film played an important role in modifying both the movie ratings system and the ratings system of the Catholic Legion of Decency (LOD). In the early 1960s, numerous challenges to the Motion Picture Association of America (MPAA) appeared in the form of what Murray Schumach labels "cheap movies that featured little else but bare bodies." The producers were usually not members of the MPAA, so these pictures were not submitted to the Hollywood censors, nor did they receive a seal of approval. Known as "nudies," films such as Russ Meyer's *The Immoral Mr. Teas* were usually shown in a limited number of theaters, yet they were profitable. Eventually, "'art' houses that formerly specialized in foreign films switched to 'nudies.'" The increase in such movies and in the number of theaters exhibiting them created a growing concern that led to a widespread censorship controversy over nudity in the movies.

Established Hollywood producers felt that their adherence to the MPAA code was keeping them out of the very profitable market of the "nudies." In this same period, foreign-made films like *La Dolce Vita*, generally called "quality films," were entering the U.S. market and showing audiences more bare skin than was permitted in movies that met the MPAA standards. Rather than agree that these were quality or art films, Hollywood producers simply saw them as "just excuses to show larger areas of lush females and more concentrated sex than anything the censors would approve in Hollywood." *La Dolce Vita* evoked the same mixed reaction. In an April 24, 1961, review of the film, a *Box Office Magazine* reviewer wrote,

> Whether the viewer regards "La Dolce Vita" as being shocking, sordid, sexy or moralistic, there can be no denial that it is a picture that reaches perfection in its technical and artistic presentation. The attention paid to the slightest detail to attain realism is almost astounding. And, too, nobody can deny that it is controversial and probably will cause considerable controversy when seen by all strata of society. Rarely, if ever, has a picture reflected decadence, immorality and sophistication with such depth, bringing into sharp focus the nobleman, the prostitute, the homosexual, the intellectual, the nymphomaniac, all woven into a series of satiric panoramas of life today. In this picture, the locale is Rome, but the events probably could take place in any large city, and very likely do.

The same mixed reaction met the film in the United States, where the LOD remained indecisive about how to handle the film, although all agreed that it was strictly for adults. In Italy, where the picture had drawn mixed opinions, the clergy both condemned and lauded the film. Some priests told their parishioners not to view the film while others stressed its Christian aspects that showed the shallowness of most public piety that is not based in true faith. Reviews of the film in the United States also stressed this duality, but most acknowledged, as did *Box Office*, that the film "will be patronized for its entertainment values—by adults, of course, and very broadminded adults at that."

The increasing tolerance for adult movies filmed in good taste and the new popularity among American audiences for foreign films that treated sex and morality in a mature fashion made the LOD reconsider its position. Schumach points out that "Catholics as well as Protestants were saying that the legion had fallen behind the times. The legion became increasingly aware that outside the church it was becoming a subject of some derision." To avoid ridicule, the legion amended its regulations in 1957 and 1963 and created special classifications to accommodate such films as *La Dolce Vita*. Thus, instead of simply assigning a film an "A" (morally unobjectionable for general patronage), "B" (morally objectionable in part for all) or "C" (condemned), the LOD added three new levels of the "A" rating. To the original "A" (now "A-1") were added: "A-2" (morally unobjectionable for adults and adolescents), "A-3" (morally unobjectionable for adults) and "A-4" (morally unobjectionable for adults with reservations). By assigning an A-4 rating to *La Dolce Vita*, the LOD could make its views known without having to condemn the film outright and risk ridicule. As the text accompanying the revisions to the code stated, "in deciding the ratings of the films, no consideration is given to artistic, technical or dramatic values. Only moral content is weighed."

The LOD was not the only ratings entity to observe this change. In a 1963 interview, Elwood L. Gebhart, the executive assistant to the Motion

Picture Censor Board of Maryland, expressed a concern regarding such foreign films as *La Dolce Vita* and stated that he thought the board should be a little stricter. He admitted that "foreign films do have different problems. They don't make nudist films where everyone stands around posing. Their use of nudism arises out of lovemaking situations." For this reason, the Maryland board could not identify reasons valid within Maryland statutes to ban *La Dolce Vita*, although the board seriously considered doing so. After passing the film for exhibition, the board received complaints from municipalities and "*La Dolce Vita* stirred up some letter writing" but no formal bans. The Chicago board of censors also expressed ambivalence regarding the film, and Sergeant Robert E. Murphy, overseer of the six-member board, admitted in a 1963 interview that *La Dolce Vita* also slipped through their regulations: "Our job is to provide legal guidance in a mature fashion. Of course, we make mistakes. You take *La Dolce Vita*. We should have cut out some parts of this or limited it to an adults only audience." The fact remains that the board was unable to isolate and identify portions of the film that were clearly objectionable as defined in the Chicago censorship ordinance.

FURTHER READING

Box Office Magazine Archives: http://www.boxofficemagazine.com/archives. April 24, 1961.

Carmen, Ira H. *Movies, Censorship and the Law.* Ann Arbor: University of Michigan Press, 1966.

Ebert, Roger. "*La Dolce Vita.*" *The Chicago Sun Times*, September 19, 1999, p. C1.

Schumach, Murray. *The Face on the Cutting Room Floor.* New York: William Morrow, 1964.

Shapiro, Walter. "Sad Picture Worth a Thousand Words." *USA Today*, September 5, 1997, p. A1.

Wilmington, Michael. "Fellini's *La Dolce Vita* Coined a Term and Created a Character Whose Amoral Image Endures." *Chicago Tribune*, September 12, 1997, p. 5.

DON JUAN

Country and date of production: Austria, 1955 (as *Don Giovanni*)
Production company/distributor: Akkond Film (Austria)/Times Film (United States, 1956)
Format: Sound, color (Agfacolor)
Running time: 89 minutes
Language: German
Producer: Walter Kolm-Veltée
Director: Walter Kolm-Veltée
Screenwriters: Ernst Henthaler, Walter Kolm-Veltée, Alfred Uhl, Lorenzo da Ponte (libretto of the opera *Don Giovanni*)
Awards: None

Genre: Adventure

With: Cesare Danova (Don Giovanni), Josef Meinrad (Leporello), Evelyn Cormand (Zerlina), Hans von Borsody (Masetto), Lotte Tobisch (Donna Elvira), Jean Vinci (Don Ottavio), Marianne Schönauer (Donna Anna), Fred Hennings (Commendatore), Senta Wengraf (Elvira's Maid)

SUMMARY

The film is an adaptation of the opera *Don Giovanni*, composed in 1787 by Wolfgang Amadeus Mozart to a libretto by Lorenzo da Ponte. The movie uses the music from the opera for much of its score. The plot concerns the adventures of a young Spanish nobleman who pursues women unscrupulously and obsessively. While the story has many variations, the version that appears in the opera and in the film *Don Juan*, the American title of the Austrian film, has its origin in Tirso de Molina's *El Burlador De Sevilla* (The Trickster of Seville), written in 1630. In this version, the dissolute young lover duels with and kills the father of one of the women with whom he has had a relationship. Don Juan later pulls the beard off a stone effigy of the man and invites the figure to dinner. The statue accepts and then returns the invitation by inviting Don Juan to a festivity in his tomb, where another stone figure strangles Don Juan. The young lover's soul is carried off to hell.

CENSORSHIP HISTORY

Litigation regarding the right of a distributor to exhibit *Don Juan* in Chicago, Illinois, forced the United States Supreme Court to rule on the issue of prior restraint in *Times Film Corp. v. City of Chicago*, a ruling that tested the permissibility of local censorship of motion pictures. Cities and states had long asserted their right to demand that distributors of movies obtain a permit from the local board of licensing or board of censors before they could exhibit their films in local theaters. In 1961, the Times Film Corporation decided to test this right in the city of Chicago, where the company applied to the board for a permit but refused to allow the board to view the film *Don Juan*. Despite the relatively innocuous content of the film, the board refused to issue a permit for exhibition because the company had refused to provide a copy of the movie. The distributor then approached the mayor of Chicago and claimed that the board had violated the rights of the company and had effectively pre-censored the film by not issuing the permit. When this argument failed to produce the permit to exhibit, the distributor then went to court to force the city to grant a license to show *Don Juan*.

Attorneys for Times Film Corporation argued before the U.S. District Court for the Northern District of Illinois that the ordinance requiring censorship was unconstitutional and contradicted the intentions of the First and Fourteenth Amendments, which prohibited a prior restraint on the freedom of expression. They asked the court to restrain Chicago from interfering with the exhibition of the film. Because the board of censors had not seen the film and, therefore, had not made their decision to deny the permit based on the nature of the film, the district court in *Times Film Corporation v. City of Chicago*, 180 F. Supp. 843 (1959), dismissed the complaint. In the decision, Chief Judge William J. Campbell wrote that a controversy appropriate for judicial determination existed. The distributor appealed the decision in the U.S. Court of Appeals for the Seventh Circuit, which affirmed the decision of the lower court. In his decision, Judge Schnackenberg wrote that the case "presented merely an abstract question of law" because the contents of the film had not been made a part of the proceedings. He dismissed the constitutional claims as only a "theoretical remedy of prevention" and expressed the opinion that the damage resulting from the exhibition of a film "could never be repaired." In example, he wrote, "A film which incites a riot produces that result almost immediately after it is shown publicly. Likewise, the effect upon the prurient mind of an obscene film may result harmfully to some third person within hours after the film has been shown."

The case was then argued before the U.S. Supreme Court in *Times Film Corporation v. City of Chicago*, 365 U.S. 43 (1961). In a decision split 5 to 4, the Court ruled that cities and states do have the right to require distributors to obtain a permit before being allowed to exhibit the film. In writing the majority opinion, Justice Tom C. Clark asserted that the only question that the Court was deciding was whether "constitutional protection includes complete and absolute freedom to exhibit, at least once, any and every kind of motion picture." The ruling disagreed with the basis upon which the distributor had brought suit and noted that the issue in this case was not freedom of expression, but instead the basic authority of a censor. Clark wrote:

> Petitioner claims that the nature of the film is irrelevant, and that even if this film contains the basest type of pornography, or incitement to riot, or forceful overthrow of orderly government, it may nonetheless be shown without prior submission for examination. The challenge here is to the censor's basic authority. . . . Petitioner would have us hold that the public exhibition of motion pictures must be allowed under any circumstances. The State's old remedy, it says, is the invocation of the criminal process under the Illinois pornography statute . . . and then only after a transgression.

The decision observed that the section of the Chicago ordinance that required films to be examined by the board of censors before public showing did constitute "prior restraint," but the distributor's complaint had not questioned the validity of the standards set by the ordinance, nor did any description of the film appear in the court record. The ruling stated that the content of the film was, indeed, important, for the "capacity for evil may be relevant in determining the permissible scope of community control," and asserted that motion pictures were not "necessarily subject to the precise rules governing any other particular method of expression."

In the lengthy and rambling dissenting opinion, Chief Justice Earl Warren wrote that the decision posed a "real danger of eventual censorship for every form of communication, be it newspapers, journals, books, magazines, television, radio, or public speeches." The dissent noted that the decision in this case was contrary to precedents already set by the Court in handing down decisions related to censorship and noted that "the question here presented is whether the City of Chicago—or, for that matter, any city, any State or the Federal Government—may require all motion picture exhibitors to submit all films to a police chief, mayor or other administrative official, for licensing and censorship prior to public exhibition within the jurisdiction." With blunt clarity, the dissenting justices wrote the following warning:

> Let it be completely clear what the Court's decision does. It gives official license to the censor, approving a grant of power to city officials to prevent the showing of any moving picture these officials deem unworthy of a license. It thus gives formal sanction to censorship in its purest and most far-reaching form, to a classical form of licensing that, in our country, most closely approaches the English licensing laws of the seventeenth century which were commonly used to suppress dissent in the mother country and in the colonies.

FURTHER READING

Carmen, Ira H. *Movies, Censorship, and the Law.* Ann Arbor: University of Michigan Press, 1966.

Giglio, Ernest David. *The Decade of the The Miracle, 1952–1962: A Study in the Censorship of the American Motion Picture.* Doctor of Social Sciences Dissertation, Syracuse University, 1964.

Nimmer, Melville B. "The Constitutionality of Official Censorship of Motion Pictures." *University of Chicago Law Review* 25 (1958): 639–640.

Times Film Corporation v. City of Chicago, 180 F. Supp. 843 (1959).

Times Film Corporation v. City of Chicago, 272 F. 2d 90 (1959).

Times Film Corporation v. City of Chicago, 365 U.S. 43 (1961).

DRACULA

Country and date of production: United States, 1931
Production company/distributor: Universal Pictures
Format: Sound, black and white
Running time: 75 minutes
Language: English, Hungarian
Producers: Tod Browning, Carl Laemmle, Jr.
Director: Tod Browning
Screenwriters: John L. Balderston and Hamilton Deane (play), Louis Bromfield, Garrett Fort, Dudley Murphy (additional dialogue), Louis Stevens, Bram Stoker (novel)
Awards: None
Genre: Horror

With: Bela Lugosi (Count Dracula/Coach Driver), Helen Chandler (Mina Seward), David Manners (John Harker), Dwight Frye (Renfield), Edward Van Sloan (Professor Abraham Van Helsing), Herbert Bunston (Dr. Jack Seward), Frances Dade (Lucy Weston), Joan Standing (Maid), Charles K. Gerard (Martin)

SUMMARY

The film begins with the appearance of a horse-drawn carriage winding down a steep, narrow road through the jagged Carpathian Mountains of Transylvania in Eastern Europe. The coach finally comes to a halt at an old inn at dusk. One passenger announces his plans to proceed farther. The nervous inn proprietor tells him that the coach driver is afraid to continue and that they should wait until sunrise. Undaunted, the real estate agent named Renfield isn't superstitious or afraid of the warning, so the journey to Borgo Pass commences as the fearful townspeople watch the coach depart. Darkness falls as the coach presses on through the mountains. As Dracula's castle comes into sight, the audience has its first glimpse of Dracula's coffin, from which he emerges. Elegantly dressed in a black tuxedo, he slowly descends a massive staircase and then motions for his guest to climb the castle's great stone staircase behind him, as wolves howl in the distance. Dracula tells Renfield that he has chartered a ship to take them to England to finalize a real estate investment, "leaving tomorrow eve - n - ing." The vampire pours some "very old wine" for his guest. As Renfield becomes light-headed and dizzy, Dracula crouches at Renfield's neck, enveloping him in his cloak.

A few days later, the sailing ship *Vesta* is bound for England and carries Dracula and his coffins. When the ship finally drifts into an English harbor at Whitby, it is a ghost ship filled with corpses. Renfield emerges from the hold of the ship, giggling and totally insane.

In his new place of residence, Dracula pursues human blood to satisfy his hunger. Dressed in an opera cape and top hat, he strides through the foggy London streets at night and preys on women. One night, during a performance of the London Symphony at the Opera House, Dracula finds a way to meet Dr. Seward and introduces himself as Count Dracula, the new neighbor in the leased Carfax Abbey conveniently located next to Seward's sanitarium. Dr. Seward introduces his daughter Mina Seward, her friend Lucy Weston, and Mina's fiancé, John Harker. Called to examine Renfield, an eminent, white-coated scientist named Van Helsing declares that he will secure proof that Renfield is "undead"— the mortal slave of a vampire. As Mina sleeps that night, Dracula flies into her room as a bat and preys on her. The next morning, Van Helsing overhears a conversation between Mina and her fiancé, then asks to examine her throat and finds two telltale bite marks. Just then, Count Dracula is introduced by a maid as a visitor. As Dracula talks directly next to Mina, John opens a small cigarette box with a mirror inside its lid, and Van

Helsing notices that Dracula does not cast a reflection. Van Helsing opens the mirrored box right in front of Dracula, who immediately slaps it out of his hands. After Dracula makes a hasty exit, Van Helsing identifies him as a vampire. A loud scream is heard, and a maid rushes into the house, crying that Mina's body is lying "dead" on the lawn, but Mina is alive and under Dracula's spell and influence.

In the predawn hours, Dracula returns to Mina's bedroom and leads Mina, his intended bride, away from the estate to his subterranean chambers in the abbey, as Van Helsing and Harker follow the mad Renfield to Carfax Abbey where they expect to locate Dracula's box of earth. Dracula is greeted by Renfield who has escaped his cell. Believing that Renfield has betrayed him, Dracula kills him, takes Mina in his arms and flees to the cellar crypt, where he is found at sunrise by Van Helsing. Van Helsing prepares a sharp wooden stake to drive into Dracula's heart. In another part of the subterranean cellar, Mina feels his agonizing death pains and screams as Dracula is impaled. As John rushes to her and hugs her, Mina appears to come out of her trance—released from Dracula's powers and curse.

CENSORSHIP HISTORY

Dracula was proposed as a film project in 1930 by Carl Laemmle, Jr., the heir apparent of his father's Universal Pictures, who had to fight even his father to make the picture. Studio executives had sent copies of the Bram Stoker novel and the successful stage play by John L. Balderston and Hamilton Deane to Colonel Jason S. Joy, the administrator of the Production Code Administration (PCA). E. M. Asher, associate producer at Universal, wrote to Joy, asking for his "censorship angles" on the story that he claimed would be filmed by Universal as a "tale of horror and mystery, with love theme for relief." Asher was especially concerned because the readers' reports on both the play and the novel had been highly negative and identified numerous areas of content that might be censored. In a report for the studio submitted on June 15, 1927, one story-department reader wrote that the story contained "everything that would cause any average human being to revolt or seek a convenient railing." In contrast to the studio concern, Joy found nothing objectionable in the script. One reason may be that supernatural films were a rarity at the time, and none had ever created a controversy. A second reason is that the Production Code contained nothing about vampires.

The movie was approved by the Motion Picture Producers and Distributors Association (MPPDA) and released in 1931 with the PCA seal, but the public seemed to be more censorious than the regulators because complaints came in almost immediately. The *Dracula* case files of the MPPDA contain letters denouncing the movie. One complainant wrote, "I cannot see one redeeming feature in this picture. It is the most horrible thing." Another wrote, "The author must have had a distorted mind and I cannot understand why it was produced. I cannot speak too strongly against this picture for children."

One writer asserted that *Dracula* represented an immediate social danger: "This picture should be protested by every previewing organization. Its insane horrible details shown to millions of impressionable children, to adults already bowed down by human misery, will do an infinite amount of harm." The Parents and Teachers Association (PTA) added to the outcry; PTA report chair Marjorie Ross Davis wrote that she was familiar in advance with the theme of the movie but "saw the first fifteen minutes of it and felt I could stand it no more. . . . It should be withdrawn from public showing, as children, [the] weak-minded and all classes attend motion pictures indiscriminately."

In a letter written to Carl Laemmle, Jr., on April 7, 1931, Joy discussed censorship of the movie both overseas and in the United States. He informed Laemmle that official censors in Singapore, British Malaya and in British Columbia had required extensive cuts in the film, including the elimination of Renfield's dialogue about the rat's blood and spiders and flies; the crying of the child in a cemetery; and the reading aloud of the newspaper article telling of the victimization of a child. Censors in both countries also demanded that the vampire women at Dracula's castle be removed from the film. In the United States, the official objections were limited to the demand by censors in Massachusetts that two brief shots be cut from the film "to enable viewing on Sundays": one scene showing part of a skeleton in a casket and another scene in which an insect emerges from a tiny coffin. The producer appears to have been especially watchful of the manner in which audiences would interpret the sexuality of Count Dracula. Laemmle's annotations to the final screenplay for the film include the note, "Dracula should only go for women and not men!" In addition to his attention to the homoerotic implications of the script, Laemmle also toned down sexual implications in general. The play by Balderston and Deane contained clear directions that Dracula was to engage in a passionate kiss on the mouth with each of his female victims before penetrating their necks with his fangs, but the script revised this to a kiss on the hand.

FURTHER READING

Asher, E. M. Correspondence to Jason S. Joy. June 26, 1930. MPPDA case file on *Dracula*. Margaret Herrick Library, Special Collections, Academy of Motion Picture Arts and Sciences, Beverly Hills, California.

Cremer, Robert. *Lugosi: The Man Behind the Cape.* Chicago: Henry Regnery Company, 1976.

Joy, Jason S. Correspondence to Carl Laemmle, Jr. April 7, 1931. MPPDA case file on *Dracula*. Margaret Herrick Library, Special Collections, Academy of Motion Picture Arts and Sciences, Beverly Hills, California.

Laemmle, Jr., Carl. "Shooting Script for *Dracula*." In *MagicImage Filmbooks Presents Dracula*, ed. Philip J. Riley. Hollywood, Calif.: MagicImage Filmbooks, 1990.

Miranda, Steve. "Reader's Report on *Dracula*." In *MagicImage Filmbooks Presents Dracula*, ed. Philip J. Riley. Hollywood, Calif.: MagicImage Filmbooks, 1990.

Skal, David J. *The Monster Show: A Cultural History of Horror.* New York: W. W. Norton, 1993.

DRESSED TO KILL

Country and date of production: United States, 1980
Production company/distributor: Warwick Associates/Filmways Pictures
Format: Sound, color
Running time: 105 minutes
Language: English
Producers: Samuel Z. Arkoff, George Litto
Director: Brian De Palma
Screenwriter: Brian De Palma
Awards: 1981 Academy of Science Fiction, Horror and Fantasy Films, Best Actress (Angie Dickinson).
Genre: Drama
With: Michael Caine (Doctor Robert Elliott), Angie Dickinson (Kate Miller), Nancy Allen (Liz Blake), Keith Gordon (Peter Miller), Dennis Franz (Detective Marino), David Margulies (Dr. Levy), Ken Baker (Warren Lockman), Susanna Clemm (Betty Luce), Brandon Maggart (Cleveland Sam)

SUMMARY

One of Brian De Palma's most divisive films, *Dressed to Kill* is a frightening movie that evokes scenes from *Psycho* and other films by Alfred Hitchcock. Kate Miller, a sexually frustrated wife and mother, visits her New York psychiatrist, Dr. Elliott, to complain about her unfulfilling erotic life. Afterward, on the way to meet her husband at a museum, she meets an anonymous man, with whom she has an afternoon of satisfying sex. Kate then discovers that the man has a venereal disease, but that information becomes a moot point when a razor-wielding blonde woman slashes Kate to ribbons in the elevator of the man's building. A blonde prostitute named Liz, who caught a glimpse of the murderer, becomes both the prime suspect and the killer's next target. With the police less than willing to believe her story, Liz joins forces with Kate's son Peter to catch the psychopath. Eventually, the murderer is revealed to be a man afflicted with multiple personality disorder who dresses in women's clothing when killing. The cross-dressing killer is overpowered before he can commit another violent act. In the film's conclusion, a psychiatrist explains the killer's psychological dementia in a lengthy monologue that attempts to evoke a feeling of sympathy from the audience.

CENSORSHIP HISTORY

Dressed to Kill was the most maligned and censored film of Brian De Palma's career. With his signature flare for visual composition and shocking gore, De Palma drew criticism for mimicking the slasher-movie convention of exploiting and then gruesomely killing women on screen.

Censorship of the film began long before its release. When the director presented the film to the Motion Picture Association of America (MPAA) Ratings Board for review and rating, the board informed him that the movie would be given an "X" rating but did not specify the cuts he could make to earn a less restrictive rating. The MPAA usually reserved the "X" designation for hard-core pornography and extreme violence; because such a rating limited the number of venues that could exhibit the film, it made commercial failure highly likely. On his own, De Palma edited scenes from the murder sequences, the nude shower scenes and every sequence that contained spurting blood. He also eliminated all frames showing pubic hair and dubbed dialogue to delete expletives. De Palma then resubmitted the film to the MPAA Ratings Board, which granted an "R" rating to the film: viewers under the age of 17 could not see it unless accompanied by an adult. The director protested this rating, arguing that controversy over CRUISING earlier in the year had increased the scrutiny of his film by the ratings board. The response he received from Jack Valenti, president of the MPAA, was that the board had originally assigned an "X" to *Dressed to Kill* because of cultural politics: "The political climate in this country is shifting from left to right, and that means more conservative attitudes toward sex and violence. But a lot of creative people are still living in the world of revolution."

Filmways Pictures used lurid advertisements and posters to market the movie, using copy that labeled De Palma the "master of the macabre" and that invited viewers "to an evening of extreme terror" or to see "the latest fashion . . . in murder." A third advertisement that appeared in daily newspapers contained a woman holding a straight razor that reflected the image of Angie Dickinson screaming, and the caption, "The second before she screams will be the most frightening moment of your life." The combination of slick advertising, the ratings controversy, and initially positive reviews resulted in high box-office profits in the first few weeks that the film was exhibited. Within a few months, however, a backlash against the film began. Writers such as Andrew Sarris accused De Palma of "simply cashing in on the current market for 'grunge,' a term connoting the dispensing of blood and gore like popcorn to the very young." When asked in a *Newsday* interview if he agreed that his movie was misogynist, De Palma stated that he believed that filmmakers should be able to make films "about anything. Should we get into censorship because we have movies that are going to upset some part of the community?"

The film, which opened in 660 theaters nationwide on July 25, 1980, earned $15 million in gross receipts in only 19 days, but protests did not begin until late August. The film was criticized for its treatment of transsexuals: Gay and transgendered groups protested that the resolution was an offense to transgendered people everywhere. They admitted that individuals suffering from bi-gendered disassociated personality disorder may exist but argued that the film should have portrayed the condition with more accuracy. Feminist groups protested that the rape fantasy scene was misogynistic. Other groups found the scene of the prostitute being pursued by street thugs to be racist and the slow-motion scenes excessive and melo-dramatic.

Feminist antipornography campaigns reached an intense pitch in Boston, Los Angeles, and San Francisco. In New York City, the group Women Against Pornography (WAP) mobilized members of several feminist groups to picket the 57th Street Playhouse, where the film was playing. Nearly 150 women chanted and carried placards bearing such slogans as "Murder of women is not erotic," "*Dressed to Kill* is a racist and sexist lie" and "Women's slaughter is not entertainment but terrorism." They also called for a boycott of the film. In San Francisco, members of Women Against Violence and Pornography in Movies (WAVPM) distributed leaflets to theatergoers reminding them that "If this film succeeds, killing women may become the greatest turn-on of the Eighties!" The result of these efforts was the opposite of the protestors' intended effect: During the height of the protests the film "rose from third to first place on *Variety*'s weekly listing of top-grossing films."

FURTHER READING

Asselle, Giovanna, and Behroze Gandhy. "*Dressed to Kill.*" *Screen* 23 (September–October 1982): 137–143.

Canby, Vincent. "Film: *Dressed to Kill*, De Palma Mystery." *New York Times*, July 25, 1980, p. C2.

Denby, David. "Deep Threat." *New York*, July 28, 1980, p. 44.

Denby, David, Alan Dershowitz,and others. "Pornography: Love or Death?" *Film Comment* 20, no. 6 (November–December 1984): 29–47.

Kael, Pauline C. "Master Spy, Master Seducer." *New Yorker*, August 4, 1980, p. 68.

Laurence, Gerald. "Dressing 'Dressed' to Sell." *Box Office*, September 1980, p. 26.

Lester, Peter. "Redress or Undress? Feminists Fume While Angie Scores in a Sexy Chiller." *Camera* 5 (Fall 1980): 71–72, 81.

Lyons, Charles. *The New Censor: Movies and the Culture Wars.* Philadelphia: Temple University Press, 1997.

Pally, Marcia, and others. "Sex, Violence, and De Palma." *Film Comment* 21, no. 5 (September– October 1985): 9–13.

Sarris, Andrew. "Dreck to Kill." *Village Voice*, September 17–23, 1980, p. 43.

Wood, Peter. "How a Film Changes from an 'X' to an 'R'." *New York Times*, July 20, 1980, p. C1.

THE EASIEST WAY

Country and date of production: United States, 1917
Production company/distributor: Clara Kimball Young Picture Company/Lewis J. Selznick Enterprises
Format: Silent, black and white
Running time: 120 minutes
Language: English
Producer: Clara Kimball Young

Director: Albert Capellani
Screenwriters: Eugene Walter (play), Albert Capellani, Frederic Chapin
Awards: None
Genre: Drama
With: Clara Kimball Young (Laura Murdock), Louise Bates (Elfie St. Clair), Joseph Kilgour (Willard Brockton), Rockliffe Fellowes (John Madison), Cleo Desmond (Annie), George Stevens (Jim Weston), Frank Kingdon (Burgess), May Hopkins (Nellie De Vere), Walter McEwen (Jerry)

SUMMARY

The Easiest Way is the story of a young woman from an impoverished background whose effort to succeed as an actress has had only modest results. When Laura Murdock meets the wealthy Willard Brockton, she is dazzled by his generosity. She soon realizes that she no longer has to struggle if she takes the "easiest way" to survive by becoming his mistress. While enjoying the luxurious lifestyle Brockton provides for her, Laura meets struggling young writer John Madison, who accepts the truth about Laura's life because she has lived in this way only to survive. The two fall in love, and Laura promises to leave Brockton. Madison attempts to make his fortune so they can marry. Time passes, and Laura runs low on money. Faced with either taking a menial job and continuing to wait for Madison or going back to her old life, Laura returns to Brockton. Two months later, Madison returns as a wealthy man and learns what Laura has done. Recognizing her greedy nature, both men reject her and Laura sinks into despair after realizing that she either has to find another man to support her or take her own life.

CENSORSHIP HISTORY

The play caused a sensation on Broadway, and the film version caught the attention of censors who felt strongly that Laura should be more severely punished for her life as a mistress. In 1918, the distributor submitted the film to the Kansas State Board of Review (BOR) in an effort to obtain a license to exhibit *The Easiest Way* in Kansas. The BOR denied the license on the grounds that the film was "immoral" and that the portrayal of Laura made her lifestyle "too alluring" to impressionable viewers. Attorneys representing the distributor sued the BOR in Wyandotte County District Court and argued that the film is "moral and fit for exhibition." The court agreed and reversed the decision of the BOR. The state then challenged the reversal in a case heard before the Supreme Court of Kansas in *Mid-West Photo Play Corp. v. Miller*, 169 P. 1154 (1919), which reversed the decision of the district court. The court reaffirmed that the exercise of administrative power to determine if a film was "moral and fit for exhibition" had by statute been "specially conferred upon the board" and that the judgment of the court cannot replace that of the board. While the court acknowledged in its decision that the board may have acted in a mistaken manner, a judicial reexamination of the action of the board was not warranted because the distributor did not claim in its suit that the board had acted in a dishonest, capricious or arbitrary manner. As Chief Justice William A. Johnson wrote, "Fraud and dishonesty cannot be imputed to public officials unless plainly alleged and proven. We must presume that the board acted in good faith, and that the decision that the picture is immoral was an honest exercise of the best judgment of its members."

FURTHER READING

Kansas State Board of Review. *Complete List of Motion Picture Films Submitted.* Vol. 1. Topeka: Kansas State Board of Reviews, 1915–1966.
Miller, Frank. *Censored Hollywood: Sex, Sin & Violence on Screen.* Atlanta, Ga.: Turner Publishing, 1994.
Reports of the Kansas State Supreme Court, 1917–1966. Topeka: Archives of the Kansas Historical Society, Vol. 102, n.d.; p. 356.
Vieira, Mark. *Sin in Soft Focus: Pre-Code Hollywood.* New York: Harry N. Abrams, 1999.

ECSTASY

Country and date of production: Czechoslovakia, 1933 (as *Extase*)
Production company/distributor: Elektra Productions/Eureka Productions (United States, 1940)
Format: Sound, black and white
Running time: 82 minutes
Language: Czechoslovakia
Producers: Moriz Grunhut, Frantisek Horky
Director: Gustav Machaty
Screenwriters: Frantisek Horky, Jacques A. Koerpel, Gustav Machaty, Vitezslav Nezval
Awards: None
Genre: Drama/ Romance
With: Leopold Kramer (Eva's Father), Hedy Lamarr (as "Hedy Kiesler," Eva), Aribert Mog (Adam), Zvonimir Rogoz (Emile)

SUMMARY

Made in Czechoslovakia in 1933, *Ecstasy (Exstase)* is a film about sexual frustration and one young woman's efforts to overcome it. The lead female character, Eva, has just married an older man. Soon after marrying, Eva discovers that her husband is obsessed with order in his life and, furthermore, that he is impotent. Her marriage remains unconsummated and she becomes despondent about the unhappy turn her life has taken. Eva leaves her husband and files for divorce. Then she returns to her father's house. She frequently swims nude in a lake and, during one such swim, she is seen by a young man, an engineer who lives nearby who introduces himself. Almost instantaneously, the two fall in love with each other. Their sexual attraction is powerful, and when Eva runs to the young man's cottage during a rainstorm, they make love. The camera captures the look of ecstasy on Eva's face as she apparently achieves orgasm. While Eva is away, her husband becomes grief stricken at the loss of his young bride, and he becomes desperate to reestablish their marital relationship. When the two lovers meet in a neighboring town with the thought of going away together, Eva's husband appears and commits suicide, leading her to leave her lover asleep at the railroad station and to depart by train for an unknown destination.

CENSORSHIP HISTORY

Ecstasy was advertised with the following tagline: "The Most Talked About Picture in the World," a label the film earned for one nude swimming scene and another scene in which the camera closes in on Eva's face at what appears to be the instant of her sexual climax. The film was the object of censorship from its first release. The star, credited as Hedy Kiesler before her Hollywood name-change to Hedy Lamarr, married an Austrian millionaire soon after completing the film, and he tried unsuccessfully to buy all prints of the film to prevent its circulation. In 1934, the Italian leader Benito Mussolini overrode the nation's censorship law to allow a screening of the film at the Venice Film Festival, but the Vatican raised vehement objections, which critics believe may have cost it a prize. In 1935, distributor Samuel Cummins' attempt to import the film failed when United States Customs agents seized it under the 1930 Tariff Act, which allowed the seizure of any imported material thought to be obscene, pending a court decision. The seizure of *Ecstasy* was the first time customs laws were used to prevent a film from entering the United States.

Attorneys representing the distributor filed a complaint with the Second District Court of New York, which decided in *United States v. Two Tin Boxes,* 79 F. 2d 1017 (1935) that the film was "immoral" and "obscene." The distributor appealed the ruling, but federal marshals burned the film while the appeal was pending. Left with no film as physical evidence, the court dismissed the appeal. The distributor then imported another copy and made major revisions in the film to remove previously objectionable scenes, such as Eva's nude run through the woods and a scene of horses copulating and added a voiceover to announce Eva's divorce before her affair. The ending was also changed to show a baby, to suggest that Eva and the engineer had married. U.S. Customs agents allowed this version of the film into the country in 1937, but the film was refused a license for exhibition by the New York Board of Review. Attorneys representing the distributor brought suit in the United States District Court for the Southern District of New York to request an injunction to prevent the state of New York from blocking exhibition of the film. The complaint alleged that by refusing to grant the permit, the authorities would "encroach upon federal power over foreign commerce in violation of the Constitution (Article 1, paragraph 8)" because "the federal authorities had admitted the film, determining it not to be immoral" based on the Tariff Act of 1930; therefore, "exhibition in a state may not later be prohibited by the state authorities." The court refused the request in *Eureka Productions v. Byrne*, 300 N.Y.S. 218 (1937).

Eureka Productions then filed an appeal with the U.S. Court of Appeals for the Second Circuit, but the court rejected the argument of the distributor and determined that once a film enters the United States, local censorship laws prevail. *Ecstasy* enjoyed several years of limited runs in art houses throughout the United States, but it did not receive Production Code Administration approval until 1940, after the distributor made severe cuts in the film to remove all scenes of nudity. Even then, several states rejected the film or demanded further cuts. Gerald Gardner records that Massachusetts would not permit the film to be shown on Sundays, while Pennsylvania rejected it "in its entirety." Maryland eventually issued the film a permit, but only after numerous cuts were made to eliminate Eva's nude run through the woods; the exposure of her breasts while she is swimming; the scene of her husband handling a box of condoms; all scenes of the new bride lying expectantly in bed; a scene in which her husband takes an aphrodisiac; and a closeup of the nude Eva chasing a horse. The film was also one of the few foreign films to earn a "C" (condemned) rating from the Catholic Legion of Decency.

FURTHER READING

Carmen, Ira H. *Movies, Censorship, and the Law*. Ann Arbor: University of Michigan Press, 1966.
Eureka Productions v. Byrne, 300 N.Y.S. 218 (1937).
Eureka Productions v. Lehman, 17 F. Supp. 259 (1937).
Gardner, Gerald. *The Censorship Papers: Movie Censorship Letters from the Hays Office, 1934 to 1968*. New York: Dodd, Mead, 1987.
Leff, Leonard J., and Jerold L. Simmons. *The Dame in the Kimono: Hollywood, Censorship, & the Production Code from the 1920s to the 1960s*. New York: Grove Weidenfeld, 1990.
United States v. Two Tin Boxes, 79 F. 2d 1017 (1935).

EMMANUELLE

Country and date of production: France, 1974 (as *Emanuelle*)
Production company/distributor: Orphée, Trinacre/Columbia Pictures
Format: Sound, color
Running Time: 105 minutes (France)
Language: French
Producer: Yves Rousset-Rouard
Director: Just Jaeckin
Screenwriters: Emmanuelle Arsan (pseudonym for Maryat Rollet-Andriane, novel), Jean-Louis Richard

Awards: None
Genre: Adult
With: Sylvia Kristel (Emmanuelle), Alain Cuny (Mario), Marika Green (Bee), Daniel Sarky (Jean), Jeanne Colletin (Ariane), Christine Boisson (Marie-Ange)

SUMMARY

The screenplay for *Emmanuelle* was adapted from the novel of the same name written by Maryat Rollet-Andriane under the pseudonym of Emmanuelle Arsan. The plot depends heavily upon scenes of explicit sex that show the cast reveling in the joys and pleasures of uninhibited sexual freedom. The central character is the beautiful young wife of a French diplomat several years older than she. They are attached to the French Embassy in Bangkok, and they appear to have a happy marriage. Emmanuelle likes and respects her husband, Jean, because he has taught her so much sexually, and Jean is pleased with her because she has learned his lessons so well and eagerly. Despite the exotic beauty of the setting, Emmanuelle soon becomes bored with the everyday routine of the diplomatic community. Jean encourages her to find something exciting to fill her days, as he seems to have taught her all he can. Both are very tolerant regarding extramarital affairs, and Jean doesn't mind when Emmanuelle begins to spend a lot of time with Marie-Ange, who is frequently at their home and who obviously wants more than conversation from his wife. Emmanuelle is flattered by the attentions of Marie-Ange, but she is more interested in her older squash partner Bee, whom she joins on a trip into the jungle. After Emmanuelle has an affair with Bee, she becomes party to a range of more strenuous sexual adventures: She is raped in an opium den, captured and presented as the prize in a boxing match and engages in a ménage à trois with another woman and a man.

CENSORSHIP HISTORY

Emmanuelle, which inspired two sequels and numerous imitations, is a classic among European and even world erotic movies. Filmed in the mid-1970s, the film and its sequels also have historic importance because they set the tone for erotic films that followed. Never before had the European audience seen an erotic movie where a liberated couple made love to each other and every other person to whom they were sexually attracted in such beautiful, exotic cities or landscapes as Bangkok, Hong Kong and Bali. Even more surprising were the quality of the film and the acting. Unlike the dark and shadowy images and bored-looking actors of stag films and standard pornography, for the first time a well-made movie starring a beautiful young woman, played by Silvia Kristel, seduced members of the audience, who were captured by her innocent looks that belied her sexual audacity. Emmanuelle, as both film and woman, appealed to both women and men. Women claimed that the movie helped them to discover their own sexuality and desires, for Emmanuelle became the embodiment of the woman who is totally free to do whatever she wants, wherever she wants and with whomever she wants. The movie was advertised on the Paris billboards for more than a year and played in the same theater for several years. The allure of *Emmanuelle* also penetrated the former Soviet Union, where it was a favorite among Soviet leaders who routinely viewed officially banned films that were illegally smuggled into the country for them but forbidden to the general population.

Despite its wide acceptance in France, the film was banned by President Georges Pompidou when it first came out. Pompidou died in April 1974 and President Giscard d'Estaing, who succeeded him, later released the film for exhibition. In the United States, the film was granted an "X" rating by the Motion Picture Association of America (MPAA), which limited exhibition to art theaters and independent venues. On July 14, 1977, the Covina city manager notified by letter Robert Pringle, manager of the Covina Cinema in Covina, California, that the community had expressed concern over "the exhibition of 'X-Rated' films" at the theater. Four days later, the city attorney was instructed by the city council to draw up an "interim emergency ordinance" that would prohibit exhibition in the city of so-called "adult" films while the council studied the zoning regulations of "adult" land use. Because bookings for films had already been made, the Covina Cinema continued to exhibit films listed on its calendar through the month of September 1977. On July 26, 1977, members of the Covina Police Department attended commercial screenings of *Emmanuelle* and *The Joys of a Woman*, then forwarded misdemeanor complaints against the theater to the office of the Los Angeles County district attorney, but no legal proceedings were initiated. Business declined as a result of unfavorable publicity generated by the actions of the city.

In June 1978, the Covina city council adopted a comprehensive city zoning ordinance "prohibiting the location of 'adult entertainment businesses' within 500 feet of a residential area." In accordance with California code, 115 Cal.App.3d 155, the ordinance also declared its purpose "to insure that [the] adverse effects [arising from their 'serious objectionable operational characteristics'] will not contribute to the blighting or downgrading of the surrounding neighborhood and will not unreasonably interfere with or injure nearby properties." The municipal code was also modified to define an adult motion picture theater as "an enclosed building with a capacity of fifty or more persons used for presenting material distinguished or characterized by an emphasis on depicting or describing 'Specified Sexual Activities' or 'Specified Anatomical Areas'." The Covina municipal code defined such activities as follows:

The Municipal Code specifies anatomical areas as follows: "Specified Anatomical Areas include the following: human genitals, pubic region, buttocks, and female breasts below a point immediately above the top of the areola." (§17.04.529)
"Specified Sexual Activities" include the following:
(a) The fondling or other touching of human genitals, pubic region, buttocks, or female breasts;

(b) Ultimate sex acts, normal or perverted, actual or simulated, including intercourse, oral copulation, sodomy;

(c) Masturbation, and

(d) Excretory functions as part of or in connection with any of the activities set forth in (a) through (c) above. (§17.04.530)

The manager of the Covina Cinema and a patron of the theater sued the city, alleging that the ordinance was unconstitutional and that the city of Covina had violated their rights of equal protection, due process under the law and freedom of speech. The plaintiffs argued that in the code the terms *distinguished or characterized by an emphasis* and *used* were too vague and "chilled freedom of expression." The plaintiff further declared that the ordinance placed limits on his choice of films to exhibit in the theater, "because he cannot know what films will bring the . . . Cinema within the definition of an Adult Motion Picture Theater. . . . and consequently subject to civil and criminal sanctions for . . . violation of the Ordinance." The court denied the request for an injunction and contended that the zoning regulation was valid under a previous case, *Young v. American Mini Theatres*, 427 U.S. 50 (1976), which had upheld the prohibition against "adult entertainment establishment" within 500 feet of a residential area. The theater operator appealed the ruling before the court of appeals of California, second appellate district, on January 26, 1981, on the basis that the injunction should have been granted "because the ordinance contains impermissibly vague terms which chill freedom of expression by deterring the exhibition of films that may or may not be within its ambit." The appellate determined that the superior court should have granted a preliminary injunction and ruled that "the ordinance cannot be enforced against the Cinema unless, contrary to its representations and previous policy, the Cinema presents a preponderance of films in which the dominant theme is the depiction of the ordinance's enumerated sexual activities."

FURTHER READING

Lyons, Charles. *The New Censors: Movies and the Culture Wars.* Philadelphia: Temple University Press, 1997.

Pringle v. City of Covina, 115 Cal.App.3d 151.

Satter, David. "Private Soviet Screenings of Forbidden Films? Insane!" *The Wall Street Journal*, March 13, 1984, p. 1+.

Young v. American Mini Theatres, 427 U.S. 50 (1976).

THE EXORCIST

Country and date of production: United States, 1973
Production company/distributor: Hoya Productions/Warner Bros.
Format: Sound, color

Running time: 122 minutes
Language: English
Producers: William Peter Blatty, Noel Marshall
Director: William Friedkin
Screenwriter: William Peter Blatty (from his novel)
Awards: 1974 Academy Awards, Best Sound (Robert Knudson and Christopher Newman), Best Screenplay Based on Material from Another Medium (William Peter Blatty).
1974 Golden Globe Awards, Best Director – Motion Picture (William Friedkin), Best Motion Picture – Drama, Best Screenplay – Motion Picture (William Peter Blatty), Best Supporting Actress – Motion Picture (Linda Blair).
1974 Writers Guild of America, Best Drama Adapted from Another Medium (William Peter Blatty).
Genre: Drama/horror
With: Ellen Burstyn (Chris MacNeil), Max von Sydow (Father Merrin), Lee J. Cobb (Lieutenant Kinderman), Kitty Winn (Sharon Spencer), Jack MacGowran (Burke Dennings), Jason Miller (Father Damien Karras), Linda Blair (Regan MacNeil), Reverend William O'Malley (Father Dyer), Mercedes McCambridge (voice of Pazuzu)

SUMMARY

Adapted from the novel of the same name by William Peter Blatty, *The Exorcist* relates the story of 12-year-old Regan MacNeil, whose seemingly normal behavior gradually becomes violent and antireligious. The opening scenes of the film chart her transformation and show it to coincide with an aging Jesuit priest's discovery of an ancient devil figure in Iraq. As Regan exhibits an increasingly destructive and violent personality, her mother, a divorced movie actress, begins to fear her but tries to ignore her malicious behavior. When Mrs. MacNeil's fiancé dies in a fall down several flights of stairs, the Washington, D.C., police point to evidence that he was murdered, and suspicion turns to Regan. Her mother finally acknowledges her daughter's recent personality changes and increasingly violent actions. She suspects that Regan suffers from demonic possession. The despairing mother consults a young Roman Catholic priest, Father Damien Karras, whose mother's death has led to his growing loss of faith in God.

Father Karras agrees to meet with Regan and concludes that the only hope of saving her is through an exorcism, which can be performed only by Father Merrin, an experienced older priest. The demon that possesses Regan contorts her voice and facial features as it taunts and torments Karras with references to his mother. In one controversial scene, the demon compels the little girl to masturbate with a crucifix while she calls out the name of Jesus.

The two priests perform the exorcism, during which Merrin dies and Karras physically struggles with the girl until the demon leaves her body and enters his. Now himself possessed, the priest commits suicide by jumping to his death from a window. Freed of the devil, Regan is weak and shaken, but she remembers nothing and appears to have been restored to her former self.

CENSORSHIP HISTORY

The producers of *The Exorcist* expected controversy over the film because attempts had been made in several communities to censor the novel on which it was based. Several key scenes were cited as especially objectionable. In addition to the scene in which Regan masturbates with a crucifix, the film shows Father Karras praying in a chapel while a statute of the Virgin Mary takes on the appearance of a harlot, complete with heavy facial makeup, naked breasts and an erect, clay phallus. The Motion Picture Association of America (MPAA) board assigned the film an "R" rating, which the United States Catholic Conference criticized as too lenient, claiming that the film deserved an "X." The producers also faced efforts to ban the film in Washington, D.C.; Boston, Massachusetts; and Hattiesburg, Mississippi.

In Washington, police officers assigned to the morals division responded to complaints from members of the community. After conferring with the U.S. Attorney's Office, the police were instructed to warn managers of the Cinema Theater that they would be arrested if minors were admitted to showings of *The Exorcist*. The censors based their authority on a provision in the legal code of the District of Columbia that forbade minors from viewing scenes that depicted even simulated sexual conduct, no matter how the actors were clothed, despite the R rating that would permit the presence of minors accompanied by an adult.

An attempt to have the film banned in Boston was eventually thrown out of court. In January 1974, Mrs. Rita Warren lodged a complaint against Sack Cinema 57 Theatre Corporation, owners of the Cinema 57 Theatre, where the film had played to packed houses for a month. She demanded that Boston ban all showings of the film because it was obscene and harmful to viewers. Municipal Court Justice Theodore A. Glynn dismissed the case after viewing the movie, ruling that "it does not meet the guidelines of obscenity as laid down by the United States Supreme Court." In response to efforts to ban the film, then-president of the MPAA Jack Valenti explained in an article in the February 25, 1974, issue of the *New York Times* that the nature of *The Exorcist* is essentially that of a horror film and that its strong language and violence were not excessive because they appeared only in relation to the theme of the film.

The most extensive banning of the film occurred in Hattiesburg, Mississippi, in 1973, in response to numerous complaints from community members. The district attorney joined a justice of the peace and several police officers to attend a showing of the film at the Saenger Theater in Hattiesburg. Officials then filed affidavits and asked a judge to issue a search and arrest warrant. Police were authorized to seize the film and to arrest the theater manager and the projectionist. The court dismissed charges against them, but the city then charged and convicted the corporate owner of the theater for "publicly exhibiting an obscene, indecent and immoral motion picture." The defendant appealed the conviction and won by arguing that the statute was overly broad and that it violated the constitutional requirements that had been affirmed by the U.S. Supreme Court in *Miller v. California*, 413 U.S. 15 (1973). In *ABC Interstate Theatres v. State*, 325 So. 2d 123 (1976), the Mississippi Supreme Court ruled the statute unconstitutional because it violated the First Amendment.

FURTHER READING

ABC Interstate Theatres v. State, 325 So. 2d 123 (1976).

Bouzereau, Laurent. *Cutting Room Floor: Movie Scenes Which Never Made It to the Screen*. New York: Carol Publishing Group, 1994.

Harmetz, Aljean. "The Movies That Draw Hatred." *New York Times*, May 4, 1981, p. C3.

Miller v. California, 413 U.S. 15 (1973).

"Warner Bros. Not Happy with the Last Heretic Laugh." *Daily Variety*, June 22, 1977, p. 5.

491

Country and date of production: Sweden, 1964
Production company/distributor: Svensk Filmindustri/Janus Films
Format: Sound, color
Running time: 101 minutes
Language: Swedish
Producer: Svensk Filmindustri (SF)
Director: Vilgot Sjöman
Screenwriters: Lars Görling (novel), Vilgot Sjöman
Awards: None
Genre: Drama
With: Sven Algotsson (Jingis), Bo Andersson (Fisken), Mona Andersson (Kajsa), Jan Blomberg (Tester), Torleif Cederstrand (Butcher), Wilhelm Fricke (German Sailor), Åke Grönberg (Reverend Mild), Lars Hansson (Pyret)

SUMMARY

491, a shocking movie for its time, is likely to seem more poignant than disturbing to contemporary viewers. Adapted from the novel of the same name written by Lars Göorling (who eventually committed suicide), the story tells of six troubled young boys who are selected to go through a social experiment, living in a social worker's home under specific behavioral guidelines. They supposedly are doing this of their own free will, but in fact they have no choice because their alternative to the experiment is jail. The boys repeatedly disappoint and abuse the social worker. They also begin to run a prostitution service out of his home, selling the services of a teenage girl whom they have brought home. The movie contains scenes that were extremely shocking to the average audience of the early 1960s, including tacit allusions to sodomy between two of the boys and the inspector to whom they must report their activities and a scene depicting (out of view) the rape of the girl by a dog. The director attempted to create a stark portrait of a changing society where young people behave in ways that are unnerving and unsettling.

CENSORSHIP HISTORY

The director Vilgot Sjöman is better known in the United States for his film I AM CURIOUS–YELLOW, but his earlier film *491* also created controversy when United States Customs agents refused to allow the film entry into the country. Sjöman wanted to portray a teenage actress in the nude in his movie, but censorship limitations in the United States forced him to cover his actress in gauze in what were supposed to be nude scenes and to clothe his male lead in flesh-colored tights. The director complied but grumbled about the "Hollywood clichés" he had to satisfy. Even with the accommodations, however, the film did not pass U.S. Customs, which applied the Tariff Act of 1930 that empowered customs officers to declare *491* to be "obscene" and confiscate the film. Edward De Grazia relates that the customs officers sent the film to the office of the United States attorney, which brought suit in federal district court to declare *491* "obscene" and to force the distributor to forfeit rights to the film.

In *United States v. Film Entitled 491*, 247 F. Supp. 373 (1965), the federal district court determined that the film was obscene, despite the testimony of numerous expert witnesses, "including film critics, writers, ministers, and the executive director of Mobilization for Youth," who testified to its social importance. Attorneys for the distributor argued that the film was constitutionally protected under the principles established in *Memoirs v. Massachusetts*, 383 U.S. 413 (1966), (see CARMEN, BABY) and in the case for THE LOVERS. The distributor appealed the decision of the federal circuit court in the U.S. Court of Appeals for the Second Circuit, which reversed the decision and concluded that the film could be imported into the United States. In their decision, the justices wrote that the film "was attempting to deal with social problems which in 1966 are not only on our doorstep but very much over the threshold," which established the film as "constitutionally protected and not obscene."

FURTHER READING

De Grazia, Edward, and Roger K. Newman. *Banned Films: Movies, Censors and the First Amendment*. New York: R. R. Bowker, 1982.
United States v. Film Entitled 491, 247 F. Supp. 373 (1965).
United States v. Film Entitled 491, 367 F. 2d 889 (1966).

A FAREWELL TO ARMS

Country and date of production: United States, 1932
Production company/distributor: Paramount Pictures

Format: Sound, black and white
Running time: 80 minutes
Language: English
Producer: Edward A. Blatt
Director: Frank Borzage
Screenwriters: Oliver H. P. Garrett, Benjamin Glazer, Ernest Hemingway (novel)
Awards: 1932 Academy Awards, Best Cinematography (Charles Lang), Best Sound Recording (Harold C. Lewis).
Genre: Drama/romance
With: Helen Hayes (Catherine Barkley), Gary Cooper (Lieutenant Frederick Henry), Adolphe Menjou (Major Rinaldi), Mary Phillips (Helen Ferguson), Jack La Rue (The Priest), Blanche Friderici (Head Nurse), Mary Forbes (Miss Van Campen), Gilbert Emery (British Major)

SUMMARY

In this adaptation of Ernest Hemingway's novel, Captain Rinaldi, an Italian surgeon, tells his friend Frederick Henry, a lieutenant in the ambulance service, that he is in love with a nurse, Catherine Barkley, and tries to set up the ambulance driver with her friend Ferguson. However, Catherine, whose fiancé of eight years has been killed in the war, likes Henry. After she slaps him when he tries to kiss her, she feels bad, apologizes and asks for a kiss. When Henry is to go to the front, he says goodbye to Catherine, but Rinaldi becomes jealous and arranges for her to be transferred to Milan. While helping the wounded at the battle of Plava, Frederick is himself wounded. A regretful Rinaldi operates and tries to make up for his earlier jealousy by sending his friend to Milan to recover and to rejoin Catherine. The hospital chaplain expresses hopes that they will marry, but Catherine's friend Ferguson expresses doubts and says that they will either fight or die. After the head nurse finds empty liquor bottles, Henry is accused of being an alcoholic and sent to the front, causing Catherine to fear that they will never see each other again. Catherine goes to Switzerland and writes to Henry; he responds, but his letters come back marked "Return to Sender." Soon Henry has had 32 letters returned and decides to leave the army. After a series of war scenes of soldiers and destruction, Henry runs and is shot. When he is sent to the hospital in Milan, Ferguson calls him a deserter and tells him that Catherine is pregnant but won't tell him where she is. Rinaldi finally reveals Catherine's whereabouts, and the two are reunited. Later, when she is about to have their baby, Catherine calls for Henry, who arrives as she is about to have an operation in an attempt to save her life. Their baby is dead. As Henry prays for her life, Catherine tells him she is fine, and they make plans, but she must eventually admit that she is dying. Helpless to do anything, Henry tells her she is brave and promises that they will never part. After Catherine dies, the armistice is declared, and all that Henry can mutter is, "Peace, peace."

CENSORSHIP HISTORY

Members of the Studio Relations Committee (SRC) were long aware that the controversial novel *A Farewell to Arms* would be made into a movie by one of the major studios. In 1930, SRC reviewer Lamar Trotti reported to the then-head of the SRC that the novel contained "profanity, illicit love, illegitimate birth, desertion from the army and a not very flattering picture of Italy during the war." In 1931, Warner Bros. contacted the Hays Office (the term is used throughout the historical literature as a synonym for the office of Will Hays, the head of the Motion Picture Producers and Distributors Association [MPPDA]) with a tentative proposal to film the novel, but reviewers warned that the novel was "anti-Italian." Nobile Giacomo de Martino, the Italian ambassador stationed in Washington, D.C., already had spoken with Will Hays, the head of the Production Code Administration, and hinted that any movie made of the novel would be banned from the Italian market. Warner Bros. feared losing not only the Italian market but also lucrative markets in other countries, so they gave up the property. In contrast, Paramount was willing to take a chance, as the studio was desperate for a box-office success after suffering substantial losses on several movies, including BLONDE VENUS and *Love Me Tonight*. The studio ousted production head B. P. Schulberg and vice president Jesse Lasky and replaced them with Cecil B. DeMille and Emanuel Cohen and then purchased rights to Hemingway's novel.

As SRC reviewer Lamar Trotti wrote in a July 19, 1932, memo to Will Hays, the new executives were expending everything they had to turn the studio around; they were going to "live or die by this picture" and planning "to be as daring as possible." Filmed in only two months at a cost of $900,000, an expensive production for the time, *A Farewell to Arms* was eagerly awaited by the public who had received carefully released information to whet their appetite for the film. The studio first had to clear the hurdle of the censors, for the film contained, as Mark Vieira describes, "an illicit love scene on the pedestal of a horseman's statue, an illicit love scene in a hospital bed, an 'unofficial marriage,' graphic scenes of childbirth, and the retreat of the Italian army, which could be the biggest problem of all."

As Paramount expected, Dr. James Wingate, a former member of the New York State board of censors and new leader of the SRC, rejected the film. Although the studio had told Wingate's predecessor Jason Joy that their screenwriters would work directly with the Italian consul in Los Angeles to resolve potential censorship problems, they did not inform Wingate—and they did not show him the version of the film that contained the ending approved by the Italian consul. The studio quickly replaced the first ending with an alternate ending shot to placate the Italian Embassy, in which the film ends by announcing a great Italian victory, and appealed the SRC ruling by submitting the film to the Association of Motion Picture Producers (AMPP) jury, the West Coast branch of the MPPDA. To alleviate some of the illicit romance charges, the filmmakers turned the film into a morality tale by making Catherine's best friend Nurse Ferguson disapprove of the affair.

Wingate and the SRC did not feel that Paramount had made enough changes; they believed the romance remained too explicit, while the childbirth scene was specifically prohibited by the Production Code. When Paramount adamantly refused to make further changes, Wingate demanded that the film be judged by a jury of Hollywood producers. Carl Laemmle, Jr., of Universal, Sol Wurtzel of Fox and Joe Schenck of United Artists screened the film and approved it. In its report dated December 7, 1932, the jury wrote, "because of the greatness of the picture and the excellence of direction and treatment the childbirth sequence was not in violation of Article II of the Production Code." When the Catholic Legion of Decency (LOD) began nationwide efforts to remove all films that the organization deemed objectionable, in early 1934 *A Farewell to Arms* was placed on the condemned list; in July 1934, Joe Breen, Wingate's assistant on the SRC and now head of the newly created Production Code Administration, demanded that it be removed from circulation. Among the new requirements that films would have to meet to earn approval was the demand that more than one character express disapproval of "illicit" behavior. "No longer would one character voice disapproval—as in *A Farewell to Arms*, for example, where Fergie reminds Catherine and Henry of their mistakes while the rest of society pays little attention. Now the entire film would be used to paint a picture of complete societal condemnation. From the first reel to the last the sinners would suffer."

Breen kept the film in storage for four years, until Paramount approached the New York office of the MPPDA and asked for permission to make cuts in the film in order to reissue it. The studio was willing to make any cuts needed to accomplish its task, knowing that audiences from four years earlier would flock to see the film without concern for the editing. Thus, as Miller explains, Paramount cut major segments from the love scenes and edited discussions of the illicit relationship. The studio also inserted frames picturing a man's hand placing a wedding ring on a woman's finger: "The new version was moral enough to earn a Seal, followed by a scene in which Cooper and Hayes discuss their plans to get married."

FURTHER READING

Black, Gregory D. *Hollywood Censored: Morality Codes, Catholics and the Movies.* New York: Cambridge University Press, 1994.

Lawrence, Frank M. *Hemingway and the Movies.* Jackson: University of Mississippi Press, 1981.

Maltby, Richard. "'To Prevent the Prevalent Type of Book': Censorship and Adaptation in Hollywood 1924–1934." *American Quarterly* 44 (December 1992): 554–616.

McNicholas, John T. "Pastorals and Statements by Members of the American Hierarchy on the Legion of Decency." *Catholic Mind* 32 (September 8, 1934): 113–119.

Miller, Frank. *Censored Hollywood: Sex, Sin and Violence on Screen.* Atlanta, Ga.: Turner Publishing, 1994.

Vieira, Mark A. *Sin in Soft Focus: Pre-Code Hollywood.* New York: Harry N. Abrams, 1999.

Yeaman, Elizabeth. "The Catholic Movie Censorship." *New Republic* 96 (October 5, 1938): 233–235.

FLAMING CREATURES

Country and date of production: United States, 1963
Production company/distributor: Jack Smith/Jonas Mekas
Format: Sound, black and white
Running time: 45 minutes
Language: English
Producer: Jack Smith
Director: Jack Smith
Screenwriter: Jack Smith
Awards: None
Genre: Short subject
With: Frances Francine (Himself), Sheila Bick (Delicious Dolores), Joel Markman (Our Lady of the Docks), Dolores Flores, aka Mario Montez (The Spanish Girl), Arnold Rockwood (Arnold), Judith Malina (The Fascinating Woman), Marian Zazeela (Maria Zazeela)

SUMMARY

Flaming Creatures employs a transvestite cast to mock the conventions of classic film and to explore the implications of shifting gender. The first three and a half minutes of the film consists of credits, accompanied by scenes from the 1944 movie *Ali Baba and the 40 Thieves*, which starred Maria Montez, complete with an especially written soundtrack of gongs and drum rolls. The opening is offered in contrast to one of the Characters in *Flaming Creatures*, the Spanish Girl, who is portrayed by a man who named himself Mario Montez. After the credits, the screen erupts into chaos with close-up shots of puckered mouths, wagging tongues and an occasional penis, punctuated by the random appearance of an odd assortment of "creatures." As performers dart back and forth, a bare-chested masked man wraps a woman in his cloak and ducks out of sight. The scene cuts to a frame containing Frances Francine, wearing a brocade turban and matching white gown, and, in a separate frame, Delicious Dolores, a young woman of ample proportions, wearing a clingy black slip and floppy hat, in front of a painting of an outsized white vase of flowers. Dolores dances slowly to the popular 1930s rumba "Amapola (Pretty Little Poppy)," with her exposed back and ample backside turned to the camera. Francine waves and enters the frame, and the pair flutter their fans, air kiss and insincerely pinch each other's cheeks.

The film then moves to a sequence that mocks lipstick commercials of the time, in which Francine, Dolores and the angular Joel Markman, who wears a false nose and a ragged negligee, apply lipstick, sometimes in close-up, to the accompaniment of a mock radio advertisement, complete with corny music, for a "new heart-shaped lipstick [that] shapes your lips as you color them." The background music continues, complete with the sound of amplified lip-smacks, as the camera pans numerous men with unshaven faces, heads thrown back, studiously painting their lips, followed by a brief tableau of half-naked bodies, then a longer shot of the outrageously made-up and clothed bodies to match the faces collapsing in slow motion. Without warning, Francine begins to chase Dolores back and forth before the painting of the great vase until Francine seizes Dolores from behind and hurls her to the ground. Dolores cries out, and her breast bounces out of her gown. As a horde of Smith's creatures descend on her, Dolores struggles, and beats her fan on the gang of creatures who are now pinning her down, jiggling her breasts, poking their noses in her armpit and otherwise exploring her body. A skinny, male creature, wearing a black wig and slip, is held down beside Dolores and feigns a campy panic. The camera shakes and plaster dust rains down on the tumultuous mix of eyes, legs, hands and genitalia. When the orgy ends, Dolores staggers dramatically to her feet and then swoons into the arms of the smiling Fascinating Woman, who wears pearls around her neck and has a flower clenched between her teeth. As the women kiss, flower petals fall on them and a veil drifts idly in the breeze.

The camera then focuses on empty space and a fly crawling on a wall. Our Lady of the Docks, a transvestite vampire dressed and make up like Marilyn Monroe, enters the scene of the orgy and prowls among the comatose creatures. She kneels over Frances Francine and attacks her neck, rolling her eyes back in sated delight. Church bells toll, and Francine's eyes open in extreme close-up watching as Our Lady lifts her own dress and shows that she has a penis. This is a signal for the creatures to rise and stage a carnival. In the movie's longest sequence, Our Lady foxtrots with Francine, and neither seems certain which one should lead. *Flaming Creatures* ends with an extended series of dance numbers followed by several minutes of curtain calls. In a final scene, the Everly Brothers' version of "Be-Bop-a-Lula" provides the background to a flurry of last-minute kisses and swoons, which give way to shots of a leg dangling a high-heeled pump, the image of Our Lady being groped, an inverted flower, the end title, and a final close-up of a jiggling breast.

CENSORSHIP HISTORY

Flaming Creatures is an avant-garde film that is part of the free-wheeling, experimental filmmaking of the 1960s, which tested sexual taboos and mocked the rigid views that mainstream society held sacred. *The Oxford History of World Cinema* states that the film "visually celebrates the orgy as *opéra bouffe* shot on grainily pallid outdated stock," and it presents outrageously sexual elements in a self-mocking manner. When *Flaming Creatures* debuted at the Gramercy Arts Theater in New York City in October 1963, theater owner Jonas Mekas did not charge admission: It would have been illegal, because the film had not been submitted to the New York State Board of Regents for licensing. To obtain compensation, Mekas solicited contributions for the Love and Kisses to Censors Film Society, a group loosely made up of viewers determined to defy the censors and whose membership changed with each showing. On December 7, 1963, he rented the Tivoli Theater and planned to present the director, Jack Smith, with the annual Independent Filmmaker Award. Shortly before the awards, the city bureau of licenses pressured the theater manager to cancel the show, so Mekas held the ceremony in the street.

A month later, Mekas was invited to serve as a judge at an experimental film festival held in Knokke-le-Zout, Belgium. When the festival refused to screen *Flaming Creatures*, Mekas resigned from the jury and organized a series of special screenings in his hotel room. On New Year's Eve, he took control of the festival theater projection booth, causing a small riot that the Belgian minister of justice, who also was the honorary head of the festival, tried to end. When the minister arrived, Mekas projected *Flaming Creatures* into the minister's face. Most of the jurors reportedly thought *Flaming Creatures* was a documentary. "A wild image of America we left in Knokke-le-Zout, I tell you," Mekas said afterward.

On March 3, 1964, the film was shown at Mekas's new site for screening underground films in New York City, the New Bowery Theater on St. Mark's Place in the East Village. Two detectives sent by the office of the district attorney stopped the screening and impounded the film along with the film projector and screen. The detectives also arrested Mekas and Kenneth Jacobs, the projectionist. Mekas and Jacobs went to trial in the Criminal Court of New York City, where a three-judge bench convicted them of violating section 1141 of the Penal Law of New York, which makes anyone "who sells, lends, gives away, distributes, shows or transmutes" an "obscene, lewd, lascivious, filthy, indecent, sadistic or masochistic" motion picture guilty of a misdemeanor and imposes a sentence of from 10 days to one year upon conviction.

In this lengthy court battle, academic experts testified in favor of the film in terms similar to those used by Susan Sontag in an article published in *The Nation* that called *Flaming Creatures* "a brilliant spoof of sex and at the same time full of the lyricism of erotic impulse." The judges failed to agree that the film had merit and sentenced Mekas and Jacobs to 60 days in the New York City Workhouse. The sentences were suspended, but the convictions for showing obscene films remained on record, which meant that the equipment seized during the arrests was subject to forfeiture and that the department of licensing could suspend their motion picture license. Mekas appealed the conviction before the United States Supreme Court, which dismissed the appeal on June 12, 1967, on the basis that, under New York State law, "the maximum time during which appellants could have had their suspended sentences revoked and replaced by prison sentences was one year from the date of the original sentences." Based on this understanding and expressing the

Court's decision to affirm the decision of the lower court, Justice Brennan wrote, "this appeal is moot because more than one year has run from August 7, 1964, and appellants are under no present threat of imprisonment. Moreover, the State contends that neither New York law nor federal law imposes any further penalty for conviction of the misdemeanor involved in this case." In a dissenting opinion, Justice Douglas wrote, "Since I believe this appeal cannot be dismissed as moot, I believe the Court must consider this case on the merits. I am satisfied that these convictions should be affirmed. Under the standards set out by the Court in *Roth v. United States*, 354 U.S. 476 (1957), this film is not within the protections of the First Amendment."

Justice Fortas asserted that he would reverse the decision of the lower court, a move that would haunt him the following year when he was nominated by President Lyndon Johnson for the position of chief justice of the Supreme Court. During hearings, James Clancy, a representative of a group named Citizens for Decent Literature (CDL), testified regarding the damage that could be done by the literature and films that were involved in recent cases in which Judge Fortas had voted to reverse the decisions of lower courts. Clancy made a 30-minute documentary, *Target Smut*, that contained scenes from a range of movies freed by Judge Fortas in the cases, including *Flaming Creatures*. With the assistance of Senator Strom Thurmond of South Carolina, Clancy showed the film repeatedly to the press corps and anyone else on Capitol Hill who wished to see it. After President Johnson spoke out against the filibuster that Thurmond and other senators were conducting, Thurmond responded: "If President Johnson would take the necessary time to review four films—*Flaming Creatures*, 'O-7,' 'O-12,' and 'O-14'—or any of them, it would be interesting to know if he still favors Mr. Fortas' appointment to the second most important office in the United States." On May 15, 1969, Justice Abe Fortas became the first Supreme Court justice in history to resign "under pressure of public opinion."

Flaming Creatures was also an object of police attention in other states. In November 6, 1966, police confiscated a copy of the film being screened at a Students for a Democratic Society (SDS) event at the University of Texas in Austin. On January 20, 1967, police at the University of Michigan in Ann Arbor confiscated a print of the film from another SDS chapter function. In January 1968, a copy of the film shipped from Vancouver, British Columbia, to New York City was confiscated by United States Attorney Robert Morganthau.

FURTHER READING

De Grazia, Edward. *Girls Lean Back Everywhere: The Law of Obscenity and the Assault on Genius.* New York: Random House, 1992.

Hoberman, J., and Jonathan Rosenbaum. *Midnight Movies.* New York: Harper & Row, 1983.

"Jack Smith's Flaming Creatures: With the Tweak of an Eyebrow." *Film Culture* 63–64 (1977): 51–56.

Sitney, P. Adams. "Film Censorship: United States." *Censorship* 2 (Spring 1965): 48–50.

Sontag, Susan. "Feast for Open Eyes." *The Nation* 198 (April 13, 1964): 374–376.
Tyler, Parker. *Screening the Sexes: Homosexuality in the Movies.* New York: Holt, Rinehart and Winston, 1972.

THE FOX

Country and date of production: United States, 1968
Production company/distributor: Motion Pictures International/Claridge
Format: Sound, color
Running time: 109 minutes
Language: English
Producers: Steve Broidy, Raymond Stross
Director: Mark Rydell
Screenwriters: Lewis John Carlino, Howard Koch, D. H. Lawrence (story)
Awards: 1968 Golden Globe Award, Best English-language Foreign Film.
Genre: Drama
With: Sandy Dennis (Jill Banford), Keir Dullea (Paul Renfield), Anne Heywood (Ellen March), Glyn Morris (Estate Agent)

SUMMARY

The Fox, an adaptation of a short story of the same name written by D. H. Lawrence, contains only four main characters. The story centers on two women, Jill Banford and Ellen March, who met in college and who live together on an isolated farm in Canada. Jill assumes the traditional woman's role of caring for the house and cooking, while Ellen takes on the traditional male duties of doing the work around the farm and serving as a protector to Jill. Each dresses to accommodate her duties, making Jill the more feminine-appearing of the two. The film takes Lawrence's creation of an unconsciously lesbian attraction between the women and turns it into an intense and obsessive lesbian affair: Audiences even see the two women in bed, kissing and embracing passionately.

The women have developed a comfortable life together, but this harmony is disrupted by a fox that threatens their henhouse. Ellen attempts several times to kill the fox, but she is unsuccessful. The animal, which disrupts their lives and which cannot be routed, is a metaphor for the man who soon enters and disrupts their lives and who will not be routed. Paul Renfield, the grandson of the farm's late owner, is a sailor on leave who decides to visit the scene of many happy childhood memories. When he meets the two women, Jill exhibits an obvious attraction toward him and asks him to stay, but Renfield is more strongly drawn to Ellen, whom he eventually asks to marry him. Ellen seems agreeable about marrying Paul, but she does not want to hurt Jill, who is highly dependent upon her. Near the end of the film, Ellen and Renfield cut down a tree. As it falls, Jill moves into its path, is struck and dies—freeing Ellen to marry Renfield and to leave her lesbian life behind.

In *The Celluloid Closet*, Vito Russo wrote that American critics were confused by the ending because Renfield is attracted to the woman who wore the pants in the relationship: "Martin Gottfried, writing in *Women's Wear Daily*, expressed disbelief that Paul could be attracted to Ellen ('the bulldyke') over Jill ('the female lesbian'). 'How,' he asked, 'could the feminine one be the real lesbian?' Pauline Kael, in a telling query, revealed that she could not conceive of a woman's preferring other women. 'If Ellen isn't afraid of sex with men, what's she doing playing house in the woods with that frumpy Jill?'" *The Fox* is a typical bisexual triangle film in which, given an even fight between a heterosexual man and a lesbian, the man will win out every time, thereby restoring the "natural order." As Andrea Weiss writes, "Heterosexuality triumphs over homosexuality; man triumphs over woman. . . . lesbian characters are frequently killed off in any film's conclusion (*The Fox, The Children's Hour*)."

CENSORSHIP HISTORY

The film was not contracted to play in many general-audience theaters simply because of the "Mature Audiences Only" rating granted to it by the Motion Picture Association of America (MPAA). In 1968, two Jackson, Mississippi, police officers, accompanied by the city attorney, bought tickets to view the film "as paid guests" at a public showing in a local theater. Immediately following the showing, without a warrant, the law officers seized the film and arrested the theater operators, charging them with having violated a Mississippi state law that made the exhibition of an obscene "moving picture show" subject to punishment. The theater operators were tried before a police justice of the peace in magistrate's court and convicted after pleading "no contest" to the charges. Attorneys for the operators and the theater corporation, charged with the same violations as the operators, requested and received a jury trial in Hinds County county court. The case was retried and the theater operators were acquitted, but a mistrial was granted in the case of the theater corporation. Attorneys for the theater corporation and operators then took the case before the U.S. District Court for the Southern District of Mississippi, in which they sought a permanent injunction against the state to prevent further prosecution and petitioned the court for return of the confiscated film. In a decision for *McGrew v. City of Jackson*, 307 F. Supp. 754 (1969), Judge Harold Cox wrote that the film is "sordid and bizarre" and contains scenes that are "extremely repulsive and offensive [and] contaminate the show as an entirety." He characterized the film as "a classic case of hard-core pornography wherein sex is pandered solely for profit. . . . solely as a box office pitch to the morbidly curious," containing "lurid and carnal scenes. . . . which so exceeded all bounds of propriety, and common decency." Despite so subjective an assessment, the court held that the film was obscene and, consequently, refused to reverse the decisions of the lower court. The strenuous effort to suppress the film and the language used in the court decision reveals the depth of fear that lesbian topics motivated in the 1960s.

FURTHER READING

McGrew v. City of Jackson, 307 F. Supp. 754 (1969).
Russo, Vito. *The Celluloid Closet*. New York: HarperCollins Publishers, 1981.
Weiss, Andrea. *Vampires and Violets: Lesbians in the Cinema*. London: Jonathan Cape, 1992.

FRANKENSTEIN

Country and date of production: United States, 1931
Production company/distributor: Universal Pictures
Format: Sound, black and white
Running time: 70 minutes
Language: English
Producer: Carl Laemmle, Jr.
Director: James Whale
Screenwriters: Mary Shelley (novel), Peggy Webling (play), John L. Balderston (adaptation), Francis Edward Faragoh, Garrett Fort, Robert Florey, John Russell
Awards: None
Genre: Horror
With: Colin Clive (Henry Frankenstein), Mae Clarke (Elizabeth), John Boles (Victor Moritz), Boris Karloff (The Monster), Edward Van Sloan (Doctor Waldman), Frederick Kerr (Baron Frankenstein), Dwight Frye (Fritz), Lionel Belmore (The Burgomaster), Marilyn Harris (Little Maria)

SUMMARY

In a prologue before the credits are shown, a tuxedoed gentleman (Edward van Sloan, who plays Dr. Waldman in the film) steps from behind a closed curtain and delivers a "friendly warning" to the audience:

> How do you do? Mr. Carl Laemmle [the producer] feels it would be a little unkind to present this picture without just a word of friendly warning. We are about to unfold the story of Frankenstein, a man of science who sought to create a man after his own image without reckoning upon God. It is one of the strangest tales ever told. It deals with the two great mysteries of creation—life and death. I think it will thrill you. It may shock you. It might even—horrify you. So if any of you feel that you do not care to subject your nerves to such a strain, now's your chance to . . . uh . . . well, we warned you.

After the warning, the credits play against an eerie set of rotating eyes, and the film begins with a close-up of a pair of hands hauling up a rope. The camera pans across a group of weeping and wailing mourners and priests conducting a funeral service around a gravesite, with a statue of a skeletal Grim Reaper in the background. Young Henry Frankenstein and his humpbacked assistant Fritz dig up the corpse and later cut down a hanged man but still need to find a brain for their creation. After watching a local physician and university instructor, Dr. Waldman, teach his class the difference between a normal brain and that of a criminal, Fritz steals the criminal brain (after dropping the normal brain). The audience learns that Frankenstein has left the university in order to continue his advanced experimental attempts to recreate human life. Frankenstein's friends Victor Moritz and Dr. Waldman believe Frankenstein to be morbidly crazy, without a chance of success. The young experimenter aims to prove them wrong. He uses electricity and a powerful storm to stimulate life in a body he has put together from various corpses. When the creature's hand moves, Frankenstein believes he has recreated life, but Dr. Waldman warns him of the danger and recommends that the creature be closely guarded. Fritz frightens the monster with a torch, and the monster must be restrained in chains. After enduring various forms of torture at the hands of his creator, the monster breaks free. Frightened of what they have unleashed, Waldman and Frankenstein decide to give the monster a lethal injection, but the monster lives on. Dr. Waldman decides to dissect the creature, but when the procedure begins, the monster strangles the doctor and escapes.

Despite all that has happened, Frankenstein marries his fiancee, Elizabeth. At the same time, in the country, a lonely girl tries to play with the monster. Mimicking the actions of girl who is throwing daisies into the water, the monster throws the girl into the lake and drowns her. The father of the drowned girl rouses the town, and the burgomaster organizes three torch-carrying search parties to find and destroy the monster. Frankenstein locates him in the hills; after a struggle, the monster carries Frankenstein up the mill tower and throws him down. The angry crowd sets fire to the mill, destroying it and the monster.

CENSORSHIP HISTORY

The story of *Frankenstein* hardly causes a reaction among most viewers today, but audiences who viewed the film when it was first released found it too violent, and many people protested that viewing the film would be traumatizing for children. The film was first previewed on October 29, 1931, at the Granada Theatre in Santa Barbara, California. In a biography of the director, a Paramount producer who accompanied Whale to the screening relates that the movie made the audience nervous: "As it progressed, people got up, walked out, came back in, walked out again." Their reaction upset Carl Laemmle, Jr., the producer, who became frightened, declared the film a disaster and told Whale, "Jesus, God, we've got to do something!" In his panic, Laemmle tried to second-guess the reaction of the Catholic Legion of Decency (LOD). He invited Martin Quigley to the second preview of the film to review it for the newly created LOD organ, *The Motion Picture Herald*. Quigley's review was negative and stirred up unfavorable pre-release publicity: "I don't know what it might do to children, but I know I wouldn't want my kids to see it. And I won't forgive Junior Laemmle or James Whale for permitting the Monster to drown a little girl before my very eyes." Negative publicity did not hurt the film, however, when it opened at the Mayfair Theatre in New York City on December 4, 1931. The film made $53,000 in the first week, a startling amount for that depression time.

State boards of review were less accepting of the film than New York City reviewers. State censors in New York, Massachusetts, Pennsylvania and Kansas demanded a range of cuts before they would issue permits for the film to be shown. Film censors in New York, Massachusetts and Pennsylvania excised the scene in which the monster drowns the little girl. They also found the following words spoken by Henry Frankenstein to be blasphemous, and cut them: "In the name of God! Now I know what it feels like to *be* God!" Once the cuts were made, the film was exhibited in these three states, but the Kansas Board of Review demanded more than a dozen cuts before it would issue the film a permit.

A frantic Universal sent a request on December 10, 1931, to the head of the Production Code Administration (PCA), Jason Joy, asking him to do anything that he could to have the requested cuts reconsidered. In addition to the cuts made for other states, before granting the film a license for exhibition, Kansas reviewers called for modifications to a grave-robbing scene at the beginning and changes in various scenes that show Frankenstein attempting to play God in the laboratory.

In 1937, Universal planned to re-release *Frankenstein*, and submitted the film to the Motion Picture Producers and Distributors Association (MPPDA) for clearance. On June 9, 1937, the MPPDA ordered that Universal cut the end of the sequence in which the little girl is drowned by the monster. The segment was kept out of the film for nearly 50 years, until MCA-Universal restored the missing frames in 1986. David Skal reports that MCA found the scene largely intact at the British Film Institute and used the material to restore to videodisc a version of Frankenstein, but it "still lacks close-ups of the child sinking, etc.—details the English censors marked for excision."

FURTHER READING

Curtis, James. *James Whale*. Metuchen, N.J.: Scarecrow Press, 1982.
————. *James Whale: A New World of Gods and Monsters*. Boston: Faber and Faber, 1998.
Kansas State Board of Review. *Disapproved Features and Shorts, 1917–1961*. Box 35–6–5–12. Kansas State Historical Society Archives, Topeka, Kansas.
Quigley, Martin. "Frankenstein." *The Motion Picture Herald*, November 14, 1931. Quoted in Curtis, *James Whale*, p. 155.
Sklar, David J. *The Monster Show: A Cultural History of Horror*. New York: W. W. Norton, 1993.

Vieira, Mark. *Sin in Soft Focus: Pre-Code Hollywood.* New York: Harry N. Abrams, 1999.

FREAKS

Country and date of production: United States, 1932 (also released as *Forbidden Love* and *Nature's Mistakes*)
Production company/distributor: MGM (Metro-Goldwyn-Mayer)
Format: Sound, black and white
Running time: 64 minutes
Language: English
Producer: Tod Browning
Director: Tod Browning
Screenwriters: Al Boasberg, Willis Goldbeck, Leon Gordon, Clarence Aaron "Tod" Robbins (short story, "Spurs"), Edgar Allan Woolf
Awards: None
Genre: Drama/horror
With: Wallace Ford (Phroso), Leila Hyams (Venus), Olga Baclanova (Cleopatra), Roscoe Ates (Roscoe), Henry Victor (Hercules), Harry Earles (Hans), Daisy Earles (Frieda)

SUMMARY

The source of the idea for the film has been variously attributed to the German midget Harry Earles, who had played a major role in director Browning's film *The Unholy Three*, and to MGM production head Irving Thalberg. The first attribution asserts that Earles suggested that Browning adapt the short story "Spurs," written by Clarence Aaron "Tod" Robbins (author of *The Unholy Three*), which tells of a full-size woman who marries a wealthy dwarf, only to find that he savagely terrorizes and subjugates her. In the alternate version of the film's genesis, related in an authorized Thalberg biography, *Freaks* was created by MGM to capitalize on the recent popularity of horror films such as DRACULA and FRANKENSTEIN. Production head Irving Thalberg claimed in interviews that he wanted a film for Tod Browning, who had returned to the studio after his success in directing *Dracula*, and Thalberg ordered writer Willis Goldbeck to come up with a treatment of the short story that would be "even more horrible" than the earlier two films. The result was even more upsetting than Thalberg anticipated. The casting calls brought hundreds of photographs and résumés from hundreds of self-described "freaks," but the studio eliminated the more prosaic tattooed actors and summoned men and women with "spectacularly photogenic deformities." The movie includes a long written preface that explains the history of social attitudes toward such people. In serious tones, the voiceover explains how fear and paranoia among "normal" people have resulted in their cruelty toward such as will appear in the film.

Hans, a dwarf, is attracted to the beautiful trapeze artist and full-size woman Cleopatra, and his midget fiancée Frieda becomes jealous. When Venus, the seal tamer, walks out on the strong man Hercules and complains about men to the clown Phroso, Cleopatra uses the opportunity to become intimate with Hercules. Cleopatra also responds to the attentions of Hans after she learns that he has a fortune. Cleopatra decides to marry Hans, expecting that he will get sick. At the wedding feast she puts poison in his wine; then Hercules kisses Cleopatra in front of Hans, and Frieda cries and walks away. The crisis occurs when everyone chants, "Gooble-gobble, gooble, gobble, one of us, one of us, now she is like one of us," but Cleopatra says no and calls them freaks. Hans passes out. The doctor says he has been poisoned, and Venus commands Hercules to have Cleopatra tell the doctor what she put in the wine.

After Hans has been in bed for a week, he asks Cleopatra's forgiveness and manages not to swallow the medicine she gives him; then he mutters to a humpbacked dwarf, "Tonight." As the carnival wagons travel in the rain, Hans, with his friends present, asks Cleopatra for the little black bottle from which she has been pouring his poison. In a scene immediately following Phroso saves Venus from an attack by Hercules and fights him. On a thundering, stormy, rainswept night as the circus wagons travel to the next town, the freaks attack Cleopatra and Hercules, crawling and slithering through the rain and mud to their overturned wagon in one of the most amazing scenes in horror cinema. In an off-camera sequence they mutilate Cleopatra, who is shown as a squawking, legless, broken-nosed and partially blind, chickenlike creature. In the rarely seen original ending, they also castrate Hercules, who is shown singing in a high-pitched voice. In the attempt to alleviate the objections of censors, MGM filmed an alternate ending in which a wealthy Hans has seen no one at his home in years. Phroso and Venus bring in Frieda, who consoles him and tells him she loves him.

CENSORSHIP HISTORY

Freaks was marketed with an eye toward exploiting its controversial content, with such taglines as: "Can a full grown woman truly love a MIDGET?" "Do the Siamese Twins make love?" "Do the Pinheads think?" "What sex is the half-man, half-woman?" It was released to much controversy because of its use of truly misshapen and malformed people instead of actors with make-up. The final cast featured the most remarkable assemblage of circus freaks to appear in one movie: Prince Randian, "The Living Torso," a limbless British Guianan who rolls and lights a cigarette with his teeth in the film; Pete Robinson, "The Living Skeleton"; Olga Roderick, "The Bearded Lady"; Martha Morris, "The Armless Beauty"; and Joseph/Josephine, the "half-man/half-woman." Five "pinheads" (microcephalics) also appeared in the picture: Zip, Pip, Elvira Snow and her sister, Jenny Lee Snow, and Schlitzie. Browning encouraged further hysteria toward the film with a stream of quotations that pointed up the exotic nature of midgets and professed to show an intimate knowledge of their "gibberish language."

During filming, a group of MGM executives sympathized with the complaints of employees who were severely disturbed by the numerous and severe physical malformations of the cast and wanted the film stopped. President Louis B. Mayer is reported to have been furious that Thalberg had approved the film, and producer Harry Rapf headed a group of MGM employees who tried to convince Thalberg to stop filming, reporting that "People run out of the commissary and throw up." Thalberg was adamant about making the film and vowed to take the blame if it proved to be a mistake. That it promised to be a box-office mistake seemed evident at the preview, which MGM arranged in a theater on the outskirts of Los Angeles. Savada and Skal quote art director Merrill Pye regarding the audience reaction to the film: "Halfway through the preview, a lot of people got up and ran out. They didn't walk out. They ran out." Thalberg oversaw the cutting of 25 minutes from the film before premiering it in Los Angeles, but box-office receipts were low and MGM pulled *Freaks* from the theater after only two weeks. In an effort to save the film, Browning shot alternate endings, even one happy ending that was tacked onto the prints sent to cities across the nation, but most banned the film outright without previewing it. The Atlanta Board of Review banned the film after viewing a copy, labeling it "loathsome, obscene, grotesque, and bizarre." Censors in San Francisco and Great Britain banned as well. In New York State, the board of censors required that MGM submit the film twice and then demanded that the company cut 30 minutes from the film before they would approve a license. The financial failure of the film marked the end of Browning's career in Hollywood, with only four more films to follow.

The film was given new life in the early 1960s when the avant-garde film scene, fueled largely by Andy Warhol's factory, discovered *Freaks* and found a kindred film vision. In 1962 the Venice Film Festival selected *Freaks* as its horror film representative, and cinema purists and scholars praised the movie in intellectual film journals throughout Europe with such adjectives as "sensitive" and "compassionate." In 1967 *Freaks* was shown at the Museum of Modern Art in New York, and in 1986 MGM-UA home video proudly released *Freaks*—the same film Louis B. Mayer had banished from distribution more than a half-century earlier.

FURTHER READING

Doherty, Thomas. *Pre-Code Hollywood: Sex, Immorality, and Insurrection in American Cinema, 1930–1934.* New York: Columbia University Press, 1999.

Hoberman, J., and Jonathan Rosenbaum. *Midnight Movies.* New York: Harper & Row, 1983.

Marx, Samuel. *Mayer and Thalberg: The Make-Believe Saints.* New York: Random House, 1975.

Savada, Elias, and David Skal. *Dark Carnival: The Secret World of Tod Browning*. New York: Anchor Books, 1995.

Skal, David J. *The Monster Show: A Cultural History of Horror*. New York: W. W. Norton, 1993.

Thomas, Bob. *Thalberg: Life and Legend*. Garden City, N.Y.: Doubleday, 1969.

THE GAME OF LOVE

Country and date of production: France, 1954 (as *Le Blé en herbe*)
Production company/distributor: Franco London Films/Times Film Corp.
Format: Sound, black and white
Running time: 108 minutes
Language: French
Producer: Louis Wipf
Director: Claude Autant-Lara
Screenwriters: Jean Aurenche, Claude Autant-Lara, Pierre Bost, Colette (novel *Le Blé en herbe*)
Awards: None
Genre: Drama
With: Nicole Berger (Vinca), Pierre-Michel Beck (Phillippe), Edwige Feuillère (Madame Dalleray)

SUMMARY

The film, based upon the 1933 novel by Colette, *Le Blé en herbe*, deals with the experiences of two cousins, 16-year-old Phillippe and his younger cousin Vinca, as they navigate the confusing and often troubling teenage years. The two have grown up together and think of each other more as brother and sister than as cousins. Their families also are close, and for many years have spent each summer together in a house in Brittany. *The Game of Love* chronicles the increasing sexual awareness of the cousins, as well as their difficult first explorations in love and the different paths that each takes in maturing. Their closeness is tested when Phillippe meets a beautiful and seductive older woman who seeks to alleviate her loneliness by inviting him to her mansion. The infatuated young man yields easily to the sensual Madame Dalleray, who arouses his desire and becomes his sexual teacher. Their illicit relationship is brief, but Phillippe "becomes a man" through his experience with the older woman and, while their leavetaking is bittersweet, he returns to Vinca with a more mature understanding of love.

CENSORSHIP HISTORY

In 1956, the Chicago board of censors refused to issue Times Film Corp. a permit to exhibit the film. The board decided that the film was "immoral and obscene" because its content was "not acceptable to standards of decency, with immorality featured and dialogue unfit." The distributor appealed the decision before the mayor, who agreed with the board of censors and denied the license as well, citing as authority Section 155–4 of the municipal code, which stated a film could be denied a license if the assessing body believed it to be "immoral or obscene."

Times Film Corp. then brought suit in the U.S. District Court for the Northern District of Illinois, which affirmed the decision of the censors in *Times Film Corp. v. City of Chicago*, 139 F. Supp. 837 (1956), and concluded that the Chicago censorship ordinance was constitutional because the Chicago authorities had "properly exercised their police power." In its decision, the court emphasized the responsibility of the state for determining the morality of the people and wrote that "the State's police power in the area of health and morals, which has always had constitutional protection, [would] be seriously invaded and reduced by the film industry" if the local ruling were to be reversed. Labeling the dominant focus of the film to be "sexuality," the court wrote that the major element of the plot is Phillippe's "illicit relationship with an adventurous adult woman, and later with Vinca. The film appears to casually write off this unconventional behavior as a mere interlude in the maturing process of the young hero. The Court is unable to detect any purpose other than an emphasis upon its sexuality."

The case then went before the United States Court of Appeals for the Seventh Circuit, which in a unanimous vote upheld the decision of the censorship board. The court determined that the board had carried out proceedings in accordance with its authority, using as a measure a properly drawn ordinance that stated a movie could be banned if "when considered as a whole, its calculated purpose or dominant effect is substantially to arouse sexual desires, and if the probability of this effect is so great as to outweigh whatever artistic or other merits the film may possess." Citing the precision of pertinent terms in the statute "obscene" and "immoral," the court refused to agree with the argument by attorneys for Times Film Corp. that the law was "void for vagueness." Thus, the court concluded in *Times Film Corp. v. Chicago*, 244 F. 2d 432 (1957), "we think these determinations are supported by the effect which this film would have upon the normal, average person."

When the case next went before the United States Supreme Court, this measure of "the normal, average person" was used to obtain a reversal of the lower court decisions in *Times Film Corp. v. City of Chicago*, 355 U.S. 35 (1957). Times Film Corp. attorney Felix J. Bilgrey reminded the censors that the standard for obscenity set by the Illinois Supreme Court was that "to be ruled obscene material must arouse sexual desires of normal persons," which reflected the conclusions of the justices in a recent case before the Supreme Court, *Alberts v. California*, 354 U.S. 46 (1957). Bilgrey questioned if *The Game of Love* had aroused the lust of the censors. They admitted that it had not, but they still considered it to be obscene. In response, Bilgrey then questioned if the board had, thus, either ignored the standard or if this determination reflected on their "capacity to censor." The Supreme Court reversed the judgment of the U.S. Court of Appeals for the Seventh Circuit without rendering a written decision and citing only the authority of *Alberts v. California*, 354 U.S. 476. The case assumed a special importance in the struggle against the censorship of films because this was the first time that the Supreme Court decided that a particular artistic work was not obscene but was entitled to constitutional protection from suppression.

FURTHER READING

Carmen, Ira H. *Movies, Censorship and the Law.* Ann Arbor: University of Michigan Press, 1966.

De Grazia, Edward, and Roger K. Newman. *Banned Films: Movies, Censors & the First Amendment.* New York: R. R. Bowker, 1982.

Mikva, Abner J. "Chicago: Citadel of Censorship." *Focus/Midwest* 2 (March–April 1963): 16–17.

Schumach, Murray. *The Face on the Cutting Room Floor.* New York. William Morrow, 1964.

Times Film Corp. v. Chicago, 244 F. 2d 432 (1957).

Times Film Corp. v. City of Chicago, 139 F. Supp. 837 (1956).

GARDEN OF EDEN

Country and date of production: United States, 1956
Production company/distributor: Excelsior Pictures Corp.
Format: Sound, color
Running time: 67 minutes
Language: English
Producers: Walter Bibo, Norval E. Packwood (supervising)
Director: Max Nosseck
Screenwriters: Max Nosseck, Nat Tanchuck
Awards: None
Genre: Drama
With: Jamie O'Hara (Susan Latimore), Mickey Knox (Johnny Patterson), R. G. Armstrong (J. Randolph Latimore), Karen Sue Trent (Joan Latimore), John Gude (John Roy)

SUMMARY

Garden of Eden relates the experiences of Susan Latimore, a young widow, and Joan, her daughter, in a Florida nudist camp. The two have been living with the widows's tyrannical father-in-law, J. Randolph Latimore, but they can no longer stand his overbearing, manipulative personality. They escape by car when the opportunity arises, but the car stalls. Inhabitants of a nearby nudist colony come to their rescue and invite the young mother and daughter to stay at the colony until the car is repaired. At first, Susan is horrified at the naked bodies that surround her, and she is especially uncomfortable that Joan is subjected to this view. Within a short time, however, Susan realizes how wholesome the nudist lifestyle is and joins in the life of the colony. When Latimore arrives to take his granddaughter and daughter-in-law home, he experiences the same change of mind about the nudist lifestyle and also joins the camp, which makes him a much kinder person. Although the film shows men and women nude and together, it carefully avoids fully exposing any adult body.

CENSORSHIP HISTORY

Garden of Eden did not attract large audiences, nor was it shown in large numbers of theaters nationwide, but it holds an important place in film censorship history for its role in increasing legal acceptability of nudity in all films. When the distributor submitted the film to the Regents of the University of the State of New York Board of Censors in 1956, the board insisted that the distributor remove scenes containing nude people engaging in daily activities at the secluded and private nudist camp. The board agreed that the film was not obscene, as nothing in the film appealed to prurient interests, but some board members found it "indecent" according to a section of the state penal law that labeled as a crime any person's willful exposure of "his private parts in the presence of two or more persons of the opposite sex whose private parts are similarly exposed." Equating the term *obscene* with their determination of *indecent*, the board of censors therefore refused to issue a permit to exhibit the film.

Excelsior filed a complaint with the Appellate Division of the New York State Supreme Court, which in *Excelsior Pictures Corp. v. Regents of the University of the State of New York*, 156 N.Y.S. 2d 800, 2 A.D. 2d 941 (1956), reversed the decision of the board and ordered that New York grant *Garden of Eden* a license for exhibition. The case then entered the New York Court of Appeals, which affirmed the decision in a four-to-three vote in *Excelsior Pictures Corp. v. Regents of the University of the State of New York*, 144 N.E. 2d 31, 165 N.Y.S. 2d 42, 3 N.Y. 237 (1957). In reversing the censor, the court wrote that "nudity in itself and without lewdness or dirtiness, is not obscenity in law or in common sense." The decision reflected the thinking of *Roth v. United States*, 354 U.S. 476 (1957), which established the test for obscenity as "whether to the average person, applying contemporary community standards, the dominant theme of the material taken as a whole appeals to prurient interest." In the *Excelsior* decision, Judge Charles S. Desmond wrote, "'indecent,' standing alone and read literally, is much too broad and vague a term to make a valid censorship standard. . . . To say that representation of criminal activity is criminal is to abolish the drama and the novel at one stroke. . . . The showing of crimes in a book, play or cinema is evil only when it is done in a dirty way or when it glories the criminal act. So to characterize *The Garden of Eden* is impossible."

The reversal of the ban in New York State influenced decisions in other states. In Massachusetts, the supreme judicial court reversed a lower court ban on exhibiting the film in the state in *Commonwealth v. Moniz*, 143 N.E. 2d 196 (1957) and 155 N.E. 2d 762 (1959). In Kansas City, Missouri, the Court of Appeals asserted in *Dickinson Operating Co. v. City of Kansas City*, 317 S.W. 2d 638 (1958), that it did not have the jurisdiction to enforce a municipal ordinance banning the exhibition of lewd, obscene and indecent films. In 1960, the Federal District Court for the Northern District of Illinois in *Excelsior Pictures Corp. v. City of Chicago*, 182 F. Supp. 400 (1960), reversed the refusal of the Chicago board of censors to grant to the distributor a license to show the film. The result made clear to future censors that nudity alone could not be sufficient grounds for suppressing a film.

FURTHER READING

Carmen, Ira H. *Movies, Censorship and the Law*. Ann Arbor: University of Michigan Press, 1966.
Commonwealth v. Moniz, 143 N.E. 2d 196 (1957), 155 N.E. 2d 762 (1959).
Dickinson Operating Co. v. City of Kansas City, 317 S.W. 2d 638 (1958).
Excelsior Pictures Corp. v. City of Chicago, 182 F. Supp. 400 (1960).
Excelsior Pictures Corp. v. Regents of the University of the State of New York, 156 N.Y.S. 2d 800, 2 A.D. 2d 941 (1956).
Excelsior Pictures Corp. v. Regents of the University of the State of New York, 144 N.E. 2d 31, 165 N.Y.S. 2d 42, 3 N.Y. 237 (1957).
Klafter, Samuel. "Education Law—Censorship of Motion Pictures—N.Y. Licensing Statute—Indecency." *Albany Law Review* 22 (January 1958): 186–191.
Roth v. United States, 354 U.S. 476 (1957).
Schumach, Murray. *The Face on the Cutting Room Floor*. New York: William Morrow, 1964.

THE GREAT DICTATOR

Country and date of production: United States, 1940
Production company/distributor: United Artists
Format: Sound, black and white
Running time: 126 minutes
Language: English, Esperanto
Producer: Charles Chaplin
Director: Charles Chaplin
Screenwriter: Charles Chaplin
Awards: 1941 New York Film Critics Circle Award, Best Actor (Charles Chaplin).
Genre: Comedy
With: Charles Chaplin (Hynkel, Dictator of Tomania/A Jewish Barber), Jack Oakie (Napaloni, Dictator of Bacteria), Reginald Gardiner (Schultz), Henry Daniell (Garbitsch), Billy Gilbert (Herring), Grace Hayle

(Madame Napaloni), Carter DeHaven (Bacterian Ambassador), Paulette Goddard (Hannah), Rudolph Anders (as Robert O. Davis)

SUMMARY

The Great Dictator, Charles Chaplin's first talking film, marked his return to filmmaking after a hiatus of five years that followed the release of *Modern Times,* his final silent film, in 1936. One of only two American films that condemned Adolf Hitler and the Nazi Party prior to U.S. involvement in World War II, this movie had a serious basis to its comedy. The film opens with the disclaimer, "Any resemblance between Hynkel the dictator and the Jewish barber is purely coincidental," and is built upon a case of mistaken identity in which a Jewish barber is mistaken for a dictator. Intended as a satire on Germany's Nazi leader Adolf Hitler, whose Third Reich was still little known in the United States, the film details the rise of Adenoid Hynkel, a lowly soldier in World War I, who becomes the ruthless dictator of a country called Tomania. The vulgar Hynkel wears a toothbrush mustache and creates an aggressive, anti-Semitic war machine. We first see Hynkel addressing the Tomanian nation, giving a speech that involves much arm-saluting, nonsense English that makes use of the phrase *sour kraut,* and embittered rages that descend into coughing fits. In contrast, Chaplin also plays the Jewish Barber, hero of the Jewish ghetto, where everyone is friendly, humane and brave. After a duck-hunting accident, the amnesiac barber is mistaken for Hynkel and, in that role, manages to make a lengthy speech in favor of democracy.

The United States did not enter the war for another year after this film was released, and many in America, Chaplin among them, did not yet understand the full horror of Hitler's reign. So his dictator is silly, hapless and human. Napaloni, the dictator of Bacteria (modeled on the Italian dictator Mussolini, Hitler's ally), is similarly oafish rather than fearful—leaving the audience to speculate that if fools are running the totalitarian regimes, they cannot be too dangerous. Some of the most amusing slapstick takes place when Hynkel meets his fellow dictator Napaloni and tries to impress him by acting the greater intellectual in all their meetings. In a gag that has appeared in more than one Bugs Bunny cartoon, the two "dictators" crank themselves up to ever-greater heights on barber's chairs. Chaplin's experience with silent film shows in such gags as a character staggering up and down the street semiconscious, or the pantomime of the coins placed in pudding as well as in such comedy set-pieces as a knockabout scrapping with the stormtroopers, the barber shaving a man to the accompaniment of Brahms and the globe ballet in which Hynkel dances and tosses around a giant balloon of the world that bursts when he thinks he has it in his grasp.

CENSORSHIP HISTORY

The Great Dictator was a thinly veiled attack on Adolf Hitler and his Nazi regime that created upset on both sides of the Atlantic even before it was filmed. The British Film Center Board and the German Consul both contacted the Hays Office after entertainment newspapers announced that Chaplin was going to burlesque Hitler in a movie. In a letter received on October 31, 1938, by Joseph Breen, head of the Production Code Administration, Dr. George Gyssling, the German chief consul, threatened that if reports of the proposed film were true, it would lead to "serious trouble and complications." Breen had not yet been informed of the plans for filming but promised in his reply dated November 2, 1938, that he would send a copy of Gyssling's letter to Chaplin's manager and ask for clarification. (Even as Breen was forwarding the letter from Gyssling to Chaplin, Hitler had invaded Czechoslovakia, sanctioned the persecution of Jews and begun a campaign of horror in Germany.) Britain also contacted Breen with concerns that the announced film might interfere with the nation's attempt to negotiate appeasement with Hitler. Brook Wilkinson, the head of the British Film Censors Board, sent a cable to Breen about the film and asked for an outline of the story. Wilkinson wrote of the "delicate situation that might arise" in England if Hitler were attacked on screen and expressed the desire "not to give offense." In the United States, people sent letters to the Senator Robert Reynolds, a member of the Senate Committee on Foreign Relations, to protest what some saw as Chaplin's private grievance against Germany and suggested that the federal government examine the English-born resident alien's motives "before the film had a chance to 'antagonize certain . . . governments.'"

The film was also banned in Peru, Spain and Japan, which stated in its official rejection, "All anti-Nazi pictures are banned in Japan." The satire of Hitler created most of the sensationalism, but the most serious controversy resulted from Chaplin's final speech in the film:

The way of life can be free and beautiful, but we have lost the way. Greed has poisoned men's souls—barricaded the world with hate—has goosestepped us into misery and bloodshed. . . . Our knowledge has made us cynical; our cleverness, hard and unkind. We think too much and feel too little. More than machinery, we need humanity. More than cleverness, we need kindness and gentleness. Without these qualities, life will be violent and all will be lost.

FURTHER READING

Gardner, Gerald. *The Censorship Papers: Movie Censorship Letters from the Hays Office, 1934 to 1968.* New York: Dodd, Mead, 1987.
Schumach, Murray. *The Face on the Cutting Room Floor.* New York: William Morrow, 1964.
Times Film Corp. v. Chicago, 365 U.S. 43 (1961).

I, A WOMAN

Country and date of production: Denmark/Sweden, 1965
Production company/distributor: Europa Film, Nordisk Film (Denmark), Novaris Film/Audubon Films (United States, 1966)

Format: Sound, black and white
Running time: 95 minutes
Languages: Danish, Swedish
Producer: Fritz Ruzicka
Director: Mac Ahlberg
Screenwriters: Peer Guldbrandsen, Agnethe Thomsen (novel, as by "Siv Holm")
Awards: None
Genre: Drama
With: Essy Persson (Siv), Jørgen Reenberg (Dr. Dam), Preben Mahrt (Heinz), Preben Kørning (Sven), Frankie Steel (Erik)

SUMMARY

I, A Woman is the first of three films based on the best-selling novel of the same name by Swedish author Agnethe Thomsen writing as Siv Holm. The others, *I, A Woman II* and *I, A Woman III*, were released in Denmark, Sweden and the United States from 1968 to 1970. This film relates in flashback the sexual escapades of a young nurse who has successfully hidden her past adventures from her religiously devout parents and an impotent boyfriend. As the film begins, Siv is waiting for a date to arrive. She is barely acquainted with the man, but thinking about him resurrects memories of her past sexual experiences. As Siv waits, she recalls three sexual relationships in graphic detail, which results in scenes that entail substantial nudity. Siv's memories began with her seduction by a wealthy patient while she was a student nurse. An apparent innocent, she is sexually awakened by the older man, after which she is eager to continue her exploration. She engages in two further sexual relationships with men who express their desire to marry her, but she chooses to only enjoy the sexual attentions of the sailor and the physician without any serious view toward a future with either. Siv learns that she enjoys men too much to become attached to only one. When her fantasies end and her new date arrives, she realizes that she has met a man whose philosophy matches hers.

CENSORSHIP HISTORY

The film was banned in Finland from 1965 to 1968, but the film entered the United States with no objections from U.S. Customs officials. When city censorship boards in Memphis, Tennessee; Providence, Rhode Island; Boston, Massachusetts; and Hartford, Connecticut, refused to grant a license to exhibit the film, the distributor appealed the decisions in the local courts, which, in all cases, determined that *I, A Woman* was not obscene. In Chicago, the board of censors required that four deletions exhibiting sexual activity be made in the film before approving it for exhibition, yet the cut version of *I, A Woman* failed to satisfy law-enforcement officials in Indiana.

On October 25, 1967, police officers seized copies of the film at drive-in theaters located in Marion County, Indiana, and Indianapolis, Indiana, where it was being shown. Without judicial warrants, the police arrested four people operating the theaters while the film was being shown and confiscated the films. Prior to the beginning of the criminal trial, the Marion County municipal court ordered that the films be retained by either the Indianapolis police or the Marion County Sheriff's Office and permitted only the attorney for the distributor to make use of a copy to show intended witnesses, with the understanding that the film was "required to be returned immediately upon demand." Attorneys for the distributor appealed to the federal circuit court and asked for a temporary injunction to prevent the office of the Marion County prosecutor and the Marion County sheriff from interfering with the exhibition of the movie. The attorneys also asked that the prosecutor and sheriff's offices retain only one copy of the film for use during the criminal trials and that the remaining copies be returned to the distributor. The court agreed, a decision that the federal court of appeals for the Seventh Circuit affirmed. The film was eventually freed for exhibition in *Metzger v. Pearcy*, 393 F. 2d 202 (1968) because the police officers had violated the constitutional rights of the theater operators in seizing the film and preventing its exhibition without holding a prior adversary judicial hearing to determine whether or not the film was actually obscene. The court cited in its decision the 1964 U.S. Supreme Court case *A Quantity of Copies of Books v. Kansas*, 378 U.S. 205 (1964), in which the Court ruled that publications or movies that have only been alleged to be obscene should not to be treated the same way as narcotics, gambling paraphernalia, and other contraband, which must be confiscated immediately. Instead the court ruled that the absence of a hearing before seizure of the film was unconstitutional

In a less publicized case in Kentucky in 1968, a theater operator named David Cain was convicted by the state for showing the movie. When attorneys for the distributor took the case before the U.S. Supreme Court, the body ruled in *Cain v. Kentucky*, 397 U.S. 1081 (1970) that the lower courts had been in error in issuing the criminal conviction. The Supreme Court reversed judgment without providing a written opinion and cited as its authority an earlier Supreme Court ruling in *Redrup v. New York*, 386 U.S. 767, in which the Court determined that "the materials [books] could not constitutionally be adjudged obscene by the States, thus rendering adjudication of the other issues unnecessary. In short, the Court disposes of the cases on the issue that was deliberately excluded from review, and refuses to pass on the questions that brought the cases here." In other words, what is obscene is determined by the Supreme Court, and that is the standard that states must apply in evaluating books or films.

FURTHER READING

Cain v. Kentucky, 397 U.S. 1081 (1970).
De Grazia, Edward, and Roger K. Newman. *Banned Films: Movies, Censors & the First Amendment.* New York: R. R. Bowker, 1982.

Metzger v. Pearcy, 393 F. 2d 202 (1968).
Redrup v. New York, 386 U.S. 767.

I AM CURIOUS–YELLOW

Country and date of production: Sweden, 1967 (as *Jag är Nyfiken–Gul*)
Production company/distributor: Sandrews, 1967; Grove Press (United States, 1969)
Format: Sound, black and white
Running time: 121 minutes
Language: Swedish
Producer: Göran Lindgren
Director: Vilgot Sjöman
Screenwriter: Vilgot Sjöman
Awards: 1968 Guldbagge Award (Main Swedish film industry award), Best Actress (Lena Nyman).
Genre: Documentary/drama
With: Lena Nyman (Lena), Vilgot Sjöman (Vilgot Sjöman), Börje Ahlstedt (Börje, Lena's boyfriend), Peter Lindgren (Lena's Father), Chris Wahlström (Rune's Woman), Marie Göranzon (Marie, Börje's mistress), Magnus Nilsson (Magnus, Lena's school friend), Ulla Lyttkens (Ulla, Lena's friend)

SUMMARY

I Am Curious–Yellow creates the impression of being almost entirely improvised. It includes random musical numbers, commercials, contests to enter by mail, and a host of other innovations that punctuate the heroine's search for truth. Lena, age 22, wants to know all she can about life and reality. Her quest focuses on moral, social, political and sexual questioning of the world surrounding her. She fantasizes about carrying on a conversation with Martin Luther King; demonstrates against the Vietnam War; and interviews men and women in the streets of Stockholm, Sweden, while carrying on an affair with a married man, Börje, who sells cars. The two engage in sexual activity in a variety of locations, including a balcony at the Royal Palace and in a tree. Lena is insatiably curious about everything and collects information in huge boxes organized alphabetically. The first 40 minutes of the movie primarily show her interviewing people on the streets about whether Sweden has a class structure, if women have the same job opportunities as men and so on. Lena stores her findings in an enormous archive while she experiments with relationships, political activism and meditation. The movie functions as a film within a film, and Lena's probing of issues gives it the quality of a documentary.

Although the film is known for its sexual content, it is more than a racy, X-rated creation. It is possible to watch this film as though it were a video diary: Lena makes dated entries, and the director never lets us forget that a film is nothing more than an idea in the mind of its creator. The actors, director and film crew are shown in a humorous parallel plot about the making of the film and their reactions to the story and to each other. At the same time, the sexual questioning in the film demands attention because it contains ample nudity and sex scenes, most centered on Lena's lovemaking with her married lover. The sexual activity includes what the attorney general of Maryland listed in presenting the case before the Supreme Court as cunnilingus, "intercourse in a variety of usual and unusual settings," nudity, fantasized castration and obscene dialogue. The film has entered censorship history for these segments rather than for its social and political commentary.

CENSORSHIP HISTORY

I Am Curious–Yellow inspired hundreds of newspaper and magazine articles and reviews in the United States and in Europe when it was first released. Such disparate publications as the *London Financial Times* and *New Leader*, in addition to the *Saturday Review*, *Time*, *The New York Times*, *Variety* and *Box Office*, debated the film's impact on international cinema. In retrospect, critics contend that this film was responsible for "fanning the flames of a racy new era in Hollywood." Grove Press publisher Barney Rosset, who had engaged in earlier court battles to bring the novels *Tropic of Cancer* by Henry Miller and *Lady Chatterley's Lover* by D. H. Lawrence into the country, tried to import copies of the film. U.S. Customs seized the first copies, using the Tariff Act of 1930 as their authority (see *491*), them and held until a federal court would decide if the film were obscene. In a jury trial, the film was found obscene, but Rosset appealed the decision in the U.S. Court of Appeals for the Second Circuit, which reversed the earlier decision.

In rendering a decision in *United States v. "I Am Curious–Yellow,"* 404 F. 2d 196 (1968), the court wrote that "under the standards established by the Supreme Court," the movie was not obscene and "the showing of the picture cannot be inhibited." This ruling emerged despite the sexual explicitness of the film, which motivated federal circuit court judge Henry Friendly to write that, although the film did have a claim to the protection of the First Amendment, "It seems to be conceded that the sexual content of the film is presented with greater explicitness than has been seen in any other film produced for general viewing. . . . Several scenes depict sexual intercourse under varying circumstances. . . . There are scenes of oral-genital activity. . . . [and a] number of scenes which show the young girl and her lover nude." In making the decision that allowed entry of the film into the United States, the court applied the "three-fold test" that had been used in *Jacobellis v. Ohio*, 378 U.S. 184, to determine that THE LOVERS was not obscene, and in *Memoirs of a Woman of Pleasure v. Attorney General*, 865 Ct. 975 (1966):

> Three elements must coalesce: it must be established that (a) the dominant theme of the material taken as a whole appeals to the prurient interest in sex; (b) the material is patently offensive because it affronts contemporary

community standards relating to the description or representation of sexual matters; and (c) the material is utterly without redeeming social value. The court applied the test to the movie and did not find it obscene, "although sexual conduct is undeniably an important aspect of the picture and may be thought of as constituting one of its principal themes, it cannot be said that 'the dominant theme of the material taken as a whole appeals to prurient interest in sex.'" In explaining its decision, the court wrote that the film "does present ideas and does strive to present these ideas artistically. It falls within the gambit of intellectual effort that the First Amendment was designed to protect." Before making a decision, the court called numerous witnesses who testified to its sociological importance, including the author Norman Mailer, who characterized the film as "one of the most important pictures I have ever seen."

The decision by the U.S. Court of Appeals for the Second Circuit freed *I Am Curious–Yellow* for entrance into the United States, but it did not mandate how city and state censorship boards would view the film. More than 125 theaters throughout the United States exhibited the film, either without contest or after local challenges were removed by municipal courts, but numerous other cities, including Boston, Spokane, Kansas City and Baltimore, banned the film. The film was challenged in court in San Jose, California; Denver, Colorado; Atlanta, Georgia; Detroit, Michigan; Albuquerque, New Mexico; Cleveland, Ohio; Philadelphia, Pennsylvania; Norfolk and Virginia Beach, Virginia; and in Livingston, Linden and Woodbridge, New Jersey. Numerous witnesses were called upon to testify to the sociological significance of the movie, but not all courts were convinced that *I Am Curious–Yellow* was not obscene. In Jefferson County, Alabama, the county sheriff arrested an employee of a theater that showed the movie, and the employee enjoined the court to prevent further prosecution and arrest on the ground that the film was constitutionally protected. The trial court disagreed and the case went to the Supreme Court of Alabama, which decided, in *Cooper v. Sheriff of Jefferson County*, 257 So. 2d 332 (1972), to uphold the decision of the lower court in the belief that each court has the duty to examine and to decide the issue of obscenity, which it could not do because a copy of the film had not been included in the transcript on appeal. In a consolidated hearing in New Jersey that combined three cases, the trial judge in *Lordi v. UA Theatres*, 259 A. 2d 734 (1969), decided that the film was constitutionally protected because the parties bringing the challenge had not proved the film to be "utterly without redeeming social value." Instead, the judge wrote that the witnesses for the exhibitor, which included *New Leader* film critic and university professor John Simon, who also served as the drama critic for *Commonweal*, a liberal Catholic weekly magazine, were "clearly more persuasive" in defending the social value of the film than those brought by the government, which included Father Morton Hill, the president of the moral action organization Morality in Media.

After applying the three-fold test, the Supreme Court of Arizona determined in *NGC Theatre Corp. v. Mummert*, 489 P. 2d 823 (1971), that the film was obscene because, in the eyes of the court, it did appeal to prurient interest and was patently offensive. In *Evans Theatre Corp. v. Slaton*, 180 S.E. 2d 712 (1971), the Georgia Supreme Court declared the film to be obscene and wrote in its decision that "if the film does not go substantially beyond the customary limits of candor in representing sexual matters, then there are no limits of candor in this country." In Boston, a theater operator argued in *Karalexis v. Byrne*, 306 F. Supp. 1363 (1969) that, because he had shown the film to an "adults-only" audience that had been alerted in advance to the sexual content in the film, the exhibition should be constitutionally protected. The federal district court agreed and dropped charges against the operator.

The issue of whether the film was obscene would have been unconditionally clear had the issue been decided before the U.S. Supreme Court when the film was first confiscated by U.S. Customs in 1967. Even when the case finally reached the high court, the 4 to 4 division of the Court left the determination of the film's constitutional protection in doubt. In 1968, the Maryland board of censors refused to grant a permit to exhibit the film, and the case went before the Maryland Supreme Court, which determined in *Wagonheim v. Maryland*, 258 A. 2d 240 (1969), that the pretense of social and political inquiry was "patently strained and contrived" and the film obscene. The distributor took the case before the U.S. Supreme Court in *Grove Press v. Maryland Board of Censors*, 401 U.S. 480 (1971). Despite the briefs filed by friends of the court urging reversal filed by Felix J. Bilgrey, for the International Film Importers and Distributors of America, Inc.; Louis Nizer, for the Motion Picture Association of America, Inc.; Leon Friedman and Lester Pollack, for the National Association of Theater Owners, Inc.; and Stanley Fleishman and Sam Rosenwein, for the Adult Film Association of America, Inc., the Court seemed to be more impressed by the evidence presented in the brief filed by Francis J. Rudolph for Morality in Media, Inc., and affirmed the lower court decision in a split (4 to 4) decision.

FURTHER READING

Cooper v. Sheriff of Jefferson County, 257 So. 2d 332 (1972).
Evans Theatre Corp. v. Slaton, 180 S.E. 2d 712 (1971).
Grove Press v. Maryland Board of Censors, 401 U.S. 480 (1971).
Jacobellis v. Ohio, 378 U.S. 184.
Karalexis v. Byrne, 306 F. Supp. 1363 (1969).
Lordi v. UA Theatres, 259 A. 2d 734 (1969).
Memoirs of a Woman of Pleasure v. Attorney General, 865 Ct. 975 (1966).
NGC Theatre Corp. v. Mummert, 489 P. 2d 823 (1971).
Sjoman, Vilgot. *I Am Curious Yellow*. New York: Grove Press, 1968.
United States v. "I Am Curious–Yellow", 404 F. 2d 196 (1968).
Wagonheim v. Maryland, 258 A. 2d 240 (1969).
Weiner, Caren. "Curious Under Fire." *Entertainment Weekly*, March 6, 1998, p. 92.

IDIOT'S DELIGHT

Country and date of production: United States, 1939
Production company/distributor: Metro-Goldwyn-Mayer (MGM)
Format: Sound, black and white
Running time: 107 minutes
Languages: English, Esperanto
Producers: Clarence Brown, Hunt Stromberg
Director: Clarence Brown
Screenwriter: Robert Sherwood (based on his play)
Awards: None
Genre: Comedy
With: Norma Shearer (Irene Fellara), Clark Gable (Harry Van), Edward
    Arnold (Achille Weber), Charles Coburn (Dr. Hugo Waldersee), Joseph
    Schildkraut (Captain Kirvline), Burgess Meredith (Quillary), Laura Hope
    Crews (Madame Zuleika)

SUMMARY

Robert Sherwood originally wrote *Idiot's Delight* as a stage play, which won a
Pulitzer Prize in 1936 and became the basis for the last antiwar film made by
MGM studios before the outbreak of World War II in Europe. The film is set
in a small Italian hotel near the Swiss border, which suddenly erupts into
activity when the Italian government closes the border and launches a surprise air attack on Paris to start the Second World War—a perceptive
prophecy by Sherwood. The formerly peaceful hotel suddenly fills with people trying to leave Italy and cross over into Switzerland. The mix of guests
includes a German scientist; an American entertainer traveling with six chorus girls; a French pacifist; a young English artist on his honeymoon; and an
American munitions manufacturer with his mistress Irene, who may or may
not be Russian. The outbreak of war changes the lives of all the guests except
that of the munitions manufacturer, who expected the war because he con-
spired to start it and will reap significant profits. The German scientist, who
was traveling to Switzerland to develop a cure for cancer, must return to Germany to use his scientific knowledge for the war effort, while the English
artist vows to return to England and to enlist in the army. The French pacifist
becomes the first victim of the senseless war when he is arrested and shot by a
firing squad after taunting Italian soldiers who are staying in the hotel. The
American entertainer, Harry Van, is unconcerned about the political implications of the conflict and hopes only that he and his troupe can leave the hotel
in time to make their next engagement. When Irene is refused an exit visa by
the Italian government at the urging of her lover, the munitions manufacturer who worries that she knows too much about his business, she admits to
Van that she is an American entertainer with whom he had a brief affair in
Omaha, Nebraska, years before. Harry and Irene remain at the hotel when
the border opens and everyone is free to leave. As they drink champagne and

make plans for the future, the French begin to bomb the area. The lovers are killed when a stray bomb destroys the hotel.

CENSORSHIP HISTORY

The story behind the filming of *Idiot's Delight* demonstrates the fear Hollywood had of making politically strong statements and exposes the extent to which a film might be censored before its release. Critics had charged in 1936 that the play was not only antiwar but also anti-Italian in its numerous references to the incompetence of modern Italy. Sherwood added the following postscript to the play:

> The megalomaniac, to live, must inspire excitement, fear and awe. If, instead, he is greeted with calmness, courage and ridicule, he becomes a figure of supreme insignificance. . . . By refusing to imitate the Fascists in their policies of heavily fortified isolation, their hysterical self-worship and psychopathic hatred of others, we may achieve the enjoyment of peaceful life on earth, rather than degraded death in the cellar.

In early 1936, both Warner Bros. and Pioneer Studios expressed interest in making the play into a film and asked Joseph Breen, the head of the Production Code Administration (PCA), to evaluate the possibility. In a strongly worded memorandum meant to discourage both studios, Breen wrote that he did not believe the play could be filmed because it "would be banned widely abroad and might cause reprisals against the American company distributing it. The play is fundamentally anti-war propaganda, and contains numerous diatribes against militarism, fascism and the munitions ring." The following month, when other studios expressed interest in filming *Idiot's Delight*, Frederick Herron, vice president of the Motion Picture Producers and Distributors Association (MPPDA), contacted Breen, who wrote on April 11, 1936, that four studios had discussed the possibility with him "and all seem to feel that it is too dangerous an undertaking at this time." Despite Breen's warnings that the play was dangerous and that the industry policy was adverse to filming it, MGM made plans in December 1936 to film the play.

The Italian Embassy brought pressure on MPPDA President Will Hays to stop the project, and Breen was directed to inform MGM that unless considerable changes were made, the studio would see "all their pictures banned in Italy and France, and there will be trouble all over the rest of the world." In a memorandum written on January 7, 1937, Herron told Breen to "keep your eyes on the production if and when it occurs because it is full of dynamite." The Italian ambassador pressured the MPPDA into hiring as technical adviser Mr. R. Caracciolo, the Italian consul assigned to Los Angeles, to whom MGM pledged that they would not make the picture if "'there is any likelihood of . . . being denied the Italian market.'"

Breen's negotiations with the Italian government to obtain approval for elements in the film took 15 months. In the first round of talks, Breen agreed to all of the demands made by Italian consul Caracciolo, including the demand that the movie script have no connection with the original play and contain nothing offensive to Italy, as well as the demand that the title be changed in all of the Italian prints of the final film and that Sherwood's name also not appear in the credits on any print shown in Italy. MGM objected to Breen's decisions. Hunt Stromberg, the producer, insisted that the film retain some of the original antiwar sentiment but also promised that the film would be a love story, not an antifascist statement. To appease Robert Sherwood and to persuade him to turn his political protest into a steamy love story, MGM explained the importance of keeping the foreign market. The loss of Italy's market would also mean that Germany, Spain and Argentina would ban the film. National censorship laws in France, Switzerland and Australia also severely restricted the political content of films.

The studio offered Sherwood an additional $135,000 to make the changes, which he completed by May 1938. The new script placed the emphasis on a love story between Henry Van and Irene, changed the setting from Italy to an unnamed Central European country, and changed the language from Italian to Esperanto. In a memorandum written on May 13, 1938, to MGM head Louis B. Mayer, Breen declared the subject matter to have been "cunningly handled." Some Central European nations may not like the film, he noted, but their reactions would "cause no serious worry" because Central Europe was not a major movie market.

The Italian government finally approved the project on June 20, 1938, after Benito Mussolini judged the script acceptable. When the film premiered, critics lambasted Hollywood for having made such drastic changes to appease Italy, and critics in such publications as *Newsweek*, *New Republic* and *The North American Review* accused MGM of deleting all material that might offend Italy. Despite the changes, *Idiot's Delight* did not do well financially in Europe as censors in Italy, Spain, France, Switzerland and Estonia rejected the film, despite earlier approval for the project by the Italian government.

FURTHER READING

Black, Gregory D. *Hollywood Censored: Morality Codes, Catholics, and the Movies.* New York: Cambridge University Press, 1994.

Brown, John Mason. *The Worlds of Robert Sherwood.* New York: Harper & Row, 1965,

Internal Memo—"Idiot's Delight." *Idiot's Delight* file. Production Code Administration Files, March 26, 1936.

Memorandum from Joseph Breen to Frederick Herron. *Idiot's Delight* file. Production Code Administration Files, April 11,1936.

Memorandum from Joseph Breen to Louis B. Mayer. *Idiot's Delight* file. Production Code Administration, May 13, 1938.

Memorandum from Frederick Herron to Joseph Breen. *Idiot's Delight* file. Production Code Administration Files, January 7, 1937.

Nowell-Smith, Geoffrey, ed. *The Oxford History of World Cinema.* New York: Oxford University Press, 1996.

Production Code Administration Files. Margaret Herrick Library, Academy of Motion Picture Arts and Sciences (AMPAS), Beverly Hills, California. Varying dates.

Sherwood, Robert E. *Idiot's Delight.* New York: Charles Scribner's Sons, 1936.

I'M NO ANGEL

Country and date of production: United States, 1933
Production company/distributor: Paramount Pictures
Format: Sound, black and white
Running time: 87 minutes
Language: English
Producer: William LeBaron
Director: Wesley Ruggles
Screenwriters: Lowell Brentano (suggestions), Harlan Thompson (story), Mae West (also story, dialogue)
Awards: None
Genre: Comedy
With: Mae West (Tira), Cary Grant (Jack Clayton), Gregory Ratoff (Benny Pinkowitz), Edward Arnold (Big Bill Barton), Ralf Harolde (Slick Wiley), Kent Taylor (Kirk Lawrence), Gertrude Michael (Alicia Hatton), Russell Hopton (Flea Madigan, the Barker), Libby Taylor (Libby, Maid)

SUMMARY

I'm No Angel opens with Tira, played by Mae West, sauntering out into a crowd and singing "Sister Honky Tonk" in a sexy gown. Tira works for a carnival called Big Bill Barton's Wonder Show. As the barker tempts a crowded audience to enter, a carnival pickpocket named Slick Wiley works the crowd. One of the main attractions is the sideshow carnival queen and dazzling circus performer, Tira the Incomparable, whose charms the barker hails to lure middle-aged male patrons into the show:

> Over there, Tira, the beautiful Tira, dancing, singing, marvel of the age, supreme flower of feminine pulchritude, the girl who discovered you don't have to have feet to be a dancer.

Tira accepts gifts from various men and wants nothing more than to find, fool and then forget them. She entertains a chump from Dallas until Slick comes in, tries to shake him down for money, and then knocks him out with a bottle when he resists. Slick steals the man's diamond ring and then is arrested for the theft. Tira calls her lawyer, Benny Pinkowitz, but cannot afford the fees, so she is forced to ask Barton for the money. When he refuses, she promises to add to her act by putting her head in a lion's mouth. Excited by the prospect of large audiences at such an event, he gives her $2,000. Tira enters the ring

157

on an elephant and commands the lions, putting her face in one's mouth. After the show she talks with society people; throws water on society girl Alicia, who has criticized her behavior; and agrees to go out with Kirk Lawrence, another suitor who has sent her expensive gifts. Alicia then tells Tira that she is engaged to Kirk and asks her to leave him alone. When Alicia offers money, Tira pushes her out. Slick returns from jail, and Tira offers to help him as long as he stops stealing. Wealthy, handsome admirer Jack Clayton asks Tira if she loves Kirk and tells her not to count on marriage. Tira consults her horoscope and gives the fascinating Jack her framed photo. She calls Jack, and they begin to see each other. She says, "When I'm good, I'm very good; but when I'm bad, I'm better." Tira sings "I Want You" and then tells Barton she is quitting the circus to marry Jack. Barton arranges for Jack to find Slick alone in Tira's apartment in his bathrobe and prompts Slick to say that he is back with her. Upon seeing this, Jack becomes despondent and plans to leave town. Meanwhile, oblivious to Barton's sabotage, Tira tries on a wedding gown, then receives a note and learns that Jack is gone. She tells Pinkowitz to sue him for breach of promise and asks for a large cash settlement. In court, Tira testifies that she has known many men, and her lawyer says the case is lost. Jack, however, has a change of heart and offers to give Tira whatever she asked for. He later calls on Tira and asks her if she loves him. She tears up his check, and he kisses her. Tira then sings "I'm No Angel."

CENSORSHIP HISTORY

Appearing just before restrictions were imposed on motion pictures by the Production Code Administration, *I'm No Angel* initially provided Mae West with an excellent venue in which to exhibit her comic talents: quotable wise-cracks one-liners, racy double entendres in her dialogue and suggestive songs. Critics claimed to be shocked by her suggestive body language, especially when she performs "Sister Honky Tonk." Another target of criticism was Tira's talent to hustle and to attract the attention of wealthy, diamond-ringed spectators personally with her erotic costumes and shimmying, as well as her philosophy to "Take all you can get and give as little as possible" and to "Find 'em, fool 'em and forget 'em." Martin Quigley, a Catholic layperson, publisher of the conservative *Motion Picture Herald* and a force behind the Catholic Legion of Decency (LOD), described the film as "A vehicle for notorious characterization of a scarlet woman whose amatory instincts are confined exclusively to the physical. There is no more pretense here of romance than on a stud-farm . . . its sportive wise-cracking tends to create tolerance if not acceptance of things essentially evil." When Dr. James Wingate, head of the Studio Relations Committee, reviewed the film in September 1933, he wrote in his report that it "contained no particularly objectionable sex scenes" and that he believed the film was within the code.

Film critics praised West's rapid-fire wit and characterized the film as enjoyable. Even the drama critic of the conservative *Motion Picture Herald*, published by Quigley, wrote that theater owners should "blaze the star's name all over the marquee." In contrast, ministers in Haverhill, Massachusetts, condemned the film, which they called "demoralizing, disgusting, suggestive and indecent" and called for it to be removed from local theaters, but the mayor and the city council did not agree. In Plymouth, Massachusetts, the Reverend Paul G. Macy labeled the film "the lowest" he had ever seen. The Catholic LOD placed the film on its condemned list. West might have offended some viewers, but her films were popular in both urban areas and in small towns. As D. W. Fiske, the owner-operator of a theater in Oak Grove, Louisiana, noted after reporting that he "did the best business of the year" with this film, "Whether they like her or not, they all come out to see her. The church people clamor for clean pictures, but they all come out to see Mae West and stay away from the clean, sweet pictures."

When the Motion Picture Producers and Distributors Association (MPPDA) unveiled its new production code on June 13, 1934, however, more stringent standards classified *I'm No Angel* as a Class I film, which meant that it was pulled immediately and the order given that it would not be re-released. As Paramount's Adolph Zukor pointed out, even though more than 20 million fans had seen the movie by the end of 1933 and West was ranked eighth as a Hollywood box-office attraction, she became one of the main casualties of the new production code.

FURTHER READING

Black, Gregory D. *Hollywood Censored: Morality Codes, Catholics, and the Movies.* New York: Cambridge University Press, 1994.

Fiske, D. W. "I'm No Angel." *Motion Picture Herald*, February 24, 1934, p. 52.

"I'm No Angel." *Motion Picture Herald*, October 7, 1933, p. 38.

Memorandum from Dr. James Wingate to Will Hays. *I'm No Angel* file. Production Code Administration Files, September 20, 1933.

Production Code Administration Files. Margaret Herrick Library, Academy of Motion Picture Arts and Sciences (AMPAS), Beverly Hills, California. Varying dates.

Quigley, Martin *Decency in Motion Pictures.* New York: Macmillan, 1937.

Zukor, Adolph, with Dale Kramer. *The Public Is Never Wrong.* New York: G. P. Putnam, 1953.

THE JAMES BOYS IN MISSOURI

Country and date of production: United States, 1908
Production company/distributor: Essanay Film Manufacturing Co.
Format: Silent, black and white
Running Time: 15 minutes
Language: English titled
Producer: O. T. Crawford
Director: O. T. Crawford

Screenwriters: Unknown
Awards: None
Genre: Western
With: Not available

SUMMARY

The James Boys in Missouri was the first film to be made about the lives and adventures of the 19th-century outlaws Frank and Jesse James. The notoriety of the James gang and the range of their activities, both real and imagined by the authors of countless dime novels, provided the film with a ready audience.

CENSORSHIP HISTORY

The 1908 banning in Chicago of *The James Boys in Missouri* and *Night Rider*, another film named in the same court action, represents the first official incident of local film censorship in the United States and resulted in the first movie censorship controversy to appear in the courts. In 1907, Chicago passed the first movie censorship ordinance in the nation, using as its authority Illinois state statutes that permitted each city and town to "license, tax, regulate or prohibit . . . theatricals and other exhibitions, shows, and amusements; . . . license, tax and regulate all places for eating or amusement" (*Illinois Rev. Stat.*, Ch. 24, Sects. 23–54 and 23–57). The Chicago ordinance required anyone who wanted to exhibit a film publicly to obtain a permit from the superintendent of police, who had to first preview the film and levy a charge of three dollars per one thousand feet of film reviewed. The ordinance instructed the superintendent of police to refuse to license any film that "is immoral or obscene, or portrays depravity, criminality or lack of virtue of a class of citizens of any race, color, creed or religion or exposes them to contempt, derision or obloquy, or tends to produce a breach of the peace or riots, or purports to represent any hanging, lynching or burning of a human being" (*Rev. Chicago Code*, Sects. 1952–61 [1931]). If the superintendent of police refused an exhibitor a license, the distributor could appeal the decision before the mayor of Chicago, whose decision would be binding. The ordinance also contained a means of classifying films according to the age of their viewers, and provided that

> in all cases where a permit . . . has been refused . . . because the movie tends towards creating a harmful impression on the minds of children, where such tendency as to the minds of adults would not exist if exhibited only to persons of mature age, the Commissioner of Police may grant a special permit limiting the exhibition of such picture . . . to persons over the age of twenty-one years; provided such picture or pictures are not of such character as to tend to create contempt or hatred for any class of law abiding citizens.

The Chicago board of censors refused to grant distributors of the films a permit to exhibit them, based on the determination that the films were immoral, as provided for in the Chicago city ordinance.

Jake Block, one of the proprietors of what were called five-and-ten-cent theaters that showed kinetoscope images, nonetheless exhibited the film in Chicago and went to court to argue in *Block v. City of Chicago*, 87 N.E. 1011, 239 Ill. 251 (1909), that the ordinance was void because it deprived him of "rights under the Constitution" and "discriminates against the exhibitors of moving pictures, delegates discretionary and judicial powers to the chief of police, takes the property of complainants without due process of law, and is unreasonable and oppressive." Block further defended the films as having ties with legitimate theater because the movies had been adapted "from plays and dramas" and they were "moral and in no way obscene." The court failed to agree with Block's arguments and dismissed his complaint.

The case then went before the Supreme Court of Illinois, which upheld the constitutional validity of the Chicago ordinance. In making a determination to affirm the decision of the lower court, Chief Justice James H. Cartwright wrote that the law was required "to secure decency and morality in the moving picture business, and that purpose falls within the police power. It is designed as a precautionary measure to prevent exhibitions criminal in their nature and forbidden by laws." The decision also made particular note of the venues in which the films were being shown, the low-priced five-and-ten-cent theaters that drew different audiences than the stage theaters, including children and "those of limited means." According to Cartwright, these audience members' "age, education, and situation in life specially entitle them to protection against the evil influence of obscene and immoral representations." The decision in *Block v. City of Chicago*, 87 N.E. 1011, 239 Ill. 251 (1909), disagreed with Block's assertion that the film could not be considered immoral because it represented a segment of the history of the United States. Instead, Chief Justice Cartwright wrote, "Pictures which attempt to exhibit that career [outlaw] necessarily portray exhibitions of crime, and pictures of the *Night Riders* can represent nothing but malicious mischief, arson, and murder." The court concluded that both films were, thus, immoral and their exhibition "would necessarily be attended with evil effects upon youthful spectators. . . . if the other pictures for which permits were refused were of similar character, the chief of police is to be commended for the refusal."

FURTHER READING

Block v. City of Chicago, 87 N.E. 1011, 239 Ill. 251 (1909).
Carmen, Ira H. *Movies, Censorship and the Law*. Ann Arbor: University of Michigan Press, 1966.
Illinois Rev. Stats., Ch. 24, Sects. 23–54 and 23–57.
Rev. Chicago Code, Sects. 1952–61 (1931).

THE KILLING OF SISTER GEORGE

Country and date of production: England, 1968
Production company/distributor: American Broadcasting Company (ABC), Palomar Pictures/Cinerama
Format: Sound, color
Running time: 138 minutes
Language: English
Producers: Robert Aldrich, Edgar J. Scherick
Director: Robert Aldrich
Screenwriters: Lukas Heller, Frank Marcus (play)
Awards: None
Genre: Drama
With: Beryl Reid (June Buckridge), Susannah York (Alice "Childie" McNaught), Coral Browne (Mercy Croft), Ronald Fraser (Leo Lockhart), Patricia Medina (Betty Thaxter)

SUMMARY

The plot of *The Killing of Sister George* centers on June Buckridge, a middle-aged soap opera actress for a long-running BBC series, who learns that her character, a matronly nurse named Sister George, is to be killed off after many years. Buckridge is outrageous, sadistic and dominating toward Childie, her passive live-in girlfriend; she enjoys ritualistically punishing her girlfriend for breaking the rules she has created but refuses to admit blame when she is the violator. The couple's relationship is rocky at best, and Buckridge's abusive behavior increases when she realizes that she can no longer get decent acting work in times that value fashion and sex appeal. The couple's relationship is further strained when a chic television executive named Mercy Croft enters the couple's life. Croft is a polished professional woman who is attempting to live as a lesbian in a straight world. Buckridge and Childie's relationship begins to fall apart when Childie becomes romantically involved with Croft. Their love affair, while healthy for Childie, brings Buckridge to the point of a mental and emotional collapse. This, along with the impending death of her soap opera character, sends Buckridge into a fit of depression, as she sees her life fall apart around her.

CENSORSHIP HISTORY

Based on the stage play of the same name, *The Killing of Sister George* gained notoriety both for its lesbian theme and for its depiction of the first lesbian love scene in a feature movie. Critics focused their attention on the somewhat graphic scene between Childie and Croft. In reviewing the film, the critic Pauline Kael titled her column "Frightening the Horses" and expressed shock over the "119 seconds of footage showing exactly what lesbians could do." Leo Mishkin wrote in his review, which appeared in the December 17,

1968, issue of the British newspaper *Morning Telegraph*, "To make the point perfectly plain the film includes a scene of this program director making love to the blonde girl in the privacy of the latter's bedroom." Overall, however, producer Robert Aldrich takes an evenhanded approach to handling the very controversial-for-its-time topic of lesbian relationships in London of the 1960s. However, while the film initially was thought to champion gay rights, its portrayal of lesbians as sick, depraved or unhappy realized the lesbian community's worst fears. Lesbian viewers also objected to the stereotyped portrayal of June Buckridge as overly masculine so that "[h]er straining after male postures is a source of humour."

The film was granted an "X" rating by the Motion Picture Association of America (MPAA) because of its lesbian theme. Many cities banned the film entirely and "in other cities an entire reel was deleted so that the film could be shown." Connecticut and Massachusetts required that the seduction scene be cut before the film was granted a permit for exhibition. The advertising for the film was censored by the *Los Angeles Times*, which altered the drawing of a female figure and deleted references to the lesbian relationships from the submitted advertising copy. The producer filed a complaint in federal district court requesting that the court stop the newspaper from censoring advertisements for the movie, but the request was denied in *Associates & Aldrich Co. v. Times Mirror Co.*, 440 F. 2d 133 (1971), on the ground that the newspaper was a private enterprise whose freedom of expression was constitutionally guaranteed. Attorneys for the producer appealed the decision, but the dismissal was affirmed. Today, the film has attained a camp status for its stereotyped depictions of lesbian roles.

FURTHER READING

Associates & Aldrich Co. v. Times Mirror Co., 440 F. 2d 133 (1971).
Dyer, Richard. *Gays and Film*. New York: Zoetrope, 1984.
Mishkin, Leo. "The Killing of Sister George." *Morning Telegraph*, December 17, 1968, p. B2.
Russo, Vito. *The Celluloid Closet*. New York: HarperCollins, 1981.
Weiss, Andrea. *Vampires and Violets: Lesbians in the Cinema*. London: Jonathan Cape, 1992.

LADY CHATTERLEY'S LOVER

Country and date of production: France, 1955 (as *L'Amant de lady Chatterley*)
Production company/distributor: Orsay Films, Régie du Film (France)/ Kingsley International (United States, 1959)
Format: Sound, black and white
Running time: 101 minutes
Language: French

Producers: Gilbert Cohen-Seat, Claude Ganz
Director: Marc Allégret,
Screenwriters: Marc Allégret, Gaston Bonheur and Philippe de Rothschild (play), D. H. Lawrence (novel)
Awards: None
Genre: Drama
With: Danielle Darrieux (Constance Chatterley), Erno Crisa (Oliver Mellors), Leo Genn (Sir Clifford Chatterley), Berthe Tissen (Mrs. Bolton), Janine Crispin (Hilda), Jean Murat (Baron Leslie Winter), Gérard Séty (Michaelis), Jacqueline Noëlle (Bertha Mellors)

SUMMARY

Lady Chatterley's Lover is based on the 1928 novel of the same name by D. H. Lawrence, which gained notoriety during the 30 years the banned work was smuggled into the United States in pirated and expurgated editions, and the play written by Gaston Bonheur and Philippe de Rothschild from the novel. In an account of his defense of the book in a landmark 1959 censorship case, Charles Rembar observes that the novel was so widely banned because *"Lady Chatterley's Lover* presented the forbidden acts in forbidden detail, and described them in forbidden language."

The movie retains some of the original flavor of the novel but does present forbidden acts in significantly less detail, while the graphic language used to describe the genitals and the bodily functions has been excised. The plot, however, remains the same. Connie Chatterley is a young noblewoman married to a tyrannical baronet, Clifford Chatterley, who is paralyzed from the waist down and sexually impotent after being wounded in World War I. Seemingly in love with her husband, yet still young and in her sexual prime, Connie has a brief and unsatisfying affair with someone in their social circle. She is, nonetheless, repulsed at first by her husband's suggestion that she have an affair and become pregnant to produce an heir to his estate. The lonely young woman eventually falls in love with the young, virile estate gamekeeper, Oliver Mellors, whose tender and natural lovemaking awaken her sexually and emotionally. When Chatterley learns of the affair, he is furious with her—not because she is having an affair, but because she has become involved with a man who is socially inferior to the baronet. Connie asks the baronet for a divorce, which he spitefully refuses to grant, so she leaves him and prepares to live with Mellors.

CENSORSHIP HISTORY

Lawrence's novel had been of interest to Hollywood producers for many years, despite its notoriety and banning by the U.S. Postal Department. Producer Nicholas Schenck had been blocked by the personal intervention of Will Hays when he tried to register the title in 1932, and a script submitted by David O. Selznick in 1950 was rejected by Joe Breen, head of the Production Code Administration. When the French writer-director Marc Allégret acquired the property, the plot of the script remained relatively similar to the novel. Adultery remained a theme: The reasons for the adultery and Chatterley's initial encouragement of his wife's activity are in the movie. The actual love scenes, however, are significantly less graphic than the descriptions in the novel. In 1957, the film entered the United States and passed through U.S. Customs. Kingsley International, the distributor, submitted the film to the Motion Picture Division of the New York Education Department, the state motion picture censorship agency, to obtain a license to exhibit. The division found three isolated scenes "'immoral' within the intent of our Law" and denied the distributors the license unless the three scenes were excised. The agency ordered that

> distributors eliminate all views of Mellors and Lady Chatterley in the cabin lying on a cot together in a state of undress as well as all views of Mellors caressing Lady Chatterley's buttocks and all views of him unzipping her dress and caressing her bare back. They were also ordered to eliminate both spoken (in French) dialogue and the English subtitles accompanying these actions.

The distributor refused to make the changes and petitioned the Regents of the University of the State of New York to review the decision, based on a provision in the New York Education Law that granted the right. The decision of the Regents was to uphold the denial based on the Education Law and the broader objection that "the whole theme of this movie is immoral under said law, for that theme is the presentation of adultery as a desirable, acceptable and proper pattern of behavior."

Attorneys representing Kingsley International argued the case before the appellate division, which reversed the decision of the Regents and directed that the license be issued to exhibit the film. The case then entered the New York Court of Appeals, which reversed the decision of the appellate division and affirmed, in 4 N.Y. 2d 349, 151 N.E. 2d 197 and 175 N.Y.S. 2d 39, the refusal by the Regents to license the film. But only three of the justices were certain that the denial of a license was constitutionally permissible. In the prevailing opinion in this decision, written by Chief Judge Conway, the decision emphasized only those parts of the New York State Education Law that dealt with the denial of licenses to exhibit for motion pictures "which are immoral in that they portray acts of sexual immorality . . . as desirable, acceptable or proper patterns of behavior." The New York Court of Appeals interpreted that language to express "a precise purpose of the New York State Legislature to require the denial of a license to a motion picture because its subject matter is adultery presented as being right and desirable for certain people under certain circumstances."

The case was next heard before the United States Supreme Court, which reversed the decision of the New York Court of Appeals in a unanimous decision that New York State had violated constitutional limits. Justice

Potter Stewart wrote in the ruling that New York State had not denied the license to exhibit because the film contained "obscenity" or "pornography," nor had the lower courts "suggested that the film would itself operate as an incitement to illegal action." Therefore, he argued, in its attempt to prevent the exhibition of a *Lady Chatterley's Lover* because it advocates an idea—that adultery under certain circumstances may be proper behavior—New York "has thus struck at the very heart of constitutionally protected liberty." Justices William O. Douglas and Hugo Black concurred with the decision and also felt compelled to state their opposition to the censorship of movies in general. Justice Douglas, with whom Justice Black joined, asserted, as he had in the decision regarding the film *M*, "that censorship of movies is unconstitutional, since it is a form of 'prior restraint' . . . at war with the First Amendment. . . . I can find in the First Amendment no room for any censor whether he is scanning an editorial, reading a news broadcast, editing a novel or a play, or previewing a movie."

As the justices wrote their decision, the novel was about to become the subject of *Grove Press Inc. v. Christenberry*, 175 F. Supp. 488 (S.D.N.Y. 1959), a landmark obscenity case in the United States that led to a signal freedom for the work not only in the United States but also in Great Britain.

FURTHER READING

Berry, Dean L. "Validity of Motion Picture Licensing Statute." *Michigan Law Review* 58 (November 1959): 134–137.

Carmen, Ira H. *Movies, Censorship and the Law*. Ann Arbor: University of Michigan Press, 1966.

Friedman, Samuel. "Constitutional Law—Motion Picture Censorship." *Brooklyn Law Review*, 26 (December 1959): 112–117.

Graham, Arthur F. "Film Censorship Upheld." *Ohio State Law Journal* 20 (Winter 1959): 161–164.

Haimbaugh, George D., Jr. "Film Censorship Since Roth-Alberts." *Kentucky Law Journal* 51 (Summer 1963): 656–666.

Kingsley International Pictures Corporation v. Regents of the University of the State of New York, 165 N.Y.S. 2d 681 (1957).

Kingsley International Pictures Corporation v. Regents of the University of the State of New York, 151 N.E. 2d 197 (1958).

Kingsley International Pictures Corporation v. Regents of the University of the State of New York, 360 U.S. 684 (1959).

Lederman, Lorna F. "New York Statute Censoring 'Sexual Immorality' in Motion Picture Film Held Unconstitutional." *Temple Law Quarterly* 33 (Winter 1959): 242–246.

McAnay, P. D. "Motion Picture Censorship and Constitutional Freedom." *Kentucky Law Journal* 50 (Summer 1962): 427–458.

Mondschein, Morris. "Constitutional Law: Motion Picture Censorship." *Cornell Law Quarterly* 44 (Spring 1959): 411–419.

Randall, Richard. *Censorship of the Movies*. Madison: University of Wisconsin Press, 1968.

Rembar, Charles. *The End of Obscenity: The Trials of Lady Chatterley's Lover, Tropic of Cancer & Fanny Hill by the Lawyer Who Defended Them.* New York: Random House, 1968.

THE LAST PICTURE SHOW

Country and date of production: United States, 1971
Production company/distributor: BBS Productions, Inc./Columbia Pictures Corporation
Format: Sound, black and white
Running time: 118 minutes
Language: English
Producers: Stephen J. Friedman, Bert Schneider
Director: Peter Bogdanovich
Screenwriters: Peter Bogdanovich, Larry McMurtry (from his novel)
Awards: 1971 Academy Awards, Best Supporting Actor (Ben Johnson), Best Supporting Actress (Cloris Leachman).
1973 British Academy Awards, Best Screenplay (Peter Bogdanovich, Larry McMurtry), Best Supporting Actor (Ben Johnson), Best Supporting Actress (Cloris Leachman).
1972 Golden Globes, Best Supporting Actor–Motion Picture (Ben Johnson), Best Director–Motion Picture (Peter Bogdanovich), Best Motion Picture–Drama.
1971 National Board of Review Awards, Best Supporting Actor (Ben Johnson).
1972 National Society of Film Critics Awards, USA, Best Supporting Actress (Ellen Burstyn).
1971 New York Film Critics Circle Awards, Best Screenplay (Peter Bogdanovich, Larry McMurtry), Best Supporting Actor (Ben Johnson), Best Supporting Actress (Ellen Burstyn).
Genre: Drama
With: Timothy Bottoms (Sonny Crawford), Jeff Bridges (Duane Jackson), Cybill Shepherd (Jacy Farrow), Ben Johnson (Sam the Lion), Cloris Leachman (Ruth Popper), Ellen Burstyn (Lois Farrow), Eileen Brennan (Genevieve), Clu Gulager (Abilene), Sam Bottoms (Billy)

SUMMARY

Adapted with director Bogdanovich by Larry McMurtry from his own novel of the same name, *The Last Picture Show* remains true to its source, and in nearly every aspect the film follows the book almost literally. As in the novel, the story tells of the desperation and claustrophobia of small-town life, where generation after generation undergo the same rites of passage, living out the same lives of frustration and unrealized dreams. Set in tiny Anarene, Texas, in the years between World War II and the Korean War, the film chronicles a brief period in the lives of Sonny and Duane, best friends who pass their time playing basketball, going to the movie house and chasing girls. Duane's steady girlfriend, the flirtatious Jacey, is wanted by every boy in school, and she flaunts her attractiveness. Her father has made his money in oil, and his wealth makes her even more attractive, so most people in Anarene feel that whoever wins Jacey's heart will be set for life.

Despite some prosperity, however, Anarene is a town dying a slow death as most of the younger townspeople head for the big cities to make their livings and rear their children. Duane and Sonny, a star on the high school basketball team, are torn between choosing an uncertain future somewhere beyond Anarene or staying in the economically battered town with its rundown pool hall and decrepit movie house. High school graduation approaches, and all the characters learn some difficult lessons about love, loneliness and jealousy. The vulnerable Sonny is seduced by the wife of his basketball coach, and the two confront each other months after the incident to find that a void remains between them. Jacey questions whether she wants a life with Duane and becomes involved with Lester Marlow, the son of a rich man. At a pool party with Lester's upscale friends, Jacey learns how far she must go to conform. When attendance falls off at the movie house that shows second-run features, the time comes for the last picture show. As the young characters contemplate the closing of the movie house, they feel that a stage of their lives is closing as well. As *The Last Picture Show* ends, Sonny is about to see *Red River*, the last showing of a film in Anarene, before leaving for military service in Korea.

CENSORSHIP HISTORY

The Last Picture Show was generally shown throughout the United States without incident because of the "R" rating (restricted to audiences 18 years and older, except when accompanied by an adult) assigned to it by the Classification and Rating Administration. The rating warned theater operators and viewers that the film included sexual content, nudity and language. In reality, the sexual content is simply verbal, the language contains swearing and anatomical references that are inherent to the characters portrayed, and the nudity consists of one scene in which Cybill Shepherd prepares to swim at a nude pool party; viewers can see her hesitation as she acknowledges what she must do to conform. However, the one attempt to censor the film that did enter the federal courts exhibits the extent to which the courts had changed their perceptions of "obscenity" by 1973.

After receiving complaints from residents regarding the exhibition of *The Last Picture Show* at the local drive-in theater, the city attorney of Phoenix, Arizona, wrote to the theater manager that the film violated the terms of the state obscenity statute and could be seen by people traveling "upon the public way." The city attorney warned the theater operator to "cease exhibiting the film" or to risk prosecution. The exhibition of the film could continue only if the distributor would agree to delete a "four-second segment of total frontal nudity of a female swimmer," a demand to which the distributor and producer objected. They brought suit in federal district court, arguing that the state obscenity statute was unconstitutional and that the actions of the prosecutor had violated their civil rights. In making his case, the prosecutor charged that the four-second segment violated a state statute that prohibited "publicly displaying pictorial depictions of 'human genitalia.'" The court determined that the prosecutor's "clear and unequivocal threats . . . directly caused the cessation of the exhibition of the Film," an action that was "tantamount to an official suppression . . . resulting in injury with no opportunity to obtain a judicial test of the constitutional issues."

In an unusual move, the court disagreed with the prosecutor's perception of what constitutes "female genitalia" and recommended that he peruse *Dorland's Illustrated Medical Dictionary*, 23rd edition, "for a view of exterior female genitalia and the names of the components." The three-judge court wrote in their decision in *BBS Productions, Inc. v. Purcell*, 360 F. Supp. 801 (1973), that "The challenged segment of film shows 'total frontal nudity of a female swimmer' walking forward and climbing the steps, completely straight, legs together, and from knee deep in the pool to the top of the pool's rim, much reminiscent of the early twentieth-century household picture entitled 'September Morn.' We find as an anatomical fact that such a portrayal is not a display of exterior female genitalia." Rebutting the prosecutor's stipulation that "the term 'genitalia' in the statute reaches total front male and female nudity," the court wrote that "common knowledge tells that is not necessarily so in the case of a female" and the judges did not accept that "the Mount of Venus, revealed by the triangular area of pubic hair, is any component of exterior female genitalia."

FURTHER READING

BBS Productions, Inc. v. Purcell, 360 F. Supp. 801 (1973).

De Grazia, Edward, and Roger K. Newman. *Banned Films: Movies, Censors and the First Amendment*. New York: R. R. Bowker, 1982.

Mast, Gerald, and Bruce F. Kawn. *A Short History of the Movies*, 7th ed. Boston: Allyn and Bacon, 1996.

LAST TANGO IN PARIS

Country and date of production: Italy (as *Ultimo Tango a Parigi*), 1972/ France (as *Le Dernier Tango à Paris*), 1972

Production company/distributor: Les Productions Artistes Associés (France), Produzioni Europee Associati (PEA) (Italy)/United Artists (United States, 1973)

Format: Sound, color

Running time: 136 minutes

Languages: English, French
Producer: Alberto Grimaldi
Director: Bernardo Bertolucci
Screenwriters: Bernardo Bertolucci (story), Franco Arcalli, Agnès Varda (additional dialogue)
Awards: 1973 Italian National Syndicate of Film Journalists, Best Director (Bernardo Bertolucci).
1974 National Society of Film Critics Awards, Best Actor (Marlon Brando).
1973 New York Film Critics Circle Awards, Best Actor (Marlon Brando).
Genre: Drama
With: Marlon Brando (Paul), Maria Schneider (Jeanne), Maria Michi (Rosa's Mother), Giovanna Galletti (Prostitute), Gitt Magrini (Jeanne's Mother), Catherine Allégret (Catherine), Luce Marquand (Olympia), Marie-Hélène Breillat (Monique), Catherine Breillat (Mouchette), Dan Diament (TV Sound Engineer), Catherine Sola (TV Script Girl), Mauro Marchetti (TV Cameraman), Jean-Pierre Léaud (Tom), Massimo Girotti (Marcel)

SUMMARY

Last Tango in Paris relates the unusual sexual and emotional relationship that develops between Jeanne, a beautiful young Parisienne who will be married in two weeks, and Paul, a mysterious American expatriate mourning his wife's recent suicide. The two meet accidentally in a vacant Paris flat while apartment hunting. They are instantly drawn to each other and engage in passionate and stormy sexual intercourse. At Paul's instigation, they agree to meet regularly to continue their passionate sexual activity, but they agree that neither will reveal personal information, including their names, to each other. Although their sex is anonymous, the relationship deeply affects both of them, helping Paul to deal with his wife's suicide and preparing Jeanne to marry her fiancé, Tom, a film director making a *cinema-verité* documentary about her. Paul seems to use the mindless physical passion to bury his sense of hurt and betrayal, while Jeanne responds to the authenticity of his emotion, even when its power becomes painful to her because it serves as an antidote to the insipidness of her boyfriend and prattling mother. Whatever Paul and Jeanne derive from their interaction is obviously confined to the apartment and is not meant to follow them into the real world of their daily lives. The music and the slow tracking shots of the camera, moving across the walls of the apartment and the bodies of Jeanne and Paul, emphasize the joyless efficiency of their sexual interaction and evoke feelings of remoteness, not sensual pleasure. Once Paul has become whole, as the result of his meetings with Jeanne, he realizes that they have shared an experience that binds them forever. He breaks their pact by opening himself to her. He hopes to alert her to his change of heart by taking part in a tango contest. In a scene that is both haunting and poignant, Paul destroys what little they have shared by engaging in drunken banality. After he pursues Jeanne to her mother's apartment, his passion frightens her and she shoots him.

CENSORSHIP HISTORY

Rated X (for sexuality, nudity and language) in 1972, *Last Tango in Paris* broke new ground, primarily because its kind of violent, uninhibited passion had never before been shown so clearly in a feature film. Unlike the soft-focus couplings that appeared in most other films, the extreme frankness in sexual physicality here made some viewers uncomfortable.

According to Roger Ebert, many movie critics saw *Last Tango* as "the banner for a revolution that never happened." He notes that the movie critic Pauline Kael voiced what many thought: "The movie breakthrough has finally come. Bertolucci and Brando have altered the face of an art form." She predicted that the date of the premiere, October 14, 1972, would become "a landmark in movie history comparable to the night in 1913 when Stravinsky's 'Rites of Spring' was first performed, and ushered in modern music." The prediction was incorrect because *Last Tango in Paris* did not lead to an adult art cinema. Instead, writes Ebert, "The movie frightened off imitators, and instead of being the first of many X-rated films dealing honestly with sexuality, it became almost the last. Hollywood made a quick U-turn into movies about teenagers, technology, action heroes and special effects."

From 1972 to 1987 the film was banned in Italy, where in 1972 federal authorities filed charges of obscenity against Marlon Brando, Maria Schneider, Bernardo Bertolucci, Alberto Grimaldi and United Artists. Although they were acquitted the following year, the ban on the film remained until 1987. Italy also revoked Bertolucci's right to vote, making him feel, in his own words, "like a martyr. . . . But the suspension of civil rights was painful, because I felt like a second class citizen." In Portugal, the government banned the film from 1973 to 1974, and the United Kingdom granted the film an "X" certification that did not change until 2000, when the film was re-rated "18" (suitable for viewers 18 and older).

In the United States, the film was re-rated in 1997 to the newly created "NC-17" (no one under 17 admitted under any circumstances) rating. The "X" rating kept *Last Tango in Paris* out of mainstream theaters and allowed it to play only in art houses unless individual states and cities certified that it was not obscene and agreed to issue permits for its exhibition. Most local theaters were not willing to risk showing a film rated "X," so few legal challenges resulted.

In Montgomery, Alabama, the operator of a local theater made an agreement with the distributor United Artists to show the film without first submitting it to the state board of censors for evaluation. Alerted to the upcoming exhibition, the Montgomery police chief warned the theater operator that showing the film without first receiving a judicial determination that it was not obscene would violate state law and subject the operator to prosecution. The theater operator contacted United Artists, and the distributor brought suit against the city of Montgomery in federal district court, asking that the statute be declared unconstitutional and that the restraints on showing the film be lifted. The court complied and, in *United Artists v. Wright*, 368 F. Supp. 1034 (1974), determined that the Alabama law was unconstitutional "on its face" because it failed to place the burden on the state government to prove that a film was obscene, nor did the statute provide for a definite time frame with which the courts must handle such incidents.

In 1973, police in Shreveport, Louisiana, arrested the manager of a theater showing the film and confiscated the film the second time that it was shown. Freed on bail, the manager then obtained a second copy of the film and exhibited it the following day. He was again arrested, and the second copy of the film was confiscated. Attorneys for the parent company of the theater filed a request with the courts for a temporary restraining order to prevent further arrest of the manager and seizure of the film, "until there could be a final judicial determination of the obscenity issue in an adversary hearing." The request was granted. When the case went to court, the district judge determined that *Last Tango in Paris* was obscene and barred the distributor and the theater manager from exhibiting it. In a review, the state supreme court in *Gulf State Theatres of Louisiana v. Richardson*, 287 So. 2d 480 (1974), reversed the decision of the lower court and declared unconstitutional the state laws used to prevent exhibition of the film because they involved prior restraint.

In 1987, the Miami-Dade County Library included *Last Tango in Paris* in a film series on past targets of censorship, only to find its series become a target of would-be censors. The Reverend Rick Patterson, leader of the Florida-based 900-member Jesus Fellowship, a religious group, called upon the county commission to ban the films and to make plans for establishing community standards "for such films." Although the films were purchased with private funds, the group objected "to public funds being spent for their display," but Commissioner Harvey Ruvin refused to agree and stated, "It's important that we stand up for the First Amendment." The film series continued without further interruption.

FURTHER READING

"The Ban Is Lifted on *Last Tango* in Italy." *Variety*, February 11, 1987, pp. 2–3.

De Quine, Jeanne. "Pastor Wants Censorship—Series Films Banned." *USA Today*, June 2, 1987, p. A3.

Ebert, Roger. "*Last Tango in Paris* Revisited." *Chicago Sun-Times*, August 11, 1995, p. C4.

Gulf State Theatres of Louisiana v. Richardson, 287 So. 2d 480 (1974).

Hoberman, J. "*Last Tango in Paris* Directed by Bernardo Bertolucci." *The Village Voice*, March 21, 1995, pp. 47+.

"Italy Acquits Brando of Obscenity in Film." *Los Angeles Times*, March 3, 1973, p. B3.

Keets, Heather. "Dancing Up a Storm (Bernardo Bertolucci's Controversial 1973 Film *Last Tango in Paris*)." *Entertainment Weekly*, January 28, 1994, p. 76.

Miller, Frank. *Censored Hollywood: Sex, Sin & Violence on Screen*. Atlanta, Ga.: Turner Publishing, 1994.

United Artists v. Wright, 368 F. Supp. 1034 (1974).

THE LAST TEMPTATION OF CHRIST

Country and date of production: United States, 1988
Production company/distributor: Cineplex Odeon Films/Universal Pictures
Format: Sound, color
Running time: 164 minutes
Language: English
Producers: Barbara De Fina, Harry J. Ufland
Director: Martin Scorsese
Screenwriters: Nikos Kazantzakis (novel), Paul Schrader
Awards: None
Genre: Drama
With: Willem Dafoe (Jesus), Harvey Keitel (Judas), Paul Greco (Zealot), Steve Shill (Centurion), Verna Bloom (Mary, Mother of Jesus), Barbara Hershey (Mary Magdalene), Roberts Blossom (Aged Master), Barry Miller (Jeroboam), Gary Basaraba (Andrew, Apostle), Irvin Kershner (Zebedee), Victor Argo (Peter, Apostle), Michael Been (John, Apostle), Paul Herman (Phillip, Apostle), John Lurie (James, Apostle), Leo Burmester (Nathaniel, Apostle), Andre Gregory (John the Baptist), Peggy Gormley (Martha, Sister of Lazarus), Randy Danson (Mary, Sister of Lazarus), Robert Spafford (Man at Wedding), Doris von Thury (Woman with Mary, Mother of Jesus), Tomas Arana (Lazarus/Voices in Crowd), Alan Rosenberg (Thomas, Apostle), Del Russel (Money Changer), Nehemiah Persoff (Rabbi), Donald Hodson (Saducee), Harry Dean Stanton (Saul/Paul), Peter Berling (Beggar), David Bowie (Pontius Pilate), Juliette Caton (Girl Angel)

SUMMARY

The Last Temptation of Christ, based on the 1948 novel of the same name by the Greek writer Nikos Kazantzakis, seeks to display both the divine and the human sides to Christ. The novel was roundly criticized in Greece; the Greek Orthodox Church excommunicated the author and later denied him a Christian burial rite. The English translation of the novel resulted in a spate of negative reviews in the United States, and libraries in the 1960s faced demands from religious groups to remove the book.

Those involved with plans for making a movie of the novel expected an even greater outcry should the film ever reach theaters, and their expectations came to fruition. Martin Scorsese used the working title *Passion* in the early stages of making the film, which provides a clue to his representation of the story. The Christ of this film is very much a man, not a one-dimensional paragon. The film shows that even Jesus might have had difficulty in meeting the requirements for salvation and that he might have been tempted by worldly concerns. Once he has accepted his destiny to die a martyr and has refused to yield to the "last temptation" of living life as an ordinary family man, Scorsese's (and Kazantzakis's) Christ becomes isolated from human life. He expresses convictions through physical pain and intense language in ways that differ little from other Scorsese characters whose lives are marked by suffering and confusion.

In the film, Christ is employed as a cross-maker, collaborating with the Romans in their persecution of the rebellious Israelites. His reason for this, he says, is to make God hate him: "God loves me and I can't stand the pain." He goes as far in his efforts to alienate his Father as to hold the feet of the rebels as they are crucified and their blood spurts into his face. Scorsese succeeds in conveying Christ's pain, but at the same time he alienates us from his hero. The Savior here is a troubled man, fighting with a duality he does not quite understand. This Christ is wracked with doubt over his destiny. He can't be certain if the voices he hears are those of God or the Devil. Hating his own weakness and cowardice and susceptibility to temptation, Jesus excoriates his flesh, wearing a nail-studded belt around his waist. Christ contends that fear, not holiness, controls him: He would rebel against God and give in to temptation if he weren't such a coward. His transformation comes in the desert, where he purifies himself, becoming first the God of Love, then the God of the Sword, waging war on the Devil in all his worldly guises.

Christ's enemy, however, is as much the Jewish hierarchy and the strictures of Jewish law as it is the Romans. When he arrives in Jerusalem to pray, he is offended by the money-changers in the temple and in a fit of rage disrupts their operations, overturning their scales and tossing their money into the air. The film's most controversial scenes are in the final segment: In a dream or in delirium, Christ, with the guidance of a guardian angel, seems to have been taken down from the Cross and relieved of His suffering. In this long passage, Christ's last temptation is acted out. Still wearing the crown of thorns and covered with blood, he is told that he is not the Messiah and that the future awaiting him is one of happy domesticity. Out of a green valley, Mary Magdalene approaches him, dressed in white for their wedding, and afterward they make love in a discreetly filmed scene. Then the vision ends and Christ rejects the temptation and resigns himself to his fate.

CENSORSHIP HISTORY

The film was delayed for 10 years as Scorsese searched for a studio willing to risk the wrath of Christian fundamentalist groups who had used intimidating tactics against studio officials. Plans for the film were announced in 1983, but Paramount Pictures canceled production plans after receiving a deluge of letters from right-wing Christian fundamentalists "expressing outrage that an artist would be 'allowed' to make such a film." The studio secretly distributed copies of the script to religious leaders, but members of the Moral Majority and the Evangelical Sisterhood, as well as other fundamentalist groups, sent out a newsletter organizing a major protest against Gulf and Western, the parent company of Paramount Pictures. Five hundred protesters arrived each day for a month at Gulf and Western offices, which led Barry Diller, the company chairman of the board of directors, to drop the film project. Scorsese reported to biographers that Diller confronted him and stated, "I don't feel enthusiastic enough to undergo all the problems I would have to undergo." The protests were based, in part, on false reports, one asserting that Scorsese planned to portray Jesus Christ as a homosexual and others predicting scenes of graphic sex. Paramount reportedly decided against the project in fear that vehement protesters would disrupt filming and hinder exhibitions of the film. Other Hollywood studios, also fearing retaliation from religious extremists, refused to touch the project. Scorsese planned to turn to European backers, but his schedule made him postpone plans for several years.

When Universal Studios decided to take a chance on a changed climate back the film in 1987, they hired Tim Penland, a Christian marketing consultant, to help them make appropriate overtures to the concerned religious groups, but Penland quit after the studio refused to listen to his objections and he later joined in the protest against the film. The Reverend Donald Wildmon, leader of the Mississippi-based American Family Association, demanded that Universal cancel plans to release the film and told United Press International reporters that the film "is absolutely the most perverted, distorted account of the historical and Biblical Jesus I have ever read."

Wildmon's organization mailed out 2.5 million action packets to 170,000 ministers and obtained secured agreements from all the theaters in San Antonio, Texas, not to show the movie. Other religious groups placed full-page advertisements encouraging its destruction. In an interview with the *Los Angeles Times*, religious leaders representing Campus Crusade for Christ, Church of the Way and Hollywood Presbyterian Church claimed that the film "portray[ed] Jesus Christ as a mentally deranged and lust-driven man" and "represent[ed] a frightening example of a major film studio's setting aside public responsibility for financial gain." On July 15, 1988, Bill Bright, the president and founder of the Campus Crusade for Christ, contacted Universal and offered to reimburse the studio for all costs to date related to the filming in return for receiving all prints of the film, which he promised to destroy. On July 16, 1988, 200 members of the Fundamentalist-Baptist Tabernacle in Los Angeles picketed outside the studios and then four days later picketed outside the home of Lew Wasserman, MCA chair. They carried banners and signs with such phrases as "Universal is like Judas Iscariot" and "Wasserman Fans Anti-Semitism" and chanted, "Jewish Money, Jewish Money."

Additional protests followed and editorials both in favor and against the film appeared in numerous magazines and newspapers. In his July 24, 1988, column, Roger Ebert asked, "Why is it that censors seem to attack the serious works of art, and ignore the trivial ones?" Although the film was not due to be released until September 23, 1988, Christian radio broadcasters such as Pat Robertson, Mother Angelica, Pat Buchanan and Paul Crouch urged their approximately 11 million listeners to boycott MCA products and to protest the film. The Christian fundamentalist groups became increasingly aggressive in their demand that Universal cancel the film. An article published in *Variety* (July 27, 1988) quoted the Reverend Wildmon, after he was told that Universal planned to go ahead with the planned release date, borrowing a line from the film *Dirty Harry:* "Go ahead . . . make my day." The Reverend Jerry Falwell declared war on Universal Pictures and addressed the National Press Club about the film, calling it "pure blasphemy and morally reprehensible." Two days before the film's release, the United States Catholic Church joined the opposition and rated the film "O" ("morally offensive") and advised the nation's 53 million Catholics that the film distorted Christian values. On August 11, 1988, the day before the release of the film, an ad hoc coalition of religious groups staged a massive protest at Universal Studios. Twenty-five thousand people of different religions, carrying Bibles, crosses and placards, chanted in protest while leaders declared, "We're unleashing a movement. . . . Christian-bashing is over."

When Universal decided to move up the release of the film by six weeks to August 12, 1988, the protests increased in intensity, and theater owners became nervous. James Edwards, Jr., owner of the 150 Edwards Theaters nationwide, warned Universal that unless "certain changes" were made he would not exhibit the film in his theaters. The head of the United Artists chain of 2,000 theaters and the General Cinema Corporation chain of 1,339 theaters announced that they would not show the film under any circumstances.

Protesters appeared at every theater in the nine cities in which Universal premiered the film: Los Angeles, New York, San Francisco, Washington, D.C., Chicago, Seattle, Minneapolis, Montreal and Toronto. Theaters hired extra security in anticipation of the protests. In Los Angeles, a protester sprayed yellow paint on a poster and one of the theater windows before a showing, and 400 demonstrators handed out biblical tracts. Hundreds of protesters also appeared at major theaters in each of the other cities.

The release of the film resulted in major controversy throughout the United States. Marjorie Heins characterizes the reaction as "probably the most virulent outbreak of religious hatred, deteriorating at times to violence, that America had seen in recent times." The majority of the protesters objected to scenes that they had heard were included in a film they had not even seen; many fundamentalist movement leaders supported the protests, however uninformed, because they lent strength to a structure that had been damaged by recent revelations of wrongdoing: "With the embarrassing public exposure and subsequent convictions of televangelists Jimmy Swaggart and Jim Bakker, conservative religious groups came to see their campaign against *Last Temptation*, for example, as not just a protest against cinematic transgression but a struggle for the survival of their coalition and for its members' 'Vision' for America."

When Universal Studios opened *The Last Temptation of Christ* in 35 more cities, the protest continued but in decreased numbers. In New Orleans, Louisiana, and Santa Ana, California, city councils voted to ban the film from exhibition. In New Orleans, the ban was enforced by a police jury in two districts, but the theater in Santa Ana ignored the ban and continued to show the film. In Montgomery, Alabama, the insurance carrier for the Capri Theatre threatened to cancel coverage if the film were shown. Alabama's Governor Guy Hunt supported a ban, as did the city council, mayor and publisher of the local newspaper, but citizens clamored for the film and prevailed so the film was exhibited. A more successful ban occurred in Oklahoma City, where Oklahoma State University regents canceled plans to show the film after determining that it could cause "extensive damage to the public interest of the University" and would "highly offend a major segment of the Oklahoma citizenry." In Salt Lake City on August 27, 1988, thieves stole a print due to be shown at the Cineplex Odeon Center Theater and the theater screen was slashed, while in Los Angeles vandals slashed seats and spray-painted threats against Lew Wasserman and promised to "decimate all Universal property. This message is for your insurance company."

FURTHER READING

Braun, Jess. "Hundreds at Mall Protest Screening of 'Temptation.'" *Los Angeles Times*, August 20, 1988, sec. 2.

Broeske, Pat A. "Universal Asked to 'Destroy' Scorsese's Film about Christ." *Los Angeles Times*, July 13, 1988, sec. 6.

Dart, John. "Church Declares 'Last Temptation' Morally Offensive." *Los Angeles Times*, August 10, 1988, sec. 2.

Dawes, Amy. "Offer to Buy Pic: Christians Protest U's *Christ*." *Variety*, July 18, 1988, pp. 1–6.

———. "Protest Continues: Wasserman Picketed Over *Temptation*." *Variety*, July 21, 1988, pp. 6–15.

———. "'Tempt' Protests Continue: Vandals Damage Hollywood House." *Variety*, September 7, 1988, p. 1.

Ebert, Roger. "Censors Should Resist 'Temptation.'" *New York Post*, July 22, 1988, sec. D.

———. "*Last Temptation* Censorship Lacks Divine Inspiration." *Chicago Sun-Times*, July 24, 1988.

Galbraith, Jane, and Richard Gold. "Scorsese Defends *Temptation* on TV." *Variety*, July 27, 1988, pp. 3–19.

Harmetz, Aljean. "Film on Christ Brings out Pickets, and Archbishop Predicts Censure." *New York Times*, July 21, 1988, p. C19.

———. "*The Last Temptation of Christ* Opens to Protests but Good Sales." *New York Times*, August 13, 1988.

———. "Scorsese *Temptation* Gets Early Release." *New York Times*, August 5, 1988.

———. "7,500 Picket Universal Over Movie About Jesus." *New York Times*, August 12, 1988, p. C4.

Heins, Marjorie. *Sex, Sin, and Blasphemy: A Guide to America's Censorship Wars*. New York: New Press, 1993.

Kelly, Mary Pat. *Martin Scorsese: A Journey*. New York: Thunder's Mouth, 1991.

Killackey, Jim, and Michael McNutt. "Regents Block Controversial Film at OSU." *Oklahoman & Times*, September 23, 1988.

London, Michael. "Film Clips: Paramount Decides to Resist *Temptation*." *Los Angeles Times Calendar*, January 6, 1984, pp. 1–10.

Lyons, Charles. *The New Censors: Movies and the Culture Wars*. Philadelphia: Temple University Press, 1997.

Mast, Gerald, and Bruce F. Kawin. *A Short History of the Movies*, 7th ed. Boston: Allyn & Bacon, 1996.

Miller, Frank J. *Censored Hollywood: Sex, Sin, & Violence on the Screen*. Atlanta: Turner Publishing, 1994.

"Minister Blasts Universal Movie as 'Perverted.'" United Press International, July 12, 1988.

"MPAA Supports Universal's 'Temptation.'" *Variety*, July 27, 1988, p. 26.

Robbins, Tim. "*The Last Temptation* War Rages on: Exhibs Pressured, Italy Quakes." *Variety*, August 3, 1988, p. 6.

Russo, Vito. *The Celluloid Closet*. New York: HarperCollins, 1987.

Schwartz, Amy E. "A Personal View: The *Temptation* Resistance." *San Francisco Chronicle*, August 8, 1999, p. E1.

Theim, Rebecca, and Chris Cooper. "St. Bernard, Kenner Officials: Don't Be Tempted by Movie." *Times-Picayune*, August 18, 1988, p. 33.

LOLITA (1962)

Country and date of production: United States, 1962
Production company/distributor: Harris-Kubrick Productions, Seven Arts Productions, Transwood/MGM
Format: Sound, black and white
Running time: 152 minutes
Language: English
Producer: James B. Harris
Director: Stanley Kubrick
Screenwriters: Vladimir Nabokov (novel and screenplay), Stanley Kubrick
Awards: None
Genre: Drama
With: James Mason (Professor Humbert Humbert), Shelley Winters (Charlotte Haze), Sue Lyon (Dolores "Lolita" Haze/Mrs. Richard Schiller), Peter Sellers (Clare Quilty)

SUMMARY

Lolita, Stanley Kubrick's sixth film, is an adaptation of Vladimir Nabokov's celebrated yet controversial 1953 novel that relates the tragic story of a middle-aged male college professor's sexual obsession for a precocious, seductive prepubescent girl. In the novel, Dolores "Lolita" Haze is 12, but in the effort to deter censors, she is portrayed as 14 in the movie. Despite this change, production of the film occurred under the threat of censorship, and Kubrick feared that the Motion Picture Association of America (MPAA) would deny the film a Seal of Approval. The film was the first of Kubrick's films to be made independently in England, and it began with a long casting search for an actress who would be old enough to prevent outcry, yet look young enough to fit the character as conceived by Nabokov. He also interested Nabokov in writing the screenplay for his own lengthy novel.

In the film's opening scene, the camera slowly sweeps over satiny drapes, then reveals the bare left foot and leg of a young girl with the word "Lolita" seemingly written on the top of the foot. A man's left hand, wearing a wedding band, holds the foot while a right hand carefully paints the toenails with bright polish, stopping sporadically to slip cotton between the toes. From this scene, the film moves to depict the incidents described in the epilogue of the novel—the killing of another man who had carelessly seduced Lolita—then returns to the events four years earlier that led to the killing.

In the 10-minute prologue, viewers see a sordid confrontation between two pedophiles. One is Humbert Humbert, a well-educated and polished, if obsessive, lover who is constantly justifying his desires. The other is Clare Quilty, a well-known playwright whose dissipated life is evident in the appearance of his old, dusty yet enormous and luxurious mansion: Empty liquor bottles are strewn throughout the house, and various articles of furniture in the cluttered rooms are draped in dustcovers. After verbally grilling Quilty to make him remember the seduction of Lolita, the emotionally pained Humbert is hurt and outraged by Quilty's vapid, uncaring answer. He hands Quilty a piece of paper on which he has written a poem that describes his pain, referring to himself as "Adam-Naked . . . before a Federal Law and all its stinging stars" and making other allusions to his transgression with the young girl. The poem also alludes to Quilty's action with Lolita, a line that Quilty mocks, noting that the poem is "getting to be kind of smutty." Humbert asks if Quilty has any last words before he dies and, after a few more minutes in which Quilty puts on boxing gloves and spars with Humbert, plays the piano and then runs from the room, Humbert fires a gun several times and hears its empty click as Quilty runs. Humbert reloads, stalks Quilty up the stairs, and empties the six rounds of the gun into Quilty, who has taken cover behind a portrait propped up against the wall in the hallway—a Victorian, Gainsborough-style painting of an 18th-century young woman.

The film then fades into flashback, four years earlier, when Professor Humbert Humbert, who narrates the novel and the film, arrived in New England. The voiceover tells viewers that he plans to stay the summer in New Hampshire before moving west in the fall. Friends have given him the names of several homes in which he might rent a furnished room, and the first to which is goes is the Haze home, a house with a white picket fence in Ramsdale, owned by the matronly and pretentious widow Charlotte Haze. Charlotte announces clearly that she is lonely after seven years of being a widow, and she slips sexual innuendo, punctuated by a raucous laugh and a bawdy manner, into her tour of the house. When Humbert seems about to decide against renting the room, Charlotte shows him her garden, where her daughter, Dolores (Lolita), is sunning herself. All thoughts of leaving escape Humbert's mind as he views the young girl sunbathing on a blanket on the lawn. Smitten, he moves into the Haze home, romances and then marries Charlotte, although he despises her, and insinuates himself into the family. Humbert takes every opportunity to make physical contact with Lolita, whom he secretly calls his "nymphet," holding her against his groin, pressing against her as they pass, staying up late with her to watch television on the couch so that they can "accidentally" touch. While he makes no overt sexual moves toward her, he rhapsodizes nightly in his journal, detailing his obsession.

While Lolita is away at summer camp, Charlotte finds his journal, becomes hysterical and runs out of the house and into the street, where she is struck by a car and dies before she can reveal the secret. After making arrangements, Humbert drives to the camp to collect Lolita and to tell her of her mother's death. Humbert and Lolita then begin an odyssey across the United States. They travel as father and daughter. At one overnight stop at a motel named the Enchanted Hunters, Humbert tries to seduce Lolita, but she puts him off until the morning. When she proposes that they do what she and a boy at camp once did, Humbert laments in the voiceover, "I was not even her first lover." In the ensuing months, as the pair moves from town to town, stopping for a time long enough for Humbert to register Lolita at school, Lolita never again makes sexual overtures to him. When she appears to have become sexually involved with a boy at school, Humbert uproots her and they move on, while Quilty pursues them. The playwright had once seen Lolita when he presented a lecture to her mother's Great Books club, and he recognizes her when they meet again. Lolita becomes ill; Humbert places her in the hospital, then is shocked to learn the next morning that her "uncle" has signed her out. Three years pass, during which Humbert has a relationship with a woman named Rita, but he continues his obsession with Lolita. When he receives a letter from her, he is overjoyed, but when he goes to her home, he finds her married, pregnant, living in a hovel and in need of money. He asks her to leave with him, but when she refuses, but he gives her a check nonetheless. Afterward, he rushes to find and to kill Quilty, which the viewer has already seen in the prologue, and the film ends with Humbert in prison, finishing his account in a cell.

CENSORSHIP HISTORY

Publicity posters for the film included the tagline, "How did they ever make a film of *Lolita?*" and a picture of Lolita wearing heart-shaped sunglasses and licking a red lollipop. The opening credits to the film contain some of the most overtly erotic images of the entire film, and they set its tone: the fade-in on satiny drapery, a young girl's bare left foot and leg ceremoniously cradled in a man's hand and the slow, sensuous, caressing motion as he paints her toe-nails in a vibrant-colored polish.

Lolita originally received a "C" (Condemned) rating from the Catholic Legion of Decency (LOD). According to Monsignor Thomas F. Little, executive secretary of the LOD in the 1960s, after private negotiations between the producer and the LOD, the film underwent "'changes of a vital nature' in order to avoid a 'Condemned' rating." This practice was known in the industry, and many other films, including SPARTACUS, were the subject of the same type of negotiation. Monsignor Little revealed that the producers usually made the first move toward the LOD in order to avoid risking a box-office failure should a film receive a "C" rating, which would lead Catholics to boycott it.

The producer and the director also met with Geoff Shurlock, who succeeded Joseph Breen as the director of the Production Code Administration (PCA), and insisted that they would have Humbert and Lolita marry in Kentucky and "draw innocent humor from the conflict between a mature man and a gum-snapping adolescent." Shurlock warned them that "a twelve-year-old bride who looked twelve years old could block a Seal." After promising to make a film that would earn PCA approval, however, the filmmakers had to find a distributor for the film, and many studios were wary. Warner Bros., United Artists and Columbia Pictures refused to make a deal with Kubrick, fearing that the final result would not receive a PCA seal of approval and, therefore, could not be exhibited in mainstream theaters throughout the United States. When Seven Arts studios agreed to distribute the film, Kubrick and Harris went to work, and Shurlock began to worry how he would deal with the film in the increasingly liberal 1960s. "Kubrick agreed to revise scenes involving the murder of Clare Quilty, the seduction at the motel, and Lolita's age. He could not change the theme of pedophilia, however, nor could he change the growing liberal climate in this country.

The solution came when the PCA decided to make the "sexual perversion" clause of the production code, which dealt with such themes as homosexuality and pedophilia, less stringent. The film was rated "R" under the Motion Picture Association of America (MPAA) rating system, which meant that the film was restricted to persons over 18 unless accompanied by an adult. In 1962, the LOD reviewed the film and nine of 12 board members voted to condemn the film, but the vocal objections of the dissenters led the body to award *Lolita* a "Special Classification" with the demand that the LOD would have the right to approve all advertising for the film. In addition, the LOD required that all advertisements for the film would contain two captions: "This movie has been approved by the M. P. P. A. [sic]" and "For persons over 18 only." Eric Johnston, the president of the MPAA, reluctantly agreed with the demands but insisted that the statement indicate that the PCA, the censorship wing of the industry, should be specified instead of the trade wing to place the blame on the appropriate party. The resulting film did not suffer major challenges after release, because of the extensive censorship and resulting modifications that occurred before its release. Eight years after the film, Kubrick reflected upon what he should have done differently: "I would have stressed the erotic component of their relationship with the same weight Nabokov did. But that is the only major area where I believe the film is susceptible to valid criticism."

FURTHER READING

Appel, Alfred, Jr. "The End of the Road: Dark Cinema and *Lolita.*" *Film Comment* 10, no. 5 (1974): 25–31.

"Cinema: Humbert Humdrum and Lullita." *Time*, June 22, 1962, p. 94.

Gelmis, Joseph. *The Film Director as Superstar.* Garden City, N.Y.: Doubleday and Company, 1970.

Lawrenson, Helen. "The Man Who Scandalized the World." *Esquire*, August 1960, pp. 70–73.

Leff, Leonard J., and Jerold L. Simmons. *The Dame in the Kimono: Hollywood, Censorship, & the Production Code from the 1920s to the 1960s.* New York: Grove Weidenfeld, 1990.

Nabokov, Vladimir. *Lolita.* New York: G. P. Putnam, 1955.

Nabokov, Vladimir. *Lolita: A Screenplay.* New York: McGraw-Hill, 1975.

Schumach, Murray. *The Face on the Cutting Room Floor.* New York: William Morrow, 1964.

LOLITA (1997)

Country and date of production: United States and France, 1997
Production company/distributor: Chargeurs SA, Pathé/Samuel Goldwyn Company (United States)
Format: Sound, color
Running time: 137 minutes
Language: English
Producers: Mario Kassar, Joel B. Michaels
Director: Adrian Lyne
Screenwriters: Vladimir Nabokov (novel), Stephen Schiff
Awards: 1999 Young Artist Awards, Best Performance in a TV Movie/Pilot/Mini-Series or Series–Leading Young Actress (Dominique Swain).
Genre: Drama
With: Jeremy Irons (Humbert Humbert), Melanie Griffith (Charlotte Haze), Frank Langella (Clare Quilty), Dominique Swain (Dolores "Lolita" Haze)

SUMMARY

The version of *Lolita* that completed filming in April 1997 maintains the same plot as both the novel and the 1962 film version (see page 178), but differs from the earlier film in ways that are worthy of note. Instead of the sensual opening of Kubrick's version, the viewer is exposed to a sense of tragic doom: Humbert is first seen driving down a picturesque country road, with soft music playing in the background, when the car suddenly begins to weave, nearly hitting a hay wagon. The camera then pans to a gun in the car and to Humbert's face, which is splashed with blood. The rest of the film shows how Humbert has reached this point. This version of *Lolita* is less sexually explicit for its time than Kubrick's film was for 1962, although Lyne, like Kubrick, increased Lolita's age from 12 to 14. Lyne, however, set the film in the decade of Nabokov's novel, the 1940s, while Kubrick placed it in the late 1950s. Unlike Kubrick, Lyne made his movie a combination of love story, sex story and horror story about two people who simply do not get along. Even at her best, Lolita is only teasing Humbert or negotiating with him, trading sexual favors for more allowance money or an afternoon off to rehearse the school play. At her worst she takes on the persona of her late mother, screaming over and over at him, "Murder me like you murdered my mother!" In looks and tone, she becomes a miniature Charlotte Haze, with all the accumulated faults.

While Kubrick put some of the film's best material into the opening scenes, Lyne saves his best moments for two climactic scenes at the end. Although the blood on Humbert's face at the opening reveals his action, the viewer does not see the actual murder until the end of the film, when Humbert manages to eliminate his rival Quilty. After the murder, Humbert is distracted and drives off the road into a field, barely avoiding a cow that briefly blocks his path. The film, like the novel, concludes as Humbert hears the sound of children at play, which he identifies in the voiceover: "an almost articulate spurt of vivid laughter, or the crack of a bat, or the clatter of a toy wagon . . . and then I knew that the hopelessly poignant thing was not Lolita's absence from my side, but the absence of her voice from that concord." He confesses, at least to himself, that he, not Quilty, kidnapped Dolores "Lolita" Haze both from her childhood and from any chance at innocence.

CENSORSHIP HISTORY

The open censorship of films in past decades, through boycotts encouraged by the Catholic Legion of Decency, refusals by boards of censors to grant permits to exhibit or the decisions of the courts to apply local and state ordinances, were in some ways preferable to today's more subtle yet equally effective means of banning a film—when the studios themselves may refuse to distribute a film that seems likely to alienate members of the population and lose money at the box office. *Lolita* (1997) appeared in a more sophisticated time than either the book or the 1962 film, yet it aroused greater apprehension among studio executives and disdain among the viewing public than had the earlier version. During the 1990s, the United States had become fixated on the issues of child molestation and child pornography. By unhappy misfortune (for the film) Congress passed the Child Pornography Prevention Act of 1996, a law that forbade images that appear to be of children, even if they are not. Even using a body double, as in *Lolita*, would be prohibited if it contained simulated sexual conduct that appears to involve a minor. A second misfortune to strike the film, only four months before its completion, was the highly publicized murder of the six-year-old beauty pageant queen JonBenet Ramsey in Colorado at Christmas of 1996. The photographs of the sensuously clothed and made up child filled the print and film news media for months, and the case, still unsolved in 2000, kept outrage against the sexual exploitation of children prominent in the public consciousness. As John Blades wrote in an article for the *Chicago Tribune*, "they may have chosen the wrong moment for a graphic remake of a novel about pedophilia, even one as perversely funny and as sensuously written as *Lolita*."

The producer also realized, after the fact, that the moral climate in this nation had changed by the time the movie was completed. In a 1999 interview he said, "I wasn't really prepared for the sort of paranoia that surrounded the subject matter. I think the climate in America was different three years ago. Everybody now talks about violence, but at that time, because of the JonBenet Ramsey case, there was an obsession with pedophilia. So there was a certain amount of paranoia." The Motion Picture Association of America (MPAA) considered the film controversial, but rather than rating it "NC-17" (no one under the age of 17 admitted), the MPAA rated the film "R" (no one under 17 admitted without an adult) for "aberrant sexuality, a strong scene of violence, nudity and some language."

All precautions appear to have been taken to prevent the reactions that the final film faced. The project began in 1990 when Carolco Pictures bought the rights to the book and hired Lyne as director. Three screenwriters were engaged, including playwrights Harold Pinter and David Mamet, before Lyne turned to Stephen Schiff, a writer for the *New Yorker* magazine. After seeking to make the screenplay viable and filming with an eye toward censors, Lyne sat at an editing table for six weeks with a lawyer at his side, scrutinizing every frame of the work. The producers then tried to sell the film to distributors, but they received rejections from Time Warner Inc.'s Warner Bros., Sony Corp.'s Sony Pictures, Viacom Inc.'s Paramount Pictures, News Corp.'s Fox and Seagram Co.'s Universal. The excuses for declining to purchase distribution rights ranged from too high a price tag for a movie "with a rancorous tone and no top stars" to simple fear of the pedophile theme.

After movie studios in the United States refused to pick up distribution rights to the film, the producer was forced to exhibit it in Europe, where it received lukewarm reviews. The film was finally shown several times in the United States on the Showtime cable television network, premiering on August 2, 1998, after which Samuel Goldwyn Films planned to distribute the movie to theaters nationwide. *Lolita* played mainly in art movie houses where the patrons knew and approved of its controversial nature. During the week before its television debut, starting on July 26, 1998, *Lolita* was also screened theatrically in Los Angeles to make it eligible for the Academy Awards. When the film finally was released in the United States, the few critics who wrote about the theater showings generally called it inferior in quality to the earlier effort and less true to the novel, although movie critics for the *New York Times* expressed approval of Lyne's adaptation and wrote that "the film's mostly unalloyed subtlety (except in its opening and closing sections) rewards a closer view. Mr. Lyne's direction is the best work of his career." Another critic for the *New York Times* viewed the story as filmed by Lyne to be "a morality tale with a tragic vision." The release to theaters in September 1998 did not result in large box-office earnings because the film played mainly in art houses, and it earned only $1.06 million during the first four months and little more since. When the film was first released for sale on videotape early in 1999, it was available only in Blockbuster Video stores, and other stores did not decide to stock it until October of that year.

FURTHER READING

Bertin, Joan. "Pornography Law Goes Too Far: 1st Amendment: The Broad Ban on Images That Only Appear to Involve Children Won't Stop Sexual Abuse and Exploitation." *Los Angeles Times*, October 17, 1997, p. B9.

Blades, John. "The Trouble with Lolita: A New $40 Million Movie Version of Nabokov's Has Been Shunned by Distributors. The Filmmakers Apparently Picked the Wrong Time for a Film about Pedophilia." *Chicago Tribune*, April 13, 1997, p. 7.

Bordo, Susan. "True Obsessions: Being Unfaithful to *Lolita*." *The Chronicle of Higher Education*, July 24, 1998, pp. B7–B8.

Campbell, Bob. "In the Shadow of the Censor's Knife." *The Sunday Star-Ledger*, August 2, 1997, sec. 4–11.

Corliss, Richard. "Lolita: From Lyon to Lyne." *Film Comment* 34 (September–October 1998): 34–39.

Healy, Michelle. "Screening *Lolita*." *USA Today*, July 9, 1998, sec. D-1.

Holden, Stephen. "Movie Guide—*Lolita*." *New York Times*, October 9, 1998, subsec. 1–16.

James, Caryn. "TELEVISION REVIEW: *Lolita*: Revisiting a Dangerous Obsession." *New York Times*, July 31, 1998.

King, Susan. "Two Years After Fuss, Lyne's *Lolita* Goes on Sale." *Los Angeles Times*, October 14, 1999, p. 52.

Leonard, John. "The New Puritanism." *The Nation*, November 24, 1997, pp. 11–15.

Lippman, John. "Remake of *Lolita* Is Rebuffed by Distributors." *Wall Street Journal*, April 30, 1997, pp. B1–B3.

Murray, Steve. "Movies—A Conversation with . . . Adrian Lyne 'It's been an iffy sort of ride.'" *Atlanta Journal/The Atlanta Constitution*, October 9, 1998, p. 8.

Ringel, Eleanor. "Movies Latest *Lolita* Short on Steam." *Atlanta Journal/Atlanta Constitution*, October 9, 1998, p. 8.

Schaefer, Stephen. "Irons' *Lolita* Still on Hold in USA." *USA Today*, September 18, 1997, p. D2.

Seitz, Matt Zoller. "Sex, Death and Storytelling: A New Look at Lolita." *Sunday Star-Ledger*, August 2, 1998, sec. 4–1, 10.
Wakin, Daniel J. "Lolita Strictly Foreign Fare." *Record*, September 28, 1997.
Weiner, Rex. "Lolita Gets Old Waiting for Date." *Variety*, June 2–8, 1997, pp. 1, 8.
Wilimington, Michel. "New *Lolita* Doesn't Stand Up to Original Film, Book." *Chicago Tribune* (North Sports Edition), November 13, 1998, Friday section, p. K.

LORNA

Country and date of production: United States, 1964
Production company/distributor: Eve Productions
Format: Sound, color
Running time: 78 minutes
Language: English
Producer: Russ Meyer
Director: Russ Meyer
Screenwriters: James Griffith, Russ Meyer (story)
Awards: None
Genre: Drama
With: Lorna Maitland (Lorna), Mark Bradley (The Convict), James Rucker (Jim), Hal Hopper (Luther), Doc Scortt (Jonah), Althea Currier (Ruthie), F. Rufus Owens (Ezra), Frank Bolger (Silas), Ken Parker (The Fisherman), James Griffith (The Man of God)

SUMMARY

Filmed by Russ Meyer, called the "King of the Nudies" for such films as *Vixen* (1968) and *Ultravixens* (1979) as well as for the decreasing the amount of clothing worn by his leading ladies in each successive film, *Lorna* was Meyer's first serious attempt to create a film with a discernible plot. It also marks the first time that he made violence a significant part of a film. He also injects moralizing into film in the form of a mysterious stranger, who appears twice: at the beginning of the film, to warn that everyone must deal with the results of their actions, and at the end, to remind viewers that people must pay for their sins.

Lorna is a housewife who is bored by both her life and her marriage to her muscular but dull husband. On their anniversary, while he goes to work at his job in the salt mines, Lorna goes for a nude swim in the bayou, showing off her improbably full bosom. When she leaves the water, an escaped convict is waiting and rapes her. She resists for a time but then invites the man back to her shack for more sexual activity. When her husband arrives home after receiving a half-day off from work for his anniversary, he is in a bad mood over a fight with a coworker who made leering remarks that Jim is not man enough for Lorna. When Jim arrives home and discovers his wife with the convict, he starts another fight and kills the lovers. The bearded hellfire-and-brimstone stranger turns up to rail about their immoral lives and eternal damnation.

CENSORSHIP HISTORY

Lorna appeared after the United States Supreme Court removed most of the restrictions on the making and showing of films through such decisions as *Burstyn v. Wilson*, 343 U.S. 495 (see THE MIRACLE). The "sexploitation" epics of the 1960s that took advantage of this decision led the way for the hard-core pornography that would be openly exhibited in many neighborhood theaters in the 1970s. *Lorna* was one of several movies by producer-director Russ Meyer, each "a step closer to the ultimate pornographic feature film, but he stopped short of actual sexual intercourse on the screen."

In 1964, the Maryland board of censors voted to deny the distributor of *Lorna* a permit for exhibition in the state on the grounds that the film was obscene. Attorneys for the distributor appealed that decision before the Circuit Court of Baltimore, arguing that the censorship board had denied the permit to exhibit without proving that the film was obscene, as was required. The circuit court affirmed the decision of the board. When the case went before the Maryland Court of Appeals, the court ruled that the board had failed to fulfill its constitutional obligation to prove that *Lorna* was obscene and, thus, could not legally refuse a permit to the film. In its decision, the court wrote that the film was "tiresome, boring, cheap, often vulgar, and sometimes revolting," but members of the court did "not feel qualified to say by virtue of a viewing of the picture only [that] the dominant theme of *Lorna* was an appeal to prurient interest, or that the picture exceeded customary limits of candor in its representations of sex or the sexual mores of the community pictured or that it was utterly without redeeming social importance or literary artistic value." As a result, the appellate court ruled on October 1, 1965, to reverse the order of the lower court and to permit the distributor to exhibit *Lorna* in the state of Maryland.

FURTHER READING

Grove, Martin A., and William S. Ruben. *The Celluloid Love Feast.* New York: Lancer Books, 1971.

Jowett, Garth. *Film, the Democratic Art: A Social History of Film.* Boston: Little, Brown, 1976.

"*Lorna*—Film & TV: Scanlines." *Austin Chronicle*, December 7, 1998.

Rotsler, William. *Contemporary Erotic Cinema.* New York: Random House, 1973.

Turan, Kenneth, and Stephen F. Zito. *Sinema.* New York: Praeger Publishers, 1974.

THE LOVERS

Country and date of production: France, 1958 (as *Les Amants*)
Production company/distributor: Nouvelles Éditions de Films (France)/ Zenith International (United States, 1959)
Format: Sound, black and white
Running time: 90 minutes

Language: French
Producer: Irénée Leriche
Director: Louis Malle
Screenwriters: Louis Malle, Louise de Vilmorin, Dominique Vivant (novel, *Point de Lendemain*)
Awards: 1958 Venice Film Festival, Special Jury Prize (Louis Malle).
Genre: Drama
With: Jeanne Moreau (Jeanne Tournier), Jean-Marc Bory (Bernard Dubois-Lambert), Judith Magre (Maggy Thiebaut-Leroy), José Luis de Villalonga (Raoul Flores, as Jose Villalonga), Gaston Modot (Coudray), Alain Cluny (Henri Tournier)

SUMMARY

The film is based on the 19th-century novel *Point de Lendemain*, written by Dominique Vivant, but the film sets the story in the 20th century. Thirty-year-old Jeanne Tournier, the bored wife of a wealthy publisher, feels trapped and restless living in the province of Lyon, and she is unhappy in her marriage to Henri Tournier, a busy man who ignores her. On the advice of her friend Maggy, she begins an affair in Paris with Raoul Flores, a cultured and attractive Argentine playboy whose shallow nature soon bores Jeanne. Before the affair ends, Tournier becomes suspicious and invites Maggy and Flores to spend the weekend in Lyon. While Jeanne drives back to the province from Paris, her car stalls. Bernard Dubois-Lambert, a handsome young archaeologist with radical social ideas, rescues her and drives her home. He is contemptuous of the Tourniers' lifestyle and society, and dinner is uncomfortable, but he is invited to spend the night at the estate. Neither Jeanne nor Dubois-Lambert can sleep, and they meet by accident as Jeanne is taking a walk around the estate in the moonlight. The two make love in a slowly drifting boat, in Jeanne's bed and in a bathtub, while everyone else on the estate remains asleep. When morning arrives, Jeanne can no longer face her former existence and does not want to give up her new love. The film ends as Jeanne and Dubois-Lambert leave the estate together: Jeanne abandons her friends, her home and her family for the uncertainty of life with the younger man. In tears, Jeanne insists passionately, "I will never regret it," but the way in which Dubois-Lambert looks at Jean and the way in which the two interact suggest that the relationship might not last long.

CENSORSHIP HISTORY

The Lovers is intensely sensual, but the primary objection to the film was not its romanticized view of adultery. Instead, boards of censors in the states of New York, Virginia and Maryland, and the cities of Memphis, Tennessee; Portland, Oregon; Providence, Rhode Island; Boston, Massachusetts; and Chicago, Illinois, objected to the prolonged love scene in the last 20 minutes of the film. Although nudity is kept to a minimum, the married, 30-year-old mother and the obviously younger archaeologist participate in what Miller labels "an exercise in eroticism" that was quite controversial in its day. In Virginia and Maryland, state censorship boards presented theater owners with lists of deletions that would have to be made before the film could receive a permit for exhibition; rather than make the excisions, theaters canceled their contracts to show the film. In New York, the distributor had to remove approximately 30 seconds of action in the final 20 minutes of the film to receive an exhibition license. In Memphis, Boston and Providence, shortened versions of the film were shown without several minutes of the final, intense lovemaking.

The most influential ruling occurred in *Jacobellis v. Ohio*, but before this decision by the United States Supreme Court, attempts to show the film also resulted in court trials in Chicago and in Cuyahoga County and Dayton, Ohio. In Chicago, after the city board of censors refused to grant the distributor a license to exhibit the film, Zenith International Corporation brought suit in the Illinois Circuit Court of Appeals, which reversed the decision of the board of censors in *Zenith International Film Corp. v. Chicago*, 291 F. 2d 785 (1961). In Dayton, a theater manager was convicted in a jury trial of having possession of an obscene film. The manager appealed his conviction before the Supreme Court of Ohio, which reversed the conviction in *State v. Warth*, 179 N.W. 2d 772, 173 Ohio St. 15 (1962), and declared unconstitutional the statute that made it a crime for a person to possess an obscene film, without any evidence of his knowledge of the film's character. In 1959, another theater manager in Cuyahoga County was convicted in the criminal division of the Cuyahoga County Court of Common Pleas on a charge of exhibiting an obscene film, after showing the previously contracted-for and scheduled film *The Lovers*. The case of *State v. Gevaras*, 165 N.E. 2d 6522, was appealed before the Supreme Court of Ohio, which affirmed the decision of the lower court on the ground that the case did not involve a "debatable constitutional issue."

The case of *Jacobellis v. Ohio*, 378 U.S. 184 (1964), however, would change such rulings forever. In 1959, Nico Jacobellis, the manager of an art theater in Cleveland Heights, Ohio, was arrested on charges of possessing and exhibiting an obscene film. When the case went to trial in the Cuyahoga Court of Common Pleas, the state's objections were based wholly on the explicit love scene near the end of the film. Jacobellis was fined $500 on the first count and $2,000 on the second count and threatened with a sentence in the workhouse if he did not pay the fines. The case was appealed before an intermediate appellate court, which upheld the conviction in *State v. Jacobellis*, 175 N.E. 2d 123, 115 Ohio App. 226 (1961). This decision also was affirmed by the Supreme Court of Ohio in *State v. Jacobellis*, 173 Ohio St. 22, 179 N.E. 2d 777. The case was then argued before the United States Supreme Court, which decided on June 22, 1964, in *Jacobellis v. Ohio*, 378 U.S. 184, that the film *The Lovers* "was not obscene within the standards set in *Roth v. United*

States and *Alberts v. California*," cases that stated that a book that has socially redeeming value is not obscene. This decided, the film was thus "entitled to the protection for free expression that is guaranteed by the First and Fourteenth Amendments," and the conviction of Nico Jacobellis was reversed. The case has had lasting impact because such rulings would never again be a debatable issue.

FURTHER READING

Anderson, Robert L. "Free Speech and Obscenity; A Search for Constitutional Procedures and Standards." *UCLA Law Review* 12 (January 1965): 532–560.
Jacobellis v. Ohio, 378 U.S. 184 (1964).
Miller, Frank. *Censored Hollywood: Sex, Sin & Violence on Screen.* Atlanta, Ga.: Turner Publishing, 1994.
O'Meara, Joseph, and Thomas L. Shaffer. "Obscenity and the Supreme Court: A Note on Jacobellis v. Ohio." *Notre Dame Lawyer* 40 (December 1964): 1–12.
Pilpel, Harriet F. "Firm Restrictions Placed on Pre-Publication Censorship." *Publishers Weekly* 180 (September 25, 1961): 30–31.
State v. Gevaras, 165 N.E. 2d 6522, 170 Ohio St. 404 (1962).
State v. Jacobellis, 175 N.E. 2d 123, 115 Ohio App. 226 (1961).
State v. Jacobellis, 173 Ohio St. 22, 179 N.E. 2d 777.
State v. Warth, 179 N.W. 2d 772, 173 Ohio St. 15 (1962).
"Supreme Court Decision Limits Censorship." *Publishers Weekly* 186 (July 6, 1964): 48–49.
Zenith International Film Corp. v. Chicago, 291 F. 2d 785 (1961).

M

Country and date of production: United States, 1951
Production company/distributor: Superior Film/Columbia Pictures Corporation
Format: Sound, black and white
Running time: 88 minutes
Language: English
Producer: Seymour Nebenzal
Director: Joseph Losey
Screenwriters: Leo Katcher, Norman Reilly Raine, Waldo Salt
Awards: None
Genre: Film noir
With: David Wayne (Martin Harrow), Howard Da Silva (Carney), Luther Adler (Langley), Martin Gabel (Marshall), Steve Brodie (Lt. Becker), Raymond Burr (Pottsy), Glenn Anders (Riggert), Karen Morley (Mrs. Coster), Norman Lloyd (Sutro), John Miljan (Blind Vendor)

SUMMARY

The 1951 version of *M* is an Americanized remake of the 1931 German thriller of the same title, which was also produced by Seymour Nebenzal but directed by Fritz Lang. The plot remains the same in both versions, but the critical reception was vastly more favorable to the earlier version. Based on true incidents involving the pedophile and psychopathic killer Peter Kurten, whom the newspapers of the time labeled the "Vampire of Düsseldorf," the plot relates the search by police for this tortured murderer, who claimed that he had no control over the evil within him and who blamed his actions on voices that commanded him to kill. In the film, the child murderer Martin Harrow has killed several little girls, whose shoes he steals after the crime. He eludes the police so effectively that they place extra law-enforcement officers on the case and canvass the entire city continuously in a desperate effort to prevent further murders. The heightened police presence has a paralyzing effect on other members of the criminal community, who decide to curtail their activities until the child killer is caught. The criminal underworld also views the killer's crimes as particularly heinous, so they join the police to stalk him. The only person to have a clue to the killer's identity is a blind beggar, who has heard whistling at times appropriate to the crime. When the blind beggar, who has joined other of the city beggars in the hunt, is once more in the killer's presence and recognizes the whistling sound, he uses chalk to mark the letter "M" on the coat of the whistler, which leads the criminal pursuers to find Harrow before the police do. The killer is trapped in the end by both the underworld and the police and faces their combined justice.

CENSORSHIP HISTORY

Distributors submitted the film to the Division of Film Censorship of the Ohio State Department of Education with a request for review and approval as required by the state statute, which had been declared constitutional four decades before in *Mutual Film Corporation v. Industrial Commission of Ohio*, 236 U.S. 230 (1915). With the statute as its authority, the board rejected the film on grounds that it would have "an adverse effect on unstable persons of any age because it could lead to the commission of immoral and criminal acts by such people." The board members further decided that the film presented both the actions and the emotions of the psychopathic killer as well as his "complete perversion," and it does so "without serving any valid educational purpose." Instead, the board determined, such an approach "creates sympathy rather than a constructive plan for dealing with perversion." Superior Pictures took the case before the Ohio Supreme Court, which affirmed by a vote of five to two the decision by the censorship board. In the majority opinion for the case, Justice Hart wrote:

> In these times of alarming rise in juvenile delinquency . . . attributed by social agencies, at least in part, to the character of the exhibitions put on in the show

houses of the country, criminal prosecution after the fact is a weak and ineffective remedy to meet the problem at hand.

The decision also decried the film's "portrayal of evil conduct" and concluded that a motion picture of this sort would appeal to "the great majority of a promiscuous audience, including children" who would be drawn to this evil. The court further determined that the criteria for licensing films in Ohio, as set forth in the statute, required that the film be of a "moral, educational, or amusing or harmless character," which *M* was not, so the board was within its authority to ban the film.

The distributor took the case before the U.S. Supreme Court, which reversed the decision in *Superior Film v. Department of Education of State of Ohio*, 346 U.S. 587 (1954). Citing *Burstyn v. Wilson*, 343 U.S. 495 (1952), in which the Supreme Court declared that the film THE MIRACLE fell under the protection of the First and the Fourteenth Amendments, the Court ruled that the exhibition of a movie may not be prevented because it is "immoral," inasmuch as this term, like some others (not including *obscene*), is too vague and uncertain a standard for censorship. The Court wrote that the state "cannot vest such unlimited restraining control over motion pictures in a censor."

FURTHER READING

Burstyn v. Wilson, 343 U.S. 495 (1952).

Carmen, Ira C. *Movies, Censorship, and the Law.* Ann Arbor: University of Michigan Press, 1966.

Leggett, Robert D. "Motion Picture Censorship." *University of Cincinnati Law Review* 23 (Spring 1954): 259–263.

"Motion Picture Censorship—A Constitutional Dilemma." *Maryland Law Review* 12 (Summer 1954): 284–298.

O'Neill, James M. "Catholics and Censorship," in *Catholics in Controversy*, ed. James M. O'Neill. New York: McMullen Publishing, 1954.

Sabsay, David. "The Challenge of the 'Fisk Report.'" *California Libraries* 20 (October 1959): 222–223.

Superior Films v. Department of Education of State of Ohio, 112 N.E. 2d 311, 159 Ohio St. 315 (1953).

Superior Film v. Department of Education of State of Ohio, 346 U.S. 587 (1954).

THE MAN WITH THE GOLDEN ARM

Country and date of production: United States, 1955
Production company/distributor: Carlyle Productions/United Artists
Format: Sound, black and white
Running time: 119 minutes
Language: English
Producer: Otto Preminger

Director: Otto Preminger
Screenwriters: Nelson Algren (novel), Walter Newman, Lewis Meltzer
Awards: None
Genre: Drama
With: Frank Sinatra (Frankie Machine), Eleanor Parker (Zosh Machine), Kim Novak (Molly), Arnold Stang (Sparrow), Darren McGavin (Louie), Robert Strauss (Schwiefka), John Conte (Drunky), Doro Merande (Vi), George E. Stone (Sam Markette), George Mathews (Williams), Leonid Kinskey (Dominiwski), Emile Meyer (Bednar)

SUMMARY

The film, based on Nelson Algren's novel of the same name, presents a stark and unglamorous look at the world of the heroin addict Frankie Machine, a man who refers to his addiction as "a 35-pound monkey on my back." Machine has for years been a respected professional card dealer in illegal poker games in the Chicago slums. After spending time in prison, where he has supposedly become cured of his drug habit, he returns to his Chicago neighborhood to make a fresh start. He expects to rebuild his life by becoming a professional drummer, but the old life draws him back. Old acquaintances pull him back into dealing cards again, and a former heroin connection lures him back to the drug. His wife has for years pretended to be paralyzed to keep him from leaving her, and he turns to an attractive young woman named Molly for comfort and strength. By locking him in her room, Molly forces Machine to go "cold turkey" and to kick the habit, after which he learns that he has been accused of a murder of which he is innocent. In an unguarded moment, his wife shows that she can walk quite well; once exposed as a fraud, she runs out of the apartment and falls to her death, knowing that she no longer has any hold on him. With the help of Molly, Machine also clears himself of the murder charges. The film ends with the expectation that he and Molly will build a happy life together.

CENSORSHIP HISTORY

The Man with the Golden Arm courted rejection by the Production Code Administration (PCA) from the outset because the code clearly forbade any film to deal with drug addiction, yet director/producer Otto Preminger felt that this was a film that had to be made whether or not it would earn a seal of approval. The Catholic Legion of Decency granted the film a "B" ("not suitable for all audiences") rating, and the film was critically and financially successful despite the lack of PCA approval. More important, Preminger's decision to release the film without the seal of approval signaled a new attitude on the part of some filmmakers who were willing to take this risk, even if it would reduce the number of theaters that would exhibit the film. The decision drove United Artists to withdraw its membership from the PCA because of its objection to the film, and both Preminger and UA fought to change the code so that other films could deal with the issues of narcotics addiction. In their fight, they pointed out that this restriction on movies had outlived its usefulness and acted as an obstacle to making films on a subject that had become an important social problem and that was dealt with frequently in newspapers and magazines. As a result of their stand, and in conjunction with changing social mores, the production code underwent extensive revisions in 1956. After changes were made to the code to allow movies about drug addiction, as well as greater sexual liberality, United Artists restored its MPAA membership. In 1962, studio heads requested that the film be reconsidered for a seal of approval, long after it had completed its runs in numerous theaters across the United States. Because the 1956 revisions to the code had eliminated the original objections to *The Man with the Golden Arm,* the PCA quietly granted the seal in July 1962, which allowed United Artists to show the film without restriction in all theaters across the nation and on military bases, as well as to lease rights to television.

Before 1962, the film was effectively kept out of all theaters that adhered to the MPAA code requiring that they exhibit only films having the PCA seal of approval, but many more sites remained. Because of these other venues, fewer challenges than might be expected emerged to the film and the film was screened without problem in many states, but not in Maryland, where the Maryland State Board of Censors demanded that the distributor excise a scene of approximately two minutes in which Machine prepares to inject himself with heroin. The board alleged that the scene violated a Maryland statute against any film that "advocates or teaches the use of, or the methods of use of, narcotics or habit-forming drugs." The distributor of the film appealed the decision in the Baltimore city court, which affirmed the decision of the censors. United Artists then appealed the decision in the court of appeals of Maryland. In *United Artists Corporation v. Maryland Board of Censors,* 124 A. 2d 292 (1956), the appellate court determined that the statute applied by the censorship board required that a film "advocate" the use of narcotics to be banned, but that *The Man with the Golden Arm* only "discussed" such use. The court of appeals found "strong and convincing" evidence that the film was more likely to have "a beneficial effect as a deterrent from the use of narcotics." Favorable opinions from health, government and education experts regarding the film appear in the written decision. One particularly powerful defense for the film was expressed by a New York City health education coordinator: "The picture presented an accurate portrayal of the many problems facing the drug addict and the responsibility of society." The appellate court reversed the decisions of the lower court and of the board of censors.

FURTHER READING

Carmen, Ira C. *Movies, Censorship, and the Law.* Ann Arbor: University of Michigan Press, 1966.

Gardner, Gerald. *The Censorship Papers: Movie Censorship Letters from the Hays Office, 1934 to 1968.* New York: Dodd, Mead, 1987.

Schumch, Murray. *The Face on the Cutting Room Floor.* New York: William Morrow, 1964.

United Artists Corporation v. Maryland Board of Censors, 124 A. 2d 292 (1956).

MARTIN LUTHER

Country and date of production: United States, 1953
Production company/distributor: De Rochemont, Luther Filmgesell-shaft GmbH/Lutheran Church in America
Format: Sound, black and white
Running time: 105 minutes
Language: English
Producer: Louis De Rochemont
Director: Irving Pichel
Screenwriters: Allan Sloane, Lothar Wolff
Awards: None
Genre: Drama
With: Annette Carell (Katherine von Bora), Alexander Gauge (Tetzel), David Horne (Duke Frederick), Alastair Hunter (Carlstadt), Fred Johnson (Prior), Philip Leaver (Pope Leo X, as "Phillip Leaver"), Hans Lefebre (Charles V), Pierre Lefevre (Spalatin), Niall MacGinnis (Martin Luther), Irving Pichel (Brueck), John Ruddock (Vicar von Staupitz), Egon Strohm (Cardinal Alexander), Guy Verney (Melanchthon), Leonard White (Emissary)

SUMMARY

The film tells the story of Martin Luther (1483–1546), German theologian and founder of the Protestant Reformation in Europe. Originally an Augustinian monk with the Roman Catholic Church, Luther became disillusioned with Catholicism after a trip to Rome, where he became convinced that the church was corrupt and vowed to fight against that corruption for the rest of his life. *Martin Luther* details Luther's campaign against the church, which reached a high point in 1517 when he nailed his Ninety-five Theses publicly to the doors of the Wittenberg Church. The theses denounced various practices of the Roman Catholic Church, especially the selling of indulgences, which were written forms of forgiveness that were purchased from pardoners representing the church and paid for according to the extent of the sin. In the film, Roman Catholic leader Pope Leo X, who is shown to be infuriated by Luther's audacity, orders the arrest of Luther and the consistent and comprehensive banning and burning of all pamphlets and books written by Luther and his followers. The Roman Catholic hierarchy is portrayed in the film as merciless in dealing with Luther, denouncing him as a heretic in May 1521, and later excommunicating him and banning him from church activities. The film also examines Luther's criticisms of Roman Catholic rite and tradition, particularly the reduction of the seven sacraments to only two, baptism and communion, which Luther said were the only two instituted by Jesus Christ; the move from the use of Latin to the vernacular in worship; and the encouragement of congregational participation in worship.

CENSORSHIP HISTORY

Martin Luther was among a group of films, including LA DOLCE VITA, ANATOMY OF A MURDER and LOLITA (1962), that forced a growing leniency in the classification system of the Catholic Legion of Decency (LOD) in the 1950s. Such films would have earned a "C" (Condemned) rating in the past, but in the 1950s, when society and the LOD were "showing an increasing tolerance for adult movies done in good taste," such a rating would have made the LOD a subject of derision. To avoid this, and to lessen tensions with Hollywood, the LOD amended its regulations "to permit itself to give special classifications to such movies." *Martin Luther* generated debate within the LOD because it contained extensive criticism of the Roman Catholic Church, albeit in a historical context. The legion finally decided to give the film one of its newly developed ratings, "A-4": "morally objectionable for adults with reservations." Thus, in the spirit of protecting Catholics, the rating was designed to keep impressionable children from viewing attacks on their faith and to forewarn adults that the material contained in the movie might be detrimental to them, as well. The Roman Catholic press in the United States characterized the historically accurate material in the film as "unfair" and claimed that it was "designed to perpetuate known falsehoods about the Catholic Church."

The film did not attract large crowds of any particular faith to the theaters, and no cause for concern emerged until 1956 when the independent television station WGN-TV, in the predominantly Roman Catholic city of Chicago, planned to air the film. Chicago's Roman Catholic diocese organized a massive telephone campaign, deluging the offices of the television station with calls in the days before the planned showing. In response to the pressure and what it called the "emotional reaction" to its plans, WGN-TV canceled the world television premiere of the award-winning film.

FURTHER READING

Lee, Robert E. A. "Censorship: A History." *Christian Century* 74 (February 6, 1957): 163–165.
Schumach, Murray. *The Face on the Cutting Floor*. New York: William Morrow, 1964.
"TV Station Yields to Catholic Pressure." *Christian Century* 74 (January 2, 1957): 4, 12.

Welch, Robert G. "The *Martin Luther* Film." *America* 96 (March 23, 1957): 698–700.

THE MIRACLE

Country and date of production: Italy, 1948
Production company/distributor: Finecine/Canton-Weiner (United States, subtitled)
Format: Sound, black and white/color
Running time: 41 minutes
Language: Italian
Producers: Pierre Braunberger, Roberto Rossellini
Director: Roberto Rossellini
Screenwriters: Federico Fellini (story, "Il Miracolo"), Tullio Pinelli, Roberto Rossellini
Awards: 1949 Italian Syndicate of Film Journalists, Best Actress (Anna Magnani).
1950 New York Film Critics Award, Best Foreign Language Film (Roberto Rossellini).
Genre: Drama
With: Sylvia Bataille (Henriette), Charles Blavette (Antonin), Jacques B. Brunius (Rudolph), Federico Fellini (The Stranger), Gabrielle Fontan (Grandmother), Anna Magnani (Nanni), Jane Marken (Madame Dufour), Henri Poupon (Fonse), Jean Renoir (Innkeeper), A. Robert (Teacher), Odette Roger (Marie), Vincent Scotto (Jofroi), Georges St. Saens (Henry), Annie Toinon (Jofroi's wife Barbe)

SUMMARY

The brief film *The Miracle* (*Il Miracolo*) relates the story of Nanni, a poor, simple-minded peasant woman who tends a herd of goats to earn her living. She is devoutly religious and daydreams of being transported to heaven, an escape from her dreary, difficult existence. When seemingly out of nowhere a bearded stranger appears, played by Federico Fellini with a skillful mix of gentleness and cunning, Nanni imagines him to be Saint Joseph, her favorite saint, and begs him to take to her heaven. The stranger gives her wine, and the more wine Nanni drinks the more frenzied her behavior becomes until she seems to reach a state of religious rapture. The film then discreetly suggests that the stranger seduces the simple woman. Nanni awakens to find the stranger gone. Her perception clouded by the wine, she questions if he even existed at all, and she appears to have no recollection of the seduction. An old priest in whom she confides agrees that she might have experienced the vision of a saint, but his younger counterpart is skeptical.

A few months pass, during which Nanni remains devoutly religious. When she faints while playing caretaker for the children whose mothers are picking grapes, the women tend to her and learn that Nanni is pregnant, which at first frightens and bewilders her. After a short while, she calls out, "It is the grace of God!" before becoming emotionally agitated and running into the church, where she throws herself to the ground in front of the statue of Saint Joseph. In the months that follow, because Nanni believes herself to be carrying Christ, she refuses to perform menial work. The older women of the village pity her and humor her behavior, but the younger people jeer at her and mock her. In one disturbing scene, a group of younger villagers first play to her fantasy, then physically push her around and hit her, before placing a metal wash basin on her head in mockery of a halo. Nanni runs away, taking with her the rags that are her only possessions, and lives by herself in a cave until she is about to give birth. When the time arrives, she walks toward the village but then changes her mind as memories of her abuse arise. Instead, she goes to a church located high on a hill and, finding it locked, is about to despair until a goat appears to lead her to an open side door. Once inside the church, she begins to experience labor pains. The film does not show the birth. Instead, the screen image dissolves from Nanni's sad face to one transformed by the happiness brought by her new child. As the audience hears the cry of a baby, Nanni passionately calls out, "My son! My love! My flesh!"

CENSORSHIP HISTORY

The film drew mixed reactions in Italy and in the United States, but the Catholic censors in the United States took strong action while their Italian counterparts only voiced their disapproval. The film raised no serious objections when it was first shown in August 1948 at the Venice Film Festival, paired with *L'Umano Voce* (*The Human Voice*) in a production named *Amore*. The director of the festival later declared in an affidavit that the Venice Film Festival Committee would have barred the film had it been "blasphemous." Piero Regnoli, the film critic of the Vatican publication *L'Osservatore Romano*, expressed support for Rossellini's body of work but called the film pretentious and suggested that it would motivate "serious questions of a religious nature." An article that appeared in the February 11, 1951, issue of the *New York Times* related that, in October 1948, a month after the premiere of the film in Rome, the Catholique Cinematographic Centre, the Vatican's censorship agency, determined that *The Miracle* "constitutes in effect an abominable profanation from religious and moral viewpoints," yet the Italian government censors cleared the film to be shown throughout Italy. The Christian Democratic Party, in essence the Catholic party in Italy, praised the film in the party newspaper *Il Popolo* as a "beautiful thing, humanly felt, alive, true and without religious profanation as someone has said, because in our opinion the meaning of the characters is clear and there is no possibility of misunderstanding." Even Regnoli, in a second review on November 12, 1948, praised Rossellini's artistry, although he criticized the "carnality" of the film and its representation of unwed motherhood. None of the Italian critics, Catholic or otherwise, charged that the film was sacrilegious.

Joseph Burstyn, an American film distributor and entrepreneur who specialized in foreign films and the management of art theaters, imported *The Miracle*, which came through U.S. Customs without difficulty and in March 1949 passed the scrutiny of the Motion Picture Division of the New York State Education Department, which granted it a license to be shown without English subtitles. Burstyn did not exhibit the film until after he had packaged it with two other short films, Jean Renoir's *A Day in the Country* and Marcel Pagnol's *Jofroi*, and submitted the trilogy with English subtitles under the title *Ways of Love*. The new title was also granted a license for exhibition by the Motion Picture Division of the New York State Education Department on November 30, 1950. The film opened on December 12, 1950, at the Paris Theatre on 58th Street in Manhattan and by December 24, 1950, it had become the object of protests organized by members of the Catholic Legion of Decency (LOD). Yielding to pressure, Edward T. McCaffrey, commissioner of licenses for New York City, informed the operator of the Paris Theatre that he found *The Miracle* "officially and personally blasphemous" and said he would revoke the theater's license unless the film were removed. McCaffrey claimed that "there were hundreds of thousands of citizens whose religious beliefs were assailed by the picture." The theater complied. The distributor, however, secured a temporary injunction against the commissioner and brought action before the New York Supreme Court, which ruled on January 5, 1951, that no municipal official had the right to interfere with the exhibition of a motion picture that had been officially licensed by the state.

The Paris Theatre resumed showing the film. On Sunday, January 7, 1951, after Cardinal Spellman, head of the New York archdiocese, read a statement at all masses in St. Patrick's Cathedral calling upon Catholics to boycott the film and all theaters that showed it, hundreds of people picketed the Paris Theatre every evening for three weeks. The New York Board of Regents reported that it had received numerous complaints about the film and, in February 1951, after viewing *The Miracle*, revoked the license to exhibit the film on the grounds that it was "sacrilegious."

Burstyn withdrew the film from the Paris Theatre and then filed an appeal with the appellate division of the New York Supreme Court, which upheld the Regents' decision in *Joseph Burstyn, Inc. v. Wilson*, 104 N.Y.S. 2d 740 (1951). (Wilson was the education commissioner for the state of New York who had rescinded the license.) The appellate division held that the banning of a film "that may fairly be deemed sacrilegious to the adherents of any religious group . . . is directly related to public peace and order" and not a denial of religious freedom. Attorneys for Burstyn filed a motion in the New York Court of Appeals, arguing that the decision violated the First and Fourteenth Amendments, impinged upon the free exercise of religion and applied the vague term *sacrilegious*, which "provided no guidelines for the scope of administrative authority." The court affirmed in a vote of 5 to 2 the decisions of the Board of Regents and the appellate division and, in *Joseph Burstyn, Inc. v. Wilson*, 101 N.E. 2d 665 (1951), held that "sacrilegious" was a valid standard for censorship.

Burstyn's attorneys then filed an appeal for the case to be heard before the United States Supreme Court, where it was argued on April 24, 1952. After examining the evidence and reviewing related cases, the justices wrote, "we conclude that expression by means of motion pictures is included within the free speech and free press guaranty of the First and Fourteenth Amendments." In a lengthy decision, the justices examined numerous standard dictionaries, "successive editions of the *Encyclopaedia Britannica* over nearly two centuries up to the present day" and other works to determine "a judicial definition of sacrilege." They concluded, "It is the impossibility of knowing how far the form of words by which the New York Court of Appeals explained 'sacrilegious' carries the proscription of religious subjects that makes the term constitutionally vague." Because the State of New York had in its cases against the film made the term *sacrilegious* the sole standard under attack, the Court determined "it is not necessary for us to decide, for example, whether a state may censor motion pictures under a clearly drawn statute designed and applied to prevent the showing of obscene films. That is a very different question from the one now before us. We hold only that under the First and Fourteenth Amendments a state may not ban a film on the basis of a censor's conclusion that it is 'sacrilegious.'"

The decision in this case, and decisions in the cases that immediately followed, provided the movie industry with the constitutional guarantees of freedom of speech and press that it had been denied by the Supreme Court decision in *Mutual Film Corporation v. Ohio Industrial Commission*, 236 U.S. 230 (1915), that declared a motion picture is not constitutionally protected as free speech. In a unanimous decision, the Court in that case wrote:

> It cannot be put out of view [that film exhibition] is a business pure and simple, originated and conducted for profit, like other spectacles, not to be regarded . . . as part of the press of the country or as organs of public opinion. They are mere representations of events, of ideas and sentiments published and known, vivid, useful and entertaining no doubt, but . . . capable of evil, having power for it, greater because of their attractiveness and manner of exhibition.

After its decision in the *Miracle* case, the Supreme Court issued five court opinions to reverse rulings in state supreme court cases that had supported decisions made by censorship boards to ban given films. Citing their decision in *Burstyn v. Wilson*, 343 U.S. 495 (1952), the *Miracle* case, the justices changed the basis for movie censorship by striking down all but one ("obscenity") of the censorship criteria that had been used for nearly five decades by city and state censorship boards to refuse permits to distributors to exhibit their films. The Supreme Court decisions in censorship cases involving the films LA RONDE, M, PINKY, THE MOON IS BLUE and NATIVE SON suggested that all of the previous applications of the terms *immoral* or tending to *corrupt morals; other than moral, educational, amusing or harmless; of such character as to be prejudicial to the best interests of the people of said City; cruel, obscene, indecent, or immoral, or such as tend to debase or corrupt morals;* or conducive to crime were too broad to function as significant criteria to ban the exhibition of films.

FURTHER READING

Cianfarra, Camille M. "The Miracle." *New York Times,* February 11, 1951, p. 4.

Clancy, William P. "The Catholic as Philistine." *Commonweal* 53 (March 16, 1951): 567–569.

———. "Freedom of the Screen." *Commonweal* 59 (February 1954): 500–502.

Crowther, Bosley. "The Strange Case of *The Miracle.*" *Atlantic Monthly* 187 (April 1951): 35–39; 188 (July 1951): 15–16.

Harris, Albert W., Jr. "Movie Censorship and the Supreme Court: What Next?" *California Law Review* 42 (Spring 1954): 122–138.

Joseph Burstyn, Inc. v. McCaffrey, 101 N.Y.S. 2d 892.

Joseph Burstyn, Inc. v. Wilson, 104 N.Y.S. 2d 740 (1951).

Joseph Burstyn, Inc. v. Wilson, 101 N.E. 2d 665 (1951).

Joseph Burstyn, Inc. v. Wilson, 343 U.S. 2d 485 (1952).

Kasson, Constantine D. "Constitutional Law-Due Process—Freedom of Expression—Moving Picture Censorship." *Michigan Law Review* 52 (February 1954): 599–602.

Lewis, Thomas P. "Freedom of Speech and Motion Pictures—the *Miracle* Decision." *Kentucky Law Journal* 41 (January 1953): 257–264.

McAnany, P. D. "Motion Picture Censorship and Constitutional Freedom." *Kentucky Law Journal* 50 (Summer 1962): 427–458.

Moore, Donald P. "Chicago Censorship Ordinance Held Enforceable." *University of Illinois Law Forum* 54 (Winter 1954): 678–684.

Morse, Howard N. "A Critical Analysis and Appraisal of *Burstyn v. Wilson.*" *North Dakota Law Review* 29 (January 1953): 38–41.

"Motion Picture Censorship: The Aftermath of Burstyn v. Wilson." *Northwestern University Law Review* 49 (July–August 1954): 390–399.

Mutual Film Corporation v. Industrial Commission of Ohio, 236 U.S. 230 (1915).

Pfeffer, Leo. "Heresy, American Democracy and The Miracle." *Jewish Frontier* 17 (August 1951): 14–18.

Reiner, Donald F. "Motion Picture Censorship Re-examined." *Albany Law Review* 23 (January 1959): 152–168.

Seldes, Gilbert. "Pressures and Pictures." *Nation* 172 (February 3, 1951): 104–106; 172 (February 10, 1951): 132–134.

Walters, Fred. "The Supreme Court Ruling on *The Miracle* and *Pinky.*" *Theatre Arts* 36 (August 1952): 74–77.

Westin, Alan F. *The "Miracle" Case: The Supreme Court and the Movies.* University: University of Alabama Press, 1961.

Wiener, Stanley. "Final Curtain Call for the Motion Picture Censor?" *Western Reserve Law Review* 4 (Winter 1953): 148–158.

MISS JULIE

Country and date of production: Sweden, 1951 (as *Fröken Julie*)
Production company/distributor: Sandrews (Sweden)/Sandrew-Baumanfilm, Trans Global (United States, 1952)
Format: Sound, black and white
Running time: 90 minutes
Language: Swedish
Producer: Rune Waldekranz (uncredited)
Director: Alf Sjöberg
Screenwriters: Alf Sjöberg, August Strindberg (play)
Awards: 1951 Cannes Film Festival, Grand Prize of the Festival (Alf Sjöberg).
Genre: Drama
With: Anita Björk (Miss Julie), Ulf Palme (Jean), Märta Dorff (Kristin, cook), Lissi Alandh (Countess Berta, Julie's mother), Anders Henrikson (Count Carl, Julie's father), Inga Gill (Viola), Åke Fridell (Robert), Kurt-Olof Sundström (Julie's fiancé), Max von Sydow (Hand), Margareta Krook (Governess), Åke Claesson (Doctor), Inger Norberg (Julie as a child), Jan Hagerman (Jean as a child)

SUMMARY

The film is based on the long one-act play of the same name by August Strindberg, which centers on the love-hate relationship between men and women and in the social relationship between the upper and the lower classes. Miss Julie, the daughter of a count, has been taught by her mother to hate men and to dominate them as a way of showing her contempt for them. She had been engaged, but her fiancé broke off the engagement after she forced him to jump over a horsewhip at her command. As the play opens, the 20-year-old Miss Julie had been left home while her aging father and mother are away, and she joins the servants in a midsummer's eve party. She flirts with Jean, a footman, and the two spend most of the evening talking together, after which they slip into Jean's room to avoid being seen by the others. Jean seduces her and then is disappointed when she succumbs to him, which makes her feel as if she has wasted herself on him. Feeling disgraced afterward, Miss Julie finds herself unable to live, and she commits suicide.

CENSORSHIP HISTORY

Miss Julie was released in the United States in 1952 with English subtitles and inspired no official controversy except in the city of Cambridge, Massachusetts, which refused to permit a theater manager to show the film on Sunday. The theater manager had applied to both the state commissioner of public safety and the city manager of Cambridge to obtain permission, as the law required, but he was refused on the authority of a state statute that specified that only the following public entertainment was permitted on Sunday: "a concert of sacred music, or a free open air concert . . . unless such public entertainment shall be in keeping with the character of the day and not inconsistent with its due observance and be duly licensed." After being refused by both the state commissioner and the city manager, the theater manager brought suit against them in the Superior Court of Middlesex County, claiming his constitutional right to exhibit the film on Sunday. The court refused to reverse the decision of the commission and dismissed the suit. The theater manager then appealed the decision in the Supreme Judicial Court of Massachusetts, which reversed the decisions of the commissioner and of the lower court. The court ruled that the state law was unconstitutional, based on decisions rendered in relation to earlier films such as THE MIRACLE, PINKY, M and NATIVE SON, in cases in which states had sought to ban films on the grounds that they were "sacrilegious" or "immoral" or in which state laws allowed the issuance of permits to exhibit only "moral, educational, or amusing and harmless" films. In rendering the final decision of the court, Justice Raymond S. Wilkins declared that it was unthinkable that religious considerations would impact on newspapers or public addresses.

FURTHER READING

Brattle Films v. Commissioner of Public Safety, 127 N.E. 2d 891 (1955).
Commercial Pictures Corporation v. Regents, 346 U.S. 587 (1954).
Crowther, Bosley. "Miss Julie." *New York Times*, April 8, 1952.
Gelling v. Texas, 343 U.S. 960 (1952).
"Miss Julie." *Films in Review*, May 1952, 242.
Superior Films, Inc. v. Department of Education, 346 U.S. 587 (1954).

MOM AND DAD

Country and date of production: United States, 1945
Production company/distributor: Hygienic Productions, Inc.
Format: Sound, black and white
Running time: 87 minutes
Language: English
Producers: Kroger Babb, J. S. Jossey
Director: William Beaudine
Screenwriter: Mildred Horn
Awards: None
Genre: Drama/documentary
With: June Carlson (Joan Blake), Lois Austin (Sarah Blake), George Eldredge (Dan Blake), Jimmy Clark (Dave Blake), Hardie Albright (Carl Blackburn), Bob Lowell (Jack Griffith), Willa Pearl Curtis (Junella, the maid), Jimmy Zaner (Allen Curtis), Jane Isbell (Mary Lou Gardner),

Robert Filmer (Superintendent McMann), Forrest Taylor (Dr. John D. Ashley), John Hamilton (Dr. Burnell), Virginia Vane (Virginia Van), Kaye Renard (Nightclub Singer), Wheeler Oakman (Bourbon drinker on train)

SUMMARY

Mom and Dad is similar in approach to the highly popular propaganda films or social problem films, such as DAMAGED GOODS, that flourished in England and the United States earlier in the century. Such films dealt with topics that were risqué for their times, such as venereal disease, unmarried pregnancy and "inversion" (homosexuality) in the guise of educational and sociological contexts that awarded them more liberal review by the censors, although their profit-minded producers frequently attempted to show them in commercial theaters.

This film relates the simple story of a high school student who becomes pregnant by an airplane pilot, who dies in a plane crash. When the young woman is several months pregnant she confides in her high school teacher, who alerts the student's parents, the Blakes. Unwilling to blame themselves at first for not having discussed sex with their daughter, the Blakes get the teacher fired on the grounds that she answered sex hygiene questions in class. Mrs. Blake and her daughter then go away to another town until the baby is born. The original version of the film, which was edited for rerelease in 1957, contained an intermission during which attendants dressed as nurses would pass out booklets about sexual hygiene, and in some theaters Elliott Forbes, billed by the producers as a "famous hygiene commentator," would give lectures while copies of his books on the topic were sold to the audience. After the intermission, the teacher is rehired and starts a class on hygiene, which gives the filmmakers an excuse to include segments of school sex-education sessions on the devastation of venereal disease. In the movie, experts show films on childbirth and venereal disease in the school to instruct students (and the audience). This segment contains one short sequence of a human birth. The ending of *Mom and Dad* is somber, as the audience learns that Joan Blake has given birth to a stillborn child.

CENSORSHIP HISTORY

The first release of the film was sensationalized by the distributors who showed the film separately to male and female audiences and who employed attendants dressed as nurses to hand out booklets on sexual hygiene. These actions made *Mom and Dad* the most notorious as well as the most successful exploitation/sex hygiene film ever made: The film cost $65,000 to make and earned over $22 million in just under 11 years. The reason was not its subject matter or its production values, but came as the result of the aggressive marketing techniques, carnival-barker like showmanship and unwavering promotion of the producer Howard W. "Kroger" Babb. Babb used to advantage the fact that the nature of the film baffled censors. Some considered it to be an educational film that should be shown only under noncommercial conditions, while others considered it a commercial film that should be subject to the same censorship restraints as other entertainment films. In an April 1963 interview conducted by Ira Carmen with Mrs. Minter S. Hooker, chairman of the Memphis Board of Film Censors, Hooker revealed that, among other films, *Mom and Dad* was one of the "films we wouldn't allow a permit." No legal action appears to have been taken by the distributor in that instance, but contention arose in other cities, such as Newark, New Jersey, and Chicago, Illinois, as well as in New York State.

In 1948, the distributor sought to increase profits on the film by exhibiting it in a commercial theater in Newark, New Jersey, but the showing of the film was halted when the city director of public safety objected that the film was suitable only for noncommercial exhibition as an educational movie. He warned the theater operator that he would revoke the operating license of the establishment if the film were shown. The distributor, Hygienic Productions, Inc., took the case before the New Jersey Superior Court, which reversed the decision of the city director. The court determined that the city director had exceeded his power in threatening to revoke the license of a theater that showed in a commercial setting a film that was not considered objectionable if shown in a noncommercial setting.

The film was revised to remove objectionable scenes and edited for a planned rerelease in 1957, so the new distributor of the film, Capitol Enterprises, submitted it for review in late 1956 to the New York State Board of Regents censorship board. The body refused to grant the distributor a permit to exhibit the film, which in its new version contained what the board termed "a biological demonstration," the birth of a baby within a clinical setting. The distributor appealed the decision before the appellate division of the New York State Supreme Court, which viewed the film and ruled that the censorship board had violated the requirements of "prior restraint." The court declared that the board had not shown that the film was "obscene," which was the sole ground upon which a film could be banned since the United States Supreme Court had eliminated other grounds in its decisions regarding THE MIRACLE, NATIVE SON and LA RONDE. In its written decision, the court cautioned that to apply the terms *indecent* or *obscene* as "constitutionally valid standards for prior restraint, the words must be given a narrow and restricted interpretation," which the court decided was "clearly not applicable" in regard to the film *Mom and Dad*. In concluding, the court wrote that merely treating the film as "indecent" failed to provide grounds for refusing the permit to exhibit.

In 1958, the chief of police of the city of Chicago refused to issue a permit to the distributor to exhibit the film, and did not state grounds for the denial. Capitol Enterprises brought suit against the city in federal district court, where the judge agreed with the decision of the police chief and found the film to be "obscene and immoral if exhibited for entertainment." In an appeal before the U.S. Court of Appeals, the distributor was granted the right to exhibit the film when that body reversed the decision of the federal district court and wrote in its decision in *Capitol Enterprises v. City of Chicago*, 260 F. 2d 670 (1958), that it could not find a sound basis for banning the film. Instead, wrote the court, "the absence of any reasons by the censors for their classification is a foreboding guise for arbitrary censorship running afoul of the First and Fourteenth Amendments. . . . This censorship results in a curb on free expression."

FURTHER READING

Burstyn v. Wilson, 343 U.S. 495 (1952).
Carmen, Ira H. *Movies, Censorship, and the Law*. Ann Arbor: University of Michigan Press, 1966.
Capitol Enterprises v. City of Chicago, 260 F. 2d 670 (1958).
Capitol Enterprises v. Regents, 149 N.Y.S. 2d 150 (1948).
Commercial Pictures Corporation v. Regents, 346 U.S. 587 (1954).
De Grazia, Edward, and Roger K. Newman. *Banned Films: Movies, Censors & the First Amendment*. New York: R. R. Bowker, 1982.
Hygienic Productions, Inc. v. Keenan, 62 A. 2d 150 (1948).
Kuhn, Annette. *Cinema, Censorship, and Sexuality, 1909–1925*. New York: Routledge, 1988.
Superior Films v. Department of Education of Ohio, 346 U.S. 587 (1954).

MONTY PYTHON'S LIFE OF BRIAN

Country and date of production: United Kingdom, 1979
Production company/distributor: Handmade Films, Ltd./Warner Bros. (United States)
Format: Sound, color
Running time: 94 minutes
Language: English
Producers: John Goldstone, Tim Hampton, George Harrison, Denis O'Brien
Director: Terry Jones
Screenwriters: Graham Chapman, John Cleese, Terry Gilliam, Eric Idle, Terry Jones, Michael Palin
Awards: None
Genre: Comedy
With: Graham Chapman (Wise Man #2/Brian/Biggus Dickus), John Cleese (Wise Man #1/Reg/Jewish Official/Centurion/Deadly Dirk/Arthur), Terry Gilliam (Man #2/Jailer/Blood and Thunder Prophet/Frank), Eric Idle (Mr. Cheeky/Stan/Loretta/Harry the Haggler/Culprit Woman/Warris/Youth/Jailer's Assistant/Otto/Mr. Frisbee III), Terry Jones (Mandy/Colin/Simon the Holy Man/Saintly Passer-by), Michael Palin (Wise Man #3/Mr. Big Nose/Francis/Mrs. A/Ex-Leper/An-

nouncer/Ben/Pontius Pilate/Boring Prophet/Eddie/Shoe Follower/Ni-
sus Wettus), Terence Bayler (Gregory), Carol Cleveland (Mrs. Gregory),
Kenneth Colley (Jesus)

SUMMARY

The film might never have been made had not the rock musician and former
Beatle George Harrison provided the needed money to produce the film under the company he created especially for the purpose, Handmade Films,
Ltd. The comedy group Monty Python had run into financial difficulty after
their production of *Monty Python and the Holy Grail*, a spoof of the Arthurian
legends. Financial backers were not eager to assist Python Pictures, Ltd., but
Harrison wanted to see the film produced. Working titles for the film included *Brian of Nazareth* and *Jesus Christ: Lust for Glory*, but the filmmakers
finally settled on the title *Life of Brian* for their story of the reluctant messiah,
Brian Cohen, whose life parallels that of Jesus Christ, and their satiric look at
his followers. When Brian Cohen is born in the stable next door to where
Jesus is born, three wise men charge in upon him first and then see the supernatural glow from the adjoining stable and head there. When the wise men
reenter the Cohen stable, it is only to rob Brian's mother of the family gold,
frankincense and myrrh. Time passes, and in A.D. 33, Brian is seen listening to
the Sermon on the Mount, as around him come murmurs of "Blessed are the
cheesemakers? Who are the cheesemakers?"

History is subjected to the skewed lens of Monty Python as viewers see
an Israel that is desperate for a savior to deliver it from the Romans. As revolutionary groups form, rival factions emerge: The People's Front of Judea
and the Judean People's Front are bitter rivals, and they are joined by the
Popular Front of Judea, a splinter group that consists of only one man. Brian
joins the People's Front of Judea, and the group of anti-Roman revolutionaries mistakenly identify him as the messiah. From that point, he is hounded
by their adoration. He tells them to act as individuals rather than to behave
as so many sheep, and they reply in unison, "We will be individuals." In exas-
peration, Brian tells the followers, "Fuck off," and they ask him in what
manner he would like them to do so. The Python version of Pontius Pilate is
a man with a speech impediment who orders his guards. "Stwike him, cen-
tuwion!" The movie satirizes not Jesus Christ, but instead the followers who
may have gotten his message all wrong, blindly following when they should
have been thinking for themselves. At the end, Brian, like Jesus, is crucified,
but the scene is typical of most chaotic Monty Python endings, filled with
song as a choir of crucifixion victims heartily sing "Always Look On the
Bright Side of Life."

CENSORSHIP HISTORY

The filmmakers made no secret of the controversy that they expected the film
to generate upon its release in 1979, and they emphasized its provocative

nature with such taglines as "See the movie that's controversial, sacrilegious, and blasphemous. But if that's not playing, see *The Life of Brian.*" As Bill McLochlin observed, "Despite the fact that Christianity is only the third-ranked religion in number of followers worldwide, Christians seem to be the loudest critics of modern film." And they did make their views about *Life of Brian* known loudly. The film was banned in Norway for the first year after its release, and Italy banned the film until 1991. As recently as July 2000, Ireland retained the film on its list of movies that are banned from exhibition, although, as David D'Arcy points out, "Pub and club owners make a killing by charging people to watch the film on video tape, which is not covered by the legislation of the time. Censorship beaten by the VCR."

In the United States, religious leaders of various faiths picketed and protested the showing of *Life of Brian* at theaters in individual cities, particularly in the South, and "incensed Bible Belters picketed the film's U.S. distributor, Warner Brothers. The six members of Monty Python were called heathens, heretics, godless atheists, and worse." In Valdosta, Georgia, outraged citizens asked the court to stop the exhibition of the movie, and a local judge granted an injunction against showing the film. He lifted the court order the following day because the courts could not support a legal challenge to the film on religious grounds. Such a move would have been ruled unconstitutional based on the United States Supreme Court decision in *Burstyn v. Wilson*, 343 U.S. 495 (see THE MIRACLE) that movies are entitled to constitutional protection from state censorship and could not be banned simply because censors considered them to be blasphemous or sacrilegious.

The film has remained controversial. In 1996, dialogue from the film became the object of an internet censorship effort in Munich, Germany, when German prosecutors investigated a user of the FidoNet bulletin board server for anti-Jewish propaganda. After searching the server to find the user's address, the server user was directed to go to a Munich police station, where he was questioned for having posted the following lines from the movie: "Down with the Judean People's Front! Long live the People's Front of Judea!" In 1998, in what represented a major victory for British filmmakers seeking control over how their product would be edited in later years for ancillary markets including television and video, a British court returned to Python Pictures, Ltd., the rights to *Life of Brian* after finding the distributors in breach of contract. In the original contract with Harrison's Handmade Films, the group was granted approval of any ancillary sales and any cuts made in the film. When Handmade sold the film in 1994 to Paragon Entertainment Corp., the distributor licensed the film to a British television station without the restrictions. The court ruled that the failure nullified the deal and required that rights to the film be reverted to the Pythons.

FURTHER READING

Chesworth, Amanda. "Godless Creations: The Irreverent Monty Python." *Secular Humanist Bulletin* 15 (Summer 2000). Reprinted at the Council for Secular

Humanism site. http://www.secularhumanism.org/library/shb/chesworth_15_4. html.

D'Arcy, David. "Comment." *ComputerScope*, April 1998. Reprinted at *Tech Central.IE.* http://www.techcentral.ie/cgi-bin/SiteWrapper.pl?template=/magazines/com.../ Opinions-O.htm.

De Grazia, Edward, and Roger K. Newman. *Banned Films: Movies, Censors and the First Amendment.* New York: R. R. Bowker, 1982.

McLochlin, Bill. "Hollywood vs. Holy Good." *TNT Rough Cut Features.* July 14, 2000. http://www.roughcut.com/features/stories/dogma.html.

"Munich.prosecutors.071096.txt." EEF "Global Internet Censorship" Archive. Maintained by Declan McCullagh. July 22, 1996. http://www.eff.org/pub/ Censorship/GII_NII/Dispatches.

"Pythons Get Life." *Movie & TV News.* http://www.IMDb.com. May 22, 1998.

THE MOON IS BLUE

Country and date of production: United States, 1953
rProduction company/distributor: Carlyle Productions/United Artists
Format: Sound, black and white
Running time: 99 minutes
Language: English
Producer: Otto Preminger
Director: Otto Preminger
Screenwriter: F. Hugh Herbert (from his play)
Awards: 1954 Golden Globe Awards, Best Actor–Musical/Comedy (David Niven).
Genre: Comedy
With: Dawn Addams (Cynthia Slater), Fortunio Bonanova (Television performer), William Holden (Donald Gresham), Maggie McNamara (Patty O'Neill), David Niven (David Slater), Gregory Ratoff (Taxi Driver), Tom Tully (Michael O'Neill)

SUMMARY

One of the most famous cases of movies released without the Production Code Administration (PCA) seal of approval, *The Moon Is Blue*, based on a play of the same title also written by F. Hugh Herbert, today seems an innocuous and somewhat dated comedy. Patty O'Neill, a struggling and naïve young television actress, meets Donald Gresham, a young but jaded architect, at the Empire State Building. He asks her to have dinner with him at the Stork Club, to which she agrees, but in the taxi he asks if they could stop at his apartment so that he can sew on a missing button. Patty asks Gresham if he will try to seduce her or if his intentions are honorable, and he mildly reprimands her for being too blunt. While they are at Gresham's apartment, his neighbor arrives from the apartment upstairs to chastise Gresham but decides, instead, to try his luck at cavalierly seducing Patty, who appeals to his cynicism regarding women who protest too much about their virginity. As both men pursue her, ridiculing her sexual innocence throughout, comedy emerges in the series of complications and misunderstandings that result. After both have exhausted all of their charm, Patty still has her virginity and she has acquired a fiancé, Donald Gresham.

CENSORSHIP HISTORY

The Moon Is Blue was denied a seal of approval from because of its light-hearted handling of the subject of adultery, even though no act of adultery takes place in the film. The Catholic Legion of Decency (LOD) rated the film "C" (condemned). The importance of this film is in its effect upon the Hollywood censors, who expected the producer and distributor to lose money on the film if they released it without a seal. Instead, the film, which cost $450,000 to make, was eventually exhibited in 4,200 theaters and earned gross receipts of $6 million in its first release. This success weakened the powers of the PCA and made other studios take note, especially when United Artists withdrew from membership in the Motion Picture Association of America (MPAA) in support of the film. A few years later, after the PCA had revised the standards extensively, United Artists rejoined the MPAA and, in 1962, long after the film had completed its run in theaters, studio heads requested that the film be reconsidered for a seal of approval. The head of the PCA, Geoff Shurlock, said he had no objection for *The Moon Is Blue*, and the PCA quietly granted the seal in July 1962, which allowed United Artists to show the film without restriction in all theaters across the nation and on military bases, as well as to lease rights to television.

The original controversy over the film was intentional. Otto Preminger knew that the script he submitted to the Production Code Administration (PCA) office in December 1952, which contained most of the dialogue from the original play, had already been turned down twice and in such resounding terms that both Warner Bros. and Paramount had given up the project. The prospect of challenging the code with what would be his first independent production intrigued Preminger. When the film was completed in April 1953, PCA head Joseph Breen rejected the movie, complaining that it showed an "unacceptably light attitude toward seduction, illicit sex, chastity and virginity." The PCA board also rejected the film and refused to grant it their seal of approval. A delegation of 10 evaluators from Catholic LOD, led by Monsignor Patrick Masterson, screened the film just before Preminger began his publicity campaign, and the evaluators voted to rate the film "B" (morally objectionable in part for all), but Monsignor Masterson and LOD leader Monsignor Thomas Little overruled the evaluators and told the LOD to issue a "C" to the movie. They acquiesced, but the LOD failed in its call for Catholics to boycott the film based on the "C" rating and thus became starkly aware of changing public attitudes. The lack of the censor's approval seemed to increase viewers' curiosity and encourage them to see what all the furor was about.

The film initially was barred from exhibition in many parts of the United States, but most of the challenges were overturned. In Birmingham, Alabama, when censors sought to remove a seduction scene from the film and to restrict attendance to people over the age of 21, members of several of the women's clubs in the city protested that the film provided "a good moral lesson to teenagers." When Memphis, Tennessee, censors banned the film from their city, a theater 30 miles away in Holly Springs, Mississippi, played to standing room only audiences. In Wisconsin, the Milwaukee Motion Picture Commission refused to allow the picture to be exhibited, so drive-in theaters, located in the suburbs beyond the legal reach of the city, showed the film and made significant profits from the crowds they drew. The Catholic archdiocese of New York labeled the film "an occasion of sin," but Catholic viewers flocked to the theaters anyway. The archbishop of Philadelphia failed in a similar manner when he tried to keep the film out of city theaters.

In Kansas, the state board of review refused to issue a permit for exhibition to the distributors of the film for the following reasons: "Sex theme throughout, too frank bedroom dialogue: many sexy words; both dialogue and action have sex as their theme." The board also determined that the film violated Kansas General Statute 1949, Sect. 51–103, which forbade anything "obscene, indecent and immoral, and such as tends to debase or to corrupt morals," all statutory ground for refusing the permit. The distributor appealed the decision of the board in a case lodged with the Wyandotte County District Court, which reversed the decision of the board on the grounds that the guidelines in the statute had been so broadly construed as to rob them of any precision. The case then went before the Supreme Court of Kansas, which unanimously reversed the decision of the lower court and ruled that the board was constitutionally empowered with the right to determine whether films may be exhibited in the state. In writing the decision, the court quoted from the United States Supreme Court decision in *Near v. Minnesota*, 230 U.S. 697 (1931), which stated that censorship of the press by the states was unconstitutional unless the periodical could be found "obscene" and "offensive to morals, order and good govern-ment." Justice Robb wrote that the Supreme Court of Kansas observed that the Kansas State Board of Review had found the film to be "obscene" and no evidence had been presented to challenge that finding. The distributor then took the case before the United States Supreme Court, which reversed the ruling of the Supreme Court of Kansas, using as its authority U.S. Supreme Court cases decided in relation to M, THE MIRACLE and LA RONDE, which found that the wording of the statute upon which the board of censors based its decision was too vague and indefinite to support the decision.

In Maryland, the Maryland State Board of Censors refused to license the film, claiming that it contained "obscenity, corruption of morals, and incitement to crime." The distributor appealed the decision before the Baltimore City Court, which reversed the decision in *United Artists Corp. v. Maryland State Board of Censors*, Baltimore City Court, Docket 16, Folio 295 (1955). Based on a law passed in 1916, the board was barred from appealing the decision to a higher court. Attempts to ban the film in New Jersey and Ohio succeeded only temporarily.

FURTHER READING

"Binford Ban Backfires; *Moon* Shines With SRO in His Native State." *Variety*, September 9, 1953, p. 1.

"Chains Flout Code, Book *Blue*." *Variety*, June 30, 1953, p. 1.

Corliss, Lamont. *Freedom Is as Freedom Does: Civil Liberties Today.* New York: Horizon Books, 1956.

Holmby Productions v. Vaughn, 177 Kansas 728 (1955).

Holmby Productions v. Vaughn, 282 P. 2d 412, 177 Kansas 728 (1955).

Holmby Productions v. Vaughn, 350 U.S. 870 (1955).

Jowett, Garth. *Film: The Democratic Art.* Boston: Little, Brown, 1976.

Leff, Leonard J., and Jerold L. Simmons. *The Dame in the Kimono: Hollywood, Censorship, and the Production Code from the 1920s to the 1960s.* New York: Grove Weidenfeld, 1990.

"*Moon* Cab Scene Cut, Plays Alabam'; St. Paul Solons Hold Nose, O.K. It." *Variety*, July 29, 1953, p. 1.

Schumach, Murray. *The Face on the Cutting Room Floor.* New York: William Morrow, 1964.

United Artists Corp. v. Maryland State Board of Censors, Baltimore City Court, Docket 16, Folio 295 (1955).

NAKED CAME THE STRANGER

Country and date of production: United States, 1975
Production company/distributor: Catalyst Productions/VCA Pictures
Format: Sound, color
Running time: 89 minutes
Language: English
Producer: L. Sultana
Director: Radley Metzger (as Henry Paris)
Screenwriter: Penelope Ashe (novel), Jake Barnes
Awards: None
Genre: Adult
With: Kevin Andre, Gerald Grant, Helen Madigan, Darby Lloyd Rains (Gilian Blake), Levi Richards (William Blake), Mary Stuart (Phyllis)

SUMMARY

The novel on which the screenplay for the film was based was written by 12 staff writers of *Newsday*, a newspaper in Long Island, New York, who used the pseudonym "Penelope Ashe" for their sole collaborative fiction effort. The story, which capitalizes on the sexually liberal climate of the 1970s, contains a range of sexual behavior involving a husband-and-wife radio talk-show team who have affairs outside of marriage. When Gilian Blake discovers her husband, William, in a sexually compromising position with his secretary, she becomes angry and decides to do some sexual exploration of her own. After a series of sexual flings with various men, she becomes intimately involved with her husband's secretary, the same woman with whom she had caught him before beginning her sexual odyssey. The novelty of the lesbian affair wears off quickly, however, and she returns to her husband. The two celebrate their reunion with exuberance, providing viewers what *Film Bulletin* called "a moral climax when the two spouses get together again in a very athletic sex scene at the end."

CENSORSHIP HISTORY

The film was assigned an "X" (suitable only for adults) rating by the Motion Picture Association of America (MPAA), and its run was largely in independent and art theaters. On August 27, 1975, representatives of the Oakland County prosecutor's office appeared with judicial warrants and ordered law enforcement officers to arrest a theater manager and to seize the copy of the film being shown. While out on bail the following day, the manager showed another copy of the film, and law-enforcement officers, acting under the authority of the Oakland County prosecutor's office, arrested the manager again and seized the second copy of the film. At an adversary judicial hearing in which opposing parties are present, the film was found to be obscene, but the judge dismissed the second prosecution and ordered the prosecutor's office to return the second copy of the film. The prosecutor refused and, instead, warned the manager that he would confiscate a copy of the film each day that the manager exhibited it. Claiming prosecutorial harassment, the manager sought an injunction that would prevent further interference by the prosecutor's office. The prosecutor also went to court with the request that the court declare the film a "nuisance" and issue an injunction to prevent further exhibition of the film, as well as a court order that would expedite the removal of the fixtures, furniture and contents of the theater. A circuit judge agreed with the prosecutor and issued a temporary order to prevent the manager from showing the film anywhere in the country. The manager made an emergency appeal to the court of appeals, which vacated the previous order after determining that it had been "a forbidden prior restraint on activities presumptively protected by the First Amendment by enjoining the showing of the named motion picture film without first having conducted an adversary proceeding . . . to determine whether said film is 'obscene.'" The manager then returned to exhibiting the film, but the county prosecutor obtained a judicial warrant and, once again, seized a copy of the film and arrested and jailed the manager, overnight this time. Upon his release, the manager exhibited a fourth copy of the film, and the prosecutor obtained another search warrant. Law enforcement officers arrested the manager, seized another copy of the film, and confiscated the film projector.

The prosecutor justified the repeated arrests and seizures on the grounds that each showing of the film represented a separate crime. The theater manager appealed to the federal district court, which disagreed with the actions of the prosecutor and ordered that the theater manager could not be arrested again for exhibiting the same film and that the film projector must be returned to the theater. The court based its opinion on the fact that only one copy of the film was required for evidence, and eyewitness by law-enforcement officers was sufficient evidence of the repeated showings. The court further determined that following the suggested procedure "would not only be less restrictive of First Amendment freedoms but possibly less expensive to the government than repeated raids upon the theater."

FURTHER READING

De Grazia, Edward, and Roger K. Newman. *Banned Films: Movies, Censors, and the First Amendment.* New York: R. R. Bowker, 1982.
Llewelyn v. Oakland County Prosecutor's Office, 402 F. Supp. 1379 (1975).
"Naked Came the Stranger." *Film Bulletin,* June 1975.

THE NAKED TRUTH

Country and date of production: United States, 1924 (also released as *T.N.T.*)
Production company/distributor: Public Welfare Pictures
Format: Silent, black and white
Running time: 75 minutes
Language: English titles
Producer: Samuel Cummins
Directors: None identified
Screenwriter: George D. Walters (story)
Awards: None
Genre: Documentary
With: Jack Mulhall (Bob), Helene Chadwick (Mary), Leo Pierson (Bob's Playmate), Charles Spere (Another Playmate), Irene Davis (Isobel), Emmett King (Dr. Brown)

SUMMARY

The plot of *The Naked Truth* is similar to that of DAMAGED GOODS and other films that sought to reach large crowds while conveying a public health message. The film relates the fates of three young men, all friends and each taking a different path in his social life. Bob is the paragon of virtue, who has chosen to avoid premarital sex. When he marries, he has built a good career as an attorney with great chance for success and appears destined for a happy future. His two friends are not so wise. One is encouraged by his father to have sex with a woman of dubious reputation, and he becomes infected with a venereal disease. Ashamed of himself and unwilling to delay his marriage, he goes first to an unscrupulous doctor who fails to cure him. When he finally decides to visit a legitimate doctor, he is forced to postpone his wedding and reveal his secret to his fiancée. The results of sexual experimentation have even more dire consequences for Bob's second friend, who contracts a venereal disease and allows only an unscrupulous doctor to treat him. He does not tell his fiancée and they marry, but he eventually loses his mind because of the disease and kills his wife. Bob then steps forward and represents his old friend in court, freeing him on a plea of insanity.

CENSORSHIP HISTORY

The film was shown in commercial theaters in various cities throughout the United States, but New Jersey and New York sought to limit exhibitions of the film to noncommercial venues, such as church or school buildings or the Y.M.C.A. The film was banned from exhibition in Newark, New Jersey, after the board of censors, consisting of the chief of the city's board of health and two police officers, reviewed the film, along with "a number of ladies" whom the board had invited. The board had been appointed by the commissioner of Newark's department of public safety, William J. Brennan (whose son and namesake would become a U.S. Supreme Court justice). The board determined that the film was not suitable for general exhibition but agreed to approve it for exhibition in a noncommercial venue. Brennan conveyed the board's decision to the distributor and warned Public Welfare Pictures Films Corporation not to exhibit the film because he would support the decision of the board and "prevent the production by force, would revoke the theater license, and arrest all persons connected with the exhibition." The distributor appealed to the court to stop the commissioner and the city from interfering with attempts to show the film, claiming that the company would suffer "great monetary loss if . . . not allowed to produce it." The city did not file a response, so the Court of Chancery granted the injunction in *Public Welfare Pictures Corporation v. Brennan*, 134 A. 868 (1926). The court made a clear in its decision that the ruling expressed no opinion "as to the morality or immorality of this production." Instead, the court wrote that "by no stretch of the imagination can it be held that the director of public safety of a municipality can delegate to a policeman or a policewoman or a voluntary committee of women or to all combined the authority to say whether a certain play should or should not be produced."

Two years later, the New York State board of censors refused the distributor a permit to exhibit the film after determining that it was "obscene and indecent." The board based its decision on a scene in the film that shows a man and a woman together in the nude, "and, among other things, the progress of different venereal diseases and the effects thereof." The distributor took the case to the appellate division of the New York State Supreme Court, which upheld the decision of the board without viewing the film. In its decision, the court wrote that the law did not require the court to review decisions made by the board of censors if the plaintiff has not alleged that the denial was "in bad faith, arbitrary, capricious, or without reasonable ground."

FURTHER READING

De Grazia, Edward, and Roger K. Newman. *Banned Films: Movies, Censors, and the First Amendment.* New York: R. R. Bowker, 1982.
Public Welfare Pictures Corporation v. Brennan, 134 A. 868 (1926).
Public Welfare Pictures Corporation v. Lord, 230 N.Y.S. 137 (1928).

NATIVE SON

Country and date of production: Argentina/United States, 1951
Production company/distributor: Classic Pictures
Format: Sound, black and white
Running time: 91 minutes
Language: English
Producers: Walter Gould, James Prades
Director: Pierre Chenal
Screenwriters: Pierre Chenal, Richard Wright (novel)
Awards: None
Genre: Drama
With: Richard Wright (Bigger Thomas), Gloria Madison (Bessie Mears), Willa Pearl Curtis (Mrs. Hannah Thomas), Nicholas Joy (Henry Dalton), Ruth Robert (Helen Dalton), Charles Cane (Det. Britten), George Green ("Panama"), Jean Wallace (Mary Dalton), Georges Rigaud (Farley, a reporter), Leslie Straugh (Buddy Thomas), Lidia Alves (Vera Thomas), Charles Simmonds (Ernie)

SUMMARY

African-American novelist Richard Wright played the lead role in the film version of his novel *Native Son,* the tale of Bigger Thomas, a poor black youth from the Chicago slums who works as a chauffeur for the daughter of a rich, white family. After he brings the girl home drunk one night and takes her to her room, he panics, fearing that her blind mother might discover him there. In a fit of irrational fear, he accidentally kills the girl and then runs away. The remainder of the story relates the struggle that Thomas wages against racism and the difficulties that he faces in the ghetto existence in which he is trapped. When Thomas is captured and placed on trial, his liberal lawyer appears to be the only character sympathetic to his plight. Wright portrays Thomas as a man trapped by society in a life that he cannot escape—and, at the end, he cannot escape death in the electric chair.

The movie, produced on a very small budget in Europe, features poor acting, low-level production skills and an amateur tone; yet it is of interest for the casting of Wright as Bigger Thomas. Wright was the first to break from the literary ghetto that confined most African-American writers, and he won mainstream critical of acclaim. Because he had earned a prestigious name in literature, his poorly played role in the movie came as a shock to viewers who had difficulty accepting the middle-aged author in the role of 19-year-old Bigger Thomas.

CENSORSHIP HISTORY

The board of censors in the state of Ohio refused three different times to grant the distributor a permit to exhibit the film. After each refusal by the board, Classic Pictures deleted specified material related to language and cut segments depicting or suggesting sexuality in the film that the board found offensive. In its initial denial of a permit, the board denounced the intent of the film and stated that it "contributes to racial misunderstanding, presenting situations undesirable to the mutual interests of both races . . . undermining confidence that justice can be carried out [and presenting] racial frictions at a time when all groups should be united against everything that is subversive." Classic Pictures appealed to the court, asking that it require the board to issue a permit for exhibition of the film in the state. The trial court refused, and the distributor appealed to the Supreme Court of Ohio, which affirmed the decision of the lower court in *Classic Pictures v. Department of Education*, 112 N.E. 2d (1953). Despite the recent decisions involving THE MIRACLE, PINKY and LA RONDE, which left obscenity as the only ground on which a film could be banned, the Supreme Court of Ohio wrote that it believed "there remained a limited field in which decency and morals may be protected from the impact of an offending motion picture film by prior restraint under proper criteria." The U.S. Supreme Court did not agree, and in a decision that also overturned the denial of a permit to the film *M*, the Court determined that the Ohio motion picture censorship statute was "unconstitutionally vague and indefinite, and contrary to the requirements of the First Amendment due process, insofar as it authorized the censorship of films believed to be harmful or conducive to immorality or crime."

FURTHER READING

Classic Pictures v. Department of Education, 112 N.E. 2d (1953).

Crowther, Bosley. "*Native Son:* A Review." *New York Times*, June 24, 1951.

De Grazia, Edward, and Roger K. Newman. *Banned Films: Movies, Censors, and the First Amendment*. New York: R. R. Bowker, 1982.

Green, Jonathan. "Native Son," in *The Encyclopedia of Censorship*. New York: Facts On File, 1990.

Superior Films, Inc. v. Department of Education, Classic Pictures v. Department of Education, 346 U.S. 587 (1954).

NATURAL BORN KILLERS

Country and date of production: United States, 1994

Production company/distributor: Ixtlan Productions, J D Productions, New Regency Pictures, Warner Bros./Warner Bros.

Format: Sound, color/black and white

Running time: 118 minutes

Language: English

Producers: Jane Hamsher, Arnon Milchan, Thom Mount, Don Murphy, Clayton Townsend, Rand Vossler

Director: Oliver Stone

Screenwriters: Richard Rutowski, Oliver Stone, Quentin Tarantino (story), David Veloz

Awards: 1994 Venice Film Festival, Best Actress (Juliette Lewis), Special Jury Prize (Oliver Stone).

Genre: Drama/action

With: Woody Harrelson (Mickey Knox), Juliette Lewis (Mallory Wilson Knox), Robert Downey, Jr. (Wayne Gale), Tommy Lee Jones (Dwight McClusky), O-Lan Jones (Mabel), Ed White (Pinball Cowboy), Richard Lineback (Sonny), Lanny Flaherty (Early Hickey), Carol-Renee Modrall (Short Order Cook), Rodney Dangerfield (Ed Wilson), Edie McClurg (Mrs. Wilson), Sean Stone (Kevin Wilson), Jared Harris (Lancon Boy), Balthazar Getty (Jimmy Lupont)

SUMMARY

Natural Born Killers is the story of Mickey and Mallory, two mass murderers who go on a killing spree across America, making certain that everybody knows their names so they get credit for their crimes. More than their killings, however, the film deals with the way in which the public and the media turn them into folk heroes. As one teenager in the film tells the TV cameras, "Mass murder is wrong. But if I were a mass murderer, I'd be Mickey and Mallory!" The killers inspire a media feeding frenzy, and during their rampage, they are the most famous people in America. Mickey and Mallory fan clubs spring up, and T-shirts bearing their faces are hawked everywhere. Tabloid television wants to interview them, and a reporter is so thrilled by their fame that he almost wants to embrace them. Even the members of law enforcement seem thrilled to be handling the case and to experience the little brush with celebrity. Viewers do not see as much actual violence as they think they do in this movie, but the characters' rapid movements and tone convey a more violent impression than is actually shown. Oliver Stone also gives his mass murderers some reason for their behavior. In a view of Mallory's childhood, shot in the style of a lurid TV sitcom, Rodney Dangerfield plays her drunken, piggish father who shouts and threatens violence. He ridicules Mallory's frightened mother, grabs his daughter and makes lewd suggestions, while a television laugh track echoes in the background. Above all, the film is a satire of American society. Reporter Wayne Gale, with his Robin Leach accent, tries to turn the murder spree into entertainment, and he is so thrilled to be able to interview the famous killers that he hardly cares what happens—even in the final, bloody showdown, when he seems to think he is immune because he has the camera.

CENSORSHIP HISTORY

The outcry over *Natural Born Killers* began before it was released, when the Motion Picture Association of America (MPAA) classification board review panel threatened the film with an "NC-17" ("no one under 17 allowed") rating. After the distributor made five appeals and agreed to cut several segments in order to profit from the lucrative teenage market, the MPAA relented and changed the "NC-17" to "R" ("no one under 17 allowed without an adult"). For good measure, however, the MPAA attached to advertisements for the movie a parental warning: "For extreme violence and graphic carnage, for shocking images, and for strong language and sexuality." The movie has been condemned more for its suggestion and encouragement of violence and sexuality rather than for their actual presence. The loud music and throbbing rhythms combined with flashing images create tension in the film to suggest more action than is actually displayed. Sounds rather than visual images of guns going off indicate murders. Even the fantasy rape scene displays no nudity, and as the film bombards viewers with some of the advertising world's favorite images, cars with sex and violence, the effect is not pornographic. In fact, there was no nudity in the film's theatrical release, and only one topless shot, of the prostitute Jack kills, in the director's cut (standard fare for R-rated films)." Although the director has characterized the movie as an indictment of violence, critics contend that "it is too violent to be an indictment of violence."

In the United States, at least, the film has been used as an excuse by murderers who claim to have been motivated by the movie to commit their violent actions, which marks attempts to censor this film as different from attempts related to earlier films. The Supreme Court of Georgia convicted Ronnie Jack Beasley of murder in *Beasley v. State*, No. S98A0265 (July 13, 1998), and

Angela Crosby of murder in *Crosby v. State*, No. S98A0243 (April 13, 1998), both of whom claimed that they were influenced by *Natural Born Killers* to kidnap and murder two men in separate incidents and murder one. They revealed that they had sometimes used the names of Mickey and Mallory and "wanted to be like the characters in that movie [*Natural Born Killers*]," and Beasley further revealed that he had watched the movie 19 or 20 times. The prosecution showed the trial jury the film in its entirety, and the pair were convicted. The defense attorney claimed that the trial court erred in allowing the movie to be shown to the jury, but in the majority opinion, Judge Hugh P. Thompson wrote, "We conclude that the movie was relevant to show Beasley's state of mind." In their dissent, Justices Norman S. Fletcher, Robert Benham and Leah J. Sears argued against showing the movie to the jury: "Whatever relevance the motion picture had to the defendant's state of mind or motive, viewing the movie in its entirety did nothing more than mislead the jury and prejudice the defendant by blurring the distinction between Ronnie Beasley, the person on trial, and Mickey Knox, the fictional character in the movie."

The film has been implicated in numerous other violent incidents as viewers have misunderstood the directors intent. Young people reported watching the movie dozens of times and said things like 'I'm a natural born killer!" when arrested. Rather than perceive the movie as a satiric look at the American media's cynical exploitation of violence to maximize profits, viewers saw a how-to manual. This charge was the basis for a Louisiana lawsuit, which the state appeals court ordered to trial, filed on behalf of a store clerk who was shot during a 1995 holdup during a shooting spree carried out by Sarah Edmondson, niece of the Oklahoma attorney general and the daughter of a district court judge, and her boyfriend, Ben Carrus. The two defendants claimed that on March 5, 1995, they each consumed a large dose of LSD and then went to Edmondson's parents' vacation cabin. "There they picked up her father's .38 Smith and Wesson and watched *Natural Born Killers*, a film they had already seen multiple times, usually when they were tripping. The next day they were driving east." Along the way, they fantasized about carrying out some of the murders they had seen in the movie. They stopped at a cotton gin in Mississippi, where they killed the manager, William Savage. They drove to Louisiana, where Sarah shot a convenience store clerk, Patsy Byers, who became a quadriplegic. The pair were caught three months later and sentenced to long prison terms for the murders.

In an interesting twist, the author and attorney John Grisham, who wrote *A Time to Kill* and numerous other thrillers, was a friend of Savage, one of the victims. Grisham learned that Edmondson and Darrus may have been influenced by *Natural Born Killers* and then suggested in articles that appeared in *Vanity Fair* and *The Oxford American*, of which he is part-owner, that Oliver Stone and Time-Warner might hold some responsibility for the murders. Joseph Simpson, attorney for Patsy Byers, filed a civil suit against the killers and added Stone and Time-Warner as defendants. When the case first appeared before the circuit court in January 1997, the judge dismissed the case, but in May 1998, the U.S. Court of Appeals for the First Circuit Court in Louisiana agreed to reinstate the case. In October 1998, the Louisiana Supreme Court refused to hear the case, so Simpson took the case before the U.S. Supreme Court. Backed by a brief endorsed by the Writers Guild of America, West, the MPAA, the National Association of Broadcasters, the Freedom to Read Foundation and others, attorneys for Stone and Time-Warner requested that the case be dismissed. On March 8, 1999, the U.S. Supreme Court refused the appeal, which sent the case back to the Louisiana Supreme Court. To win the suit, attorneys for Byers had to "show that Stone and the production companies attempted to incite, and intended for the viewers of the movie to engage in, the type of crimes that were committed against Byers." The case remains unresolved.

Viewers have been denied the right to see the film in the United Kingdom as well. In the parish of Forest Constables, Guernsey, in the Channel Islands, the constables of the area were permitted to screen the film in advance of the dates that it was scheduled to be exhibited in the two theaters located in the parish. The film was given an "18 cert." rating by the British board of censors, which allows only people 18 and older to view the film. The film has not been given a video rating in the U.K. In another incident, after a gunman massacred 16 elementary school children and their teacher in Dunblane, Scotland, in March 1996, Warner Home Video voluntarily stopped distributing the videotape of *Natural Born Killers* in the U.K. and some other areas.

FURTHER READING

American Booksellers Foundation for Free Expression. "ABFFE Opposes *Natural Born Killers* Lawsuit." *ABFFE Update.* Http://www.abffe.com/updatel-4.htm.

"Correction." *The ew York Times*, April 28, 1996, pp. 9–10.

Douglas, Susan. "The Devil Made Me Do It: Is *Natural Born Killers* the Ford Pinto of Movies? Motion Picture That Inspired Copycat Murders Sued as Unprotected Speech." *The Nation*, April 5, 1999, pp. 50+.

Ebert, Roger. "Natural Born Killers." *Chicago-Sun Times*, August 26, 1994.

Swerczek, Mary. "Copycat Killing Suit Is Facing Test." *Times-Picayune*, March 22, 1999, pp. A1+.

Wills, Garry. "Dostoyevsky Behind the Camera: Oliver Stone Is Making Great American Novels on Film." *Atlantic Monthly* 280 (July 1997): 96+.

NEVER ON SUNDAY

Country and date of production: Greece, 1960 (as *Pote tin Kyriaki*)
Production company/distributor: Melinafilm/Lopert Pictures Corporation
Format: Sound, black and white
Running time: 91 minutes
Languages: English, Greek
Producer: Jules Dassin

Director: Jules Dassin
Screenwriter: Jules Dassin
Awards: 1960 Academy Awards, Music, Best Song (Manos Hadjidakis).
1960 Cannes Film Festival, Best Actress (Melina Mercouri; tied with Jeanne
   Moreau for *Moderato cantabile.*
1961 Golden Globe Awards, Best Film.
Genre: Drama/comedy
With: Melina Mercouri (Ilya), Jules Dassin (Homer), George Foundas
   (Tonio), Titos Vandis (Jorgo), Mitsos Liguisos (The Captain), Despo
   Diamantidou (Despo), Dimitris Papamichael (A Sailor)

SUMMARY

Never on Sunday was written, directed and produced by Jules Dassin, a leading
Hollywood producer and director who emigrated from the United States to
France in the early 1950s after he was blacklisted during the anticommunist
witch hunts conducted by the House Un-American Activities Committee
(HUAC) in Washington, D.C. Even with the success of this film, which was
made for $150,000 and earned gross receipts of $6 million ($2 million in the
United States and $4 million abroad), Dassin "remained unemployable in
Hollywood" a decade after the HUAC hearings.

The plot of *Never on Sunday* revolves around the lively and vivacious prostitute Ilya, who happily practices her profession from Monday through Saturday and makes Sunday her day of rest. She is an independent contractor of
sorts and refuses to work for a pimp named Noface, who has made her
repeated offers. When she meets Homer, an American scholar who is on
vacation in Greece, his dry and serious nature seems to challenge her. As they
attend performances of Greek tragedies and spend free time together, Homer
decides to "save" Ilya from her profession, which he convinces her to leave,
and promises to teach her about philosophy and to appreciate music and art.
At this time, Noface appears surreptitiously and offers to join Homer in paying for Ilya's education, using the false reason that he wants to keep her off
the streets so that she won't act as competition for his girls. The naïve Homer
takes the offer but then becomes the victim of Ilya's wrath when she learns of
his plan. After throwing what Homer has given her out of the window, Ilya
storms out to return to her old life. Once she is gone, Homer realizes that his
preoccupation with the past has been a means of escaping the present and
that Ilya made him truly enjoy life. He vows to stop hiding in the past and to
really live life in the present.

CENSORSHIP HISTORY

The United States distributor for *Never on Sunday* did not apply for the MPAA
seal of approval. Had the effort been made, the film would likely have had a
difficult time gaining approval because—unlike other films about prostitutes
such as *Butterfield 8*, in which the heroine sins and later dies—although Ilya

refuses to work on Sunday, she also shows no remorse for plying her trade the other six days of the week. The MPAA censors demanded "moral compensation" in the films to which they gave approval. The industry body had expected that Lopert Pictures Corporation would apply for a seal, and Production Code Administration (PCA) leader Geoff Shurlock wrote to MPAA head Eric Johnston on May 25, 1961, that "he was 'in terror' that the producers of Never on Sunday would apply for a Seal" (Leff and Simmons 227). He voiced this concern soon after the film was banned in Atlanta, Georgia, and stated further, "'But the horrible part is that, in rejecting it, we would probably have to adduce perforce exactly the same reason as did the Atlanta censor board'" (Leff and Simmons 227). Shurlock feared having the public associate the actions of the PCA what was still viewed as Southern provincialism.

The film played mostly in art theaters throughout the United States, and it did not face a serious challenge until the distributor applied for a license to exhibit the film in Atlanta, Georgia. The Atlanta motion picture censor, a librarian named Christine Smith Gilliam, demanded that certain cuts including references to Ilya's profession and her relaxed morality be made in the film before it could receive a license. The distributor made an administrative appeal to the city's board of censors, comprised of members of the Atlanta Public Library Board of Trustees, who ruled that even with the deletions specified by Gilliam the film could not be shown in Atlanta because it "would be harmful to the average child who might view the film and because [it] presented an unacceptable idea." When the distributor went to court to request an injunction to prevent the board of censors from interfering with exhibition of the movie, the Superior Court of Fulton County ruled that the film was not obscene and granted the injunction on the grounds that the Atlanta censorship law violated the free speech provisions of the constitutions of Georgia and the United States. The city board of censors appealed the decision, which was reversed by the Supreme Court of Georgia in *City of Atlanta v. Lopert Pictures Corporation*, 122 S.E. 2d 916 (1961). In the opinion, Justice Joseph D. Quillian wrote that the distributor should have applied to the superior court by writ of certiorari (an order made by a higher court to a lower court to provide records regarding a case that will allow the superior court to correct any excess or errors) if it wanted to have the decision of the board of censors reviewed. Instead, the distributor had petitioned the court for an injunction, and Justice Quillian would not allow the substitution. "In other words, once plaintiff had begun to make use of an appeals system that was part of the usual legal proceeding in such cases he could not then exercise the option of changing horses in mid-stream by asking for equitable relief."

FURTHER READING

Alverson, Luther. *A Movie Censorship Decision.* Columbia: Freedom of Information Center, School of Journalism, University of Missouri, 1961.

Carmen, Ira H. *Movies, Censorship and the Law.* Ann Arbor: University of Michigan Press, 1966.

City of Atlanta v. Lopert Pictures Corporation, 122 S.E. 2d 916 (1961).

Crosby, John. "Movies Are Too Dirty." *Saturday Evening Post*, November 10, 1962, pp. 10, 11.

Leff, Leonard J., and Jerold L. Simmons. *The Dame in the Kimono: Hollywood, Censorship, & the Production Code from the 1920s to the 1960s.* New York: Grove Weidenfeld, 1990.

Schumach, Murray. *The Face on the Cutting Room Floor.* New York: William Morrow, 1964.

THE NEWCOMERS

Country and date of production: United States, 1972
Production company/distributor: Ander Productions
Format: Sound, color
Running time: 70 minutes
Language: English
Producer: Gerry Bronson
Director: William Logan
Screenwriter: William Logan
Awards: None
Genre: Adult
With: Linda Marena, Alan Randall, Anne Sargent, David Strange

SUMMARY

The Newcomers, a brief film with little plot beyond the standard effort to titillate viewers, contains what a review in the September 6, 1972, issue of *Variety* described as "now conventional straight hardcore elements: mixed couplings, a dash of lesbian activity and an orgy." The setting for all of this activity is a college campus. Six young college students, played by actors whose names do not appear in the credits, are invited to the home of their social hygiene professor. The professor and his wife then encourage the students to explore their sexuality, which they do so enthusiastically that *Variety* was moved to state, "That sensual expedition . . . presumably rates them all A+ in the professor's social hygiene class."

CENSORSHIP HISTORY

The Motion Picture Association of America board of censors gave the film an "X" rating (only for adults) for its sexual content. Had the case motivated by the film not resulted in a state court interpreting a state statute in such a way as to bring it into conformity with the U.S. Constitution, the film would have slipped into obscurity, as did many other sexually explicit films during this same period. In 1973, the film was the target of a civil action brought by the corporation counsel for New York City and the New York County district attorney who sought to prevent its exhibition at theaters in New York City.

The counsel requested that the court issue search warrants to use in seizing prints of this film and four others, including BEHIND THE GREEN DOOR, as well as other evidence that might be used in prosecuting the manager of the Capri Cinema, Inc., for violating the New York State obscenity law. While the trial was pending, the city corporation counsel and the New York County district attorney requested that the court issue an order that would prevent the exhibitors from showing the film, as the state censorship statute provided. The New York Supreme Court heard the case and refused the requests of the corporation counsel, ruling in *Redlich v. Capri Cinema, Inc.*, 347 N.Y.S. 2d 811 (1973), that the censorship statute was not clearly defined. The attorneys for New York appealed the decision in the appellate division of the New York Supreme Court, which reversed the ruling and granted a temporary injunction in *Redlich v. Capri Cinema, Inc.*, 349 N.Y.S. 2d 697 (1973). The distributors of the film filed an appeal of the decision with the Supreme Court's appellate division, which upheld the constitutionality of the action in *Redlich v. Capri Cinema, Inc.*, 309 N.E. 2d 136 (1974), and declared that the New York statute was not overly broad when judged by the standards set by the Supreme Court in the landmark case of *Miller v. California* which required that a work be judged as a whole and according to community standards. The court concluded in its decision that film contained "multiple and variegated ultimate acts of sexual perversion [that] would have been regarded as 'obscene' by the community standards of Sodom and Gomorrah."

FURTHER READING

De Grazia, Edward, and Roger K. Newman. *Banned Films: Movies, Censors, and the First Amendment.* New York: R. R. Bowker, 1982.
"The Newcomers." *Variety,* September 6, 1972.
Redlich v. Capri Cinema, Inc., 347 N.Y.S. 2d 811 (1973).
Redlich v. Capri Cinema, Inc., 349 N.Y.S. 2d 697 (1973).
Redlich v. Capri Cinema, Inc., 309 N.E. 2d 136 (1974).

THE NORTH STAR

County and date of production: United States, 1943
Production company/distributor: Goldwyn Pictures Corporation/RKO Radio Pictures
Format: Sound, black and white
running time: 106 minutes
Language: English
Producer: Samuel Goldwyn
Director: Lewis Milestone
Screenwriter: Lillian Hellman
Awards: None
Genre: Drama

With: Dana Andrews (Kolya), Charley Bates (Petya), Anne Baxter (Marina), Walter Brennan (Karp), Ann Carter (Olga), Esther Dale (Anna), Farley Granger (Damian), Paul Guilfoyle (Iakin), Ann Harding (Sophia), Walter Huston (Dr. Kurin), Dean Jagger (Rodion), Martin Kosleck (Doctor Max Richter), Erich von Stroheim (Dr. Otto Von Harden)

SUMMARY

The North Star is a relic of its time, one of several World War II propaganda films created by Hollywood to reflect the new relationship between the United States and Russia after the 1941 German invasion transformed Russia from an ally of Hitler to an ally of the United States. These films, which also included Warner Brothers' *Mission to Moscow*, RKO's *Days of Glory* and MGM's *Song of Russia*, were made to help the U.S. war effort, even at the sacrifice of box-office profits. Samuel Goldwyn pulled together an impressive creative team, from Lewis Milestone, whose *All Quiet on the Western Front* had earned universal praise, to the Popular Front writer and playwright Lillian Hellman, and a cast that included some of the best-known young actors of the time. The prominent composer Aaron Copeland wrote the score, and the popular lyricist Ira Gershwin supplied lyrics for what were portrayed as folk songs in the film. Instead of following other propaganda films in exploring the Soviet experiment, Goldwyn Pictures focused on the ordinary lives of ordinary people, as the publicity for the film stated: "a picture about average Russians for average Americans."

The story takes place in a Ukrainian farming village and begins with extensive scenes of village life before war breaks out. The images suggest that life in the village is an endless round of singing, dancing, picnicking and accordion-playing. Everyone is happy, well-fed and in high spirits. The scenes are devoid of any sign that this is Soviet Russia, where industrialization and collectivization predominate. As Diana Davies observed, "One can't help thinking that if the Disney corporation were to create a new theme park called 'Russialand,' it would look something like this. A 'Russian folk song' with music by Aaron Copeland and words by Ira Gershwin says it all." The film changes dramatically for the worse once war breaks out. Most of the film consists of extended battle sequences, and the idyllic village scenes turn to a devastated landscape of burning buildings and wheat fields, dead bodies and constant, dull gray smoke. The film avoids the dark politics of Stalin and the burdens under which ordinary Russians labored in the 1920s and 1930s, and instead focuses on the horror and the tragedy of the war. The final words of the film, spoken by a character named Marina, are the final judgment on war: "None of us will be the same. Wars do not leave people as they are. All people will learn that and come to see that wars do not have to be. We will make this the last war; we will make a free world for all men."

CENSORSHIP HISTORY

The film does not have a standard censorship history in that it was not banned by boards of censors or by law. Instead, pieces of the screenplay and, eventually, of the film were removed over time to change the message from friendly cooperation between the United States and Russia in the war years to an anticommunist narrative renamed *Armored Attack* and aimed at the 1956 Soviet invasion of Hungary. The dilution of the message of the screenplay began at the outset of filming, when the studio edited or wrote out much of Hellman's material regarding Soviet life and her mention of such issues as collectivization. After arguing that her best material was being edited out of the daily screenings or changed in the script, Hellman eventually bought out her contract for $30,000, although her name stayed on the film as screenwriter and published the original screenplay through Viking Press. She did this to guarantee that her version of the screenplay would be a matter of public record and would not be confused with the eventual version that would appear on screen. In the eyes of some observes, the studio version avoided an in-depth treatment of any of the problems involved in the building of a socialist society and the contradictions of an alliance between a capitalist and a communist country in its version. Even with the many changes, the film attracted negative attention from conservatives who could not forget that these happy villagers were actually the Soviet Russians. As Representative Marion T. Bennett, a congressman from Missouri, said in a speech before the House:

> Hollywood, in its usual extreme style, has apparently lost its head and gone completely overboard in its attempt to make Communism look good. Our temporary military alliance with Russia must not cause us to forget that, except insofar as treatment of Jews is concerned, there is no difference between Communism and nazi-ism as it affects the common man.

The newspaper magnate William Randolph Hearst was particularly rancorous toward *The North Star*, and he ordered his editors to qualify all mention of that film with the phrase "Bolshevist propaganda." After World War II, those involved with the making of such pro-Russian films found themselves under close scrutiny by the House Un-American Activities Committee. *The North Star* and other films about Russia were used by politicians in the late 1940s and early 1950s to beat Hollywood. Because attitudes of both Hellman and Milestone toward the committee remained defiant, both she and the director were quietly "gray-listed" by the industry. Thus, unlike outright blacklisting, which would have marked their films as clearly unacceptable, Hellman and Milestone experienced a more subtle ostracism.

FURTHER READING

Ceplair, Larry, and Steven Englund. *The Inquisition in Hollywood: Politics in the Film Community, 1930–1960.* Garden City, N.Y.: Anchor Press, 1980.

Davies, Diana. *"The North Star."* *Film Notes.* New York State Writers Institute. Http://www.albany.edu/writers-inst/filmnote.html#N.

Hagopian, Kevin. *"The North Star."* *Film Notes.* New York State Writers Institute. Http://www.albany.edu/writers-inst/filmnote.html#N.

Millichap, Joseph. *Lewis Milestone.* Boston: Twayne Publishers, 1981.

Moody, Richard. *Lillian Hellman, Playwright.* New York: Pegasus, 1972.

OCTOBER

Country and date of production: Soviet Union, 1927 (as *Oktyabr* or *Oktiabr*)

Production company/distributor: Amkino Corporation (United States, as *Ten Days That Shook the World*, 1928)

Format: Silent, black and white

Running time: 106 minutes

Language: Russian (English subtitles in United States)

Producer: Grigori Aleksandrov

Directors: Sergei M. Eisenstein, Grigori Aleksandrov

Screenwriters: Grigori Aleksandrov, Sergei M. Eisenstein, John Reed (book, *Ten Days That Shook the World*)

Awards: None

Genre: Drama

With: Layaschenko (Minister)

SUMMARY

After major success with his 1925 film *Battleship Potemkin*, Eisenstein was called upon by Sovkino, the Soviet film agency, to make a film to commemorate the tenth anniversary of the October Revolution. Eisenstein first titled the film *Ten Days that Shook the World* and used the popular 1919 book of the same name by John Reed to write the script, translating Reed's account into cinema terms and experimenting with what Eisenstein called "intellectual montage," or the use of metaphorical devices to elaborate certain ideas within the medium of film. John Reed, born in 1917, was a United States journalist who served as a correspondent during the Mexican War (1916 to 1917) and then reported on World War I, which led him to Petrograd in 1917 at the beginning of the Bolshevik (October) Revolution. He then returned to the United States and helped to found the Communist Party there. The reproduction of battles and the scenes of bridge building and destruction with thousands of people and visual effects were difficult to create with the limited technical knowledge and resources of the time.

The movie, filmed in documentary style, relates the events of the Russian Revolution with a tendency to support the communist side, although it retains a factual stance in a number of areas, such as the dedication of many to the cause and the suffering endured. Eisenstein reenacts events in Petrograd from the end of the czarist monarchy in February 1917 to the end of the provisional government and the decrees of peace and of land in November of that year.

Following the actual historical timeline, the film opens with the view of a crowd toppling a huge statue of Czar Alexander III. Portrayed next is the return of Lenin in April, the suppression by counterrevolutionaries of a spontaneous revolt in July and the ordering of Lenin's arrest. In the film, the Bolsheviks are ready to strike by late October and to begin 10 days that will shake the world. As had occurred 10 years earlier, the Mensheviks in the film vacillate, and an advance guard infiltrates the palace. The leader of the attack is Anatov-Oveyenko, who signs the proclamation dissolving the provisional government. In *October*, Eisenstein used newsreel footage of actual events filmed in 1917 and also featured participants of the 1917 conflict. He also used many of the same buildings where the events of 1917 occurred.

CENSORSHIP HISTORY

Eisenstein was able to complete only six films in his lifetime—and most of them only with major revisions and under the eyes of the Stalinist censors. *Potemkin* (1925) was the last film over which Eisenstein was to have complete control, and it gained a high level of respect from Hollywood studio executives. In contrasts, the Hollywood hierarchy considered *October*, a history of the 1917 revolution made at the height of the Soviet fight against the bureaucracy by the Left Opposition, too supportive of the communist philosophy. Because the political climate changed in the U.S.S.R., Soviet bureaucrats instructed Eisenstein—in the last stages of editing the film—to slice out of *October* summarily many of the leading participants in the revolution, most notably Leon Trotsky. Because of government demands that Eisenstein rewrite history, he removed an estimated one-third of the film. He also removed much of the newsreel footage. Eisenstein's long-time collaborator Aleksandrov reported that late one night, during the last stages of editing the film, Stalin unexpectedly came by the studios and was shown certain sequences, including a speech by Lenin. Stalin ordered that sequence, amounting to about 3,000 feet, to be cut, saying, "Lenin's liberalism is no longer valid today." The film was released in the United States and England in a shortened and simplified version. The satire of the original, shown in a montage of icons—crosses, statues of Buddha and wooden figures of primitive goods—was cut. The film did not receive wide play in the United States because of its strong support for communism.

FURTHER READING

Barna, Yon. *Eisenstein*. Boston: Little, Brown, 1973.

Carr, Jay. "After the Revolution: It's Time to Reevaluate Sergei Eisenstein." *Boston Globe*, January 10, 1993, p. B32.

Jukovsky, Martin. "Eisenstein." *Labour Review*, September 1978; reproduced at http://www.wsws.org.

Kenez, Peter. "Film Review—October (Oktiabr) Directed by Sergei Eisenstein." *The Russian Review* 50 (October 1991): 487.

Mailer, Martin. "Success and Failure of the Soviet Cinema." *Marxist* 6, no. 1 (1967): 4–6.

Mast, Gerald, and Bruce F. Kawin. *A Short History of the Movies.* Boston: Allyn & Bacon, 1996.

"*Oktyabar [October]*: A Review." *Variety* 333 November 30, 1988 p. 23.

OF HUMAN BONDAGE

Country and date of production: United States, 1934
Production company/distributor: Radio Pictures/RKO Pictures
Format: Sound, black and white
Running time: 83 minutes
Language: English
Producer: Pandro S. Berman
Director: John Cromwell
Screenwriters: W. Somerset Maugham (novel), Lester Cohen
Awards: None
Genre: Drama
With: Leslie Howard (Philip Carey), Bette Davis (Mildred Rogers), Frances Dee (Sally Athelny), Kay Johnson (Norah), Reginald Denny (Harry Griffiths), Alan Hale (Emil Miller), Reginald Sheffield (Cyril Dunsford), Reginald Owen (Athelny), Desmond Roberts (Dr. Jacobs)

SUMMARY

Of Human Bondage, adapted from the novel of the same name written by W. Somerset Maugham, relates the story of Philip Carey, a sensitive young man with a club foot whose first dream is to become an artist. In France a painting instructor tells Carey that he lacks the skill to become a great painter, so he decides to study medicine in London. A friend asks Carey to help him get to know a waitress named Mildred, but Carey becomes infatuated with her. When he asks her out, he asks her not to say, "I don't mind," which seems to signal her lack of enthusiasm, but she does so anyway. When Carey's friend, Emil Miller, decides that he wants Mildred, he tells Carey that he is too artistic, then convinces Mildred to cancel her date with Carey and go out with him instead. Unaware that Mildred is cheating on him, Carey tries to study for his medical examination but cannot keep his mind off her, and he subsequently fails his exam. He finally recognizes his infatuation, buys an engagement ring and asks Mildred to marry him. He is too late, however, because she has agreed to marry Miller, who makes more money. Although losing Mildred is painful, Carey reluctantly gets on with his life and meets Norah, who writes romance stories. She falls in love with Carey and becomes a good influence on him, making him study. Just when Carey appears to have found happiness with Norah, Mildred returns, saying her husband has left and that she is pregnant. Carey assists her financially and then confronts Miller and tells him to take care of her. Miller, however, denies he and Mildred are married. Realizing that he is still infatuated with Mildred, who promises that she will do anything to please him if he'll help take care of her, Carey ends his relationship with Norah. She and Carey express regrets that one always loves more than the other.

Carey is bound to Mildred as Norah is to Carey and as Mildred was to Miller. Mildred gives her baby into the care of a nurse. Carey then invites a friend, Harry Griffiths, to spend time with them so that Mildred won't be bored, but the two begin to fall in love. Carey, obviously upset with this turn of events, calls Mildred cheap and vulgar, and the infuriated Mildred leaves for Paris with Griffiths. While at a hospital Carey meets Sally, whose father invites him to dinner. Later, Carey visits Sally and her father occasionally, until Mildred reappears with her baby. He takes them in but soon is sickened to discover that Mildred has stolen the securities he was using for his tuition. After Carey loses his apartment, Sally's father takes him in. Meanwhile, Mildred's baby has died. Distraught and ill, Mildred dies soon thereafter. In the final scene, Carey and Sally decide to get married right away.

CENSORSHIP HISTORY

RKO advertised *Of Human Bondage* with the following tagline: "The Love That Lifted a Man to Paradise . . . and Hurled Him Down." The provocative advertising reflected the subject of the movie, which dealt with the obsessive love of a young medical student for a prostitute. When RKO first submitted the script based on Maugham's book, Joseph Breen, the head of the Production Code Administration (PCA), warned that the subject matter was "highly offensive" because in the novel the slatternly Mildred becomes infected with syphilis. Breen demanded that the studio change her affliction to tuberculosis. The studio also directed to make the character of Mildred less slatternly and to portray her as married to Miller. After RKO made all of the changes that Breen required, the film received the seal of approval from the PCA. But the final version did not meet the standards of the Catholic Legion of Decency (LOD) chapters in Detroit, Pittsburgh, Omaha and Chicago, and the film was condemned for Catholic viewers in those cities.

Although the LOD had been extremely effective in banning earlier films, *Of Human Bondage* seemed to exert a stronger pull on the imaginations of Catholics. Lupton "Lup" A. Wilkinson, an employee of Will Hays, the head of the Motion Picture Producers and Distributors Association (MPPDA), was sent by Hays to tour 20 U.S. cities from late July to mid-September 1934 and to assess the impact of the LOD. When Wilkerson arrived in Baltimore in August, the Hippodrome Theater was exhibiting *Of Human Bondage*, which had been banned by the Chicago LOD, and he arrived to find delegations of local priests picketing the theater. "The result was that *Of Human*

Bondage broke all attendance records at the theater. More than five hundred people had been turned away opening night. The movie critic for the *Baltimore Sun*, Norman Clark, told Wilkinson that because of the Catholic protest against the movie 'he had scarcely been able to get into a theater during the past three weeks.'" In Chicago, where the LOD had condemned the movie and forbade Catholics to view it, "*Of Human Bondage* played to huge crowds at the RKO Palace. After an opening week of sellouts, the film was still going strong after four weeks at the Palace." Wilkinson was able to report the same of Buffalo, Cleveland, Boston, Detroit, Pittsburgh and Newark. In mid-1935, despite acceptance throughout the country, Breen included *Of Human Bondage* in the list of films that he reinspected and requested changes in, as a condition for allowing the film to be screened should RKO decide to rerelease it.

FURTHER READING

Black, Gregory D. *Hollywood Censored: Morality Codes, Catholics, and the Movies.* Cambridge, England: Cambridge University Press, 1994.

Leff, Leonard J., and Jerold L. Simmons. *The Dame in the Kimono: Hollywood, Censorship, and the Production Code from the 1920s to the 1960s.* New York: Grove Weidenfeld, 1990.

Vieira, Mark. *Sin in Soft Focus: Pre-code Hollywood.* New York: Harry N. Abrams, 1999.

THE ORDEAL

Country and date of production: United States, 1914
Production company/distributor: Life Photo Film Corp.
Format: Silent, black and white
Running time: 75 minutes
Language: English Titles
Producer: Life Photo Film Corp.
Director: William S. Davis
Screenwriter: Edward M. Roskam
Awards: None
Genre: Drama/ war
With: Sue Balfour (The patriot's mother), Barbara Castleton, George De Carlton (The father), Anna Laughlin (The patriot's sweetheart), Beulah Poynter, Harry Springler (The patriot [as Harry Spingler]), William H. Tooker (The general), Margot Williams (The patriot's sister)

SUMMARY

Set during the Franco-Prussian War, *The Ordeal* is built on the concept of a dream in which a young patriot sees himself going off to fight. Edward De Grazia reports that the story is based on a poem written long before World

War I, but no poet has been identified. As many a soldier before him, the patriot must say goodbye to those he leaves behind: his mother, father, sister and sweetheart. The patriot is taken prisoner on the battlefield, but when he is interrogated by an officer wearing a German uniform, he staunchly refuses to reveal where the rest of the soldiers in his company are hiding. To taunt him, the officer condemns the young man's mother, sister and sweetheart to be shot to death as he agonizes in silence. When the dream ends and the young man awakens, he finds his family is alive and happy, and he recognizes that he has been dreaming. The film was reissued in 1918 under the title *The Mothers of Liberty*.

CENSORSHIP HISTORY

The beginning of World War I made the United States particularly sensitive about its relations with Germany; also alert was the National Board of Review (NBR) of Motion Pictures, formed as the National Board of Censorship of Motion Pictures in 1909 but renamed in 1915, which was the earliest attempt at movie industry self-regulation. Fearing that the portrayal of the cruel German officer "might occasion racial differences at this particular time," this group of public-spirited citizens was encouraged by Ephraim Kaufmann, a New York City deputy commissioner of licenses, to call upon George Bell, the New York commissioner of licenses, to stop *The Ordeal*'s exhibition. After the movie had been screened several times at Hammerstein's Lexington Avenue Opera House, Bell warned the theater owner that he must stop exhibiting the film or risk having his operating license revoked. The commissioner further warned the distributor of the film, Life Photo Film Corporation, that the film was banned from exhibition in any theater in New York City, based on the request by the NBR and the deputy commissioner who "feared the disapproval of foreigners." The distributor filed a request with the New York State Supreme Court to grant an injunction to prevent Bell from revoking the theater's license, at least as long as the contract for the exhibition of the film. When the case went to trial, the commissioner admitted that he found nothing objectionable in the film and had made the earlier decision based solely on the judgment of the NBR and of his deputy commissioner. The court granted the distributor the injunction and wrote in its decision that the film "to a sensible and ordinary mind could in no way create racial strife . . . even if some supersensitive Teutonic might consider it . . . an unfair characterization and a misrepresentation of the German army, but, as a matter of fact, this is not so." Moreover, the court asserted in *Life Photo Film Corporation v. Bell*, 90 Misc. 469 (1915) (N.Y.), that whether or not the film displayed "an officer of the German army in a cruel and inhuman light during the Franco-Prussian war," that alone was not enough to support banning the film because the commissioner and his deputy had testified that the film contained nothing "that could offend Americans."

FURTHER READING

De Grazia, Edward, and Roger K. Newman. *Banned Films: Movies, Censors, and the First Amendment.* New York: R. R. Bowker, 1982.

Leuchtenberg, William E. *The Perils of Prosperity, 1914–1932.* Chicago: University of Chicago Press, 1958.

Life Photo Film Corporation v. Bell 90 Misc. 469 (1915) (N.Y.).

Soderburgh, Peter A. "'Aux Armes': The Rise of the Hollywood War Film, 1916–1930." *South Atlantic Quarterly* 65 (1966): 512.

THE OUTLAW

Country and date of production: United States, 1941
Production company/distributor: United Artists/RKO Pictures
Format: Sound, black and white
Running time: 106 minutes
Language: English
Producer: Howard Hughes
Directors: Howard Hawks (uncredited), Howard Hughes
Screenwriters: Jules Furthman, Howard Hawks (uncredited), Ben Hecht (uncredited)
Awards: None
Genre: Western
With: Jack Buetel (Billy the Kid), Jane Russell (Rio), Thomas Mitchell (Pat Garrett), Walter Huston (Doc Holliday), Mimi Aguglia (Guadalupe), Joe Sawyer (Charley), Gene Rizzi (Stranger)

SUMMARY

The Outlaw recounts the relationships among Doc Holliday, Billy the Kid (William Bonney), Sheriff Pat Garrett and Rio, a half-Native American woman who is Doc Holliday's girlfriend. Garrett is the newly appointed sheriff of Lincoln, New Mexico. He learns that an old friend, Doc Holliday, is coming to town. While Doc has a reputation for causing some troubles with the law, Sheriff Garrett is pleased by the news nonetheless. Doc arrives in Lincoln on a stagecoach. In his possession is a stolen horse, which Billy the Kid, a famous outlaw of the time, later steals. Billy and Doc, both scoundrels, form a friendship. Doc's allegiance with a notorious outlaw cools the relationship between Garrett and Doc. As Billy and Doc spend more time with each other, the bond between them strengthens, and it is cemented when Doc hides Billy at his girlfriend's house after Billy has been shot. Although Billy is rude to Doc's girlfriend, she finds herself falling for the famous outlaw, who also happens to be the best friend of her current lover. This causes strains in every possible relationship. Doc and Billy become tense with each other, but in a humorous twist Billy makes Doc an offer: the choice of his horse Red or the return of Rio. Doc chooses the horse, which leaves Billy a bit melancholy for, as he tells Doc, he had become very fond of the horse. The final scenes include a showdown in which Doc Holliday is hit by a bullet Garrett meant for Billy the Kid. Out of respect for Doc's sacrifice, Garrett allows Rio and Billy to ride safely away.

CENSORSHIP HISTORY

The Outlaw was the subject of Joseph Breen's final fight as head of the Production Code Administration: His dispute with Howard Hughes over the movie led to his resignation. Because the film was independently produced, Hughes did not have to submit the screenplay in advance to the Production Code Administration review board, but he chose to do so anyway. When Breen read the script, he listed more than 100 objections to dialogue and character interactions. He wanted all suggestions of a sexual relationship between Doc Holliday and Rio deleted, all references to cold-blooded killing by Billy the Kid removed, and all sexually suggestive dialogue excised. When Breen later screened the film, not only did he find that Hughes had ignored many of his objections, but he also saw the manner in which Hughes had exploited the assets of the well-endowed Russell. Breen wrote the following in a memo to Will Hays:

> I have never seen anything quite so unacceptable as the shots of the breasts of the character of Rio. This is the young girl whom Mr. Hughes recently picked up and who has never before, according to my information, appeared on the motion picture screen. Throughout almost half the picture the girl's breasts, which are quite large and prominent, are shockingly emphasized and, in almost every instance, are very substantially uncovered.

Hughes acquiesced to some of Breen's suggested changes and agreed to cover more of Jane Russell, but he also ignored quite a number of Breen's demands. The PCA issued a seal of approval to *The Outlaw* on May 23, 1941, but only after considerable bickering, committee meetings and excisions to the film. "After considerable bickering and the appointment of committees to make studies, changes were made and a seal of approval was issued to *The Outlaw* on May 23, 1941."

The film opened in a single theater in San Francisco on February 5, 1943, accompanied by huge images of a scantily covered Jane Russell on billboards throughout the city. The advertising caused more outcry than the movie, as religious and civic groups wrote to Hays to complain about the "very disgusting portrayal of the feminine star." Other studios also protested Hughes's advertising, which they viewed as a form of unfair competition. Hughes finally withdrew the movie from exhibition when the San Francisco police prepared arrest warrants and he was called into a conference with the city district attorney. The movie then disappeared for a few years. When World War II ended, Hughes brought out the movie again under a new advertising campaign. Using such lines as "What are the two great reasons for Jane Russell's rise to stardom?" Hughes drew public attention and angered the PCA, which revoked the seal of approval for *The Outlaw*. Hughes then sued the Motion Picture Producers and Distributors Association (MPPDA) in the U.S. District Court of New York City, charging that the association was in violation of antitrust laws and for restraint of trade. The court disagreed, and on June 27, 1946, issued its decision in *Hughes Tool Co. v. Motion Picture Assn. of America*, 66 F. Supp. 1006 (S.D.N.Y. 1946). Judge D. J. Bright wrote, "Experience has shown that the industry can suffer as much from indecent advertising as from indecent pictures. Once a picture has been approved the public may properly assume that the advertisement and promotional matter is likewise approved. The blame for improper, salacious or false advertising is placed as much at the door of the association as of the producer."

When Hughes released the film for the second time, it carried the "C" (condemned) rating from the Catholic Legion of Decency (LOD). In Philadelphia, LOD pressure forced one theater to withdraw the film after organized Catholics vowed to boycott the theater for a year if the film continued. In New Jersey, the New Jersey Conference of the Methodist Church called for the state to establish a board of censors after the film was exhibited. In New York State, although the distributor was granted a permit to exhibit the film and three theaters in New York City had contracted to show it, the New York City police commissioner and the commissioner of licenses declared the film obscene after watching it in a private screening. The commissioners warned the theater owners that they were subject to criminal prosecution and the revocation of their operating licenses if they showed the film. Howard Hughes filed a request with the court to bar the threatened criminal prosecutions and to rule that criminal proceedings for showing an allegedly obscene film were improper because the New York State censors had granted a permit for exhibition. The court denied Hughes's request in *Hughes Tool Co. v. Fielding*, 73 N.Y.S. 2d 98 (1947). Hughes appealed the decision before the appellate division of the New York State District Court, which in *Hughes Tool Co. v. Fielding*, 75 N.Y.S. 2d 287 (1947), affirmed the decision of the lower court. The New York Court of Appeals also affirmed the decision in *Hughes Tool Co. v. Fielding*, 80 N.E. 2d 540 (1948) and wrote that the penal law provided law enforcement officials with an avenue by which to appeal decisions made by the state censorship board.

Changes and deletions to the movie to satisfy both the censors and Hughes's artistic vision were not completed until 1949. When this occurred, the MPAA once again granted a seal of approval to *The Outlaw*. The LOD also reclassified the film to "B" (morally objectionable in part for all) after the morally offensive elements had been eliminated.

FURTHER READING

Carmen, Ira H. *Movies, Censorship, and the Law*. Ann Arbor: University of Michigan Press, 1964.

Gardner, Gerald. *The Censorship Papers: Movie Censorship Letters from the Hays Office, 1934 to 1968*. New York: Dodd, Mead, 1987.
Hughes Tool Co. v. Motion Pictures Assn. of America, 66 F. Supp. 1006 (S.D.N.Y. 1946).
Hughes Tool Co. v. Fielding, 73 N.Y.S. 2d 98 (1947).
Hughes Tool Co. v. Fielding, 75 N.Y.S. 2d 287 (1947).
Hughes Tool Co. v. Fielding, 80 N.E. 2d 540 (1948).
Leff, Leonard J., and Jerold L. Simmons. *The Dame in the Kimono: Hollywood, Censorship, and The Production Code from the 1920s to the 1960s*. New York: Grove Weidenfeld, 1990.
Schumach, Murray. *The Face on the Cutting Room Floor*. New York: William Morrow, 1964.

PATTERN OF EVIL

Country and date of production: United Kingdom, 1967
Production company/distributor: Chelsea Productions/Marvin Films
Format: Sound, color
Running time: 72 minutes
Language: English
Producers: George Harrison Marks, Al Weiss
Director: George Harrison Marks
Screenwriter: Larry Sanders
Awards: None
Genre: Drama /adult
With: Paul Holcombe, Yvonne Paul, Cindy Neal, Rena Bronson, Jutka Goz, Monique Devereaux, Tony Barton, David London, Howard Nelson

SUMMARY

Pattern of Evil, also known under the title *Fornicon*, is a story of industrial espionage enlivened by murder and graphic sexuality. The film opens with a view of the advertising campaign for a new perfume, Formula-69, about to be marketed by Madame LaBanca's cosmetics firm. Aiming to capitalize on the sexual associations with the product name, John Webley, the public relations manager, has focused advertising around a stripper who performs a suggestive dance in the opening scenes. As with any product with the potential for great success, Formula-69 becomes the target of competitors who try to obtain the formula, to the extent of trying to kill Webley. Instead, Webley's wife is killed, and Webley becomes the suspect. After an interrogation, Scotland Yard releases him for lack of evidence, but Webley is sure that someone he knows is the murderer. He has the opportunity to act on his suspicions a short time later while attending a party held at the home of Madame LaBanca when he suggests that all present participate in a game of "truth or consequences." He manages to trick his main suspect, Greta Marr, into having to endure "consequences": The group places her on a medieval torture rack where, after a substantial amount of writhing, she reveals the true murderer.

CENSORSHIP HISTORY

The film is notable only because it was one of the last films that the United States Customs Bureau refused admittance into the United States. The legal proceedings related to *Pattern of Evil* hold further interest because U.S. Customs lost the case when their challenge went to court and a jury disagreed with the view that the government held toward this film. In 1969, U.S. Customs agents seized the film on the grounds that it was obscene, and they began forfeiture proceedings. Marvin Films, the company that had imported the film and planned to distribute it for exhibition in the United States, requested that the court dismiss the proceedings before the case went to trial. The distributor claimed in the request that the "proceedings amounted to an unconstitutional prior restraint on freedom of expression" and that the term *obscene* as applied by the U.S. Customs Bureau was "unconstitutionally vague." Attorneys for the distributor argued further that the film was not obscene when assessed according to the constitutional procedural requirements established by the United States Supreme Court in such cases as *Freedman v. Maryland*, 380 U.S. 51 (1965), which involved the film REVENGE AT DAYBREAK. The court denied the motion to dismiss the charges, and the case went to trial before a jury. After viewing the film and applying the constitutional requirements, the jury decided that *Pattern of Evil* was not obscene.

FURTHER READING

De Grazia, Edward, and Roger K. Newman. *Banned Films: Movies, Censors and the First Amendment*. New York: R. R. Bowker, 1982.
Freedman v. Maryland, 380 U.S. 51 (1965).
United States v. A Motion Picture Entitled Pattern of Evil, 304 F. Supp. 197 (1969).

PINKY

Country and date of production: United States, 1949
Production company/distributor: 20th Century-Fox
Format: Sound, black and white
Running time: 102 minutes
Language: English
Producer: Darryl F. Zanuck
Director: Elia Kazan
Screenwriters: Philip Dunne, Dudley Nichols, Cid Ricketts Sumner (novel)
Awards: None
Genre: Drama
With: Jeanne Crain (Patricia "Pinky" Johnson), Ethel Barrymore (Miss Em), Ethel Waters (Granny), William Lundigan (Dr. Thomas Adams), Basil Ruysdael (Judge Walker), Kenny Washington (Dr. Canady), Nina Mae McKinney (Rozelia), Griff Barnett (Dr. Joe), Frederick O'Neal (Jake

Walters), Evelyn Varden (Melba Wooley), Raymond Greenleaf (Judge Shoreham)

SUMMARY

The story, adapted from the novel by Cid Ricketts Sumner, was first conceived as a movie entitled *Quality*. The story's main character is Patricia Johnson, a light-skinned black woman nicknamed Pinky, who is born in Mississippi during a time of intense racial prejudice. After finishing high school, she goes to Boston to earn a nursing degree and to work; while there, she "passes" for white. She also falls in love with a young white doctor, Dr. Thomas Adams, who knows nothing of her past or of her ancestry. After 12 years in Boston, Pinky returns to her grandmother's house in the South and tells her about the wealthy young doctor. She explains to her grandmother that she is going to return to the North as soon as possible to get married. Not certain what to make of these changes in her granddaughter's life, her grandmother persuades Pinky to stay for a while and to treat an ailing white woman, to which Pinky reluctantly agrees. At the same time, she is resentful because she believes that she is now performing the same tasks that her grandmother performed. Pinky sees her treatment of a white woman as a form of continued oppression and servitude, instead of as a way of using her education.

Pinky is emotionally torn apart by her racial identity. She wishes to be treated with dignity and respect, and she seems to wish to help others situated similarly to herself; however, when an African-American doctor asks for her help in training some African-American students, Pinky declines. As Pinky nurses Miss Em, the two slowly develop a mutual respect. Upon her death, Miss Em leaves Pinky her property. Miss Em's relatives are shocked and contest the new will in court. To raise money for the defense of the will, Pinky washes clothes by hand with her grandmother. When the court rules in Pinky's favor and allows her to keep the land, she is faced with another difficult decision. Her white fiancé Tom wants her to return to Boston, to resume life as a white woman and to marry him, but Pinky is tired of hiding her true self. She has found happiness in her new estate and in her position in Mississippi. She refuses Tom and decides to use the land to begin a clinic and nursery school.

CENSORSHIP HISTORY

The actions of the anticommunist House Un-American Activities Committee (HUAC), which investigated all instances of possible disloyalty to the government, made filmmakers nervous in the late 1940s, and "the promising trend of movies with social content came to a jarring halt." The planned film *Quality*, like other films that exposed the ugly reality of racism, was among those "which most of the Communist screenwriters saw [as] a triumphant step forward in Hollywood's 'fight against racism,'" but such movies also began to concern movie studios as HUAC became more aggressive in its investigations. A fearful 20th Century-Fox shelved its plans for the movie, which dealt in detail with the volatile topic of interracial romance, and then commissioned Philip Dunne to rewrite the script and to severely downplay the romance before renaming the movie *Pinky*. The film was exhibited in theaters all over the nation with no incidents, even in such Southern strongholds of racism as Jackson, Mississippi; Birmingham, Alabama; and Atlanta, Georgia. But it did not pass the censors in Marshall, Texas, in 1952. The town had on the books a statute that allowed local officials to act in the capacity of a "film censorship agency," empowered to preview all movies before they could be shown publicly and to reject those that were found to be "of such character as to be prejudicial to the best interests of the people of said City." In accordance with the statute, theater operators who showed films that had been denied permission or those that had no license because they had not been submitted for review were guilty of a misdemeanor. The theater operator, Gelling, showed *Pinky* with a license, but after a jury trial in the county court of Harrison County, he was convicted of a misdemeanor for violating the local statute.

Gelling appealed his conviction in the court of criminal appeals of Texas. The defense attorney argued that the local statute was invalid on its face because it violated the due process provisions of the Fourteenth Amendment of the Constitution, which protected free speech. The court refused to accept this argument and affirmed the conviction, writing in its decision in *Gelling v. State of Texas*, 247 S.W. 2d 95, 156 Tex. Cr. R 516 (1952), that it did not accept that "the motion picture industry had emerged from the business of amusement and become propagators of ideas entitling it to freedom of speech." Referring in the opinion to *Mutual Film Corporation v. Industrial Commission of Ohio* (1915), in which the U.S. Supreme Court had determined that movies were commercial enterprises and not entitled to the constitutional guarantees of freedom of speech and press, the court wrote, "We cherish the history of a federal government which has been based on a constitution as solid as the rocks and whose constancy is not shifted by changing winds." Five months later, an unanticipated shift would occur in the momentous United States Supreme Court decision regarding THE MIRACLE in *Burstyn v. Wilson*, 343 U.S. 495 (1952).

Attorneys for Gelling argued the case before the U.S. Supreme Court, where it was heard on June 2, 1952. On June 9, 1952, the Court reversed the decision of the lower courts and, while referring to the concurring opinion in *Burstyn v. Wilson*, 343 U.S. 495 (1952), declared that "this ordinance offends the Due Process Clause of the Fourteenth Amendment on the score of indefiniteness." In writing the concurring opinion, Justice William O. Douglas wrote, "the evil of prior restraint, condemned by *Near v. Minnesota*, 283 U.S. 697, in the case of newspapers and by *Burstyn v. Wilson*, 343 U.S. 495, in the case of motion pictures, is present here in flagrant form. If a board of censors can tell the American people what is in their best interests to see or to read or to hear . . . then thought is regimented, authority substituted for liberty, and the great purpose of the First Amendment to keep uncontrolled the freedom of expression defeated."

FURTHER READING

Burstyn v. Wilson, 343 U.S. 495 (1952).
Carmen, Ira H. *Movies, Censorship, and the Law*. Ann Arbor: University of Michigan Press, 1964.
Ceplair, Larry, and Steven Englund. *The Inquisition in Hollywood: Politics in the Film Community, 1930–1960*. Garden City, N.Y.: Anchor Press, 1980.
Gelling v. State of Texas, 247 S.W. 2d 95, 156 Tex. Cr. R 516 (1952).
Gelling v. State of Texas, 343 U.S. 960 (1952).
Jowett, Garth. *Film: The Democratic Art*. Boston: Little, Brown, 1976.

PROFESSOR MAMLOCK

Country and date of production: Soviet Union, 1938 (as *Professor Mamlok*)
Production company/distributor: Lenfilm/Amkino Corporation (United States)
Format: Sound, black and white
Running time: 100 minutes
Language: Russian
Producer: Lenfilm
Directors: Adolf Minkin, Gerbert Rappaport
Screenwriters: Adolf Minkin, Gerbert Rappaport, Friedrich Wolf (also play)
Awards: None
Genre: Drama
With: Sergei Mezhinsky (Prof. Mamlock), E. Nikitina (Frau Mamlock), Vladimir Chestnokov (Dr. Hellpach), Nina Shaternikova (Dr. Inge), Vasili Merkuryev (Krass)

SUMMARY

Professor Mamlock was filmed in the Soviet Union from a screenplay based on a play of the same name written by Frederick Wolf for the Works Progress Administration (WPA) and first staged at a WPA theater. The story, set in Germany after Hitler's rise to power, relates the fate of Professor Mamlock, a Jewish doctor who with his family must deal with the persecution and difficulties of the time. At the outset Mamlock is apolitical, but his son Rolf has become a member of an underground communist movement that has formed to resist the Nazis. Mamlock's religion makes him an outsider, and the officials feel free to humiliate him and force him to leave his post in the clinic. When his surgical skill is desperately needed to operate on a high-ranking Nazi official, he is reinstated temporarily and then forbidden to practice medicine once the Nazis no longer need him. The experience politicizes Mamlock, who seeks to awaken others to the dangers posed by the Nazis. While he stands before a crowd delivering a speech in defiance of the Nazi regime and praying that God may deliver Germany from tyranny, Nazi troops enter and shoot him down with machine guns. His death makes his son's defiance of the Nazis more fervent, and the film ends on an optimistic note as Rolf and others at a secret meeting of the Communist Party pledge to continue the struggle.

CENSORSHIP HISTORY

Professor Mamlock joins BLOCKADE and SPAIN IN FLAMES as films banned in various states because censors believed that they contained pro-Left or antifascist positions. In the years immediately preceding the United States's involvement in World War II, censors suppressed all films that treated communism in anything but the most unfavorable light. In other cases, as with THE GREAT DICTATOR, the U.S. desire to refrain from antagonizing Germany before World War II kept the Russian-made film, which attacks Nazi anti-Semitism, out of theaters, "on the grounds that it would 'stir up hatred and ill will and gain nothing.'" The film was released twice in the United States. First released in 1938, it was withdrawn in 1939 by the distributor when the Russo-German alliance was signed (Russian and Germany signed a pact to support each other and to not become military opponents, World War II soon ended that). The film was rereleased in July 1941 after the alliance ruptured when Germany invaded Russia and new alliances were formed. During the first release of *Professor Mamlock*, the film was banned by the Chicago board of censors and Ohio's state division of censorship, as well as in England and in Chungking, China. The Massachusetts board of censors banned exhibition of the film on Sundays.

The most contested effort to ban the film occurred in Providence, Rhode Island, in 1939. The "amusement inspector," who was part of the Rhode Island Bureau of Police and Fire, viewed the film privately, and then recommended in a report to city officials that the city prevent public exhibition in Providence because it was communistic propaganda that would not be for the public welfare. Instead, the inspector felt that the film would incite race hatred and class strife because it contained scenes of brutality and bloodshed. The inspector further asserted that the city statute that authorized a city review of films before exhibition also required that films be approved by the National Board of Review (NBR), the censoring arm of the motion picture industry, but that the distributor had not obtained such approval. Attorneys for the distributor then filed two applications for approval and requested a hearing to review approval for the film. Both applications were denied, and the city also denied the distributor's request for a hearing. The distributor then filed a petition with the Supreme Court of Rhode Island, charging that an "error of law" was the basis for the denial of the application without a hearing and that the decision to deny had been made without "competent evidence." In *Thayer Amuse-*

ment Corporation v. Moulton, 7 A. 2d 682 (1939), the court decided against the distributor, writing in its opinion that the decision as to which films are granted permits to exhibit in the state was "subject to regulation and even prohibition under the police power of the state. . . . [and it is] well-understood belief in this state to show motion pictures publicly for a price is necessarily a mere privilege and not in any sense a right of property." The court also refused the distributor's request that it view the film, writing in the decision that to do so "would be to put ourselves in the place of the bureau in determining whether [it] ought to be shown." In concluding, the court wrote that all of the questions raised by the attorneys for the distributor "are without merit."

FURTHER READING

De Grazia, Edward, and Roger K. Newman. *Banned Films: Movies, Censors and the First Amendment.* New York: R. R. Bowker, 1982.
Lyons, Charles. *The New Censors: Movies and the Culture Wars.* Philadelphia: Temple University Press, 1997.
Schumach, Murray. *The Face on the Cutting Room Floor.* New York: William Morrow, 1964.
Thayer Amusement Corporation v. Moulton, 7 A. 2d 682 (1939).

PURITY

Country and date of production: United States, 1916
Production company/distributor: American Film Company/Mutual Film Corporation
Format: Silent, black and white
Running time: 105 minutes
Language: English titles
Producer: American Film Company
Director: Rea Burger
Screenwriter: Clifford Howard
Awards: None
Genre: Drama
With: Audrey Munson (Purity/Virtue), Clarence Burton (Publisher), William A. Carroll (Evil/Luston Black), Nigel De Brulier (Thornton Darcy), Eugenie Forde (Judith Lure), Alfred Hollingsworth (Claude Lamarque)

SUMMARY

Purity is the story of the sacrifices that one beautiful and innocent young woman makes to provide money for the man she loves so that he can publish his poetry. Thornton Darcy, a struggling poet, is working on a long allegorical poem titled "Virtue," divided into two parts. The first part delineates the nature of "Virtue," which he depicts as a nude female figure, and the second part introduces the myth of Pandora and the evil she released. One day, Darcy falls asleep in the woods and awakens to find what appears to be his poetic "Virtue" in the woods with him, wearing a simple homemade dress and gathering flowers. The woman's name is Purity Worth, and she lives in a humble home deep in the woods. The two fall in love and plan to marry, but Darcy has no money and cannot publish his work unless he gives a publisher $500, which he does not have. One day, Purity is bathing alone in a stream when Claude Lamarque, a painter, sees her and asks her to pose for him; she refuses but takes his card nonetheless. Soon after, she receives word from Darcy that his final effort to publish the book of poems has been rebuffed, and he is now lying ill in bed. After tending to Darcy, she asks Lamarque for an advance payment of $500, agreeing to pose for him and for other artists to repay the money. She meets with the publisher and pays for the publication of Darcy's poems but insists that the publisher never tell her beloved what she has done. The publication of the poetry brings Darcy instant fame, and he is invited everywhere. Meanwhile, Purity has become the object of desire to Luston Black, a friend of Lamarque's. As Black is trying to force himself on Purity in Lamarque's studio, Darcy walks in and Black taunts him that Purity has been posing in the nude. A shocked Darcy refuses to listen to Purity's explanations, and he breaks off their relationship. When he later sees Lamarque's completed picture of "Virtue," with Purity as the model, he understands the truth and rushes to reunite with Purity.

CENSORSHIP HISTORY

Purity was one of several films that used the premises of antiquity, morality or art to introduce nudity into the story line "without inviting censor trouble." The film was planned around Audrey Munson, a well-known artist's model who had posed for commemorative coins and for statuary. She had also appeared nude in the 1915 film *Inspiration* as an artist's model. Local censor boards decided that the profession justified Munson's nudity. The writer and director against cast Munson as an artist's model in *Purity*, having her not only pose in the studio but also appear in various famous works of art. To make certain that no one suspected that the nudity in the film was meant to titillate, the director and writer placed the following biblical quotation (Titus 1:15) at the beginning and the end of the film: "To the pure all things are pure." The July 7, 1916, issue of *Variety* pointed out that Munson's nude body could be seen 18 times during the film, "in about the same state of undress as she would be on entering her morning tub."

The distributor, Mutual Film Corporation, marketed the film for exhibition on a state-by-state basis. The censor boards of most cities appear to have approved the film for exhibition. In New York City, however, the nudity was an issue and before the board of censors would permit exhibition of the film at the Liberty Theater, the license commissioner demanded several cuts. The distributor was required to reduce the instances of nudity to less than half the number of original scenes. Screenwriter Clifford Howard later said of the film, "Whatever may be said of the outcome as a production of art, it fulfilled the company's expectations. It was the most costly film [Mutual] had ever turned out, yet by the end of the year they were half a million dollars to the good. Some towns forbade it, and other frankly welcomed it. Critics unmercifully roasted it, and critics enthusiastically praised it. Sermons were preached about it—pro and con. It was the first time I had ever had a hand in the creating of a sensation, and I have never contributed to another."

FURTHER READING

Brownlow, Kevin. *Hollywood: The Pioneers.* London: Collins Publishing, 1979.
"Purity." *Moving Picture World*, July 29, 1916, p. 804.
"Purity." *Variety*, July 7, 1916, p. 25.
Thompson, Frank. *Lost Films: Important Movies That Disappeared.* New York: Citadel Press, 1996.

RED-HEADED WOMAN

Country and date of production: United States, 1932
Production company/distributor: MGM (Metro-Goldwyn-Mayer)
Format: Sound, black and white
Running time: 79 minutes
Language: English
Producer: Albert Lewin (uncredited)
Director: Jack Conway
Screenwriters: Katherine Brush (novel), F. Scott Fitzgerald (uncredited), Anita Loos
Awards: None
Genre: Comedy/romance
With: Jean Harlow (Lillian "Lil"/"Red" Andrews Legendre), Chester Morris (William "Bill"/"Willie" Legendre, Jr.), Lewis Stone (William "Will" Legendre, Sr.), Leila Hyams (Irene "Rene" Legendre), Una Merkel (Sally), Henry Stephenson (Charles B. "Charlie"/"C.B." Gaerste), May Robson (Aunt Jane), Charles Boyer (Albert, the Chauffeur), Harvey Clark (Uncle Fred)

SUMMARY

Red-Headed Woman is the story of Lil, a girl from a poor background who yearns to be wealthy, even as she works as a secretary. To achieve her aim she will go to any lengths and hurt anyone, and she is used to getting her way. She also likes to live somewhat dangerously: She has a bootlegging boyfriend, yet she works hard to romance her boss after offering to complete secretarial tasks for him at his house while his wife is in Cleveland. Bill Legendre makes clear to Lil that he loves his wife, but the two have a few drinks and Bill loses his head. Drinking and dancing lead to kissing. When Bill's wife Irene returns home early, he tells her that his flirtation with Lil started and will end that day. Undeterred, Lil tells her friend Sally that she intends to hook a rich man, preferably Bill. When Bill's father offers Lil a job in Cleveland to save Bill's marriage, Lil refuses to be bought off. Even when Bill tells Lil that she must go, she corners him in a phone booth and makes him promise to visit her, but Bill and Irene go home instead and make up. Lil gets drunk, then goes to Bill's house and complains of the broken date, driving Irene to lock herself in her bedroom. Bill follows Lil home and gives her money to get out of town, but she locks him in her bedroom and hides the key in her bra. Bill succumbs to Lil's charms, and Irene divorces him even though she still loves him. Bill and Lil marry, but Irene predicts Lil will lose Bill because she lured him with sex, not love.

Lil resents Bill's reluctance to take her to formal affairs because of her behavior, so she blackmails one of his wealthy friends, Gaerste, into inviting his friends to her party. He does so, and Lil is happy until she finds the departing guests are going across the street to Irene's. Lil follows and tells them off, and Bill has to carry her home. A few days later, Lil visits Gaerste and kisses him; he soon falls under her spell and proposes marriage. In love with Gaerste's chauffeur, Albert, Lil plans to marry the rich man instead and then see what follows. When Bill shows Gaerste photos that a detective took of Lil and Albert, Gaerste fires the chauffeur, who offers to take Lil to Paris. She returns to Bill, but he moves out and reconciles with Irene. Once again, Bill's father tries to pay off Lil with a check for $500. She takes the check, then stops Bill's car and shoots him. The film ends two years later in Paris, where the recovered Bill and his father see Lil romancing a rich old man in the back seat of a car Albert is driving.

CENSORSHIP HISTORY

Red-Headed Woman was the first of a large number of films that would attempt to push the limits of moral behavior as far as the censors would allow. Other studios questioned why the Motion Picture Producers and Distributors Association (MPPDA) had given MGM such leeway in making this film. Even Jason Joy, the head of the Studio Relations Committee (SRC), whose responsibility was to approve or disapprove a film for release, seemed unsure of the film's potential effect, although he did approve it. In a letter to Will Hays, head of the Motion Picture Producers and Distributors Association (MPPDA), Joy wrote, "My feeling is that the picture is either very good or very bad, dependent on the point of view of the spectator who sees is as [either] farce or as heavy sex." The head of the board of censors in Atlanta, Georgia, lobbied against the film before its public release, writing "We have been working for years for clean decent pictures, and here in 1932, we have THIS . . . Sex! Sex! Sex! the picture just reeks with it until one is positively nauseated."

After Jason Joy approved the film, Hollywood trade papers questioned his judgment, suggesting that the SRC had shown favoritism toward MGM by allowing it greater latitude in screen content than other studios had been permitted. As a result, other studios scrambled to create properties that would capitalize on what they saw as the temporary laxness of the industry censors. State censors, however, took a different view of the film. Without much fanfare and with no repercussions, censor boards in Massachusetts and Pennsylvania cut most of the scenes showing Lil's romance with the chauffeur Albert. Ohio removed the ending, which shows an unrepentant Lil beginning yet another relationship with a rich man in the back seat of a limousine, while her former husband looks on from a distance and her current lover, Albert, sits—apparently in approval—in the front seat. England banned the film entirely.

The film played to substantial audiences and remained in circulation through 1934, until the Catholic Legion of Decency (LOD) and the MPPDA joined forces to create the Hollywood Production Code Administration (PCA). Film historians cite *Red-Headed Woman* as one of 10 films, including BABY FACE, SCARFACE: SHAME OF THE NATION, SHE DONE HIM WRONG and SIGN OF THE CROSS, that were most responsible for the creation of the restrictive Code that would dominate the film production industry. In 1934, when the head of the newly created PCA, Joseph Breen, began to reclassify films currently in circulation and others that might be rereleased, *Red-Headed Woman* was one of the first films to receive his attention. He pulled the film from circulation and ordered the studio never to rerelease it. The film was never again released in theaters and emerged only in 1988, restored and packaged for the home videotape market.

FURTHER READING

Doherty, Thomas. *Pre-Code Hollywood: Sex, Immorality, and Insurrection in American Cinema, 1930–1934.* New York: Columbia University Press, 1999.

Greenberg, Joel, and Charles Higham. *The Celluloid Muse.* New York: Signet Books, 1972.

Leff, Leonard J., and Jerold L. Simmons. *The Dame in the Kimono: Hollywood, Censorship, and the Production Code From the 1920s to the 1960s.* New York: Grove Weidenfeld, 1990.

Loos, Anita. *Kiss Hollywood Good-by.* New York: Viking Press, 1974.

Miller, Frank. *Censored Hollywood: Sex, Sin, and Violence on Screen.* Atlanta, Ga.: Turner Publishing, 1994.

Thomas, Bob. *Thalberg: Life and Legend.* Garden City, N.Y.: Doubleday, 1969.

Vieira, Mark. *Sin in Soft Focus: Pre-Code Hollywood.* New York: Harry N. Abrams, 1999.

REEFER MADNESS

Country and date of production: United States, 1936 (also released as *Tell Your Children; The Burning Question; Dope Addict; Doped Youth; Love Madness*)

Production company/distributor: G&H/Motion Picture Ventures Inc.

Format: Sound, black and white

Running time: 67 minutes

Language: English

Producers: Dwain Esper, George A. Hirliman

Director: Louis J. Gasnier

Screenwriters: Paul Franklin, Arthur Hoerl, Lawrence Meade (story)

Awards: None

Genre: Exploitation

With: Dorothy Short (Mary), Kenneth Craig (Bill), Lillian Miles (Blanche), Dave O'Brien (Ralph), Thelma White (Mae), Carleton Young (Jack), Warren McCullum (Jimmy), Pat Royale (Agnes), Joseph Forte (Dr. Carroll), Harry Harvey, Jr. (Junior)

SUMMARY

First released under the title *Tell Your Children*, the film is best known as *Reefer Madness*. In a 1987 interview published in the *Los Angeles Times*, the actress Thelma White (Mae in the film) spoke of *Reefer Madness* with embarrassment: "I hide my head when I think about it. It was a dreadful film." So badly acted and filmed, it has become camp and a cult favorite in recent years. The story opens as Dr. Carroll, a high-school principal whose main concern in life is to stop the use of marijuana by his students, speaks at a meeting with local parents and warns against the dangers of the drug. To illustrate his point, he tells the story of Bill and Mary, two of his students whose lives were destroyed by the drug. The two were good students and good citizens; however, as we learn from his story, marijuana changed all that. In a sensationalist twist, the film relates that a crime ring has begun to operate within the town. The focus of the ring is to hook teenagers on marijuana. Drug gang members Mae and Jack throw local house parties where they supply marijuana to the unsuspecting teenagers. Ralph, an older student who has a crush on Mary, also attends these parties, as does Blanche, who is attracted to Bill. One day Mary's younger brother, Jimmy, takes Bill with him to Mae's apartment. Blanche, seeing the opportunity to seduce Bill, quickly hooks him on marijuana. Jimmy goes driving while high and hits and kills a pedestrian. Bill, whose mind is confused by the drug, begins an affair with Blanche. Mary goes to Mae's apartment looking for her brother and accepts a reefer from Ralph, who then tries to seduce her. As a dazed and confused Bill emerges from the bedroom, he imagines that Mary was stripping for Ralph. He attacks Ralph, and as the two fight, Jack tries to break up the scuffle by hitting Bill with the butt of his gun. The gun goes off, Mary is shot and killed and Blanche and

Jack blame Bill for the murder. Bill is arrested and put on trial. At Bill's trial, Dr. Carroll testifies that Bill's use of marijuana caused his criminal behavior. Jack and Mae, in an attempt to hide the truth, keep Ralph at Mae's apartment. Ralph, as a result of his drug use, goes insane and beats Jack to death. The police then arrest Ralph, Mae and Blanche. Mae decides to cooperate with the police and reveals all the details of the gang. After the crime ring is rounded up, Blanche decides to relieve her conscience and reveals that Bill is innocent. When Bill is released from jail, Ralph is placed into an asylum and Blanche commits suicide.

CENSORSHIP HISTORY

"Women Cry For It—Men Die For It!" During the first release of the movie, that tagline attracted viewers who thought they were about to see a documentary film of marijuana's real effects. In reality, the film was not meant to educate or instruct but only to exploit, and it left many viewers with misperceptions about the drug. In recounting her experiences in playing the role of Mae, actress Thelma White said "The director wanted us to 'hoke' it up. He wanted us to show the 'madness.'" The movie was produced as a slick commercial attempt to capitalize on the government campaign to fight "reefer madness," the increasing use of marijuana, and to support the efforts of the U.S. commissioner of narcotics, Harry J. Anslinger and the newly formed Federal Bureau of Narcotics. Newspapers of the 1920s, especially those owned by William Randolph Hearst, had run a rash of articles about "reefer madness," many written by Anslinger. In hearings held before the passage of the Marijuana Tax Act in 1937, Anslinger told half-truths to motivate passage of the law. He testified with sensational stories about people who went insane and killed their families after smoking the drug. (In at least one case, he did not tell the authorities that the killer also had been institutionalized for severe personality disorder in the year preceding.) *Reefer Madness* became the most famous of several films of the 1930s that dealt with the "killer weed." Today, mentions of *Reefer Madness* appear at many of the hundreds of Web sites that support the use of cannabis, but most of these sites mistake the date of the film's production, the people who created it, and its original purpose. Some critics and reviewers label the film a government-produced propaganda piece created as a prelude to the passage on April 14, 1937, of the Marijuana Tax Act, while others, such as the *New York Times*, claim that the film is part of "A 1930's Bureau of Narcotics campaign [that] warned that marijuana would cause teenagers to commit vicious crimes. The bureau promoted a 1936 commercial film, '*Tell Your Children*' [the first name for *Reefer Madness*] warning that marijuana caused teenagers to rape, murder and commit suicide." After playing to audiences for less than a year, the film was withdrawn from exhibition because its lack of a Production Code Administration seal of approval had limited the number of theaters in which it could be shown. The film could not hope to earn the seal because it violated several principles of the code that prohibited the depiction of drug paraphernalia and methods of drug use in any film of the time. The complete film was out of circulation until 1972, when it was rereleased under the auspices of the National Organization for the Reform of Marijuana Laws (NORML), the pro-marijuana lobby, and shown as a fundraiser for the campaign to decriminalize marijuana. In the intervening years, shortened versions of the films had appeared in independent theaters and on campuses under a range of names. Since 1972, the film has led a healthy life as a video rental and midnight feature at small theaters, but first-run houses have shown no interest.

FURTHER READING

Annas, George J. "Reefer Madness: the Federal Government's Response to California's Medical-Marijuana Law." *New England Journal of Medicine*, August 7, 1997.

Corliss, Richard. "Sex! Violence! Trash! The Exploitation Movies of a Bygone Era Had Everything but Money, and Talent, and Scruples." *Time*, July 7, 1997.

Hamilton, Denise. "Actress Recalls Days of *Reefer Madness.*" *Los Angeles Times*, February 12, 1987, p. 30.

Hoberman, J., and Jonathan Rosenbaum. *Midnight Movies.* New York: Harper & Row, 1983.

Johnson, Gary. "Forbidden Fruit: The Golden Age of the Exploitation Film." *Images: A Journal of Film and Popular Culture.* http://www.imagesjournal.com/issue08/reviews/forbiddenfruit/video s.htm.

Klein, Philippa. "The Bad Influence: Representation of Marijuana in Hollywood." http://collection-nic-bnc.ca/100/202/300/mediatribe/mtribe95/ marijuana.html.

"Marijuana: Marijuana Timeline." *Frontline.* http://www.pbs.org/wgbh/ pages/frontline/shows/dope/etc/cron.html.

Morais, Richard C. "Reefer Madness." *Forbes*, June 17, 1996, p. 118.

"Reefer Madness." *Brown Film Society Film Bulletin*, September 18, 1997.

Rothstein, Richard. "Reality Check Due in Drug Prevention." *New York Times*, September 17, 1997, p. L12.

REVENGE AT DAYBREAK

Country and date of production: France, 1952; as *La jeune folle*
Production company/distributor: Hoche Productions (France) / Times Film Corporation (United States) 1964
Format: Sound, black and white
Running time: 70 minutes
Language: French
Producers: Julien Derode, Ray Ventura
Director: Yves Allégret
Screenwriters: Cathérine Beauchamp (novel), Jacques Sigurd
Awards: None

Genre: Drama
With: Danièlle Delorme (Catherine), Henri Vidal (Steve), Nic Vogel (Tom), Maurice Ronet (Jim), Jean Debucourt (A Mysterious Man), Michèle Cordoue (Mary), Jacqueline Porel (Mother Superior), Marcel Journet (Police Chief Donovan)

SUMMARY

Revenge at Daybreak, originally titled *Desperate Decision*, is adapted from the novel *La jeune folle*, written by Catherine Beauchamp. Set in Dublin, Ireland, in 1916, the plot relates one young woman's personal losses during the Anglo-Irish struggle. The brother of convent-educated Catherine has become involved in the conflict, in which the Irish Republican Army (IRA) is using guerrilla warfare to resist the Free State movement, the British and their supporters. After he is captured and brutally executed by a Republican gang leader for informing on their activities, Catherine vows to find and kill the man responsible. Catherine becomes a revolutionary and falls in love with one of the IRA leaders without knowing that he was responsible for her brother's torture and death. After learning the truth, she becomes distraught and then carries out the revenge she had vowed long ago.

CENSORSHIP HISTORY

This film would have played out its run and disappeared had not a Baltimore theater owner named Ronald L. Freedman chosen to deliberately challenge the system of film censorship in Maryland. The decision in the U.S. Supreme Court case that ensued, *Freedman v. Maryland*, 380 U.S. 51 (1965), would later be used to launch attacks on the four state boards of censorship remaining—in Pennsylvania, Oregon, Georgia and Maryland—and on cities that continued to censor films, as well as on the inspection of imported films by the U.S. Customs Bureau. With the backing of the International Film Importers and Distributors Association (IFIDA), a group made up of importers and distributors on foreign, non-American made films and represented by attorney Felix Bilgrey, counsel to the organization and the attorney who had represented the film DON JUAN in *Times Film Corporation v. City of Chicago*, 365 U.S. 43 (1961), Freedman proceeded. Bilgrey and the IFIDA guided Freedman in selecting *Revenge at Daybreak* to test if an exhibitor who refused to submit an unobjectionable picture in advance of its public screening (an action required by the Maryland censorship law) would earn a criminal conviction. The censorship statute in Maryland required that every film exhibited in the state be "approved and licensed" by the state censorship board. To test the constitutionality of the law, Freedman simply did not submit the film to the board for approval, and exhibited the film in his Baltimore theater without a license. As he expected, the Baltimore police arrested him and charged him with violating the state statute, and the criminal court of Baltimore convicted him of the charge.

In advance of his arrest, Freedman alerted the news media and placed the following statement on his theater marquee: "Fight for Freedom of the Screen." Attorneys for Freedman appealed the case to the court of appeals of Maryland, which affirmed the decision of the lower court and wrote in its decision in *State v. Freedman*, 197 A. 2d 232, 233 Md. 498 (1964), that even though neither the court nor the state believed the movie would violate the standards of the state statute, Freedman was obligated to submit the film to the board because the statutory requirement was "valid and enforceable." The case was then heard by the U.S. Supreme Court, which decided unanimously for Freedman. The Court ruled that the Maryland system of censorship was in fact invalid because the statute as written posed a "prior restraint" on the film and failed to include provisions for judicial participation or to include procedural safeguards. The Court wrote in its determination:

> First, the burden of proving the film is unprotected must rest on the censor. . . . Second, while the State may require advance submission of all films, in order to proceed effectively to bar all showings of unprotected films, the requirement cannot be administered in a manner which would lend an effect of finality to the censor's determination whether a film constitutes protected expression. . . . The exhibitor must be assured, by statute or authoritative judicial construction, that the censor will, within a specified brief period, either issue a license or go to court to restrain showing the film. Any restraint imposed in advance of a final judicial determination on the merit must similarly be limited to preservation of the status quo for the shortest fixed period compatible with sound judicial resolution. . . . The procedure must also assure a prompt final judicial decision, to minimize the deterrent effect of an interim and possibly erroneous denial of a license.

Although it did not settle the question of whether any prior censorship was constitutional, the decision in this case led to "a wholesale reformation of movie licensing procedures, or a complete collapse of censorial legislation where such reformation proved to be impossible."

FURTHER READING

Carmen, Ira H. *Movies, Censorship and the Law*. Ann Arbor: University of Michigan Press, 1966.
De Grazia, Edward, and Roger K. Newman. *Movies, Censors and the First Amendment*. New York: R.R. Bowker, 1982.
Freedman v. Maryland, 380 U.S. 51 (1965).
Jowett, Garth. *Film: The Democratic Art*. Boston: Little, Brown, 1976.
State v. Freedman, 197 A. 2d 232, 233 Md. 498 (1964).
Times Film Corporation v. City of Chicago, 365 U.S. 43 (1961).

THE ROAD TO RUIN

Country and date of production: United States, 1928
Production company/distributor: Cliff Broughton Productions/True-Life Photoplays
Format: Silent, black and white
Running time: 90 minutes
Language: English titles
Producers: Clifton Broughton Productions
Director: Norton S. Parker
Screenwriter: Willis Kent (story)
Awards: None
Genre: Drama
With: Helen Foster (Sally Canfield), Grant Withers (Don Hughes), Florence Turner (Mrs. Canfield), Charles Miller (Mr. Canfield), Virginia Roye (Eve Terrell), Tom Carr (Jimmy), Don Rader (A1)

SUMMARY

This is a controversial, low-budget drama about the life of a young teenage girl on the "road to ruin." Sally Canfield is a 16-year-old New York City resident who, neglected by her parents, begins to smoke and drink and have sexual affairs with a series of older men. When the police raid a strip-poker game one evening, they decide to give her a chance, so they send her home. A few weeks later Sally learns that she is pregnant, and she seeks an illegal abortion. After the procedure, as she lies ill in her bed and looks close to death, the words *The Wages of Sin Is Death* inexplicably appear over her bed in fire.

CENSORSHIP HISTORY

The Road to Ruin was banned by the city of Birmingham, Alabama, in a case in which the exhibitor argued unsuccessfully that the statute used as the basis for the banning was too "vague and uncertain" to apply to his film. Although the argument failed in this case, it would become a successful defense in landmark cases involving THE MIRACLE and VIVA MARIA. In Birmingham, the requirements of the city ordinance forbade films that depicted "the human female in a nude state or condition, or draped or clothed with transparent or partially transparent garments, draperies, or clothing which shows or represents any indecent, obscene, lewd . . . or suggestive act." The ordinance further forbade "any film depicting drunkenness of any female, unless the scene is reduced to a flash" as well as any scenes "describing the plying of the trade of procurer . . . or any seduction scene . . . immoral, unlawful relations of any person or persons of either sex." When the city ordered the exhibitor to stop showing the film, attorneys for the exhibitor brought suit against the city in the Northern District of Alabama federal court, alleging that the exhibitor would lose more than $3,000 if he were not allowed to show the film and asking for an injunction against interference by the city in exhibiting the film. The suit was filed on the ground that the city ordinance was "vague and uncertain," but the court disagreed and upheld the ordinance based on a ruling that law enforcement officials have the right to determine what may have a negative impact on the public good. In the opinion in *Brooks v. City of Birmingham*, 32 F. 2d 274 (N.D. Ala. 1929), Judge Henry D. Clayton wrote, "Undoubtedly the governing authority was convinced that the business of exhibiting motion picture films might be attended with such public evil as to at once warrant and demand regulation. Here the measures adopted have reasonable relation to that end, and it is not open to the judiciary to interfere."

FURTHER READING

Brooks v. City of Birmingham, 32 F. 2d 274 (N.D. Ala. 1929).

Drew, William M. *Speaking of Silents*. Vestal, N.Y.: Vestal Press, 1989.

Munden, Kenneth W., ed. *The American Film Institute Catalog of Motion Pictures Produced in the United States: Feature Films, 1921–1930*. New York: R.R. Bowker, 1971.

Pratt, George C. *Spellbound in Darkness: A History of the Silent Film*. Greenwich, Conn.: New York Graphic Society, 1966.

LA RONDE

Country and date of production: France, 1950
Production company/distributor: Svanfilm/Commercial Pictures
Format: Sound, black and white
Running time: 95 minutes
Language: French
Producers: Ralph Baum, Sacha Gordine
Director: Max Ophüls
Screenwriters: Jacques Natanson, Max Ophüls, Arthur Schnitzler (play)
Awards: 1952 British Academy Awards, Best Film From Any Source
Genre: Drama
With: Anton Walbrook (Raconteur), Simone Signoret (Leocadie, the Prostitute), Serge Reggiani (Franz, the Soldier), Simone Simon (Maid), Daniel Gélin (Alfred), Danielle Darrieux (Emma Breitkopf), Fernand Gravey (Charles, Emma's Husband), Odette Joyeux (The Grisette), Jean-Louis Barrault (Robert Kuhlenkampf), Isa Miranda (The Actress), Gérard Philippe (The Count)

SUMMARY

La Ronde, or *The Roundabout* (carousel), is adapted from the play *Reigen*, a comedy written by Arthur Schnitzler. The movie deals in an ironic manner with promiscuity, adultery and seduction among a group of people from a range of social classes, as the characters "carry on their intrigues while . . .

hypocritically ignoring the social tensions." The setting moves between a carousel and the city of Vienna as players on the sexual merry-go-round appear and disappear from the scene, moving from the artificial sound stage of the carousel to a bedroom and other locations and then back to the carousel. An urbane and witty narrator sorts out the comic seductions and provides perspectives on the pairings. The movie does not show sexual activity, only the events that lead to and follow it and the attendant emotional reactions at each stage. Focusing on the dual aims of examining sexual desire and the lies that people tell to satisfy this desire, the film examines each character in two seduction scenes, one following on the other. The seductions begin with a prostitute and rise on the social scale so that the final seduction involves a count. The higher a character is on the social scale, the more elaborate his or her lies, but each couple seems to play the same games. At one point, the film stops and the narrator, holding a strip of film and a pair of scissors, shakes his head and decries the immorality of the scene about to occur. He then cuts several frames from the strip, and the action resumes to show what appear to be two lovers in a postcoital embrace. The pairing that begins between a prostitute and a soldier comes full circle on this carousel to end with a pairing of the prostitute with the count.

CENSORSHIP HISTORY

The film was imported from France and passed through U.S. Customs without incident. Its foreign status meant that it did not require a seal of approval to be exhibited in the United States: The decision was left to local censor boards. In 1952, New York State censors refused to issue a license to the film on the grounds that it was "immoral" and would "tend to corrupt morals." Attorneys for the distributor, Commercial Pictures, appealed the decision in the appellate division of the state supreme court, which upon review confirmed the decision of the state supreme court in *Commercial Pictures Corporation v. Regents*, 114 N.Y.S. 2d 561, 280 App. Div. 260 (1952). The case then entered the New York court of appeals, which supported the decision of the board of censors. The court determined that the movie "panders to base human emotions" and that it provided a "breeding ground for sensuality, depravity, licentiousness and sexual immorality." In its opinion rendered in *Commercial Pictures v. Regents*, 114 N.Y. 2d 502, 305 N.Y. 336 (1953), the court affirmed the decision of the lower court and wrote, "That those vices represent a 'clear and present danger' to the body social seems manifestly clear."

The case was argued before the United States Supreme Court on January 7, 1954, and the decision rendered on January 18, 1954, reversed the decisions of the lower courts. Justice William O. Douglas made a powerful argument in favor of granting protection under the First and the Fourteenth Amendments:

> Nor is it conceivable to me that producers of plays for the legitimate theater or for television could be required to submit their manuscripts to censors on pain

of penalty for producing them without approval. Certainly the spoken word is as freely protected against prior restraints as that which is written. . . . The First and the Fourteenth Amendments say that Congress and the States shall make "no law" which abridges freedom of speech or of the press. In order to sanction a system of censorship I would have to say that "no law" does not mean what it says, that "no law" is qualified to mean "some" laws. I cannot take that step.

In this Nation every writer, actor, or producer, no matter what medium of expression he may use, should be freed from the censor.

Commercial Pictures Corporation v. Regents, 346 U.S. 587 (1954)

FURTHER READING

Commercial Pictures Corporation v. Regents, 114 N.Y.S. 2d 561, 280 App. Div. 260 (1952).

Commercial Pictures Corporation v. Regents, 114 N.Y. 2d 502, 305 N.Y. 336 (1953).

Commercial Pictures Corporation v. Regents, 346 U.S. 587 (1954).

Mast, Gerald, and Bruce F. Kawin. *A Short History of the Movies.* Boston: Allyn & Bacon, 1996.

Schumach, Murray. *The Face on the Cutting Room Floor.* New York: William Morrow, 1964.

ROOM AT THE TOP

Country and date of production: United Kingdom, 1959
Production company/distributor: Remus Films/Continental Distributing
Format: Sound, black and white
Running time: 118 minutes
Language: English
Producers: James Woolf, John Woolf
Director: Jack Clayton
Screenwriters: John Braine (novel), Neil Paterson, Mordecai Richler (uncredited)
Awards: 1959 Academy Awards, Best Actress (Simone Signoret), Best Screenplay Based on Material From Another Medium (Neil Paterson).
1959 British Academy Awards, Best British Film, Best Film from Any Source, Best Foreign Actress (Simone Signoret).
1959 Cannes Film Festival, Best Actress (Simone Signoret). 1960 National Board of Review, Best Actress (Simone Signoret).
Genre: Drama
With: Laurence Harvey (Joe Lampton), Simone Signoret (Alice Aisgill), Heather Sears (Susan Brown), Donald Houston (Charles Soames), Donald Wolfit (Mr. Brown), Hermione Baddeley (Elspeth), Allan Cuthbertson (George Aisgill), Raymond Huntley (Mr. Hoylake), John Westbrook (Jack Wales), Ambrosine Phillpotts (Mrs. Brown)

SUMMARY

Room at the Top is the story of one of England's angry young men of post-World War II, Joe Lampton, an ambitious yet disillusioned and bitter man who desperately wants to escape his dirt-poor past. When he arrives in the big city by train in the opening of the film, the camera makes the symbolic statement that industry is the new religion: Church bells ring and the screen fills with factory smokestacks belching filthy smoke. When Joe arrives at his new job, he makes clear that he hopes to be in a bureaucratic position someday soon. While he seeks to reach the top echelon of power, Lampton does not let his colleagues forget his working-class origins, and he continues to hate the privileged classes. He courts Susan, the daughter of his millionaire boss, whom he sees as the quickest way to success, but he has fallen in love with Alice, an older, married Frenchwoman. Lampton meets both women when he joins a local acting troupe out of boredom, and he honestly believes that he can successfully maintain a relationship with each. The film makes clear that Lampton is most comfortable with Alice, with whom he can let down all of his defenses, but he desires all that a life with Susan offers. When Susan becomes pregnant, her father demands that she and Lampton marry. The news devastates Alice, who dies soon after in a self-induced automobile accident. The film ends with Lampton entering a passionless marriage with the vapid Susan and pretending to love her. The power structure has finally made room for him at the top.

CENSORSHIP HISTORY

Room at the Top was one of the most successful foreign movies shown in the United States in the 1950s and '60s, giving hope to distributors who handled foreign films, who often did "not even bother to seek a seal because they know it is hopeless." The film critic Leslie Halliwell wrote that this movie has been "claimed as the first British film to take sex seriously, and the first to look at the industrial north as it really was." Some viewers even found that *Room at the Top* had moral lessons to teach. In a 1962 interview with George Dugan, the editor of religious news at the *New York Times*, Reverend Malcolm Boyd, Protestant Episcopal chaplain at Colorado State University at the time, criticized the Hollywood biblical epic and found, instead, a "decided religious dimension" in such films as *Room at the Top*. He stated that churches "frequently stood by and witnessed the spectacle of churchly kudos being bestowed upon artistic and religious trash in the form of very bad movies that are dubbed religious merely because they deal with Biblical subjects or sentimentally pseudo-religious themes.

Because it did not have a seal of approval for exhibition, the film played in art theaters where managers frequently called aside parents who brought in their children and gave them a summary of the content. In this film, the sexual and moral transgressors suffer for their sins through death or unhappiness. This did not prevent *Room at the Top* from being banned in 1963 in Atlanta,

Georgia, by Christine Smith Gilliam, the motion picture reviewer for the city of Atlanta, who was the city's only full-time employee paid to review movies. In a 1964 interview with Ira C. Carmen, Gilliam stated, "Up until we censored *Never on Sunday* and *Room at the Top* we rarely had a problem. These were the first real challenges." Rather than take the route of earlier film distributors, who would make suggested cuts to films or appeal the censor's decisions "to the Library Board and from there to the courts," the distributors of NEVER ON SUNDAY and *Room at the Top* did not stop with appeals.

In 1962, the distributor of *Room at the Top*, the K. Gordon Murray Production Company, appealed an Atlanta censorship order banning the film and asked the supreme court of Georgia to grant a petition for equity on the grounds that the banning of the film constituted "free speech deprivation." The court decided that the key section of the Georgia state constitution that required interpretation was Article 1, Section 1, Paragraph 15: "No law shall ever be passed to curtail, or restrain the liberty of speech, or of the press; any person may speak, write, and publish his sentiments on all subjects, being responsible for the abuse of that liberty." In the decision, the state supreme court determined that the city charter and censorship ordinance were "void in so far as they required the prescreening of movies protected by this clause as well as those that were not so protected because they abused the privilege of free speech" (*K. Gordon Murray Productions, Inc. v. Floyd*, 217 Ga. 784 [1962]).

When the state supreme court declared the censorship ordinance unconstitutional, the Atlanta Board of Aldermen and the mayor enacted a new ordinance that established a movie rating system and required that "any movie to be shown for commercial purposes within city limits must first be previewed by a Motion Picture Reviewer who is to be appointed and to serve in office under the same rules as provided by the previous law." The three new categories were as follows: *Approved*, a motion picture without content to arouse sexual, lustful or carnal desires or appeal to prurient interests; *Unsuitable for the Young* [UY], a motion picture which, while not objectionable for the average person or for mature adult persons, would nevertheless be objectionable for children, young people or immature people because it contains content deemed immoral; *Objectionable*, an obscene movie picture, according to contemporary community standards, as applied by the average person. The ordinance made showing an obscene film unlawful under any circumstances. To exhibit any film labeled "objectionable" meant automatic arrest and a maximum fine of five hundred dollars, imprisonment for not more than thirty days, or both.

The ordinance made showing an obscene film unlawful under any circumstances. To exhibit any film labeled "objectionable" meant automatic arrest, and a maximum fine of five hundred dollars, imprisonment for not more than thirty days, or both. Under the new rating system, *Room at the Top* was classified as "UY," so it was no longer banned. Distributors realized clearly that the decision in *K. Gordon Murray Production, Inc. v. Floyd*, 217 Ga. 784 (1962), might have changed the future for one film, but the possibility that future films might be censored remained.

FURTHER READING

Carmen, Ira H. *Movies, Censorship, and the Law*. Ann Arbor: University of Michigan Press, 1966.

Halliwell, Leslie. *Halliwell's Film Guide*, 7th ed. New York: Harper & Row, 1989.

K. Gordon Murray Productions, Inc. v. Floyd, 217 Ga. 784 (1962).

Mast, Gerald, and Bruce Kawin. *A Short History of the Movies*. Boston: Allyn & Bacon, 1996.

Schumach, Murray. *The Face on the Cutting Room Floor*. New York: William Morrow, 1964.

SCARFACE: THE SHAME OF A NATION

Country and date of production: United States, 1932
Production company/distributor: Caddo/United Artists
Format: Sound, black and white
Running time: 93 minutes
Language: English
Producers: Howard Hawks, Howard Hughes
Directors: Howard Hawks, Richard Rosson
Screenwriters: W.R. Burnett, Ben Hecht, John Lee Mahin, Seton I. Miller, Armitage Trail (novel)
Genre: Drama
With: Paul Muni (Tony Camonte), Ann Dvorak (Cesca Camonte), Karen Morley (Poppy), Osgood Perkins (Johnny Lovo), C. Henry Gordon (Guarino), George Raft (Guino Rinaldo), Vince Barnett (Angelo), Boris Karloff (Gaffney)

SUMMARY

One of the first movies about organized crime, *Scarface* is based on a novel written by Armitage Trail, but the screenplay, written by Chicago native Ben Hecht, infuses the characters with the experiences of real-life mobsters Al Capone, Deanie O'Bannion, Johnny Torrio and "Big Jim" Colosimo. The film opens with a preface that claims the events depicted in the film are actual occurrences about mob activity and governmental corruption. The preface then challenges the audience by asking what they are going to do about it. The action begins with the slaying of a local crime figure and a prediction by the press of a mob war for control of the lucrative bootlegging business. In hopes of eliciting information about criminal activity, the police arrest Tony Camonte, who refuses to talk and is soon released. Tony then visits Johnny Lovo and Poppy, Lovo's girlfriend, with whom Tony is infatuated. Lovo pays Tony for not saying anything to the police. When Tony returns to his family, he plays the loving big brother and tells his sister Cesca not to let men kiss her; then he gives her money for herself and their mother, who pleads with Cesca not to be bad like Tony.

As the newspapers had predicted, a power struggle for control of the bootlegging operation erupts. Lovo takes over Costillo's gang, and Tony beats up a man who tries to leave the gang. Tony and Rinaldo force unwilling customers to buy from them by bombing and shooting those who don't. Tony invites Poppy out, but she at first refuses to date him but later relents. Tony gets a flower from Rinaldo that indicates another killing has been completed, this time of O'Hara in his flower shop. The police once again arrest Tony, but he is soon released. Gaffney, played by Boris Karloff in the year following his role in FRANKENSTEIN, introduces machine guns to the conflict and attempts a drive-by shooting of Tony and Poppy in a restaurant. After a wounded Lovo berates Tony for getting rid of O'Hara, Tony sees his chance to move up in the underworld and takes over for the injured Lovo. After a massacre of seven men on Valentine's Day, which Gaffney blames on police, law-enforcement officials try to turn the public against the gangsters by claiming that children are being killed in the streets. An editor argues for more extensive news coverage and calls for guns to be outlawed to stop organized murder. While bowling, Gaffney is shot by Tony's gang, and Tony is later shot at and driven off the road. He and Rinaldo suspect that Lovo ordered the hit, so Rinaldo kills Lovo, and Tony sees the opportunity to possess all that was Lovo's. He tells Poppy to pack and go briefly into hiding with him. While Tony is away, Tony's sister Cesca and Rinaldo become romantically involved with each other. Feeling as if his best friend had betrayed him, Tony kills Rinaldo, but Cesca later reveals to Tony that she and Rinaldo were married. The police surround the house in which Tony is hiding and accidentally kill his secretary, then Cesca emerges with a gun and is involved in the shootout with the police. The police throw tear gas into the house, forcing Tony to run outside where he is shot dead.

CENSORSHIP HISTORY

Reformers and censors often condemned films that combined entertainment with social commentary, such as *Scarface*, because even if the main characters met violent deaths at the end of the film, along the way "each movie violated the code by creating 'sympathy' for the criminal and/or taught the methods of successful crime to impressionable youth." The most dangerous of these early gangster films seems to have been *Scarface*, which one review said made "all other gangster pictures appear almost effeminate." Jason Joy, head of the Studio Relations Committee (SRC), rejected the initial idea for the film when Howard Hughes first proposed it, and he demanded that Hughes not even consider the picture: "Under no circumstances is this film to be made. The American public and all conscientious State Boards of Censorship find mobsters and hoodlums repugnant. Gangsterism must not be mentioned in the cinema. If you should be foolhardy enough to make Scarface, this office will make certain it is never released." Hughes passed the letter on to his co-producer, Howard Hawks, with the following memo attached:

"Screw the Hays Office. Start the picture and make it as realistic, as exciting, as grisly as possible."

The first version of the film was everything that Hughes wanted, but numerous changes were eventually made to appease the SRC. Despite reviewers' perceptions that the final film was exceedingly violent, film historians report that the film released to the public was a highly censored version of the original script, so much so that the movie "is a shadow of what it might have been." A biographer of the screenwriter Ben Hecht wrote that the producers directed Hecht to make the script violent, and he promised them a minimum of 25 killings; reviewers of the film contend that the body count exceeded 40. The original version of the film upset the Motion Picture Producers and Distributors Association (MPPDA) for several reasons. It showed politicians and respected citizens socializing privately with the gangsters and then publicly denouncing them. Tony's mother is fully aware that her son is a criminal yet treats him lovingly, and the conclusion shows Tony going out in a blaze of bullets as he stands up to the police with guns in both in his hands.

Before the film would even be considered for approval by the Motion Picture Producers and Distributors Association (MPPDA), the Hays Office wanted it to be a moral lesson, not a reflection of what might be reality. Will Hays began by demanding the subtitle "Shame of a Nation" to show that the film industry was indicting and not glorifying the behavior in the film. The next change required that Hawks and Hughes "clean up" the relationships between politicians and gangsters so as not to imply that government officials were corrupt—despite the public's knowledge of the extensive corruption in most major U.S. cities at the time. The final change required by the Hays Office was to modify the behavior of Mrs. Camonte toward her son so that she would clearly express disapproval of his lifestyle and state repeatedly that "he is no good." When the film was completed in 1931, the Hollywood censors refused to approve it until the producers agreed to add scenes that would show clearly that "the public, not law enforcement officials, was to blame for the existence of gangs. Hays also demanded scenes that would show the effectiveness of the justice system in combating criminals." MPPDA also required an alternate ending to be filmed in which Camonte is captured, placed on trial and sentenced to hang. Although the MPPDA gave a seal of approval to the second version, they demanded that Hughes also retain the third version with its changed ending.

Despite all of the changes and the addition of the subtitle, the first attempt to release the second version of the film brought rejections from the state boards of censors in New York, Virginia, Ohio, Kansas, Maryland and Virginia, as well as from the municipal boards in Chicago, Portland, Boston, Seattle and Detroit. The rejections so infuriated Howard Hughes that he issued a public statement against censorship that led the *New York Herald-Tribune* to praise him as "the only producer who has the courage to come out and fight this censorship menace in the open":

It has become a serious threat to the freedom of honest expression in America when self-styled guardians of the public welfare, as personified by our censor boards, lend their aid and their influence to the abortive efforts of selfish and vicious interests to suppress a motion picture simply because it depicts the truth about conditions in the United States which have been front page news since the advent of Prohibition. *Scarface* is an honest and powerful indictment of gang rule in America and, as such, will be a tremendous factor in compelling our State and Federal governments to take more drastic action to rid the country of gangsterism.

In an unusual move to protect the financial investment in the film, the MPPDA helped to get the film past the state and city boards of censors by sending SRC head Jason Joy to speak with each board. Joy showed board members the third version of the film with the alternate ending, explained that the film was not intended to glorify criminals, and convinced them that *Scarface* was actually a moral film that was meant to work against crime. His success in changing the minds of the censorship boards angered such conservative elements as the *Christian Century Magazine*, which wrote in its July 13, 1932, issue that such success showed "the grim determina-tion of the industry to defeat agencies which the public has set up to de-fend its children from vicious pictures," while the equally conservative *Harrison's Reports* wrote in its June 18, 1932, issue that the example of *Scarface* proved "censorship . . . is impotent to cure the evils of the motion picture industry."

The filmmakers' victory of which these publications wrote was not complete, however, because different versions of *Scarface* played in different states. On March 31, 1932, Hughes opened the second version of the film in New Orleans, which had a relatively lax board of censors, and the film was well attended. Hughes then obtained all copies of the third ver-sion of the film and decided to try releasing only the second version. The Ohio board of censors issued this version of the film a permit for exhibition, but the censor boards of Pennsylvania, New York and Chicago rejected it. Hughes finally gave in and released the third version of SCARFACE in New York in May 1932, while across the Hudson River in New Jersey, the second version of the film was playing without comment. The film joined others, including BABY FACE, RED-HEADED WOMAN, SIGN OF THE CROSS and SHE DONE HIM WRONG, in motivating conservative groups to call loudly for stronger measures of censorship that would eventually produce the Catholic Legion of Decency and the Production Code Administration.

FURTHER READING

Black, Gregory D. *Hollywood Censored: Morality Codes, Catholics, and the Movies.* New York: Cambridge University Press, 1994.

MacAdams, William. *Ben Hecht: The Man Behind the Legend.* New York: Charles Scribner's Sons, 1988.

Mast, Gerald. *Howard Hawks, Storyteller.* New York: Oxford University Press, 1982.

McCarthy, Todd. *Howard Hawks.* New York: Grove Press, 1997.
Thomas, Tony. *Howard Hughes in Hollywood.* Secaucus, N.J.: Citadel Press, 1985.

SCHINDLER'S LIST

Country and date of production: United States, 1993
Production company/distributor: Amblin Entertainment/Universal Pictures
Format: Sound, color/black and white
Running time: 197 minutes
Language: English, Hebrew
Producers: Kathleen Kennedy, Branko Lustig, Gerald R. Molen, Lew Rywin, Steven Spielberg
Director: Steven Spielberg
Screenwriters: Thomas Keneally (novel), Steven Zaillian
Awards: 1994 Academy Awards, Best Art Director/Set Decoration (Ewa Braun, Allan Starski), Best Cinematography (Janusz Kaminski), Best Director (Steven Spielberg), Best Film Editing (Michael Kahn), Best Music–Original Score (John Williams), Best Picture (Branko Lustig, Gerald R. Molen, Steven Spielberg), Best Screenplay Based on Material from Another Medium (Steven Zaillian), Best Actor (Liam Neeson).
1994 Boston Society of Film Critics Awards, Best Cinematography (Janusz Kaminski), Best Director (Steven Spielberg), Best Film, Best Supporting Actor (Ralph Fiennes).
1994 British Academy Awards, Best Supporting Actor (Ralph Fiennes), Best Adapted Screenplay (Steven Zaillian), Best Cinematography (Janusz Kaminski), Best Editing (Michael Kahn), Best Film (Branko Lustig, Gerald R. Molen, Steven Spielberg), Best Score (John Williams), David Lean Award for Direction (Steven Spielberg).
1994 Chicago Film Critics Association Awards, Best Cinematography (Janusz Kaminski), Best Director (Steven Spielberg), Best Picture, Best Screenplay (Steven Zaillian), Best Supporting Actor (Ralph Fiennes).
1994 Directors Guild of America Awards, Outstanding Directorial Achievement in Motion Pictures (Michael Helfand, Branko Lustig, Sergio Mimica-Gezzan, Steven Spielberg).
1994 Golden Globe Awards, Best Director–Motion Picture (Steven Spielberg); Best Motion Picture–Drama; Best Screenplay–Motion Picture (Steven Zaillian).
1995 Grammy Awards, Best Instrumental Composition Written for a Motion Picture or for Television (John Williams).
1994 Humanitas Prize, Feature Film Category.
1995 London Critics Circle Awards, British Actor of the Year (Ralph Fiennes), Director of the Year (Steven Spielberg), Film of the Year.
1993 Los Angeles Film Critics Association Awards, Best Cinematography (Janusz Kaminski), Best Picture, Best Production Design (Allan Starski).

1994 MTV Movie Awards, Best Breakthrough Performance (Ralph Fiennes), Best Movie.

1993 National Board of Review, Best Picture–English Language.

1994 National Society of Film Critics Awards, Best Cinematography (Janusz Kaminski), Best Director (Steven Spielberg), Best Film, Best Supporting Actor (Ralph Fiennes).

1993 New York Film Critics Circle Awards, Best Cinematography (Janusz Kaminski), Best Film, Best Supporting Actor (Ralph Fiennes).

1994 Norwegian International Film Festival, Best Foreign Language Feature Film (Steven Spielberg).

1994 PGA Golden Laurel Awards, Motion Picture Producer of the Year Award (Branko Lustig, Gerald R. Molen, Steven Spielberg).

1994 Political Film Society Awards, Human Rights.

1994 USC Scripter Awards, Author (Thomas Keneally), Screenwriter (Steven Zaillian).

1994 Writers Guild of America Awards, Best Screenplay Based on Material Previously Produced or Published (Steven Zaillian).

Genre: Drama/war

With: Liam Neeson (Oskar Schindler), Ben Kingsley (Itzhak Stern), Ralph Fiennes (Amon Goeth), Caroline Goodall (Emilie Schindler), Jonathan Sagall (Poldek Pfefferberg) (as Jonathan Sagalle), Embeth Davidtz (Helen Hirsch), Malgoscha Gebel (Victoria Klonowska), Shmulik Levy (Wilek Chilowicz), Mark Ivanir (Marcel Goldberg), Béatrice Macola (Ingrid), Andrzej Seweryn (Julian Scherner), Friedrich von Thun (Rolf Czurda), Krzysztof Luft (Herman Toffel), Harry Nehring (Leo John), Norbert Weisser (Albert Hujar), Adi Nitzan (Mila Pfefferberg), Michael Schneider (Juda Dresner), Miri Fabian (Chaja Dresner), Anna Mucha (Danka Dresner), Albert Misak (Mordecai Wulkan), Michael Gordon (Mr. Nussbaum), Aldona Grochal (Mrs. Nussbaum), Jacek Wójcicki (Henry Rosner), Beata Paluch (Manci Rosner), Piotr Polk (Leo Rosner), Ezra Dagan (Rabbi Menasha Levartov), Beata Nowak (Rebecca Tannenbaum), Rami Heuberger (Josef Bau) (as Rami Hauberger), Leopold Kozlowski (Investor), Jerzy Nowak (Investor), Uri Avrahami (Chaim Nowak), Adam Siemion (O.D./Chicken Boy), Magdalena Dandourian (Nuisa Horowitz), Pawel Delag (Dolek Horowitz), Shabtai Konorti (Garage Mechanic), Oliwia Dabrowska (Red Genia), Henryk Bista (Mr. Lowenstein), Tadeusz Bradecki (D.E.F. Foreman)

SUMMARY

The film is adapted from the novel of the same name written by Thomas Keneally, which is based upon real events in which a gentile German profiteer saved the lives of hundreds of German Jews during World War II. The film opens in September of 1939 in Krakow, Poland. The Jewish community is feeling the increased Nazi pressure as their freedoms are slowly eroded and even appearing on public streets has become dangerous. Oskar Schindler is a relatively poor German who comes to Krakow with a plan to capitalize on the changing political scene and, in the process, make himself a wealthy man. Allowing his greed to dictate his actions, Schindler is loyal to those who will make him the most money. For these reasons, Schindler smoothly talks business with the Nazi officials. While Schindler is getting to know, and become known by, the Nazi Party, the Jewish population of Poland is being forced into the major cities, including Krakow.

Schindler obtains a pan-manufacturing plant and stocks it with cheap Jewish labor. Besides a discounted labor supply, the Jews also offer the advantage of favorable financing, since no Jew is legally allowed to own his or her own business. Although he is initially reluctant to work with the Jews, Schindler's attitude changes with the opening of Jewish ghettos in Krakow, which make a new arrangement profitable. Soon Schindler has his workforce and the factory is making money, with Stern, the financial backer, running the business side of the operation and providing protection to favored Jews. This business continues to be profitable until the ghetto is liquidated by Nazi forces. The region's Jewish inhabitants are rounded up and either shipped off to concentration camps or executed.

Amon Goeth, the commandant of the new labor camp, where the ghetto survivors have been sent, is a devoted Nazi soldier who seems to take pleasure in the torture of his Jewish occupants. Schindler visits the labor camp, hoping to bribe the officials to let some people go back to work for him. He is able to gain the confidence of Goeth and reestablish his workforce. As Schindler learns of Goeth's mindless brutality, he begins to take pity on the Jews. As a result, Schindler also begins to take risks to keep his workers from being sent to concentration camps. The tension in the movie grows as the terror machine mounts offensive after offensive on the Jewish civilians, threatening Schindler as well.

CENSORSHIP HISTORY

Schindler's List earned critical acclaim and awards internationally, yet it was banned in some countries for ethnic and political reasons, as well as for what some officials labeled its sexual content. In Malaysia, the government board of censors banned the film as "Jewish propaganda" and claimed that "it reflects the privilege and virtues of a certain race only." Moreover, "the [Malaysian] government's film censor, Zainun Bin Saleh, said that Malaysian regulations required 25 deletions involving 'scenes of sex, cruelty, horror and obscene dialogue,'" but Spielberg refused to allow the cuts. In April 1994, the film was banned from theaters in Jordan and Lebanon. In June 1994, Egyptian censors banned the movie because it contains scenes of violence, torture and nudity. In announcing the ban, the chief censor Hamdi Sorour said that the film contravened "general order and morality." In Indonesia, a largely Muslim country, the board of censors decided to ban the film after two months of deliberation, "citing what they considered excessive violence and nudity." Before the movie was even reviewed by the board, the Committee for World Muslim Solidarity had denounced the film, labeling it "nothing but Zionist propaganda. . . . From history we can see that the Jewish people were always trying to spread their influence through the use of media, which they control." In Thailand, where hardcore pornographic videos are sold in the streets, nightclubs feature graphic sex shows and prostitution is common, the Police Censorship Board demanded the deletion of the brief lovemaking scene, which caused a major outcry and postponed the premiere of the film.

In the Philippines, the Movie and Television Review and Classification Board initially refused to allow the film to be shown without deletions of bare breasts and a scene of a couple making love. "The board explained that is was not objecting to the nude scenes in concentration camps, but to three short 'bed scenes' involving 'double breast exposure' of women. Worse, it said, one of the scenes—of Schindler in bed with a mistress—explicitly showed the 'pumping motion' during sex, followed by 'orgasm.'" Manuel Morato, former chief censor in the Philippines, supported the decision of the current board and expressed concern for the poor, "who he said are oversexed. 'Sex is detrimental to the people,' he told reporters. 'If a person is poor and he gets horny, he's just going to rape.' He suggested that those who want to see the movie watch it on video. That way, 'you can have your private orgasm in the privacy of your room.'" After Spielberg refused to cut the film and after large public outcry, "President Fidel Ramos overruled the censorship board and ordered the film released, and it played to capacity audiences."

In the United States, the Mormon Church-owned Brigham Young University in Provo, Utah, edited *Schindler's List* to provide a suitable version for campus viewing in 1994. The scenes excised from *Schindler's List* included the much-debated brief nudity and sex scenes.

FURTHER READING

"Because It's Not Nice." *Star-Ledger,* January 23, 1998, p. 3.

Branigin, William. "Manila in Agony Over Schindler's Ecstasy; 30-Second Sex Scene Has Censors Atwitter." *Washington Post,* March 8, 1994, p. B1.

"Crossing *Schindler* Off the List." *World Press Review,* August 1994, p. 47.

"Egyptian Censors Ban *Schindler's List.*" *The Jerusalem Post,* June 2, 1994, p. 5.

Hassan, Kalimullah. "KL May Review *Schindler's* Ban." *The Straits Times,* March 29, 1994, p. 2.

Holmberg, Judith. "Spielberg: Rethink Ban of All Your Films in M'sia." *The Straits Times,* May 14, 1994, p. 18.

"Malaysia Bans *Schindler's List* as Propaganda." *The Guardian,* March 24, 1994, p. 16.

Stamets, Reena Shah. "*Schindler's List* Faces Censorship in Muslim Nations." *St. Petersburg Times,* April 17, 1994, p. D1.

Wallace, Charles P. "Malaysian Censors Move to Ban *List;* Government Body in Muslim Nation Calls Spielberg's Holocaust Film 'Propaganda'—Jewish Groups Are Outraged." *Los Angeles Times,* March 24, 1994, p. F1.

Weiner, Ernest H. "Reason, Truth and Art Are Held Hostage." *San Francisco Chronicle,* April 27, 1994, p. A21.

THE SEX LURE

Country and date of production: United States, 1916 (also released as *The Girl Who Did Not Care*)
Production company/distributor: Ivan Film Productions/States Rights Pictures
Format: Silent, black and white
Running time: 90 minutes
Language: English titles
Producer: Ivan Film Productions
Director: Ivan Abramson
Screenwriters: Ivan Abramson (story), Don Dundas
Awards: None
Genre: Drama
With: James Morrison (Arthur Reynolds), Louise Vale (Laura Reynolds), Frankie Mann (Rose Bernton), Donald Hall (Clinton Reynolds), Marie Reichardt (Martha Reynolds), W. W. Black (Bill Bernton), George Henry (Col. Haldane Denby), Thomas B. Carnahan, Jr. (Arthur, as a child)

SUMMARY

The Sex Lure is the story of a young woman who uses her considerable sexual charms to destroy a family. The seemingly innocent Rose manipulates the emotions of the honest and caring Reynolds family, who take pity that she is alone in the world and invite her into their home to live with them. They soon learn that she is cunning and devious and that she had chosen them as her victims. She helps her father to kidnap the Reynolds's only son Clinton for ransom, and she lures the father, Arthur Reynolds, into being unfaithful to his wife. Although Rose believes that she has triumphed, she eventually learns that family ties are stronger than her "sex lure" when the family reunites and she is left alone.

CENSORSHIP HISTORY

The Sex Lure was banned for its provocative advertising instead of its content. The New York City commissioner of licensing threatened theaters who showed this film that they would lose their licenses because of "the title and the method of advertising." He stated for the court record that the film title and advertising were "an offense against morality, decency, and public welfare," although the contents of the film were not objectionable and were "without harmful results." The commissioner asserted that the advertising was "purely for the purpose of holding out to the public that the photoplay is of an indecent character, thus creating an immoral curiosity as to the nature of the same." After the commissioner denied the permit to exhibit, the distributor filed a request with the Supreme Court of New York State for an injunction that would prevent the city from blocking exhibition of the film, but the court met in a special session and denied the motion.

In the decision rendered in *Ivan Film Productions v. Bell*, 167 N.Y.S. 123 (1917), Judge Clarence J. Shearn acknowledged that even if the advertising of an entertainment may be "disgusting, offensively sensational, and even dishonest, either on billboards or in the newspapers or elsewhere . . . this has nothing to do with the character of the exhibition itself, and is obviously not an offense committed in the exhibition. . . . [and the licensing commissioner] has no more legal right to revoke the license of a theater on these grounds than he would have because the moral character of the author of a play or of the actors employed to produce it was bad." In this case, however, Judge Shearn denied the motion for an injunction because the distributor had come to the court "with unclean hands," having used advertising falsely to "invite the public to a prurient and disgusting performance" when the film was "a clean one." Thus, the distributor was guilty of false advertising and "is inviting the public to the theater upon false pretenses, and seeking to capitalize whatever degenerate interest there may be created by the use of this name and the posters that go with it. Furthermore, the name and the posters taken together are indecent, nasty, and offensive. Such practices result, too, in bringing odium unjustly upon the many respectable members of the important picture industry."

FURTHER READING

De Grazia, Edward, and Roger K. Newman. *Banned Films: Movies, Censors, and the First Amendment.* New York: R. R. Bowker, 1982.

Hanson, Patricia King, ed. *The American Film Institute Catalog of Motion Pictures Produced in the United States: Feature Films, 1911–1920.* Berkeley: University of California Press, 1988.

Ivan Film Productions v. Bell, 167 N.Y.S. 123 (1917).

Ramsaye, Terry. *A Million and One Nights: A History of the Motion Picture Through 1925.* New York: Simon & Schuster, 1925; reprinted in 1986.

SHE DONE HIM WRONG

Country and date of production: United States, 1933
Production company/distributor: Paramount Pictures
Format: Sound, black and white
Running time: 66 minutes
Language: English
Producer: William LeBaron
Director: Lowell Sherman
Screenwriters: Mae West (play, *Diamond Lil*), Harvey F. Thaw, John Bright
Awards: None
Genre: Comedy
With: Mae West (Lady Lou), Cary Grant (Captain Cummings), Owen Moore (Chick Clark), Gilbert Roland (Serge Stanieff), Noah Beery (Gus

Jordan), David Landau (Dan Flynn), Rafaela Ottiano (Russian Rita), Dewey Robinson (Spider Kane), Rochelle Hudson (Sally)

SUMMARY

She Done Him Wrong is one of several films in which Mae West presented snappy one-liners and innuendo and acted as an exaggerated version of contemporary screen stars. This was her second film, after *Night After Night* (1932) and the first film to give her top billing. West's play *Diamond Lil*, on which the film is based, opened on Broadway in 1928, then toured the United States during the summer of 1929, drawing large audiences despite reviews that it contained "highly censorable dialogue" and "vulgar dramatic situations." Paramount decided in 1930 that a film of the same name based on the play would be just the solution to financial problems at the studio, and West agreed. The film was given a different title to disassociate it from the "scandalous" play and to draw in a new audience.

The story mixes the politics of New York City's Bowery with West's rendition of "a turn-of-the-century bawdy-house entertainer." Dan Flynn wants to get rid of Lady Lou's boss Gus Jordan and become boss of the bawdy house or saloon so he can have Lady Lou. Lady Lou explains to her maid that she wasn't always rich and that there was a time when she didn't know where her next husband was coming from. She welcomes another entertainer Russian Rita back and is pleased to meet Rita's lover, the suave Sergei Stanieff, with whom she appears to be running a prostitution and counterfeiting ring. When a depressed young woman named Sally tries to kill herself in Jordan's bar, Lou stops her and says, "When women go wrong, men go right after them." She then hands Sally over to Russian Rita, who offers her a job on "the Barbary Coast," a veiled reference to prostitution.

The shady characters learn that "The Hawk," a new and supposedly very effective undercover federal agent, is in town and bent on cleaning up the area. He is Captain Cummings, disguised as a young missionary who runs a city mission located next to the bar. He, too, is soon under Lady Lou's spell, and it is to Cummings that West coos one of her most famous lines, "Why don't ya come up and see me sometime." The scheming Lou visits a prison, where most of the inmates seem to know her, to see Chick Clark, who has been convicted of stealing diamonds for her. He complains, but she says she'll wait for him. When the mission next door is about to close for lack of rent, Lou buys the building for $12,000 in diamonds. Chick, missing Lou and his freedom, escapes from prison.

The plot then becomes complicated. Jordan gives Russian Rita and Stanieff counterfeit money to spend. Meanwhile, the police are looking for Chick, and Chick is looking for Lou. When he finds her and climbs in her window, she throws him out. While a woman is accusing Rita of using the phony money, Sergei gives Lou a diamond pin and kisses her. Rita is furious, argues with Lou and then attempts to stab her with a knife. In the struggle, the knife is turned on

Rita and kills her. Lou and her bodyguard get rid of Rita's body. Soon after, Cummings raids the bar with a group of police officers, arrests Jordan and takes testimony from some of the girls. Lou angrily realizes that Cummings is the Hawk. Chick, feeling betrayed and trapped, is about to kill Lou when he is arrested along with her. As the film ends, Cummings and Lou are driving off in a carriage, and the viewers are not told if it is bound for the jail or elsewhere. On the ride, however, Chick gives Lou a diamond ring and says, "You're going to be my prisoner, and I'm going to be your jailer for a long, long time. You bad girl." In typical West fashion, Lou responds, "You'll find out."

CENSORSHIP HISTORY

Mae West may have done more than any other film star of the late 1920s and early 1930s to make industry censors nervous. At least two of her films, I'M NO ANGEL and *She Done Him Wrong*, are among the films that led to the formation of the Catholic Legion of Decency (LOD) and the increased restrictions of the film industry's Production Code Administration (PCA). Even though her on-screen persona seemed to mock everything that the pre-Code industry censors had tried to suppress, she succeeded in Hollywood "for one excellent reason: her early films were enormous moneymakers." When Paramount Studios head B. P. Schulberg asked permission of the Hays Office to make a film based on *Diamond Lil*, he learned "that the Hays Office had banned the play because 'of the vulgar dramatic situations and the highly censurable dialogue,' which would result in an 'unacceptable' film." The Motion Picture Producers and Directors Association (MPPDA) censors placed the play on its forbidden list, which technically meant that no studio could attempt to make a movie of it. Paramount, however, was in dire financial straits and believed the movie would be a certain moneymaker, so it began filming in violation of the MPPDA restriction. The Hays Office sensed danger: If a film not sanctioned by the industry censors became the sure-fire success that *Diamond Lil* promised to be, it could set a dangerous precedent and lead other studios to defy the code. Will Hays decided to compromise, and in a special board meeting the Hays Office formally approved the production as long as the following changes were made: The title *Diamond Lil* could not be used; Lady Lou, played by West, could not be portrayed as a "kept woman"; the crime in Lady Lou's past would be counterfeiting, not "white slavery"; counterfeiting and not "white slavery" would be the present crime practiced in the bar; and the federal agent posing as a young missionary must not be a member of the Salvation Army.

After the film was completed, James Wingate, the head of the Studio Relations Committee (SRC), predicted that censor boards would object to the unpunished murder and concealment of the body and that Paramount might have to remove the song Lady Lou sings, "A Guy What Takes His Time," because of its highly suggestive lyrics. His assessment was correct: Boards of censorship in Pennsylvania, Massachusetts, Maryland, New York and Ohio cut the song from the film before issuing permits for exhibition. The censors in Pennsylvania and Ohio also removed most of West's snappy one-liners. In Atlanta, the censors banned the film entirely, and it was similarly rejected in Austria, Australia and Finland. At the same time, huge numbers of viewers saw the film and it broke box-office records for earnings: "While ministers, women's clubs, and state and local censors condemned her as immoral, New York City policemen, who had arrested West for her theater performances, were called out to control crowds trying to buy tickets for her film." In Atlanta, theater critics chastised the decision of the municipal board of censors to ban the film, and people flocked to a small theater outside the city limits to see it. In retrospect, West once quipped, "I believe in censorship. After all, I made a fortune out of it."

The success of the film captured the attention of Father Daniel Lord and others who, within less than a year of the film opening, would create the Catholic Legion of Decency. With the backing of millions of Catholics, the LOD would force the Hays Office and the film industry to create a harsher and more restrictive self-regulating body in the Production Code Administration (PCA). When Joseph Breen, as head of the PCA, evaluated films, he created three classes, of which Class I was to contain films that would be withdrawn immediately and never again be released. He placed *She Done Him Wrong* in that category, and it remained locked away until the mid-1950s, when the major film studios opened their film libraries and sold this film and many other pre-Code films intact to television.

FURTHER READING

Black, Gregory D. *Hollywood Censored: Morality Codes, Catholics, and the Movies.* New York: Cambridge University Press, 1994.

"Confounding Censors." *Motion Picture Herald,* May 19, 1934, p. 46.

Leff, Leonard J., and Jerold L. Simmons. *The Dame in the Kimono: Hollywood, Censorship, and the Production Code from the 1920s to the 1960s.* New York: Grove Weidenfeld, 1990.

Shawell, Julia. "Mae West Curves Herself a Career." *Pictorial Review,* February 1934, p. 7.

Walker, Alexander. *The Celluloid Sacrifice.* London: Michael Joseph, 1966.

Vieira, Mark. *Sin in Soft Focus: Pre-Code Hollywood.* New York: Harry N. Abrams, 1999.

THE SIGN OF THE CROSS

Country and date of production: United States, 1932
Production company/distributor: Paramount Pictures
Format: Sound, black and white
Running time: 115 minutes
Language: English
Producer: Cecil B. DeMille

Director: Cecil B. DeMille
Screenwriters: Wilson Barret (play), Sidney Buchman, Dudley Nichols (1944 prologue), Waldemar Young
Awards: None
Genre: Drama
With: Fredric March (Marcus Superbus), Elissa Landi (Mercia), Claudette Colbert (Poppaea), Charles Laughton (Emperor Nero), Ian Keith (Tigellinus), Arthur Hohl (Titus), Nat Pendleton (Strabo), Tommy Conlon (Stephan), Joyzelle Joyner (Ancaria)

SUMMARY

The Sign of the Cross is adapted from a play by Wilson Barrett, and it presents one perspective on the persecution of Christians by Emperor Nero. Cecil B. DeMille created a massive spectacle in the film, hiring 4,000 extras and building a model of Rome in miniature. He also ordered the construction of a massive amphitheater into which he placed hundreds of animals taken from the local zoos "and scoured Hollywood for giants, dwarfs, and every kind of strange-looking 'human freak' he could find." The setting is the year 64, and Rome is burning as Nero plays his lyre. Rumors abound that Nero has started the fire, but he hopes to blame the Christians for the devastation. The film then shows the meeting of two bearded Christians, who know each other by the sign of the cross each makes on the ground. When they are arrested by soldiers and resist, the prefect of Rome, Marcus Superbus, uses his whip to stop the disturbance. He is influenced to let the Christians go when the beautiful Mercia pleads for them.

The powerful Marcus Superbus likes the virginal Mercia, but he soon becomes the object of another woman's desire. Poppaea, wife of Nero, learns about Marcus from her friend Dacia. Marcus, however, surreptitiously meets Mercia at a fountain and asks her for water, but Nero has ordered him to exterminate Christians and he learns that soldiers are waiting to arrest Mercia. Marcus visits Mercia's home to take her away. Soldiers arrest a boy named Stephan, whom they question and torture until he reveals that the Christians will meet at a grove. Marcus then arrives and revives Stephan to learn the location of the meeting. In his rush, Marcus runs over Poppaea's carriage with his chariot, and she has him followed. As the Christians converge on the grove, singing softly, Roman troops appear and begin to slaughter the Christians until Marcus arrives. He stops the killing immediately and then orders the wounded to be cared for and the rest sent to prison. He also orders his soldiers to bring Mercia to him. When Marcus visits Poppaea the next day, she tells him that she loves him, but he affirms his loyalty to Nero. After an aide reports the meeting to Nero and he confronts Poppaea, she orders him to destroy Mercia but to spare Marcus.

When Mercia visits Marcus after a feast, she pleads for the other Christians. Revelers, singing and undulating to "The Dance of the Naked Moon" and led by Ancaria, the most beautiful lesbian in Rome, break in on them. To tempt Mercia to want him sexually, Marcus allows several of the scantily clad female revelers to stroke her body, but this "lesbian dance of 'temptation'" does not work, and the Christians continue to sing on the way to the arena dungeon. Touched by the sounds of her fellow Christians, Mercia asks to go with them, but Marcus tells her that she must stay with him and live, not go with them and die. Soldiers loyal to Nero arrive and arrest Mercia, and Marcus is refused when he asks Nero for her. Nero agrees to give Mercia her freedom only if she renounces her religion, but she refuses to do so and is forced to join 100 Christians waiting to die. As the Christians wait, the arena features spectacular scenes: Gladiators fight, criminals are killed by wild animals, and women fight dwarves. Afterward, the Christians pray before they are whipped into the arena. The soldiers make Mercia wait while the lions attack the other Christians. When Marcus arrives, he asks Mercia once more to renounce her faith. When she refuses, Marcus accompanies her into the arena.

CENSORSHIP HISTORY

Director Cecil B. DeMille became one of the most successful filmmakers in evading the industry censors, an approach he learned in making *The Sign of the Cross*, through which he found that "An audience of churchgoers could enjoy having their libido stimulated, so long as the sinners were punished in the final reel by an avenging God." The mixture of "sin and sensation" meant that industry censors did not object to a scene in which Claudette Colbert (Poppaea) is filmed, bathing in a tub supposedly filled with asses' milk, "her breasts bobbing on the frothy surface like two scoops of vanilla ice cream," or a scene "in which a naked young woman is chained to a stake in the arena, about to be raped by a gorilla." The state and municipal censors were less accepting, and Catholic coalitions were pushed by this film and nine others, including I'M NO ANGEL, RED-HEADED WOMAN, SCARFACE and SHE DONE HIM WRONG, toward forming the Catholic Legion of Decency (LOD) and urging the film industry to create the more restrictive Production Code Administration (PCA).

Jason Joy, the head of the Studio Relations Committee (SRC), approved the script with only a few reservations, although he did warn that local boards of censors might take a different view of the film. A reviewer for *Variety* gleefully reported that the film contained the "boldest censor-bait every attempted" and predicted that it would "make the church element dizzy trying to figure which way to turn." The prediction was accurate, and the executive offices of Paramount were soon deluged by letters from Catholic groups such as the Knights of St. John, of Lorain, Ohio; the Daughters of Isabella, of Owensboro, Kentucky; and other groups. Some reviewers labeled the film "a damnable hypocrisy" and "downright filth," while members of the Protestant and Catholic clergy railed that it was "cheap," "disgusting," "suggestive" and "unclean." Father Daniel Lord, a driving force behind the creation of the LOD and the PCA, wrote in *Commonweal* magazine that the film was "intolerable."

State censorship boards had fewer objections, and none cut "The Dance of the Naked Moon." This led conservative publications to speculate that the scene remained because "no one knew what it meant" but that "Midwest Catholics knew impure love when they saw it. Hollywood had defiled their mythology of Christians vs. lions, and they would not forget it."

When Joseph Breen became the head of the SRC in 1933, he joined forces with leaders in the Catholic movement and delivered a condemnatory speech to the annual bishops' meeting in November 1933 in which he attacked *The Sign of the Cross* as "vile and nauseating" and exhorted the bishops to organize against Hollywood: "The pest hole that infects the entire country with its obscene and lascivious moving pictures must be cleaned and disinfected." The result was the creation of the Catholic Legion of Decency and a new industry board of censors, the Production Code Administration (PCA), which Breen would head. The first order of business was the reclassification of films into three categories and the immediate withdrawal from circulation of all films classified as the most offensive. *The Sign of the Cross* was among these films. In 1944, however, Paramount asked for permission to reissue the film, to which the PCA agreed as long as the studio would add a prologue to downplay the eroticism. The master print was crudely cut but has been restored in recent years by the UCLA Film and Television Archive.

FURTHER READING

Black, Gregory D. *Hollywood Censored: Morality Codes, Catholics, and the Movies.* New York: Cambridge University Press, 1994.

Gardner, Gerald. *The Censorship Papers: Movie Censorship Letters from the Hays Office, 1934 to 1968.* New York: Dodd, Mead, 1987.

Lord, Daniel, S.J. "The Sign of the Cross." *Commonweal* 18 (December 31, 1932): 215.

"The Sign of the Cross." *Variety*, December 6, 1932, p. 14.

Vieira, Mark. *Sin in Soft Focus: Pre-Code Hollywood.* New York: Harry N. Abrams, 1999.

SPAIN IN FLAMES

Country and date of production: Spain, 1937
Production company/distributor: Agencies of the Spanish and Soviet governments/Amkino
Format: Sound, black and white
Running time: 65 minutes
Language: English
Producers: Various agencies of the Spanish and Soviet governments
Director: Joris Ivens
Screenwriters: John Dos Passos, Ernest Hemingway
Awards: None
Genre: Documentary

SUMMARY

Spain in Flames, based on screenplays written by Ernest Hemingway and John Dos Passos and accompanied by newsreel footage, expressed the anti-Fascist sympathies popular in Hollywood at the time. The film is constructed in two parts. The first, entitled "Spain, the Fight for Freedom," examines the historical background of the Spanish Civil War. Excerpts from newsreels show the abdication of Alfonso XIII, the La Rue government of 1931 and the national general strike of 1934. The second part, entitled "No Pasaran, They Shall Not Pass," examines the civil war in all of its brutal reality. Newsreel footage filmed by Soviet cinematographers, includes scenes of Franco's troops fighting Spanish citizens and footage of the wounded and dying.

CENSORSHIP HISTORY

Spain in Flames evoked reactions similar to those in the fictional film BLOCK-ADE, which also focused on the suffering of the Spanish during the civil war. *Spain in Flames*, a documentary feature, was banned by the Pennsylvania board of censors for being "immoral" because of its pro-Loyalist leanings. The board told the distributor that it would approve the film if all references to "Fascist," "Nazi," "German" and other volatile political references were deleted. When the distributor appealed the decision in the court of common pleas, the justices ruled that the film was a newsreel and exempt from censorship under the state statute. In the majority ruling in *Spain in Flames*, 36 D. & C. 285 (1937), which reversed the decision of the censors, Judge Louis L. Levinthal wrote that the film contained "no immorality in any of the dialogue and subtitles and assuredly no immorality so great as the suppression of free speech." The film also was banned in Waterbury, Connecticut, when the chief of police refused the distributor of the film a license for exhibition, charging that it was "controversial, anti-Catholic, and opposed by the Knights of Columbus." In Ohio, the director of the Department of Education, Division of Film Censorship denied the distributor a permit to exhibit the film on the grounds that it was "not in keeping with the neutrality laws of the country . . . upon the grounds that it was harmful in stirring up race hatred and that it was antireligious." Further, they charged that although the film "did not contain any harmful propaganda . . . the dialogue of the narrator made [it] very harmful." In a deviation from most censorship cases, a group interested in the fate of the film, the North American Committee to Aid Spanish Democracy, filed a request in the Ohio supreme court to "set aside and vacate" the denial by the board of censors on the grounds that the censor's decision had been made without any hearing or trial. In rendering a decision in *North American Committee to Aid Spanish Democracy v. Bowsher*, 9 N.E. 2d 617 (1937), the court dismissed the request on a procedural technicality, stating that the petition for judicial review had not been filed within the required period.

FURTHER READING

"Censorship in Motion Pictures." *Yale Law Review Journal* 49 (November 1939): 95–100.

De Grazia, Edward, and Roger K. Newman. *Banned Films: Movies, Censors, and the First Amendment.* New York: R. R. Bowker, 1982.

Jowett, Garth. *Film: The Democratic Art.* Boston: Little, Brown, 1976.

Levinthal, Louis E. "Reminiscences of 'A Cause Célèbre.'" *Pennsylvania Bar Association Quarterly* 37 (October 1965): 39–45.

North American Committee to Aid Spanish Democracy v. Bowsher, 9 N.E. 2d 617 (1937).

SPARTACUS

Country and date of production: United States, 1960
Production company/distributor: Bryna Productions/Universal Pictures
Format: Sound, color
Running time: 161 minutes; 198 minutes (restored version, 1991)
Language: English
Producers: Kirk Douglas, Edward Lewis
Director: Stanley Kubrick
Screenwriters: Howard Fast (novel), Dalton Trumbo, Calder Willingham (battle scenes)
Awards: 1960 Academy Awards, Best Art Direction and Set Decoration–Color (Russell A. Gausman, Alexander Golitzen, Julia Heron, Eric Orbom), Best Cinematography–Color (Russell Metty), Best Costume Design–Color (Bill Thomas, Valles), Best Supporting Actor (Peter Ustinov).
1961 Golden Globe Awards, Best Motion Picture–Drama.
Genre: Drama
With: Kirk Douglas (Spartacus), Laurence Olivier (Marcus Licinius Crassus), Jean Simmons (Varinia), Charles Laughton (Sempronius Gracchus), Peter Ustinov (Lentulus Batiatus), John Gavin (Caius Julius Caesar), Nina Foch (Helena Glabrus), John Ireland (Crixus), Herbert Lom (Tigranes Levantus), John Dall (Marcus Publius Glabrus), Charles McGraw (Marcellus), Woody Strode (Draba), Tony Curtis (Antoninus)

SUMMARY

Spartacus is based on an historical figure and is the story of the rise and fall of a slave living in Rome before the birth of Jesus Christ. Spartacus is rescued from working in an open-pit mine by a gladiator trainer, Batiatus, who sees that the slave has a fire in his eye and the capacity to captivate an audience. Enrolled in a gladiator school, Spartacus is instructed on how to fight, but he is not allowed to kill. As a form of reward for good performances, the students sometimes are allowed to see women. Most of the men treat the women as their own slaves in these limited interactions and are interested only in sexual activity. Spartacus, however, refuses to treat anyone like an animal, and with Varinia he develops first a friendship and later a romantic relationship.

The Roman official Marcus Crassus visits the school, bringing with him two women who wish to see four of the trainee gladiators fight to the death. Spartacus, unfortunately, is among those chosen. Spartacus is defeated in the battle, but his opponent refuses to kill him. For the penalty of breaking with Roman tradition in gladiator wars, Spartacus's opponent is put to death. This infuriates the gladiators, who see no point in fighting each other, but who also do not want to die at the hands of the Romans. When Spartacus learns that his love interest, Varinia, has been sold to Crassus, he becomes enraged and kills one of the guards. His action sparks an uprising and the gladiators break out. Led by Spartacus, the rebellious gladiators sweep through Italy, looting villas and freeing slaves. He hopes that they will be able to escape to freedom and to return to their homelands. Crassus, however, sees the defeat of Spartacus's army as an opportunity for him to seize power in the Republic. This inevitably leads to a final battle between the slaves and the Roman army. Spartacus is portrayed as a catalyst for a new era of Roman dictatorship: By suppressing his slave rebellion, Rome sets itself irrevocably on a path away from the Republic and perhaps confirms its eventual downfall. At the end, Spartacus is crucified and dies.

CENSORSHIP HISTORY

Spartacus was censored before it was first released, and it is one of the last commercial films "in which homosexuality was removed before the code was changed." Geoff Shurlock, head of the Production Code Administration (PCA), objected to the suggestions of homosexuality in the character of Crassus and recommended in a report to Universal that "this page clearly suggests that Crassus is sexually attracted to women and men. This flavor should be completely removed. Any suggestion that Crassus finds a sexual attraction in Antoninus will have to be avoided. . . . The reason for Antoninus's frantic escape should be something other than the fact that he is repelled by Crassus's suggestive approach to him." Shurlock also warned in several scenes that "the subject of sexual perversion seems to be touched on" and recommended that the scenes be deleted from the script, and that "the loincloth costumes must prove adequate." The Catholic Legion of Decency (LOD) focused much of its attention on the violence in the film, which the organization found "too gruesome by half. The Legion was particularly perturbed about one shot in which a gladiator is dismembered." The violence of the original film had "chilling authenticity" because, in scenes in which men were dismembered and in particularly gruesome battle scenes, Stanley Kubrick employed dwarfs and armless or legless men with breakaway artificial limbs to create a greater impression of the carnage. The LOD also protested a scene in which the crucified

Spartacus writhes in pain and his beloved Varinia calls out to him, "Oh, please die, my darling." At the request of the LOD, that line of dialogue was removed and the scene edited.

Before releasing the film to the general public, Universal held a screening for representatives of the LOD and the media. In the version shown to these groups, the film clearly suggests that the Roman general Crassus is homosexual and that he wants to acquire Antoninus for his sexual gratification. The scene in question occurs when the young slave Antoninus is helping the older Crassus in bathing and the two discuss how to treat a woman. Crassus seems to suddenly change the subject:

> Crassus: Do you eat oysters?
> Antoninus: Yes.
> Crassus: Snails?
> Antoninus: No.
> Crassus: Do you consider the eating of oysters to be moral and the eating of snails to be immoral?
> Antoninus: No, master.
> Crassus: Of course not. It's all a matter of taste, isn't it?
> Antoninus: Yes, master.
> Crassus: And taste is not the same as appetite and therefore not a question of morals, is it?
> Antoninus: It could be argued so, master.
> Crassus: Um, that'll do. My robe, Antoninus. Ah, my taste . . . includes both oysters and snails.

Murray Schumach writes that "the scene was killed because of the legion. Some of the bloodiest violence was also eliminated for the same reason." Even with the cuts, the amount of bloodshed left in far outweighed that of movies not having historical or biblical backgrounds. The cut scenes, which amounted to more than a half hour, were not restored to *Spartacus* until 1991. The film also came under fire from the American Legion, which sent letters to its 17,000 posts (branches) advising members, "Don't See Spartacus!" They objected to the involvement of the blacklisted screenwriter Dalton Trumbo in the film, who had been identified in hearings conducted by the House Un-American Activities Committee as a danger to this country for his connection to the Communist Party.

FURTHER READING

Gardner, Gerald. *The Censorship Papers: Movie Censorship Letters from the Hays Office, 1934 to 1968.* New York: Dodd, Mead, 1987.
Kagan, Norman. *The Cinema of Stanley Kubrick.* New York: Continuum Books, 1989.
Russo, Vito. *The Celluloid Closet.* New York: HarperCollins, 1987.
Schumach, Murray. *The Face on the Cutting Room Floor.* New York: William Morrow, 1964.

THE SPIRIT OF '76

Country and date of production: United States, 1917
Production company/distributor: Continental Producing Company/ States Rights
Format: Silent, black and white
Running time: ca. 180 minutes
Language: English titles
Producer: Robert Goldstein
Director: Frank Montgomery
Screenwriters: Robert Goldstein, George L. Hutchin
Awards: None
Genre: Drama /war
With: Adda Gleason (Catherine Montour), Howard Gaye (Lionel Esmond), George Chesebro [Chesborough] (Walter Butler), Dark Cloud (Joseph Brant), Doris Pawn (Madeline Brant), Jack Cosgrave [Cosgrove] (George III), Norval MacGregor [McGregor] (Lorimer Steuart), Jane Novak (Cecil Steuart), William Colby (Sir John Johnson), Lottie Kruse [Cruez] (Peggy Johnson), Chief John Big Tree (Gowah), William Freeman (Lord Chatham), W. E. Lawrence (Captain Boyd), William Beery (George Washington), Ben Lewis (Benjamin Franklin), Jack McCredie [McCready] (Tim Murphy)

SUMMARY

The Spirit of '76 is a lengthy account of the American Revolution that contains many of the highlights of early American history: Patrick Henry's speech, the ride of Paul Revere, the signing of the Declaration of Independence and the winter at Valley Forge with George Washington and his troops. The film sets these historical events against an insidious plot on the part of the beautiful Catherine Montour, whose mother is Native American. Montour plots with King George III of England to marry would be American monarchist Lionel Esmond and become queen of America. Shortly before the wedding, however, Montour learns that Esmond is her brother, which destroys her credibility with George III. Hopes for the American monarchy are destroyed and the colonists revolt, leading to numerous battle scenes depicting atrocities perpetrated by the British troops on American women and children. In one scene of the Wyoming Valley massacre, a British soldier uses a bayonet to pierce the body of a baby, which he then spins around above his head. Other scenes depict British soldiers dragging women and children by the hair, and shooting and stabbing them with bayonets. After numerous scenes of violence, the film ends with the promise of freedom and views of the brave colonists bedraggled but victorious.

CENSORSHIP HISTORY

The legal objection to *The Spirit of '76* was not that it exhibited too high a level of violence, but instead that it portrayed the British in a negative light at a time when England and the United States were allies in World War I. The distributor showed the film first in Chicago in the summer of 1917. After complaints from the public, the board of censors ordered Robert Goldstein to withdraw the film from exhibition. Goldstein, who was also one of the financial backers for THE BIRTH OF A NATION, went to court and asked for an injunction against the city to permit him to continue showing the film, but the court refused his request. He then sought to exhibit the film in Los Angeles, where he removed several controversial scenes before showing it in a private screening to local and state officials. The officials raised no objections to the film and granted Goldstein permission to exhibit it in the city. Before beginning public exhibition of the film at Clune's Auditorium, the producer restored the previously removed scenes. After two days, officials from the Los Angeles area office of the United States Attorney used a search warrant to seize the film and to arrest Goldstein. When Goldstein requested that the film be returned to him, the court denied the request and wrote in its ruling that the film would remain

> . . . in the possession of the marshal until such time as, under changed conditions, it may be properly presented. . . . This is not a time for the exploitation of those things that may have a tendency or effect of sowing dissension among our people, and of creating animosity or want of confidence between us and our allies. . . . That which in ordinary times might be clearly permissible, or even commendable, in this hour of national emergency, effort, and peril, may be as clearly treasonable, and therefore properly subject to review and repression.

Goldstein was prosecuted under the Espionage Act which provided penalties for appealing to enemy sympathies in time of war. For appealing to anti-British sentiments among German Americans, he was tried in federal district court in *United States v. Motion Picture Film The Spirit of '76*, 252 F. 946 (S.D. Calif. 1917). The court convicted him for "knowingly, willfully, and unlawfully attempting to cause insubordination, disloyalty, mutiny, and reprisal of duty in the military and naval forces of the United States during war." Goldstein was sentenced to ten years in prison and a $5,000 fine. His attorneys appealed the case, but the conviction was affirmed in *Goldstein v. United States*, 258 F. 908 (9th Cir. 1919). In the final opinion, the court wrote that although the film might have been based on historical fact, and even if it would be of little interest during a time of peace, the United States was entering a war against Germany and had to motivate American troops to fight alongside the British, who are shown at bad advantage in the film. Exhibition of the film seemed to be "calculated to arouse antagonisms and to raise hatred in the minds of some . . . and to encourage disloyalty and refusal of duty or insubordination among the military and naval forces," the court wrote. The decision of the court rested, in part, upon the decision of the U.S. Supreme Court in *Mutual Film Corp. v. Industrial Commission of Ohio*, 236 U.S. 230 (1915), regarding *The Birth of A Nation*, which determined that movies were commercial enterprises and, as such, not entitled to the constitutional guar-

antees of freedoms of speech and press. Goldstein was found guilty of disloyalty during wartime and served his sentence.

FURTHER READING

Goldstein v. United States, 258 F. 908 (9th Cir. 1919).

Hanson, Patricia King, ed. *The American Film Institute Catalog of Motion Pictures Produced in the United States: Feature Films, 1911–1920.* Berkeley: University of California Press, 1988.

Isenberg, Michael T. "The Mirror of Democracy: Reflections on the War Films of
World War I, 1917–1919." *Journal of Popular Culture* 9 (1976): 879.

Lyons, Timothy J. "Hollywood and World War I, 1914–1918." *Journal of Popular Film*
1 (1972): 15.

United States v. Motion Picture Film The Spirit of '76, 252 F. 946 (S.D. Calif. 1917).

THE SPY

Country and date of production: United States, 1917
Production company/distributor: Fox Film Corporation
Format: Silent, black and white
Running time: 90 minutes
Language: English titles
Producer: William Fox
Director: Richard Stanton
Screenwriter: George Bronson Howard
Awards: None
Genre: Drama/ thriller
With: Dustin Farnum (Mark Quaintance), Winifred Kingston (Greta
Glaum), William Burress (Freiheer Von Wittzchaeft), Charles Clary
(American Ambassador), William Lowry (The Shadow), Howard Gaye
(Baron von Bergen)

SUMMARY

An American is sent to Germany to unearth the identities of German agents
operating in the United States. With the aid of his German girlfriend, he infiltrates the German secret service in an attempt to abscond with a book that
contains the names of undercover German operatives. He is caught before he
can get away, but he does manage to hide the book. His captors use torture to
make him confess. The camera focuses several long shots on the hero's ago-
nized writhings, and the effect is suitably gruesome. He is finally shot to death
by a firing squad when he refuses to reveal where he hid the book.

CENSORSHIP HISTORY

Fox Film Corporation submitted the film for review to the Chicago chief of
police in accordance with the Chicago censorship ordinance, which

required films to obtain a police permit before they could be exhibited in the city. Under the ordinance, a permit could be denied to an "immoral or obscene" film or to one that portrayed "any riotous, disorderly, or other unlawful scenes or has the tendency to disturb the public peace." After viewing the film, the police chief agreed to issue a permit that would permit exhibition only to viewers over the age of 21. The distributor filed suit in federal district court, where the police chief testified that he objected to "the horrifying nature of the tortures which are portrayed as inflicted upon the hero of the play, and his ultimate shooting by a firing squad" and felt that this made the film immoral for "children under the age of 21 years." The court ruled in *Fox Film Corporation v. Chicago*, 247 F. 231 (1917), that the ordinance did not authorize the police chief to refuse a permit on such grounds and that his doing so constituted an "abuse of discretion." The city appealed the ruling in the federal circuit court of appeal, which affirmed the decision in *City of Chicago v. Fox Film Corporation*, 251 F. 883 (1918).

FURTHER READING

Carmen, Ira H. *Movies, Censorship, and the Law.* Ann Arbor: University of Michigan Press, 1966.

City of Chicago v. Fox Film Corporation, 251 F. 883 (1918).

De Grazia, Edward, and Roger K. Newman. *Banned Films: Movies, Censors, and the First Amendment.* New York: R. R. Bowker, 1982.

Fox Film Corporation v. Chicago, 247 F. 231 (1917).

A STRANGER KNOCKS

Country and date of production: Denmark, 1959 (as *En Fremmed banker på*)
Production company/distributor: Trans-Lux Film Corporation (United States, 1963)
Format: Sound, black and white
Running time: 81 minutes
Language: Danish
Producer: Finn Methling
Director: Johan Jacobsen
Screenwriters: Annelise Hovmand, Johan Jacobsen
Awards: 1959 Bodil Festival (Denmark), Best Actor (Preben Lerdorff Rye), Best Actress (Birgitte Federspiel), Best Film (Johan Jacobsen, director).
Genre: Drama
With: Birgitte Federspiel (Vibeke), Preben Lerdorff Rye (Han), Victor Montell

SUMMARY

A Stranger Knocks takes place in an isolated area on the coast of Denmark, where the widowed Vibeke has lived alone since the Nazis killed her husband during World War II. When a man comes to her door one stormy evening, she welcomes the company and is physically drawn to him. He does not reveal that he is a fugitive from the Danish authorities and a Nazi collaborator, and she does not recognize him at the outset. During their sexual intimacy, however, Vibeke realizes that he is the man responsible for the torture and killing of her husband. She struggles to decide whether to forget the past and enjoy the company of this man to whom she is so strongly drawn or to satisfy the need for revenge that has long plagued her.

CENSORSHIP HISTORY

Attempts to censor *A Stranger Knocks* in New York led to a decision by the U.S. Supreme Court that the state censorship law, which had been used to assess nearly 18,000 films between 1929 and 1965, violated the due process clause of the Fourteenth Amendment. The distributor presented the film for review by the Board of Regents of the State of New York, which refused to issue a permit to exhibit the film on the grounds that it was obscene because it contained two scenes of sexual intercourse. Attorneys for the distributor challenged the decision in the New York State supreme court appellate division, which found in favor of the distributor and reversed the decision of the censors. The Board of Regents then appealed that decision in the New York court of appeals, which in *Trans-Lux Distributing Corporation v. Board of Regents*, 248 N.Y.S. 2d 857 (1964), reversed the decision again and declared the scenes of sexual intercourse in the film to be conduct rather than speech; as conduct, they were not protected by constitutional guarantees of free speech.

The court ruled that the board did not need to apply the test for obscenity established by the U.S. Supreme Court concerning books in *Roth v. United States*, 354 U.S. 476 (1957), which required that censors consider if the "dominant theme of the work as a whole" appeals to "prurient interest." The court wrote, "If that requirement were applicable to cases of this nature, the law would be hopeless to cope with the grossest imaginable pornography if it were included in the film as an incidental feature, collateral to the main plot." In its decision, the court described in detail the two scenes that the Board of Regents had labeled obscene:

> The first scene presents a man and a woman on a beach embracing and caressing one another, and ends in a view of the head and shoulders of the woman with facial expressions indicative of orgasmic reaction. The second scene presents the woman astride the man on a bed. Their bodily movements are unmistakably those of the sexual act and the woman's face again registers emotions concededly indicative of orgasm.

The court found no reason to allow the film to be licensed, for to do so would be to produce "the first court determination in recorded history holding to be nonobscene and constitutionally protected the portrayal on stage or a screen of the very sexual act itself."

The U.S. Supreme Court disagreed and reversed the decision in *Trans-Lux Distributing Corp. v. Board of Regents*, 380 U.S. 259 (1965), citing their decision in the case of *Freedman v. Maryland*, 380 U.S. 51 (1961), regarding REVENGE AT DAYBREAK. The Court also directed "the applicable state court to dispose of the controversy in proceedings not inconsistent with its decision," which led the New York court of appeals to declare the state censorship statute null and void in *Trans-Lux Distributing Corp. v. Regents*, 209 N.E. 2d 558 (1965).

In Maryland, the state board of censors refused to issue the distributor a license to exhibit the film, based on its decision that the film was obscene. Attorneys for the distributor asked the Circuit Court of Baltimore City to intervene, but the court confirmed the board's decision. The distributor then appealed the decision before the Court of Appeals of Maryland, which in *Trans-Lux Distributing Corp. v. Maryland State Board of Censors*, 213 A. 2d 235 (1965), reversed the decision of the lower court and the board of censors. The court ruled that no constitutional basis existed for denying the film a license for exhibition because the board of censors had not produced evidence or testimony to prove that the film was obscene within the definition established by the U.S. Supreme Court in *Roth v. U.S.* Further, the Court of Appeals of Maryland wrote in its decision that *A Stranger Knocks* is "a serious work of art, dealing with a subject of social importance, and does not appeal to prurient interests."

FURTHER READING

Carmen, Ira H. *Movies, Censorship, and the Law.* Ann Arbor: University of Michigan Press, 1966.

Freedman v. Maryland, 380 U.S. 51 (1961).

Sibley, John. "Film Censorship in State is Ended." *New York Times*, June 11, 1965, pp. 33, 61.

Trans-Lux Distributing Corporation v. Board of Regents, 248 N.Y.S. 2d 857 (1964).

Trans-Lux Distributing Corp. v. Board of Regents, 380 U.S. 259 (1965).

Trans-Lux Distributing Corp. v. Maryland State Board of Censors, 213 A. 2d 235 (1965).

Trans-Lux Distributing Corp. v. Regents, 209 N.E. 2d 558 (1965).

Weiler, A.H. "Movie Censorship Seen in New Light." *New York Times*, March 3, 1965, p. 35.

A STREETCAR NAMED DESIRE

Country and date of production: United States, 1951
Production company/distributor: Warner Bros.

Format: Sound, black and white

Running time: 121 minutes (original release); 126 minutes (rerelease, 1993)

Language: English

Producer: Charles K. Feldman

Director: Elia Kazan

Screenwriters: Oscar Saul (adaptation), Tennessee Williams (play)

Awards: 1951 Academy Awards, Best Actress (Vivien Leigh), Best Art Direction/Set Decoration–Black-and-White (Richard Day, George James Hopkins), Best Supporting Actor (Karl Malden), Best Supporting Actress (Kim Hunter).

1953 British Academy Awards, Best British Actress (Vivien Leigh).

1952 Golden Globe Awards, Best Supporting Actress (Kim Hunter).

1999 National Film Preservation Board, National Film Registry.

1951 New York Film Critics Circle Awards, Best Actress (Vivien Leigh), Best Director (Elia Kazan), Best Film.

1951 Venice Film Festival Awards, Special Jury Prize (Elia Kazan), Volpi Cup–Best Actress (Vivien Leigh).

Genre: Drama

With: Vivien Leigh (Blanche DuBois), Marlon Brando (Stanley Kowalski), Kim Hunter (Stella Kowalski), Karl Malden (Mitch), Rudy Bond (Steve), Nick Dennis (Pablo)

SUMMARY

The film was adapted from Tennessee Williams's play of the same name, which won the Pulitzer Prize and enjoyed a successful Broadway run. Director Elia Kazan used most of the stage cast in the film and made only minor changes to the play, and those only to satisfy the Production Code Administration (PCA) head Joseph Breen. *A Streetcar Named Desire*, set in the French Quarter of New Orleans in the years immediately following World War II, tells the story of Blanche DuBois, a fragile and neurotic former English teacher who has arrived at the apartment of her pregnant sister, Stella, and brother-in-law, Stanley Kowalski, from her hometown of Laurel, Mississippi. She claims that she has taken time off because of "nervous exhaustion," but she really has lost her teaching job after seducing a 17-year-old boy, whose father reported the incident to her school principal. Blanche is indigent, and she will depend upon her sister and brother-in-law for her shelter, food and liquor, but she plays the role of the refined Southern belle: She knows disdain for the Kowalskis' small apartment, for the man who works to pay for what little they have, and for her sister's apparent lust for him. Blanche claims that her condition is the result of a series of financial calamities that have claimed the family plantation, Belle Reve. Stanley is suspicious and demands to see a bill of sale, warning Blanche that "under Louisiana's Napoleonic code, what belongs to the wife belongs to the husband."

While she takes advantage of the Kowalskis' hospitality, Blanche seems determined to destroy their marriage. She is temporarily dissuaded when she meets Stanley's friend Mitch, who is as lonely as she and who soon reveres Blanche as a beautiful and refined woman. She plays the innocent with him, but her image is destroyed when rumors of her past reach New Orleans with Stanley's help. When Stanley takes Stella to the hospital to give birth, a drunken Mitch arrives and tells Blanche that he has learned the truth about her. She is in a confused state after he leaves, and her psychological state deteriorates even further when Stanley arrives, also drunk, from celebrating the birth of his child. The anger that has built up over the months finally comes to a boil: Stanley paws through Blanche's belongings, terrorizes her and eventually rapes her, telling her that they have had this "date" from the beginning. At the end of the film, Blanche is taken away to a mental institution as Stella clutches her child and whispers that she is never going back to Stanley.

CENSORSHIP HISTORY

The 1951 film version of *A Streetcar Named Desire* was the source of a bitter conflict between the censors and the director Elia Kazan and the playwright Tennessee Williams. Before filming even began, Joseph Breen, head of the Production Code Administration (PCA), told the producer that the play would not be brought to the screen without major cutting of scenes and dialogue. After reading the screenplay, Breen wrote a memo, dated April 28, 1950, to Warner Brothers that he would have to remove the "inference of sex perversion" in Blanche's reference to her young husband and "an inference of a type of nymphomania with regards to the character of Blanche herself." In addition, Breen also foresaw problems with the rape and suggested several alternatives, including having Blanche invent the rape and Stanley prove "positively" that he did not rape her. In the negotiations that followed between the industry censors and the studio, Breen eventually yielded because Kazan and Williams stood firm and Warner Brothers stood to lose the project—and its substantial investment, which the already beleaguered studio could not afford if it were to survive. However, Breen won on the important part of the rape, however, convincing Kazan to punish Stanley at the end by losing Stella's love, as she murmurs to her baby, "We're never going back. Never, never back, never back again." As Schumach notes, "Thus, the twelve-year-olds could believe Stella was leaving her husband. But the rest of the audience would realize it was just an emotional outburst of the moment."

Once the film earned Breen's approval the director moved on to other projects, but Warner Brothers then learned that the Catholic Legion of Decency (LOD) planned to rate the film "C" (condemned), which would keep many Catholics away from the film. At the request of Warner Brothers, Kazan met with a representative of the LOD, Father Patrick Masterson, who told the director that he was not a censor and not telling him to do anything. When Kazan walked away, he thought that the film would remain intact.

But there is another phase of movie censorship that neither Kazan nor Williams had apparently considered. In the movie business, the studio does not need the permission of a writer or director to make cuts in a film after it has been shot. The power to make changes in the movie after the filming is known as "the right of the final cut."

After receiving demands from the LOD, the studio made cuts from what Kazan and Williams had thought was the final version of the film. Close-ups were deleted to tone down the passionate relationship between Stella and Stanley, as were the words "on the mouth" from Blanche's invitation to the newspaper boy to kiss her. The censors also cut references to Blanche's promiscuity and Stanley's words to Blanche before raping her—"You know, you might not be bad to interfere with"—as well as a portion of the rape scene.

In a 1993 review of the restored version, the film critic Roger Ebert noted that the cuts removed five minutes in length from the original film and took away much of its impact.

When "A Streetcar Named Desire" was first released, it created a firestorm of controversy. It was immoral, decadent, vulgar and sinful, its critics cried. And that was after substantial cuts had already been made in the picture, at the insistence of Warner Bros., driven on by the industry's own censors. Elia Kazan, who directed the film, fought the cuts and lost. For years the missing footage—only about five minutes in length, but crucial—was thought lost. But this 1993 restoration splices together Kazan's original cut, and we can see how daring the film really was.

The final restrictions placed on the film came from the LOD, not from the PCA and Breen, who "had quietly loosened the Code" as a means of keeping afloat Warner Bros. studios, which desperately needed a financial success.

FURTHER READING

Ebert, Roger. "*A Streetcar Named Desire.*" *Chicago Sun-Times*, November 12, 1993.

Gardner, Gerald. *The Censorship Papers: Movie Censorship Letters from the Hays Office, 1934 to 1968.* New York: Dodd, Mead, 1987.

Leff, Leonard J., and Jerold L. Simmons. *The Dame in the Kimono: Hollywood, Censorship, and the Production Code from the 1920s to the 1960s.* New York: Grove Weidenfeld, 1990.

Schumach, Murray. *The Face on the Cutting Room Floor.* New York: William Morrow, 1964.

THERESE AND ISABELLE

Country and date of production: West Germany, 1968 (as *Therese und Isabel*)
Production company/distributor: Amsterdam Film Corp./Audubon Films
Format: Sound, black and white

Running time: 118 minutes
Language: German
Producer: Radley Metzger
Director: Radley Metzger
Screenwriters: Violette Leduc (novel), Jesse Vogel
Awards: None
Genre: Drama
With: Essy Persson (Therese), Anna Gaël (Isabelle), Barbara Laage (Therese's Mother), Anne Vernon (Mlle. Le Blanc), Simone Paris (The Madame), Maurice Teynac (Mons. Martin), Rémy Longa (Pierre), Nathalie Nort (Renee), Darcy Pulliam (Agnes), Suzanne Marchellier (Mlle. Germain), Bernadette Stern (Françoise), Martine Leclerc (Martine), Brigitte Morisan (Brigitte)

SUMMARY

Therese and Isabelle is Radley Metzger's best work and shows his abilities as a director of films that are visually rich and scenic. Told in flashbacks and filmed in a Paris monastery that passes for a French boarding school, the movie is based on the memoirs of author Violette Leduc. The story is framed by a visit to the school by the now-adult Therese and her fiancé. Therese is haunted by the memory of a long-ago romance based on loneliness that she shared with her former classmate Isabelle. The adult Therese recounts her tale mostly in voiceovers as she wanders through the mazelike halls of the now-abandoned school. The young Therese had been sent to the school against her will by her newly remarried mother, and she had gravitated toward Isabelle, with whom she could share her melancholy feelings. The growing closeness between the girls developed into a highly emotional and sexually charged relationship.

As critics have pointed out, the story is more about self-discovery than sexuality, because the girls' relationship helps Therese to gain self-confidence and a feeling of self-worth. At one point, the building emotions between the two girls lead them to a sexual expression of their bond. The experience is handled in a discreet manner, which makes the scene even more effective than if sexual acts were blatant. Soon afterward, Isabelle's mother takes her from the school, leaving Therese with only her powerful memories.

CENSORSHIP HISTORY

The film was exhibited in cities throughout the United States without incident, but community residents in Allegheny County, Pennsylvania, called the office of the district attorney to ask that exhibition be stopped because the subject matter of the film was "offensive." Acting on their requests, the district attorney asked that a judge grant a temporary injunction to prevent the Guild Theatre from showing the film, which he declared "obscene." The district attorney was granted the injunction, but it was overturned on appeal. Arguing that an injunction against exhibition of the film was necessary "to eliminate what he considered to be a public harm," the district attorney then filed suit with the local court, charging that the film was "obscene" and, as such, not constitutionally protected free expression. The local court agreed that the film was obscene and granted the district attorney permanent injunction against the film. Attorneys for the theater appealed the decision in the Supreme Court of Pennsylvania, which ruled that "the question of whether the movie was obscene or was constitutionally protected was not a matter to be decided by the district attorney, but by the supreme court itself, exercising its 'independent constitutional judgment on the facts of the case.'" Basing its decision on the ruling by the U.S. Supreme Court regarding The Lovers in *Jacobellis v. Ohio*, 378 U.S. 184 (1964), the Supreme Court of Pennsylvania determined in *Duggan v. Guild Theatre*, 258 A. 2d 858 (1969), that *Therese and Isabelle* was not obscene and reversed the decision of the lower court.

FURTHER READING

Adler, Renata. "*Therese and Isabelle.*" *New York Times*, May 15, 1968, p. C2.
De Grazia, Edward, and Roger K. Newman. *Banned Films: Movies, Censors, and the First Amendment*. New York: R. R. Bowker, 1982.
Duggan v. Guild Theatre, 258 A. 2d 858 (1969).
Jenkins, Dan. "Apollo Movie Guide's Review of *Therese and Isabelle.*" http://www.apolloguide.com/mov.
Memoirs v. Massachusetts, 383 U.S. 413 (1966).

THE TIN DRUM

Country and date of production: Germany, 1979 (as *Die Blechtrommel*)
Production company/distributor: Franz Seitz Filmproduktion/New World (United States, 1980)
Format: Sound, color
Running time: 142 minutes
Language: German
Producers: Anatole Dauman, Franz Seitz
Director: Volker Schlöndorff
Screenwriters: Jean-Claude Carrière, Günter Grass (novel), Volker Schlöndorff, Franz Seitz
Awards: 1980 Academy Awards, Best Foreign Language Film.
1980 Bodil Festival (Denmark), Best European Film (Volker Schlöndorff, director).
1979 Cannes Film Festival, Golden Palm (Volker Schlöndorff).
1979 German Film Awards, Outstanding Feature Film.
1980 Golden Screen (Germany), Golden Screen.
1980 Los Angeles Film Critics Association Awards, Best Foreign Language Film.

1980 National Board of Review, USA, Best Foreign Language Film.

Genre: Drama

With: Mario Adorf (Alfred Matzerath), Angela Winkler (Agnes Matzerath), David Bennent (Oskar Matzerath), Katharina Thalbach (Maria Matzerath), Daniel Olbrychski (Jan Bronski), Tina Engel (Anna Koljaiczek) (young), Berta Drews (Anna Koljaiczek) (old), Roland Teubner (Joseph Koljaiczek), Tadeusz Kunikowski (Uncle Vinzenz) Andréa Ferréol (Lina Greff), Heinz Bennent (Greff), Ilse Pagé (Gretchen Scheffler), Werner Rehm (Scheffler), Käte Jaenicke (Mother Truczinski), Helmut Brasch (Old Heilandt), Otto Sander (Musician Meyn), Wigand Wittig (Herbert Truczinski), Mariella Oliveri (Roswitha), Fritz Hakl (Bebra)

SUMMARY

The Tin Drum, based on the controversial novel of the same name by Günter Grass, is a surreal story of the young Oskar Matzerath, whose growing up parallels the rise to power of the Nazis in Germany. Oskar refuses to be born until Agnes, his mother, bribes him by promising that he will receive a tin drum on his third birthday. When that day arrives and Oskar receives his long-awaited present, he makes a vow to himself that he will stop growing and stay age three for the rest of his life, a decision that will rule his life for 18 years. He makes this decision because he never wants to become like the hypocritical adults in his family, and he effectively stunts his growth by throwing himself down the cellar stairs. This action is also manipulative because his father, Alfred, will forever blame himself for having left the cellar door open. As time passes, Oskar becomes obsessively attached to his drum, which he beats mercilessly whenever anything annoys him. When Alfred tries to take away the drum, Oskar discovers his other talent, an ability to scream at such a high register that his voice can shatter glass. Oskar takes pride in being a medical oddity, but he also develops physically in spite of his will to remain a child, and the film suggests in at least three points that he takes part in sexual adventures with the 16-year-old Maria while he is still a young adolescent. Oskar is the only person in Danzig who fully realizes the danger posed by the gradual rise of the Nazis, who work insidiously toward total power while the other characters watch complacently. Oskar's awareness pushes him to disrupt a fascist rally with the overwhelming beat of his instrument.

CENSORSHIP HISTORY

The Tin Drum won numerous film awards in 1979 and 1980, including an Academy Award yet in 1997, claims by an American fundamentalist religious group in Oklahoma that the film was "child pornography" led to civil abuses and the confiscation of the videotapes by law enforcement officials. The film had been freely available on videotape and widely distributed throughout the United States, including the state of Oklahoma, during which time "no government jurisdiction had ever alleged *The Tin Drum* to be obscene or child pornography" (*Video Software Dealers Association, Inc. v. Oklahoma City, et al.*) The complaint began after a citizen of Oklahoma City heard on a radio talk show about a former student of Bethel College and Seminary in Minnesota, who had objected to a class assignment to review the movies *The Tin Drum*, *Like Water for Chocolate* and *Do the Right Thing*. The student alleged that the films were pornographic and "contrary to her expectations at this Christian college and seminary," and filed a suit in *Sisam v. Bethel College & Seminary*, C5-96-10825, slip op. at 10 (Minn. Dist. ct., Ramsey Co., May 9, 1997), which the court dismissed, without addressing First Amendment issues, as "essentially an improper attack on the general quality of educational experience Bethel College provided its students."

The resident of Oklahoma City who heard the talk show went to the local library and checked out a copy of the videotape *The Tin Drum*, then submitted it to the Oklahoma City police for review and alleged that it violated Oklahoma's obscenity law. The police then went before State District Judge Richard Freeman, who determined on June 25, 1997, that the film violated the Oklahoma obscenity law that barred the depiction of children under 18 having sex. He cited three scenes in which the boy Oskar is shown as a minor "engaged in or portrayed, depicted or represented" in sex acts with the female character, 16-year-old Maria. Hours later, the city police confiscated all copies of the tape in six video stores and used the customer records at each store to track down the remaining copies. At night, the police went to the homes of individuals and demanded that they turn over the copies of the tapes.

Coincidentally, Michael Camfield, the development director for the American Civil Liberties Union (ACLU) in Oklahoma, had heard of the impending censorship of the tape and had rented the tape that day to review it. As he noted in an ACLU press release dated July 3, 1997, "I tried to explain to the officers that they were trampling on constitutional rights and this serious film was protected by the First Amendment, but they confiscated it anyway." City officials tried to intimidate those who spoke in favor of the film and made subsequent threats to press criminal charges "against anyone in possession of the film," even though such threats constituted "unconstitutional prior restraint—which has been upheld by the courts to be one of the most egregious violations of free speech" (ACLU, July 3, 1997).

As Marjorie Heins, a First Amendment authority with the national ACLU, observed, "few examples of censorship in recent years have been as astonishing as the entirely lawless actions of the Oklahoma City police and Judge Freeman" (ACLU, July 3, 1997). On October 20, 1998, a federal court ruled that *The Tin Drum* was not child pornography and was not, therefore, subject to criminal penalties imposed by the Oklahoma child pornography law. United States District Judge Ralph Thompson had ruled the year before that "the Video Privacy Protection Act was violated when defendants and police officers High, Kim and French obtained identifying customer information without a prior search warrant, grand jury subpoena or court order." He ruled further that "the Constitution requires an adversarial court hearing before police can round up forms of expression, such as films and novels, as illegal works."

The Video Software Dealers Association, the National Association of Recording Merchandisers and Southwest Video Rentals filed a civil lawsuit in the U.S. District Court for the Western District of Oklahoma against Oklahoma City, "not seeking monetary damages. . . . [but] to ensure police avoid the same unconstitutional procedures regarding customer privacy and protected works of art." The ACLU of Oklahoma development director, Michael Camfield, also became a plaintiff in a lawsuit against Oklahoma City after the three police officers confiscated his rented copy of *The Tin Drum* in June 1997. Ultimately, the Oklahoma City Council and District Attorney Bob Macy agreed to pay $575,000 to settle one lawsuit arising out of the flap. Attorneys in the federal case sought more than $360,000 in court costs from the city and DA's office, leading many citizens in Oklahoma City to question why such abuses were permitted.

FURTHER READING

American Civil Liberties Union. "ACLU Praises Summary Judgment Ruling in Oklahoma Tin Drum Litigation." Press release, October 21, 1998. http://www.aclu.org/news/n102198a.html.

———. "Tin Dream Video Seizure Sparks ACLU Lawsuit." Press release, October 21, 1998. http://www.aclu.org/issues/freespeech/tindrum.html.

Associated Press Wire Service. "Confiscation of Video Violated Federal Privacy Law." *Tulsa World*, December 20, 1998. http://www.tulsaworld.com.

———. "Settlement Considered in Tin Drum Case." *Tulsa World*, March 16, 1999. http://www.tulsaworld.com.

———. "Testimony Begins in Tin Drum Trial." *Tulsa World*, August 24, 1999. http://www.tulsaworld.com.

"Expensive Movie: Taxpayers Hit with Costly Tab." *Tulsa World*, February 17, 2000. http://www.tulsaworld.com.

Michael D. Campfield v. City of Oklahoma City. Complaint for Declaratory and for Injunctive Relief and Damages, October 13, 1998.

Nascenzi, Nicole. "Free-thought Process Defended." *Tulsa World*, September 10, 1999. http://www.tulsaworld.com.

Sisam v. Bethel College & Seminary, C5-96-10825, slip op. at 10 (Minn. Dist. ct., Ramsey Co., May 9, 1997).

Video Software Dealers Association, Inc. v. Oklahoma City, Sergeant French, Brett N. High, SE Kim, Sam Gonzales, and Robert Macy. Class Action Complaint for Declaratory Judgement and Injunctive Relief, July 11, 1997.

TITICUT FOLLIES

Country and date of production: United States, 1967
Production company/distributor: Bridgewater Film Co./Titicut Follies Film Distributing Company, Grove Press
Format: Sound, black and white

Running time: 84 minutes
Language: English
Producer: Frederick Wiseman
Director: Frederick Wiseman
Screenwriters: None
Awards: 1967 International Filmfest Mannheim-Heidelberg, Best Feature (Frederick Wiseman).
Genre: Documentary
With: Residents at the Bridgewater (Massachusetts) State Hospital for the Criminally Insane

SUMMARY

This documentary film records scenes for the mistreatment of inmates and the conditions in a state prison for the criminally insane juxtaposed against scenes from a musical performed by the patients and the staff within the same period. One of the most disturbing documentary films ever made, it is honest and unflinching in its portrayal of the horrific systemic abuses at this institution. More important, the director hoped that the film would shed light on the kind of society that would treat the least fortunate of its members in this dehumanizing and cruel way. The film opens with scenes from the musical performance, then segues into scenes from inmate life, including a forced nose-feeding of an inmate who is on a hunger strike and his later death and burial; the violent response of an inmate who is repeatedly taunted by corrections officers for the "crime" of keeping his cell dirty; strip-searches conducted on inmates to allow correction officers to search them for contraband; an interview between a psychiatrist and a young husband and father who has been diagnosed as suffering from paranoia and incarcerated for sexually molesting young children; and a heart-wrenching interview with a highly articulate young schizophrenic who complains about inappropriate treatment by the staff and the negative influence of his surroundings.

CENSORSHIP HISTORY

Titicut Follies was the only documentary shown at the 1967 New York Film Festival. It was reviewed by film critics in the *New York Times* (October 4, 1967), *Variety* (October 4, 1967) and *Cue* (October 21, 1967) and was also the subject of numerous newspaper and magazine articles that praised the courage of the filmmaker and decried the conditions he exposed. Soon after the filming was completed, however, Frederick Wiseman attempted to show the film in Massachusetts, but state legislators banned it outright when a Suffolk County judge ruled in *Commonwealth v. Wiseman*, 249 N.E. 2d 610 (1969), that the portrayals of naked inmates or those exhibiting manifestations of extreme "mental disease" constituted "a collective indecent intrusion" into the most private aspects of their lives. Attorneys for the distributor appealed the decision, and the court modified the ban to allow restricted exhibition of the film to "legislators, judges, lawyers, doctors, psychiatrists, students in those or related fields, and organizations dealing with the social problems of custodial care and mental infirmity." The film producer sought to have the case heard by the U.S. Supreme Court, but the Court denied Wiseman's petition for review in *Wiseman v. Massachusetts*, 398 U.S. 960 (1970), because of the conflicting concerns that the case represented. As Justice Harlan wrote in his dissent from the denial, the film "is at once a scathing indictment of the inhumane conditions that prevailed at the time of the film and an undeniable infringement of the privacy of the inmates filmed, who are shown nude and engaged in acts that would unquestionably embarrass an individual of normal sensitivity." The public may have the right to know about the conditions in public institutions, but this right conflicts with "the individual's interest in privacy and dignity." Thus, the refusal of the Court to review the case affirmed the limitations set by the lower court.

The officials of the Bridgewater institution also brought suit to stop the exhibition of the film on the grounds of defamation and invasion of privacy. When the case was heard in federal district court as *Cullen v. Grove Press, Inc.*, 276 F. Supp. 727 (1967), the judges ruled that *Titicut Follies* "was expression included within the free speech and free press of the First and Fourteenth Amendments" and, as such, could be suppressed only if it "amounted to a false report made with knowledge of its falsity or in reckless disregard of the truth" or if it were obscene. Because the plaintiffs could prove neither condition to exist, the court denied the injunction. Nonetheless, viewing of the film remained restricted to related professionals until 1991, when Wiseman won the right to distribute the film for commercial exhibition with the proviso that all faces of inmates and correction officers be seen as blurs, to protect individual privacy. Two years later, the film was shown on the Public Broadcasting System.

FURTHER READING

Commonwealth v. Wiseman, 249 N.E. 2d 610 (1969).
Cullen v. Grove Press, Inc., 276 F. Supp. 727 (1967).
De Grazia, Edward, and Roger K. Newman. *Banned Films: Movies, Censors, and the First Amendment*. New York: R. R. Bowker, 1982.
Hoberman, J. "Titicut Follies Unbound." *Premiere*, March 1992, p. 41.
Jeavon, Clyde. "The Films of Frederich Wiseman." In *Movies of the Seventies*, ed. Ann Lloyd. London: Orbis, 1984.
Lyons, Charles. *The New Censors: Movies and the Culture Wars*. Philadelphia: Temple University Press, 1997.
Miller, Frank. *Censored Hollywood: Sex, Sin, and Violence on Screen*. Atlanta, Ga.: Turner Publishing, 1994.
Parenti, Michael. "Preemption, Profits, and Censors." In *Make-Believe Media: The Politics of Entertainment*. New York: St. Martin's Press, 1966; pp. 182–195.

TOMORROW'S CHILDREN

Country and date of production: United States, 1934
Production company/distributor: Foy Productions Ltd./State Rights
Format: Sound, black and white
Running time: 70 minutes
Language: English
Producer: Bryan Foy
Director: Crane Wilbur
Screenwriters: Wallace Thurman (story), Crane Wilbur
Awards: None
Genre: Drama
With: Diane Sinclair (Alice Mason), Donald Douglas (Dr. Brooks), John Preston (Dr. Crosby), Carlyle Moore, Jr. (Jim Baker), Sterling Holloway (Dr. Dorsey), W. Messenger Bellis (Dr. McIntyre), Hyram A. Hoover (Spike), Constance Kent (Nurse), Lewis Gambart (Jef), Crane Wilbur (Father O'Brien), Arthur Wanzer (Mr. Mason), Sarah Padden (Mrs. Mason), Ray Corrigan (Bit)

SUMMARY

Tomorrow's Children, which was distributed in the United Kingdom under the title *The Unborn*, exposes the legal abuses that accompany orders for sterilization. It was advertised with the following tagline: "The most daring, sensational drama ever filmed!" The story focuses on the Mason family, in which the parents are alcoholic, one child is physically challenged and another is in jail; the family also has an adopted daughter who is "normal." Aggravated by the continued problems with the family, the Welfare Bureau advises that the whole family be sterilized so they will not perpetuate what it sees as their defective genes. This order meets with resistance from a Roman Catholic priest and from a young physician who loves the adopted daughter, whom no one except the Masons knows is adopted. The court order for the sterilizations is granted, but after Mrs. Mason admits that Alice is adopted, the priest and the physician try to obtain a court order to prevent Alice's sterilization. The judge to whom they first appeal refuses to listen to their calls for justice, but another judge grants the order that frees Alice just as she is placed on the surgeon's table. The film also shows that the judge who refused to free Alice yields easily to the request of a politically important senator that he discharge an order for sterilization against a repeat sex offender. This court scene emphasizes the film's message that decisions regarding sterilization were often made without the approval of the victim and without attention to due process issues. The study of eugenics in the United States resulted in grave prejudice against the physically and mentally challenged and led to sterilization of those whom scientists felt unfit to reproduce or even live.

CENSORSHIP HISTORY

The distributor applied for a permit to exhibit this film in New York State but was refused by the board of censors on the grounds that the film was "immoral" and would "tend to corrupt morals" and "incite to crime." After being refused the permit four times between May 5, 1934, and August 20, 1937, the distributor filed suit in state court to request, in *Foy Productions v. Graves*, 299 N.Y.S. 671 (1937), that the court reverse the determination of the censors. The court denied the application and sent the case to the New York State Appellate Division, where the majority ruled in *Foy Productions v. Graves*, 3 N.Y.S. 2d 573 (1938), to confirm the determination of the lower court. In a lengthy explanation of the decision, the court wrote that, although the law required that a film receive a permit for exhibition unless it "is obscene, indecent, immoral, inhuman, sacrilegious, or is of such a character that its exhibition would tend to corrupt morals or incite to crime," the court would not reverse the censor's decision: "if the verdict of a jury reaching the same conclusion would not be set aside as against the weight of evidence, the court is not at liberty to disturb his finding."

Moreover, the court decided that "the content of the picture is devoted to an illegal practice." New York State penal law prohibited the distribution of birth control information, and the court ruled that the film

> publicizes and elucidates sterilization as a means to prevent the conception of children, that it is a form of birth control, contraception without penalty, and that it is "an immoral means to a desirable end." It declares its own immorality. It tends to inculcate the fact that venal judges in court dispense injustice, and that young girls may be mutilated, unlawfully but under the forms of law, when accident does not prevent. It demonstrates the manner how and the ease with which the law may be violated. The content of the picture is devoted to an illegal practice, which is, as a matter of common knowledge, immoral and reprehensible according to the standards of a very large part of the citizenry of the state.

The two dissenting judges, Justice James P. Hill and Justice Christopher J. Heffernan, disagreed with the meaning of the word "immoral," calling it uncertain and defending the film as devoid of anything lewd or lustful. Moreover, they wrote that one would have to have "a prurient imagination to find anything of the unchaste or indecent" in the film. Addressing the suggestion that events in the film would do injury to the image of the court, the dissenting justices wrote,

> Merited and unmerited criticism is permitted against all who hold public office. It is deemed necessary and wise under our concept of freedom of speech and of the press. The judiciary, no more than the executive and legislative, are sacrosanct. The foundation and fame of our judicial system is not so unstable as to be injured by this police court scene which is neither immoral, tending to injure morals, or to incite to crime.

The distributor then appealed the decisions in the New York Court of Appeals, which confirmed the earlier decisions without writing an opinion in *Foy Productions v. Graves*, 15 N.E. 2d 435 (1938).

FURTHER READING

De Grazia, Edward, and Roger K. Newman. *Banned Films: Movies, Censors, and the First Amendment.* New York: R. R. Bowker, 1982.
Foy Productions v. Graves, 299 N.Y.S. 671 (1937).
Foy Productions v. Graves, 3 N.Y.S. 2d 573 (1938).
Foy Productions v. Graves, 15 N.E. 2d 435 (1938).

TOTO WHO LIVED TWICE

Country and date of production: Italy, 1998 (as *Totò che visse due volte*)
Production company/distributor: Instituto Luce, Lucky Red Distribuzione
Format: Sound, black and white
Running time: 93 minutes
Language: Italian
Producer: Rean Mazzone
Directors: Daniele Ciprì, Franco Maresco
Screenwriters: Daniele Ciprì, Lillo Iacolino, Franco Maresco
Awards: 1998 Catalonian International Film Festival (Sitges, Spain), Best Cinematography (Luca Bigazzi).
Genre: Drama
With: Salvatore Gattuso (Totò/Don Totò), Marcello Miranda (Paletta), Carlo Giordano (Fefè), Pietro Arciadiacono (Pitrinu), Camillo Conti (Tremmotori), Angelo Prollo (First customer/Apostle), Antonino Carollo (Don Nenè), Leonardo Aiello (Paletta's chaser), Antonino Cirrincione (Cascino), Giuseppe Pedalino (Pigs keeper), Michele Lunardo (Accordion player), Aurelio Mirino (Second customer), Rosolino Spatola (Third customer), Vincenzo Girgenti (Fourth customer), Antonino Accomando (First robber), Niccolò Villafranca (Second robber), Giuseppe Mulè (Third robber), Michele Dia (Old believer), Baldassare Catanzaro (Bastiano), Giuseppe Pepe (Zà Concetta), Antonino Aliotta (Solino), Francesco Arnao (Maddalena/Apostle)

SUMMARY

The film, set in a decimated Sicilian wasteland, is composed of three episodes that, taken together, provide an irreverent version of the gospels. The first episode is an account of the quest of Paletta, the village idiot, to find sexual satisfaction. He does not have enough money to pay for the services of the village prostitute, Tremmotori, so he steals a locket from the holy shrine owed by a Mafia don. The second episode opens with the death of Pitrinu in a rat-infested room and then provides a flashback that reveals his courtship and betrayal by his male lover, Fefe. In the third episode, Toto, a mob boss, throws a small-time criminal named Lazarus into an acid bath, but Lazarus is later raised from the dead by a bad-tempered local messiah, also named Toto and played by the same actor who plays the mob boss. The reanimated Lazarus creates major destruction throughout the town, and those in power demand an explanation. Angry with Toto-the-messiah for refusing to cure his deformity, the hunchbacked Judas betrays him and receives in exchange the favors of Maddalena, the hooker with a glass eye. This episode also contains the majority of the activity that raised the objections of the censors: the rape of an angel, a man masturbating in front of a statue of the Virgin Mary, a man having sex with a chicken, and an ending that contains crucifixions of Paletta and Fefe. As a *Variety* reviewer observed, "the presentation of any kind of sexuality seems to pose problems. Women (played by men in all the directors' films) are either toothless hags or lewd whores, and sex is depicted in emotionless paid encounters, bestiality, rape or joyless masturbation. The effect, however, is more undergraduate than subversive."

CENSORSHIP HISTORY

From its premiere in Berlin in February 1998, the film became a controversial topic and the subject of major debate about film censorship in Italy, "which has no censorship for books, music or theater." Controversy over its banning would lead Italy to abolish its board of censors, which had existed since the time of silent films.

The state commission of censors banned *Toto* from theaters throughout Italy only days before it was due to open, and a lengthy appeal ensued. The Italian film censorship commission expressed outrage that the film linked sex and religious symbols and labeled it an "offense to common decency." Leonardo Ancono, head of the censorship board, stated in a television interview that the film featured "an absence of any values. No, on the contrary—there were negative values." In defiance of the censors, the head of an Italian consumer group promised to take the same approach as it had in 1970 regarding LAST TANGO IN PARIS, when Italy ordered the master copy of the film burned; it would show the film to the public. The director of *Last Tango in Paris*, Bernardo Bertolucci, reacted to this latest attempt at censorship by calling it an "ugly flashback" to his own experience. The Italian government finally decided to strip the censors of their power to ban films entirely. The bill sent to parliament aimed "to remove the possibility of an administrative body such as the censorship committee preventing a film being screened to the public" and would allow state censors only to "determine it unfit for those under 18."

The notoriety of the film exceeded the borders of Italy. In promotional literature for the Second Annual Italian Film Festival in Toronto, organizers wrote, "Everything about this film is controversial. Initially, the directors were accused of contravening censorship laws in Italy but this was determined not to be the case. Nevertheless, the issues surrounding the film were not to end there. The directors were put on trial for blasphemy and the vatican [sic] denounced the film in a last ditch effort to have it banned." The film festival brochure also carried the following warning: "Although some viewers may find the controversy surrounding this film intriguing, even those who do not consider themselves sensitive may find the many scenes of sexual deviance, degradation and crude acts intensely offensive. We strongly do not recommend this film for sensitive viewers."

FURTHER READING

D'Emilio, Frances. "Italy Censors Ban Film About Mafia." Associated Press, March 3, 1998.

"Italian Government Responds to Film Industry." *Media Awareness Network.* http://www.reseau-medias.ca/eng/news/news/two/italy.htm.

Rooney, David. "Toto Who Lived Twice." *Variety,* March 9, 1998, p. 43–44.

"Toto Who Lived Twice." Second Annual Toronto Italian Film Festival, June 16–20, 2000. http://www.italianfilmfestival.com.

THE VIRGIN SPRING

Country and date of production: Sweden, 1960 (as *Jungfrukällan*)
Production company/distributor: Svensk Filmindustri/Janus Films (United States)
Format: Sound, black and white
Running time: 89 minutes
Language: Swedish
Producers: Ingmar Bergman (uncredited), Allan Ekelund (uncredited)
Director: Ingmar Bergman
Screenwriter: Ulla Isaksson
Awards: 1960 Academy Awards, Best Foreign Language Film. 1960 Cannes Film Festival, Special Mention (Ingmar Bergman). 1961 Golden Globe Awards, Best Foreign-Language Film.
Genre: Drama
With: Max von Sydow (Töre), Birgitta Valberg (Märeta), Gunnel Lindblom (Ingeri), Birgitta Pettersson (Karin), Axel Düberg (Thin Herdsman), Tor Isedal (Mute Herdsman), Allan Edwall (Beggar), Ove Porath (Boy), Axel Slangus (Bridge Keeper), Gudrun Brost (Frida), Oscar Ljung (Simon)

SUMMARY

The story of the film is based on a 13th-century Swedish legend popularized in such Swedish folk songs as "Tores dotte I Vange" ("The Daughter of Tore o Vange"). The tale uses two sisters to explore the concepts of good versus evil in the form of Karin, the fair-haired virginal sister, and Ingeri, the dark and moody sister who is jealous of Karin. While walking through a forest to bring candles to the church, Ingeri confuses Karin so much that the fair-haired sister becomes lost in the woods, and Ingeri leaves her without a word.

Unknown to either girl, three goatherders are lurking in the forest, and when they find that Karin is alone, all three rape and murder her. They take her cloak with them and look for shelter. As fate would have it, they reach the farmhouse where the sisters live and try to sell Karin's cloak to her father Töre for a night of shelter and for food. When Töre sees the cloak and realizes that the men have harmed his daughter, he loses all control and kills the men on the spot and then leaves the farmhouse to find her. He is anguished when he finds her naked body in the woods and kneels beside her to vow that he will build a church to her memory. As he speaks, he sees a spring gush from the ground beneath her head.

CENSORSHIP HISTORY

The major objection of censors to *The Virgin Spring* was the 90-second rape scene. In Detroit, the censorship tribunal considered themselves enforcers more than censors, stating "We are the Obscenity Enforcement Bureau. . . . We are engaged in irradicating obscenity." Although the Detroit censors had agreed to give the owners of the three art theaters in the city a relatively free hand over the movies they chose to exhibit as long as they kept people under 18 off the premises, *The Virgin Spring* became a special case. "The censors eliminated the rape scenes in *Two Women* and *The Virgin Spring* even when these pictures were shown only to adults." In New York State, the board of censors ordered two brief views of the rape scene removed "because they were too explicit. These views depicted a shepherd in a coital position with the victim's bare legs being pulled around his body by a second shepherd." In both instances, the distributor complied with the changes without an argument.

The same changes were proposed in Fort Worth, Texas, after the city board of censors invoked an ordinance that prohibited the exhibition of any film that was "indecent or injurious to the morals of the citizens of Fort Worth, or which would tend to promote or encourage indecency, immorality, or racial or sectional prejudice, or juvenile delinquency." In 1962, the censors denied permission to exhibit the film when the distributor refused to allow the excisions to the film, and an administrative board of review upheld the denial. Attorneys representing the distributor applied in the Tarrant County District Court for an injunction to prevent law enforcement officials in Fort Worth from interfering with exhibition of the film on the grounds that the city officials had "applied capricious and private standards of taste and judgment." Presiding judge Harris Brewster, who viewed the film at a Dallas theater, refused to grant the injunction in *Janus Films, Inc. v. City of Fort Worth*, 354 S.W. 2d 597 (1962). The distributor made application for a writ of error, (a writ authorizing an appeal from an inferior court, assigning error in the proceedings to matters of law only on the face of the proceedings, so that no evidence is required to substantiate or support the appeal) to the Supreme Court of Texas, claiming that Texas criminal law "generally proscribed the showing of obscene films except any film that had been 'legally imported' into the country and had been 'passed by a customs office of the United States Government at any port of entry.'" Although the film had been approved by U.S. Customs, the Supreme Court of Texas denied the application and "found no reversible error in the lower court's handling of the case" in *Janus Films, Inc. v. City of Fort Worth*, 358 S.W. 2d 589 (1962).

FURTHER READING

Carmen, Ira H. *Movies, Censorship, and the Law.* Ann Arbor: University of Michigan Press, 1966.
Crist, Judith. "The Virgin Spring." *New York Herald-Tribune*, November 13, 1960.
De Grazia, Edward, and Roger K. Newman. *Banned Films: Movies, Censors and the First Amendment.* New York: R. R. Bowker, 1982.
Janus Films, Inc. v. City of Fort Worth, 354 S.W. 2d 597 (1962).
Janus Films, Inc. v. City of Fort Worth, 358 S.W. 2d 589 (1962).

VIVA MARIA!

Country and date of production: France/Italy, 1965
Production company/distributor: Nouvelles Editions de Films–Les Productions Artistes Associes (Paris) and Vides Cinematografica (Rome)/ United Artists (United States)
Format: Sound, color
Running time: 115 minutes
Language: French
Producer: Óscar Dancigers
Director: Louis Malle
Screenwriters: Louis Malle, Jean-Claude Carrière
Awards: None
Genre: Western/comedy
With: Brigitte Bardot (Maria O'Malley), Jeanne Moreau (Maria), Paulette Dubost (Mme. Diogenes), Claudio Brook (Rudolfo), Carlos López Moctezuma (Don Rodriguez), Juan López Moctezuma (Señor Rodriguez), Poldo Bendandi (Werther), Gregor von Rezzori (M. Diogenes), Francisco Reiguera (Father Superior), Jonathan Eden (Juanito), Roberto Pedret ( ), José Ángel Espinosa (El Presidente), George Hamilton (Flores)

SUMMARY

Viva María! is a comic western that relates the adventures of a traveling circus and music hall troupe that becomes immersed in a peasant revolution in the fictitious country of San Miguel. The film features numerous comic sequences, including hand grenades dropped by a pigeon; sex kitten Brigitte Bardot swinging through trees on a rope; a billiard-playing, corrupt president of San Miguel; and inept revolutionaries whose behavior calls into question their ability to lead themselves. The film quickly sketches Maria O'Malley's revolutionary childhood, from 1891 in Ireland to 1907 in Central America, as young Maria blows up a bridge that British colonial soldiers are crossing as they attempt to reach her mortally wounded father, an Irish anarchist. She escapes from the soldiers and joins a traveling troupe in San Miguel, where she meets the older, more experienced Maria, who takes the younger woman under her protection. During one performance, Maria O'Malley accidentally performs the striptease, which increases her popularity in the small revolutionary country, and she is wined and dined by several of the nation's powerful but corrupt leaders.

Angered by the suffering and poverty the she sees, Maria O'Malley loses her temper one day and shoots the leader of a group of bandits. For this the troupe is captured and imprisoned in the hacienda of the wicked Don Rodriguez. While there, both Maria and Maria find themselves strongly attracted to the handsome young leader of the revolution, Flores, whom Rodriguez has bound and tied to a wooden yoke. In a scene that is more comic than erotic, Maria (Jeanne Moreau) engages in sexual intercourse with the bound man, who is unable to move. When both women are summoned to Rodriguez's opulent salon the next morning, they take advantage of the opportunity to destroy the room, using a machine gun that Maria O'Malley is fluent in operating. The prisoners escape and Flores is later shot in a fight, so Maria (Moreau) takes his place as leader of the revolution, aided ably by Maria (Bardot). Various fight sequences include the rebels' attack on the hacienda, which they destroy, and their humiliation of Rodriguez, whom they leave crawling along the dusty ground wearing only underwear. The people of San Miguel hail the two women as heroes and saviors, but they are eventually captured. Condemned to face a firing squad, the women are about to die when their followers rescue them and reveal that the revolutionaries have taken control of the capital city of San Miguel. The version of the film released in the United States, one minute shorter than the original, ends with dancing and celebration in San Miguel. In the original version, at 115 minutes long, the women return to Europe, where they are shown on stage, performing the story of the San Miguel revolution.

CENSORSHIP HISTORY

Viva María! did not take itself seriously, but the censors in Texas did. The distributor submitted the film to the Motion Picture Classification Board (MPCB) in Dallas, Texas, to request a permit to exhibit the film. Five members of the MPCB viewed the film, but eight members voted to classify the film as "not suitable for young persons," while the ninth member abstained. A local ordinance allowed the MPCB to make this classification if it believed, in its judgment, that a film "describes or portrays (1) brutality, criminal violence, or depravity in such a manner as likely to incite young persons to crime or delinquency or (2) sexual promiscuity or extra-marital or abnormal sexual relations in such a manners as . . . likely to incite or encourage delinquency or sexual promiscuity on the part of young persons or to appeal to their prurient interest." The law provided that if an exhibitor did not accept the board's decision, the MPCB must file suit to enjoin any exhibition of the film, then subject its determination to a second review. The exhibitor gave written notice that it did not accept the classification and the MPCB petitioned for an injunction, alleging that the classification "was warranted because of the film's portrayal of sexual promiscuity. . . . [and] several scenes portraying male-female relationships contravened 'acceptable and approved behavior.'" The trial judge at the hearing issued the injunction and concluded that there were "two or three features in the picture that look to me would be unsuitable to young people."

The exhibitor appealed the ruling in the Texas Court of Appeals in *Interstate Circuit v. Dallas*, 402 S.W. 2d 770 (1966), but the appellate court affirmed the decision. The case was then argued before the United States Supreme Court, which held that the ordinance violated the First and Fourteenth Amendments because "it lacks 'narrowly drawn, reasonable and definite standards for the officials to follow,'" which the Supreme Court had ruled in *Niemotko v. Maryland*, 340 U.S. 268, 271 (1951). In delivering the opinion of the Court, Justice Marshall expressed the opinion that, despite what may appear to be a limited sphere of influence for a case concerning one city, the implications of the case in regard to constitutional impact were vast. He decried the fact that filmmakers fearful of censorship might dilute their products and produce more inane, safe films.

The decision in regard to *Viva María!* moved the Hollywood film industry closer toward abandoning the Production Code that based ratings on maturity levels—"G" (for all audiences), "M" (suggested for mature audiences), "R" (restricted to audiences of 18 and over, except when accompanied by an adult) and "X" (restricted to audiences of 18 and over) and toward adopting an age classification system that changed "M" to "PG," added "PG-13" (parental guidance suggested for children under 13) and "NC-17" (no children under 17).

FURTHER READING

Interstate Circuit v. Dallas, 402 S.W. 2d 770 (1966).
Interstate Circuit v. Dallas, 390 U.S. 676 (1968).

THE VIXEN

Country and date of production: United States, 1968
Production company/distributor: Goldstein Films/Eve Productions
Format: Sound, color
unning time: 70 minutes
Language: English
Producer: Russ Meyer
Director: Russ Meyer
Screenwriters: Russ Meyer (story), Anthony-James Ryan (story), Robert Rudelson
Awards: None

Genre: Drama
With: Erica Gavin (Vixen Palmer), Garth Pillsbury (Tom Palmer), Harrison Page (Niles), Jon Evans (Jud), Vincene Wallace (Janet King), Robert Aiken (Dave King), Michael Donovan O'Donnell (Mr. O'Bannion)

SUMMARY

The plot of the film deals with the sexual escapades of Vixen Palmer, who owns a lodge in British Columbia with her husband, Tom. While Tom Palmer is away from home working as a bush pilot or serving as a hunting guide for lodge guests, his bored wife aggressively seeks out other men and women for sexual encounters. As a review in *Time* magazine described Vixen's activities, she has affairs with "everyone from a Royal Mountie to the wife of a visiting fisherman." The plot also seeks to deal with such contemporary issues as racism, antimilitarism, communism and airplane hijacking, which the court viewed as simply "contrived social commentary totally unrelated to the dominant theme of the picture."

CENSORSHIP HISTORY

The film was rated "X" (for adults only) by the Motion Picture Association of America (MPAA) rating system, so it could not play in commercial theaters, but it was permitted for exhibition in art theaters. In Ohio, the distributor was enjoined permanently from exhibiting the film in the state after local officials applied to the court of common pleas to obtain an injunction against the film using the authority granted by the nuisance abatement ordinance. Attorneys for the distributor took the case before the Ohio Supreme Court to request that the injunction be lifted. In *State ex rel Keating v. A Motion Picture Entitled Vixen*, 272 N.E. 2d 137 (1971), the court upheld the ban after refusing to legally distinguish between the "depiction of purported acts of sexual intercourse on the movie screen" and the performance of such acts "in a public place," and determining that both constitute "conduct, not free speech." The court also claimed that whatever social value the film might have (in its attempts to deal with contemporary issues) was negated by the evidence that "a film's exhibitor was principally motivated by the prospect of financial gain [that was] equivalent to pandering to prurient interests in sex, and so negative [*sic*] whatever social value or importance the film might conceivably have." The court ruled that, because *Vixen* displayed "sexual intercourse on the movie screen for commercial exploitation," not for an educational, social, scientific, moral or artistic purpose, the film was obscene.

FURTHER READING

De Grazia, Edward, and Roger K. Newman. *Banned Films: Movies, Censors and the First Amendment.* New York: R. R. Bowker, 1982.
State ex rel Keating v. A Motion Picture Entitled Vixen, 272 N.E. 2d 137 (1971).
"Vixen!" *Time*, June 13, 1969.

WHIRLPOOL

Country and date of production: France, 1935 (as *Remous*)
Production company/distributor: H.O. Film/Mayer-Burstyn (United States, 1939)
Format: Sound, black and white
Running time: 120 minutes
Language: French
Producer: Edmond T. Gréville
Director: Edmond T. Gréville
Screenwriters: André Doderet, Peggy Thompson (story)
Awards: None
Genre: Drama
With: Robert Arnoux, Jeanne Boitel, Lyne Clevers, Jean Galland, Jean Kolb, Maurice Maillot, Françoise Rosay, Diana Sari

SUMMARY

The film tells a story similar to that of LADY CHATTERLEY'S LOVER. A passionate young wife tries valiantly to remain faithful to her husband, who was paralyzed from the waist down in an automobile accident during their honeymoon. In time, she succumbs to her desires and has an affair with a young man, but she swears that she remains spiritually faithful to her husband. She makes her decision without much forethought and then agonizes over her infidelity in sequence after sequence. When her husband learns of the affair, he cannot live with the knowledge and commits suicide.

CENSORSHIP HISTORY

The New York board of censors took the important and not so common, step of viewing this film before deciding whether to issue a permit for exhibition. After review, the board determined that, although the wife realizes that her affair is wrong, "the movie, because it portrayed immorality, might corrupt others." The distributor challenged the decision of the board in a case heard before the appellate division of the supreme court of New York, which in *Mayer v. Byrne*, 10 N.Y.S. 2d (1939), affirmed the decision of the board and wrote in its evaluation of the film, "Such is not fit subject matter for screen display."

FURTHER READING

Carmen, Ira H. *Movies, Censorship, and the Law.* Ann Arbor: University of Michigan Press, 1966.
De Grazia, Edward, and Roger K. Newman. *Banned Films: Movies, Censors, and the First Amendment.* New York: R. R. Bowker, 1982.
Mayer v. Byrne, 10 N.Y.S. 2d 794 (1939).

WILD WEED

Country and date of production: United States, 1949 (also released as *The Devil's Weed; Marijuana, the Devil's Weed; She Shoulda Said No*)
Production company/distributor: Eureka Productions/Jewell
Format: Sound, black and white
Running time: 90 minutes
Language: English
Producers: Kroger Babb, Richard Day
Director: Sam Newfield
Screenwriters: Arthur Hoerl (story), Richard H. Landau
Awards: None
Genre: Drama
With: Lila Leeds (Anne Lester), Alan Baxter (Markey), Douglas Blackley (Lt. Mason), Michael Whalen (Jonathan Treanor), Mary Ellen Popel (Rita), David Holt (Bob Lester), Lyle Talbot (Capt. Hayes), Don Harvey (Lt. Tyne), Henry Corden (Hugo, the club manager)

SUMMARY

In this film, Anne Lester works as a chorus girl to support her brother as he attends college. At a party, Anne meets an attractive man who introduces her to marijuana and invites her to take her first puff. She soon becomes addicted to smoking marijuana and gets involved with a drug dealer, who plans to recruit her to sell drugs. While under the influence of the marijuana, Anne engages in somewhat risqué sexual behavior. When narcotics agents place the dealer under surveillance, Anne agrees to cooperate with them to break up the drug ring. At the end, she turns from her misguided ways and becomes a "good girl" once again. Mixed in with the moralizing, however, are numerous scenes of drug use and trafficking.

CENSORSHIP HISTORY

The debate in the courts of Pennsylvania over whether to license this film for exhibition in the state led to the end of the motion picture licensing law in that state. The distributor probably expected some resistance to *Wild Weed*, given that advertisements for the film carried the tagline, "How Bad Can a Good Girl Get . . . Without Losing Her Virtue and Self-Respect?" Although Finland banned the film entirely, the United States paid it little attention until the censorship board in Pennsylvania refused the distributor a license to exhibit the film at three different times when it was submitted under three different names. After the third denial, attorneys for the distributor appealed the decision in the Court of Common Pleas in Philadelphia. The court considered that the board had concluded that the film was "indecent and immoral and . . . tended to debase and corrupt morals." These criteria had been found unconstitutional in relation to THE MIRACLE in *Burstyn v. Wilson*, 343 U.S. 495 (1952), because they were too vague. Using this case as its basis, the Court of Common Pleas in *Hallmark Productions v. Pennsylvania Board of Censors,* 121 A. 2d 584 (1956), reversed the decision of the censorship board and declared the Pennsylvania Motion Picture Censorship Act unconstitutional. The board of censors then appealed to the Supreme Court of Pennsylvania, which affirmed the lower court's ruling. In the majority decision, Chief Justice Horace Stern wrote, "even if all precensorship of motion picture films were to be held invalid this would not in and of itself affect the right to suppress objectionable films, if exhibited, or to punish their exhibitor." Three years later, the Pennsylvania state legislature enacted the Motion Picture Control Act of 1959, which provided highly specific guidelines for anyone who wished to exhibit a film in the state. The charges of vagueness in language would not plague future movie screening boards because the act spelled out in detail the elements that constituted grounds for restrictions of films.

FURTHER READING

Carmen, Ira H. *Movies, Censorship, and the Law.* Ann Arbor: University of Michigan Press, 1966.

De Grazia, Edward, and Roger K. Newman. *Banned Films: Movies, Censors, and the First Amendment.* New York: R. R. Bowker, 1982.

Duggan, Shirle. *"She Shoulda Said No." Los Angeles Examiner,* September 2, 1949. *Hallmark Productions v. Pennsylvania Board of Censors,* 121 A. 2d 584 (1956).

WINDOWS

Country and date of production: United States, 1980
Production company/distributor: Mike Lobell Productions/United Artists
Format: Sound, color
Running time: 96 minutes
Language: English
Producer: Mike Lobell
Director: Gordon Willis
Screenwriter: Barry Siegel
Awards: None
Genre: Drama
With: Talia Shire (Emily Hollander), Joseph Cortese (Bob Luffrono), Elizabeth Ashley (Andrea Glassen), Kay Medford (Ida Marx), Michael Gorrin (Sam Marx), Russell Horton (Steven Hollander), Michael Lipton (Dr. Marin)

SUMMARY

Windows tells a convoluted story of obsession and sexual victimization. Shy and introverted Emily Hollander leaves her abusive husband to create a life on her own, but she is soon noticed by her neighbor Andrea, a lesbian who forms an obsessive attachment to Emily. Using a telescope, Andrea spies on Emily through their apartment windows. Despite Andrea's numerous efforts to forge a close relationship with Emily, she is unsuccessful and becomes desperate. She hires a man to rape Emily and to record the attack on tape, hoping that the shy and stuttering former wife of an abusive husband will feel only hate for men and run to her for comfort. The tactic does not work, as Emily becomes emotionally attached to the male detective assigned to investigate her case. Andrea watches through her telescope as the relationship between the two develops. Her psychopathic personality and crime against Emily are eventually revealed. As Emily appears to be headed for a happy and satisfying heterosexual future with the detective, Andrea is made to suffer for her demented obsession.

CENSORSHIP HISTORY

The release of *Windows* sparked considerable controversy among gay rights groups across the United States, who protested the stereotyping of the lesbian Andrea as a psychopathic homosexual. When the film opened on January 18, 1980, gay rights groups picketed theaters in New York and other major cities, and the film received scathing reviews that combined with the protestors' efforts to keep audiences out of the theaters. Transamerica Company, the parent company of United Artists, withdrew plans to show the film in northern California theaters after receiving serious threats of disruption and violence at the impending premiere in San Francisco. *Variety* reported on January 23, 1980, that theaters in New York City had decided to stop showing the film because of the protests and the low audience numbers. A coalition of gay rights and feminist groups, especially the Coalition Against Violence Against Women, held news conferences in New York City and Los Angeles on January 25, 1980, that called upon executives of United Artists to withdraw the film from distribution immediately and to refrain from selling the movie to television. Coalition leaders asserted that they were not advocating censorship and told reporters for the *Los Angeles Times*, "In fact, the only censorship surrounding this controversy is that which the industry has done on its own regarding positive lesbian and gay images in film." Although gay rights leaders viewed the box-office failure of the film as a victory, they soon turned their attention to another film that featured similarly negative stereotypes, CRUISING. Negative homosexual images continued in films released throughout the 1980s.

FURTHER READING

Bell, Arthur. *"Windows." Village Voice*, June 28, 1980, p. 30.
Schreger, Charles. "Gays, Feminists Protest 2 Films." *Los Angeles Times*, January 25, 1980, p. V3.
"Windows." Jump Cut, May 1980, p. 197.
"Windows Enrages NY Homosexuals." *Variety*, January 23, 1980, p. 7.

WOMEN OF THE WORLD

Country and date of production: Italy, 1963 (as *La Donna nel mondo*)
Production company/distributor: Cineriz Films/Embassy Pictures Corporation
Format: Sound, black and white/color
Running time: 110 minutes
Language: English
Producer: Cineriz Films
Directors: Paolo Cavara, Gualtiero Jacopetti, Franco E. Prosperi
Screenwriters: Paolo Cavara, Gualtiero Jacopetti, Franco E. Prosperi
Awards: None
Genre: Pseudodocumentary
With: Peter Ustinov (Narrator)

SUMMARY

This feature-length film is in the style of a documentary that examines the mores, manners, interests and amorous adventures of women in nations throughout the world. Peter Ustinov, who narrates the film throughout, described it as "a voyeur's dream come true." The film documents professional mourners on Sardinia; actresses wearing bikinis at the Cannes Film Festival; Israeli women actively engaged in combat training and bathing in the nude; and sexual behavior in a Swedish dormitory. The film is structured as if it were meant to be educational, but Ustinov's bantering narrative soon alerts the viewer that it is meant to be fun.

CENSORSHIP HISTORY

The distributor was denied a permit by the Memphis, Tennessee, board of censors, who demanded that four scenes be deleted before the board would reconsider the film. The board claimed that the film violated city charter provisions that made it unlawful to exhibit films that were "immoral, lewd, obscene, or lascivious" or were "inimical to the public safety, health, morals, or welfare." The distributor alleged that eliminating the four scenes would destroy the continuity of the movie and "diminish the artistic and commercial value" and brought suit in federal district court. In the suit, the distributor claimed that the censorship statue violated its rights of free speech under the First Amendment and the right of property under the due process clause of the Fourteenth Amendment. The distributor further argued that the board of censors had violated the distributor's constitutional rights because the film "contains nothing which can constitutionally be proscribed." The city moved to dismiss the case against the board of censors, which the court denied in *Embassy Pictures Corporation v. Hudson*, 226 F. Supp. 421 (1964). The court then granted the distributor's motion to prevent the city from interfering with the exhibition of the film.

In *Embassy Pictures Corporation v. Hudson*, 242 F. Supp. 975 (1965), the court also found the Memphis censorship ordinance to be "a system of prior restraint."

FURTHER READING

De Grazia, Edward, and Roger K. Newman. *Banned Films: Movies, Censors, and the First Amendment.* New York: R. R. Bowker, 1982.
Embassy Pictures Corporation v. Hudson, 226 F. Supp. 421 (1964).
Embassy Pictures Corporation v. Hudson, 242 F. Supp. 975 (1965).
Weiler. A. H. *"Women of the World." New York Times*, July 3, 1963.

WOODSTOCK

Country and date of production: United States, 1970
Production company/distributor: Wadleigh-Maurice/Warner Bros.
Format: Sound, color
Running time: 184 minutes
Language: English
Producer: Bob Maurice
Director: Michael Wadleigh
Screenwriter: None
Awards: 1970 Academy Awards, Best Documentary–Feature (Bob Maurice).
Genre: Documentary
With: Richie Havens, Joan Baez, Pete Townshend, John Entwistle, Roger Daltrey, Keith Moon, Joe Cocker, Country Joe McDonald, Arlo Guthrie, Graham Nash, David Crosby, Stephen Stills, Alvin Lee, John Sebastian, Jon "Bowzer" Bauman, Carlos Santana, Sly Stone, Jimi Hendrix

SUMMARY

The film documents three days of peace, music and love that took place on the Yasgar Farm in Bethel, New York, in 1969. The "Woodstock Music Art Fair" drew more than half a million people, all camping out as near as they could to the sound stage that promoters had erected on the farm. The film includes performances by such bands and singers as the Who, Jefferson Airplane and Jimi Hendrix, interspersed with scenes of the audience as they enjoy the concert and cope with the problems inevitable in such a large crowd. Aside from the music, the festival offered a unique experience. As Deac Rossell wrote of the experience in *Boston After Dark:* "The whole uniqueness of the Woodstock festival lay in its communal mood, its liberation of the individual through participation. Skinny-dipping in a pond, childishly sliding in mud, sharing a blanket, a bottle, a joint, Woodstock had that extra dimension of community."

CENSORSHIP HISTORY

Because of the nudity, drug use and language, the film was rated "R" (restricted to adults over the age of 18) by the Motion Picture Association of America (MPAA). When two adults in Kenosha, Wisconsin, brought their children and the children's friends, all of whom were under the age of 18, to a theater in the city, the children were denied entrance to view *Woodstock*. A Kenosha city ordinance specifically forbade minors to view films classified by the MPAA as either "X" or "R." The adults acting on their behalf brought suit in federal district court to ask the court to enjoin the enforcement of the ordinance on the grounds that it denied the children the right to freedom of expression. The court issued the injunction and ruled that "the ordinance amounted to an unconstitutional prior restraint on expression because there was no requirement that the city go to court immediately and prove the movie was of the type banned for minors."

FURTHER READING

Cohn, Ellen. "Woodstock." *The Villager,* April 30, 1970.
De Grazia, Edward, and Roger K. Newman. *Banned Films: Movies, Censors, and the First Amendment.* New York: R. R. Bowker, 1982.
Mast, Gerald, and Bruce F. Kawin. *A Short History of the Movies,* 7th ed. Boston: Allyn & Bacon, 2000.
Rossell, Deac. "Woodstock." *Boston After Dark,* April 1, 1970.

THE YOUTH OF MAXIM

Country and date of production: Soviet Union, 1935 (also released as *Junost Maksima; Bolshevik; Maxim Trilogy, Part 1*)
Production company/distributor: Lenfilm Studio (U.S.S.R)/Amkino Corporation (United States)
Format: Sound, black and white
Running time: 85 minutes
Language: Russian
Producer: Lenfilm Studio
Directors: Grigori Kozintsev, Leonid Trauberg
Screenwriters: Grigori Konzintsev, Leonid Trauberg
Awards: First prize for the Leningrad Studios at the Moscow Film Festival on the 15th anniversary of Soviet cinema
Genre: Drama
With: Boris Chirkov (Maksim), Stepan Kayukov (Dyoma), Valentina Kibardina (Natasha), Mikhail Tarkhanov (Polivanov)

SUMMARY

One of the early sound films to come from the Russian studios, the film traces the change in an ignorant factory worker from simple peasant to experienced revolutionary. The film is representative of the politicization of Soviet movies that occurred in the 1930s, which some critics found disturbing, because its purpose was to make Bolshevism very attractive. Planned as the first part of a trilogy, this film is set in czarist Russia during the years 1905–07 before the monarchy was overthrown and the Communist Party took control. In essence, the worker receives his education in the city as he sees his best friends victimized or killed by the police and the capitalist system; he, too, is imprisoned without legal reasons for a time and then released. He emerges from prison embittered and, filled with revolutionary zeal, joins the underground socialist movement.

CENSORSHIP HISTORY

In Detroit in 1935, the police commissioner declared that the *The Youth of Maxim* was "pure Soviet propaganda and is likely to instill class hatred of the existing government and social order of the United States." The commissioner prevented exhibition of the film on the authority of a city ordinance that allowed the banning of films if they were "immoral or indecent." The exhibitor Schuman (no first name provided) challenged the decision in a suit filed with the Wayne County circuit court and asked for a writ of mandamus to compel the commissioner to issue the permit. In a written statement, the police commissioner told the court that "protests were lodged by representatives of various religious, . . . veterans . . . and civic organizations protesting against the showing." The trial court viewed the film and refused to issue a command on the ground that there existed an "absence of proof of flagrant abuse of discretion" by the police commissioner. The exhibitor appealed the decision before the supreme court of Michigan, which reversed the prohibition because it had been illegally applied: The court refused to accept the city's argument that "immoral" could be extended to mean anything that opposes the "good order or public welfare." Instead, the court declared in *Schuman v. Pickert*, 269 N.W. 277 Mich. 255 (1936), that a motion picture exhibitor had "a constitutional property right to show a film which is not indecent or immoral. . . . No feeling against foreign political policies or forms of government should be permitted to establish the principle that a police officer may be invested with discretion to determine his own powers of suppression or change the plain terms of his authority."

FURTHER READING

Barnes, Howard. *"The Youth of Maxim."* *New York Herald-Tribune*, April 1935.
Ceplair, Larry, and Stephen Englund. *The Inquisition in Hollywood: Politics in the Film Community, 1930–1960.* Garden City, N.Y.: Anchor Press, 1980.
Hale, Wanda. *"The Youth of Maxim."* *New York Daily News*, April 19, 1935.
Schuman v. Pickert, 269 N.W. 277 Mich. 255 (1936).
Sennwald, André. *"The Youth of Maxim."* *Nation*, May 1, 1935.

BIBLIOGRAPHY

BOOKS

Abel, Richard. *French Film Theory and Criticism: A History/Analogy, 1907–1939.* Vol. 2. Princeton: Princeton University Press, 1988.

Aitken, Roy E., as told to Al P. Nelson. *The Birth of a Nation Story.* Middleburg, Va.: Denlinger Publishing, 1965.

Alexander, William. *Film on the Left: American Documentary Film from 1931 to 1942.* Princeton: Princeton University Press, 1981.

"All Quiet on the Western Front: Screenplay by George Abbott, Maxwell Anderson, and Dell Andrews; Adaptation by Dell Andrews; Dialogue by Maxwell Anderson and George Abbott (Abbott Version, November 19, 1929)." In *Best American Screenplays: First Series: Complete Screenplays,* ed. Sam Thomas. New York: Crown, 1986; pp. 13–72.

Alverson, Luther. *A Movie Censorship Decision.* Columbia, Mo.: Freedom of Information Center, School of Journalism, University of Missouri, 1961.

Atkins, Thomas R., ed. *Sexuality in the Movies.* Bloomington: Indiana University Press, 1975.

Barna, Yon. *Eisenstein.* Boston: Little, Brown, 1973.

Benson, Thomas W., and Carolyn Anderson. *Reality Fictions: The Films of Frederick Wiseman.* Carbondale: University of Southern Illinois Press, 1989.

Black, Gregory D. *Hollywood Censored: Morality Codes, Catholics, and the Movies.* New York: Cambridge University Press, 1994.

Bordwell, David. *The Cinema of Eisenstein.* Cambridge: Harvard University Press, 1993.

Bouzereau, Laurent. *Cutting Room Floor: Movie Scenes Which Never Made It to the Screen.* New York: Carol Publishing Group, 1994.

Brown, John Mason. *The Worlds of Robert Sherwood.* New York: Harper & Row, 1965.

Brownlow, Kenneth. *Behind the Mask of Innocence.* New York: Alfred A. Knopf, 1990.

———. *Hollywood: The Pioneers.* London: Collins, 1979.

Carmen, Ira H. *Movies, Censorship, and the Law.* Ann Arbor: University of Michigan Press, 1966.

Ceplair, Larry, and Steven Englund. *The Inquisition in Hollywood: Politics in the Film Community, 1930–1960.* Garden City, N.Y.: Anchor Press, 1980.

Cremer, Robert. *Lugosi: The Man Behind the Cape.* Chicago: Henry Regnery, 1976.

Crispin, Colin. *The Classic French Cinema, 1930–1960.* Bloomington: Indiana University Press, 1994.

Curtis, James. *James Whale.* Metuchen, N.J.: Scarecrow Press, 1982.

———. *James Whale: A New World of Gods and Monsters.* Boston: Faber and Faber, 1998.

De Beauvoir, Simone. *Brigitte Bardot and the Lolita Syndrome.* London: André Deutsch and Weidenfeld & Nicolson, 1961.

De Grazia, Edward, and Roger K. Newman. *Banned Films: Movies, Censors, and the First Amendment.* New York: R. R. Bowker, 1982.

———. *Girls Lean Back Everywhere: The Laws of Obscenity and the Assault on Genius.* New York: Random House, 1992.

Dershowitz, Alan M. *The Best Defense.* New York: Random House, 1982.

Doherty, Thomas. *Pre-Code Hollywood: Sex, Immorality, and Insurrection in American Cinema, 1930–1934.* New York: Columbia University Press, 1999.

Drew, William M. *Speaking of Silents.* Vestal, N.Y.: Vestal Press, 1989.

Dyer, Richard. *Gays and Film.* New York: Zoetrope, 1984.

Eberwein, Robert. *Sex Education: Film, Video, and the Framework of Desire.* New Brunswick, N.J.: Rutgers University Press, 1999.

Ernst, Morris L., and Alexander Lindey. *The Censor Marches On.* Garden City, N.Y.: Doubleday, 1940.

Facey, Paul W. *The Legion of Decency: A Sociological Analysis of the Emergence and Development of a Pressure Group.* New York: Arno Press, 1974.

Farber, Stephen. *The Movie Rating Game.* Washington, D.C.: Public Affairs Press, 1972.

Fleener-Marzec, Nickieann. *D. W. Griffith's "The Birth of a Nation": Controversy, Suppression, and the First Amendment as It Applies to Filmic Expression, 1915–1973.* Madison: University of Wisconsin, 1977.

Gardner, Gerald. *The Censorship Papers: Movie Censorship Letters from the Hays Office, 1934 to 1968.* New York: Dodd, Mead, 1987.

Gaume, Thomas Michael. *Suppression of Motion Pictures in Kansas, 1952–1975.* Unpublished thesis. Lawrence: University of Kansas, 1976.

Gidal, Peter. *Andy Warhol: Film and Paintings.* New York: Dutton, 1971.

Giglio, Ernest David. *The Decade of the Miracle, 1952–1962: A Study in the Censorship of the American Motion Picture.* Doctoral dissertation. Syracuse University, 1964. Ann Arbor, Mich.: University Microfilms International.

Gish, Lillian. "The Making of *The Birth of a Nation.*" In *The Movies, Mr. Griffith & Me.* Englewood Cliffs, N.J.: Prentice-Hall, 1959.

Gomery, Douglas, ed. *The Will Hays Papers.* Frederick, Md.: University Publications of America, 1986.

Grant, Barry Keith. *Voyages of Discovery: The Cinema of Frederick Wiseman.* Urbana: University of Illinois Press, 1992.

Green, Jonathan. *The Encyclopedia of Censorship.* New York: Facts On File, 1990.

Greenberg, Joel, and Charles Higham. *The Celluloid Muse.* New York: Signet Books, 1972.

Grove, Martin A., and William S. Ruben. *The Celluloid Love Feast.* New York: Lancer Books, 1971.

Halliwell, Leslie. *Halliwell's Film Guide,* 7th ed. New York: Harper & Row, 1989.

Hammond, Paul. *L'Age d'Or.* Bloomington: Indiana University Press, 1997.

Hanson, Patricia King, ed. *The American Film Institute Catalog of Motion Pictures Produced in the United States: Feature Films, 1911–1920.* Berkeley: University of California Press, 1988.

Heins, Marjorie. *Sex, Sin, and Blasphemy: A Guide to America's Censorship Wars.* New York: New Press, 1993.

Henderson, Robert M. *D. W. Griffith: His Life and Work.* New York: Oxford University Press, 1972.

Hoberman, J., Jonathan Rosenbaum. *Midnight Movies.* New York: Harper & Row, 1983.

Hunnings, Neville March. *Film Censors and the Law.* London: Allen & Unwin, 1967.

Inglis, Ruth A. *Freedom of the Movies: A Report on Self-Regulation from the Commission on Freedom of the Press.* Chicago: University of Chicago Press, 1947.

Jacobs, Lea. *The Wages of Sin: Censorship and the Fallen Woman Film, 1928–1942.* Madison: University of Wisconsin Press, 1991.

Jacobs, Lewis. "D. W. Griffith: *The Birth of a Nation* and *Intolerance.*" In *The Rise of the American Film.* New York: Harcourt Brace Jovanovich, 1939.

Jowett, Garth. *Film: the Democratic Art—A Social History of American Film.* Boston: Little, Brown, 1976.

Kagan, Norman. *The Cinema of Stanley Kubrick.* New York: Continuum Books, 1989.

Kansas State Board of Review. *Complete List of Motion Picture Films Submitted,* vol. 1. Topeka: Kansas State Board of Reviews, 1915–1966.

Kelly, Mary Pat. *Martin Scorsese: A Journey.* New York: Thunder's Mouth, 1991.

Kolker, Robert Phillip. *Bernardo Bertolucci.* London: British Film Institute, 1985.

Krafsur, Richard. *American Film Institute Catalog of Motion Pictures: Feature Films, 1961–1970.* New York: R. R. Bowker, 1982.

Kuhn, Annette. *Cinema, Censorship, and Sexuality, 1909–1925.* New York: Routledge, 1988.

Lamont, Corliss. *Freedom Is as Freedom Does: Civil Liberties Today.* New York: Horizon Books, 1956.

Lang, Robert, ed. *The Birth of a Nation: D. W. Griffith, Director.* New Brunswick, N.J.: Rutgers University Press, 1994.

Lawrence, Frank M. *Hemingway and the Movies.* Jackson: University of Mississippi Press, 1981.

Leff, Leonard J., and Jerold L. Simmons. *The Dame in the Kimono: Hollywood, Censorship, & the Production Code from the 1920s to the 1960s.* New York: Grove Weidenfeld, 1990.

Leuchtenberg, William E. *The Perils of Prosperity, 1914–1932.* Chicago: University of Chicago Press, 1958.

Liehm, Mira. *Passion and Defiance: Film in Italy from 1942 to the Present.* Berkeley: University of California Press, 1984.

Loos, Anita. *Kiss Hollywood Good-by.* New York: Viking Press, 1974.

Lyons, Charles. *The New Censor: Movies and the Culture Wars.* Philadelphia: Temple University Press, 1997.

MacAdams, William. *Ben Hecht: The Man Behind the Legend.* New York: Charles Scribner's Sons, 1988.

MacCann, Richard Dyer. *The People's Films: A Political History of U.S. Government Motion Pictures.* New York: Hastings House, 1973.

McCarthy, Todd. *Howard Hawks.* New York: Grove Press, 1997.

McLaughlin, Mary L. *A Study of the National Catholic Office for Motion Pictures.* Ph.D. dissertation in speech. Indiana University, 1974.

Marx, Samuel. *Mayer and Thalberg: The Make-Believe Saints.* New York: Random House, 1975.

Maryland Board of Censors. *Annual Reports.* Baltimore, Md.: The Board, 1969.

Mast, Gerald, and Bruce F. Kawin. *A Short History of the Movies,* 7th ed. Boston: Allyn & Bacon, 1996.

Millichap, Joseph. *Lewis Milestone.* Boston: Twayne Publishers, 1981.

Moody, Richard. *Lillian Hellman, Playwright.* New York: Pegasus Books, 1972.

MPPDA Case Files. Margaret Herrick Library, Special Collections, Academy of Motion Picture Arts and Sciences. Beverly Hills, California.

Munden, Kenneth W., ed. *The American Film Institute Catalog of Motion Pictures Produced in the United States: Feature Films, 1921–1930.* New York: R. R. Bowker, 1971.

Nabokov, Vladimir. *Lolita*. New York: G.P. Putnam, 1995.

———. *Lolita: A Screenplay*. New York: McGraw-Hill, 1975.

Nesteby, James R. *Black Images in American Film, 1896–1954. The Interplay Between Civil Rights and Film Culture*. Lanham, Md.: University Press of America, 1982.

North, Joseph H. *The Early Development of the Motion Picture, 1887–1909*. New York: Arno Press, 1973.

Nowell-Smith, Geoffrey, ed. *The Oxford History of World Cinema*. New York: Oxford University Press, 1996.

O'Neill, James M. "Catholics and Censorship." In *Catholics in Controversy*, ed. by James M. O'Neill. New York: McMullen, 1954.

Pennsylvania State Board of Censors (Motion Pictures). *Legal Briefs, 1915–1921*. Pennsylvania State Archives, Pennsylvania Historical and Museum Commission, RG-22, Series #22.28.

Pratt, George C. *Spellbound in Darkness: A History of the Silent Film*. Greenwich, Conn.: New York Graphic Society, 1966.

Quigley, Martin. *Decency in Motion Pictures*. New York: Macmillan, 1937.

Ramsaye, Terry. *A Million and One Nights: A History of the Motion Picture Through 1925*. New York: Simon & Schuster, 1925; reprinted in 1986.

Randall, Richard. *Censorship of the Movies: The Social and Political Control of a Mass Medium*. Madison: University of Wisconsin Press, 1968.

Rembar, Charles. *The End of Obscenity: The Trials of Lady Chatterley's Lover, Tropic of Cancer & Fanny Hill by the Lawyer Who Defended Them*. New York: Random House, 1968.

Renan, Sheldon. *An Introduction to the American Underground Film*. New York: Dutton, 1967.

Reports of the Kansas State Supreme Court, 1917–1966. Topeka: Archives of the Kansas Historical Society, n.d.

Riva, Maria. *Marlene Dietrich (by her daughter)*. New York: Alfred A. Knopf, 1993.

Rotsler, William. *Contemporary Erotic Cinema*. New York: Random House, 1973.

Russo, Vito. *The Celluloid Closet: Homosexuality in the Movies*. New York: Harper-Collins, 1981.

Savada, Elias, and David Skal. *Dark Carnival: The Secret World of Tod Browning*. New York: Anchor Books, 1995.

Schorer, Mark. *Sinclair Lewis: An American Life*. New York: McGraw-Hill, 1961.

Schumach, Murray. *The Face on the Cutting Room Floor*. New York: William Morrow, 1964.

Sherwood, Robert E. *Idiot's Delight*. New York: Charles Scribner's Sons, 1936.

Silva, Fred, ed. *Focus on "The Birth of a Nation."* Englewood Cliffs, N.J.: Prentice-Hall, 1971.

Sjoman, Vilgot. *I Am Curious–Yellow*. New York: Grove Press, 1968.

Skal, David J. *The Monster Show: A Cultural History of Horror*. New York: W. W. Norton, 1993.

Smith, Richard. *Getting Into Deep Throat*. Chicago: Playboy Press, 1973.

Sova, Dawn B. *Banned Books: Literature Suppressed on Sexual Grounds*. New York: Facts On File, 1998.

Spoto, Donald. *The Blue Angel: The Life of Marlene Dietrich*. Boston: G. K. Hall, 1993.

Starks, Michael. *Cocaine Fiends and Reefer Madness: An Illustrated History of Drugs in the Movies*. New York, 1982.

Stott, William. *Documentary Expression and Thirties America.* New York: Oxford University Press, 1973.

Thomas, Bob. *Thalberg: Life and Legend.* Garden City, N.Y.: Doubleday, 1969.

Thomas, Tony. *Howard Hughes in Hollywood.* Secaucus, N.J.: Citadel Press, 1985.

Thompson, Frank. *Lost Films: Important Movies That Disappeared.* New York: Citadel Press, 1996.

Traver, Robert. *Anatomy of a Murder.* New York: St. Martin's Press, 1958.

Turan, Kenneth, and Stephen F. Zito. *Sinema: American Pornographic Films and the People Who Make Them.* New York: Praeger, 1974.

Tyler, Parker. *Screening the Sexes: Homosexuality in the Movies.* New York: Holt, Rinehart and Winston, 1972.

Vieira, Mark. *Sin in Soft Focus: Pre-Code Hollywood.* New York: Harry N. Abrams, 1999.

Walker, Alexander. *The Celluloid Sacrifice.* London: Michael Joseph, 1966.

Warhol, Andy. *Blue Movie–Screenplay.* New York: Grove Press, 1970.

Warner, Linda K. *Movie Censorship in Kansas: The Kansas State Board of Review.* Unpublished thesis. Emporia State University, 1988.

Weiss, Andrea. *Vampires and Violets: Lesbians in the Cinema.* London: Jonathan Cape, 1992.

Wolf, William. *Landmark Films: The Cinema and Our Century.* New York: Paddington Publishers, 1979.

Youngblood, Denise James. *Soviet Cinema in the Silent Era, 1918–1935.* Ann Arbor: UMI Research Press, 1985.

Zukor, Adolph, with Dale Kramer. *The Public Is Never Wrong.* New York: G. P. Putnam, 1953.

ARTICLES

Adler, Renata. *"Therese and Isabelle."* *New York Times*, May 15, 1968, p. C2.

Alpert, Hollis. *"Carnal Knowledge."* *Saturday Review*, July 3, 1981, p. 19.

American Booksellers Foundation for Free Expression. "ABFFE Opposes *Natural Born Killers* Lawsuit." *ABFFE Update.* http://www.abffe.com/update1-4.htm.

American Civil Liberties Union. "ACLU Praises Summary Judgment Ruling in Oklahoma *Tin Drum* Litigation." Press release, October 21, 1998. http://www.aclu.org/news/n102198a.html.

———. *"Tin Drum* Video Seizure Sparks ACLU Lawsuit." Press release, October 21, 1998. http://www.aclu.org/issues/freespeech/tindrum.html.

Anderson, Robert L. "Free Speech and Obscenity: A Search for Constitutional Procedures and Standards." *UCLA Law Review* 12 (January 1965): 532–560.

Annas, George J. *"Reefer Madness:* The Federal Government's Response to California's Medical-Marijuana Law." *New England Journal of Medicine*, August 7, 1997.

"Ann Vickers." *Catholic World* 36 (February 1933): 622.

Appel, Alfred, Jr. "The End of the Road: Dark Cinema and *Lolita.*" *Film Comment* 10, no. 5 (1974): 25–31.

Aronson, Charles S. *"Candy."* *Variety*, January 14, 1969.

Asselle, Giovanna, and Behroze Gandhy. *"Dressed to Kill."* *Screen* 23 (September–October 1982): 137–143.

Associated Press Wire Service. "Confiscation of Video Violated Federal Privacy law." *Tulsa World*, December 20, 1998. http://www.tulsaworld.com.

———. "Settlement Considered in *Tin Drum* Case." *Tulsa World*, March 16, 1999. http://www.tulsaworld.com.

———. "Testimony Begins in *Tin Drum* Trial." *Tulsa World*, August 24, 1999.

"*Baby Doll.*" *Commonwealth* 65 (January 11, 1957): 372.

"*Baby Doll.*" *Variety*, January 9, 1957, p. 13.

"The Ban Is Lifted on *Last Tango* in Italy." *Variety*, February 11, 1987, pp. 2–3.

Barnes, Howard. "*The Youth of Maxim.*" *New York Herald-Tribune*, April 1935.

Battistini, Robert. "*Basic Instinct:* Revisionist Hard-On, Hollywood Trash, or Feminist Hope?" *Cinefocus* 2, no. 2 (Spring 1992): 38–43.

"Because It's Not Nice." *The Star-Ledger*, January 23, 1998, p. 3.

Berry, Dean L. "Validity of Motion Picture Licensing Statute." *Michigan Law Review* 58 (November 1959): 134–137.

Bertin, Joan. "Pornography Law Goes Too Far. 1st Amendment: The Broad Ban on Images That Only Appear to Involve Children Won't Stop Sexual Abuse and Exploitation." *Los Angeles Times*, October 17, 1997, p. B9.

"Binford Ban Backfires; *Moon* Shines With SRO in His Native State." *Variety*, September 9, 1953, p. 1.

Blades, John. "The Trouble with *Lolita:* A New $40 Million Movie Version of Nabokov's Book Has Been Shunned by Distributors. The Filmmakers Apparently Picked the Wrong Time for a Film about Pedophilia." *Chicago Tribune*, April 13, 1997, p. 7.

Bordo, Susan. "True Obsessions: Being Unfaithful to *Lolita.*" *Chronicle of Higher Education*, July 24, 1998, pp. B7–B8.

Bowman, James. "To Die in Bed (The Sex-Death Complex in Motion Pictures)." *American Spectator*, 25 (June 1992): 47–49.

Branigin, William. "Manila in Agony Over Schindler's Ecstasy; 30-Second Sex Scene Has Censors Atwitter." *Washington Post*, March 8, 1994, p. B1.

Braun, Jess. "Hundreds at Mall Protest Screening of '*Temptation.*'" *Los Angeles Times*, August 20, 1988, Sec. 2.

"Brigham Young University Bans Movie *Amistad.*" *Jet*, February 9, 1998, p. 29.

Broeske, Pat A. "Universal Asked to 'Destroy' Scorsese's Film About Christ." *Los Angeles Times*, July 13, 1988.

Bush, W. Stephen. "*Damaged Goods.*" *Moving Picture World*, October 2, 1915.

Campbell, Bob. "In the Shadow of the Censor's Knife." *Sunday Star-Ledger*, August 2, 1997, Sec. 4–11.

Campbell, Howard. "Jamaican Censors Cut Opening Slave Ship Scenes from *Amistad.*" *Associated Press*, February 17, 1998.

Canby, Vincent. "Film: *Dressed to Kill*, De Palma Mystery." *New York Times*, July 25, 1980, p. C2.

"*Candy.*" *Newsweek*, December 30, 1968.

Carr, Jay. "After the Revolution: It's Time to Reevaluate Sergei Eisenstein." *Boston Globe*, January 10, 1993, p. B32.

"Censors Cut Opening *Amistad.*" *Calgary Herald*, February 17, 1998, p. E3.

"Censors Fight Over Movie Morals." *Life*, July 18, 1938, pp. 50–55.

"Censors on the Street (Gay Activists Protest Against *Basic Instinct*)." *Time*, May 13, 1991, p. 70.

"Censorship in Motion Pictures." *Yale Law Review Journal* 49 (November 1939): 95–100.

Ceplair, Larry. "The Politics of Compromise in Hollywood: A Case Study." *Cineaste*, 8:4, pp. 2–7.

"Chains Flout Code, Book *Blue*." *Variety*, June 30, 1953, p. 1.

Chesworth, Amanda. "Godless Creations: The Irreverent Monty Python." *Secular Humanist Bulletin* 15 (Summer 2000). Reprinted at the Council for Secular Humanism site. http://www.secularhumanism.org/library/shb/chesworth_15_4.html.

Cianfarra, Camille M. *"The Miracle." New York Times*, February 11, 1951, p. 4.

"Cinema." *Time*, December 24, 1956, p. 61.

"Cinema: Humbert Humdrum and Lullita." *Time*, June 22, 1962, p. 94.

Clancy, William P. "The Catholic as Philistine." *Commonwealth* 53 (March 16, 1951): 567–569.

———. "Freedom of the Screen." *Commonwealth* 59 (February 1954): 500–502.

Cohn, Ellen. *"Woodstock." The Villager*, April 30, 1970.

"Confounding Censors." *Motion Picture Herald*, May 19, 1934, p. 46.

Corliss, Richard. *"Lolita:* From Lyon to Lyne." *Film Comment* 34 (September/October 1998): 34–39.

———. "Sex! Violence! Trash! The Exploitation Movies of a Bygone Era Had Everything but Money, and Talent, and Scruples." *Time*, July 7, 1997.

"Correction." *New York Times*, April 28, 1996, pp. 9–10.

Crist, Judith. *"The Virgin Spring." New York Herald-Tribune*, November 13, 1960.

Crosby, John. "Movies Are Too Dirty." *Saturday Evening Post*, November 10, 1962, pp. 10, 11.

"Crossing *Schindler* Off the List." *World Press Review*, August 1994, p. 47.

Crowther, Bosley. "Miss Julie." *New York Times*, April 8, 1952.

———. *"Native Son:* A Review." *New York Times*, June 24, 1951.

———. "The Strange Case of The Miracle." *Atlantic Monthly* 187 (April 1951): 35–39; Discussion, *188* (July 1951): pp. 15–16.

"Cruisin' in New Ratings Rumpus; 'R' Taken, Given." *Variety*, June 11, 1980, pp. 4, 30.

"Damaged Goods." Motography, September 5, 1915.

Danziger, Marie. *"Basic Instinct:* Grappling for Post-Modern Mind Control." *Literature/Film Quarterly*, 22:1 (1994): 7–10.

Dare, Michael. "2nd Features: *December 7th:* The Movie, Directed by John Ford/Target: Pearl Harbor." *Billboard*, 103 (October 19, 1991): 62.

Dart, John. "Church Declares *'Last Temptation'* Morally Offensive." *Los Angeles Times*, August 10, 1998, sec. 2.

Davies, Diana. *"The North Star." Film Notes.* New York State Writers Institute. http://www.albany.edu/writers-inst/filmnote.html#N.

Davis, Dave, and Neal Goldberg. "Organizing the Screen Writers Guild—An Interview with John Howard Lawson." *Cineaste* 8, no. 2, p. 10.

Dawes, Amy. "Offer to Buy Pic: Christians Protest U's Christ." *Variety*, July 18, 1988, pp. 1–6.

———. "Protest Continues: Wasserman Picketed Over *Temptation*." *Variety*, July 21, 1988, pp. 6–15.

———. "'Tempt' Protests Continue: Vandals Damage Hollywood House." *Variety*, September 7, 1988, p. 1.

Deleyto, Celestino. "The Margins of Pleasure: Female Monstrosity and Male Paranoia in *Basic Instinct*." *Film Criticism*, 21, no. 3 (Spring 1997): 20–42.

Delormé, Gérard. *"Anna and the King." Première* (France), February/March 2000, p. 56.

D'Emilio, Frances. "Italy Censors Ban Film About Mafia." Associated Press, March 3, 1998.

Denby, David. *"Deep Throat." New York*, July 28, 1980, p. 44.

———, Alan Dershowitz, and others. "Pornography: Love or Death?" *Film Comment*, 20:6 (November–December 1984): 29–47.

De Quine, Jenne. "Pastor Wants Censorship-Series Films Banned." *USA Today*, June 2, 1987, p. A3.

"Did *Cruising* Respect Ratings?" *Variety*, June 25, 1980, p. 4.

Douglas, Susan. "The Devil Made Me Do It: Is *Natural Born Killers* the Ford Pinto of Movies? Motion Picture That Inspired Copycat Murders Sued as Unprotected Speech." *The Nation*, April 5, 1999, pp. 50+.

Duggan, Shirle. "She Shoulda Said No." *Los Angeles Examiner*, September 2, 1949.

Ebert, Roger. "Censors Should Resist 'Temptation.'" *New York Post*, July 22, 1988, Sec. D.

———. *"La Dolce Vita." Chicago Sun-Times*, September 19, 1999, p. C1.

———. *"Last Tango in Paris* Revisited." *Chicago Sun-Times*, August 11, 1995, p. C4.

———. *"Last Temptation* Censorship Lacks Divine Inspiration." *Chicago Sun-Times*, July 24, 1988.

———. *"Natural Born Killers." Chicago Sun-Times*, August 26, 1994.

———. *"A Streetcar Named Desire." Chicago Sun-Times*, November 12, 1993.

"Egyptian Censors Ban *Schindler's List." Jerusalem Post*, June 2, 1994, p. 5.

"Expensive Movie: Taxpayers Hit with Costly Tab." *Tulsa World, Tulsa World*, February 17, 2000. http://www.tulsaworld.com.

"Film Censorship and Health Propaganda." *Bioscope*, December 18, 1919, p. 89.

"Films and Birth and Censorship." *Survey* 34 (April 3, 1915): 4–5.

Fiske, D. W. *"I'm No Angel." Motion Picture Herald*, February 24, 1934, p. 52.

Friedman, Samuel. "Constitutional Law—Motion Picture Censorship." *Brooklyn Law Review*, 26 (December 1959): 112–117.

Galbraith, Jane, and Richard Gold. "Scorsese Defends *Temptation* on TV." *Variety*, July 27, 1988, pp. 3–19.

Gangas, Spiros. *"L'Age d'Or." Edinburgh University Film Society Programme, 1993–1994.*

Gleiberman, Owen. *"Anna and the King* (C+)." *Entertainment Weekly* 520, no. 1 (January 7, 2000): 42.

Graham, Arthur F. "Film Censorship Upheld." *Ohio State Law Journal* 20 (Winter 1959): 161–164.

Guthmann, Edward. "The *Cruising* Controversy: William Friedkin vs. the Gay Community." *Cineaste* 10, no. 2 (Summer 1980): 2–4.

Hagopian, Kevin. *"The North Star." Film Notes.* New York State Writers Institute. http://www.albany.edu./writers-inst/filmnote.html#N.

Haimbaugh, George D., Jr. "Film Censorship Since *Roth-Alberts." Kentucky Law Journal* 51 (Summer 1963): 656–666.

Hale, Wanda. *"The Youth of Maxim." New York Daily News*, April 19, 1935.

Hamilton, Denise. "Actress Recalls Days of *Reefer Madness." Los Angeles Times*, February 12, 1987, p. 30.

Harmetz, Aljean. "Film on Christ Brings Out Pickets, and Archbishop Predicts Censure." *New York Times*, July 21, 1988, p. C10.

———. *"The Last Temptation of Christ* Opens to Protests but Good Sales." *New York Times*, August 13, 1988, p. C2.

———. "The Movies That Draw Hatred." *New York Times*, May 4, 1981, p. C3.

———. Scorsese *Temptation* Gets Early Release." *New York Times*, August 5, 1988, p. C4.

————. "7,500 Picket Universal Over Movie About Jesus." *New York Times*, August 12, 1988, p. C12.

Harris, Albert W., Jr. "Movie Censorship and the Supreme Court: What Next?" *California Law Review* 42 (Spring 1954): 122–138.

Hassan, Kalimullah. "KL May Review *Schindler's* Ban." *The Strait Times*, March 29, 1994, p. 2.

Healy, Michelle. "Screening *Lolita*." *USA Today*, July 9, 1998, Sec. D-1.

Hemblade, Christopher. "Chain Reaction." *Empire*, March 1998, pp. 74–79.

Hoberman, J. "Fantastic Projections (Criticism of Director Paul Verhoeven's Movie *Basic Instinct*)." *Sight and Sound* 2, no. 1 (May 1992): 4.

————. "*Last Tango in Paris* Directed by Bernardo Bertolucci." *Village Voice*, March 21, 1995, pp. 47+.

————. "*Titicut Follies* Unbound." *Premiere*, March 1992, p. 41.

Holmberg, Judith. "Spielberg: Rethink Ban of All Your Films in M'sia." *The Straits Times*, May 14, 1994, p. 18.

Holden, Stephen. "Movie Guide—*Lolita*." *New York Times*, October 9, 1998.

Holmlund, Chris. "Cruisin' for a Bruisin': Hollywood's Deadly (Lesbian) Dolls." *Cinema Journal* 34, no. 1 (Fall 1994): 31–51.

"I'm No Angel." *Motion Picture Herald*, October 7, 1933, p. 38.

Isenberg, Michael T. "The Mirror of Democracy: Reflections on the War Films of World War I, 1917–1919." *Journal of Popular Culture* 9 (1976): 879.

"It Ain't No Sin." *Variety*, June 13, 1934, p. 1.

"Italian Government Responds to Film Industry." *Media Awareness Network*. http://www.reseau-medias.ca/eng/news/news/two/italy/.htm.

"Italy Acquits Brando of Obscenity in Film." *Los Angeles Times*, March 3, 1973, p. B3.

"Jack Smith's *Flaming Creatures:* With the Tweak of an Eyebrow." *Film Culture* 63, no. 63 (1977): 51–56.

Jacobs, Lea. "The Censorship of the *Blonde Venus*." *Cinema Journal* 27 (Spring 1988): 21–31.

James, Caryn. "TELEVISION REVIEW: *Lolita:* Revisiting a Dangerous Obsession." *New York Times*, July 31, 1998.

Jeffries, Neil. "*Amistad*." *Empire*, October 1998, p. 131.

Jenkins, Dan. "Apollo Movie Guide's Review of *Therese and Isabelle*." http://www.apolloguide.com/mov.

Johnson, Brian D. "Killer Movies (Violence in Motion Pictures)." *Maclean's*, March 30, 1992, pp. 48–51.

Johnson, Gary. "Forbidden Fruit: The Golden Age of the Exploitation Film." *Images: A Journal of Film and Popular Culture*. http://www.imagesjournal.com/issue08/forbiddenfruit/videos.htm.

Jukovsky, Martin. "Eisenstein." *Labour Review*, September 1978. Reproduced at http://www.wsws.org.

Kael, C. Pauline. "Master Spy, Master Seducer." *New Yorker*, August 4, 1980, p. 68.

Kasson, Constantine D. "Constitutional Law—Due Process—Freedom of Expression—Moving Picture Censorship." *Michigan Law Review* 52 (February 1954): 599–602.

Kauffman. L. A. "Queer Guerrillas in Tinseltown (Protesting Movie Portrayals of Gays and Lesbians)." *Progressive* 56, no. 7 (July 1992): 36–37.

Keets, Heather. "Dancing Up a Storm (Bernardo Bertolucci's Controversial 1973 Film *Last Tango in Paris*)." *Entertainment Weekly*, January 28, 1994, p. 76.

Kenez, Peter. "Film Review—*October* (Oktiabr) Directed by Sergei Eisenstein." *Russian Review* 50 (October 1991): 487.

Khaikaew, Thaksina. "'*Anna and the King*' Challenged." Associated Press, September 28, 1999.

Killackey, Jim, and Michael McNutt. "Regents Block Controversial Film at OSU." *Oklahoma Times*, September 23, 1988.

King, Susan. "Two Years After Fuss, Lyne's *Lolita* Goes on Sale." *Los Angeles Times*, October 14, 1999, p. 52.

Klafter, Samuel. "Education Law—Censorship of Motion Pictures—N.Y. Licensing Statute— Indecency." *Albany Law Review* 22 (January 1958): 186–191.

Klein, Philippa. "The Bad Influence: Representation of Marijuana in Hollywood." http://collection-nic-bnc.ca/100/202/300/mediatribe/mtribe95/marijuana.html.

Kupferman, Theodore R., and Philip J. O'Brien. "Motion Picture Censorship—The Memphis Blues." *Cornell Law Quarterly* 36 (1951): 273–300.

LaSalle, Mick. "*Cruising* Back from the '80s." *San Francisco Chronicle*, May 12, 1995, p. C12.

Laurence, Gerald. "Dressing 'Dressed' to Sell." *Box Office*, September 1980, p. 26.

Lawrenson, Helen. "The Man Who Scandalized the World." *Esquire*, August 1960, pp. 70–73.

Ledbetter, Les. "1,000 in 'Village' Renews Protest Against Movie on Homosexuals." *New York Times*, July 27, 1979, Sec. 2 (1).

Lederman, Lorna F. "New York Statute Censoring 'Sexual Immorality' in Motion Pictures Film Held Unconstitutional." *Temple Law Quarterly*, 33 (Winter 1959): 242–246.

Lee, Robert E. A. "Censorship: A History." *Christian Century*, 74 (February 6, 1957): 163–165.

Leggett, Robert D. "Motion Picture Censorship." *University of Cincinnati Law Review* 23 (Spring 1954): 259–263.

Lemisch, Jesse. "Black Agency in the Amistad Uprising: Or, You've Taken Our Cinque and Gone." *Souls: A Critical Journal of Black Politics, Culture, and Society* 1 (Winter 1999): 57–70.

Leonard, John "The New Puritanism." *The Nation*, November 24, 1997, pp. 11–15.

Lester, Peter. "Redress or Undress? Feminists Fume While Angie Scores in a Sexy Chiller." *Camera* 5 (Fall 1980): 71–72, 81.

Levinthal, Louis E. "Reminiscences of 'A Cause Célèbre.'" *Pennsylvania Bar Association Quarterly* 37 (October 1965): 39–45.

Levy, Emanuel. "'*King*' and the Eye-Popping Pageantry." *Variety*, December 1999, pp. 83–84.

Lewis, Thomas P. "Freedom of Speech and Motion Pictures—the *Miracle* Decision." *Kentucky Law Journal* 41 (January 1953): 257–264.

Lippman, John. "Remake of *Lolita* Is Rebuffed by Distributors." *Wall Street Journal*, April 30, 1997, pp. B1–B3.

Lombardi, Fred. "Reviews—*December 7th:* the Movie, Directed by Gregg Toland and John Ford." *Variety*, December 2, 1991, p. 91.

London, Michael. "Film Clips: Paramount Decides to Resist *Temptation*." *Los Angeles Times Calendar*, January 6, 1984, pp. 1–10.

Lord, Daniel, S. J. "*The Sign of the Cross*," *Commonweal* 18 (December 31, 1932): 215.

"*Lorna*—Film & TV: Scanlines." *Austin Chronicle* December 7, 1998.

Lyons, Timothy J. "Hollywood and World War I, 1914–1918." *Journal of Popular Film* I (1972): 15.

MacQueen, Scott. "*Alibi:* Gangsters Take On Talkies." *American Cinematographer,* 72:4 (April 1991).

Mailer, Martin. "Success and Failure of the Soviet Cinema." *Marxist,* 6:1 (1967): 4–6.

"Malaysia Bans *Schindler's List* as Propaganda." *The Guardian,* March 24, 1994, p. 16.

Maltby, Richard. "The Genesis of the Production Code." *Quarterly Review of Film and Video,* 15:4 (March 1995): 5–57.

———. "'To Prevent the Prevalent Type of Book': Censorship and Adaptation in Hollywood 1924–1934." *American Quarterly* 44 (December 1992): 554–616.

"Marijuana: Marijuana Timeline." *Frontline.* http://www.pbs.org/wgbh/pages/front-line/shows/dope/etc/cron.html.

Marro, Anthony. "Prurient Interest in Memphis." *New Republic,* April 24, 1976.

Maslin, Janet. "Friedkin Defends His Cruising." *New York Times,* September 18, 1979, p. C12.

McAnay, P. D. "Motion Picture Censorship and Constitutional Freedom." *Kentucky Law Journal* 50 (Summer 1962): 427–458.

McLochlin, Bill. "Hollywood vs. Holy Good." *TNT Rough Cut Features.* http://www.roughcut.com/features/stories/dogma.html. July 14, 2000.

McNicholas, John T. "Pastorals and Statements by Members of the American Hierarchy on the Legion of Decency." *Catholic Mind* 32 (September 8, 1934): 113–119.

Mekas, Jonas. "*Un Chant d'Amour.*" *Village Voice,* December 10, 1964.

Mikva, Abner J. "Chicago: Citadel of Censorship." *Focus/Midwest* 2 (March–April 1963): 16–17.

Mishkin, Leo. "*The Killing of Sister George.*" *Morning Telegraph,* December 17, 1968, p. B2.

"Minister Blasts Universal's Movie as 'Perverted.'" United Press International, July 12, 1988.

"Miss Julie." *Films in Review,* May 1952, p. 242.

"Miss West Talks Shop." *New York Times,* February 3, 1935, p. 5.

Mondschein, Morris. "Constitutional Law: Motion Picture Censorship." *Cornell Law Quarterly* 44 (Spring 1959): 411–419.

"*Moon* Cab Scene Cut, Plays Alabam'; St. Paul Solons Hold Nose, O.K. It." *Variety,* July 29, 1953, p. 1.

Moore, Donald P. "Chicago Censorship Ordinance Held Enforceable." *University of Illinois Law Forum* 54 (Winter 1954): 678–684.

Morais, Richard C. "*Reefer Madness.*" *Forbes,* June 17, 1996, p. 118.

Morris, Gary. "*Carmen, Baby.*" *Bright Lights Journal* 26 (1999). http://www.bright-lightsfilm.com.

Morse, Howard N. "A Critical Analysis and Appraisal of *Burstyn v. Wilson.*" *North Dakota Law Review* 29 (January 1953): 38–41.

"Motion Picture Censorship—A Constitutional Dilemma." *Maryland Law Review* 12 (Summer 1954): 284–298.

"Motion Picture Censorship: The Aftermath of *Burstyn v. Wilson.*" *Northwestern University Law Review* 49 (July–August 1954): 390–399.

"MPAA Supports Universal's *Temptation.*" *Variety,* July 27, 1988, p. 26.

"Munich.prosecutors.071096.txt." EEF "Global Internet Censorship" Archive. Maintained by Declan McCullagh. http://www.eff.org/pub/Censorship/gII_NII/Dispatches. July 22, 1996.

Murray, Steve. "Movies—A Conversation with . . . Adrian Lyne: 'It's Been an Iffy Sort of Ride.'" *The Atlanta Journal/The Atlanta Constitution*, October 9, 1998, p. 8.

"Naked Came the Stranger." Film Bulletin, June 1975.

Nascenzi, Nicole. "Free-thought Process Defended." *Tulsa World*, September 10, 1999. http://www.tulsaworld.com.

"The Newcomers." Variety, September 6, 1972.

Nimmer, Melville B. "The Constitutionality of Official Censorship of Motion Pictures." *University of Chicago Law Review* 25 (1958): 639–640.

"Oktyabar (October): A Review." *Variety*, November 30, 1988, p. 23.

O'Meara, Joseph, and Thomas L. Shaffer. "Obscenity and the Supreme Court: A Note on *Jacobellis v. Ohio.*" *Notre Dame Lawyer* 40 (December 1964): 1–12.

Pally, Marica, and others. "Sex, Violence, and De Palma." *Film Comment* 21:5 (September–October 1985): 9–13.

Pfeffer, Leo. "Heresy, American Democracy and *The Miracle.*" *Jewish Frontier* 17 (August 1951): 14–18.

Picardie, Ruth. "Mad, Bad and Dangerous (Gay Film Makers and Gay Opposition to the Film *Basic Instinct*)." *New Statesman & Society*, May 1, 1992, p. 36.

Pilpel, Harriet F. "Firm Restrictions Placed on Pre-Publication Censorship." *Publishers Weekly*, September 25, 1961, pp. 30–31.

Pittman, Randy. "Video Movies—*December 7th:* The Movie." *Library Journal* 116 (November 15, 1991): 127.

Pollack, Dale. "*Cruising* Protests Intensify." *Los Angeles Times*, February 1, 1980, p. V1.

"Protests Call the Film *Cruising* Anti-homosexual." *New York Times*, July 26, 1979, p. C1.

"Purity." Moving Picture World, July 29, 1916, p. 804.

"Purity." Variety, July 7, 1916, p. 25.

"Pythons Get Life." *Movie & TV News*. http://www.IMDb.com. May 22, 1998.

Quigley, Martin. "Frankenstein." *Motion Picture Herald*, November 14, 1931.

Rabinowitz, Dorothy. "TV: A Month of Classic Documentaries—from the South Pole to the Frozen North Via the Dust Bowl." *Wall Street Journal*, November 8, 1999, p. A48.

"Reasons for Banning '*Anna and the King.*'" *The Nation*, January 7, 2000, p. 11.

"Reefer Madness." Brown Film Society Film Bulletin, September 18, 1997.

"The Regulation of Film." *The Nation*, May 6, 1915, pp. 486–487.

Reiner, Donald F. "Motion Picture Censorship Re-examined." *Albany Law Review* 23 (January 1959): 152–168.

Ringel, Eleanor. "Movies Latest *Lolita* Short on Steam." *Atlanta Journal/The Atlanta Constitution*, October 9, 1998, p. 8.

Robbins, Tim. "*Last Temptation* War Rages on: Exhibs Pressured, Italy Quakes." *Variety*, August 3, 1988, p. 6.

Rooney, David. "*Toto Who Lived Twice.*" *Variety*, March 9, 1998, pp. 43–44.

Rorty, James. "It Ain't No Sin." *Nation* (August 1, 1934): 124–127.

Rossell, Deac. "*Woodstock.*" *Boston After Dark*, April 1, 1970.

Rothstein, Richard. "Reality Check Due in Drug Prevention." *New York Times*, September 17, 1997, p. L12.

Sabsay, David. "The Challenge of the 'Fisk Report.'" *California Libraries* 20 (October 1959): 222–223.

Sangster, Jim. "*Anna and the King.*" *Film Review*, January 2000, p. 24.

Sarris, Andrew. "Dreck to Kill." *Village Voice*, September 17–23, 1980, p. 43.

Satter, David. "Private Soviet Screenings of Forbidden Films? Insane!" *Wall Street Journal*, March 13, 1984, p. 1+.

Sauter, Michael. "Video: *Anna and the King.*" *Entertainment Weekly*, June 23, 2000, p. 76.

Schaefer, Stephen. "Irons' *Lolita* Still on Hold in USA." *USA Today*, September 18, 1997, p. D2.

Schickel, Richard. "*Amistad:* A Paean to Past Agony." *The Arts/Culture* 150, no. 25 (December 15, 1997).

Schwartz, Amy E. "A Personal View: The *Temptation* Resistance." *San Francisco Chronicle*, August 8, 1999, p. E1.

Scott, Barbara. "Motion Picture Censorship and the Exhibitor." *Film Comment* 2, no. 4 (Fall 1965): 56–60.

Scott, Michael. "The Highbrow Railings of Gore Vidal." *Rolling Stone*, May 15, 1980.

Seitz, Matt Zoller. "Sex, Death and Storytelling: A New Look at *Lolita.*" *Sunday Star-Ledger*, August 2, 1998, Sec. 4–1, 10.

Seldes, Gilbert. "Pressures and Pictures." *The Nation*, February 3, 1951, pp. 104–106.

Sennwald, André. "*The Youth of Maxim.*" *The Nation*, May 1, 1935.

Shapiro, Walter. "Sad Picture Worth a Thousand Words." *USA Today*, September 5, 1997, p. A1.

Sharrett, Christopher. "Hollywood Homophobia (Column)." *USA Today*, July 1992, p. 93.

Shawell, Julia. "Mae West Curves Herself a Career." *Pictorial Review*, February 1934, p. 7.

Sibley, John. "Film Censorship in State Is Ended." *New York Times*, June 11, 1965, pp. 33, 61.

"*The Sign of the Cross.*" *Variety*, December 6, 1932, p. 14.

Simpson, Janice C. "Out of the Celluloid Closet: Gay Activities Are on a Rampage Against Negative Stereotyping and Other Acts of Homophobia in Hollywood." *Time*, April 6, 1992, p. 65.

Sitney, P. Adams. "Film Censorship: United States." *Censorship* 2 (Spring 1965): 48–50.

Smith, Mark Chalon. "War Film a Morale Dilemma Movie: *December 7th* Was Deemed a Propaganda Film and Shelved." *Los Angeles Times*, December 9, 1991, p. 28.

Soderburgh, Peter A. "'Aux Armes': The Rise of the Hollywood War Film, 1916–1930." *South Atlantic Quarterly* 65 (1966): 512.

Sontag, Susan. "Feast for Open Eyes." *The Nation*, April 13, 1964, pp. 374–376.

Stamets, Reena Shah. "*Schindler's List* Faces Censorship in Muslim Nations." *St. Petersburg Times*, April 17, 1994, p. D1.

Starks, Michael. *Cocaine Fiends and Reefer Madness: An Illustrated History of Drugs in the Movies.* New York: Carol Publishing Group, 1982.

Stephens, Bob. "Lasting Images of *Cruising.*" *San Francisco Examiner*, May 12, 1995, p. C5.

"Supreme Court Decision Limits Censorship." *Publishers Weekly* 186 (July 6, 1964): 48–49.

Swerczek, Mary. "Copycat Killing Suit Is Facing Test." [New Orleans] *Times-Picayune*, March 22, 1999, p. A1+.

Talbot, Frans X., S.J. "More on Smut." *America* 48 (February 25, 1933): 500–501.

Taylor, Winchell. "Secret Movie Censors." *The Nation*, July 9, 1938, pp. 38–40.

Theim, Rebecca, and Chris Cooper. "St. Bernard, Kenner Officials: Don't Be Tempted by Movie." [New Orleans] *Times-Picayune*, August 18, 1988, p. 33.

"Too Much Anatomy." *Richmond News Ledger*, August 5, 1959, p. 50.

"Toto Who Lived Twice." Second Annual Toronto Italian Film Festival. June 16–20, 2000. http.//www.italianfilmfestival.com.

Trillin, Calvin. "Trying *Green Door.*" *New Yorker*, February 11, 1974, pp. 23–29.

"TV Station Yields to Catholic Pressure." *Christian Century* 74 (January 2, 1957): 4, 2.

Velie, Lester. "You Can't See That Movie: Censorship in Action." *Collier's*, May 6, 1950, pp. 11–13, 66.

Wakin, Daniel J. *"Lolita* Strictly Foreign Fare." *Record* (Bergen City, N.J.), September 28, 1997.

Walker, Alexander. *"Bunny Lake Is Missing."* *London Evening Standard*, December 8, 1999.

Wallace, Charles P. "Malaysian Censors Move to Ban List; Government Body in Muslim Nation Calls Spielberg's Holocaust Film 'Propaganda'—Jewish Groups Are Outraged." *Los Angeles Times*, March 24, 1994, pp. F1.

Walters, Fred. "The Supreme Court Ruling on *The Miracle* and *Pinky.*" *Theatre Arts* 36 (August 1952): 74–77.

"Warner Bros. Not Happy with the Last Heretic Laugh." *Variety*, June 22, 1977, p. 5.

Wedin, Carolyn. "How the NAACP Fought the Worst Great Movie." *American Legacy*, 2:4 (Winter 1997): 37–42.

Weiler, A. H. *"Women of the World."* *New York Times*, July 3, 1963.

Weiner, Caren. "Curious Under Fire." *Entertainment Weekly*, March 6, 1998, p. 92.

Weiner, Ernest. "Reason, Truth and Art Are Held Hostage." *San Francisco Chronicle*, April 27, 1994, p. A21.

Weiner, Rex. "Lolita Gets Old Waiting for Date." *Variety*, June 2–8, 1997, pp. 1, 8.

Wiener, Stanley. "Final Curtain Call for the Motion Picture Censor?" *Western Reserve Law Review* 4 (Winter 1953): 148–158.

Welch, Robert G. "The *Martin Luther* Film." *America* 96 (March 23, 1957): 698–700.

Wills, Garry. "Dostoyevsky Behind the Camera: Oliver Stone Is Making Great American Novels on Film." *Atlantic Monthly* 280 (July 1997): 96+.

Wilmington, Michael. "Fellini's *La Dolce Vita* Coined a Term and Created a Character Whose Amoral Image Endures." *Chicago Tribune*, September 12, 1997, p. 5.

———. "New *Lolita* Doesn't Stand Up to Original Film, Book." *Chicago Tribune* (North Sports Edition), November 13, 1998, Friday section, page K.

Wood, Peter. "How a Film Changes from an 'X' to an 'R.'" *New York Times*, July 20, 1980, p. C1.

Wyman, Mark. *"The Blue Angel."* *Film Review*, November 1997, p. 26.

Yeaman, Elizabeth. "The Catholic Movie Censorship." *New Republic*, 96 (October 5, 1938): 233–235.

APPENDIX I

DIRECTORS' PROFILES

ABRAMSON, IVAN (1869–1934)

Abramson's films helped to shape Jewish intellectual life in the United States through his casting of stars from Yiddish theater, such as Molly Picon, in such popular films as *East and West* (1923). He also made many financially successful melodramas, among them *Forbidden Fruit* (1915), *Enlighten Thy Daughter* (1917), *Child for Sale* (1920) and THE SEX LURE (1916).

ALDRICH, ROBERT (1918–1983)

The films of this flamboyant producer and director have earned a sizable cult following. After a long stint as an assistant director to Charles Chaplin and Jean Renoir, he directed several tough, gritty films in the 1950s, including *Kiss Me Deadly* (1955), *The Big Knife* (1955) and *Attack!* (1956). His more colorful side soon asserted itself with such crowd-pleasers as *What Ever Happened to Baby Jane?* (1962), *The Dirty Dozen* (1967), THE KILLING OF SISTER GEORGE (1968) and *The Longest Yard* (1974). The profits from *Dozen* allowed him to buy an entire studio, which he dubbed Associates & Aldrich.

ALLEGRET, MARC (1900–1973)

Older brother of the director Yves Allegret, his first film was the 1927 documentary *Voyage Au Congo*, about a trip to Africa undertaken by his uncle, the author André Gide. Allegret went on to assist the directors Robert Florey and Augusto Genina. In 1931 he completed *Le Blanc Et Le Noir* for Florey and co-directed *Les Amants De Minuit*. That same year he made his solo directing debut, launching a 40-year career that includes such notable films as the Josephine Baker musical *Zou-Zou* (1934), the documentary *Avec André Gide* (1952) and the D. H. Lawrence adaptation LADY CHATTERLEY'S LOVER (1955).

ANDERSON, ROBERT (N.D.)

Anderson directed such soft-core pornography films as CINDY AND DONNA (1970), *The Young Graduates* (1971) and *The Hoax* (1972).

AUTANT-LARA, CLAUDE (1901–2000)

This French director *Claude Autant-Lara* was taken to England during World War I by his mother, the actress Louise Lara, whose strong pacifist stance forced her to flee France. He returned to his native country in 1919, first studied art and then worked as a set and costume designer for the major French filmmakers of the 1920s. In 1923 he directed the surrealistic short *Fait Divers* (1923), worked for three years in collaboration with fellow director René Clair, and then returned to solo filmmaking in 1926.

Autant-Lara flourished during the years of the Occupation (1940–1944), specializing in romantic, nostalgic productions. His first international success was *Le Diable au Corps* (also released as *The Devil in the Flesh;* 1946). In the mid-1950s he was attacked by the New Wave critics for his too-traditional approach, but his 1954 film THE GAME OF LOVE was well received. Autant-Lara's last film, *Gloria*, appeared in 1977, after which he served as a member of the European Parliament. He was forced to resign in 1989 after a speech in which he suggested that the Holocaust had never happened.

BARKER, REGINALD (1886–1945)

Born in Scotland, Barker arrived in the United States in 1896 and made his first acting appearance in a Los Angeles stock company. Hired as a general-purpose actor, Barker worked his way up to assistant director in 1913 for the producer Thomas Ince, who took most of the credit for Barker's work in this period. After guiding the Western star William S. Hart through his first major film *On the Night Stage* (1914), Barker's success was assured, and he began to work on a greater number of feature film projects, including THE BRAND (1919). Only a few years after he made *Seven Keys to Baldpate* (1929), the first sound effort by RKO, Barker's popularity waned and his work with the larger studios decreased. His final film was *Forbidden Heaven* (1935).

BEAUDINE, WILLIAM (1892–1970)

William Beaudine began his long career working for director D. W. Griffith on silent films and directed many of the top silent stars in numerous films. Once he made the transition to sound, Beaudine gained the nickname "One Shot" Beaudine for his rapid filmmaking techniques, which were often disparaged, even by the director himself. In later years, Beaudine made numerous exploitation films, such as MOM AND DAD (1948), and later served as one of the principal directors for the *Lassie* TV series of the late 1950s and early '60s. He also directed episodes for numerous other television series, including *Broken Arrow, Naked City* and *The Mickey Mouse Club's* "Spin and Marty." When Beaudine retired in 1967 he was the oldest active director in Hollywood.

BENNETT, RICHARD (1872–1944)

Bennet directed such social propaganda films as *And the Law Says* (1916) and both the original and the revised versions of DAMAGED GOODS (1914, 1917). Also a distinguished actor, he was the father of actresses Constance and Joan Bennett.

BERGER, REA (N.D.)

Berger directed seven films in 1916, including PURITY (1916), and two films in 1918. Berger's first name is credited as "Rhea" for the first film, *The Overcoat* (1916), but as "Rea" in the remaining eight films. His name is not associated with any film after *Danger Within* (1918).

BERGMAN, INGMAR (1918–   )

Noted for pictures that probe the inner reaches of human emotion, Bergman has served as a model for generations of filmmakers around the world. His primary artistic concerns are spiritual conflict and the fragility of the psyche. He made his directorial debut with *Kris* (1945), but the prototypical Bergman picture, filled with the the-matic and stylistic innovations that were to become the director's trademark, would not appear until 1949. It was followed by a series of pictures that marked Bergman's maturation as an artist, among these *Sommaren Med Monika* (1953). Bergman contin-ued to strike out into new narrative and thematic areas with *The Magician* (1958), an examination of the role of the artist; THE VIRGIN SPRING (1959), another medieval morality play; *The Devil's Eye* (1960); and the disturbing "trilogy" of *Through a Glass, Darkly* and *Winter Light* (both 1962), and *The Silence* (1963). Bergman had his biggest U.S. success with *Cries and Whispers* (1972). Bergman was nominated for Academy Awards, five times for best screenplay and three times for best director.

BERTOLUCCI, BERNARDO (1941–)

Bertolucci, the Italian director whose films are known for their colorful visual style, was born in Parma, Italy, in 1941. He served as assistant director for the 1961 film *Accatone* (1961) and directed *La Commare secca* (1962) in 1962. His second film, *Prima della rivoluzione* (1962), gained him recognition as a director who updated literary clas-sics and added political thought to his work. Bertolucci received an Academy Award nomination as best director for LAST TANGO IN PARIS (1973) and the best director and best screenplay awards for *The Last Emperor* (1987).

BOGDANOVICH, PETER (1939–)

Many French cineasts and film critics went on to become major filmmakers, but in America only one such critic made that transition. Peter Bogdanovich, a lifelong film buff, wrote dozens of articles, books and program notes about Hollywood before set-tling there in the mid-1960s. After one of his greatest successes, THE LAST PICTURE SHOW (1971), he made two big hits: *What's Up, Doc?* (1972) and *Paper Moon* (1973), which brought an Academy Award for best supporting actress to the young newcomer Tatum O'Neal. After a period of self-imposed exile from film making, he began to work again, although his output has been small: *Mask* (1985), *Noises Off* (1992) and the Nashville-based *The Thing Called Love* (1993).

BORZAGE, FRANK (1893–1962)

Borzage worked primarily in the arena of romantic melodrama, and at his peak in the late 1920s, his soft-focus style was much admired and imitated. He began in show business as an actor at age 13. During the 1920s, Borzage alternated Westerns with melodrama. He concentrated for a time on comedy but also won the first best director Oscar for *Seventh Heaven* (1927). Returning to freelancing, he directed such diverse films as A FAREWELL TO ARMS (1932), *Little Man, What Now?* (1934), *No Greater Glory* (1934), *Flirtation Walk* (1934), *Shipmates Forever* (1935), *Desire* (1936) and *Hearts Divided* (1936).

BRASS, TINTO (1933–)

Italian-born, Brass began directing films in the early 1960s, starting with *Ça ira il fiume della rivolta* (*Tell It Like It Is*) in 1964. He has directed 24 films, and his most recent, *Angelo nero* (*Black Angel*), is due out in 2001. Although many of his films have been well received, none has gained the notoriety of CALIGULA (1980).

BROWN, CLARENCE (1890–1987)

After graduating from the University of Tennessee at 19 with a degree in engineering, Brown worked first as a mechanics expert with the Stevens Duryea Company and then founded the Brown Motor Car Company. In 1913, he left engineering and became involved in motion pictures, beginning as assistant director at the Peerless Studio at Fort Lee, New Jersey, under the tutelage of the French-born director Maurice Tourneur, whom Brown thanked for his success. He later had the good fortune to direct Greta Garbo and became her favorite director. Brown and Garbo collaborated on such films as *Flesh and the Devil* (1927), *A Woman of Affairs* (1928) and *Anna Christie* (1930), Garbo's first sound film. From 1925 through 1952, Brown directed almost exclusively at MGM, where he made IDIOT'S DELIGHT (1939). After retiring, Brown became a sought-after lecturer on film topics.

BROWNING, TOD (1882–1962)

The man who made DRACULA (1931), Browning was once dubbed "the Edgar Allan Poe of the cinema" for his use of supernatural and eerie elements in his productions. He ran away from home at age 16 to join the circus, which would provide background for *The Show* (1927), *The Unknown* (1927) and FREAKS (1932). He became a director in 1917, heading production on many nondescript pictures before being teamed with monster film veteran Lon Chaney. Among the more than 60 films that Browning directed, none achieved the notoriety of *Freaks*. He retired after directing *Miracles for Sale* (1939), a routine whodunit with supernatural trappings.

CAPELLANI, ALBERT (1870–1931)

French-born, Capellani began his career as a theatrical actor and administrator before directing short comedies for Pathé in 1905. He soon turned to adaptations of classic literature, directing such epic-length movies as the five-hour-long *Les Miserables* in 1912. Critics hailed Capellani's work as an example of film as true art, and he was invited to work in the United States in 1915, where he directed numerous works, including THE EASIEST WAY (1917). He returned to France in 1923, after suffering paralysis due to a stroke.

CAVARA, PAOLO (1926–1982)

The Italian-born Cavara made a career largely of exploitation films, beginning in 1962 with *Mondo Cane* (*A Dog's Life*). He achieved a modest level of critical acclaim with *La cattura* (*The Ravine*) in 1969 and *La tarantola dal ventre nero* (*Black Belly of the Tarantula*) in 1972, but most of his 13 films, including his second, *La donna nel mondo* (WOMEN OF THE WORLD) in 1963, generated little cinematic interest.

CHAPLIN, CHARLES (1889–1977)

Best known by moviegoers for his remarkable character portrayals, such as "the tramp," English-born Chaplin appeared in his first movie, *Making a Living*, in February 1914 and made his first full-length film, *The Kid*, in 1921. In 1923, Chaplin produced and directed *A Woman of Paris*, released by United Artists. In 1929 he won a special award at the first Academy Awards "for versatility and genius in writing, acting, directing and producing" the 1928 film *The Circus*. His films *City Lights* (1931) and

Modern Times (1936) are cinema classics. Chaplin went on to star in and direct a number of works, including THE GREAT DICTATOR (1940), a satire on the fascist political climate of the time. Tired of political and moralistic controversies and plagued by tax collectors, he left the United States for Switzerland in 1952. He was named Knight Commander of the British Empire in 1975.

CHRISTIE, AL (1881–1951)

Although he directed nearly 70 films, including the controversial BIRTH OF A BABY (1938), Christie is best known for a piece of Hollywood real estate. What is now Studio City, California, grew out of a joint venture between Al Christie and Mack Sennett, who began as rival filmmakers before they joined forces to make a deal with a real estate development company to build a new up-to-the-minute sound studio, along with a residential and commercial district to support the economic growth of their new city. The consortium they founded in 1929 was named the Central Motion Picture District Inc.

CIPRI, DANIELE (1962–   )

Italian-born Cipri began working with Franco Maresco in 1986 filming short videos and experimental programs for a television station in Palermo. In 1990, Cipri worked on *Blob Cinico TV* and, with Maresco, won the Aristophanes prize for satirical comedy. The director of only three feature films to date, beginning with *Lo zio di Brooklyn* (*The Uncle from Brooklyn*) in 1995, Cipri created a sensation when Italy banned the 1998 *Toto che visse due volte* (TOTO WHO LIVED TWICE).

CLARKE, SHIRLEY (1919–1997)

Although she trained as a choreographer, Clarke began as a director in 1953, filming short subjects on dance for a limited audience, and then moved to documentary-style films such as *Bridges Go Round* (1959) and *Skyscraper* (1959). In 1960 Clarke filmed her first feature, *The Connection* (1961), which the New York State film censors banned. Shortly after, Clarke established her own production company, Film-Makers Cooperative, and won an Academy Award for her 1962 documentary *Robert Frost: A Lover's Quarrel with the World*. Clarke later turned to moviemaking on videotape and taught film courses at UCLA.

CLAYTON, JACK (1921–1995)

Clayton became a film editor just before World War II began and entered the British military to serve during the war in the Royal Air Force Film Division. When the war ended, he worked as production manager for producer Alexander Korda. The 1959 feature film ROOM AT THE TOP established Clayton in his career and marked him as one of the "Angry Young Men" of Britain's entertainment world. He later varied his film output to include psychological horror and marital drama and then took a break from moviemaking between 1967 and 1974. He returned to film with *The Great Gatsby* (1974).

CONWAY, JACK (1887–1952)

Conway, a former stage actor, became an assistant to D. W. Griffith in 1909 and in 1913 turned his talents to directing films. In the 1930s and 1940s at MGM, he directed comedies, action films and historical dramas. Because of sexual innuendo and overt sexuality, his RED-HEADED WOMAN (1932) is credited as one of the films that pushed Hollywood toward strengthened film standards in the early 1930s.

CROMWELL, JOHN (1888–1979)

A longtime stage performer who had already produced and directed many plays by the time he got to Hollywood in 1929, Cromwell made his movie debut as an actor in *The Dummy* (1929). He shared directorial responsibilities with Edward Sutherland on *Close Harmony* (1929) and *The Dance of Life* (1929), learning the mechanics of film directing before striking out on his own with ANN VICKERS (1930) and *OF HUMAN BONDAGE* (1934). For the most part Cromwell eschewed flashy camera moves or other stylistic flourishes that might, in his view, distract from the story or the performances. Late in life he appeared in front of the cameras again, playing bit parts for Robert Altman in *3 Women* (1977) and *A Wedding* (1978).

DASSIN, JULES (1911–   )

Dassin made his stage debut at the Yiddish Theater in New York City but soon moved into directing at MGM in Hollywood. His first short-subject film was an adaptation of Edgar Allan Poe's "The Tell-Tale Heart" (1941). He later directed numerous feature films, moving to Universal in the late 1940s where he directed *Brute Force* (1947) and *The Naked City* (1948). Dassin's political leanings caused him difficulty in Hollywood, and he was blacklisted after being identified as a member of the Communist Party in the 1950s. He moved to France, where he made the extremely influential crime movie *Rififi* in 1954. Living in Greece in 1959, Dassin directed his second wife Melina Mercouri in NEVER ON SUNDAY (1960), a successful comedy that brought Dassin back to the attention of Hollywood and led to his return in the mid-1960s. His later political films were directed at limited audiences and did not achieve box-office success, but his reputation remained intact nonetheless.

DAVIS, WILL S. (1882–1920)

From 1913 through 1919, Davis directed 35 films, several as William S. Davis. When THE ORDEAL was first released in 1914, officials called for its withdrawal because it was anti-German, but no objection was made when the film was reissued in 1918 under the title of *Mothers of Liberty*. He died of peritonitis.

DEMILLE, CECIL B. (1881–1959)

To a generation of moviegoers, Cecil B. DeMille was the very image of a Hollywood producer-director. Early features like *The Warrens of Virginia and The Cheat* (both 1915), *Maria Rosa* (1916), *Joan the Woman and The Little American* (both 1917) and *The Whispering Chorus* (1918) are still impressive today. In the mid-1920s he launched his own production company, for which he supervised a slate of films and directed *The Road to Yesterday* (1925, featuring the first of many DeMille train wrecks), *The Volga Boatman* (1926) and other "run of the DeMille" pictures. DeMille hit his stride once more when he returned to Paramount, where he would remain for the rest of his career. He drew on prior experience to mix historical drama with sex in THE SIGN OF THE CROSS (1932) and *Cleopatra* (1934). DeMille continued to direct for the next 20 years.

DE PALMA, BRIAN (1940–   )

De Palma remains one of the most controversial filmmakers on the contemporary screen. His early features were 1960s satires. De Palma invented the telekinetic-teen horror genre with *Carrie* (1976), an adaptation of a Stephen King novel, with contains both genuine shocks and clever humor. *The Fury* (1978) takes the premise of shock and humor to the point of ridiculousness but contains some impressive cinematic and special effects pyrotechnics. DRESSED TO KILL (1980), De Palma's take on *Psycho*, was jolting for both its violence and sexual content. He also updated the 1930s gangster classic *Scarface* (1983) to contemporary Miami, with Al Pacino as a drug-crazed Cuban hero. Just as his career seemed commercially irredeemable, he directed the popular hit *The Untouchables* (1987) from a script by playwright David Mamet. He returned to familiar territory for the shocker *Raising Cain* (1992) and then took on a more ambitious project with Al Pacino in *Carlito's Way* (1993).

DIETERLE, WILHELM (1893–1972)

Dieterle began his career as a stage actor in Germany and Switzerland and then entered the movies in 1913, where he remained an actor for 10 years. In 1923, he directed himself in a series of films in Germany, including *Sex in Chains* (1928). When he moved to Hollywood in 1930, Dieterle directed German-language versions of films, but his true Hollywood success began at Warner Bros., where he began with feature films and then created prestigious biopics of Louis Pasteur, Emile Zola and Benito Juarez. He also directed BLOCKADE (1938), which was challenged for its political content. This was followed by a move to RKO and a series of well-received feature films. In the late 1950s Dieterle returned to Europe and directed films in Italy and Germany.

FELLINI, FEDERICO (1920–1993)

So distinctive and original is the vision of this Italian filmmaker that the adjective "Felliniesque," used to describe bizarre, colorful personages and events, has become almost commonplace. A friendship with Italian actor Aldo Fabrizi led Fellini into the theater, and during the 1940s he worked as a radio and film scriptwriter. *La Strada* (1954) is generally acknowledged to be Fellini's first great film, and it won him his first Academy Award for best foreign language film. LA DOLCE VITA (1960) marked the beginning of a period in which the director's skewed sensibilities would be fully realized. In the 1970s critics began to accuse Fellini of self-parody, and indeed some of his films seemed like pale imitations of earlier works, but his vivid and nostalgic reminiscence, *Amarcord* (1974), was a great success and earned him his fourth Academy Award.

FINDLAY, MICHAEL (?–1977)

Findlay directed, wrote and produced films under a variety of names: J. Ellsworth, Michael Fenway, Richard Jennings, Julian Marsh, Richard West, Robert West and Robert Wuesterwurst. Their status as mainly erotic horror, such as *Shriek of the Mutilated* (1974), *Snuff* (1976) and BODY OF A FEMALE (1965), on which he listed the two fictitious directors J. Ellsworth and Julian Marsh, largely kept them out of the mainstream theaters. Findlay died in a helicopter crash while filming a movie that his widow Roberta left unfinished.

FORBIDDEN FILMS

FORD, JOHN (1894–1973)

Among the most honored of all American movie directors, John Ford was lauded by critics for his poetic vision. The early days of talkies saw Ford, like many other silent film directors, groping for a command of the new storytelling techniques imposed by the addition of sound on film. In the 1930s Ford further developed a distinctive style, which he honed both on commercial, work-for-hire movies and on modest, more personal productions. He won back-to-back Academy Awards for *The Grapes of Wrath* (1940) and *How Green Was My Valley* (1941), both of which centered on tight-knit families surviving in the face of adversity. World War II intervened and Ford, serving in the Field Photographic Branch of the OSS, turned out several documentaries; two of them, *The Battle of Midway* (1942) and DECEMBER 7TH (1943), won Academy Awards. In the late 1940s Ford and producer Merian C. Cooper formed Argosy Productions, a partnership that produced some of Ford's best pictures. *Fort Apache* (1948), *She Wore a Yellow Ribbon* (1949) and *Rio Grande* (1950) comprised Ford's unofficial cavalry trilogy. His 1950s films vary in quality, although many film fans and critics single out *The Searchers* (1956), starring John Wayne, as the definitive Ford film.

FRIEDKIN, WILLIAM (1939–   )

Friedkin first earned recognition when he directed *The French Connection*, (1971) known for its gritty realism and justifiably famous car chase. After THE EXORCIST (1973), however, Friedkin lost ground. His next film, *Sorcerer* (1977), failed to excite audiences, and *The Brink's Job* (1978), CRUISING (1980), *Deal of the Century* (1983), *To Live and Die in L.A.* (1985), *Stalking Danger* (1986) and *Rampage* (1987) gave him a string of box-office nonperformers. He also directed a pair of TV movies, *C.A.T. Squad* (1986) and *C.A.T. Squad: Python Wolf* (1988). *The Guardian* (1990) brought Friedkin back to supernatural suspense, and *Blue Chips* (1994) put him back in the mainstream.

GASNIER, LOUIS J. (1875–1963)

French-born Louis J. Gasnier was a stage actor, director and producer in Paris when he was hired by Pathe to direct comedy shorts. Like many silent-film directors, however, Gasnier couldn't successfully make the transition to sound. Many of his sound films were made for the low-budget independent market, and he often required the collaboration of dialogue directors (who received co-director credit) to handle the actors' line readings. Gasnier's most famous film is the cult classic REEFER MADNESS (1936), an unintentionally hilarious antimarijuana polemic.

GENET, JEAN (1910–1986)

Genet was saved from imprisonment for theft by the intervention of Jean Cocteau, the famous writer, filmmaker and artist who, on the basis of Genet's first poem, declared him a literary genius and helped to obtain his release. Genet, while in prison, would steal paper from the prison workshop on which he would then write his poems and stories. He was also a playwright. Many of Genet's gay-themed works excited controversy in America and were not issued in France and the rest of Europe. UN CHANT D'AMOUR (1950) was Genet's only cinematic directorial work.

334

GREEN, ALFRED E. (1889–1960)

One of the more prolific American directors, Alfred E. Green entered the film indus-try in 1912 as an actor for the Selig Polyscope Co. He became an assistant to the director Colin Campbell and started directing two-reelers (of approximately 30 min-utes) turning to features in 1917. Although his career lasted into the mid-1950s, his output was mostly routine, but there were some gems among them. Among his more controversial films was BABY FACE (1933), which explored the forbidden world of sex-ually opportunistic women. Mary Pickford chose him to direct several of her pictures in the 1920s, and he had several hits with Wallace Reid and Colleen Moore. He directed Bette Davis in her Academy Award-winning performance in *Dangerous* (1935) and was responsible for the commercial and critical success *The Jolson Story* (1946). It was followed by a string of routine B pictures, however, and Green retired from films in 1954 after suffering for many years from arthritis. He spent the remain-der of his career directing TV series episodes.

GRIFFITH, D. W. (1875–1948)

Griffith was born in rural Kentucky to Jacob "Roaring Jake" Griffith, a Confederate army colonel and Civil War hero. He grew up with his father's romantic war stories and with melodramatic 19th-century literature, which eventually molded his black-and-white view of human existence and history. In 1897, Griffith set out to pursue a career acting and writing for the theater but for the most part was unsuccessful. Griffith even-tually was offered a job at the financially struggling American Biograph Company, where he directed more than 450 short films and experimented with the storytelling techniques he would later perfect in his epic THE BIRTH OF A NATION (1915). Griffith and his personal cinematographer G. W. Bitzer collaborated to create and perfect such cinematic devices as the flashback, the iris shot, the mask and crosscutting.

HARRIS, JAMES B. (1928–   )

Born in New York City, Harris has worked as a producer and screenwriter as well as a director in the drama, action, spy film and crime genres. He started out producing films for Stanley Kubrick and worked with him on *The Killing* (1956), *Paths of Glory* (1957) and LOLITA (1962), before his directorial debut in THE BEDFORD INCIDENT (1965). His most recent film is *Boiling Point* (1993), on which he served as both writer and director.

HUGHES, HOWARD (1905–1976)

A millionaire businessman, banker, aviation pioneer, film producer and film director, Hughes was born in Houston, Texas. In 1926 he ventured into films, producing *Hell's Angels* (1930), SCARFACE: SHAME OF THE NATION (1932) and THE OUTLAW (1941). Throughout his life he shunned publicity, eventually becoming a recluse while still controlling his vast business interests from sealed-off hotel suites, thus giving rise to endless rumor and speculation.

JACOBSEN, JOHAN (1912–1972)

This Danish-born producer and director made 30 films, but only three have been released with English subtitles in the United States: *Den usynlige haer* (*The Invisible*

Army, 1945), *Soldaten og Jenny* (*Jenny and the Soldier*, 1947) and *En freemed banker på* (A STRANGER KNOCKS, 1959).

JACOPETTI, GUALTIERO (1919–   )

Jacopetti is one of the founders of "shockumentary" cinema: lurid, sensational documentary-style films that display social taboos, horrors and vulgarities from around the world. A journalist and magazine editor early in his career, in the late 1950s he wrote commentary for documentaries and such pseudodocumentaries as *Mondo Cane* (1962) and WOMEN OF THE WORLD (1962).

JAECKIN, JUST (1940–   )

French-born Jaeckin has been both a screenwriter and director, and he has filmed in both France and Germany. His first directorial effort, EMMANUELLE (1974), was followed in 1975 by *The Story of O*, and his later films, notably *Lady Chatterley's Lover* (1981), contain similarly sensual themes.

JONES, TERRY (1942–   )

Terry Jones was born in Colwyn Bay, North Wales and studied at St. Edmund Hall College, Oxford University. In 1965, with his friend Michael Palin, he made *The Love Show* for television, which was his first success. He wrote for many other TV shows, such as *The Kathy Kirby Show* and *Late Night Lineup* (with Michael Palin), but Jones's greatest successes have been zany comedies, such as MONTY PYTHON'S LIFE OF BRIAN (1969).

KAZAN, ELIA (1909–   )

From the first film Kazan directed, *A Tree Grows in Brooklyn* (1945), he showed an ability to coax great performances from his actors; star James Dunn and child actress Peggy Ann Garner both won Academy Awards for their turns in this lovely, evocative film. Kazan had another success with PINKY in 1949. A STREETCAR NAMED DESIRE (1951) not only earned Kazan another Academy Award nod for best director, but it also made a full-fledged screen star of Marlon Brando, a leading exponent of the "Method" acting technique taught at Lee Strasberg's Actors' Studio, which Kazan cofounded. He went abroad to make *Man on a Tightrope* (1953), the story of a circus troupe's escape from behind the Iron Curtain. Kazan picked up yet another nomination for *East of Eden* (1955), in which he did for newcomer James Dean what he'd done for Brando a few years earlier. The wildly provocative BABY DOLL (1956), *A Face in the Crowd* (1957), *Wild River* (1960) and *Splendor in the Grass* (1961) all bore Kazan's stamp of quality but didn't quite match his earlier successes.

KOLM-VELTEE, WALTER (1910–1999)

Austrian-born Kolm-Veltee was a screenwriter and director at different times in his career. He was lauded for a brilliantly presented *Franz Schubert* (1953), as well as for *Don Giovanni* (1955), known as DON JUAN in the United States, where it generated controversy.

KOZINTSEV, GRIGORI (1905–1973)

Born in Czarist Russia, in Kiev, Kozintsev filmed dramas in the U.S.S.R. and was among the founders of the notorious Factory of Eccentric Actors, an improvisational group. In collaboration with director Leonid Trauberg, he made such films as the satirical *New Babylon* (1931) and the *Maxim* trilogy, which included THE YOUTH OF MAXIM (1935), released in the United States. Kozintsev and Trauberg continued to work together until after they produced the postwar drama *Plain People* (1945), banned by the Russian government until the mid-1950s. Kozintsev later became known for making faithful film adaptations of classic literature, including *Hamlet* (1964), *King Lear* (1970) and *Don Quixote* (1957).

KUBRICK, STANLEY (1928–1999)

Few directors have inspired as much controversy as this unpredictable artist and innovative craftsman, whose output spans many film genres. After making a couple of documentary shorts, he obtained financing for a short feature, *Fear and Desire* (1953), which he wrote, produced, edited and photographed. Kirk Douglas was impressed enough by Kubrick to place him in the director's chair for the literate costume epic SPARTACUS (for which Douglas was executive producer and star), replacing Anthony Mann. Director and star clashed mightily during production; the experience reportedly was so unpleasant for Kubrick that he left Hollywood altogether and moved to London. His first project there was an intermittently successful screen version of Nabokov's novel LOLITA (1962). His next projects were *2001: A Space Odyssey* (1970) and the cynical, savagely violent *A Clockwork Orange* (1971). Kubrick's Vietnam war film, *Full Metal Jacket* (1987), uses history to depict Kubrick's own increasing disillusionment with the human race. Controversy stalked Kubrick to the end with his posthumously released film *Eyes Wide Shut.*

LA CAVA, GREGORY (1892–1952)

A former cartoonist, Gregory La Cava entered films during World War I as an animator for Walter Lantz on such animated films as *The Katzenjammer Kids* (1916). La Cava switched to live-action films in the 1920s and began directing two-reel shorts. Graduating to features, he gained a reputation as a surefooted comedy director, responsible for such classics as *My Man Godfrey* (1936), THE AFFAIRS OF CELLINI (1934) and *She Married Her Boss* (1935). La Cava was equally proficient in other genres as well, turning out the drama *Stage Door* (1937) and the bizarre political fantasy *Gabriel Over the White House* (1933).

LOSEY, JOSEPH (1909–1984)

Losey started making short documentary films for the Rockefeller (educational) Foundation in 1938. In Hollywood, he managed to imbue mainstream movies with provocative social commentary, as in his debut, *The Boy With Green Hair* (1948); *M* (1951); and *The Lawless* (1950), which explores the plight of Chicano fruit pickers in Southern California. The political climate of the times was destined to affect Losey's life and career. Screenwriter Leo Townsend, while testifying before the House Un-American Activities Committee, was the first to publicly name Losey and his wife, Louise, as Communist Party members. In order to avoid a subpoena to testify before

HUAC, Losey fled to England in 1951 and was summarily blacklisted. He spent the next decade directing mostly forgettable features. Losey came into his own with *The Servant* (1963), a symbolic psychological drama focusing on the complex involvement between a young, upper-class man and his manservant. Even as the blacklist era faded, Losey chose not to return to America.

LYNE, ADRIAN (1941–)

Born in Peterborough, England, the director began by making commercials for television and later used the same quick-cut techniques in such films as *Foxes* (1980) and *Flashdance* (1983). Lyne clashed creatively with editors in the making of *9 1/2 Weeks* (1986) and *Fatal Attraction* (1987): As he tried to retain the erotic content of the films, editors sought to trim the material to achieve an "R" rating. In both cases, theater audiences saw a different version of the film from the one released on videotape. In LOLITA (1997), although Lyne showed restraint in handling the subject matter, the film was banned from the United States for two years.

MACHATY, GUSTAV (1901–1963)

Born in Prague, then a part of the Austro-Hungarian Empire, Machaty filmed in Czechoslovakia, France and the United States. He made his acting debut at the age of 17 after playing the piano in movie theaters. He moved to Hollywood in the early 1920s, where he worked for four years as an apprentice director for D. W. Griffith and Erich Von Stroheim, before returning to Prague to make his own films. Machaty gained international renown for two erotically charged films, *Erotikon* (1929) and *Extase* (ECSTASY, 1933).

MALLE, LOUIS (1932–1995)

One of France's most acclaimed directors, Malle rose to prominence during the New Wave and maintained a remarkably consistent critical and popular reputation with an extraordinary variety of films. He served as an assistant to the explorer Jacques Cousteau, with whom he codirected the Academy Award-winning documentary *The Silent World* (1956), then made short films on his own and assisted Robert Bresson on *A Man Escaped* (1956) before writing and directing his first feature, *Frantic* (1957), starring a young Jeanne Moreau. Malle's next film, THE LOVERS (1958), caused a scandal with its beautifully photographed and highly sensual depiction of a bored wife's extramarital affair. It firmly established Malle's reputation and made Moreau a star. Malle also faced controversy with the 1965 release of *VIVA MARIA!*. He also directed the documentaries *Humain, trop humain* (1972) and *Place de la Republique* (1973) and contributed the "William Wilson" episode to the 1968 *Spirits of the Dead*.

MANN, DELBERT (1920–)

Born in Lawrence, Kansas, Mann worked as a salesman, bomber pilot and theatrical director before starting in live television in the early 1950s. His handling of the original Goodyear Playhouse production of *Marty* (1953) led him to direct the Academy Award-winning film version of the teleplay. Mann then directed the film version of DESIRE UNDER THE ELMS (1958) and such film hits as *Separate Tables* (1958), *Lover Come Back* (1961) and *That Touch of Mink* (1962). He later returned to television when film work became scarce and made such made-for-television films as *David Copperfield* (1970), *Jane Eyre* (1971) and *All Quiet on the Western Front* (1979).

MARESCO, FRANCO (1958–)

Italian-born Maresco began working with Daniele Cipri in 1986 filming short videos and experimental programs for a television station in Palermo. In 1990, Maresco worked on *Blob Cinico TV* and, with Cipri, won the Aristophanes prize for satirical comedy. The codirector of three feature films to date, beginning with *Lo zio di Brooklyn* (*The Uncle from Brooklyn*, 1995), Maresco created a sensation when Italy banned the 1998 *Toto che visse due volte* (TOTO WHO LIVED TWICE).

MARKS, GEORGE HARRISON (1926–1997)

Marks began his film career as a photographer of nudes and producer of "naturist" films, such as *As Nature Intended* (1961) and PATTERN OF EVIL (in conjunction with wife Pamela Green) in 1967. After the relaxation of U.K. film censorship made his soft porn uncommercial, because feature films too began to contain soft-porn sequences. Marks turned to hardcore, illegal material with such titles as *Naughty Schoolgirls' Revenge* (1994) and *The Spanking Game* (1993).

MARQUAND, CHRISTIAN (1927–2000)

Marquand was an actor and director born in Marseilles, France, who appeared in 49 films during the 1940s, 1950s and 1960s, including *And God Created Woman* (1957) and *Behold a Pale Horse* (1964), as well as the cult classic *I Spit on Your Grave* (1959). Marquand directed only two films, *Of Flesh and Blood* (1962) and the cameo-filled satire CANDY (1968).

MCCAREY, THOMAS LEO (1898–1969)

Hired by Hal Roach Studios in 1923, McCarey initially wrote gags for "Our Gang" and studio stars and then produced and directed shorts, including a string of inventive and hilarious two-reelers. He was instrumental in teaming and establishing the comic foundation for Stan Laurel and Oliver Hardy. In the sound era McCarey ventured into feature-film directing, and after some tentative early efforts he got the knack. He subsequently worked with many of the greatest comedic talents in movies, including Eddie Cantor and W. C. Fields, and directed Mae West in BELLE OF THE NINETIES (1934). He also directed such films as *Going My Way* (1944) and *The Bells of St. Mary's* (1945), as well as *An Affair to Remember* (1957), which gained new life when it became a prominent part of the plot in the 1995 film *Sleepless in Seattle*. A fierce anticommunist, McCarey was involved in many squabbles with fellow filmmakers during hearings held by the House Un-American Activities Committee in the 1950s. In 1952 he wrote and directed *My Son John*, a hysterical portrait of one American family's struggle against the influence of the Red Menace, which earned him an Academy Award nomination for best screenplay.

METZGER, RADLEY (1929–)

Renowned as a stylish director of erotica in the late 1960s and early 1970s, Metzger worked as an assistant director immediately upon graduating college. He first attracted attention by importing and distributing I, A WOMAN (1966), a Scandinavian sex film that was enormously successful. His visually sumptuous films, which include THERESE AND ISABELLE (1968), CARMEN, BABY (1967) and *Camille 2000* (1969), were mostly shot in Europe. Metzger turned to hard-core (under the pseudonym Henry Paris) in the 1970s, and added his distinguished touch to such films as *The Private Afternoons of Pamela Mann* (1975), NAKED CAME THE STRANGER (1975) and *The Opening of Misty Beethoven* (1976). Later he directed a relatively distinguished international cast (including Wendy Hiller, Edward Fox, Olivia Hussey, Honor Blackman, Daniel Massey and Carol Lynley) in the fourth screen version of *The Cat and the Canary* (1979).

MEYER, RUSS (1922–)

The son of a policeman and a nurse, Russ Meyer made amateur films in his early teens. He spent World War II in Europe as a newsreel cameraman and then became a professional photographer, shooting some of the earliest *Playboy* centerfolds. He made his film debut in 1959 with *The Immoral Mr. Teas*, the first soft-core sex film to make a profit, which led to a string of self-financed films that gradually became more bizarre, violent and cartoonish. In 1964–65 he established his style in a "Gothic period" quartet of black-and-white films, including the controversial LORNA (1964). After *Faster, Pussycat! Kill! Kill!* (1965), and the blockbuster VIXEN (1968), he was hired by 20th Century-Fox to make studio pictures. The first of these, *Beyond the Valley of the Dolls* (1970), was an enormous hit, but after the lukewarm reception of the uncharacteristically serious *The Seven Minutes* (1972), Meyer returned to the sex-and-violence films that made his name, culminating in the delirious *Beneath the Valley of the Ultravixens* (1979).

MILESTONE, LEWIS (1895–1980)

Born Lewis Milstein in Chisineau, Ukraine, Russia, Milestone directed drama, comedy, adventure and crime films. He came to the United States as a teenager and served in the U.S. Army during World War I as an assistant director of army training films. After military service, he went to Hollywood, where he worked as a film editor and then directed his first feature, *Seven Sinners* (1925), for Howard Hughes. He made other films, but he gained major recognition for his 1930 adaptation of the novel ALL QUIET ON THE WESTERN FRONT, which he followed with several lighthearted comedies. During the 1940s, Milestone directed more serious subjects that reflect the war era, including *The Purple Heart* (1944) and THE NORTH STAR (1943), which would later be brutally edited and rereleased as *Armored Attack*. Milestone's last directorial effort was *Mutiny on the Bounty* (1962).

MOMPLET, ANTONIO (1899–1974)

Momplet directed 25 films, including AMOK (1944).

MONTGOMERY, FRANK (1870–1944)

Montgomery directed two films, *The Rajah's Sacrifice* (1915) and THE SPIRIT OF '76 (1917).

NEWFIELD, SAM (1899–1964)

Born Samuel Neufeld in New York City, he began directing comedy shorts, such as *Jane's Engagement Party* and *Jane's Predicament*, in 1926. In 1933, Newfield directed the full-length features *Reform Girl* and *Important Witness*, and he quickly found a niche with the growing B-movie production houses of the era. He began to direct so many films that he adopted two pseudonyms, Sherman Scott and Peter Stewart. Newfield, who directed nearly 200 films between 1933 and 1958, was a specialist in fast, low-budget filmmaking, relying heavily on stock footage that he repeatedly reused. His output includes western, crime and action films, as well as serious drama (*I Accuse My Parents*, 1945) and such exploitation films as WILD WEED (1949) and horror or science-fiction vehicles (*The Monster Maker*, 1944; *Dead Men Walk*, 1943; *The Lost Continent*, 1951). Made quickly and always within a low budget, Newfield's films were popular program fillers, and his science fiction and horror films are among the most familiar in the B-movie category. *The Terror of Tiny Town* (1938) has become a cult classic.

NICHOLS, MIKE (1931–   )

Nichols made a highly acclaimed film directorial debut with his 1966 adaptation of a successful theatrical property, *Who's Afraid of Virginia Woolf?* His next film, *The Graduate* (1967), gave voice to the disaffected youth of the late 1960s; it was enormously successful and influential and earned Nichols an Academy Award. He took on riskier and more offbeat projects in the years that followed. The Joseph Heller adaptation *Catch-22* (1970) was highly anticipated but proved to be a critical disappointment. Nichols captured attention with CARNAL KNOWLEDGE (1971), a startlingly frank examination of sexual mores, attitudes and behavior. He spent most of the next decade working with great success on Broadway and directing an occasional television special. Nichols's films since the 1980s have not been groundbreakers, but they are marked by intelligence, top-quality craftsmanship and high-caliber talent on both sides of the camera.

NOSSECK, MAX (1902–1972)

The German-born Nosseck left Europe when the Nazis rose to power; he relocated to Hollywood, where he directed several well-received crime dramas, some under the pseudonym Alexander M. Norris. Critics have praised *Dillinger* (1945) as a classic in the crime genre for its innovative use of expressionist techniques, although the atmospheric thriller *The Brighton Strangler* (1956) is usually identified as his best film for its effective use of atmosphere. The versatile Nosseck also directed *Black Beauty* (1946), which was his biggest hit, although he never considered this film representative of his style, and THE GARDEN OF EDEN (1954).

OPHÜLS, MAX (1902–1957)

Born Max Oppenheimer in Saarbrücken, Germany, Ophüls began his career as a stage actor and director in the 1920s. In the early 1930s, he discovered the movie world in France and began to work as an assistant director for Anatole Litvak. In 1941 he immigrated to the United States where he worked for a period of 10 years before he went back to France in 1950, where he directed the controversial LA RONDE.

PARKER, NORTON S. (1920–1969)

American-born Parker directed only two films, THE ROAD TO RUIN (1928) and *The Pace That Kills* (1928). He is better known as a screenwriter for numerous western films, including *The Last Stand* (1936), *Young Bill Hickock* (1940) and *Rio Grande Raiders* (1946) and for his dialogue contributions to the quasi-documentary film *Tundra* (1936).

PERKINS, HAROLD (N.D.)

A director of soft-core pornography, Perkins's films include *Help Wanted, Female* (1968), THE ALIMONY LOVERS (1968), *Baby Vickie* (1969), *Baby Rosemary* (1975), *Hot Lunch* (1978) and *Working Girls* (1985).

PREMINGER, OTTO (1906–1986)

A former law student, onetime assistant to Viennese stage director Max Reinhardt and a juvenile lead on the stage, Preminger directed a few German films before coming to America to stage plays on Broadway. He was spotted as a potential film director and signed by 20th Century-Fox in 1936. His 1949 work, *Whirlpool*, was one of Preminger's first pieces to cause controversy within the political climate of the period. Suspended from directing, the imposing-looking Preminger could always turn to acting. In 1953 Preminger turned independent producer, working outside the studio system for most of the remainder of his career. His first film was the disarmingly benign romantic comedy THE MOON IS BLUE. Preminger's own films ran an amazing gamut of subjects and treatments, from the all-black musicals *Carmen Jones* (1954) and *Porgy and Bess* (1959) to THE MAN WITH THE GOLDEN ARM (1955), a harrowing portrait of drug addiction starring Frank Sinatra. In subsequent years Preminger made increasingly bigger, more ambitious projects, like the sizzling courtroom melodrama ANATOMY OF A MURDER (1959). In his later years, Preminger directed a number of other films, including the controversial BUNNY LAKE IS MISSING (1965).

RAPPAPORT, GERBERT (1908–1983)

Also known as Herbert Rappaport, the Russian-born filmmaker is best known in his native country for musical films and those that have ballet at their core. His earliest directorial effort was PROFESSOR MAMLOCK (1938), which was followed by several controversial films such as *This Is the Enemy* (1942) and *Song Over Moscow* (1963), in addition to *Krug* (1972). He relocated to Estonia at the end of World War II and worked primarily there until his death.

RUGGLES, WESLEY (1889–1972)

After a brief acting career as a Keystone Kop and a supporting player at Essanay with Charles Chaplin's company, the American-born Ruggles directed nearly 60 films, many of them romantic comedies starring some of the top stars of the 1930s and 1940s. He directed Clark Gable and Carole Lombard in *No Man of Her Own* (1932), their only film together, as well as Bing Crosby in his first singing film role, in *College Humor* (1933). Ruggles also directed Mae West in I'M NO ANGEL (1933), and he had the daring to include stripper Sally Rand's fandance in *Bolero* (1934). Ruggles's film *Cimarron* (1931) won the Academy Award for best picture.

RYDELL, MARK (1934–)

A former jazz musician and actor, Rydell won critical kudos for his first directorial effort, THE FOX (1968), and has enjoyed considerable success ever since. The picaresque Faulkner story *The Reivers* (1969) remains one of his best films, and *Cinderella Liberty* (1973) told its offbeat love story with refreshing candor and credibility. He moved in front of the camera to play vicious gangster Marty Augustine for Robert Altman in *The Long Goodbye* (1973) and has been persuaded to act again from time to time, as in *Punchline* (1988) and *Havana* (1990).

SHERMAN, LOWELL (1885–1934)

Lowell Sherman was one of several respected silent-film actors who later turned to directing. Critics believe that, had he lived longer, he would have been a great director. He directed early films for Constance Bennett and Katharine Hepburn. Shortly before his death in 1934, Sherman directed the controversial SHE DONE HIM WRONG, starring Mae West.

SJÖBERG, ALF (1903–1980)

Sjöberg developed an early career in live theater as a director of the Royal Dramatic Theatre in Stockholm, from 1927 through the 1930s. With *Den Starkaste* in 1929, he began to direct films on a sporadic basis. In 1942, *Himlaspelet* (*The Road to Heaven*) earned him international acclaim, and Sjöberg began to act as a mentor to a young screenwriter named Ingmar Bergman, who would later identify Sjöberg as his primary inspiration. Sjöberg directed his best work in the 1950s, with works such as *Fröken Julie* (*Miss Julie*, 1951) and *Barabbas* (1953) earning him international acclaim.

SJÖMAN, VILGOT (1924–)

Controversial Swedish film director made famous for his depictions of outrageous sexual acts. While the majority of his films, including 491 (1964) and I AM CURIOUS— YELLOW (1968), are known primarily for their shock value, Sjöman is viewed as one of the pioneers of cinematic sexual expression.

SMITH, JACK (1931–1989)

Mainly a playwright and an actor in underground films of the 1960s and 1970s, Smith often appeared in the films of Andy Warhol and other avant-garde New York filmmakers. He directed the offbeat *Buzzards Over Baghdad* (1951) and in 1963 directed FLAMING CREATURES, an homage to actress Maria Montez starring an all-transvestite cast. Made for $300, using black and white film stock, the film was labeled obscene and confiscated when it first appeared and did not reappear until the late 1970s.

STANTON, RICHARD (N.D.)

Between 1914 and 1925, this American silent film director helmed 24 films, including THE SPY (1914), *Love Thief* (1917), *Rough and Ready* (1918) and *McGuire of the Mounted* (1923).

SPIELBERG, STEVEN (1946–   )

Spielberg is probably the most commercially influential director of all time, with a handful of his films listed among the top-ten moneymakers of all time. A moviemaker since boyhood, Spielberg launched his professional career at Universal Studios. His films, such as *E.T., the Extra-Terrestrial* (1982) and *Jurassic Park* (1993), combine a childlike sense of wonder with the expert craftsman's sure-handed manipulation of the medium's most effective and evocative image-making techniques. As Spielberg has matured as a filmmaker, he has also taken on larger issues. In 1993, Spielberg presented the world with SCHINDLER'S LIST. The director, an American Jew, had never dealt with his ethnicity on film before, and critics, who never thought him capable of anything so dark or wrenching, were impressed by the results. Spielberg once again delved into the topic of ethnic relations in 1997 with the release of AMISTAD. In 1998, he filmed the World War II epic *Saving Private Ryan*.

STERNBERG, JOSEF VON (1894–1969)

As an apprentice filmmaker, from around 1916 to the early 1920s, Sternberg developed a lasting contempt for most of the directors and producers for whom he worked, because he was sure that he could improve on their product. For the next few years, he struggled for recognition. His commercial breakthrough was *Underworld* (1927), the prototypical Hollywood gangster film; behind the scenes, Sternberg successfully battled Ben Hecht, the writer, for creative control. With *The Last Command* (1928), starring the equally strong-willed Emil Jannings, Sternberg began a period of almost a decade as one of the most celebrated artists of world cinema. Both his film career and his personal life were transformed in the making of THE BLUE ANGEL (1930). Von Sternberg went on to produce a number of other films, including the controversial 1932 classic BLONDE VENUS.

STONE, OLIVER (1946–   )

This controversial filmmaker blends a flamboyant style with passionate, issue-oriented storytelling. His first feature was *Seizure* (1974), a Canadian shocker with a cast full of cult favorites. Stone placed his focus on the subject of Vietnam and won an Oscar as best director for the emotionally wrenching *Born on the Fourth of July* (1989). Some critics, however, began to accuse him of being mired in the sixties, an impression that he reinforced with *The Doors* (1991) and *JFK* (also 1991), which gained instant notoriety for its examination of Jim Garrison and the various conspiracy theories surrounding the assassination of John F. Kennedy. Stone made a sharp turn to dark comedy in NATURAL BORN KILLERS (1994). Stone has also produced or coproduced such films as *Reversal of Fortune* and *Blue Steel* (both 1990), *Iron Maze* (1991), *South Central* and *Zebrahead* (both 1992), *The Joy Luck Club* (1993), *The New Age* (1994) and the 1993 television miniseries *Wild Palms*.

TENNANT, ANDY (?–   )

Tennant began his career as a dancer and soon turned to acting. After a modest success in front of the camera, Tennant began writing screenplays and directing movies. Beginning with television programs, Tennant worked his way through the ranks to direct made-for-television movies and finally to direct feature films on the silver screen. Among his more popular works are *Fools Rush In* (1997) and ANNA AND THE KING (1999).

TOLAND, GREGG (1904–1948)

American-born Toland was the most sought-after cinematographer in the film industry in the 1930s, as well as the most influential and innovative cinematographer of the sound era. He won an Academy Award for cinematography in *Wuthering Heights* (1939) and was nominated in that category for five additional times. Toland's major advance in sound film production was his invention of a soundproof camera housing that blocked the sound of winding film from the recording equipment. He was praised for his innovative work in deep-focus photography and techniques that added clarity and detail to filmed scenes. His innovative work with Orson Welles on *Citizen Kane* (1941) led Welles to place Toland's name alongside his own in the closing credits, but the sole effort for which Toland received credit as director is DECEMBER 7TH (1943).

VADIM, ROGER (1928–2000)

Vadim was a New Wave director at least as well known for his romantic liaisons with his female stars as for the films in which he directed them. A former stage actor and journalist, he burst upon the international cinema scene with the sexually charged AND GOD CREATED WOMAN (1956), which catapulted his then-wife Brigitte Bardot to worldwide fame. He enjoyed international notoriety when he directed his second wife, Jane Fonda, in the sexy comic strip adaptation *Barbarella* (1968). He made an effective Hollywood debut with the sexy black comedy *Pretty Maids All in a Row* (1971), but it was to be his only American film of note. He wrote a 1975 autobiography, *Memoirs of the Devil*, and a 1987 memoir modestly titled *Bardot, Deneuve, Fonda: My Life With the Three Most Beautiful Women in the World*.

VERHOEVEN, PAUL (1938–   )

This creator of violent, big-budget crowd pleasers got his filmmaking start as a documentarian for the Royal Dutch Navy. After working for Dutch television he took his first feature assignment, *Business Is Business* (1971). His second film, the sexy *Turkish Delight* (1973), starred fellow countryman and frequent collaborator Rutger Hauer, who also played the lead in *Keetje Tippel* (1975). Verhoeven's initial stateside exposure—with the release here of the war saga *Soldier of Orange* (1979), the erotic thriller *The Fourth Man* (also 1979) and the sexually frank *Spetters* (1980)—won him contracts to direct films in America. His next three films were all ultraviolent fantasies: *Flesh + Blood* (1985), *RoboCop* (1987) and *Total Recall* (1990). These action melodramas confirmed Verhoeven's talent as a creator of muscular, fast-moving films. But the box-office success of BASIC INSTINCT (1992), a gritty, sexually explicit thriller, allowed Verhoeven the freedom to pick and choose his next projects. His next was *Showgirls* (1995).

WADLEIGH, MICHAEL (N.D.)

American director Wadleigh also worked in the film industry as a cinematographer, editor and screenwriter in drama, comedy, experimental and avant-garde films. In addition to directing the documentary WOODSTOCK (1970), he served as cinematographer on *Who's That Knocking on My Door?* (1968), *My Girlfriend's Wedding* (1969) and other films, as well as director and screenwriter on *Wolfen* (1981).

WARHOL, ANDY (1928—1987)

Andy Warhol started directing films in 1963, although the word *directing* is used loosely because most of his early work such as BLUE MOVIE (1969) consisted simply of pointing the camera at something (a man asleep, the Empire State Building) and leaving it running, often for hours. His films gradually grew more sophisticated, with scripts and soundtracks, although they were generally performed by assorted groupies with little acting talent. After a near-fatal shooting by an unstable fan, Warhol retired from direct involvement in filmmaking, and under former assistant Paul Morrissey the Warhol films became increasingly commercial. Warhol died in 1987 after a routine gall-bladder operation.

WEST, ROLAND (1885–1952)

Roland West directed over 10 films from 1916 to 1931, including the banned film, ALIBI. West's films are often crime thrillers, which take place at night and are visually influenced by German Expressionism. This is exactly the same combination of conditions that gave rise to *film noir* in the 1940s. Unlike the approach of *noir*, West's films tend not to have a single viewpoint character or characters through whose eyes most of the action is seen, as with the great majority of noirs. Instead, his movies have an omniscient narrating camera, allowing the audience to see the action as a participant.

WHALE, JAMES (1883–1957)

Theater work took Whale to the London stage, then Broadway, and later to a contract with Paramount. He began his contribution to the horror film genre with his move to Universal, directing Boris Karloff in FRANKENSTEIN (1931), followed by *The Invisible Man* (1933) and *Bride of Frankenstein* (1935). As horror movies lost favor, he retreated to a more private and hedonistic life that included painting and all-male pool parties. After suffering several strokes, Whale committed suicide by drowning in his pool.

WILBUR, CRANE (1886–1973)

The American-born Wilbur began work as a stage actor and then entered the movies as the costar of *The Perils of Pauline* (1914) and other serial films of the silent era. He directed several films, including the controversial TOMORROW'S CHILDREN (1934), and then moved on to become a screenwriter. Despite his early success as an actor, most of his 57 film credits are as the screenwriter of such classic crime thrillers as *House of Wax* (1953), *The Bat* (1959) and *Mysterious Island* (1961).

WILLIS, GORDON (1931–)

Renowned as a cinematographer, Willis's only directorial attempt was the critical and box-office failure WINDOWS (1980). Before directing the film, Willis had already worked with Woody Allen on such films as *Annie Hall* (1977), *Interiors* (1978), *Manhattan* (1979) and *Stardust Memories* (1980), as well on *The Godfather* (1972), *The Godfather Part II* (1974) and *All the President's Men* (1976), among 22 films. After the failed directorial effort, Willis returned to working as a cinematographer, making 15 more films and winning cinematography awards for *Zelig* (1983) and *The Godfather Part III* (1990).

REASONS FOR BANNING

The films dicussed in this book are listed below according to the charges or court decisions made in efforts to ban or censor them. Several films appear in two categories because of the different grounds upon which they were censored. For the purpose of clarification, "social" reasons for banning, censoring and challenging films include protests against the mention or inclusion of racism, miscegenation, abortion, birth control, cohabitation, drug use, homosexuality and childbirth. Violent content rates its own category because it has so often been the reason a film has been banned.

SEXUAL CONTENT

The Affairs of Cellini
The Alimony Lovers
Anatomy of a Murder
And God Created Woman
Baby Doll
Behind the Green Door
The Blue Angel
Blue Movie
Body of a Female
Caligula
Candy
Carmen, Baby
Carnal Knowledge
Un Chant d'Amour
Cindy and Donna
Deep Throat
Desire Under the Elms
The Devil in Miss Jones
Ecstasy
Emmanuelle
491
The Flaming Creatures
The Game of Love
Garden of Eden

I, A Woman
I Am Curious—Yellow
The Killing of Sister George
Lady Chatterley's Lover
The Last Picture Show
Last Tango in Paris
Lolita
Lorna
The Lovers
Miss Julie
The Moon Is Blue
The Newcomers
The Outlaw
Pattern of Evil
La Ronde
Room at the Top
The Sex Lure
She Done Him Wrong
A Stranger Knocks
A Streetcar Named Desire
Therese and Isabelle
The Virgin Spring
Viva Maria!
The Vixen
Women of the World

SOCIAL CONTENT

The Alibi
Amok
Ann Vickers
Baby Face
Basic Instinct
Belle of the Nineties
The Birth of a Baby
The Birth of a Nation
Blonde Venus
The Brand
Un Chant d'Amour
The Connection
Cruising
Curly
Damaged Goods
Dressed to Kill
The Easiest Way
A Farewell to Arms
Flaming Creatures
The Fox
Freaks
I'm No Angel
The James Boys in Missouri
The Killing of Sister George
M
The Man with the Golden Arm
Mom and Dad
The Naked Truth
Native Son
Never on Sunday
Of Human Bondage
Red-Headed Woman
Reefer Madness
The Road to Ruin
She Done Him Wrong
Spartacus
The Tin Drum
Titicut Follies
Tomorrow's Children

Whirlpool
Wild Weed
Woodstock

POLITICAL CONTENT

All Quiet on the Western Front
Anna and the King
The Bedford Incident
Blockade
December 7th
The Great Dictator
The North Star
October
The Ordeal
Revenge at Daybreak
Schindler's List
Spain in Flames
The Spirit of '76
The Spy
The Youth of Maxim

RELIGIOUS CONTENT

La Dolce Vita
The Exorcist
The Last Temptation of Christ
Martin Luther
The Miracle
Monty Python's Life of Brian
The Sign of the Cross
Toto Who Lived Twice

VIOLENT CONTENT

The Alibi
Amistad
Dressed to Kill
Frankenstein
Natural Born Killers
Scarface: The Shame of a Nation

125 ADDITIONAL CHALLENGED, CENSORED AND BANNED FILMS

The following list of films is extensive but not exhaustive, yet its length provides a clearer view of how broad the reach of the censor has been. In some cases, movie industry regulators or city and state censorship boards excised portions of a film before approving its exhibition, while in other cases exhibition of a film was banned entirely. Many of the films are known to the general viewing public in only their censored forms, but recent restorations have given film buffs the opportunity to see the original. Too many films will never be seen in their original form because the portions excised were destroyed and no master copies kept. Whatever the case, the loss of each frame from each movie represents a measure of freedom lost.

The Adventures of Tarzan (1922)
The Advocate (1994)
American Pie (1999)
The Amorous Adventures of Moll Flanders (1965)
Angel Heart (1987)
The Battle Cry of Peace (1915)
Below the Dead Line (1929)
The Bicycle Thief (1948)
Biography of a Bachelor Girl (1935)
Blade Runner (1982)
Bliss (1997)
Body of Evidence (1993)
Bonnie and Clyde (1967)
Boogie Nights (1997)
Brewster's Millions (1945)
The Bride of Frankenstein (1935)
Cape Fear (1962)
Cat on a Hot Tin Roof (1958)
The Chapman Report (1962)

The Children's Hour (1962)
A Clockwork Orange (1971)
Close Encounters of the Third Kind (1977)
Coming Soon (1999)
Convention City (1933)
Crimes of Passion (1984)
Crouching Tiger, Hidden Dragon (2000)
The Crying Game (1992)
Damage (1992)
Darling (1965)
Dead End (1937)
Detective Story (1951)
Eraserhead (1978)
Eyes Wide Shut (1999)
Fanny Hill (1964)
Fingers (1978)
Flesh (1968)
The French Line (1954)
From Here to Eternity (1953)

The Fugitive Kind (1960)
Golden Boy *(1938)*
Gone with the Wind (1939)
Hail Mary (1985)
Happy Anniversary (1959)
Hard Target (1993)
Hot Pepper (1933)
Human Wreckage (1923)
If You Love This Planet (1982)
Imitation of Life (1934)
Inherit the Wind (1960)
Island of Lost Souls (1933)
John Barleycorn (1914)
Johnny Got His Gun (1971)
Kids (1995)
King of Kings (1927)
Kindling (1915)
Klondike Annie (1936)
Legend (1985)
The Libertine (1969)
The Life of Vergie Winters (1934)
Little Caesar (1930)
Lost Boundaries (1949)
The Lover (1992)
Loving Couples (1965)
Madame du Barry *(1934)*
*The Magic Garden of Stanley
    Sweetheart* *(1970)*
The Mask of Fu Manchu (1932)
The Merry Widow (1934)
Midnight Cowboy (1969)
Missing (1982)
Mondo Cane (1962)
Mystery of the Wax Museum (1933)
Night After Night (1932)
9 1/2 Weeks (1986)
Our Boys (1981)
Paris Is Burning (1991)
The Pawnbroker (1965)
The Phantom of the Opera (1925)
Pink Flamingos (1972)
Poetic Justice (1993)
Poison (1991)

The Postman Always Rings Twice (1981)
The Priest (1995)
The Prince of Egypt (1998)
The Program (1993)
Psycho (1960)
The Racket (1928)
Rampage (1963)
Rebel Without a Cause (1955)
Reservoir Dogs (1992)
RoboCop (1987)
Rules of Engagement (1999)
Salo: 120 Days of Sodom (1975)
Saturday Night and Sunday Morning
    (1960)
Scarface (1983)
Scorpio Rising (1966)
The Servant (1963)
She's Gotta Have It (1986)
The Silence of the Lambs (1991)
Sliver (1993)
Snuff (1976)
Soldier Blue (1970)
The Southerner (1945)
South Park: Bigger, Longer & Uncut
    (1999)
Storm Center (1956)
The Story of Temple Drake (1933)
Straw Dogs (1971)
Summer of Sam (1999)
Taxi Driver (1976)
Tea and Sympathy (1956)
Too Hot to Handle (1960)
To the Victor (1948)
Tropic of Cancer (1970)
Two-Faced Woman (1941)
Walk on the Wild Side (1962)
Where Eagles Dare (1969)
Where Love Has Gone (1964)
Who's Afraid of Virginia Woolf? (1966)
The Wild Bunch (1969)
Woman of the Dunes (1964)
The Year of Living Dangerously (1982)
The Year of the Dragon (1985)

INDEX

Note: **Boldface** page numbers indicate the primary discussion of a film.

**** (film) 59

A

ABC Interstate Theatres v. State 124
Abramson, Ivan 327
ACLU *See* American Civil Liberties Union
ACT UP, on *Basic Instinct* 34
adult entertainment, zoning for 120–121
adultery
  in *Amok* 15–16
  in *And God Created Woman* 19–21
  in *Ann Vickers* 23–26
  in *Baby Doll* 26–29
  in *Baby Face* 29–33
  in *Blonde Venus* 53–55
  in *The Brand* 61–63
  in *I Am Curious–Yellow* 150–153
  in *Lady Chatterley's Lover* vi, 163–167
  in *Lorna* 186–187
  in *The Lovers* 187–190
  in *The Moon Is Blue* 210
  in *Naked Came the Stranger* 213
  in *Whirlpool* 305
advertisements
  for *Baby Doll* 28–29
  for *Belle of the Nineties* 42
  for *Dressed to Kill* 113
  for *Freaks* 139
  for *The Killing of Sister George* 163
  for *Lolita* (1962) 180, 181
  for *Natural Born Killers* 219
  for *Of Human Bondage* 231
  for *The Outlaw* 235–236
  for *Reefer Madness* 249

  for *The Sex Lure* 267–268
  for *Wild Weed* 306
The Affairs of Cellini **2–3**
  censorship history of 2–3
  summary of 2
L'Âge d'Or **3–5**
  censorship history of 5
  summary of 4
Aimée, Anouk 102
Alabama
  I Am Curious–Yellow in 152
  Last Tango in Paris in 171–172
  The Last Temptation of Christ in 177
  The Moon Is Blue in 211
  The Road to Ruin in 253–254
Albany, Georgia, *Carnal Knowledge* in 76
Alberts v. California 142, 143
Aldrich, Robert 163, 327
Aleksandrov, Grigori 229
Algren, Nelson 193
Ali Baba and the 40 Thieves 129
The Alibi **5–8**
  censorship history of 7
  summary of 6
The Alimony Lovers **8–9**
  censorship history of 8–9
  summary of 8
Allegret, Marc 165, 327
Allen, Woody 346
All Quiet on the Western Front (film) **9–12**
  censorship history of 11–12
  summary of 10–11
All Quiet on the Western Front (Remarque) 10
American Civil Liberties Union (ACLU)
  on *Baby Doll* 29

  on freedom of opinion *vs.* moral censorship v
  on *God of Vengeance* v
  on LOD boycotts 29
  on *The Tin Drum* 291–292
American Committee on Maternal Welfare 43–44
American Family Organization 175
American Legion 278
American Mini Theatres, Young v. 121
Amistad **12–15**
  censorship history of 14–15
  summary of 13–14
Amok **15–16**
  censorship history of 16
  summary of 15–16
"Der Amokläufer" (Zweig) 15
Amore 198
Anatomy of a Murder **17–18**
  censorship history of 18
  summary of 17–18
Ancono, Leonardo 298
Anderson, John, Jr. 38, 64
Anderson, Robert 327
And God Created Woman **19–21**
  censorship history of 20–21
  summary of 19–20
Andy Warhol Garrick Theater 59
Angelica, Mother 176
Anger, Kenneth 78
Anna and the King **21–23**
  censorship history of 22–23
  summary of 22
Anna and the King of Siam 22, 23
Ann Vickers (film) **23–26**

censorship history of
24–26
summary of 24
Ann Vickers (Lewis) 24, 25
Anslinger, Harry J. 249
Arizona
I Am Curious–Yellow in
153
The Last Picture Show in
168–169
Armored Attack 227
Arsan, Emmanuelle (pseudo-
nym) 119
Asch, Sholem v
Ashe, Penelope (pseudonym)
212–213
Asher, E. M. 110
*Associates & Aldrich Co. v.
Times Mirror Co.* 163
Astin, John 69
Atlanta, Georgia
Caligula in 67–68
Freaks in 140
Never on Sunday in 223
Room at the Top in
257–258
She Done Him Wrong in
271
*Attorney General, Memoirs of a
Woman of Pleasure v.*
151–152
Aurora, Illinois, *Baby Doll* in
29
Australia, *She Done Him
Wrong* in 271
Austria, *She Done Him Wrong*
in 271
Autant-Lara, Claude
327–328
Aznavour, Charles 69

B

Babb, Howard W. 204–205
Baby Doll **26–29**
censorship history of
28–29
summary of 27–28
Baby Face **29–33**
censorship history of
31–32
summary of 30–31
*Bainbridge v. City of Minneapo-
lis* 50
Bakker, Jim 176
Balderston, John L. 110, 111
Baldwin, Roger v
Baltimore, Maryland
Of Human Bondage in
231–232

Revenge at Daybreak in
251–252
Bardot, Brigitte 19, 301, 345
Barker, Reginald 328
Barrett, Wilson 272
Basic Instinct **33–37**
censorship history of
34–36
summary of 33–34
Battleship Potemkin 228, 229
BBS Productions, Inc. v. Purcell
169
Beach, Rex 62
Beasley, Ronnie Jack
219–220
Beasley v. State 219–220
Beatty, Marion 38, 64
Beauchamp, Catherine 251
Beaudine, William 328
The Bedford Incident **37–39**
censorship history of
38–39, 64
summary of 37–38
Behind the Green Door **39–41**
censorship history of 40
summary of 39–40
Belgium, *Flaming Creatures* in
131
Bell, George 233
Bell, Ivan Film Productions v.
268
*Bell, Life Photo Film Corpora-
tion v.* 233
Belle of the Nineties **41–43**
censorship history of
42–43
summary of 41–42
Benham, Robert 220
Bennett, Marion T. 227
Bennett, Richard 90, 328
Berger, Rea 328
Bergman, Ingmar 328–329,
343
Bertolucci, Bernardo vii, 171,
298, 329
*Bethel College & Seminary,
Sisam v.* 291
Bhumibol, King of Thailand
23
Bilgrey, Felix 142–143, 153,
251
Binford, Lloyd 89
Birmingham, Alabama
The Moon Is Blue in 211
The Road to Ruin in
253–254
The Birth of a Baby **43–46**
censorship history of
44–45
summary of 43–44

The Birth of a Nation **46–51**
censorship history of x,
48–50
summary of 46–48
Black, Gregory 57
Black, Hugo 166
Blades, John 184
Blatty, William Peter 122
Le Blé en herbe (Colette) 141
Block, Jake 161
Blockade **51–53**
censorship history of
52–53
summary of 51–52
Block v. City of Chicago 161
Blonde Venus **53–56**
censorship history of
54–55
summary of 53–54
The Blue Angel **56–58**
censorship history of
57–58
summary of 56–57
Blue Movie **58–60**
censorship history of 59
summary of 58–59
*Board of Censors of City of
Memphis, United Artists
Corporation v.* 89
*Board of Regents, Trans-Lux
Distributing Corporation v.*
283–284
Body of a Female **60–61**
censorship history of 61
summary of 60–61
Bogdanovich, Peter 167, 329
Bonheur, Gaston 164
Borzage, Frank 329
Boston, Massachusetts
The Birth of a Nation in
49
Caligula in 67
Deep Throat in 96
The Exorcist in 123
I, A Woman in 148
I Am Curious–Yellow in
153
The Lovers in 188–189
Boston After Dark (Rossell)
310
Bouras, James 73
*Bowsher, North American Com-
mittee to Aid Spanish
Democracy v.* 275
Boyd, Malcolm 257
The Brand **61–63**
censorship history of
62–63
summary of 62

Brando, Marlon 69, 171, 336
Brass, Tinto 329
Breen, Joseph xi
  on *The Affairs of Cellini* 3
  on *All Quiet on the Western
    Front* 12
  on *Ann Vickers* 25
  on *Baby Face* 31, 32
  on *Belle of the Nineties* 42
  on *Blonde Venus* 55
  on *A Farewell to Arms* 128
  on *The Great Dictator* 147
  on *Idiot's Delight* 155–156
  on *Lady Chatterley's Lover*
    164–165
  on *The Moon Is Blue* 210
  on *Of Human Bondage*
    231, 232
  on *The Outlaw* 235
  on *Red-Headed Woman*
    247
  on *She Done Him Wrong*
    271
  on *The Sign of the Cross*
    274
  on *A Streetcar Named
    Desire* 286, 287
*Brennan, Public Welfare Pic-
  tures Corporation v.* 215
Brennan, William J. 215
Brennan, William J., Jr. 77,
  82–83, 132
Brewster, Harris 300
Brieux, Eugène 90
Brigham Young University
  Amistad at 15
  Schindler's List at 266
Bright, Bill 175
Bright, D. J. 236
British Columbia, *Dracula* in
  111
Broder, James 76
Broderick, Vincent L. 67
Brooks v. City of Birmingham
  254
Brown, Clarence 330
Browning, Tod 138,
  139–140, 330
Brownlow, Kevin 91
Brynner, Yul 22
Buchanan, Pat 176
Bunny Lake Is Missing **63–65**
  censorship history of 38,
    64
  summary of 63–64
Buñuel, Luis 3–5
El Burlador De Sevilla
  (Molina) 106
Burstyn, Joseph vi, 199–200

Burstyn v. Wilson vi, xi, 200,
  240
Burton, Richard 69
Butler v. Michigan 99
Butterfield 8 222
Byers, Patsy 220–221
Byrne, Eureka Productions v.
  118
Byrne, Karalexis v. 153
Byrne, Mayer v. 305

C

Cain, David 149
Cain v. Kentucky 149
California
  Behind the Green Door in
    40
  The Birth of a Nation in
    50
  The Blue Angel in 58
  Un Chant d'Amour in
    79–80
  Cruising in 87
  Dressed to Kill in 114
  Emmanuelle in 120–121
  Frankenstein in 136
  Freaks in 140
  *The Last Temptation of
    Christ* in 176, 177
  obscenity in, definition of
    80
  The Outlaw in 235
  The Spirit of '76 in 280
  Windows in 308
California, Alberts v. 142, 143
California, Miller v. 40, 59, 66
Caligula **65–68**
  censorship history of
    66–68
  summary of 65–66
Cambridge, Massachusetts,
  Miss Julie in 202–203
Camelots du Roi, Les 5
Camfield, Michael 291, 292
Campbell, William J. 107
Campus Crusade for Christ
  175
Canada
  Basic Instinct in 36
  Dracula in 111
  Toto Who Lived Twice in
    298–299
Candide (Voltaire) 69
Candy (film) **68–71**
  censorship history of
    70–71
  summary of 69–70
Candy (Southern and Hoffen-
  berg) 69

Capellani, Albert 330
*Capitol Enterprises v. City of
  Chicago* 206
Capri Cinema, Redlich v. 40,
  225
CARA *See* Code and Rating
  Administration
Caracciolo, R. 155–156
Carmen (film) vi
Carmen (Mérimée) 71
Carmen, Baby **71–74**
  censorship history of
    72–74
  summary of 71–72
Carmen, Ira 205, 258
Carnal Knowledge **74–77**
  censorship history of vii,
    76–77
  summary of 75–76
Carrie 333
Carrington, Elaine S. 6
Carrus, Ben 220
Cartwright, James H. 161
Catholic Church
  on *The Affairs of Cellini* 3
  on *L'Âge d'Or* 5
  on *Ann Vickers* 25
  on *Basic Instinct* 36
  on *Belle of the Nineties* 42
  on *Caligula* 67
  on *La Dolce Vita* 103
  films recommended by xi
  on *The Last Temptation of
    Christ* 176
  in *Martin Luther* 195–196
  on *The Miracle* 198–199
  on *The Moon Is Blue* 211
  on *Power of the Cross* xi
  on *The Sign of the Cross*
    273–274
Catholic Legion of Decency
  (LOD)
  on *The Affairs of Cellini* 3
  on *And God Created
    Woman* 20
  on *Ann Vickers* 26
  on *Baby Doll* 28–29
  on *Baby Face* 32
  on *Belle of the Nineties* 42
  on *The Birth of a Baby* 44
  on *Blockade* 52
  on *Blonde Venus* 55
  on *La Dolce Vita* 103, 104
  on *Ecstasy* 118
  establishment of xi, 270,
    271, 274
  on *A Farewell to Arms* 128
  on foreign films 104, 118
  on *Frankenstein* 136–137

on *I'm No Angel* 159
influence of xi, 3, 181
on *Lolita* 181
on *The Man With the
Golden Arm* 193
on *Martin Luther* 196
on *The Miracle* 199
on *The Moon Is Blue* 210
on *Of Human Bondage*
231–232
on *The Outlaw* 236
on *Red-Headed Woman*
247
revision of classifications
of 104
on *Spartacus* 277–278
on *A Streetcar Named
Desire* 286–287
Cavara, Paolo 330
CDL *See* Citizens for Decent
Literature
Cellini, Benvenuto 2
The Celluloid Closet (Russo)
86, 134
Censored Hollywood (Miller)
31
Ceplair, Larry 52
Chalker, Ray 34
Chambers, Marilyn 40
Un Chant d'Amour **77–81**
censorship history of
79–80
summary of 78–79
Chaplin, Charles
The Great Dictator vi,
145–147
profile of 330–331
Chatri, Prince of Thailand
23
*Chicago, Fox Film Corporation
v.* 282
Chicago, Illinois
The Affairs of Cellini in 3
The Alibi in 7
Anatomy of a Murder in
18
Belle of the Nineties in 43
The Birth of a Nation in
49
Body of a Female in 61
censorship ordinance of
61, 98–99, 107,
160–161
Desire Under the Elms in
98–99
La Dolce Vita in 105
Don Juan in 106–108
The Game of Love in
141–143

Garden of Eden in 145
I, A Woman in 148
The James Boys in Missouri
in 160–161
LOD influence in xi, 3
The Lovers in 189
Martin Luther in 196
Mom and Dad in 205–206
Night Rider in 160
Of Human Bondage in 232
prior restraint in v–vi,
106–108
The Spirit of '76 in 280
The Spy in 281–282
*Chicago, Zenith International
Film Corp. v.* 189
Child Pornography Preven-
tion Act 184
*Christenberry, Grove Press Inc.
v.* 166
Christian fundamentalists, on
*The Last Temptation of
Christ* 174–177
Christie, Al 331
Church of the Way 175
Cincinnati, Ohio, *The Birth of
a Baby* in 44
Cindy and Donna **81–83**
censorship history of
81–83
summary of 81
Cipri, Daniele 331, 339
Citizens for Decent Litera-
ture (CDL) 132
*City of Atlanta v. Lopert Pic-
tures Corporation* 223
City of Birmingham, Brooks v.
254
City of Chicago, Block v. 161
*City of Chicago, Capitol Enter-
prises v.* 206
*City of Chicago, Excelsior Pic-
tures Corp. v.* 145
*City of Chicago, Paramount
Film Distributing Corpora-
tion v.* 98–99
*City of Chicago, Times Film
Corp. v.* (on *Don Juan*)
106–108
*City of Chicago, Times Film
Corp. v.* (on *The Game of
Love*) 142
*City of Chicago v. Fox Film
Corporation* 282
*City of Fort Worth, Janus
Films, Inc. v.* 300–301
City of Jackson, Hosey v. 70–71
City of Jackson, McGrew v.
134–135

*City of Kansas City, Dickinson
Operating Co. v.* 145
*City of Minneapolis, Bainbridge
v.* 50
Civiletti, Benjamin R. 66
Clancy, James 132
The Clansman (Dixon) 46
Clark, Norman 232
Clark, Tom C. vi, 107
Clarke, Shirley 331
*Classic Pictures v. Department
of Education* 217
Clayton, Henry D. 254
Clayton, Jack 331
Coalition Against Violence
Against Women 308
Coburn, James 69
Coburn, Tom viii
Cocteau, Jean 78, 334
Code and Rating Administra-
tion (CARA) xii
Cohen, Emanuel 127
Colbert, Claudette 273
Colette 141
Colorado
Behind the Green Door in
40
The Birth of a Nation in
49
1900 in vii
*Commercial Pictures Corpora-
tion v. Regents* 255–256
Committee for World Mus-
lim Solidarity 266
Commonwealth v. Moniz 145
Commonwealth v. Wiseman
293–294
Connecticut
I, A Woman in 148
The Killing of Sister George
in 163
Spain in Flames in 275
The Connection **83–84**
censorship history of 84
summary of 83–84
Connection Company, Regents v.
84
*Connection Company v. Regents
of the University of the State
of New York* 84
Conway, Jack 331–332
Cooper, Merian 25
*Cooper v. Sheriff of Jefferson
County* 152
Copeland, Aaron 226
Cousteau, Jacques 338
Covina, California,
Emmanuelle in 120–121
Cowan, C. V. 58

Cox, Harold 134
Coxe, Tench C. 76
Cromwell, John 332
Crosby, Angela 220
Crosby v. State 220
Crouch, Paul 176
Cruising **84–88**
    censorship history of
        86–87
    summary of 85–86
Cullen v. Grove Press, Inc. 294
Cummins, Samuel 117
Curley **88–90**
    censorship history of vi,
        89–90
    summary of 88–89
Cusack, Teitel Film Corp. v. 61
Cusack v. Teitel Film Corp. 61
Customs Act 67

D

Dalí, Salvador 4, 5
Dallas, Interstate Circuit v.
    303
Dallas, Texas, *Viva Maria!* in
    vii, 302–303
Damaged Goods **90–92**
    censorship history of
        91–92
    summary of 90–91
The Dame in the Kimono (Leff
    and Simmons) 100
Damiano, Gerald 95, 99
Dangerfield, Rodney 219
D'Arcy, David 208
Dassin, Jules 222, 332
Davies, Diana 226
Davis, Marjorie Ross 111
Davis, Will S. 332
A Day in the Country 199
Days of Glory 226
Dayton, Ohio, *The Lovers* in
    189
Deane, Hamilton 110, 111
December 7th **92–94**
    censorship history of 94
    summary of 93
Deep Throat **94–97**
    censorship history of
        95–97
    summary of 95
de Grazia, Edward 7, 40, 68,
    70, 96, 125, 232
DeMille, Cecil B. 127, 272,
    273, 332
Denver, Colorado, *The Birth
    of a Nation* in 49
De Palma, Brian 112–113,
    333

*Department of Education, Clas-
    sic Pictures v.* 217
Deren, Maya 78
Dershowitz, Alan 97
Desire Under the Elms (film)
    97–99
    censorship history of
        98–99
    summary of 98
Desire Under the Elms
    (O'Neill) 98
Desmond, Charles S. 144
*Desperate Decision See Revenge
    at Daybreak*
Detroit, Michigan
    The Virgin Spring in 300
    The Youth of Maxim in
        312
The Devil in Miss Jones
    99–101
    censorship history of
        100–101
    summary of 99–100
*The Devil's Weed See Wild
    Weed*
Diamond Lil (West) 269, 270
*Dickinson Operating Co. v. City
    of Kansas City* 145
Dieterle, Wilhelm 333
Dietrich, Marlene 56, 57, 58
Diller, Barry 175
directors, profiles of 327–346
District of Columbia, *The
    Exorcist* in 123
Dixon, Thomas, Jr. 46
La Dolce Vita **101–105**
    censorship history of
        103–105
    summary of 102–103
Don Giovanni (Mozart) 106
Don Juan **105–108**
    censorship history of
        106–108
    summary of 106
Do the Right Thing 291
Dos Passos, John 275
Douglas, Kirk 337
Douglas, Michael 35
Douglas, William O. 132,
    166, 240–241, 255–256
Dracula **108–111**
    censorship history of
        110–111
    summary of 109–110
Dressed to Kill **112–114**
    censorship history of
        112–114
    summary of 112
drive-in theaters 72–74

drug use
    in *The Connection* 83–84
    in *The Man With the
        Golden Arm*
        192–195
    in *Reefer Madness*
        248–250
    in *Wild Weed* 305–306
due process clause 240, 283
Dugan, George 257
Duggan v. Guild Theatre 289
Dunn, James 336
Dunne, Irene 22
Dunne, Philip 240
Dwyer, William L. 73

E

Earles, Harry 138
The Easiest Way **114–116**
    censorship history of
        115–116
    summary of 115
Ebert, Roger 171, 176, 287
Ecstasy **116–118**
    censorship history of
        117–118
    summary of 116–117
Edmondson, Sarah 220
educational films
    The Birth of a Baby **43–46**
    Damaged Goods **90–92**
    Mom and Dad 203–206
    The Naked Truth 214–216
Edwards, James, Jr. 176
Egypt, *Schindler's List* in 265
Eisenstein, Sergei M.
    228–229
Ekberg, Anita 102
Elam, Harry 67
*Embassy Pictures Corporation v.
    Hudson* 309–310
Emmanuelle (Arsan) 119
Emmanuelle (film) **118–121**
    censorship history of
        119–121
    summary of 119
England *See* United King-
    dom
Englund, Steven 52
Espionage Act 280
Estonia, *Idiot's Delight* in 156
Eszterhaus, Joe 35–36
Eureka Productions v. Byrne
    118
Evangelical Sisterhood, on
    *The Last Temptation of
    Christ* 175
Evans Theatre Corp. v. Slaton
    153

Excelsior Pictures Corp. v. City of Chicago 145
Excelsior Pictures Corp. v. Regents of the University of the State of New York 144
The Exorcist (Blatty) 122, 123
The Exorcist (film) **121–124**
  censorship history of 123–124
  summary of 122–123
Eyes Wide Shut viii

F

Falwell, Jerry 176
A Farewell to Arms **125–129**
  censorship history of 127–128
  summary of 126
federal government, and *Deep Throat* 95–97
Federal Motion Picture Commission x
Feinstein, Diane 87
Fellini, Federico
  La Dolce Vita 101–105
  The Miracle 197
  profile of 333
FidoNet bulletin board 208
Fielding, Hughes Tool Co. v. 236
Film Entitled 491, United States v. 125
Findlay, Michael 333
Finland
  I, A Woman in 148
  She Done Him Wrong in 271
  Wild Weed in 306
The Firebrand (Meredyth) 2
Fisher, Harry M. 7
Fisher, James B. 11–12
Fiske, D. W. 159
Flaming Creatures **129–133**
  censorship history of 130–132
  summary of 129–130
Fleishman, Stanley 73, 153
Fletcher, Norman S. 220
Florey, Robert 327
Florida, *Last Tango in Paris* in 172
Floyd, K. Gordon Murray Productions, Inc. v. 258
Forbes, Elliott 204
Ford, John 93, 94, 334
Fording, Landau v. 80
foreign films, ratings for 104–105, 118
Fornicon See Pattern of Evil

Fortas, Abe 132
Fort Worth, Texas, *The Virgin Spring* in 300–301
491 (film) **124–125**
  censorship history of 125
  summary of 124–125
491 (Göorling) 124
The Fox (film) **133–135**
  censorship history of 134–135
  summary of 133–134
The Fox (Lawrence) 133
Fox Film Corporation, City of Chicago v. 282
Fox Film Corporation v. Chicago 282
Foy Productions v. Graves 296–297
France
  Candy in 70
  Emmanuelle in 120
  Idiot's Delight in 156
Francine, Frances 129–130
Franco, Francisco 51, 52
Frankenstein **135–138**
  censorship history of 136–137
  summary of 135–136
Freaks **138–141**
  censorship history of 139–140
  summary of 138–139
Freedman, Ronald L. 251–252
Freedman, State v. 252
Freedman v. Maryland 9, 38, 251–252
Freeman, Richard vii, 291
Friedkin, William 86–87, 334
Friedman, Leon 153
Friendly, Henry 151
Fuck See Blue Movie
Fundamentalist-Baptist Tabernacle 175
fundamentalists, on *The Last Temptation of Christ* 174–177
The Fury 333

G

The Game of Love **141–143**
  censorship history of 141–143
  summary of 141
Garbo, Greta 330
Garden of Eden **143–145**
  censorship history of 144–145
  summary of 143–144

Gardner, Gerald 118
Garner, Peggy Ann 336
Gasnier, Louis J. 334
Gebhart, Elwood L. 104–105
Gelling v. State of Texas 240–241
Genet, Jean 78, 80, 334
Genina, Augusto 327
Georgia
  Behind the Green Door in 40
  Caligula in 67–68
  Carnal Knowledge in 76
  Freaks in 140
  I Am Curious–Yellow in 153
  Monty Python's Life of Brian in 208
  Natural Born Killers in 219–220
  Never on Sunday in 223
  obscenity statute of 76
  Room at the Top in 257–258
  She Done Him Wrong in 271
Germany
  The Blue Angel in 57, 58
  The Great Dictator and 147
  Monty Python's Life of Brian in 208
Gershwin, Ira 226
Gevaras, State v. 189
Gide, André 327
Gielgud, John 66
Gilliam, Christine Smith 223, 258
The Girl Who Did Not Care See The Sex Lure
Giscard d'Estaing, Valéry 120
Glynn, Theodore A. 123
God of Vengeance (Asch) v
Goldbeck, Willis 138
Goldstein, Robert 280–281
Goldstein v. United States 280–281
Goldwyn, Samuel 226
Göorling, Lars 124
Gottfried, Martin 134
government, federal, and *Deep Throat* 95–97
Grass, Günter vii, 290
Graves, Foy Productions v. 296–297
Great Britain *See* United Kingdom
The Great Dictator **145–147**

censorship history of vi,
146–147
summary of 146
Greece, *The Last Temptation of
Christ* in 173
Greek Orthodox Church, on
*The Last Temptation of
Christ* 173
Green, Alfred E. 335
Green, Jonathan 40
Gregory, Herbert B. 45
Griffith, D. W.
The Birth of a Nation x,
46–51
profile of 335
Grimaldi, Alberto 171
Grisham, John 220
Grove Press, Inc., Cullen v.
294
*Grove Press Inc. v. Christen-
berry* 166
*Grove Press v. Maryland Board
of Censors* 153
Grutman, Roy 97
Guccione, Bob 66, 68
Guild Theatre, Duggan v. 289
*Gulf State Theatres of
Louisiana v. Richardson*
172
Guthmann, Edward 87
Gyssling, George 147

H
Hacker, Andrew 67
Halliwell, Leslie 257
*Hallmark Productions v. Penn-
sylvania Board of Censors*
307
Hammond, Hall 9
Harlan, John Marshall 294
Harris, James B. 181, 335
Harrison, George 207
Harrison, Rex 22
Hart, William S. 328
Hartford, Connecticut, *I, A
Woman* in 148
Hattiesburg, Mississippi, *The
Exorcist* in 123–124
Haverhill, Massachusetts, *I'm
No Angel* in 159
Hawks, Howard 260–261
Hays, Will xi
on *Ann Vickers* 25–26
A Farewell to Arms and
127
on *Idiot's Delight* 155
on *Lady Chatterley's Lover*
164
The Outlaw and 235

Red-Headed Woman and
246
on *Scarface: The Shame of a
Nation* 261
on *She Done Him Wrong*
270
Hays Production Code vii,
55
Hearst, William Randolph
227, 249
Hecht, Ben 259, 261
Heffernan, Christopher J.
296
Heins, Marjorie 176, 291
Heller, People v. 59
Heller v. New York 59
Hellman, Lillian 51, 226,
227
Hemingway, Ernest 51, 126,
275
Henderson, Floyd M. 89
Herbert, F. Hugh 209
Herron, Frederick 155
*Hewitt v. Maryland State
Board of Censors* 9
Hill, James P. 16, 296
Hill, Morton 152
Hitchcock, Alfred 112
Hitler, Adolf 58, 146–147
Hoffenberg, Mason 69
Holly Springs, Mississippi,
The Moon Is Blue in 211
Hollywood Presbyterian
Church 175
Holm, Siv (pseudonym) 148
homosexuality
in *Basic Instinct* 33–36
in *Un Chant d'Amour*
78–80
in *Cruising* 85–87
in *Dressed to Kill*
112–114
in *The Fox* 133–135
in *The Killing of Sister
George* 162–163
in *Naked Came the
Stranger* 213
in *The Sign of the Cross*
273
in *Spartacus* 277–278
in *Therese and Isabelle*
288–289
in *Windows* 308
Hooker, Minter S. 205
Hosey v. City of Jackson 70–71
House Un-American Activi-
ties Committee (HUAC)
xii, 222, 227, 239, 278
Howard, Clifford 245

HUAC *See* House Un-
American Activities Com-
mittee
*Hudson, Embassy Pictures Cor-
poration v.* 309–310
Hugenberg, Alfred 57
Hughes, Howard
The Outlaw 235–236
profile of 335
*Scarface: The Shame of a
Nation* 260–262
Hughes Tool Co. v. Fielding
236
*Hughes Tool Co. v. Motion Pic-
ture Assn. of America* 236
Hunt, Guy 177
Huston, John 69

I
I, A Man 59
I, A Woman **147–150**
censorship history of
148–149
summary of 148
I, A Woman II 148
I, A Woman III 148
I Am Curious–Yellow **150–153**
censorship history of
151–153
summary of 150–151
"*I Am Curious–Yellow," United
States v.* 151–152
IATSE *See* International
Alliance of Theatrical
Stage Employees
Idiot's Delight **154–157**
censorship history of
155–156
summary of 154–155
IFIDA *See* International Film
Importers and Distribu-
tors Association
Illinois
The Affairs of Cellini in 3
The Alibi in 7
Anatomy of a Murder in
18
Baby Doll in 29
Belle of the Nineties in 43
The Birth of a Nation in
49
Body of a Female in 61
Desire Under the Elms in
98–99
La Dolce Vita in 105
Don Juan in 106–108
The Game of Love in
141–143
Garden of Eden in 145

I, A Woman in 148
The James Boys in Missouri in 160–161
The Lovers in 189
Martin Luther in 196
Mom and Dad in 205–206
Night Rider in 160
Of Human Bondage in 232
The Spirit of '76 in 280
The Spy in 281–282
immorality
    state censorship laws on xi–xii
    Supreme Court on 201
The Immoral Mr. Teas 103
I'm No Angel **157–159**
    censorship history of 158–159
    summary of 157–158
Ince, Thomas 328
indecency, *vs.* obscenity 144
Indiana, *I, A Woman* in 148–149
Indianapolis, Indiana, *I, A Woman* in 148–149
Indonesia, *Schindler's List* in 265–266
Industrial Commission of Ohio, Mutual Film Corporation v. x, 191
Inspiration 244
International Alliance of Theatrical Stage Employees (IATSE) 52–53
International Film Importers and Distributors Association (IFIDA) 251
internet, *Monty Python's Life of Brian* on 208
Interstate Circuit v. Dallas 303
Ireland, *Monty Python's Life of Brian* in 208
It Ain't No Sin See Belle of the Nineties
Italian Film Festival in Toronto, Second Annual, *Toto Who Lived Twice* in 298–299
Italy
    La Dolce Vita in 104
    Ecstasy in 117
    A Farewell to Arms in 127
    and *Idiot's Delight* 155–156
    Last Tango in Paris in 171, 298
    The Miracle in 198–199
    Monty Python's Life of Brian in 208

Toto Who Lived Twice in 298
Ivan Film Productions v. Bell 268

J

Jackson, Mississippi
    Candy in 70
    The Fox in 134–135
Jacobellis, Nico 189, 190
Jacobellis, State v. 189
Jacobellis v. Ohio 151–152, 189–190
Jacobs, Kenneth 131
Jacobsen, Johan 335–336
Jacopetti, Gualtiero 336
Jaeckin, Just 336
Jamaica, *Amistad* in 14–15
The James Boys in Missouri **159–161**
    censorship history of 160–161
    summary of 160
Janus Films, Inc. v. City of Fort Worth 300–301
Japan, *The Great Dictator* in 147
Jenkins, Billy 76
Jesus Fellowship 172
La jeune folle (Beauchamp) 251
Jeunesses Patriotiques, Les 5
Jofroi 199
Johnson, Lyndon 132
Johnson, William A. 116
Johnston, Eric 181, 223
Jones, Terry 336
Jordan, *Schindler's List* in 265
Joseph Burstyn, Inc. v. Wilson 199–200
Joy, Jason
    on *All Quiet on the Western Front* 11
    on *Blonde Venus* 55
    on *The Blue Angel* 57–58
    on *Dracula* 110, 111
    Frankenstein and 137
    on *Red-Headed Woman* 246–247
    on *Scarface: The Shame of a Nation* 260, 262
    on *The Sign of the Cross* 273
Joyce, James v
The Joys of a Woman 120

K

K. Gordon Murray Productions, Inc. v. Floyd 258

Kael, Pauline 134, 162, 171
Kahane, B. B. 25–26
Kansas
    The Bedford Incident in 38–39
    The Birth of a Nation in 49
    Bunny Lake Is Missing in 64
    The Easiest Way in 115–116
    Frankenstein in 137
    March of Time in vi
    The Moon Is Blue in 211
Kansas, A Quantity of Copies of Books v. 149
Kansas City, Missouri, *Garden of Eden* in 145
Karalexis v. Byrne 153
Karloff, Boris 260
Kaufmann, Ephraim 233
Kazan, Elia 28, 285–287, 336
Kazantzakis, Nikos 173
Keneally, Thomas 264
Kenosha, Wisconsin
    Schindler's List in vii–viii
    Woodstock in 311
Kenton, Maxwell (pseudonym) 69
Kentucky
    Cindy and Donna in 81–83
    I, A Woman in 149
Kentucky, Cain v. 149
Kerr, Deborah 22
Kiesler, Hedy *See* Lamarr, Hedy
The Killing of Sister George **162–163**
    censorship history of 162–163
    summary of 162
The King and I 22, 23
King of Kings 89
Kingsley International 20–21
Koch, Ed 86
Kolm-Veltee, Walter 336
Kozintsev, Grigori 337
Kris 329
Kristel, Silvia 119
Kubrick, Stanley
    Eyes Wide Shut viii
    Lolita 178–183
    profile of 337
    Spartacus 277
Ku Klux Klan, in *The Birth of a Nation* x, 46–51
Kurten, Peter 191

L

La Cava, Gregory 337

Lady Chatterley's Lover (film) **163–167**

censorship history of vi, 164–166

summary of 164

Lady Chatterley's Lover (Lawrence) vi, 151, 164, 166

Laemmle, Carl, Jr.

Dracula 110, 111

on *A Farewell to Arms* 128

Frankenstein 135, 136–137

Lamarr, Hedy 117

Landau, Saul 79–80

Landau v. Fording 80

Lang, Fritz 191

Lara, Louise 327

Larsen, Ralph 45

Lasky, Jesse 127

The Last Picture Show (film) **167–169**

censorship history of 168–169

summary of 167–168

The Last Picture Show (McMurtry) 167

Last Tango in Paris **169–173**

censorship history of 171–172, 298

summary of 170–171

The Last Temptation of Christ (film) **173–178**

censorship history of 174–177

summary of 173–174

The Last Temptation of Christ (Kazantzakis) 173

law enforcement

portrayal in *The Alibi* 7

seizure by (*See* seizure)

Lawrence, D. H.

The Fox 133

Lady Chatterley's Lover vi, 151, 164, 166

Lawson, John Howard 51–52

Lebanon, *Schindler's List* in 265

Leduc, Violette 288

Leff, Leonard J. 100

The Leopard's Spots (Dixon) 46

Levinthal, Louis L. 275

lewdness, *vs.* obscenity 100–101

Lewis, Sinclair 24, 25

libraries vii

Last Tango in Paris in 172

The Last Temptation of Christ in 173

The Tin Drum in vii, 291

licensing standards, prior restraint through v, vii, 106–108, 252

Life (magazine), *The Birth of a Baby* and 45

Life of Brian, Monty Python's 206–209

Life Photo Film Corporation v. Bell 233

Like Water for Chocolate 291

Limphapayom, Thepmontree 23

Little, Thomas F. 181, 210

LOD *See* Catholic Legion of Decency

Lolita (1962 film) **178–182**

censorship history of 180–182

summary of 178–180

vs. 1997 version 182–183

Lolita (1997 film) **182–186**

censorship history of 183–185

summary of 182–183

Lolita (Nabokov) 178–179, 182–183

Londerholm, Robert 38, 64

Lopert Pictures Corporation, City of Atlanta v. 223

Lord, Daniel xi, 24–25, 271, 273–274

Lordi v. UA Theatres 152

Lorna **186–187**

censorship history of 187

summary of 186

Los Angeles, California

Freaks in 140

The Last Temptation of Christ in 176, 177

The Spirit of '76 in 280

Losey, Joseph 337–338

Louisiana

Last Tango in Paris in 172

The Last Temptation of Christ in 177

Natural Born Killers in 220–221

Scarface: The Shame of a Nation in 262

Love and Kisses to Censors Film Society 131

Lovelace, Linda 95

The Lovers **187–190**

censorship history of vii, 188–190

summary of 188

Ludwig, Curtis 73

Luther, Martin 195–196

Lynchburg, Virginia, *The Birth of a Baby* in 44–45

Lyne, Adrian 183, 184, 185, 338

Lyons, Charles 35

M

M (1931 film) 191

M (1951 film) **190–192**

censorship history of 166, 191–192

summary of 191

Machaty, Gustav 338

MacLeish, Archibald 51

Macy, Bob 292

Macy, Paul G. 159

"The Madness Lover" (Zweig) 15

Mahoney, Roger 36

Mailler, Norman 152

Malaysia, *Schindler's List* in 265

Malle, Louis

The Lovers vii, 187–190

profile of 338

Viva Maria! vii

Mamet, David 184

Mann, Delbert 338–339

The Man With the Golden Arm (Algren) 193

The Man With the Golden Arm (film) **192–195**

censorship history of 193–194

summary of 193

March of Time vi

Maresco, Franco 331, 339

marijuana

in *Reefer Madness* 248–250

in *Wild Weed* 305–306

Marijuana Tax Act 249

Markman, Joel 129–130

Marks, George Harrison 339

Marquand, Christian 339

Marshall, Texas, *Pinky* in 240–241

Marshall, Thurgood 82–83, 303

Martin Luther **195–197**

censorship history of 196

summary of 195–196

Martino, Nobile Giacomo di 127

Maryland

The Alimony Lovers in 8–9

censorship law in 8–9

La Dolce Vita in 105
Ecstasy in 118
I Am Curious–Yellow in 153
Lorna in 187
The Lovers in 188–189
The Man With the Golden Arm in 194
The Moon Is Blue in 211–212
Of Human Bondage in 231–232
Revenge at Daybreak in 251–252
A Stranger Knocks in 284
Maryland, Freedman v. 9, 38, 251–252
Maryland, Niemotko v. 303
Maryland, Wagonheim v. 153
Maryland Board of Censors, Grove Press v. 153
Maryland Board of Censors, United Artists Corporation v. 194
Maryland State Board of Censors, Hewitt v. 9
Maryland State Board of Censors, Trans-Lux Distributing Corp. v. 284
Maryland State Board of Censors, United Artists Corp. v. 212
Massachusetts
The Birth of a Nation in 49
Caligula in 67
Deep Throat in 96
Ecstasy in 118
The Exorcist in 123
Frankenstein in 137
Garden of Eden in 145
I, A Woman in 148
I Am Curious–Yellow in 153
I'm No Angel in 159
The Killing of Sister George in 163
The Lovers in 188–189
Miss Julie in 202–203
Red-Headed Woman in 247
Titicut Follies in 293–294
Massachusetts, Memoirs v. 70, 76
Massachusetts, Wiseman v. 294
Masterson, Patrick 210, 286
Matthau, Walter 69, 70
Maugham, W. Somerset 230
Mayer, Louis B. 140, 156

Mayer v. Byrne 305
McAuliffe, Hinson 67–68
McAuliffe, Penthouse v. 68
McCaffrey, Edward T. 199
McCarey, Thomas Leo 339
McDowell, Malcolm 66
McGrew v. City of Jackson 134–135
McLochlin, Bill 208
Medved, Michael 36
Mekas, Jonas 130–132
Memoirs v. Massachusetts 70, 76
Memoirs of a Woman of Pleasure v. Attorney General 151–152
Memphis, Tennessee
Curley in vi, 89–90
I, A Woman in 148
King of Kings in 89
The Lovers in 188–189
Mom and Dad in 205
The Moon Is Blue in 211
The Southerner in vi, 89
Women of the World in 309–310
Mercouri, Melina 332
Meredyth, Bess 2
Mérimée, Prosper 71
Merrifield, Charles W. 79
Metzger, Radley 72, 288, 339–340
Metzger v. Pearcy 149
Meyer, Russ 103, 186–187, 340
Michigan
The Devil in Miss Jones in 100–101
Flaming Creatures in 132
The Virgin Spring in 300
The Youth of Maxim in 312
Michigan, Butler v. 99
Mid-West Photo Play Corp. v. Miller 115–116
Milestone, Lewis 226, 227, 340
Miller, Frank 31, 50, 128, 189
Miller, Henry 151
Miller, Mid-West Photo Play Corp. v. 115–116
Miller v. California 40, 59, 66
Miller Standard 59, 66, 77
Miner, Julius H. 18
Minneapolis, Minnesota, *The Birth of a Nation* in 49–50
Minnesota, *The Birth of a Nation* in 49–50

Minnesota, Near v. 211
The Miracle **197–201**
censorship history of vi, xi, 198–201
summary of 197–198
Mishkin, Leo 162–163
Mission to Moscow 226
Mississippi
Candy in 70
The Exorcist in 123–124
The Fox in 134–135
The Moon Is Blue in 211
Miss Julie (film) **202–203**
censorship history of 202–203
summary of 202
Miss Julie (Strindberg) 202
Missouri
The Birth of a Nation in 49
Garden of Eden in 145
Modell, Marryam 63
Modern Times 146
Molina, Tirso de 106
Mom and Dad **203–206**
censorship history of 204–206
summary of 204
Momplet, Antonio 340
Moniz, Commonwealth v. 145
Montez, Maria 129
Montgomery, Alabama
Last Tango in Paris in 171–172
The Last Temptation of Christ in 177
Montgomery, Frank 340
Monty Python and the Holy Grail 207
Monty Python's Life of Brian **206–209**
censorship history of 207–208
summary of 207
The Moon Is Blue (film) **209–212**
censorship history of 210–212
summary of 209–210
The Moon Is Blue (Herbert) 209, 210
Morality in Media
on *Caligula* 66–67
on *Carmen, Baby* 73
on *I Am Curious–Yellow* 152, 153
Moral Majority, on *The Last Temptation of Christ* 175
Morato, Manuel 266

Moreau, Jeanne 338
Morganthau, Robert 132
Mormon Church, on *Amistad* 15
The Mothers of Liberty See The Ordeal
Motion Picture Assn. of America, Hughes Tool Co. v. 236
Motion Picture Association of America (MPAA)
on *Dressed to Kill* 113
on *The Exorcist* 123
on *Lolita* (1962) 181
on *Lolita* (1997) 184
on *Natural Born Killers* 219
on *Never on Sunday* 222–223
on *The Newcomers* 224
"nudies" and 103–104
on *The Outlaw* 235–236
rating system of vii, viii, xii
Motion Picture Control Act (Pennsylvania) 307
A Motion Picture Entitled Vixen, State ex rel Keating v. 304
Motion Picture Film The Spirit of '76, United States v. 280
Motion Picture Producers and Distributors Association (MPPDA) xi
Moulton, Thayer Amusement Corporation v. 242–243
Mozart, Wolfgang Amadeus 106
MPAA *See* Motion Picture Association of America
MPPDA *See* Motion Picture Producers and Distributors Association
Mummert, NGC Theatre Corp. v. 153
Mundelein, George W. 3
Munich, Germany, *Monty Python's Life of Brian* in 208
Munson, Audrey 244
Murphy, Robert E. 105
Mussolini, Benito 117, 146, 156
Mutual Film Corporation v. Industrial Commission of Ohio x, 191

N

NAACP *See* National Association for the Advancement of Colored People

Nabokov, Vladimir 178–179, 182–183
Naked Came the Stranger **212–214**
censorship history of 213–214
summary of 212–213
The Naked Truth **214–216**
censorship history of 215–216
summary of 214–215
National Association for the Advancement of Colored People (NAACP), on *The Birth of a Nation* 48
National Association of Theatre Owners, Inc. (NATO) 73
National Board of Censorship of Motion Pictures 48
National Board of Review of Motion Pictures x, 233
National Film Registry, *The Birth of a Nation* in 50
National Gay Task Force, on *Cruising* 86–87
National Organization for the Reform of Marijuana Laws (NORML) 250
National Organization for Women (NOW), on *Basic Instinct* 35
Native Son (film) **216–218**
censorship history of 217
summary of 216–217
Native Son (Wright) 216
NATO *See* National Association of Theatre Owners, Inc.
Natural Born Killers **218–221**
censorship history of 219–221
summary of 218–219
NC-17 rating xii
for *Last Tango in Paris* 171
for *Natural Born Killers* 219
Near v. Minnesota 211
Nebenzal, Seymour 191
Nebraska, *The Birth of a Baby* in 44
Never on Sunday **221–224**
censorship history of 222–223
summary of 222
Newark, New Jersey
Mom and Dad in 205
The Naked Truth in 215

The Newcomers **224–225**
censorship history of 224–225
summary of 224
Newfield, Sam 340–341
New Garrick Theater 58–59
New Jersey
I Am Curious–Yellow in 152
Mom and Dad in 205
The Moon Is Blue in 212
The Naked Truth in 215
The Outlaw in 236
Scarface: The Shame of a Nation in 262
New Orleans, Louisiana
The Last Temptation of Christ in 177
Scarface: The Shame of a Nation in 262
New York
Amok in 16
Baby Doll in 28
Behind the Green Door in 40
The Birth of a Baby in 45
The Birth of a Nation in 49
Blue Movie in 58–59
Caligula in 66–67
The Connection in 84
Cruising in 86–87
Deep Throat in 95
Dressed to Kill in 114
Ecstasy in 117–118
Education Law of 165
Flaming Creatures in 130–132
Frankenstein in 137
Freaks in 140
Garden of Eden in 144–145
Lady Chatterley's Lover in vi, 165–166
The Lovers in 188–189
The Miracle in vi, 199–200
Mom and Dad in 205
The Moon Is Blue in 211
The Naked Truth in 215–216
The Newcomers in 224–225
The Ordeal in 233
The Outlaw in 236
Purity in 244–245
La Ronde in 255–256
Scarface: The Shame of a Nation in 262

The Sex Lure in 267–268
A Stranger Knocks in
    283–284
Tomorrow's Children in
    296–297
The Virgin Spring in 300
Whirlpool in 305
Windows in 308
New York, Heller v. 59
New York, Redrup v. 149
New York City
    Baby Doll in 28
    Behind the Green Door in
        40
    The Birth of a Nation in 49
    Blue Movie in 58–59
    Caligula in 66–67
    Cruising in 86–87
    Deep Throat in 95
    Dressed to Kill in 114
    Flaming Creatures in
        130–132
    Frankenstein in 137
    The Newcomers in
        224–225
    The Ordeal in 233
    The Outlaw in 236
    Purity in 244–245
    The Sex Lure in 267–268
    Windows in 308
New York Film Festival, *Titi-
    cut Follies* at 293
*NGC Theatre Corp. v. Mum-
    mert* 153
Nichols, Mike vii, 341
Niemotko v. Maryland 303
Night Rider 160, 161
Nightstick (Carrington,
    Nugent, and Wray) 6
1900 vii
Nizer, Louis 73, 76, 153
Noailles, Charles de 5
NORML *See* National Orga-
    nization for the Reform of
    Marijuana Laws
North American Committee
    to Aid Spanish Democ-
    racy 275
*North American Committee to
    Aid Spanish Democracy v.
    Bowsher* 275
The North Star **225–228**
    censorship history of 227
    summary of 226
Norway, *Monty Python's Life of
    Brian* in 208
Nosseck, Max 341
NOW *See* National Organi-
    zation for Women

Nowell-Smith, Geoffrey 79
"nudies" 103–104
nudity
    in *Garden of Eden* 143–145
    in *The Last Picture Show*
        168–169
    vs. obscenity 144–145,
        168–169
    in *Purity* 243–245
Nugent, J. C. 6
nuisances, public, theaters as
    100–101
Nye, W. G. 49–50

O

obscenity
    exhibition site and 72–74
    vs. indecency 144
    in language 84
    vs. lewdness 100–101
    vs. nudity 144–145,
        168–169
    state censorship laws on
        xi–xii
    Supreme Court on xi–xii,
        59, 66, 76
    three-fold test for
        151–153
October **228–230**
    censorship history of 229
    summary of 228–229
Odets, Clifford 51
Of Human Bondage (film)
    230–232
    censorship history of
        231–232
    summary of 230–231
Of Human Bondage
    (Maugham) 230
Ohio
    *All Quiet on the Western
        Front* in 12
    The Birth of a Baby in 44
    The Birth of a Nation in
        49
    Carmen in vi
    The Lovers in 189–190
    M in 191–192
    The Moon Is Blue in 212
    Native Son in 217
    Red-Headed Woman in 247
    *Scarface: The Shame of a
        Nation* in 262
    She Done Him Wrong in
        271
    Spain in Flames in 275
    The Vixen in 304
Ohio, Jacobellis v. 151–152,
    189–190

Oklahoma
    *The Last Temptation of
        Christ* in 177
    The Tin Drum in vii,
        290–292
Oklahoma City, Oklahoma
    *The Last Temptation of
        Christ* in 177
    The Tin Drum in vii,
        291–292
Oklahoma State University
    177
Omaha, Nebraska, *The Birth
    of a Baby* in 44
*One Book Called "Ulysses,"
    United States v.* v
O'Neill, Eugene 98
*One Reel of Film, United States
    v.* 96
Ophüls, Max 341
The Ordeal **232–234**
    censorship history of 233
    summary of 232–233
Oshima, Nagisa 78
O'Toole, Peter 66
Otsep, Fyodor 15
The Outlaw **234–237**
    censorship history of
        235–236
    summary of 234–235
Oxnard, California, *The Birth
    of a Nation* in 50

P

Pagnol, Marcel 199
Palin, Michael 336
paparazzi 102
*Paramount Film Distributing
    Corporation v. City of
    Chicago* 98–99
Paramount Pictures, *The Last
    Temptation of Christ* and
    174–175
Parents and Teachers Associa-
    tion (PTA), on *Dracula*
    111
Parker, Norton S. 341–342
Parrish, Larry 96–97
Pasadena, California, *The
    Blue Angel* in 58
Pattern of Evil **237–238**
    censorship history of
        238
    summary of 237
Patterson, Rick 172
PCA *See* Production Code
    Administration
Pearcy, Metzger v. 149
Penland, Tim 175

Pennsylvania
And God Created Woman
in 20–21
The Birth of a Nation in
49
The Brand in 62–63
Carmen in vi
Ecstasy in 118
Frankenstein in 137
Motion Picture Control
Act of 307
The Outlaw in 236
Red-Headed Woman in
247
She Done Him Wrong in
270–271
Spain in Flames in 275
Therese and Isabelle in
288–289
Wild Weed in 306–307
*Pennsylvania Board of Censors,
Hallmark Productions v.*
307
Penthouse magazine 66,
67–68, 97
Penthouse v. McAuliffe 68
People v. Heller 59
*The Perfect Alibi See The
Alibi*
Perkins, Harold 342
Perlman, Nathan D. 45
Peru, *The Great Dictator* in
147
Philadelphia, Pennsylvania
And God Created Woman
in 20–21
The Outlaw in 236
Philippines, *Schindler's List* in
266
Phillips, George W., Jr.
79–80
Phoenix, Arizona, *The Last
Picture Show* in 168–169
Pickert, Schuman v. 312
Pinky **238–241**
censorship history of
239–241
summary of 239
Pinter, Harold 184
Pittsburgh, Pennsylvania, *The
Birth of a Nation* in 49
Plymouth, Massachusetts, *I'm
No Angel* in 159
Point de Lendemain (Vivant)
188
police force
portrayal in *The Alibi* 7
seizure by (*See* seizure)
political content

of *All Quiet on the Western
Front* 10–12
of *Anna and the King*
22–23
of *The Bedford Incident*
37–39
of *Blockade* 51–53
of *December 7th* 93–94
of *The Great Dictator*
146–147
of *The North Star*
226–227
of *October* 228–229
of *The Ordeal* 232–233
of *Professor Mamlock*
241–243
of *Revenge at Daybreak*
250–252
of *Schindler's List* 264–266
of *Spain in Flames*
274–276
of *The Spirit of '76*
279–281
of *The Spy* 281–282
of *The Youth of Maxim*
311–312
Pollack, Lester 153
Pompidou, Georges 120
Ponte, Lorenzo da 106
POPism (Warhol) 59
porno art 39, 100
pornography, *Deep Throat* as
94–97
Portugal, *Last Tango in Paris*
in 171
Power of the Cross xi
Preminger, Otto 18, 193,
210, 342
Pringle, Robert 120
prior restraint, Supreme
Court on v, vii, 106–108,
240–241, 252
Production Code Administration (PCA) xi
on *Baby Doll* 28
establishment of 247, 274
on *The Man With the
Golden Arm* 193–194
on *The Moon Is Blue* 209,
210
on *The Outlaw* 235–236
on *Red-Headed Woman*
247
revisions in 194
Professor Mamlock (film)
241–243
censorship history of
242–243
summary of 241–242

Professor Mamlock (Wolf) 241
propaganda films
Damaged Goods **90–92**
December 7th **92–94**
The North Star 225–228
Providence, Rhode Island
I, A Woman in 148
The Lovers in 188–189
Professor Mamlock in
242–243
Psycho 112
PTA *See* Parents and Teach-
ers Association
*Public Welfare Pictures Corpo-
ration v. Brennan* 215
Purcell, BBS Productions, Inc. v.
169
Purity **243–245**
censorship history of
244–245
summary of 243–244
Pye, Merrill 140

Q

Quality See Pinky
*A Quantity of Copies of Books v.
Kansas* 149
Queer Nation, on *Basic
Instinct* 34, 35
Quigley, Martin xi
on *Blockade* 52
on *Frankenstein* 136–137
and Hays Production
Code 32, 55
on *I'm No Angel* 158
Quillian, Joseph D. 223

R

racial relations/strife
in *Amistad* 13–15
in *The Birth of a Nation* x,
46–50
in *Curley* vi, 88–90
in *Native Son* 216–217
in *The Ordeal* 233
in *Pinky* 239–241
Ramos, Fidel 266
Ramsey, JonBenet 184
Rapf, Harry 140
Rappaport, Gerbert 342
rating system
for foreign films
104–105, 118
MPAA vii, viii, xii
Red-Headed Woman
245–247
censorship history of
246–247
summary of 245–246

Redlich v. Capri Cinema 40, 225
Redrup v. New York 149
Reed, John 228
Reefer Madness **248–250**
 censorship history of 249–250
 summary of 248–249
Reems, Harry 96–97
Regents, Commercial Pictures Corporation v. 255–256
Regents v. Connection Company 84
Regents of the University of the State of New York, Connection Company v. 84
Regents of the University of the State of New York, Excelsior Pictures Corp. v. 144
Regnoli, Piero 198–199
Regusis, Constantine 73
Rehnquiest, William H. 77
Reigen (Schnitzler) 254
religious content
 of *La Dolce Vita* 101–105
 of *The Exorcist* 121–124
 of *The Last Temptation of Christ* 173–178
 of *Martin Luther* 195–196
 of *The Miracle* vi, 197–201
 of *Monty Python's Life of Brian* 206–209
 of *The Sign of the Cross* 272–274
 of *Toto Who Lived Twice* 297–299
Remarque, Erich Maria 10
Rembar, Charles 164
Renoir, Jean 199
Rent-a-Gril 61
Revenge at Daybreak **250–252**
 censorship history of 9, 38, 251–252
 summary of 251
Reynolds, Robert 147
Rhode Island
 I, A Woman in 148
 The Lovers in 188–189
 Professor Mamlock in 242–243
Richardson, Gulf State Theatres of Louisiana v. 172
Richland, Washington, *Carmen, Baby* in 72–74
The Road to Ruin **253–254**
 censorship history of 253–254
 summary of 253

Robbins, Clarence Aaron 138
Robertson, Pat 176
Rollet-Andriane, Maryat 119
La Ronde **254–256**
 censorship history of 255–256
 summary of 254–255
Room at the Top **256–259**
 censorship history of 257–258
 summary of 257
Roosevelt, Eleanor 44
Rosenwein, Sam 73, 153
Rossell, Deac 310
Rossellini, Roberto vi, 197–201
Rosset, Barney 151
Rothschild, Philippe de 164
Roth v. United States 18, 74, 80, 144, 283
Rudolph, Francis J. 153
Ruggles, Wesley 342
Russell, Jane 235–236
Russia
 Emmanuelle in 120
 in *The North Star* 225–228
 in *October* 228–229
 in *The Youth of Maxim* 311–312
Russo, Vito 86, 134
Ruvin, Harvey 172
Rydell, Mark 343

S

sacrilege *See also* religious content
 in *The Miracle* vi, 199–200
 Supreme Court on vi, xi–xii, 200, 208
St. Louis, Missouri, *The Birth of a Nation* in 49
Saleh, Zainun Bin 265
Salt Lake City, Utah, *The Last Temptation of Christ* in 177
San Antonio, Texas, *The Last Temptation of Christ* in 175
San Francisco, California
 Un Chant d'Amour in 79–80
 Cruising in 87
 Dressed to Kill in 114
 Freaks in 140
 The Outlaw in 235

Santa Ana, California, *The Last Temptation of Christ* in 177
Santa Barbara, California, *Frankenstein* in 136
Sarris, Andrew 113
Sataman, Prakat 22–23
Savada, Elias 140
Savage, William 220
Scarface: The Shame of a Nation **259–263**
 censorship history of 260–262
 summary of 259–260
Schenck, Gilbert V. 45
Schenck, Joe 128
Schenck, Nicholas 164
Schiff, Stephen 184
Schindler's List (film) **263–266**
 censorship history of vii–viii, 265–266
 summary of 264–265
Schindler's List (Keneally) 264
Schneider, Maria 171
Schnitzler, Arthur 254
schools
 1900 in vii
 Schindler's List in vii–viii
Schorer, Mark 25
Schroder, William H., Jr. 76
Schulberg, B. P. 54–55, 127, 270
Schumach, Murray 103, 104, 278, 286
Schuman v. Pickert 312
Scorsese, Martin 173–178
SDS *See* Students for a Democratic Society
Sears, Leah J. 220
seizure, by law enforcement
 of *Cindy and Donna* 82–83
 of *Ecstasy* 117
 of *The Fox* 134
 of *I, A Woman* 148–149
 of *Pattern of Evil* 238
 Supreme Court on 82–83, 149
Selznick, David O. 164
Sennett, Mack 331
The Sex Lure **267–268**
 censorship history of 267–268
 summary of 267
sexual content
 in *The Affairs of Cellini* 2–3
 in *The Alimony Lovers* 8–9
 in *Anatomy of a Murder* 17–18

in *And God Created Woman* 19–21
in *Baby Doll* 26–29
in *Baby Face* 29–33
in *Behind the Green Door* 39–41
in *The Blue Angel* 56–58
in *Blue Movie* 58–60
in *Body of a Female* 60–61
in *Caligula* 65–68
in *Candy* 68–71
in *Carmen, Baby* 71–74
in *Carnal Knowledge* 74–77
in *Un Chant d'Amour* 77–81
in *Cindy and Donna* 81–83
in *Cruising* 84–88
in *Deep Throat* 95–97
in *Desire Under the Elms* 98–99
in *The Devil in Miss Jones* 99–101
in *Dressed to Kill* 112–114
in *Ecstasy* 116–118
in *Emmanuelle* 118–121
in *Flaming Creatures* 129–132
in *491* 124–125
in *The Fox* 133–135
in *The Game of Love* 141–143
in *Garden of Eden* 143–145
in *I, A Woman* 147–150
in *I Am Curious–Yellow* 150–153
in *The Killing of Sister George* 162–163
in *Lady Chatterley's Lover* vi, 163–167
in *The Last Picture Show* 167–169
in *Last Tango in Paris* 169–173
in *Lolita* (1962) 178–182
in *Lolita* (1997) 182–186
in *Lorna* 186–187
in *The Lovers* 187–190
in *Miss Julie* 202–203
in *Mom and Dad* 203–206
in *The Moon Is Blue* 209–212
and MPAA ratings viii
in *Naked Came the Stranger* 212–214
in *Never on Sunday* 221–224

in *The Newcomers* 224–225
in *The Outlaw* 234–236
in *Pattern of Evil* 237–238
in *The Road to Ruin* 252–253
in *La Ronde* 254–256
in *Room at the Top* 257–258
in *The Sex Lure* 267–268
in *She Done Him Wrong* 269–271
in *A Stranger Knocks* 283–284
in *A Streetcar Named Desire* 285–287
in *Therese and Isabelle* 287–289
in *Toto Who Lived Twice* 297–299
in *The Virgin Spring* 299–301
in *Viva Maria!* 301–303
in *The Vixen* 303–304
in *Windows* 307–308
in *Women of the World* 309–310
Shaw, Irwin 98
Shearn, Clarence J. 268
She Done Him Wrong **268–271**
censorship history of 270–271
summary of 269–270
Shepherd, Cybill 168
Sheriff of Jefferson County, Cooper v. 152
Sherman, Lowell 343
Sherwood, Robert 154–156
She Shoulda Said No See Wild Weed
Shreveport, Louisiana, *Last Tango in Paris* in 172
Shurlock, Geoff 181, 210, 223, 277
The Sign of the Cross **271–274**
censorship history of 273–274
summary of 272–273
Simmons, Jerold L. 100
Simon, John 152
Simpson, Joseph 220–221
Singapore, *Dracula* in 111
Sisam v. Bethel College & Seminary 291
Sjöberg, Alf 343
Sjöman, Vilgot 125, 343
Skal, David 137, 140
Sklar, Robert 68

Slaton, Evans Theatre Corp. v. 153
Smith, Jack 131, 343
social content 347
of *The Alibi* 6–7
of *Amok* 15–16
of *Ann Vickers* 24–26
of *Baby Face* 30–32
of *Basic Instinct* 33–36
of *Belle of the Nineties* 41–43
of *The Birth of a Baby* 43–45
of *The Birth of a Nation* 46–50
of *Blonde Venus* 53–55
of *The Brand* 62–63
of *Un Chant d'Amour* 78–80
of *The Connection* 83–84
of *Cruising* 85–87
of *Curley* 88–90
of *Damaged Goods* 90–92
of *Dressed to Kill* 112–114
of *The Easiest Way* 115–116
of *A Farewell to Arms* 126–128
of *Flaming Creatures* 129–132
of *491* 124–125
of *The Fox* 133–135
of *Freaks* 138–140
of *I'm No Angel* 157–159
of *The James Boys in Missouri* 160–161
of *The Killing of Sister George* 162–163
of *M* 191–192
of *The Man With the Golden Arm* 193–194
of *Mom and Dad* 204–206
of *The Naked Truth* 214–216
of *Native Son* 216–217
of *Never on Sunday* 222–223
of *Of Human Bondage* 230–232
of *Red-Headed Woman* 245–247
of *Reefer Madness* 248–250
of *The Road to Ruin* 253–254
of *She Done Him Wrong* 269–271
of *Spartacus* 276–278

of *The Tin Drum*
290–292
of *Titicut Follies* 293–294
of *Tomorrow's Children*
295–297
of *Whirlpool* 305
of *Wild Weed* 306–307
of *Woodstock* 310–311
Solanis, Valerie 59
A Song of Love See *Un Chant d'Amour*
Song of Russia 226
Sontag, Susan 131
Sorour, Hamdi 265
Southern, Terry 69
The Southerner vi, 89
Soviet Union See Russia
Spain
   The Great Dictator in 147
   Idiot's Delight in 156
Spain in Flames **274–276**
   censorship history of 275
   summary of 275
Spanish Civil War 51, 275
The Spanish Earth 51
Spartacus **276–278**
   censorship history of
   277–278
   summary of 276–277
Spellman, Francis vi, 28, 199
Spielberg, Steven
   profile of 344
   Schindler's List vii–viii,
   265, 266
The Spirit of '76 **279–281**
   censorship history of
   279–281
   summary of 279
"Spurs" (Robbins) 138
The Spy **281–282**
   censorship history of
   281–282
   summary of 281
SRC See Studio Relations
   Committee
Stalin, Joseph 229
Stanton, Richard 343
Stark, Harold 94
Starr, Ringo 69
*State, ABC Interstate Theatres
   v.* 124
State, Beasley v. 219–220
State, Crosby v. 220
*State ex rel Keating v. A
   Motion Picture Entitled
   Vixen* 304
State of Texas, Gelling v.
   240–241
State v. Freedman 252

State v. Gevaras 189
State v. Jacobellis 189
State v. Warth 189
Stern, Horace 307
von Sternberg, Josef
   Blonde Venus 54
   The Blue Angel 56, 57
   profile of 345
Stewart, Potter 82–83,
   165–166
Stoker, Bram 110
Stone, Oliver 219, 220–221,
   344
Stone, Sharon 35
A Stranger Knocks **282–284**
   censorship history of
   283–284
   summary of 283
A Streetcar Named Desire
   284–287
   censorship history of
   286–287
   summary of 285–286
Strindberg, August 202
Strode, Aubrey E. 45
Stromberg, Hunt 156
Students for a Democratic
   Society (SDS) 132
Studio Relations Committee
   (SRC) xi
   on *All Quiet on the Western
      Front* 11–12
   on *Ann Vickers* 25–26
   on *Belle of the Nineties* 42
   on *Blonde Venus* 55
   on *The Blue Angel* 57–58
   on *A Farewell to Arms*
      127–128
   on *Red-Headed Woman*
      246–247
   on *Scarface: The Shame of a
      Nation* 260–261
Sumner, Cid Ricketts 239
Supreme Court
   on *Body of a Female* 61
   on *Carnal Knowledge*
      76–77
   on censorship, history of
      v–vii, x, xi–xii
   on *Un Chant d'Amour* 80
   on *Cindy and Donna*
      82–83
   on exhibition sites 74
   on *The Game of Love*
      142–143
   on *I, A Woman* 149
   on *I Am Curious–Yellow*
      153
   on immorality 201

   on *Lady Chatterley's Lover*
      vi, 165–166
   on *The Lovers* 189–190
   on *M* 192, 217
   Miller Standard of 59, 66,
      77
   on minority opinions vi
   on *The Miracle* xi,
      200–201
   on *The Moon Is Blue* 211
   on *Native Son* 217
   on *The Newcomers* 225
   on obscenity xi–xii, 59,
      66, 76
   on *Pinky* 240–241
   on prior restraint v, vii,
      106–108, 240–241,
      252
   on *Revenge at Daybreak* 9,
      38, 251–252
   on *La Ronde* 255–256
   on sacrilege vi, xi–xii,
      200, 208
   on seizure 82–83, 149
   on *A Stranger Knocks* 284
   on *Titicut Follies* 294
   on *Viva Maria!* 303
Sutherland, Edward 332
Swaggart, Jimmy 176
Switzerland, *Idiot's Delight* in
   156

T

Target Smut 132
Tariff Act 117, 118, 125, 151
Taylor, Winchell 52, 53
Teitel Film Corp., Cusack v.
   61
Teitel Film Corp. v. Cusack 61
television
   Lolita on 184–185
   Martin Luther on 196
   ratings for viii
   Schindler's List on viii
Tell Your Children See *Reefer
   Madness*
Ten Days That Shook the World
   (Reed) 228
Tennant, Andy 344
Tennessee
   Curley in vi, 89–90
   I, A Woman in 148
   King of Kings in 89
   The Lovers in 188–189
   Mom and Dad in 205
   The Moon Is Blue in 211
   The Southerner in vi, 89
   Women of the World in
      309–310

Texas
  Behind the Green Door in
    40
  Deep Throat in 95–96
  Flaming Creatures in 132
  *The Last Temptation of
    Christ* in 175
  Pinky in 240–241
  The Virgin Spring in
    300–301
  Viva Maria! in vii,
    302–303
Thailand
  Anna and the King in
    22–23
  Schindler's List in 266
Thalberg, Irving 138, 140
*Thayer Amusement Corporation
  v. Moulton* 242–243
Therese and Isabelle **287–289**
  censorship history of
    288–289
  summary of 288
Thompson, Hugh P. 220
Thompson, Ralph 291–292
Thomsen, Agnethe 148
Thurmond, Strom 132
*Times Film Corp. v. City of
  Chicago* (on *Don Juan*)
  106–108
*Times Film Corp. v. City of
  Chicago* (on *The Game of
  Love)* 142
*Times Mirror Co., Associates &
  Aldrich Co. v.* 163
Time-Warner, *Natural Born
  Killers* and 220–221
The Tin Drum (film)
  289–292
  censorship history of vii,
    290–292
  summary of 290
The Tin Drum (Grass) vii,
  290
Titicut Follies **292–294**
  censorship history of
    293–294
  summary of 293
Toland, Gregg 93, 94, 345
Tomorrow's Children **295–297**
  censorship history of
    296–297
  summary of 295
Toronto, *Toto Who Lived Twice*
  in 298–299
Toto Who Lived Twice
  297–299
  censorship history of
    298–299
  summary of 297–298

Townsend, Leo 337
Trail, Armitage 259
*Trans-Lux Distributing Corp.
  v. Maryland State Board of
  Censors* 284
*Trans-Lux Distributing Corpo-
  ration v. Board of Regents*
  283–284
Trauberg, Leonid 337
Traver, Robert 17
Tropic of Cancer (Miller) 151
Trotti, Lamar 54, 127
Trumbo, Dalton 278
Twentieth Century Pictures
  2
*Twenty-Seven Wagons Full of
  Cotton* (Williams) 27
Two Tin Boxes, United States v.
  117
Two Women 300

U

UA Theatres, Lordi v. 152
Ultravixens 186
Ulysses (Joyce) v
L'Umano Voce 198
*The Unborn See Tomorrow's
  Children*
The Unholy Three 138
United Artists 2
*United Artists Corp. v. Mary-
  land State Board of Censors*
  212
*United Artists Corporation v.
  Board of Censors of City of
  Memphis* 89
*United Artists Corporation v.
  Maryland Board of Censors*
  194
United Artists v. Wright 172
United Kingdom
  Damaged Goods in 91–92
  Freaks in 140
  The Great Dictator and
    147
  Last Tango in Paris in 171
  Natural Born Killers in 21
  Red-Headed Woman in
    247
  in *The Spirit of '72*
    79–280
United States, Goldstein v.
  280–281
United States, Roth v. 18, 74,
  80, 144, 283
United States Supreme Court
  See Supreme Court
*United States v. Film Entitled
  491* 125

*United States v. "I Am Curi-
  ous–Yellow"* 151–152
*United States v. Motion Picture
  Film The Spirit of '76*
  280
*United States v. One Book
  Called "Ulysses"* v
*United States v. One Reel of
  Film* 96
United States v. Two Tin Boxes
  117
*Universal Amusement Co. v.
  Vance* 95–96
*Universal Amusement Co.,
  Vance v.* 96
Universal Studios, *The Last
  Temptation of Christ* and
  175–177
An Unsatisfying Supper
  (Williams) 27
Ustinov, Peter 309
Utah
  Amistad in 15
  *The Last Temptation of
    Christ* in 177
  Schindler's List in 266

V

Vadim, Roger 345
Valdosta, Georgia, *Monty
  Python's Life of Brian* in
  208
Valenti, Jack 113, 123
*Vance, Universal Amusement
  Co. v.* 95–96
*Vance v. Universal Amusement
  Co.* 96
van Sloan, Edward 135
v-chip viii
venereal disease
  in *Damaged Goods* 90–92
  in *The Naked Truth*
    215–216
Venice Film Festival
  Ecstasy in 117
  Freaks in 140
  The Miracle in 198
Verhoeven, Paul 36, 345
Vidal, Gore 65, 66
Video Privacy Protection Act
  291
Vieira, Mark 127
violence
  in *The Alibi* 6–7
  in *Amistad* 13–15
  in *Dressed to Kill* 112–114
  in *Frankenstein* 135–137
  in *Natural Born Killers*
    218–221

in *Scarface: The Shame of a Nation* 259–262
in *Spartacus* 276–278
Virginia
  The Birth of a Baby in 44–45
  The Lovers in 188–189
The Virgin Spring **299–301**
  censorship history of 300–301
  summary of 299–300
Viva Maria! **301–303**
  censorship history of vii, 302–303
  summary of 301–302
Vivant, Dominique 188
The Vixen **303–304**
  censorship history of 186, 304
  summary of 304
Voltaire 69
Voyage Au Congo 327

W

Wadleigh, Michael 345
Wagonheim v. Maryland 153
Walker, Gerald 87
Wallis, Hal 32
Wanger, Walter 51
WAP *See* Women Against Pornography
Warhol, Andy
  **** 59
  Blue Movie 58–60
  and *Freaks* 140
  I, a Man 59
  profile of 346
Warner, Jack 32
Warren, Earl v, vii, 107–108
Warren, Rita 123
Warth, State v. 189
Washington, *Carmen, Baby* in 72–74
Washington, D.C., *The Exorcist* in 123
Wasserman, Lew 175, 177
Waterbury, Connecticut, *Spain in Flames* in 275
WAVPM *See* Women Against Violence and Pornography in Movies
The Ways of Love vi, 199
Webley, Stanford 14

Weintraub, Jerry 86
Weiss, Andrea 134
Wellford, Harry W. 97
West, Mae
  Belle of the Nineties 41–43
  I'm No Angel 157–159
  She Done Him Wrong 268–271
West, Roland 346
Whale, James 136, 346
Whirlpool **305**
  censorship history of 305
  summary of 305
White, Thelma 248, 249
Wilbur, Crane 346
Wildmon, Donald 175, 176
Wild Weed **306–307**
  censorship history of 306–307
  summary of 306
Wilkins, Raymond S. 203
Wilkinson, Brook 147
Wilkinson, Lupton A. 231–232
Williams, Tennessee
  Baby Doll 26–29
  A Streetcar Named Desire 285–287
  Twenty-Seven Wagons Full of Cotton 27
  An Unsatisfying Supper 27
Willis, Gordon 346
Wilson, Burstyn v. vi, xi, 200, 240
Wilson, Joseph Burstyn, Inc. v. 199–200
Wilson, Woodrow x, 48
Windows **307–308**
  censorship history of 308
  summary of 307–308
Wingate, James
  on *Ann Vickers* 25
  on *Baby Face* 32
  on *A Farewell to Arms* 127–128
  on *I'm No Angel* 158
  on *She Done Him Wrong* 270
Wisconsin
  The Moon Is Blue in 211
  Schindler's List in vii–viii
  Woodstock in 311
Wiseman, Commonwealth v. 293–294

Wiseman, Frederick 293–294
Wiseman v. Massachusetts 294
Wolf, Frederick 241
Women Against Pornography (WAP), on *Dressed to Kill* 114
Women Against Violence and Pornography in Movies (WAVPM), on *Dressed to Kill* 114
Women of the World **309–310**
  censorship history of 309–310
  summary of 309
Woodstock **310–311**
  censorship history of 311
  summary of 310
Wray, John Griffith 6
Wright, Richard 216–218
Wright, United Artists v. 172
Wurtzel, Sol 128

X

X rating
  for *Dressed to Kill* 113
  for *Emmanuelle* 120
  for *The Killing of Sister George* 163
  for *Last Tango in Paris* 171
  for *Naked Came the Stranger* 213
  vs. NC-17 rating xii
  for *The Newcomers* 224
  for *The Vixen* 304

Y

Young v. American Mini Theatres 121
The Youth of Maxim **311–312**
  censorship history of 312
  summary of 311–312

Z

Zanuck, Darryl F. 2–3, 32
Zenith International Film Corp. v. Chicago 189
zoning, for adult entertainment 120–121
Zukor, Adolph 159
Zweig, Stefan 15